Learning SQL Server Reporting Services 2012

Get the most out of SQL Server Reporting Service 2012, both Native and SharePoint Integrated modes

Jayaram Krishnaswamy

[PACKT] enterprise
PUBLISHING
professional expertise distilled

BIRMINGHAM - MUMBAI

Learning SQL Server Reporting Services 2012

Copyright © 2013 Packt Publishing

All rights reserved. No part of this book may be reproduced, stored in a retrieval system, or transmitted in any form or by any means, without the prior written permission of the publisher, except in the case of brief quotations embedded in critical articles or reviews.

Every effort has been made in the preparation of this book to ensure the accuracy of the information presented. However, the information contained in this book is sold without warranty, either express or implied. Neither the author, nor Packt Publishing, and its dealers and distributors will be held liable for any damages caused or alleged to be caused directly or indirectly by this book.

Packt Publishing has endeavored to provide trademark information about all of the companies and products mentioned in this book by the appropriate use of capitals. However, Packt Publishing cannot guarantee the accuracy of this information.

First published: March 2009

Second edition: June 2013

Production Reference: 1170613

Published by Packt Publishing Ltd.
Livery Place
35 Livery Street
Birmingham B3 2PB, UK.

ISBN 978-1-84968-992-2

www.packtpub.com

Cover Image by Prashant Timappa Shetty (sparkling.spectrum.123@gmail.com)

Credits

Author
Jayaram Krishnaswamy

Reviewers
Satya Jayanty
Ritesh Shah
Maria Zakourdaev

Acquisition Editor
Mary Jasmine Nadar

Lead Technical Editor
Azharuddin Sheikh

Technical Editors
Mausam Kothari
Amit Ramadas
Varun Pius Rodrigues
Lubna Shaikh

Project Coordinator
Apeksha Chitnis

Proofreader
Ting Baker

Indexer
Rekha Nair

Graphics
Abhinash Sahu

Production Coordinator
Manu Joseph

Cover Work
Manu Joseph

About the Author

Jayaram Krishnaswamy studied at the Indian Institute of Science in Bangalore and Madras University in India and taught at the Indian Institute of Technology in Madras. He went to Japan on a Japanese Ministry of Education Research scholarship to complete his PhD in Electrical Engineering at Nagoya University. He was a Post-Doctoral Fellow at Sydney University in Australia; a Government of India Senior Scientific Officer at the Indian Institute of Science in Bangalore and Indian Institute of Technology at Kanpur; a visiting scientist at the Eindhoven Institute of Technology in Netherlands; a visiting professor of Physics at the Federal University in Brazil; an associate research scientist at a government laboratory in Sao Jose dos Campos in Sao Paulo, Brazil; and a visiting scientist at the National Research Council in Ottawa, Canada, before coming to USA in 1985. He has also taught and worked at the Colorado State University in Fort Collins and North Carolina State University in Raleigh, North Carolina. He worked with Northrop Grumman Corporation on a number of projects related to high energy electron accelerators / free electron lasers. These projects were undertaken at the Brookhaven National Laboratory in Long Island and in the Physics Department at Princeton University. He has over 80 publications in refereed and non-refereed publications and 8 issued patents. He is fluent in Japanese and Portuguese and lives in Honolulu, Hawaii, USA.

He has been working in IT related fields since 1997. He was once a Microsoft Certified Trainer in Networking and a Siebel Certified developer. He has worked with several IT related companies, such as Butler International in their Siebel practice; and with several IBM subcontractors and smaller companies. Presently he is active in writing technical articles in the IT field to many online sites such as `CodeProject.com`, `APSFree.com`, `DevShed.com`, `DevArticles.com`, `OfficeUsers.org`, `ASPAlliance.com`, `Egghead Café`, `SSWUG.org`, `Packt Article Network`, `databasedev.co.uk`, `cimaware.com`, and many others. Between 2006 and 2010 he wrote more than 400 articles mostly related to database and web-related technologies covering Microsoft, Oracle, Sybase, ColdFusion, Sun, and other vendor products.

He has written four books all published by Packt related to Microsoft database and application development, namely, *SQL Server Integration Services Using Visual Studio 2005*, *Learning SQL Server Reporting Services 2008*, *Microsoft SQL Azure, Enterprise Application Development*, and *Microsoft Visual Studio Lightswitch Business Application Development*. He regularly writes on his four blogs on Blogger `http://Hodentek.blogspot.com`, `http://HodentekHelp.blogspot.com`, `http://HodentekMobile.blogspot.com`, and `http://HodentekMSSS.blogspot.com`. He received the 2011 Microsoft Community Contributor award.

I would like to thank Packt Publishing for giving me this opportunity to write the second edition of my book *Learning SQL Server Reporting Services 2012*. Dilip Venkatesh, the Senior Acquisition Editor, my early contact for this book was most helpful and without his guidance this book would not have been possible. I am most grateful for his advice.

I would like to thank Mary Nadar, the Acquisition Editor, for help with this book, in its early stages. I am obliged to Apeksha Chitnis, the Project Coordinator, for having monitoring the flow of correspondence successfully and for her timely reminders. I also would like to thank Lead Technical Editors Sharvari Tawde in the early stages, Azharuddin Sheikh for having stayed with this book to the end, and Chalini Victor. I would like to thank the Technical Editors Varun Pius Rodrigues, Mausam Kothari, and Lubna Shaikh for their excellent support and detailed editing and patience. I would also like to record the help of many others at Packt at different stages of production.

I sincerely thank the reviewers for their valuable time and effort. Satya Shyam K Jayanty, Maria Zakourdaev, Ritesh Shah (SQLHub.com), and Bihag Thacker (MsSQLBlog.com) have contributed enormously to the book. Their pointed questions and well directed advice have made portions of this book more readable and clear and I am most thankful to them. I particularly would like to thank Satya Shyam K Jayanty who meticulously went through the book and provided very valuable advice both technical and organizational.

I would like to thank my parents who would have shared my joy. I thank my brothers and sisters, and the whole hearted support of our Subbagiri family. I cannot sufficiently thank my wife, Michiko Fukumoto, my son, Krishna Jayaram, and his wife, Jannet Jayaram, for their continuous encouragement and their dog, Oliver, who sat by my side and gave me his company during the writing.

Last but not the least I would like to thank Microsoft Corporation for making available evaluation software without which this book would not exist. I am most indebted to the MSDN forums specially related to SQL Server Reporting Services 2012 and SharePoint 2010, their moderators and mentors from whom I have received unstinted support.

About the Reviewers

Satya Jayanty is a Subject Matter Expert (Technical and Data Architect and DBA) with more than 21 years of experience in the IT field that includes a wide range of industries such as the stock exchange, insurance, tele-communications, financial, insurance, retail, and manufacturing sectors among others. He has been a **Microsoft Most Valueable Professional** (**MVP**) (Architecture – SQL Server) since the year 2006. He was a Director and Principal Architect at DBIA Solutions Limited.

His Twitter handle is `@SQLMaster`.

He is also the author of the book *Microsoft SQL Server 2008 R2 Administration Cookbook* (May 2011). More information on the book can be found at `http://tinyurl.com/SJ-SQL2K8R2AdminCookBook` from Packt Publishers. He was also a co-author on the book *MVP Deep Dives Volume II – SQL Server* (October 2011). More information on this book can be found at `http://manning.com/delaney` from Manning Publications. He has also been a technical reviewer and provided a foreword for three books related to high availability and disaster recovery topics. He has worked as an item writer and technical reviewer for *SQL Server 2008, 2008 R2, and 2012 Microsoft ITPRO and DEV certification exams*. He has written a foreword for *SQL Server 2008 High Availability* and was a technical reviewer for the book *SQL Server Denali – The Definitive Guide*. He is currently working on *SQL Server 2012 Analysis Services Cube Security – Microbook* and has completed the draft for the same.

He is a regular speaker and SME volunteer at major technology conferences such as Microsoft Tech-Ed (Europe, India, and North America), SQL PASS (Europe and North America), SQL Bits – UK and manages Scottish Area SQL Server user group based in Scotland.

D B I A Solutions Limited – Europe : an experienced consulting company delivering manageable solutions for the customers across the Europe (a few other parts in the globe).

> I want to thank my wife first for letting (helping) me complete the review in time and my kids for relieving the stress in my day-to-day schedule.
>
> I give my appreciation for all the help and support from the Packt Publishing team in completing the technical review.

Ritesh Shah is data professional with more than 10 years of experience in Microsoft technology from SQL Server 2000 to the latest version and has worked on Visual Basic 6.0 to .NET Framework 4.0. He has deployed many medium-scale as well as large-scale projects using Microsoft technology.

He has authored a book called *Microsoft SQL Server 2012 Performance Tuning Cookbook* with Packt Publication. He also writes articles on technology at blog, `Extreme-Advice.com` and `SQLHub.com`.

> I would sincerely like to thank Packt Publishing, for showing their confidence in me and providing the invaluable opportunity of being a part of this book. Individuals at Packt whom I am deeply grateful to, are Apeksha Chitnis and Rukmini Iyer. They have been very co-operative and supportive at all the stages of this book.
>
> Without my family support, a task such as reviewing a book would not have been achievable, especially when you are committed to other professional projects also. I would like to heartily thank my parents, Mr. Ashwin Shah and Mrs. Divya Shah. It is because of them that I exist, and I cherish their blessings, which are always with me.

Maria Zakourdaev has more than 13 years experience working with SQL Server. She is currently working at one of the most successful Israel startup company called Conduit. She is in charge of the company's large scale and very dynamic SQL Server environment. She has extensive knowledge in Microsoft replication solutions, table partitioning, and advanced query tuning techniques. Prior to Conduit, she had worked at many different companies, benchmarking different SQL Server features and flows, such as partitioning, data import, indexes impact on DML flows, star transformations in RDBMS, and Hierarchic queries and custom OLAP-like aggregations. She was a speaker in the Microsoft Teched (Israel) on the SQL Server track. She frequently delivers sessions on different local conferences is and an active member of the Israel SQL Server Users Group.

www.PacktPub.com

Support files, eBooks, discount offers and more

You might want to visit www.PacktPub.com for support files and downloads related to your book.

Did you know that Packt offers eBook versions of every book published, with PDF and ePub files available? You can upgrade to the eBook version at www.PacktPub.com and as a print book customer, you are entitled to a discount on the eBook copy. Get in touch with us at service@packtpub.com for more details.

At www.PacktPub.com, you can also read a collection of free technical articles, sign up for a range of free newsletters and receive exclusive discounts and offers on Packt books and eBooks.

PACKTLIB

http://PacktLib.PacktPub.com

Do you need instant solutions to your IT questions? PacktLib is Packt's online digital book library. Here, you can access, read and search across Packt's entire library of books.

Why Subscribe?

- Fully searchable across every book published by Packt
- Copy and paste, print and bookmark content
- On demand and accessible via web browser

Free Access for Packt account holders

If you have an account with Packt at www.PacktPub.com, you can use this to access PacktLib today and view nine entirely free books. Simply use your login credentials for immediate access.

Instant Updates on New Packt Books

Get notified! Find out when new books are published by following @PacktEnterprise on Twitter, or the *Packt Enterprise* Facebook page.

Table of Contents

Preface   **1**

Chapter 1: Overview and Installation – SQL Server Reporting Services 2012   **9**
   SQL Server 2012 – mission statement by Microsoft   9
   Overview of Reporting Services 2012   11
   Installing software used in the book   14
      SQL Server 2012 installation requirements   15
         Operating system requirements (64-bit)   15
         Hardware requirements   16
         Software requirements   16
      Configuring the hardware used for the book   17
      Hands-on exercise 1.1 – installing SQL Server 2012   18
         Downloading the source file   18
         Installation steps   18
      Hands-on exercise 1.2 – verifying the installation   33
         Installation choices and notes   37
   Configuring SQL Server Reporting Services   37
      Hands-on exercise 1.3 – configuring SQL Server 2012 Reporting Services in Native mode   38
         Report Server – configuration options   50
   Installing sample databases   55
      Downloading files and running scripts   55
   SharePoint Server 2010 Enterprise Edition   56
      Installing SharePoint Server 2010 Enterprise Edition on Windows 7 (64-bit)   56
   Installing Reporting Services 2012 in SharePoint Integrated mode   60
      Reporting Services add-in for SharePoint 2010   61
      Installing and starting the Reporting Services SharePoint Service   62

Hands-on exercise 1.4 – installing the Reporting Services SharePoint Service	63
Creating the Reporting Services Service application	65
Activating the Power View site collection feature	71
Summary	**72**

Chapter 2: SQL Server Reporting Services 2012 Projects with Visual Studio 2012 — 73

What is business intelligence?	**73**
Introduction to SQL Server Data Tools	**74**
BI Projects on SSDT	77
Report Server Project	78
Report Server Project Wizard	78
Creating reports using SSDT	**79**
Hands-on exercise 2.1 – creating a report using the Report Server Project Wizard	79
Hands-on exercise 2.2 – deploying the report to the Report Server	87
Hands-on exercise 2.3 – creating a report using the Report wizard in SSDT	90
Hands-on exercise 2.4 – modifying the report in Project RSPW2012 using an expression	96
Report formats supported in Report Server Reports	98
Report-related projects in Visual Studio 2012	**99**
Creating reports using Visual Studio 2012	**100**
Software and hardware requirements	100
Hands-on exercise 2.5 – creating a report for a Windows Form application using Report Viewer Control	101
Hands-on exercise 2.6 – creating a report using Report Viewer Control for the Web	115
Hands-on exercise 2.7 – using Report Viewer Control in the remote mode	121
Hands-on exercise 2.8 – converting an RDLC to a RDL file	123
Microsoft Report Viewer Runtime	**129**
Summary	**130**

Chapter 3: Overview of SQL Server Reporting Services 2012 Architecture, Features, and Tools — 131

Structural design of SQL servers and SharePoint environment	**132**
Native mode	134
SharePoint Integrated mode	136
Reporting Services configuration	**139**
Native mode	139

SharePoint Integrated mode	142
Hands-on exercise 3.1 – modifying the configuration file in Native mode	143
Turn on/off the Report Server Web Service	144
Turn on/off the scheduled events and delivery	145
Turn on/off the Report Manager	145
Hands-on exercise 3.2 – turn the Reporting Service on/off in SSMS	146
Salient features of Reporting Services 2012	**147**
Report definition	148
XML-based report definition (the `.rdl` file)	148
Power View report contents	150
Creating reports	150
Report data	151
New toolbox items in Report Builder 3	153
Report parts and their reusability	153
Customizing reports	154
Saving and deploying reports	155
Report validation	156
Viewing reports	157
Managing reports	158
Report scheduling	158
Subscriptions and delivery	160
Features new in RS2012 SharePoint Integrated	162
Power View	163
Data Alerts	164
Implementing security – authentication and authorization	166
Authentication	166
Authorization	170
URL access	171
Reporting Services extensions	172
Reporting Services tools	173
Tools for Report Server administration	173
Tools for report authoring	174
Tools for report content management	174
Summary	**175**
Chapter 4: Working with Report Manager	**177**
Tasks performed using Report Manager	178
Starting Report Manager	179
Starting Report Manager for the URL	180
User access to Report Server (Report Manager)	180
Considerations for giving user access to the Report Server	180
First step – deploying reports	181

Table of Contents

Report Manager user interface	**182**
Customizing Report Manager	185
Hands-on exercise 4.1 – creating, modifying, moving, and deleting folders	185
Navigating through the folders	186
Creating a folder and a subfolder	187
Moving an item into a folder	190
Configuring permissions from Report Manager	191
Configuring role-based security	192
Hands-on exercise 4.2 – assigning a Windows user to the System Administrator role	193
Creating a Windows user	193
Assigning RSMax to the RS System Administrator role	195
Assigning users to item-level roles	196
Review users on a Reporting Services database	198
Hands-on exercise 4.3 – assigning a user to a Custom role	198
Hands-on exercise 4.4 – creating a permission to a specific report	200
Report data sources	**202**
An embedded data source	202
A shared data source	203
Hands-on exercise 4.5 – creating a shared data source on Report Manager	203
Hands-on exercise 4.6 – creating a data model from a data source	205
Viewing, searching, and printing reports	**211**
Hand-on exercise 4.7 – view, print, and search on Report Manager	212
Viewing reports	212
Printing reports	213
Search	215
Uploading and downloading files from the Report Server to the filesystem	**217**
Uploading a report on the computer to the Report Server	217
Hands-on exercise 4.8 – uploading a report to the Report Server	217
Hands-on execise 4.9 – downloading and reviewing a report definition file from the Report Server	218
Report subscription and delivery	**220**
Hands-on exercise 4.10 – creating an event-driven report subscription for delivery by an e-mail	222
Hands-on exercise 4.11 – creating an event-driven report subscription for delivery to a file share	227
Hands-on exercise 4.12 – creating data-driven report subscription for delivery to a file share	229

Create a Subscribers database in SQL Server	230
Creating the data-driven Subscription and testing it	231
Report caching	**237**
Report processing options	238
Cache refresh options	239
Hands-on exercise 4.13 – creating a cache refresh plan by preloading the cache	240
Snapshot and snapshot history	**242**
Hands-on exercise 4.14 – creating a snapshot and snapshot history	242
Summary	**244**
Chapter 5: Working with Report Builder 3.0	**245**
Report authoring with Report Builder	**246**
Downloading and installing Report Builder	**246**
Report Builder 3.0 user interface	**248**
Report authoring	**248**
Hands-on exercise 5.1 – creating a report with an embedded data source	249
Hands-on exercise 5.2 – creating a report from a shared data source	259
Creating a List report	263
Parameterized reports	267
Subreports	267
Hands-on exercise 5.3 – creating a report that has a subreport	268
Creating the subreport	268
Creating the main report	270
Embedding the subreport in the main report	272
Report with groups	275
Hands-on exercise 5.4 – setting up a group and creating a document map	276
Bring up the report from the previous hands-on exercise and remove parameter	276
Adding a group to the data	277
Adding a Document Map to the report	280
Configuring page breaks	281
Adding interactive sorting	282
Drill-through and drill-down reports	284
Drill-through reports	285
Hands-on exercise 5.5 – Creating a drill-through report	285
Source report	285
Destination report	286
Set up the drill-through action	287
Drill-down report	288
Hands-on exercise 5.6 – Creating a drill-down report	289

Linked reports — 291
Hands-on exercise 5.7 – creating linked reports — 291
Customizing the linked report in the France folder — 292
Creating a report with XML data sources — 293
Creating a well-formed XML data — 294
Displaying data with sparklines, maps, data bars, and indicators — 297
Hands-on exercise 5.8 – creating a report and highlighting data with data bars — 297
Displaying data with sparklines — 300
Hands-on exercise 5.9 – creating reports with sparklines — 301
Creating a table — 301
Creating a report and inserting sparklines — 302
Indicators — 304
Hands-on exercise 5.10 – creating reports using indicators — 304
Reports with map — 307
Hands-on exercise 5.11 – creating reports with embedded maps — 307
Report parts — 314
Hands-on exercise 5.12 – creating report parts and reusing an item — 314
Saving report as report parts — 315
Reusing the report parts items — 319
Summary — 323

Chapter 6: Power View and Reporting Services — 325
What is Power View? — 325
Helpful resources — 326
What do you need to author a Power View report? — 327
Creating a tabular model — 328
Hands-on exercise 6.1 – creating a tabular model — 328
Brief review of SSDT ribbon — 330
Creating a connection to the Northwind database — 331
Getting tables from the database — 332
Default field set and table behavior — 337
Adding measures — 339
Deploying the model — 340
Hands-on exercise 6.2 – deploying the model — 340
Tabular model permissions — 341
Hands-on exercise 6.3 – creating a role in SQL Server Data Tools — 341
Creating a Power View — 344
Hands-on exercise 6.4 – connecting to model from SharePoint Server 2010 — 344
Connecting to the model — 347
Creating a data source using the model as the source — 347
Creating a Power View report using the data source — 349

Hands-on exercise 6.5 – exploring a Power View report	350
Creating the first view of the Power View report	351
Creating a chart showing sales orders from NW Employees shipped from cities	355
Adding a second view to the Power View report	357
Highlighting of data	360
Displaying data as a card	360
Using tiles	362
Slicing the data	363
Advanced filtering	365
Scatter and bubble charts	366
Animation with Power View	368
Navigating the views of the Power View report	370
Save, do, undo, and refresh	370
Saving to PowerPoint	371
Summary	**372**
Chapter 7: Self-service Data Alerts in SSRS 2012	**373**
Getting ready for data alerts	**374**
Granting permissions to work with data alerts	377
Creating a report and saving to the Report Server	**385**
Creating a report in Report Builder and saving it to the Documents library	**386**
Hands-on exercise 7.1 – creating a report in Report Builder and saving it to the SharePoint site	387
Giving permission to a report	**389**
Hands-on exercise 7.2 – giving full control of a report to a user	390
Creating a data alert	**393**
Hands-on exercise 7.3 – creating a data alert in Data Alert Designer	394
Editing data alerts	398
Troubleshooting	**402**
Using PowerShell to review the log file	404
Alert logs and alerting database	406
Summary	**408**
Chapter 8: Reporting Services and Programming	**409**
Overview of programming interfaces and utilities	**409**
URL access	**410**
Hands-on exercise 8.1 – URL access, Native mode Report Server	411
Accessing the Report Server	411
Listing contents of a folder	412
Accessing a component in report parts	412
Rendering a report	413
Accessing the contents of a data source	413
Exporting to supported formats	414
Rendering a report with the report parameter	414

Hands-on exercise 8.2 – URL access and SharePoint Integrated mode Report Server	415
Accessing the Report Server in SP-integrated implementation	415
Accessing a report on the Report Server in SP-integrated implementation	416
ReportViewer control	**417**
Hands-on exercise 8.3 – using URL access and ReportViewer controls with Web applications	418
Report Server Web Services API	**422**
Hands-on exercise 8.4 – rendering a report on the native mode Report Server into different formats	423
Reporting Services in SharePoint Integrated mode	430
Hands-on exercise 8.5 – accessing SharePoint management endpoints	431
PowerShell	**434**
Hands-on exercise 8.6 – a quick review of basics	435
PowerShell and reporting services with SharePoint Integration	437
Hands-on exercise 8.7 – exploring reporting services in SharePoint Integrated mode	438
Getting help about help	438
Application server of the Reporting Services Service Application	438
Finding all cmdlets related to Reporting Services SharePoint Integration	439
Proxy URL of the Report Server	440
SP service application pool	440
PowerShell and Native mode Reporting Services 2010	441
Hands-on exercise 8.8 – exploring Native mode Reporting Services	441
The Native mode Report Server	441
Native mode Report Server configuration	442
Extensions supported on a Windows Forms ReportViewer	444
Windows Management Instrumentation	445
Hands-on exercise 8.9 – exploring the native mode Report Server programmatically	446
Providing access permission to WMI	446
Report Server properties using WMI	448
Reporting Services command prompt utilities	**451**
The RSS utility	452
What can rs.exe do?	452
Hands-on exercise 8.10 – creating a data source on the report server using rs.exe and a script file	453
The Rskeymgmt utility	456
Rsconfig	457

Incorporating custom code into reports	**458**
Hands-on 8.11 – inserting custom code into a report	458
Summary	**460**
Chapter 9: Windows Azure SQL Reporting	**461**
What is Windows Azure SQL Reporting?	**462**
Hands-on exercise 9.1 – accessing the Windows Azure portal	463
Creating content for reports and viewing them	**468**
Preparing to author reports	468
Hands-on exercise 9.2 – creating a report using SSDT and deploying it to the Windows Azure Reporting on the Cloud	469
Creating a SQL database on Windows Azure	469
Creating a table for the report	474
Populating the table in SSMS	476
Creating a SQL Reporting Service in Windows Azure	478
Creating a report based on the Skyblue database on the Windows Azure Platform	480
Deploying the report to the SQL Reporting Services on Windows Azure	484
Viewing the report on the SQL Reporting Web server	486
Hands-on exercise 9.3 – using the Windows Azure SQL Reporting Services to create folders, share data sources, and upload reports	488
Creating a shared data source in the portal	489
Managing your reports and users is easy	491
Managing users	492
Managing reports	493
Managing the report Dashboard	494
Status of activities	495
Managing permissions	496
Report viewing	496
Using Report Builder to view reports	497
Making changes to the report and placing it on the Report Server	500
URL access to reports on the Report Server	502
Accessing the server and running a report	502
Do gadgets like indicators and data bars work?	502
SQL Server 2012 Reporting Services – Known Issues	503
Hands-on exercise 9.4 – migrating a table on an on-premise SQL Server 2012 to the Windows Azure SQL database	505
Summary	**506**
Chapter 10: Applications Accessing Report Servers	**507**
Hands-on exercise 10.1 – accessing the Native mode Report Server using SSIS	508
Creating the Report Server Web Service WSDL file	513

Providing the WSDL file to the Web Service Task	513
Adding a File System Task to the Control Flow page	515
Accessing reports from a Windows Presentation Foundations classes project	**517**
Hands-on exercise 10.2 – accessing Report Server URLs in a WPF project	518
Accessing Native Report Server reports from SharePoint Web parts	**524**
Hands-on exercise 10.3 – viewing reports on the Native mode Report Server using SharePoint Web parts	524
Accessing the Web parts	**525**
Summary	**532**
Index	**533**

Preface

From Microsoft SQL Server Reporting Services 2008 to Microsoft SQL Server Reporting Services 2012 there have been many great changes. The landscape of computing itself has changed with a proliferation of devices of various shapes and sizes. As you might have already learned, and I am sure you will learn from reading this book, Reporting Services has changed a lot especially as it relates to integration with SharePoint, another great product from Microsoft.

The initial motivation to write the 2nd edition of *Learning SQL Server 2008 Reporting Services* came from Packt. In my 1st edition, I had bypassed the part related to SharePoint. SharePoint Integration with SQL Server 2012 becoming much more robust leading to some great interactive features motivated me further. I wanted to experience the thrill of investigating what these new features are and communicate it to my readers. Also, Report Builder 3 came after the 1st edition, and the new features that came with it compelled me to write this book.

The style of writing this edition is very similar to the first edition, which my readers enjoyed. This style makes learning a pleasure, removing the drudgery of reading a lot of text before tackling what is essential for the task. The task is made easier because of Microsoft's wizard-based program flow, a keenly honed **Rapid Application Development (RAD)** technology. The content of the book is not just GUI-based, there is enough coding, but is kept to a minimum. All code has been tested and is available for download at the Packt site. The background material, a condensate of Microsoft documentation, is carefully added to each chapter giving it an entry point. Sometimes entire portions of Microsoft documentation has been added to leave out ambiguities. This is then followed by graded hands-on exercises supported by screenshots with concluding remarks highlighting what is learned. In each chapter there are a number of links to material on Microsoft sites (mostly); some of them may be broken by the time the reader may reach out, however these links are meant mostly for those who seek information beyond the book to further the understanding of a particular item. I plan to present a list of all links in the book on my blog `http://hodentek.blogspot.com`.

I recommend readers start with *Chapter 1, Overview and Installation – SQL Server Reporting Services 2012*, and follow through. *Chapter 1, Overview and Installation – SQL Server Reporting Services 2012*, is mandatory as the book depends on the environment created in in this chapter. In *Chapter 2, SQL Server Reporting Services 2012 Projects with Visual Studio 2012*, the report viewer controlling both desktop and web applications will be described with examples. *Chapter 3, Overview of SQL Server Reporting Services 2012 Architecture, Features, and Tools*, is a summary of available documentation regarding architecture and features. *Chapter 4, Working with Report Manager*, describes the various tasks you can perform with Report Manager. In *Chapter 5, Working with Report Builder 3.0* (also part of *Chapter 10, Applications Accessing Report Servers*) you will work with Report Builder 3.0 and the new gadgets. *Chapter 6, Power View and Reporting Services*, is entirely devoted to Power View, new and interesting in SQL Server 2012, and so is *Chapter 7, Self-Service Data Alerts in SSRS 2012*, on Self-Service Data Alerts, both of which launched from the SharePoint Site. A large number of programming tools are presented in *Chapter 8, Reporting Services and Programming*, with a brief introduction to Power Shell in as much detail as it is essential for configuring SharePoint Reporting Services service. *Chapter 9, Windows Azure SQL Reporting*, describes fully the way to get acquainted with the new Windows Azure SQL Reporting. Three applications accessing Report Servers are described in *Chapter 10, Applications Accessing Report Servers*, which in addition to those in the first edition completes the picture.

I am not new to reporting software and I have seen and worked with many. I believe that Microsoft SQL Server Reporting Services is one of the best as it delivers what is promised. Microsoft has tested and tried the various components that go into Reporting Services over many years to make this happen such as Windows, .NET Framework from v1.1 to v4.5, Microsoft SQL Server, Windows Azure, Microsoft SharePoint, and Silverlight to mention only a few and I have a feeling that I might have left out many others. Microsoft documentation has the last word and I would recommend readers to access the MSDN/TECHNET forums and the Microsoft Connect site to further their learning experience.

Writing this book was somewhat of a challenge. Windows 7 platform is not a recommended platform for SharePoint. Installing and configuring SharePoint on a Windows 7 platform was not easy. Two malware attacks during the writing period made it lot worse. My educational and research background over 25 years in academia has helped me a lot in delivering a book whose sole purpose is to take a reader with little initial background to be productive in a relatively short time. I do sincerely hope this has been achieved and that readers enjoy this book as much as I have enjoyed writing it.

Preface

Editors and reviewers have contributed a great deal of time and effort both technically and otherwise to make this book possible. One could say, editors write the book. However, I hold myself totally responsible for any errors and omissions. I will be looking forward to hearing from my readers to share with me their learning experience.

What this book covers

Chapter 1, Overview and Installation – SQL Server Reporting Services 2012, provides step-by-step instructions supported by detailed screenshots for installing/configuring SQL Server 2012 Enterprise in Native and SharePoint Integrated mode, configuring Reporting Services 2012 in Native mode, installing sample databases used in the book, guidance to install SharePoint 2010 on Windows 7, and installing Reporting Services 2012 in SharePoint Integrated mode.

Chapter 2, SQL Server Reporting Services 2012 Projects with Visual Studio 2012, gives details about Microsoft Business Intelligence projects, including an introduction to **SQL Server Data Tools (SSDT)**, creating BI projects in SSDT, creating reports using SSDT, and creating reports using Visual Studio suite.

Chapter 3, Overview of SQL Server Reporting Services 2012 Architecture, Features, and Tools, provides readers a summary of Microsoft documentation related to SSRS 2012 regarding structural design of the environment, architecture of Native mode and SharePoint Integrated mode of Reporting Services, Reporting Services Configuration, and salient features of Reporting Services 2012. The reader will learn to work with Reporting Services operational features and configuration files.

Chapter 4, Working with Report Manager, describes how to work with Report Manager and administer the Report Server. Specifically the reader will learn all aspects of reports that include management, viewing, security, and permission for reports. The reader will also learn scheduling and delivery of reports, uploading/downloading reports/resources, creating data models, and so on, which are all described with examples.

Chapter 5, Working with Report Builder 3.0, describes all aspects of Report Builder 3.0 with examples. Readers will learn to author reports using this one-stop tool for Reporting Services. In the process the reader will learn to access Native/SharePoint mode Report Servers; author different types of reports, including embedded and shared data sources, column grouping and document maps, subreports, drill-down/drill-through reports, linked reports, reports based on XML data; and the use of additional visual analytic gadgets/features not described in the first edition such as maps, data bars, sparklines, and report parts.

Preface

Chapter 6, Power View and Reporting Services, describes Power View as a new feature in SSRS 2012 that does ad-hoc reporting accessible to all levels of expertise in the business from data analysts to business decision makers, but depends on a model built using SSAS (or PowerPivot). Readers will install SQL Server 2012 instance to support Tabular Model, create model/models using **SQL Server Analysis Services (SSAS)**, and use the model to create data source in SharePoint site that has a Reporting Services service running. Readers will create Power View reports using this data source and experience a full dose of interactivity and fun.

Chapter 7, Self-Service Data Alerts in SSRS 2012, describes another new feature of SSRS 2012 when implemented in SharePoint Integrated mode that helps with monitoring data changes on a report, very useful for any proactive organization. Readers will learn details of Data Alert workflow and learn how to use the interfaces in SharePoint. Reader will also learn details of Data Alerts including Data Alert designers and Data Alert managers.

Chapter 8, Reporting Services and Programming, describes several programming and interfaces used with SSRS 2012 that include URL Access, Report Viewer Controls, Reporting Services Web Services APIs, PowerShell support for Native and SharePoint Integrated mode implementation, Windows management instrumentation, Reporting Services utilities, and incorporating custom code in reports that are described with working examples.

Chapter 9, Windows Azure SQL Reporting, describes Windows Azure SQL Reporting as Microsoft Reporting Services in the cloud. The readers will learn how to begin using Windows Azure SQL Reporting Services and create reports using SSDT and deploy them to Azure SQL Reporting Services. In doing so, readers will learn to work with Windows Azure Portal, Windows Azure SQL Databases, and viewing reports on the cloud-based Report Server. All aspects of creating, viewing, and managing reports are discussed.

Chapter 10, Applications Accessing Report Servers, describes working through three examples of accessing Report Servers via applications. In the first, SQL Server Integration Services access the Report Server using a Web Service task; in the second, a Windows Foundation Project accesses Report Servers, both native and SharePoint Integrated mode using an embedded web browser control and in the third, SharePoint web parts are used to access a Native mode Report Server.

Appendix, Reference, provides useful references that have been used in the book. You can download this appendix from `http://www.packtpub.com/sites/default/files/downloads/9922EN_Appendix_References.pdf`.

What you need for this book

You need the following:

- Windows 7 64-bit (Ultimate edition is used in the book) computer (laptop was used) that meets the specifications described in *Chapter 1, Overview and Installation – SQL Server Reporting Services 2012* (note 32-bit will not do).
- SQL Server 2012 Enterprise Edition (evaluation edition will do).
- SharePoint 2010 Enterprise (evaluation edition will do). Note that the reader may have to install multiple instances of SQL Server 2012.
- Access to Northwind, AdventureWorks Databases available from CodePlex sites described in *Chapter 1, Overview and Installation – SQL Server Reporting Services 2012*.
- IIS 7.5 Version (a part of Windows 7 installation).
- IE 9.0 browser or the version specified in *Chapter 1, Overview and Installation – SQL Server Reporting Services 2012*.
- Visual Studio 2010 or 2012 Ultimate (evaluation edition will do).

Who this book is for

This book is for anyone who is new to SQL Server 2012 Reporting Services and needs to create and deploy/publish reports. This book will be useful for authors creating/administering reports for Native as well as SharePoint Integrated mode implementations. Report Server DBAs will greatly benefit by the administrative topics discussed in the book. This book is suitable for autodidacts, computer programming trainers, report developers, data analysts, and non-programmer type decision makers.

A basic but not necessarily specialist knowledge of SQL Server is assumed. Basic working knowledge of SharePoint will be very helpful.

Conventions

In this book, you will find a number of styles of text that distinguish between different kinds of information. Here are some examples of these styles, and an explanation of their meaning.

Preface

Code words in text, database table names, folder names, filenames, file extensions, pathnames, dummy URLs, user input, and Twitter handles are shown as follows: "Double-click on the `SQLFULL_x64_ENU_Install.exe` file, which begins the installation"

A block of code is set as follows:

```
<Service>
  <IsSchedulingService>True</IsSchedulingService>
  <IsNotificationService>True</IsNotificationService>
  <IsEventService>True</IsEventService>
  <PollingInterval>10</PollingInterval>
  <WindowsServiceUseFileShareStorage>False
    </WindowsServiceUseFileShareStorage>
  <MemorySafetyMargin>80</MemorySafetyMargin>
  <MemoryThreshold>90</MemoryThreshold>
  <RecycleTime>720</RecycleTime>
  <MaxAppDomainUnloadTime>30</MaxAppDomainUnloadTime>
  <MaxQueueThreads>0</MaxQueueThreads>
  <UrlRoot>
  </UrlRoot>
  <UnattendedExecutionAccount>
    <UserName></UserName>
    <Password></Password>
    <Domain></Domain>
  </UnattendedExecutionAccount>
  <PolicyLevel>rssrvpolicy.config</PolicyLevel>
  <IsWebServiceEnabled>True</IsWebServiceEnabled>
  <IsReportManagerEnabled>True</IsReportManagerEnabled>
  <FileShareStorageLocation>
    <Path>
    </Path>
  </FileShareStorageLocation>
</Service>
```

New terms and **important words** are shown in bold. Words that you see on the screen, in menus or dialog boxes for example, appear in the text like this: "clicking the **Next** button moves you to the next screen".

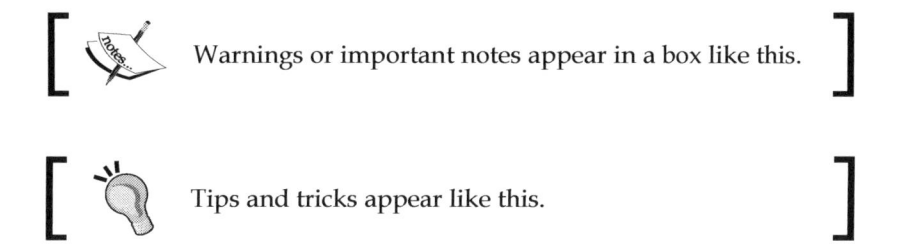

> Warnings or important notes appear in a box like this.

> Tips and tricks appear like this.

Reader feedback

Feedback from our readers is always welcome. Let us know what you think about this book—what you liked or may have disliked. Reader feedback is important for us to develop titles that you really get the most out of.

To send us general feedback, simply send an e-mail to feedback@packtpub.com, and mention the book title via the subject of your message.

If there is a topic that you have expertise in and you are interested in either writing or contributing to a book, see our author guide on www.packtpub.com/authors.

Customer support

Now that you are the proud owner of a Packt book, we have a number of things to help you to get the most from your purchase.

Downloading the example code

You can download the example code files for all Packt books you have purchased from your account at http://www.packtpub.com. If you purchased this book elsewhere, you can visit http://www.packtpub.com/support and register to have the files e-mailed directly to you.

Errata

Although we have taken every care to ensure the accuracy of our content, mistakes do happen. If you find a mistake in one of our books—maybe a mistake in the text or the code—we would be grateful if you would report this to us. By doing so, you can save other readers from frustration and help us improve subsequent versions of this book. If you find any errata, please report them by visiting http://www.packtpub.com/submit-errata, selecting your book, clicking on the **errata submission form** link, and entering the details of your errata. Once your errata are verified, your submission will be accepted and the errata will be uploaded on our website, or added to any list of existing errata, under the Errata section of that title. Any existing errata can be viewed by selecting your title from http://www.packtpub.com/support.

Piracy

Piracy of copyright material on the Internet is an ongoing problem across all media. At Packt, we take the protection of our copyright and licenses very seriously. If you come across any illegal copies of our works, in any form, on the Internet, please provide us with the location address or website name immediately so that we can pursue a remedy.

Please contact us at copyright@packtpub.com with a link to the suspected pirated material.

We appreciate your help in protecting our authors, and our ability to bring you valuable content.

Questions

You can contact us at questions@packtpub.com if you are having a problem with any aspect of the book, and we will do our best to address it.

1
Overview and Installation – SQL Server Reporting Services 2012

In this chapter, an overview of Reporting Services 2012 is presented, highlighting the latest enhancements to SQL Server Reporting Services. This chapter is really about setting up the reader with the necessary installations so that he/she can follow the contents of the book. We will install the following applications/software in this chapter and a few others in the other chapters, where they are required:

- SQL Server 2012 with Reporting Services in Native Mode
- Configuring the Reporting Services using Reporting Services Configuration Manager
- Sample databases used in the book
- Guidance to install SharePoint Server 2010 on Windows 7 operating system
- Reporting Services 2012 in SharePoint Integrated mode

A description of the computer used in the preparation of this book is also given.

SQL Server 2012 – mission statement by Microsoft

The amount of information available on SQL Server 2012 is very large, so we will not be looking at the several groundbreaking developments in this area. Just browsing for SQL Server 2012 brings 10 to 50 million pages on an Internet search.

The highlights of SQL Server 2012 as perceived by Microsoft highlights these three major aspects (all in Microsoft's own words). It may be mentioned that SQL Server 2012 is a major revision of SQL Server 2008:

- Mission-critical confidence with greater uptime, blazing-fast performance, and enhanced security features for mission-critical workloads:
    - Enhancements to audit and security and manageability for compliance with PC and HIPAA
    - Use of the **AlwaysOn** feature to build for high availability and disaster recovery
    - New T-SQL enhancements with best practices
    - New tool, known as the **Distributed Replay**, to test real application loads for mission-critical scenarios
    - Faster failover support with enhanced **AlwaysOn Failover Cluster** instances, making improvements to high availability service level agreement and performance
    - Active secondary option in high availability to offload reporting, and logging tasks to improved use of resources
    - Enhancements to the extended events infrastructure provide a deep insight to events using the events engine and the `XEvents` management namespace

- Breakthrough insight with managed, self-service data exploration and stunning interactive data visualizations capabilities
    - Ad-hoc exploration and interactive presentation of data using the business intelligence semantic model
    - Expanding the reach to data by non-programmer business users
    - Self-servicing data-driven alerts
    - Effortless visualization of data in myriad ways by mere clicks of a mouse with power views

- Cloud on your own terms by enabling the creation and extension of solutions across on-premises and public Cloud
    - The extension of Windows Azure Services to Reporting Services
    - Use of tools such as SQL Server SysPrep, Microsoft Assessment and Planning, the Hyper-V virtualization of SQL Server, and Self Service Portals.
    - Hybrid public and private Cloud to contend with security concerns

Overview of Reporting Services 2012

SQL Server Reporting Services (SSRS) has changed by a quantum leap from its 2000 version. From 2000 to 2012, it has gone through 2005, 2008, and 2008 R2 versions of SQL Server. It is not attempted to describe here all the changes that have taken place in details, as it would take volumes, but to highlight the major ones that have changed since the first edition of this book in 2008.

Visual Studio **Business Intelligence (BI)** has changed over to **SQL Server Data Tools (SSDT)**, wherein the Visual Studio Shell is endowed with only BI project templates that are installed with SQL Server 2012. This translates to not needing a separate license for Visual Studio in order to create BI projects. Visual Studio 2012 (for example, the Ultimate edition) does not have templates of BI projects, but is used to create reports using Report Viewer Controls. This said, if you have both SQL Server 2012 and Visual Studio 2012, you will find the templates for BI projects in Visual Studio. SSDT installs when you install SQL Server 2012.

Major enhancements in SSRS 2012 are, taking ad-hoc reporting to the next level of experience, by leveraging the **Business Intelligence Semantic Model (BISM)** and tying it up with SharePoint Server to render, by the now famous, Power Views, and **Data Alerts**. **Power View** reports can be exported to PowerPoint maintaining the interactive features while connected to SharePoint Server, adding an extra dimension of interest to the stake holders.

The server-based SSRS in the SQL Server 2012 platform provides the following enhancements:

- Comprehensive reporting functionality, including the services of SharePoint
- Data acquisition from a variety of data sources
- A complete set of tools for reports from creation to delivery
- APIs that help developers to integrate and/or extend custom reporting
- Complete integration with Microsoft Visual Studio and SharePoint Server environments
- In practical terms one can create interactive, tabular, graphical or free-form reports from relational, multidimensional, or XML data sources
- Rich data visualization of data from the preceding sources is possible, including charts, sparkline, data bars, and maps
- Publish immediately, or schedule reports, or access reports on-demand
- Support for several report view formats—capability of exporting to Excel and subscribing to published reports are possible

- Reports can be accessed over the Web or from a SharePoint site
- Data alert feature when used with reports published to SharePoint can send e-mail alerts

Data extensions built in SQL Server 2012 can work with the data sources shown, and with OLE DB and ODBC included; many other sources can be accessed as well:

- Microsoft SQL Server
- Microsoft SharePoint List
- Windows Azure SQL Database
- Microsoft SQL Server Parallel Data Warehouse
- OLE DB
- Oracle
- SAP NetWeaver BI
- Hyperion Essbase
- Teradata
- XML
- ODBC

Ad-hoc reporting gained popularity as it made it possible for non-programmer type, but business-wise information workers to create reports critical to the business. In SQL Server 2008, the Report Model Projects provided the underpinning data for creating ad-hoc reports using the Report Builder.

In SQL Server 2012, Microsoft took ad-hoc reporting to the next level in RS 2012, by creating the BISM as the core for all BI under Microsoft's umbrella. Ad-hoc reporting uses the BISM as its backbone, and uses it very effectively in creating Power View Reports in SharePoint. At the time of writing, there are two ways Power View reports can be authored—through the SharePoint with Reporting Services add-in using the BISM created with SQL Server Analysis Services, or through the Power Pivot add-in using Excel. In either case, Power View is not a substitute if one is after very complex queries on the underlying archived data, but for creating a quick and astonishingly flexible report connected to live data.

One of the biggest features new in SQL Server 2012 is Power View. Power View a browser based with Silverlight working in the background, addressing interactive data exploration and visualization features capable of presenting multiple views of data in a single report.

Although originally Power View relied on models created by what are called Analysis Services Tabular Models, Microsoft has quickly extended it to even multi-dimensional models, which are still in the Community Technology Preview stage. We will create tabular models, and using the Share Point site learn the basics of creating the Power View. In *Chapter 6, Power View and Reporting Services*, we will learn how to go about creating the model and using it to create Power Views.

Besides Power View for interactive data exploration, self-service Data Alerts is another important feature, which came about in SQL Server 2012. Data Alerts are alerts set up by users in a SharePoint site to alert (a third party) about changes that have occurred to a data in a report. This feature provides a pervasive insight to corporate data by being very proactive. The end user can easily configure and manage data-driven alerts by setting up what he/she wants to see and when, with the alert information being delivered by e-mails. In *Chapter 7, Self-Service Data Alerts in SSRS 2012*, the reader will learn about setting up this alert, managing it, and monitoring it.

Report Builder 3.0 is the reporting component of SQL Server 2008 R2 with visualizations such as maps, sparklines, and data bars, which were not a part of Report Builder 2 (introduced in SQL Server 2008). The report part gallery was also introduced in SQL Server 2008 R2 and continues in SQL Server 2012. The report part gallery enables users to re-use the existing parts of a report known as Report Parts, where the author can pick up the report part from the gallery and use it in his new report. Also, enhancements to performance while interacting with servers can be achieved. Bugs fixes are periodically applied, and the latest download of Report Builder 3.0 with SQL Server 2012 SP1 has the bugs of the previous build fixed. The enhancements to Report Builder 3.0 that started with SQL Server 2008 R2 can be summarized as follows:

- Adding maps, sparklines, and indicators to reports
- Rotate text 270 degrees
- Control page breaks
- Create report parts
- Create shared datasets and save them to the Report Server
- New data sources have been added—SharePoint Lists, Microsoft SQL Azure, and SQL Server parallel data warehouse
- Enhanced aggregation and exporting to Excel
- Report-based data feeds
- Feature enhancements specific to SQL Server 2012 in Report Builder 3.0 are Excel and Word Rendering for versions 2007 to 2010, and the recent version 2013 of Microsoft Office Suite

Installing software used in the book

The number of software programs and their modes used in the preparation of this book is large. Although SQL Server 2012 Enterprise Evaluation Edition is the main data engine product used in the book, the Reporting Services Component is installed both in the Native mode as well as in the SharePoint Integrated mode to describe fully the features of **Reporting Services 2012** (hereafter referred to simply as **RS2012**). The Enterprise evaluation edition with an evaluation period of 120 days supports most of the feature sets needed, and therefore used.

In the same vein, the SharePoint 2010 Enterprise Evaluation provides the correct match of SharePoint to describe the two specific features of RS 2012's SharePoint Integrated mode of installation, namely Power View and Data Alerts. Another restriction imposed by Power View was that it required a tabular data model for creating it (although this restriction has been lifted in a recent CTP, not considered in this book), which required the installation of SQL Server Analysis Services to support generating a tabular model using SSDT.

In this chapter we will look at the following:

- SQL Server 2012 Enterprise Evaluation database engine (x64-bit) with Reporting Services in Native mode and Analysis Services to support tabular models
- Installing sample databases using scripts
- Installing SharePoint Server 2010 Enterprise Evaluation on Windows 7 Ultimate(x 64-bit)

> Windows 7 is not the recommended OS to install SharePoint Server 2010, but it is, however, allowed by adopting special procedures described in this chapter. However, this installation is not production worthy, and can only be used for testing such as what is contemplated here.

- Installing SQL Server instance with Reporting Services 2012 in SharePoint Integrated mode

In summary, the main criterion was to create an environment to enable the reader to create Power View reports and explore other such features of Reporting Services 2012. Since SharePoint Server 2010 was chosen, the x 64-bit architecture choice was already made as SharePoint 2010 can only be installed on a Windows 7, 64-bit machine. SQL Server 2012 Enterprise was also on 64-bit, and therefore all the software used adopted this basic (x64-bit) architecture.

Chapter 1

Another criterion was the choice of the server editions, which was not too difficult since the Evaluation Enterprise editions support all the needed features and the only one available as a free download.

SQL Server 2012 installation requirements

We will describe the operating system requirements followed by the hardware and software requirements. There are a large number of SQL Server 2012 versions, and they can be installed on a number of Windows operating systems. The list is quite large and some of it is summarized here for the 64-bit version.

Operating system requirements (64-bit)

The following table (copied from the Microsoft documentation) shows the supported OS for the 64-bit version, and there is an even larger set for 32-bit SQL servers.

SQL Server Edition	Windows Operating System 64-bit platform
SQL Server Enterprise 2012	Windows Server 2012, 64-bit Data Center
	Windows Server 2012, 64-bit Standard
	Windows Server 2012, 64-bit Essentials
	Windows Server 2012, 64-bit Foundation
SQL Server Standard 2012	Windows Server 2012 64-bit Data Center
	Windows Server 2012 Standard
	Windows Server 2012 Essentials
	Windows Server 2012 Foundation
	Windows 8 64-bit
	Windows 8 x64-bit Professional
	Windows 7 SP1 64-bit Ultimate
	Windows 7 SP1 64-bit Enterprise
	Windows 7 SP1 64-bit Professional
	Windows Vista x64-bit Ultimate
	Windows Vista x64-bit Enterprise
	Windows Vista x64-bit Business
SQL Server Web 2012	Windows Server 2012 64-bit Datacenter
	Windows Server 2012 64-bit Standard
	Windows Server 2012 64-bit Essentials
	Windows Server 2012 64-bit Foundation

While the preceding table shows only a small subset (x64) of the principle editions of SQL Server, the reader should obtain complete details from Microsoft's MSDN website or the home site for SQL servers.

The edition used in this book is indeed the evaluation edition (as only the evaluation edition is available for free download). In addition to these, Microsoft also has other special and custom editions, the details of which may be found at http://msdn.microsoft.com/en-us/library/ms144275.aspx.

Hardware requirements

The following are the minimum requirements, and depend upon the components installed:

- **Hard disk space requirement**: A minimum of 6 GB is required, out of which more than 1.5 GB is required for client components, excluding the Book on Line and Integration Services tools, and only about 800 MB is required for the database engine.

During installation, the program checks for available space.

- **Data file storage**: Local Disk, Shared Storage, and SMB File Share
- **DVD drive**: This is required if you are planning to install from an ISO image
- **Monitor and pointing device**: Super VGA (800 x 600) or a higher resolution, and a mouse
- **Processor speed**: This should be a minimum of 1.4 GHZ; 2.0 GHZ or higher recommended
- **Memory**: This should be a minimum of 1 GB for 64-bit; 4 GB recommended
- **Processor type for a 64-bit processor**: AMD Opteron, AMD Athlon 64, Intel Xeon with Intel EM64T support, and Intel Pentium IV with EM64T support

Software requirements

Besides the OS described previously, you require the following (if they are not already installed); these will be checked during installation:

- .NET 3.5 SP1 for most of the SQL Server components; it is not installed during SQL Server 2012 installation. NET 4 is required; it will be installed during SQL Server 2012 installation.

- Windows Power Shell 2.0 is required. It is preinstalled for Windows 7 but not for Windows 2008 Server and Windows Vista (http://msdn.microsoft.com/en-us/library/ff637750(v=azure.10).aspx).
- Supported network protocols are TCPIP, shared memory, named pipes, and VIA (deprecated in the future)
- Virtualization is limited to Hyper-V role in Windows servers.
- Browser support includes IE 7.0 or later for Microsoft Management Console, SSDT and Report Designer Component of Reporting Services, and HTML help.
- WOW support is needed for management tools.

Configuring the hardware used for the book

A Toshiba laptop (Satellite P775) is used with the following specifications:

- 8 Core processor (Intel Core i7-2670QM at 2.20 GHZ, RAM (8 GB), 64-bit version
- No pen or touch input
- Clean install of Windows 7 Ultimate 64-bit with the SP1 operating system
- Free disk space of 350 GB with all the needed servers (described in this chapter) installed
- Monitor display having a resolution of 1600 x 900 pixels, a mouse, and a DVD/CD-ROM drive
- The Internet Explorer 9.0 browser

> If you are not sure of how many processor cores are there, follow this link: http://hodentekhelp.blogspot.com/2013/01/how-do-i-find-number-of-cores-in.html.

This configuration meets the requirements for installing the SQL Server 2012 software and running Reporting Services, and SharePoint 2010.

Hands-on exercise 1.1 – installing SQL Server 2012

As the space available is limited, the number of installation screenshots shown is limited. Here, the major steps and some key screenshots, which are new for this version of the product, will be presented.

Downloading the source file

The installation source files for SQL Server 2012 64-bit Enterprise Evaluation can be downloaded from the following URL:

`http://www.microsoft.com/en-us/download/details.aspx?id=29066`

> First, search for `http://www.microsoft.com/en-us/download/default`. Then. search for the servers on that page.

Read the *System requirements* section before downloading the source files. You can download a single ISO file (the first one in the bullet list) or the evaluation CAB file:

- `ENU\SQLFULL_ENU.iso`, 4.2 GB
- `ENU\x64\SQLFULL_x64_ENU_Core.box`, 1.8 GB
- `ENU\x64\SQLFULL_x64_ENU_Install.exe`, 94 KB
- `ENU\x64\SQLFULL_x64_ENU_Lang.box`, 655.8 MB

Installation steps

1. Double-click on the `SQLFULL_x64_ENU_Install.exe` file, which begins the installation. After processing the request, the **SQL Server Installation Center** window will be displayed, as shown in the following screenshot:

Chapter 1

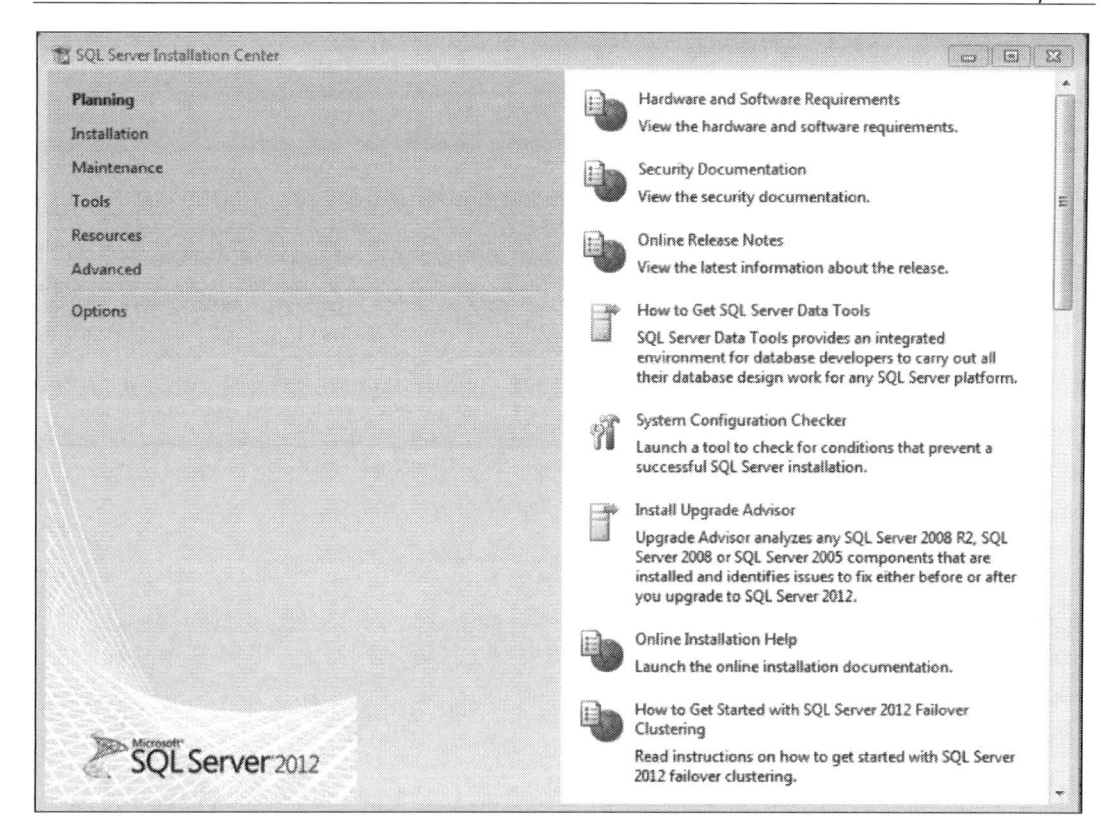

This **Planning** pane of the **Installation** center has many more linked items than displayed. The ones you would see when you scroll down are the following:

- **How to Get Started with a SharePoint Standalone Server Installation**
- **How to Get Started with Reporting Services SharePoint Integration on a Standalone Server**
- **Upgrade documentation**
- **Install SQL Server Migration Assistant (SSMA)**
- **How to apply SQL Server updates**

2. Clicking on **Installation** displays the following window:

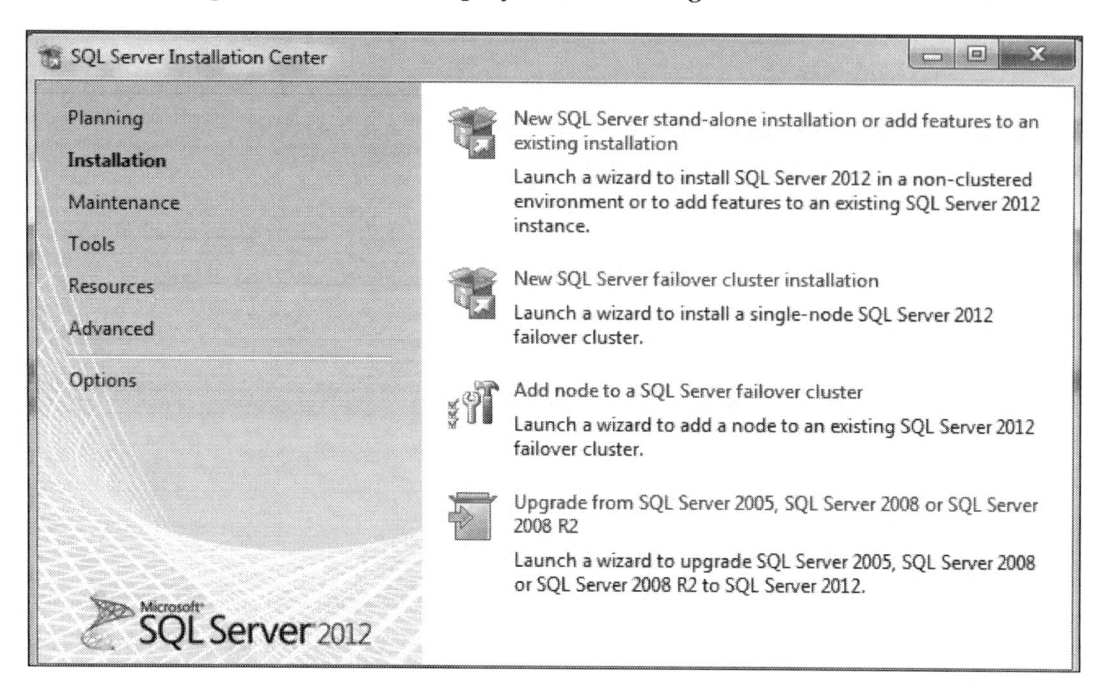

3. As we will be installing a single SQL Server 2012 named `instance`, click on the first option—**New SQL Server stand-alone installation or add features to an existing installation**.
4. In the next screen, you will be asked to specify the architecture of SQL Server 2012 to install and specify the location (where your product files are stored on your computer) of the SQL Server Installation media. There will be two options; choose the radio button for **x64**. You may need to browse to **Installation Media Root Directory**, as shown in the screenshot. The choice of x64-bit was made when a decision was taken to install SharePoint 2010 on the same machine.

[SharePoint 2010 does not install on a 32-bit operating system.]

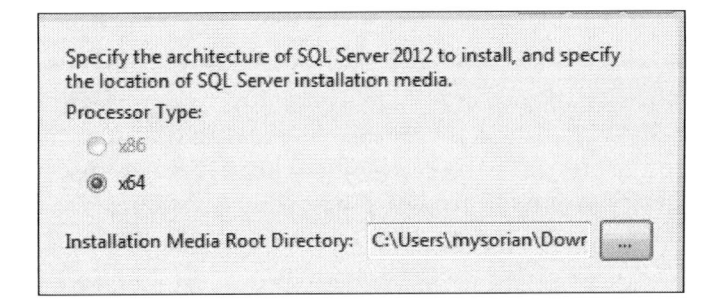

Chapter 1

> Specify the architecture of SQL Server 2012 to install, and specify the location of SQL Server installation media.
>
> Processor Type:
> - ○ x86
> - ⦿ x64
>
> Installation Media Root Directory: C:\Users\mysorian\Dowr [...]

5. In the next **Setup Rules** page problems are identified and flagged. The installation can proceed only after the verification passes all the rules. In the present installation, eight rules were checked. This following screenshot shows a list of rules that passed the verification:

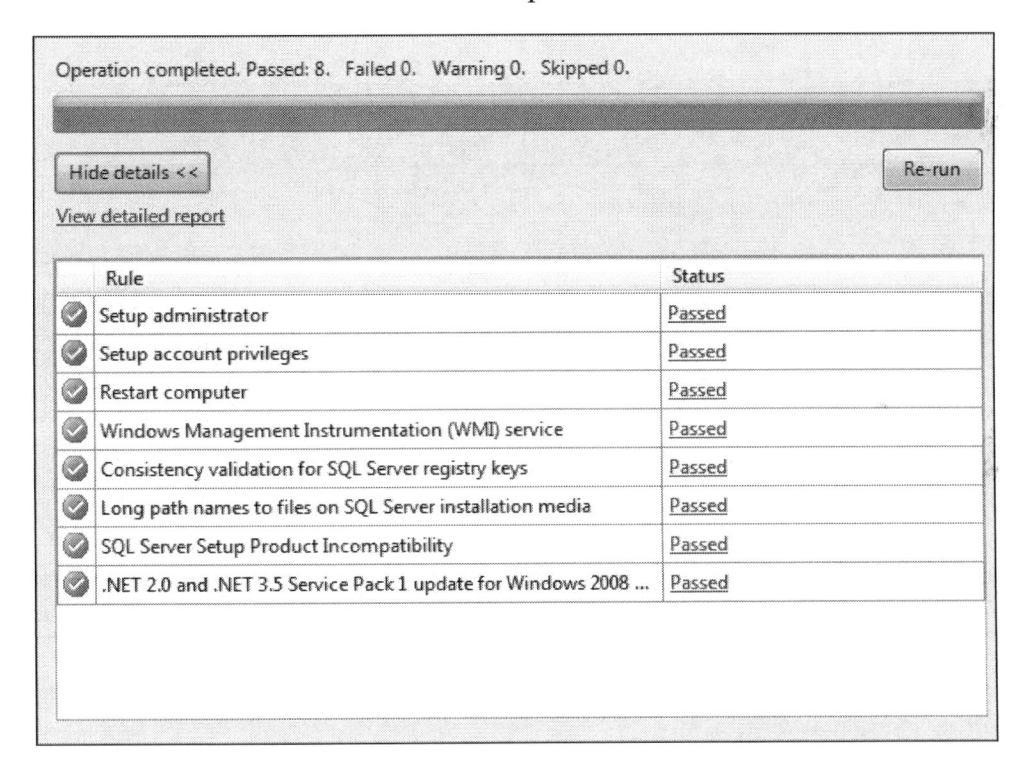

> Operation completed. Passed: 8. Failed 0. Warning 0. Skipped 0.
>
> [Hide details <<]   [Re-run]
> View detailed report
>
> | Rule | Status |
> |---|---|
> | Setup administrator | Passed |
> | Setup account privileges | Passed |
> | Restart computer | Passed |
> | Windows Management Instrumentation (WMI) service | Passed |
> | Consistency validation for SQL Server registry keys | Passed |
> | Long path names to files on SQL Server installation media | Passed |
> | SQL Server Setup Product Incompatibility | Passed |
> | .NET 2.0 and .NET 3.5 Service Pack 1 update for Windows 2008 ... | Passed |

6. Clicking on **OK** takes us to the next **Product Key** page. In this page, you need to choose the edition of SQL Server 2012 to install. There are two options, one of which is for the evaluation edition. This edition expires in 180 days, after which you need a product key. This edition has the largest feature set.

[21]

Overview and Installation – SQL Server Reporting Services 2012

7. Click on **Next**. This will take you to the **License Terms** page, where you place check marks for the two checkboxes to signify that you agree to the terms.

8. Click on **Next**. The **Product Updates** page is displayed with a default to include SQL Server product updates with **KB2674319** in the **More Information** column. You may want to learn about the updates by using the link at the bottom of this window.

> Hitherto using Slip Stream ISO images did not install the SQL Server 2012 SP1 as it was originally designed to, and hence the link was provided to directly install SP1 without the assistance of Slip Stream.

9. Click on **Next**. The **Install Setup Files** page will be displayed. The updates are scanned; the setup files are then downloaded and extracted. The **Setup Support Rules** page identifies problems that may crop up; any failure must be addressed. In the present installation, only one warning is issued, as shown in the following screenshot:

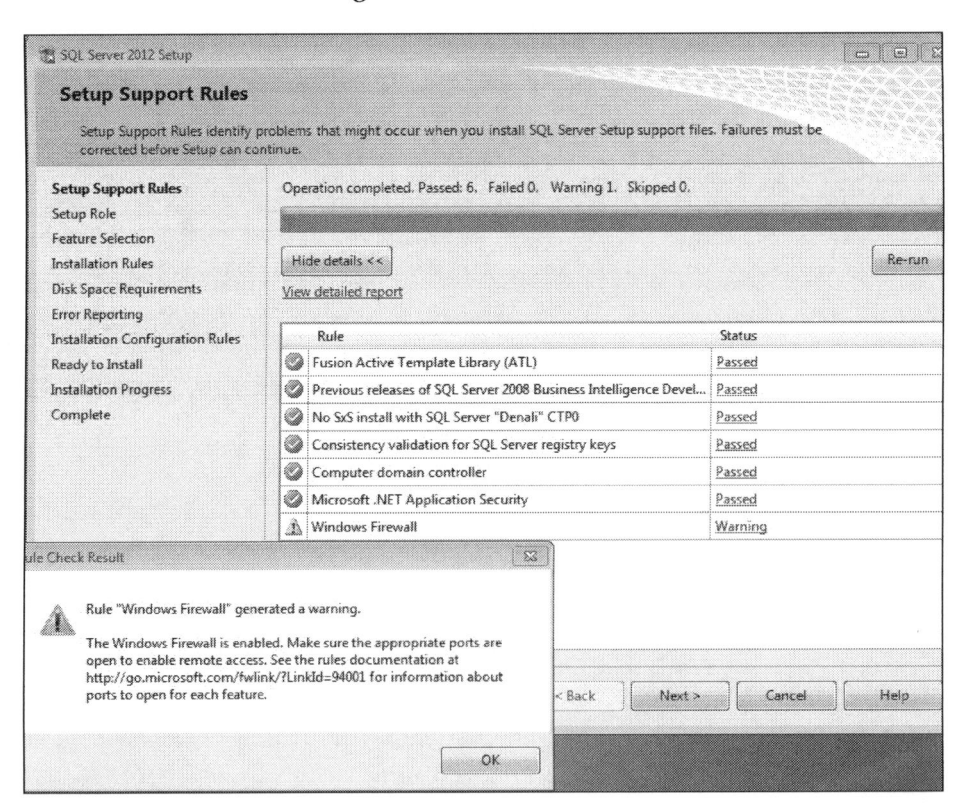

10. Click on **Next**. This brings you to the **Setup Role** page. Please read the information at the top of this page. The next image is a cut-out of the **Setup Role** page. As shown, all the features are chosen to be installed with default values for the service account:

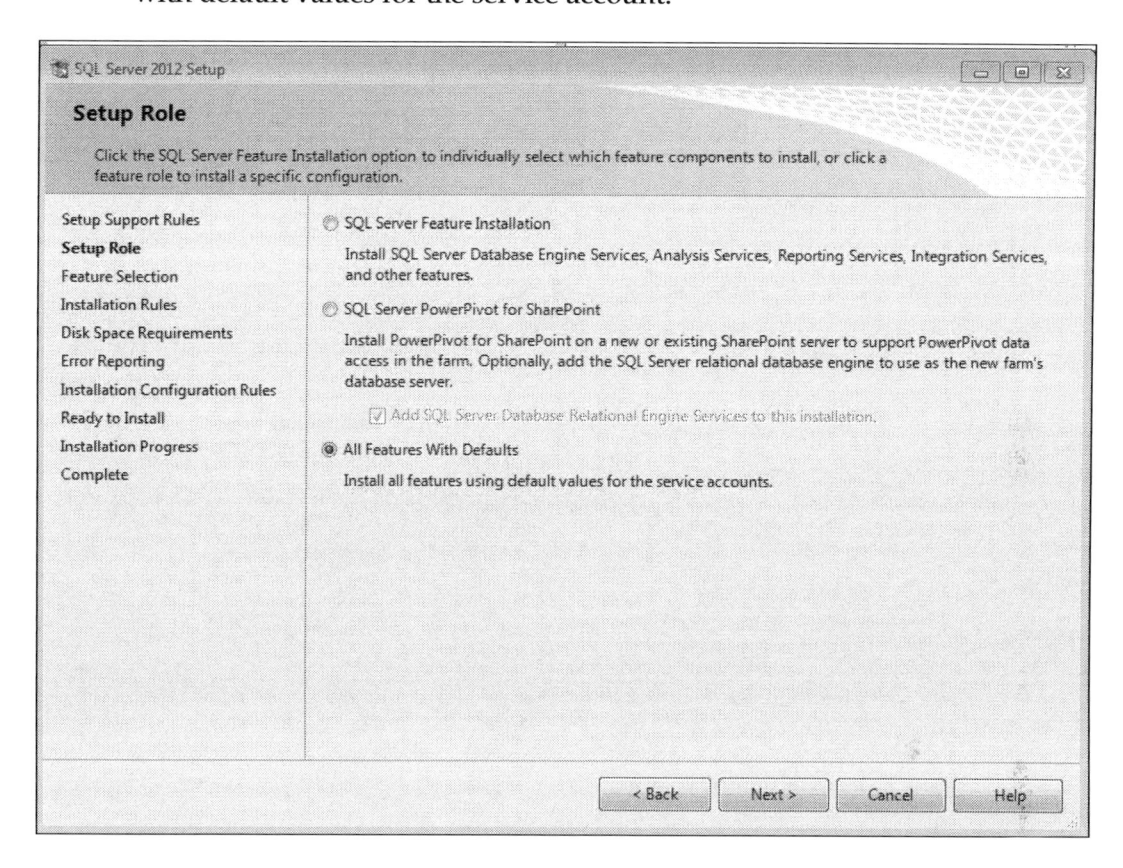

Overview and Installation – SQL Server Reporting Services 2012

11. Click on **Next** at the bottom of the preceding page. The **Feature Selection** page will be displayed. Here, all the features are chosen, as shown in the next screenshot:

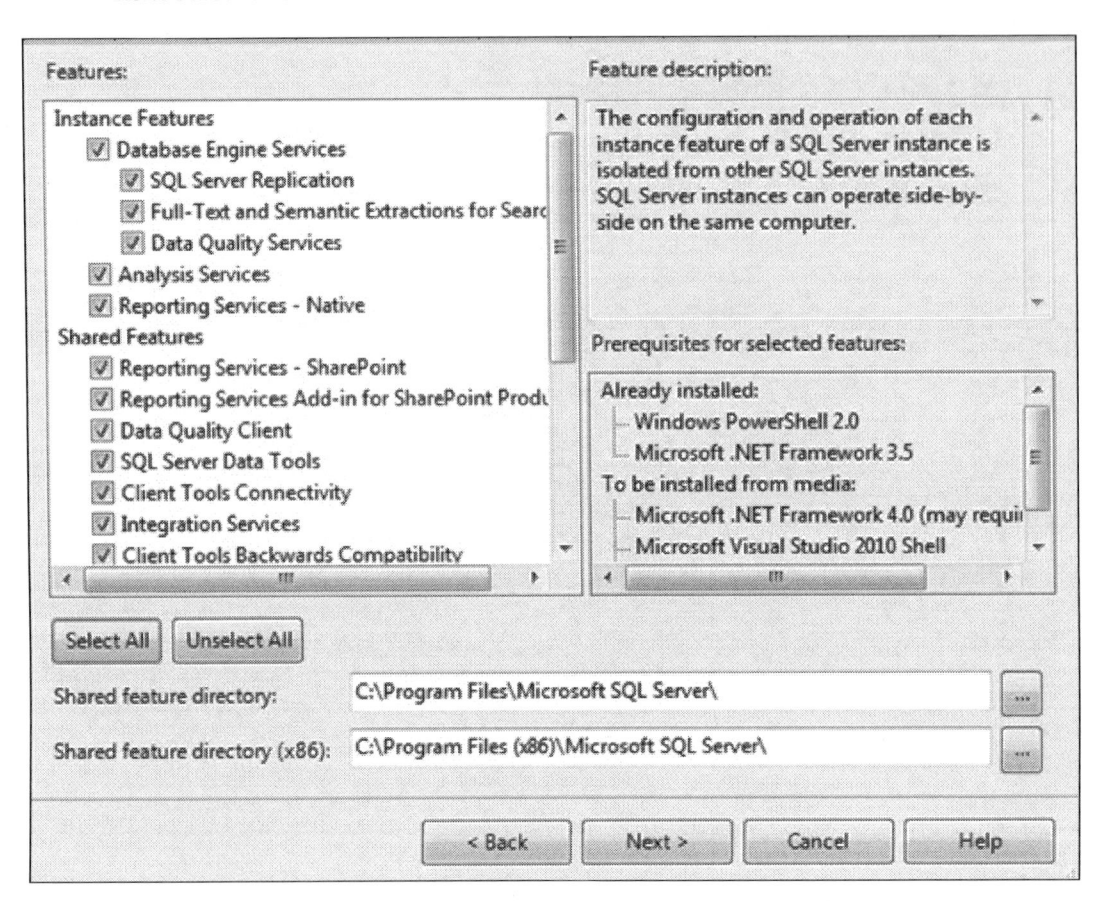

> Although the installation sequence is described here, it is always possible to come back and add features such as Reporting Services and Analysis Services separately. However, there are restrictions, such as you cannot have Native mode and SharePoint Integrated mode with the same SQL Server Instance. You may remove features as well if you want to.

Chapter 1

Note that Reporting Services Native as well as Reporting Services SharePoint and the Reporting Services add-in for SharePoint products are installed as shared features. Please follow this link to the MSDN forum to review the options with SharePoint Integration: `http://technet.microsoft.com/en-us/library/hh213532.aspx`. Also note that more details about the pre-requisites are also shown on the right side of this pane.

12. Click on **Next** at the bottom of the preceding window. The installation rules will be displayed to determine if there are any blocking issues before the product is installed. In the present installation, all the three installation rules were checked without any problem. Here is a cut-out of the screenshot showing the relevant portion. If the test fails, you may fix the failed items and do a re-run. After there are no more issues, the program takes you to the next page.

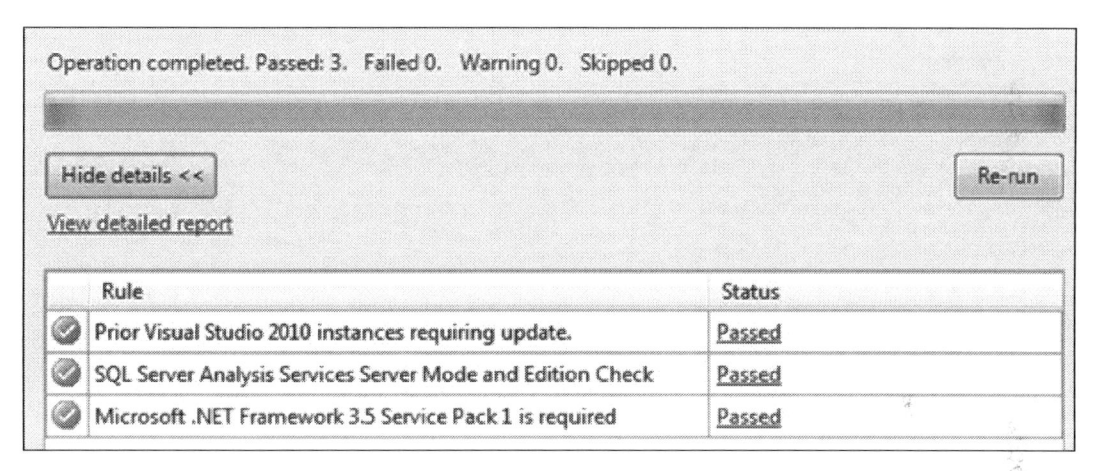

Operation completed. Passed: 3. Failed 0. Warning 0. Skipped 0.

Hide details <<   Re-run

View detailed report

Rule	Status
Prior Visual Studio 2010 instances requiring update.	Passed
SQL Server Analysis Services Server Mode and Edition Check	Passed
Microsoft .NET Framework 3.5 Service Pack 1 is required	Passed

13. Click on **Next**. This brings you to the **Instance Configuration** page. As indicated on the next image, a named instance with the name `Kailua` is chosen. Note that there are no installed instances as yet. Also notice the directories for the SQL Server, Analysis Services, and Reporting Services since we selected all the features earlier. Although it is recommended to install on disks instead of the operating system, herein all software worked off the same machine; in this case a laptop computer.

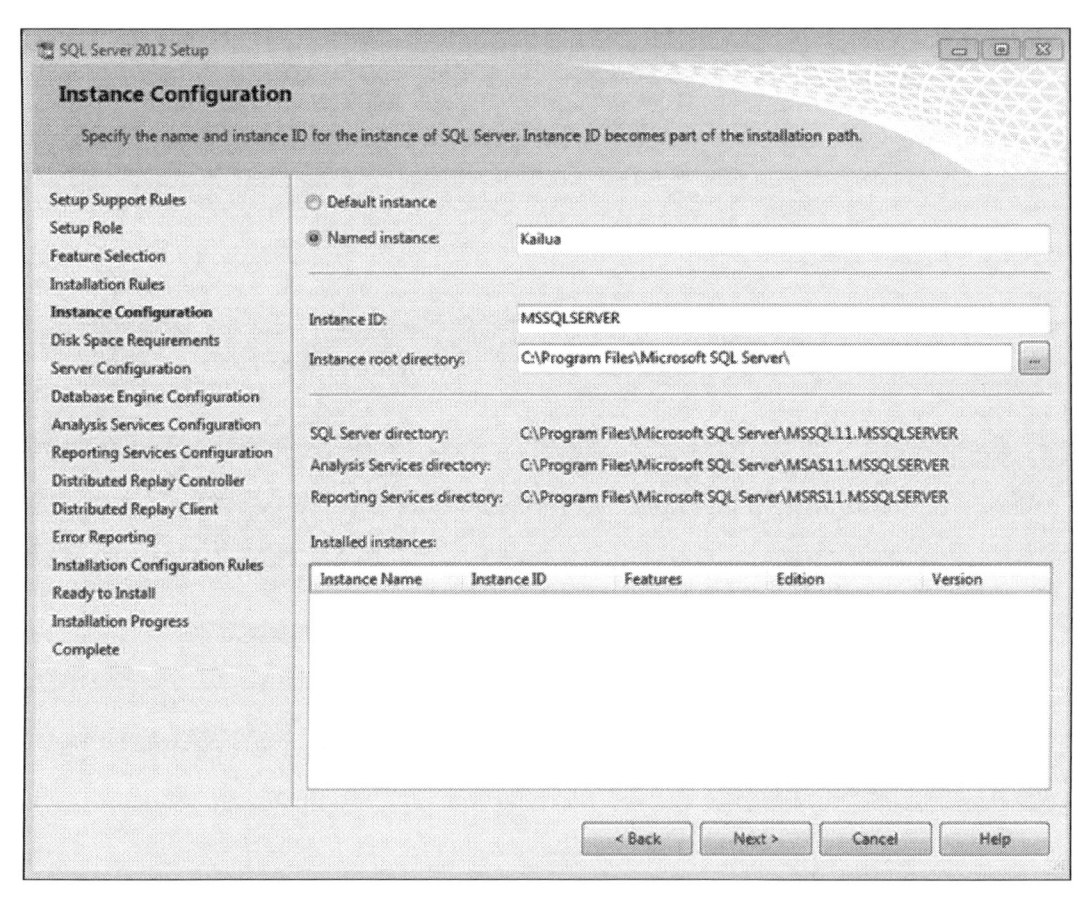

14. Click on **Next**. The **Disk Space Requirements** page will be displayed to verify if space is available for the choices made. The page shows that the program required 8916 MB and the available space was 354,111 MB, which includes (for this particular installation) both the instance directory as well as the shared install directory.

15. Click on **Next**. This brings you to the **Server Configuration** page, as shown, where **Service Accounts** as well as **Collation** are configured. Since we agreed the default values at the beginning, all of the features have the same value for **Account Name**, and a number of them start up automatically. Make a note of the ones that are to start manually:

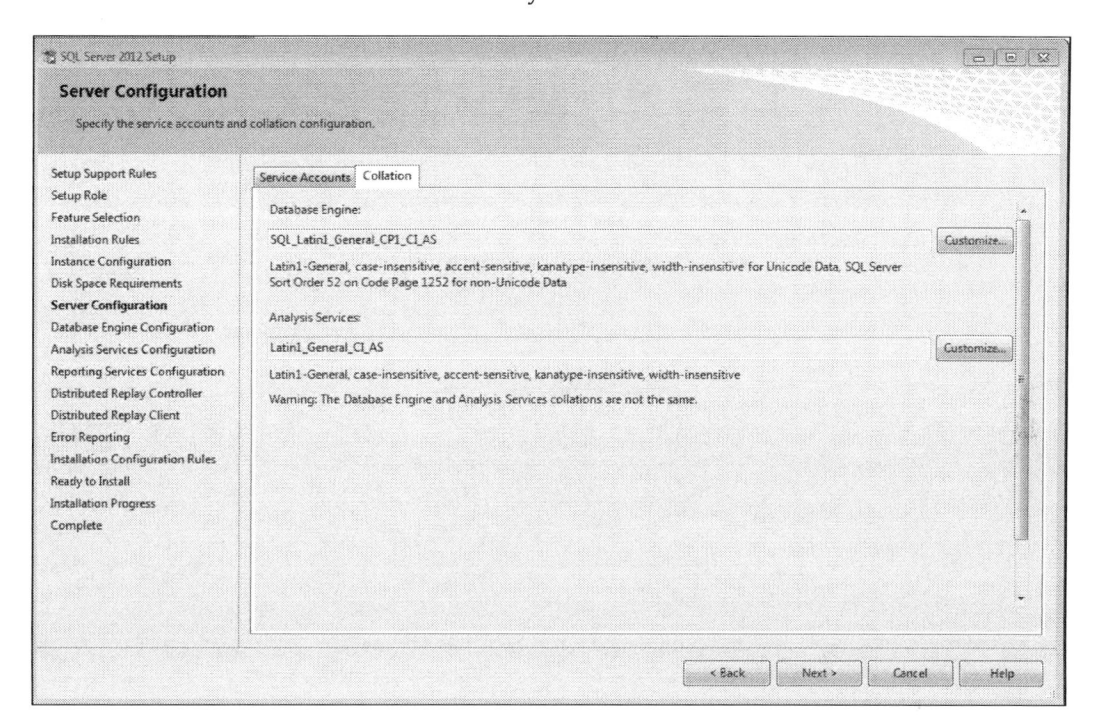

In the **Collation** tabbed page, the default choice is as shown in the cut-out for both SQL Server and the Analysis Server:

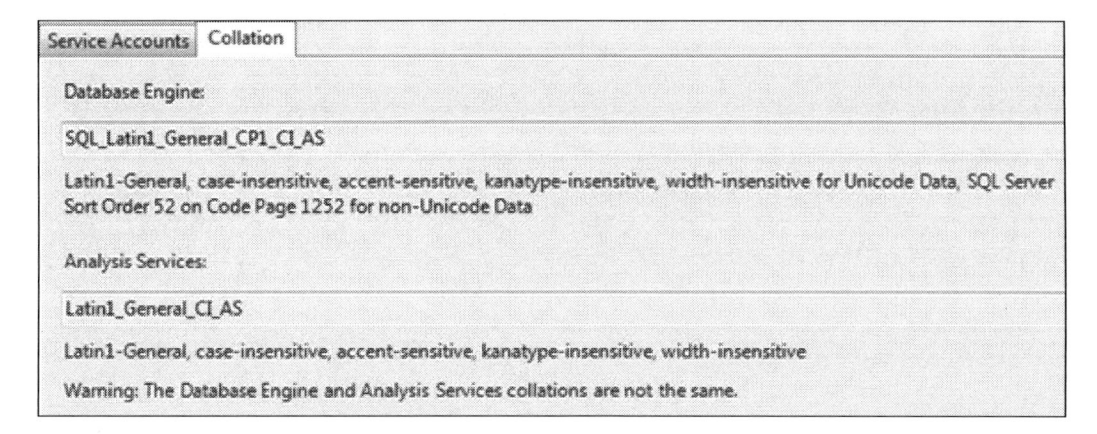

> **Collation** refers to rules governing the proper use of characters to use with different languages (Greek, Russian, Arabic, and so on). Western European languages use `Latin1_General`, which is usually the default. The default collation for US (English) is `SQL_Latin1_General_CP1_CI_AS`.

16. Click on **Next**. This brings you to the **Database Engine Configuration** page. You need to specify the Database Engine authentication, choice of **Data Directories** locations (if other than the defaults), and the choices for **FILESTREAM**. You can also specify SQL Server administrators on this page. Here, the Windows user (in this case, the administrator) will be chosen as the SQL Server administrator and he/she can be added by using **Add Current User** and the interactive windows that show up. The details of this page are as shown in the next image. You can add more than one administrator by repeatedly hitting on the **Add...** button. In the same screen, you can remove an administrator as well:

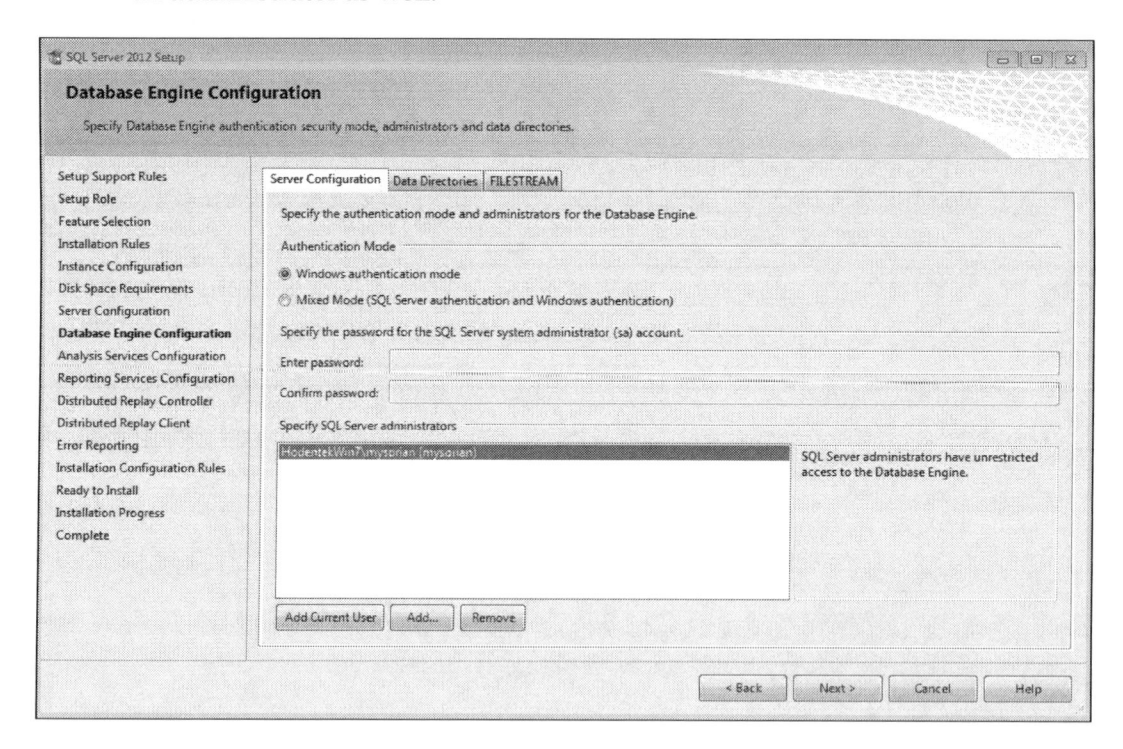

Chapter 1

The default directories were accepted for data, and all the choices on the **FILESTREAM** tabbed page were enabled. As they are not going to be used, you may skip that tabbed page if you like.

17. Click on **Next**. The **Analysis Services Configuration** page will be displayed. Here, instead of the default, **Tabular Mode** was selected, and the current user was added as the administrator, as shown. Again, the default directories were accepted:

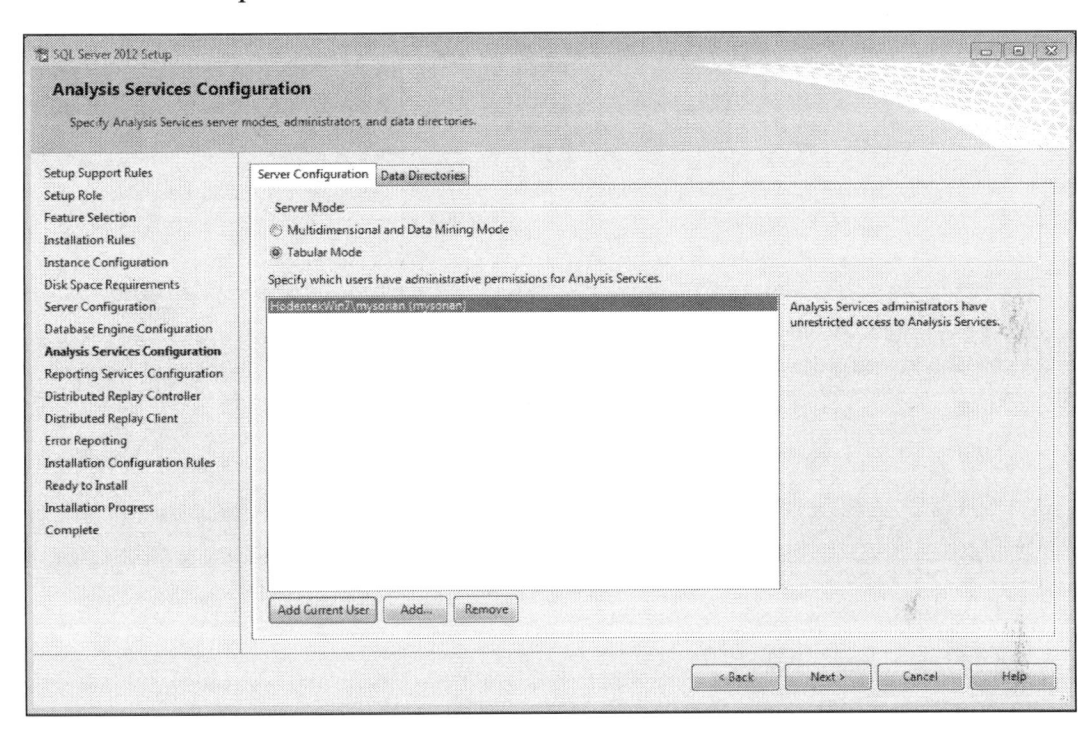

18. Click on **Next**. This takes you to the **Reporting Services Configuration** page shown in the next image. Here, there are two options—**Reporting Services Native Mode** with two options (**Install Only** and **Install and Configure**) and **Reporting Services SharePoint Integrated mode** with the **Install only** option. Here, the **Install and Configure** option in the Native mode is accepted:

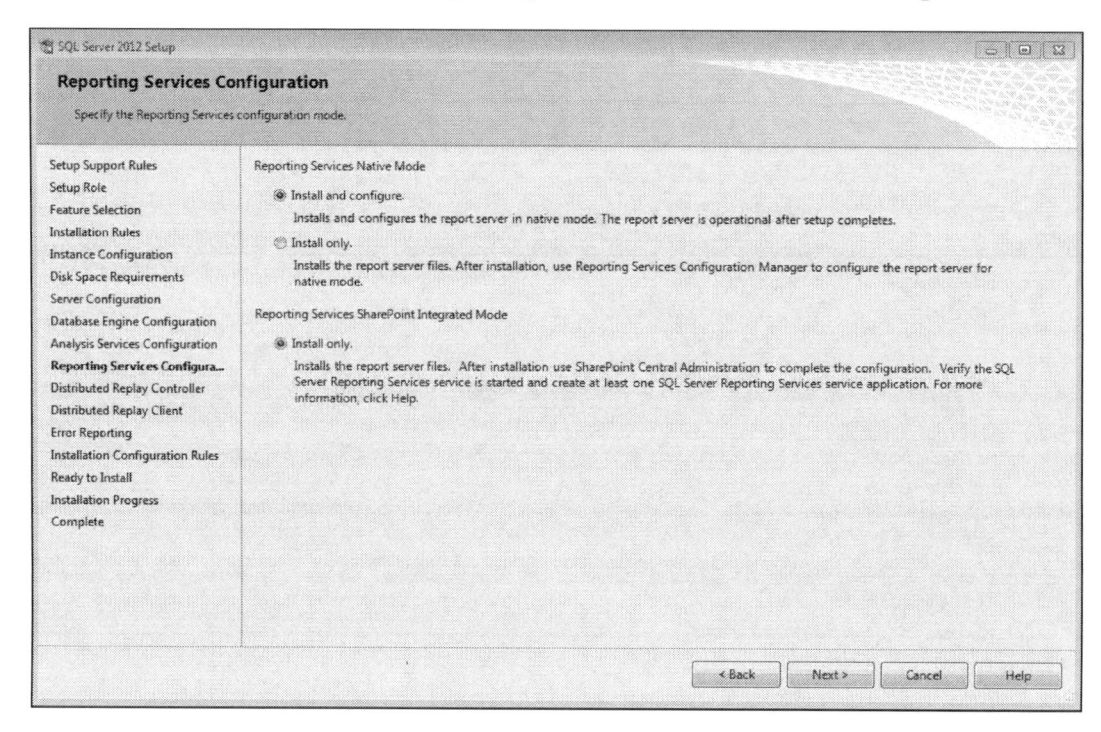

Native mode is chosen in this section, because the chapters immediately following will use the Native mode installation. However, in *Chapter 6, Power View and Reporting Services*, where Power View is discussed, the installation has to be in the SharePoint Integrated mode.

19. Click on **Next**. This brings up the **Distributed Replay Controller** page. The Distributed Replay Controller is very much similar to SQL Profiler, but is more scalable and used in scenarios of upgrades, hardware changes, and so on. Although, for this installation, the current user is added as the user of the preceding service, you may skip it. Follow this link to learn more on this subject: http://msdn.microsoft.com/en-us/library/ff878183(v=SQL.110).aspx. Clicking on **Next** brings up the **Distributed Replay Client** page; you need to specify the value for **Controller Name** and directories, as shown in the following screenshot:

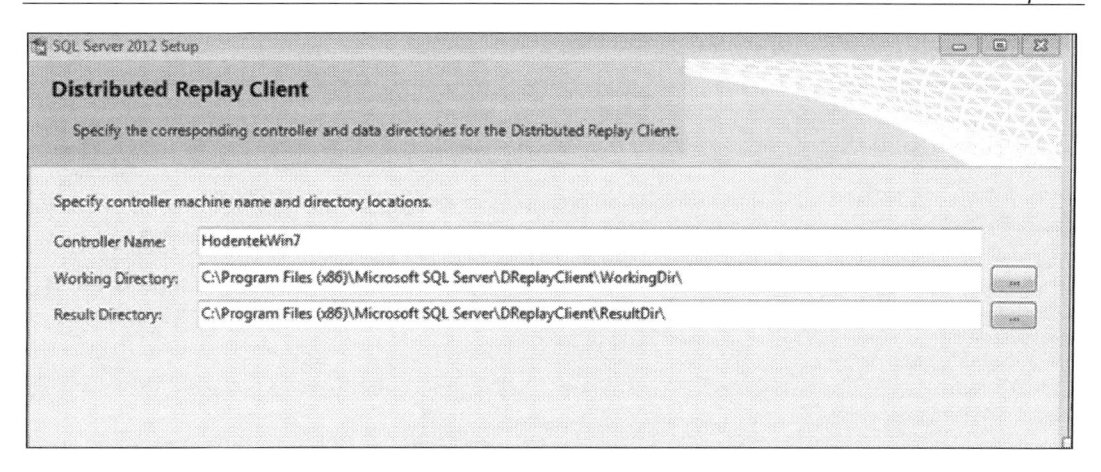

Chapter 1

SQL Server 2012 Setup

Distributed Replay Client

Specify the corresponding controller and data directories for the Distributed Replay Client.

Specify controller machine name and directory locations.

Controller Name:	HodentekWin7
Working Directory:	C:\Program Files (x86)\Microsoft SQL Server\DReplayClient\WorkingDir\
Result Directory:	C:\Program Files (x86)\Microsoft SQL Server\DReplayClient\ResultDir\

20. Click on **Next**. The **Error Reporting** page will be displayed. Accepting this would improve the software and is highly recommended. Click on **Next**.

> The software is in the evaluation period and likely to have problems, and I believe it is better that Microsoft knows about it, since the message will also carry machine-specific information. In a corporate environment, this must be deferred to the discretion of the administration.

The **Installation Configuration rules** page is displayed. This is also a pass/fail and warn page. It is to verify if there are any issues preventing an installation. The lists of rules checked are shown in the following screenshot:

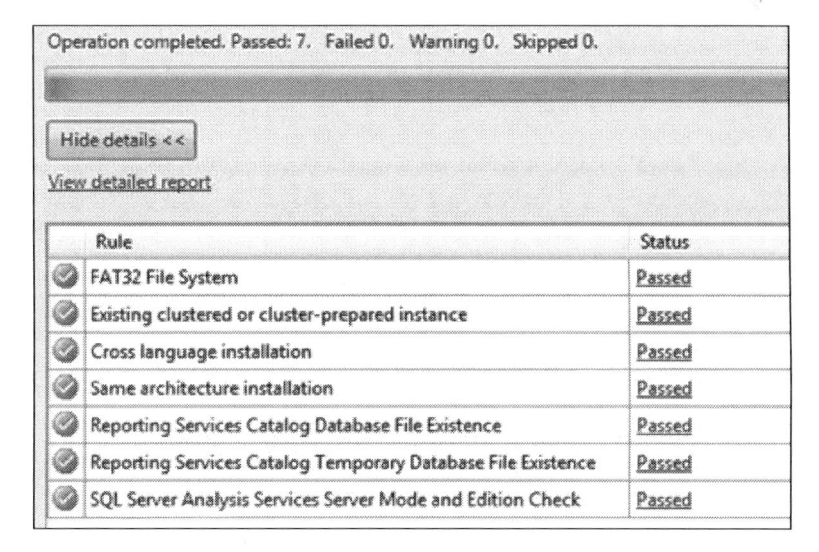

Operation completed. Passed: 7. Failed 0. Warning 0. Skipped 0.

Hide details <<

View detailed report

Rule	Status
FAT32 File System	Passed
Existing clustered or cluster-prepared instance	Passed
Cross language installation	Passed
Same architecture installation	Passed
Reporting Services Catalog Database File Existence	Passed
Reporting Services Catalog Temporary Database File Existence	Passed
SQL Server Analysis Services Server Mode and Edition Check	Passed

[31]

Overview and Installation – SQL Server Reporting Services 2012

21. Clicking on **Next** brings up the **Ready to Install** page, where all the features to be installed are displayed. It is possible to back off by using the **Back** button to go and correct if some modification is needed. Here is the image showing the details of this installation:

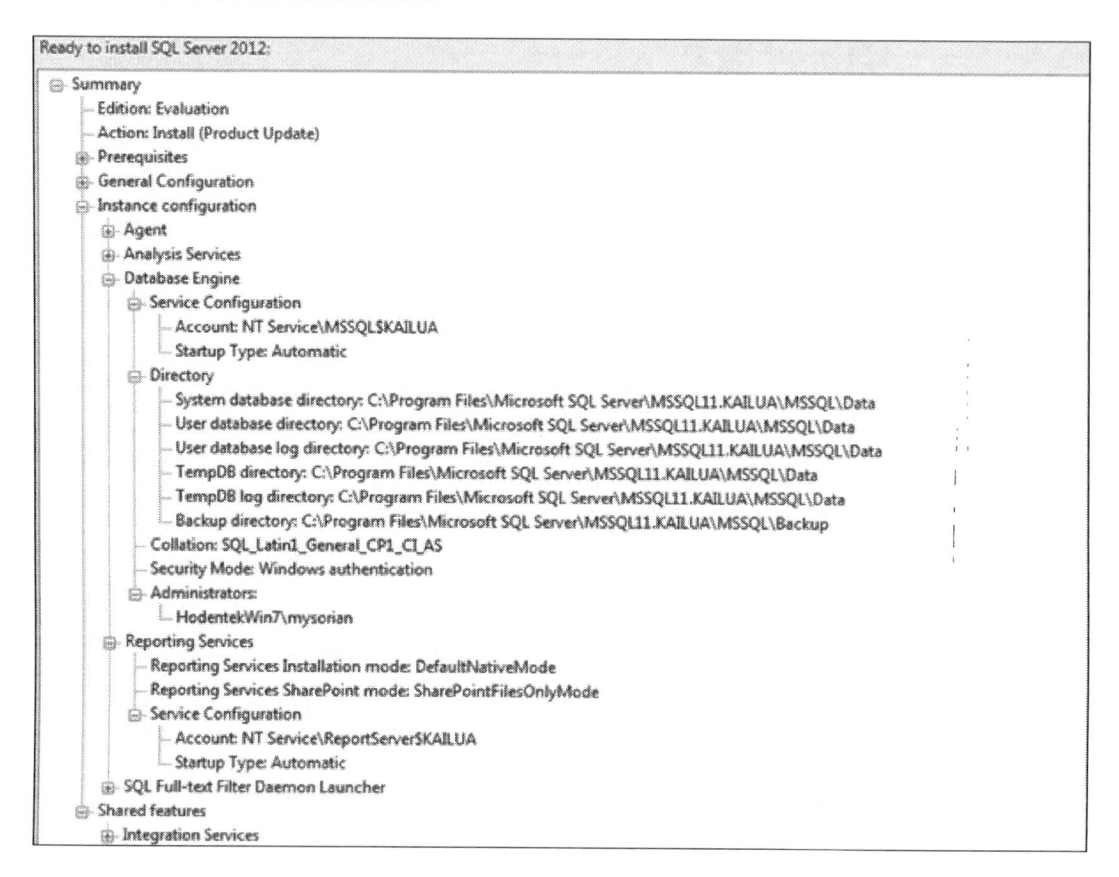

```
Ready to install SQL Server 2012:
└─ Summary
   ├─ Edition: Evaluation
   ├─ Action: Install (Product Update)
   ├─ Prerequisites
   ├─ General Configuration
   ├─ Instance configuration
   │  ├─ Agent
   │  ├─ Analysis Services
   │  ├─ Database Engine
   │  │  ├─ Service Configuration
   │  │  │  ├─ Account: NT Service\MSSQL$KAILUA
   │  │  │  └─ Startup Type: Automatic
   │  │  ├─ Directory
   │  │  │  ├─ System database directory: C:\Program Files\Microsoft SQL Server\MSSQL11.KAILUA\MSSQL\Data
   │  │  │  ├─ User database directory: C:\Program Files\Microsoft SQL Server\MSSQL11.KAILUA\MSSQL\Data
   │  │  │  ├─ User database log directory: C:\Program Files\Microsoft SQL Server\MSSQL11.KAILUA\MSSQL\Data
   │  │  │  ├─ TempDB directory: C:\Program Files\Microsoft SQL Server\MSSQL11.KAILUA\MSSQL\Data
   │  │  │  ├─ TempDB log directory: C:\Program Files\Microsoft SQL Server\MSSQL11.KAILUA\MSSQL\Data
   │  │  │  └─ Backup directory: C:\Program Files\Microsoft SQL Server\MSSQL11.KAILUA\MSSQL\Backup
   │  │  ├─ Collation: SQL_Latin1_General_CP1_CI_AS
   │  │  ├─ Security Mode: Windows authentication
   │  │  └─ Administrators:
   │  │     └─ HodentekWin7\mysorian
   │  ├─ Reporting Services
   │  │  ├─ Reporting Services Installation mode: DefaultNativeMode
   │  │  ├─ Reporting Services SharePoint mode: SharePointFilesOnlyMode
   │  │  └─ Service Configuration
   │  │     ├─ Account: NT Service\ReportServer$KAILUA
   │  │     └─ Startup Type: Automatic
   │  └─ SQL Full-text Filter Daemon Launcher
   └─ Shared features
      └─ Integration Services
```

22. Clicking on **Install** begins the installation showing the installation progress. When it is completed, you should see a **Complete** page showing that the installation succeeded, as shown in the following screenshot. Review the list of what was installed. In the lower-half of this page, some very useful information is provided with links; make sure you pay attention to them:

Chapter 1

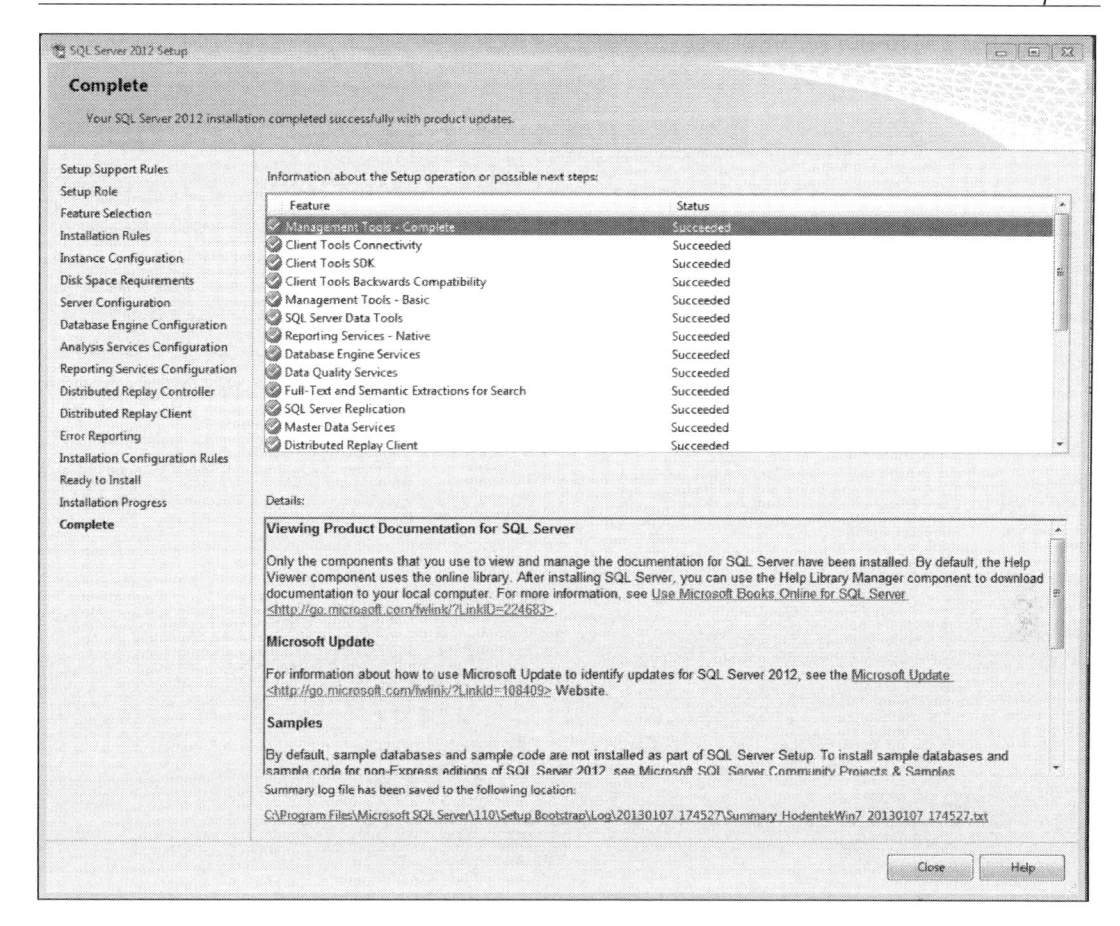

> Although rebooting was not necessary, it is possible that you may have to reboot, especially if you get a message to that effect.

Hands-on exercise 1.2 – verifying the installation

After any installation, it is a good practice to check out if everything that you wanted in the SQL Server is installed. Make yourself familiar with where to look if something did not go well.

Review the following in your computer:

> Note that the **Always On** features are available only when SQL Server 2012 is installed on a Windows server.

1. Verify that the shortcuts are added to **All Programs**, as shown in the following screenshot:

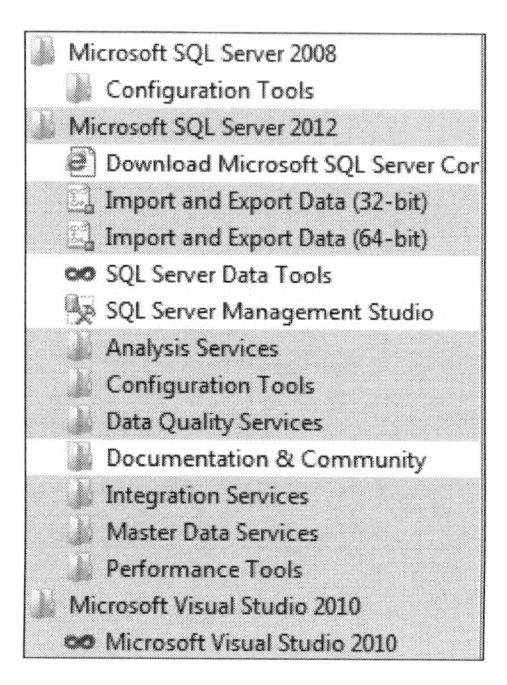

   - Microsoft SQL Server 2008
     - Configuration Tools
   - Microsoft SQL Server 2012
     - Download Microsoft SQL Server Cor
     - Import and Export Data (32-bit)
     - Import and Export Data (64-bit)
     - SQL Server Data Tools
     - SQL Server Management Studio
     - Analysis Services
     - Configuration Tools
     - Data Quality Services
     - Documentation & Community
     - Integration Services
     - Master Data Services
     - Performance Tools
   - Microsoft Visual Studio 2010
     - Microsoft Visual Studio 2010

   Further down in **All Programs**, you will see the following shortcut:

   - Data Quality Client

2. Click on **Start | All Programs | Control Panel | Programs | Programs and Features**. Review the items installed during this installation. The following were installed on this computer:

Chapter 1

Microsoft SQL Server 2012 Management Objects (x64)	Microsoft Corporation	1/7/2013	25.6 MB	11.0.2100.60
Microsoft SQL Server Data Tools – Database Projects ...	Microsoft Corporation	1/7/2013	201 KB	10.3.20116.0
Microsoft System CLR Types for SQL Server 2012 (x64)	Microsoft Corporation	1/7/2013	1.77 MB	11.0.2100.60
Microsoft Visual Studio Tools for Applications x64 Ru...	Microsoft Corporation	1/7/2013	1.15 MB	10.0.40220
Microsoft System CLR Types for SQL Server 2012	Microsoft Corporation	1/7/2013	1.15 MB	11.0.2100.60
Microsoft SQL Server 2012 Policies	Microsoft Corporation	1/7/2013	996 KB	11.0.2100.60
Microsoft SQL Server 2012 Management Objects	Microsoft Corporation	1/7/2013	14.3 MB	11.0.2100.60
Microsoft SQL Server 2012 T-SQL Language Service	Microsoft Corporation	1/7/2013	6.13 MB	11.0.2100.60
Microsoft SQL Server System CLR Types	Microsoft Corporation	1/7/2013	2.53 MB	10.51.2500.0
Microsoft Visual C++ 2008 Redistributable - x86 9.0.3...	Microsoft Corporation	1/7/2013	599 KB	9.0.30729.4974
Microsoft SQL Server 2008 Setup Support Files	Microsoft Corporation	1/7/2013	39.4 MB	10.1.2731.0
Adobe Reader XI	Adobe Systems Incorporated	1/7/2013	120 MB	11.0.00
Microsoft SQL Server 2012 Setup (English)	Microsoft Corporation	1/7/2013	49.6 MB	11.1.3000.0
Microsoft Report Viewer 2012 Runtime	Microsoft Corporation	1/7/2013	26.2 MB	11.0.2100.60
Prerequisites for SSDT	Microsoft Corporation	1/7/2013	6.36 MB	11.0.2100.60
Microsoft SQL Server 2008 R2 Management Objects	Microsoft Corporation	1/7/2013	15.2 MB	10.51.2500.0
Visual Studio 2010 Prerequisites - English	Microsoft Corporation	1/7/2013	23.3 MB	10.0.40219
Microsoft Visual C++ 2010 x86 Runtime - 10.0.40219	Microsoft Corporation	1/7/2013	15.9 MB	10.0.40219
Microsoft Visual Studio Tools for Applications Design...	Microsoft Corporation	1/7/2013	33.3 MB	10.0.40220
SQL Server Browser for SQL Server 2012	Microsoft Corporation	1/7/2013	9.88 MB	11.0.2100.60
Microsoft Visual Studio Tools for Applications x86 Ru...	Microsoft Corporation	1/7/2013	939 KB	10.0.40220
Microsoft SQL Server 2012 Transact-SQL ScriptDom	Microsoft Corporation	1/7/2013	4.53 MB	11.0.2100.60
Microsoft Help Viewer 1.1	Microsoft Corporation	1/7/2013	3.97 MB	1.1.40219

3. Review **Windows Services**. Click on **Start | All Programs | Control Panel | System and Security | Administrative Tools | Services**. In **Services (Local)**, you will find the following:

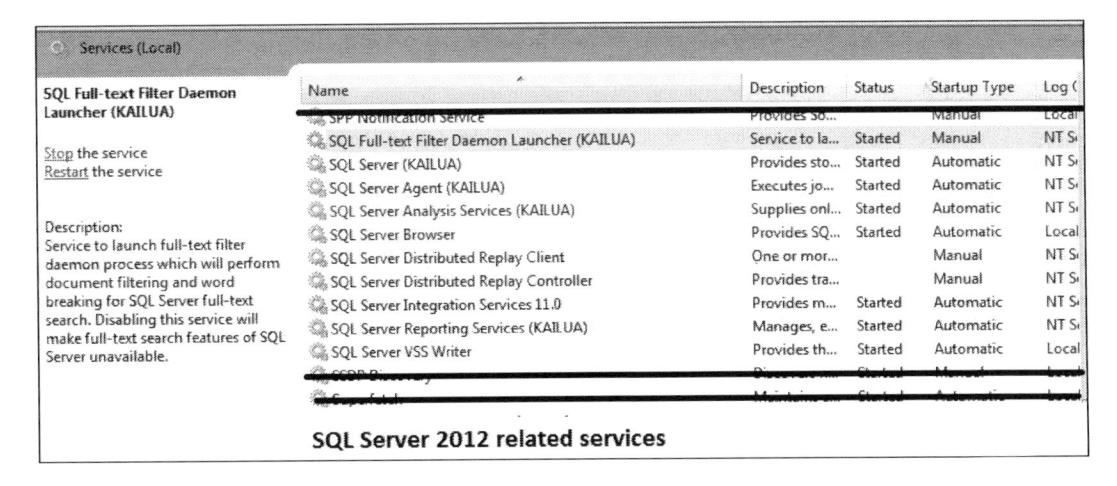

SQL Server 2012 related services

While you are on this page, make sure you can start/stop the SQL Server Services (Database Engine, Analysis Services, and so on). Since some of them are automatic, their status should be **Start**.

[35]

4. Review the services in the SQL Server Configuration Manager by going to **Start | All Programs | Microsoft SQL Server 2012 | Configuration Tools | SQL Server Configuration Manager**. You should find the following (you should be able to start/stop services from here as well):

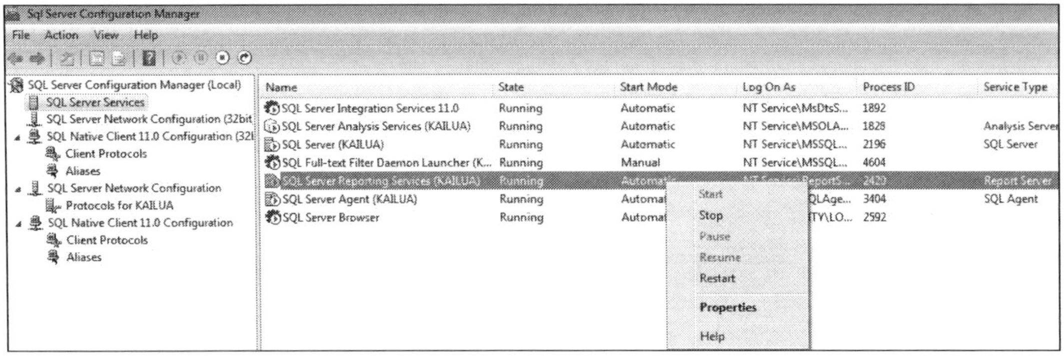
Sql Server Configuration Manager
File Action View Help
SQL Server Configuration Manager (Local)
SQL Server Services
SQL Server Network Configuration (32bit
SQL Native Client 11.0 Configuration (32
Client Protocols
Aliases
SQL Server Network Configuration
Protocols for KAILUA
SQL Native Client 11.0 Configuration
Client Protocols
Aliases
Name
State
Start Mode
Log On As
Process ID
Service Type
SQL Server Integration Services 11.0
SQL Server Analysis Services (KAILUA)
SQL Server (KAILUA)
SQL Full-text Filter Daemon Launcher (K...
SQL Server Reporting Services (KAILUA)
SQL Server Agent (KAILUA)
SQL Server Browser
Running
Automatic
Manual
NT Service\MsDtsS...
NT Service\MSOLA...
NT Service\MSSQL...
1892
1828
2196
4604
2420
3404
2592
Analysis Server
SQL Server
Report Server
SQL Agent
Start
Stop
Pause
Resume
Restart
Properties
Help

Also make sure the SQL Browser Service has started before trying to connect to the installed instance.

5. In the preceding window, right-click on **SQL Server Report Services (Kailua)**. A new window (as displayed in the next screenshot) will be displayed.

   The Reporting Services in Native mode has not been completely configured. The reason for this is, during SQL Server installation, Reporting Services is enabled but not configured completely. It is to be configured by using the Reporting Services Configuration Manager:

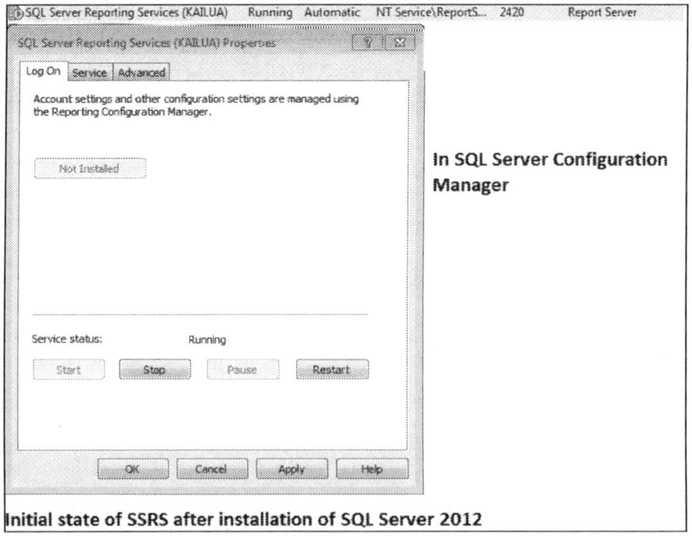
SQL Server Reporting Services (KAILUA) Running Automatic NT Service\ReportS... 2420 Report Server
SQL Server Reporting Services (KAILUA) Properties
Log On
Service
Advanced
Account settings and other configuration settings are managed using the Reporting Configuration Manager.
Not Installed
Service status:
Running
Start
Stop
Pause
Restart
OK
Cancel
Apply
Help
In SQL Server Configuration Manager
Initial state of SSRS after installation of SQL Server 2012

Installation choices and notes

Since this installation is just for working with basic reporting services and savoring the features of SharePoint Integration by a single user on a single machine, the same service account was used for all of the services. During installation, the username and password chosen are of the author on this particular custom environment, as it makes meaningful screen capture easier. It is not a recommended practice to make public the security arrangement, except for a demo environment such as the one used here.

If you want to customize, you may want to choose the locations for the data and log files but for this book, however, the default locations are adequate. However, for a production environment, this is not recommended; you may have to choose proper locations for data and log files, preferably not on drives with operating system files.

Windows authentication was chosen for both the database engine as well as all the services to keep it simple. Also, to make it simple, the current user of the machine was made the sysadmin. If necessary, one may add, other SQL Server administrators using the related **Database Engine** page or the **Analysis Services** page. While configuring the database engine, the defaults were used for data directories, but these can be customized as well.

Regarding the choices for the Reporting Services configuration mode, there are three possible choices from two different modes—Native mode or SharePoint Integrated mode. For Reporting Services with SQL Server 2012, the choice of Native mode was made and most of the Report Builder reports deploy them to the Report Server.

The installation should proceed as described, without any problem. The order in which the various software items were installed closely follows the installation steps in the hands-on exercise, but is simply listed here:

- SQL Server 2012 (x64) Enterprise Evaluation
- Configuration of Reporting Services 2012 in Native mode
- Installation of SharePoint 2010 Server Enterprise Evaluation
- Installation of Reporting Services in SharePoint Integrated mode

Configuring SQL Server Reporting Services

In this section, we will consider configuring the Reporting Services in Native mode as against configuring in SharePoint Integrated mode. It may be useful to remember that Reporting Services SharePoint Integration provides two ways to work with reports (for details, refer to the link at http://msdn.microsoft.com/en-us/library/cc281311.aspx and Hands-on exercise 10.3).

Hands-on exercise 1.3 – configuring SQL Server 2012 Reporting Services in Native mode

The option of installing Reporting Services in Native mode was made during the SQL Server 2012 installation, as described earlier. When this is configured, the Reporting Services Report Server as well as the Report Manager can be accessed by authenticated users. Reports generated using Report Builder (version 3) can be deployed to the Report Server and handled by the frontend Report Manager.

1. Click on **Start | All Programs | Microsoft SQL Server 2012 | Configuration Tools | Reporting Services Configuration Manager**.

   The **Reporting Services Configuration Manager** window opens and the installed Report Server is automatically discovered, as shown in the modal window:

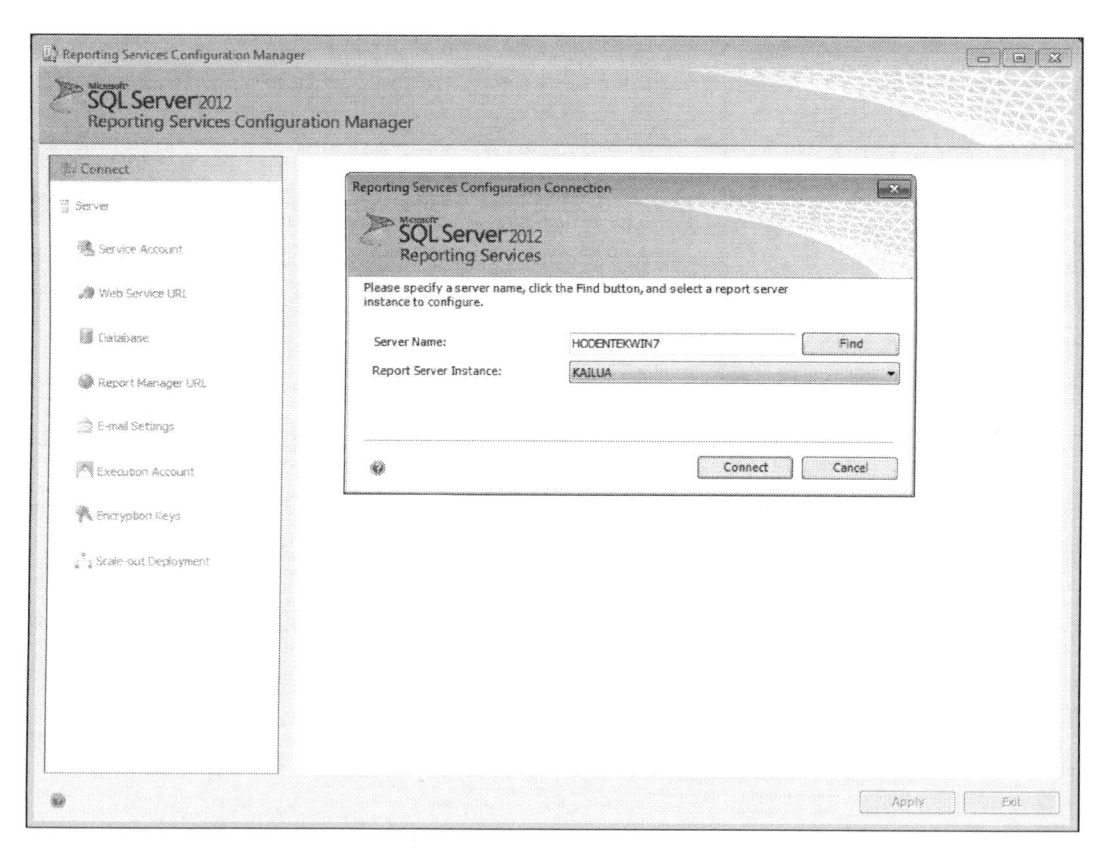

2. Click on **Connect**. The connection is established to the server, as shown in the following screenshot; read the provided information:

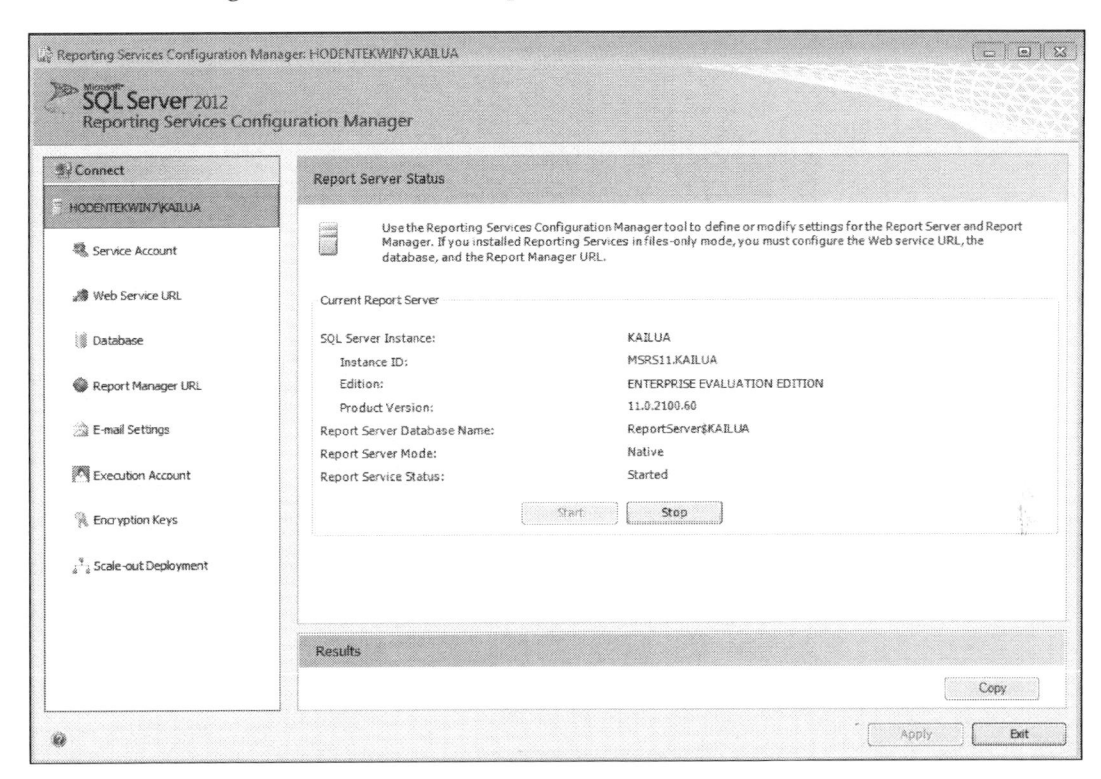

You can start/stop the Report Server from the preceding window.

Overview and Installation – SQL Server Reporting Services 2012

3. Click on **Service Account** on the left. The **Service Account** page opens with the default built-in account, as shown in the following screenshot:

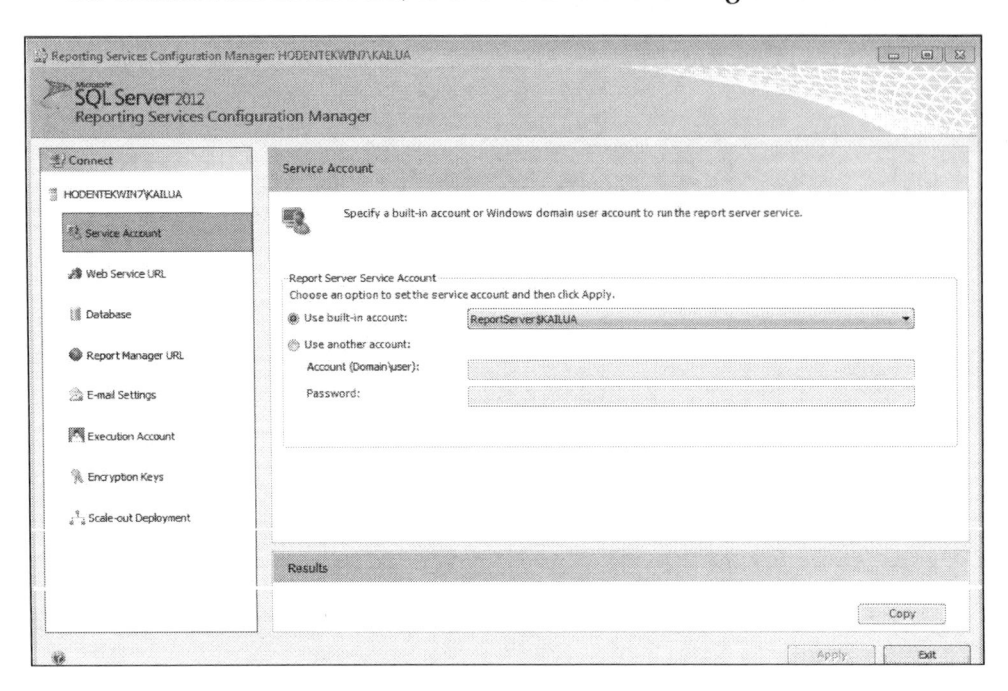

4. Click on **Use another account**. Add the Windows domain user account with the current user as `HodentekWin7\mysorian` and password as xxxxxxx. The **Apply** button gets enabled, as shown in the following screenshot:

Chapter 1

5. Please consult this link for security-related aspects of SQL Server installation at `http://msdn.microsoft.com/en-us/library/ms144228.aspx`. In this demo installation, many of the best practices are not followed just to make it easier to work with exploring the features. Also, mostly the computer administrator is the only entity interacting with the SQL Servers, the SharePoint Server, and other services, and therefore the same account (that of the administrator) is used for everything, again not the best practice. However, since Reporting Services on both Native and SharePoint Integrated Report Servers are accessed by users who assume other roles (but still Windows users), the Windows authentication is mostly used. Click on **Apply**; the **Backup Encryption Key** window will be displayed, as shown in the following screenshot:

6. Click on on the ellipsis button for **File Location** and browse your computer for a location to save your key file. Saving the key is essential to recover the service, in case something untoward happens. For example, the author experienced a hacking incidence and he was able to get back to his servers. It should be deemed as one of the best practices.

    The file location chosen is `C:\Users\mysorian\Desktop\Booksnarticles\SSRS\Jan-08-2013.snk`.

7. Provide a password and confirm it. In the present case, it was xxxxxx. The **SQL Server Connection Dialog** window opens, as shown in the following screenshot:

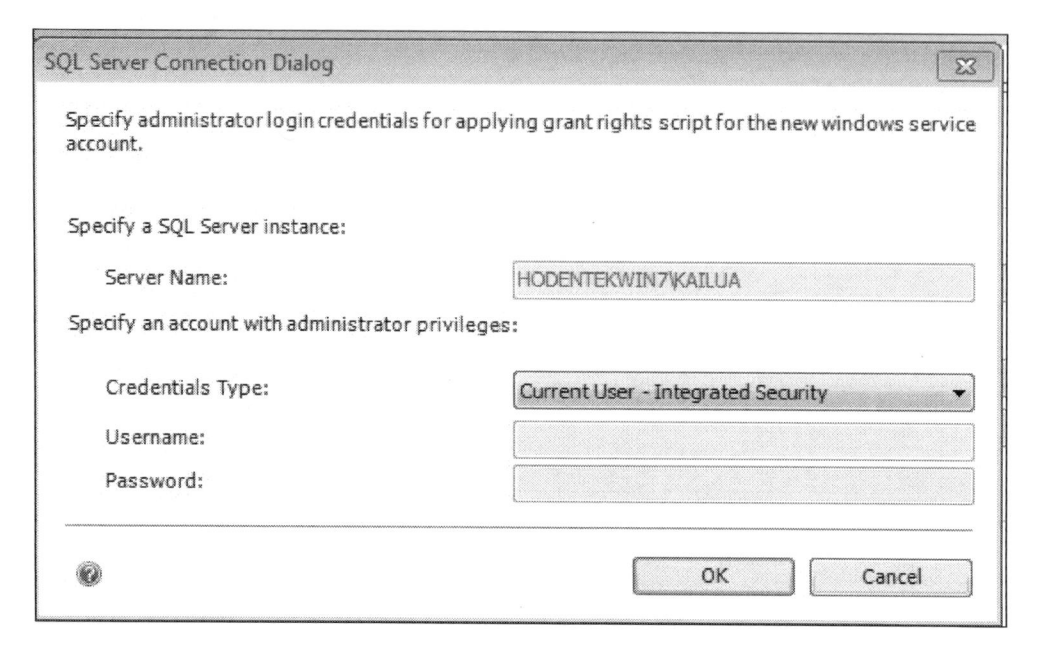

8. Click on **OK**. The current user can connect to the SQL server instance with the instance name `Hodentekwin7\Kailua`.

9. Click on **OK**. Some processing takes place (watch the **Results** window for the changes made). The service account now looks similar to the following screenshot:

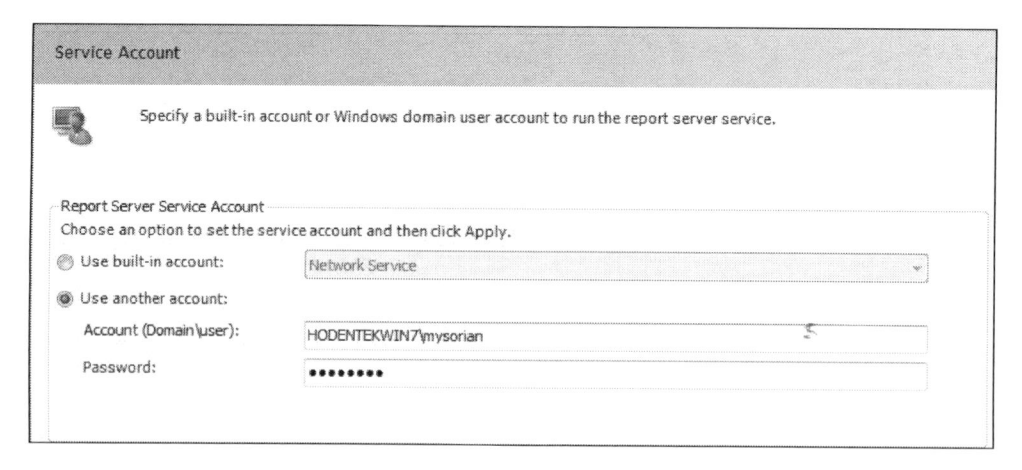

You will see the following in the **Results** window:

> **Results**
> - Creating Encryption Key Backup
> - Stopping report server "KAILUA" on HODENTEKWIN7.
> - Setting Windows Service Identity to Windows Account
> - Creating a Grant Rights script for HODENTEKWIN7\mysorian
> - Assigning Reporting Services Rights to User
> - Starting report server "KAILUA" on HODENTEKWIN7.
> - Removing url http://+:80
> - Reserving url http://+:80
> - Removing url http://+:80
> - Reserving url http://+:80
> - Restoring Encryption Key

10. Click on **Web Service URL** in the left navigation pane. **The Web Service URL** page opens, as shown in the following screenshot:

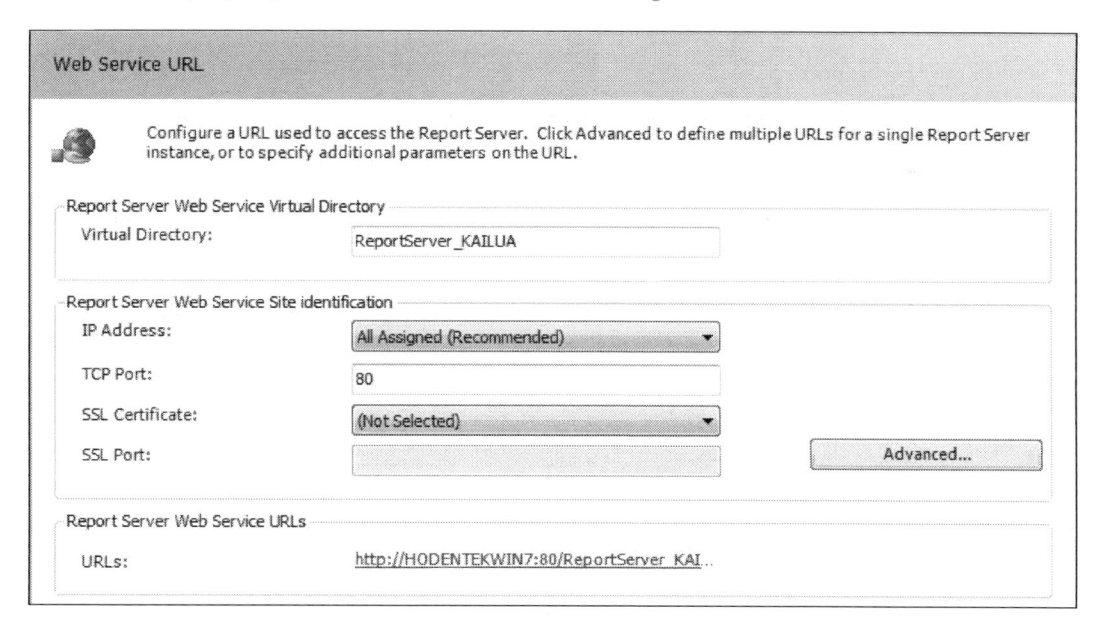

Web Service URL

Configure a URL used to access the Report Server. Click Advanced to define multiple URLs for a single Report Server instance, or to specify additional parameters on the URL.

Report Server Web Service Virtual Directory
- Virtual Directory: ReportServer_KAILUA

Report Server Web Service Site identification
- IP Address: All Assigned (Recommended)
- TCP Port: 80
- SSL Certificate: (Not Selected)
- SSL Port: [Advanced...]

Report Server Web Service URLs
- URLs: http://HODENTEKWIN7:80/ReportServer_KAI...

Overview and Installation – SQL Server Reporting Services 2012

The hyperlink at the bottom of the preceding window is the Report Server Web Service URL. The **Advanced...** button provides you access to create multiple HTTP/SSL identities for the RS Web service.

Click on the hyperlink on the **Web Service URL** window. The **Windows Security** login authentication window will be displayed (note that this window may go behind the larger **Configuration Manager** window; go, look for it). The username is not case sensitive as it responds to `Hodentekwin7\mysorian`:

11. Click on **OK** after entering the credentials. You may get a page with an error, as follows:

12. Arrange to set up the IE 9 browser to open with administrator's credentials. If you want to know how to set it up follow this link: `http://hodentekhelp.blogspot.com/2013/01/how-to-start-ie-browser-with.html`. Click on the URL once again after this, to display the following window:

[44]

Chapter 1

> If you try to access the Report Server without the elevated administrator permissions, you would get a display that would not display an error message. The information you get is often misleading, without pointing to the main reason. However, when you access it with elevated permission, you get connected right away.

13. Click on **Database** in **Reporting Services Configuration Manager**. The **Report Server Database** page will be displayed as follows:

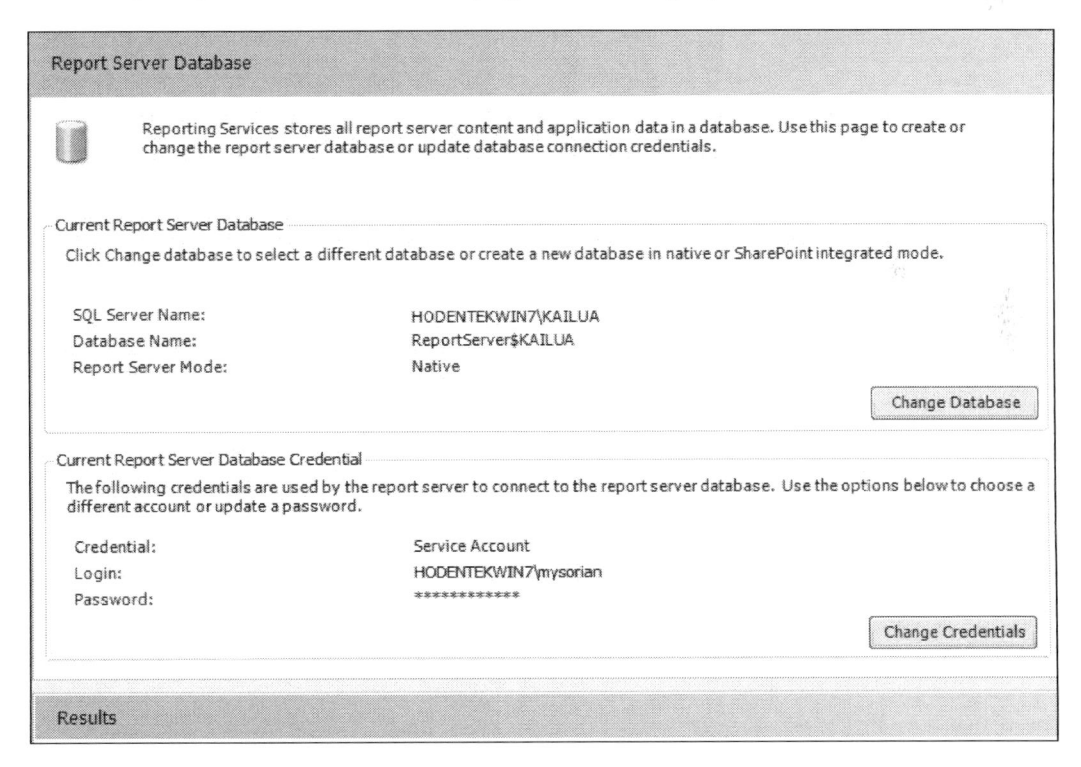

[45]

14. Make sure you read the information on this page. The current Report Server database can be changed or even a new one can be created either in the Native or SharePoint Integrated mode.

    This statement on the Configuration Manager is not entirely correct. Once it is in the Native mode, you cannot change or create a new one in the SharePoint Integrated mode.

    You can also modify the credentials for the current Report Server database. This is something that Microsoft should take care of. As of SQL Server 2012, the SharePoint Integration configuration is only via SharePoint Central Administration and not by using the Reporting Services Configuration Manager. I believe this needs changing.

15. Click on **Report Manager URL** on the left to open its page, as shown in the following screenshot:

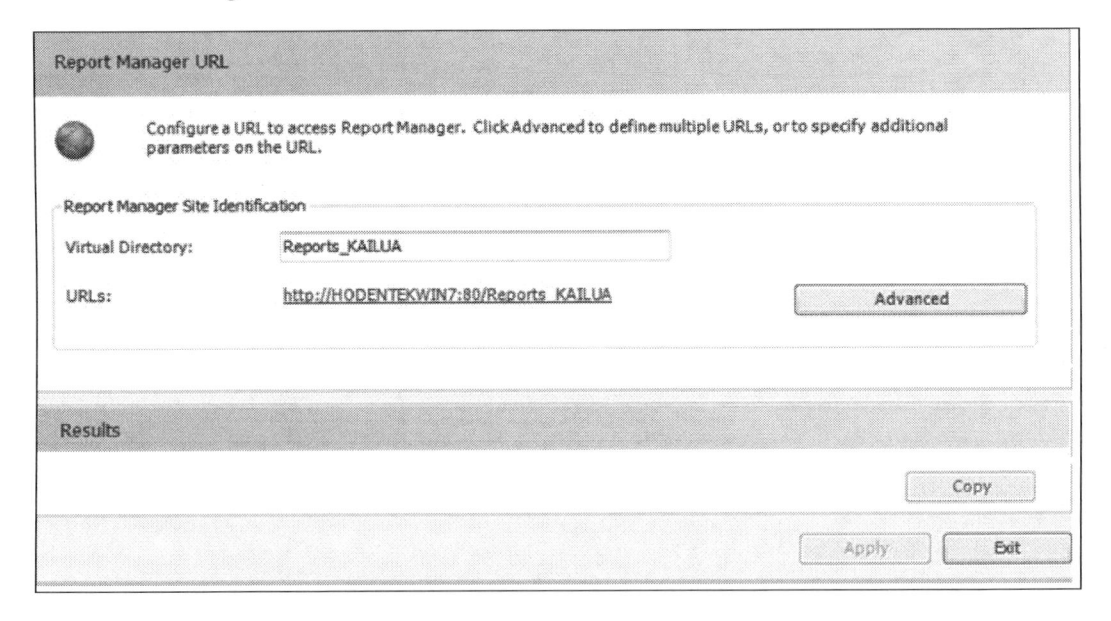

    The **Advanced** button in the **Report Manager URL** window opens the **Multiple Site Configuration** page just like in the case of the **Report Server URL** page. Make no changes.

16. Click on the hyperlink to test.

The Home of the Report Manager opens as shown:

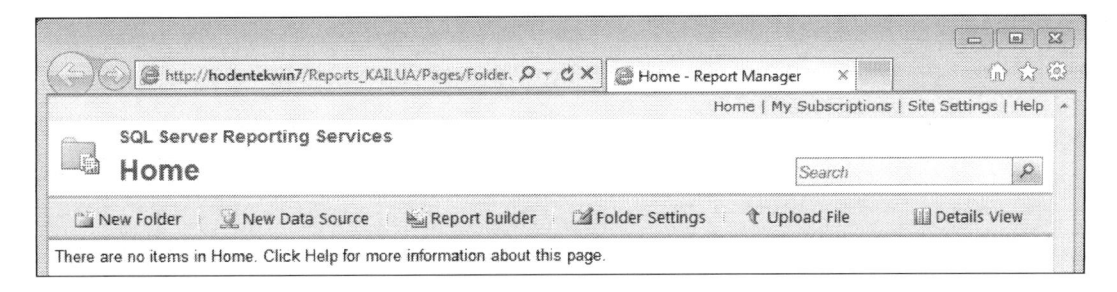

Presently, there are no items showing, as reports have been neither authored nor imported.

17. Click on **E-mail Settings** on the left in the **Navigation** pane. The **E-mail Settings** page will open, as shown in the following screenshot:

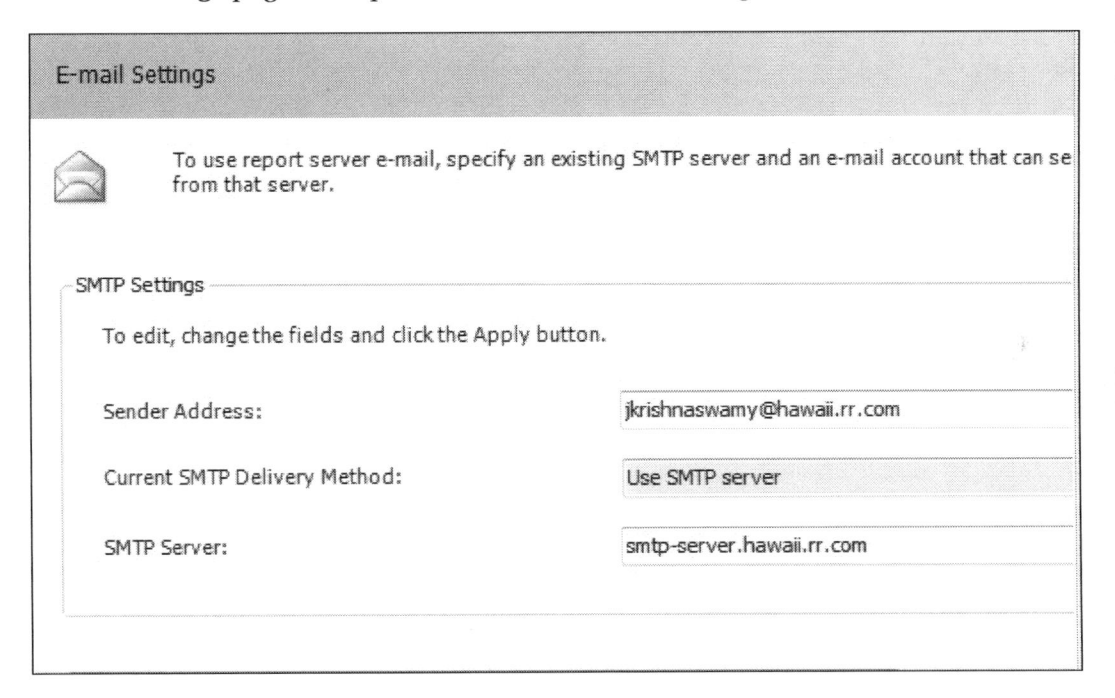

The Reporting Server uses the **Simple Mail Transfer Protocol (SMTP)**, and the SMTP server that accepts the mails is `smtp.live.com`.

[47]

18. After filling in the details, click on **Apply** at the bottom. Your SMTP provider may be different.

    After some processing, you should see the following displayed at the bottom of **Results**: "**Your Configuration has been updated with your new email settings**".

19. Click on on the **Execution Account** item in the navigation pane. The page opens as follows:

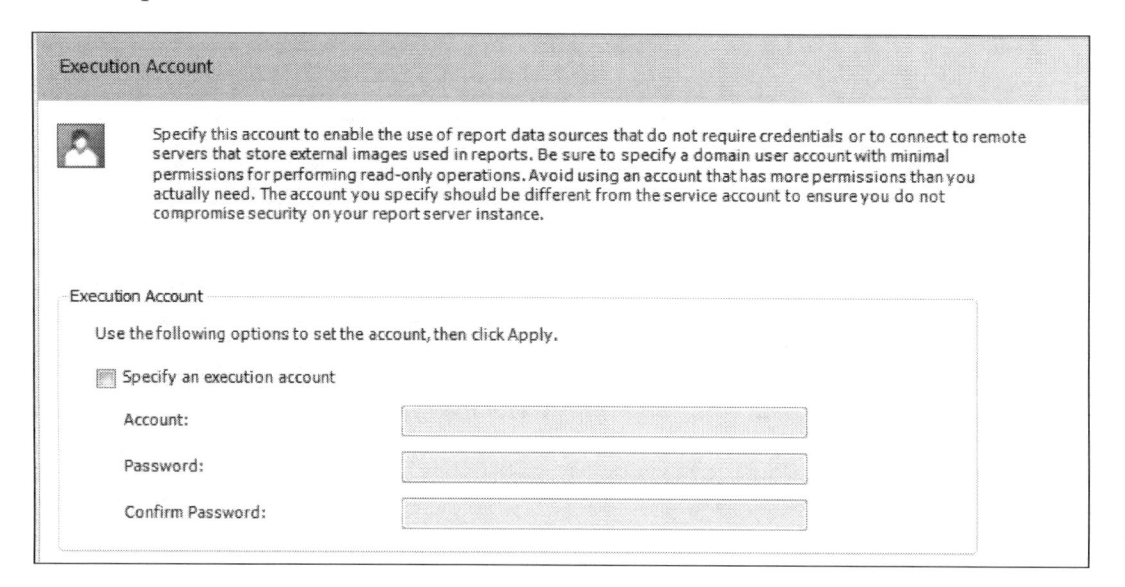

    ![Execution Account configuration screen]

    Make sure you read the information about this page. If you are accessing the file system or items stored on a remote server, which you may want to use in your reports, then you may need to provide a domain user account with just the needed minimum permission. You can also come back and make changes later, if you like. For the present, make no changes. Later, we will configure it for a user with this credential.

20. Click on the **Encryption Keys** item in the **Navigation** pane.

    The **Encryption Keys** page will open, as shown in the next screenshot. Read the information on this page. Reporting Services uses symmetric keys to encrypt sensitive material, such as passwords and connections strings. You can back up, restore, change, and delete keys information from this page:

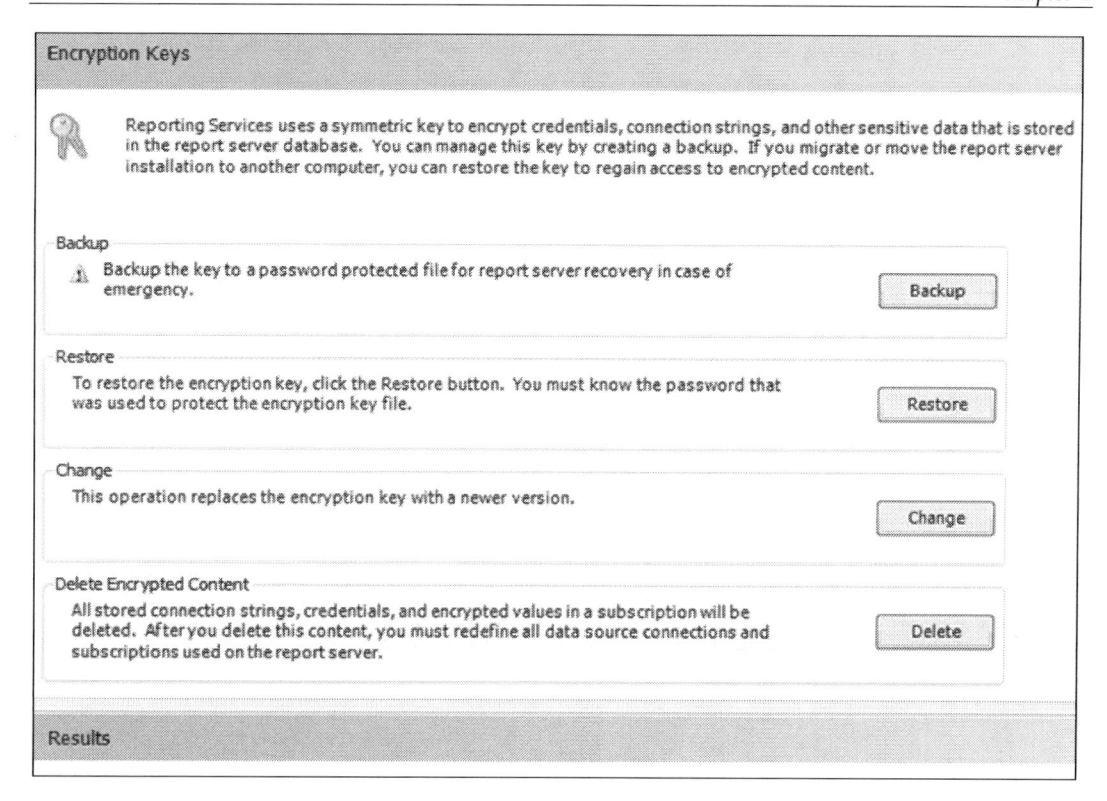

Chapter 1

Encryption Keys

Reporting Services uses a symmetric key to encrypt credentials, connection strings, and other sensitive data that is stored in the report server database. You can manage this key by creating a backup. If you migrate or move the report server installation to another computer, you can restore the key to regain access to encrypted content.

Backup
Backup the key to a password protected file for report server recovery in case of emergency. [Backup]

Restore
To restore the encryption key, click the Restore button. You must know the password that was used to protect the encryption key file. [Restore]

Change
This operation replaces the encryption key with a newer version. [Change]

Delete Encrypted Content
All stored connection strings, credentials, and encrypted values in a subscription will be deleted. After you delete this content, you must redefine all data source connections and subscriptions used on the report server. [Delete]

Results

21. Click on **Backup** to open the following page:

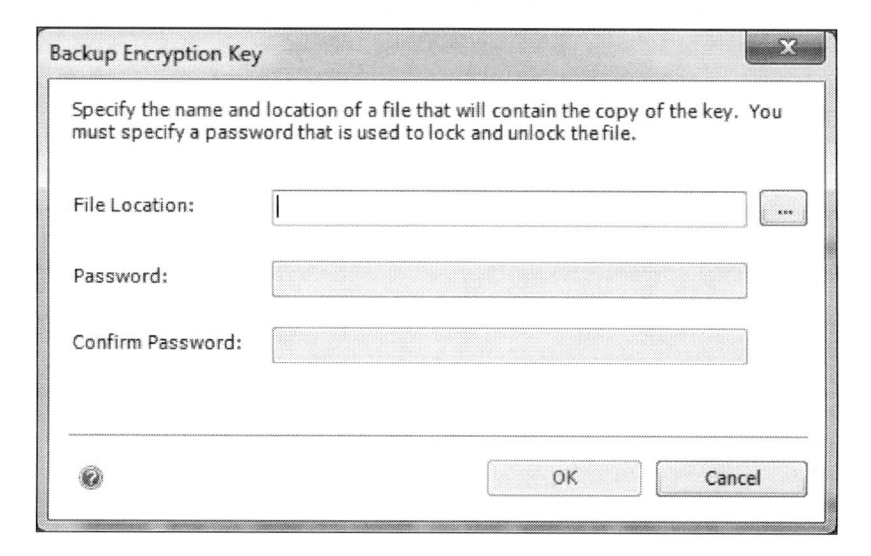

Backup Encryption Key

Specify the name and location of a file that will contain the copy of the key. You must specify a password that is used to lock and unlock the file.

File Location: [   ] [...]

Password: [   ]

Confirm Password: [   ]

[OK] [Cancel]

22. Browse and find a location that you can remember. You need to provide a password and confirm it. You can later use it to restore. A Visual Studio `Strong Key` named file with extension `SNK` is saved to the location chosen.
23. Click on **Scale-out-Deployment** in the **Navigation** pane. The **Scale-Out Deployment** page will open up. This book will not be considering scale-out deployment.
24. Click on **Exit** and the configuration of Reporting Services will be completed.

Report Server – configuration options

While configuring the Report Server, we went ahead and chose a couple of options, but the Configuration Manager provides a number of options for each of the steps. Here, the other options you could have chosen are described. What we have chosen, was for the sake of expediency rather than an example of the best practices.

You may configure multiple Report Servers. Depending upon the size of the business, there could be more than one report server. In the installation used for this book, there is only one report server named `KAILUA` (excluding the report server with SharePoint Integration). The name of the report server is the one you provided during the installation of SQL Server 2012. You may also see a report server in Native mode HI but it is just another instance of SQL Server.

The Report Server mode that you chose dictates most of what you see in the rest of the Report Server configuration, as most of the defaults will be configured at the end of the SQL Server installation, such as whether the service is started automatically when a window starts or not or the authentication details.

However, it is also possible to do the following:

- Start and stop the Report Server from the configuration tool, make changes to the authentication, access the Report Server and Report Manager URLs
- Create or change the Report Server Database
- Manage e-mail settings
- Manage encryption keys

Using the Configuration tool is the recommended (best) practice, if you need to make changes to the Report Server installation. Later on, you will see how the configuration is carried out when the Report Server is installed in the SharePoint Integrated mode.

The service account provided during installation passes to the Report Server as well. It is possible to change the password or use a different account as described previously. For the purpose of this book, the default account will be used. Also, as the Report Server will not be deployed on a network, we will not be concerned with registering a Report Server **Service Principal Name** with the domain user account. Interested readers, who may want to pursue this, should look up *Register a Service Principal Name (SPN) for a Report Server* in the Microsoft SQL Server documentation, or if you have created a local help library look for it at `C:\Program Data\Microsoft\HelpLibrary\catalogs\SQLSERVER`.

Reporting Services uses an encryption key to secure data in the Report Server database. Changing the account or password involves saving the backup encryption key-related information. We will be using the service account and password we supplied during the SQL Server installation, and do not intend to change them. However, to guard against any untoward event, we have carried out a backup of the encryption key.

Using browsers you can access the Report Server Web Service URL as well as the Report Manager URL, as seen earlier. To use any of these, at least one URL should be configured for each instance of Report Server and Report Manager. Since the Native mode for Reporting Services was chosen during the SQL Server 2012 installation, the reserved URLs are configured with default values automatically. You may also choose custom values. For this book, however, the defaults are accepted. Since Port 80 is used by the IIS 7.5 as well as the SharePoint Server site, there is a contention that can be managed by setting a different port.

Overview and Installation – SQL Server Reporting Services 2012

In addition to the Virtual Directory, the IP Address, the TCP Port, the SSL-related items are unique for each Report Server instance. The default IP address set to **All Assigned** is recommended. The SSL port and SSL certificate related information (optional) can be configured as well. These are not configured in this book. Hitting the **Advanced...** button brings up the window for configuring **Advanced Multiple Web Site Configuration**, as shown in the next image, wherein Multiple HTTP and SSL identities for the Report Server Web Service can be configured. No such identities were created for the examples in this book.

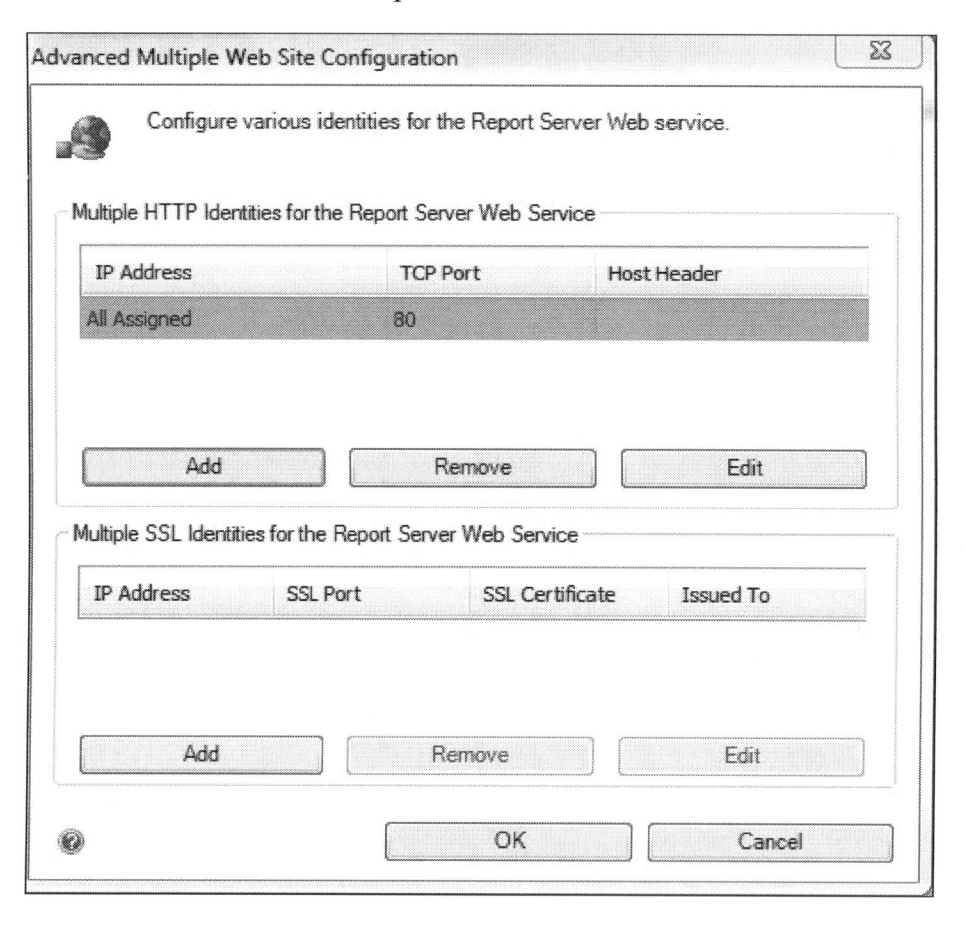

Regarding Report Server databases, the Native mode installation (install and configure) chosen during SQL Server 2012 installation creates two relational databases (together called the **Report Server Catalog**), `ReportServer` (primary) and `ReportServerTempDb` for storing Report Server metadata and objects.

> Reporting Services 2012 in Native mode has two options (refer to the installation steps of SQL Server 2012). There is an **Install and Configure** option and an **Install Only** option. In the first case, the Report Server is installed and configured for the most part, and is operational at the end of the SQL Server 2012 installation. When installed using the **Install Only** option, the user will have to configure the Report Server by using the Reporting Services Configuration Manager from scratch.
>
> However, if SharePoint Integrated mode is chosen, only the required files are installed and you need to work with SharePoint Central administration to complete the configuration.

In case this option (**Install Only**) is chosen, you need to manually create the catalog by using this page. Using the **Change Database** and **Change Credentials** buttons, you can invoke the wizards to make your desired changes. Regarding the credentials to access the Reporting Services catalog, the Windows Integrated Security login specified during SQ Server 2012 installation is used, as we have done during the SQL Server installation. The Windows user account for the local machine (domain account for remote) and SQL Server logins can also be used for the credentials.

Although SQL Server 2012 on the local machine hosts the database, the Report Server catalog can be hosted on a remote machine or on a SQL Server 2005 instance. For this book, the default databases are accepted. The catalog schema is not public, and the applications should not run queries against this catalog. The recommended procedure is to use the Reporting Services API to access the databases.

Just like the Report Server, the Report Manager can also be accessed by a URL. The virtual directory of Report Manager is very similar to the virtual directory of the Report Server and shows the instance name. Since the Native mode installation option was chosen, it is configured with the default. The **Advanced** button on the Report Manager URL would bring up the **Advanced Multiple Web Site Configuration** window, wherein you can configure various identities for Report Manager. These options are not used in the book.

Regarding the e-mail delivery, SMTP is chosen for the mail transfer, and you must supply the correct information for configuring this screen. SMTP needs a sender's address as well as an SMTP server for sending out the mail. The SMTP server can be local or remote. Using Internet SMTP servers did not work, as the Internet Web mail providers such as gmail.com, live.com, and Yahoo.com have made changes to their SMTP servers, which make it difficult to use them from Reporting Services.

Using the exchange server makes it possible to send e-mails from RS without problems. You need to fill in information appropriate to your environment. Advanced e-mail settings can be made by using the configuration file. For this book, no further configuration of e-mail is made apart from the basic configuration using this window. Also, make sure the SQL Server agent has started.

Configuration of the Execution Account is optional. The related screen in the hands-on exercise describes most of the details. This account can be ideally a Windows User account and if it is configured, it should be maintained to avoid accessing errors. For the purposes of this book, this is not configured as we neither send connection requests over networks nor try to retrieve external image files for use in the reports while making requests when logged in anonymously.

Creating a backup copy of the symmetric key used in encrypting sensitive information is an important part of Report Server configuration, although it is strictly unnecessary for the purposes of this book. You do not need to do this for the following reasons:

- We do not intend to change the Report Servers Windows Service account name or reset the password
- We do not intend to rename either the computer that hosts the instance or the name of the instance
- We do not intend to migrate the Report Server installation
- We do not expect to have a Report Server installation failure due to hardware failure

Although it was optional for the purposes of this book, encryption keys were generated during configuration, which proved of great value as the author's site had a malware attack and the encryption keys saved the day.

The scale-out-deployment model of running reporting services is needed when multiple report servers use a shared report server database. All action buttons are disabled in the related screen, as there is only one reporting service. We do not intend to use this mode of operation, since we have no intention of having multiple report servers.

The Native mode Reporting Services configuration was completed at the end of the previous hands-on exercise.

Installing sample databases

We will be working with Microsoft's `Northwind` database and sometimes with the more recent `AdventureWorks` databases in both SQL Server 2012. These database samples comes in two forms—MDF and LDF files or script files, which when run on the server install the databases. The MDF and LDF files can be used to install the samples by using either the graphic user interface (right-click on the **Databases** node in the SQL Server Management Studio and choose **Attach...**), the **Attach** menu item on SQL Server, or by using T-SQL scripts.

Downloading files and running scripts

For SQL Server 2000 database files, refer to the follow URL:
`http://www.microsoft.com/en-us/download/details.aspx?id=23654`

For Adventure Works database files, refer to the follow URL :
`http://msftdbprodsamples.codeplex.com/releases`

Make sure you get both the MDF and LDF files, as both are needed while attaching the databases; read the following comments at
`http://msftdbprodsamples.codeplex.com/workitem/19203`.

For attaching the MDF/LDF files, refer to the following URL for a step-by-step procedure:
`http://hodentek.blogspot.com/search?q=Sample+databases`

For running the script files, refer to the follow URL and following the steps as indicated:
`http://hodentekmsss.blogspot.com/2013/01/how-do-i-install-sample-database-using.html`

In addition to these files, some data and even tables may be created to describe some aspects of Reporting Services, and these will be described at appropriate places.

SharePoint Server 2010 Enterprise Edition

SharePoint Server 2010 Enterprise (herein the Evaluation Edition) is necessary for configuring Reporting Services in the SharePoint Integrated mode. The designated machine platform for SharePoint Server 2010 (hereafter SP2010) is Windows 2008 Server (x64) or Windows Server 2008 R2 (x64). It is, however, possible to install SP2010 on Windows 7 platform as long as it is 64-bit and has sufficient resources. The procedure is by no means trivial, and you will want a better and simplified installer (like a Microsoft Web installer, it does not exist except on a wish list) for installing on Windows 7 (64-bit).

For finding the right version of SQL Server to use with SharePoint Server, visit the following URL:

http://technet.microsoft.com/en-us/library/dc6a3372-db26-43f0-b7aa-f725acc635c2

For installing SP2010 on Windows 7 (64-bit), refer to the follow URL:

http://msdn.microsoft.com/en-us/library/ee554869(office.14).aspx

Installing SharePoint Server 2010 Enterprise Edition on Windows 7 (64-bit)

For hardware and software requirements, before you install SP2010, refer to the follow URL:

http://technet.microsoft.com/en-us/library/cc288751(v=office.14).aspx

1. Read the complete list of prerequisites for SharePoint 2010 to install correctly.
2. Download Microsoft SharePoint Server 2010 Trial (SharePointServer.exe, 560.5 MB) from the following URL, to a location of your choice:

   http://www.microsoft.com/en-us/download/details.aspx?id=16631

3. You need to extract the files to a folder that you create, say SharePoint. Change to the DOS command line and run the following command (make suitable changes to the command line):

Chapter 1

```
C:\Users\mysorian\Desktop\Booksnarticles\SharePoint>dir
 Volume in drive C is TI106240W0D
 Volume Serial Number is D213-A8DF

 Directory of C:\Users\mysorian\Desktop\Booksnarticles\SharePoint

01/13/2013  03:51 PM    <DIR>          .
01/13/2013  03:51 PM    <DIR>          ..
01/12/2013  03:30 PM       587,742,552 SharePointServer.exe
               1 File(s)    587,742,552 bytes
               2 Dir(s)  344,554,930,176 bytes free

C:\Users\mysorian\Desktop\Booksnarticles\SharePoint>SharePointServer /extract c:
Users\mysorian\Desktop\Booksnarticles\SharePoint\SharePointServerFiles
```

4. The Share Point Server 2010 files are now in the `SharePointServerFiles` folder.

    In this folder, locate **Files | Setup | config.xml**, and make changes to this file with a text editor so that the following XML code:

    `<Setting Id="AllowWindowsClientInstall" Value="True"/>`

    is typed below other `<Settings/>` location but not after `</configuration>`. Save the file to the same location where you found it. With this when you launch the setup file, it will not complain that your computer OS is not supported.

5. You now need to install the following prerequisite files:

    - Install `FilterPack.msi` from **SharePointServerFiles | PreRequisitesInstallerFiles | FilterPack.msi**
    - Install the Microsoft Sync Frame work 1.0(x64) from `http://go.microsoft.com/fwlink/?LinkID=141237`
    - Install Microsoft SQL Server 2008 Native Client MSI file from `http://go.microsoft.com/fwlink/?LinkId=123718`
    - Download and install the Windows `6.1-KB974405-x64.msu` file from `http://www.microsoft.com/en-us/download/details.aspx?id=17331`
    - You may also need to install Microsoft Chart Controls for Microsoft .NET Framework 3.5 (KB2500170). Read `http://support.microsoft.com/kb/2500170`

Overview and Installation – SQL Server Reporting Services 2012

- You will have to turn on some of the Windows features in **Control Panel | Programs | Programs and Features**. Click on **Turn On Windows Features** and place check marks for the needed items, as shown in the next image. Note that some of them might already have a check mark. These are needed for the Web Server Role and by application roles in SP2010.

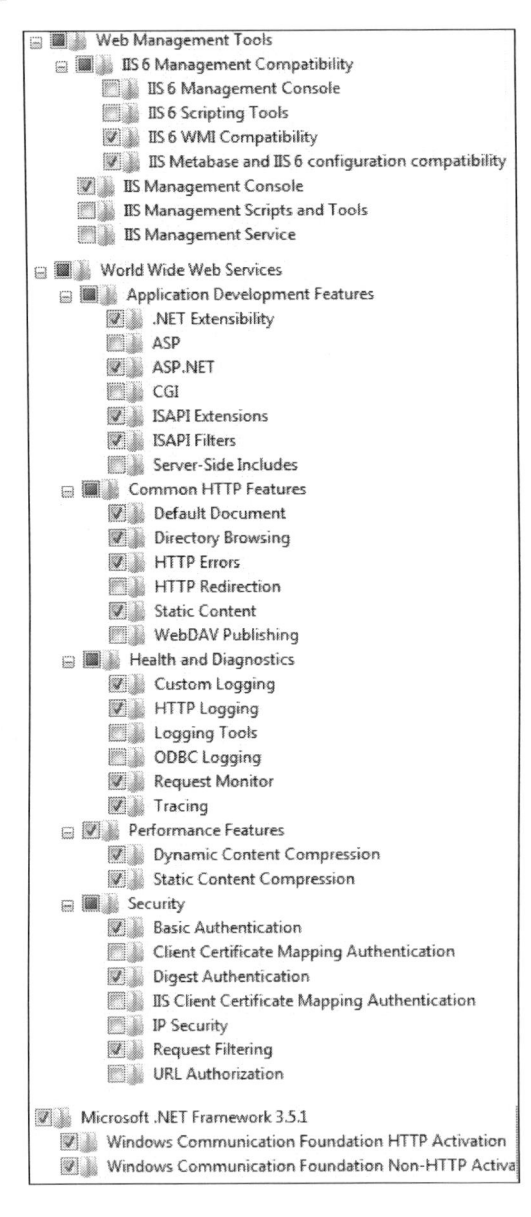

```
Web Management Tools
    IIS 6 Management Compatibility
        IIS 6 Management Console
        IIS 6 Scripting Tools
        [✓] IIS 6 WMI Compatibility
        [✓] IIS Metabase and IIS 6 configuration compatibility
    [✓] IIS Management Console
        IIS Management Scripts and Tools
        IIS Management Service
World Wide Web Services
    Application Development Features
        [✓] .NET Extensibility
            ASP
        [✓] ASP.NET
            CGI
        [✓] ISAPI Extensions
        [✓] ISAPI Filters
            Server-Side Includes
    Common HTTP Features
        [✓] Default Document
        [✓] Directory Browsing
        [✓] HTTP Errors
            HTTP Redirection
        [✓] Static Content
            WebDAV Publishing
    Health and Diagnostics
        [✓] Custom Logging
        [✓] HTTP Logging
            Logging Tools
            ODBC Logging
        [✓] Request Monitor
        [✓] Tracing
    [✓] Performance Features
        [✓] Dynamic Content Compression
        [✓] Static Content Compression
    Security
        [✓] Basic Authentication
            Client Certificate Mapping Authentication
        [✓] Digest Authentication
            IIS Client Certificate Mapping Authentication
            IP Security
        [✓] Request Filtering
            URL Authorization
[✓] Microsoft .NET Framework 3.5.1
    [✓] Windows Communication Foundation HTTP Activation
    [✓] Windows Communication Foundation Non-HTTP Activa
```

After making all these modifications, the SP 2010 setup starts with the following screen:

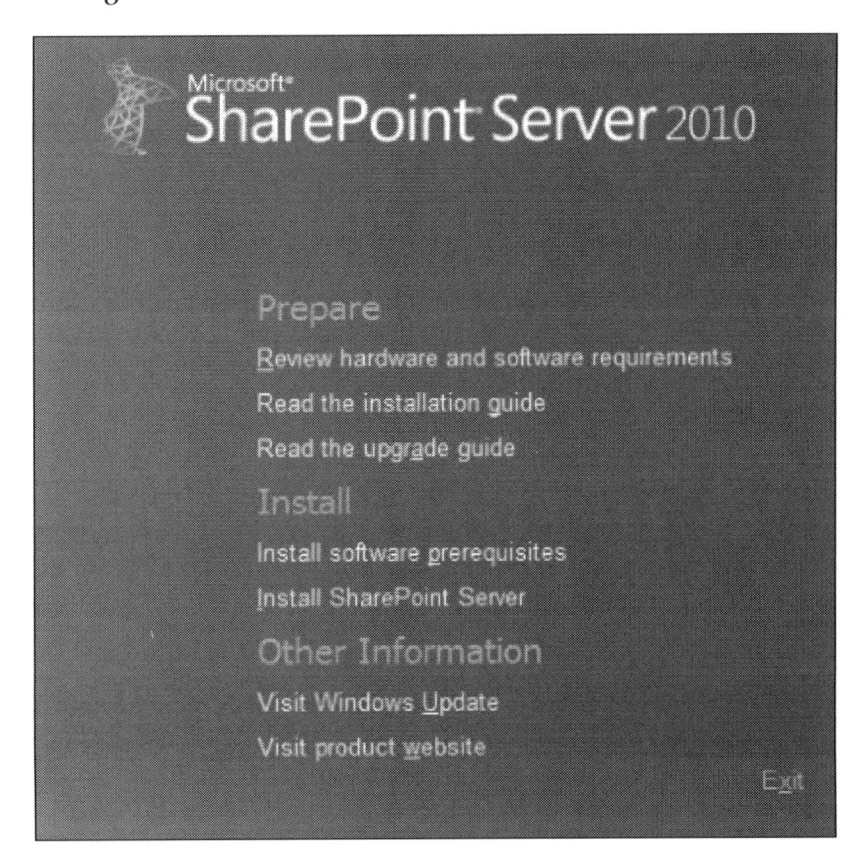

6. Click on **Install SharePoint Server**. In the **Choose Installation you want** window, choose to install standalone using default settings by clicking on the **Standalone** button. You may also need to run the configuration wizard, after which you will have the following programs added to **Start | All Programs | SharePoint 2010 Products**:

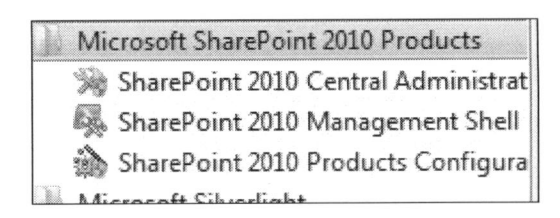

Installing Reporting Services 2012 in SharePoint Integrated mode

Installing Reporting Services 2012 in SharePoint Integrated mode consists of two basic installations:

- **Microsoft SharePoint add-in for SharePoint 2010 products**: This installs RS user interface pages/features on a SharePoint Server; the frontend for reporting services needed for Power View, administration pages in SharePoint Central Administration, and Reporting Services data alert pages.
- **Microsoft SQL Server Reporting Services in SharePoint Integrated mode**: The Report Server handles the data and report processing; rendering, subscription, and data alert features. The SharePoint report server is installed as a SharePoint Service.

In a previous hands-on exercise, we have seen how to install Reporting Services SQL Server 2012 in Native mode. In order to install in SharePoint Integrated mode, we need to make this choice during SQL Server 2012 installation, as shown in the following installation page:

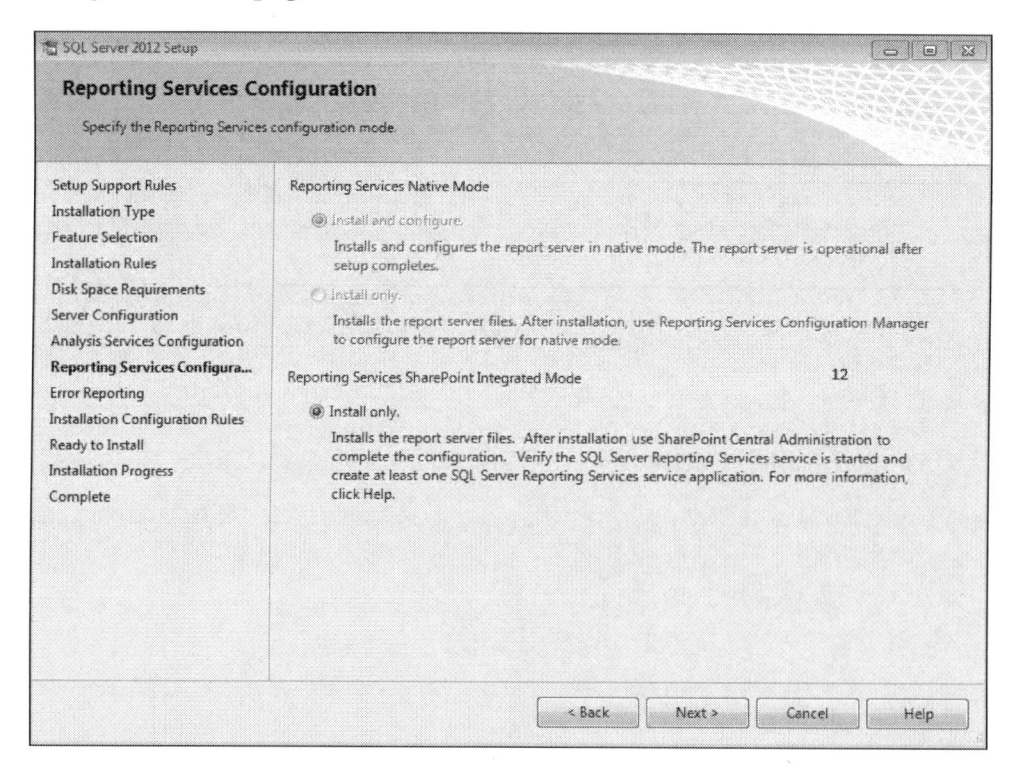

> A number of combinations of Report Server, Report Server add-in for SharePoint, and SharePoint Version support reporting services integration, for example, Reporting Services 2008 R2 can be implemented in SharePoint 2010 integrated mode but does not support Power View. However, Integration of Reporting Services 2012 with SharePoint 2010 supports Power Views and Data Alerts. Hence, the number of combinations reduces to three at present. The choice made in this book is therefore SQL Server 2012 and SharePoint 2010. Review http://msdn.microsoft.com/en-us/library/dc6a3372-db26-43f0-b7aa-f725acc635c2.

Reporting Services add-in for SharePoint 2010

SQL Server 2012 installation installs the Reporting Services add-in for SharePoint 2010 on the computer when you make the feature selection during installation. You may also verify this in the Control Panel's Add/Remove Programs.

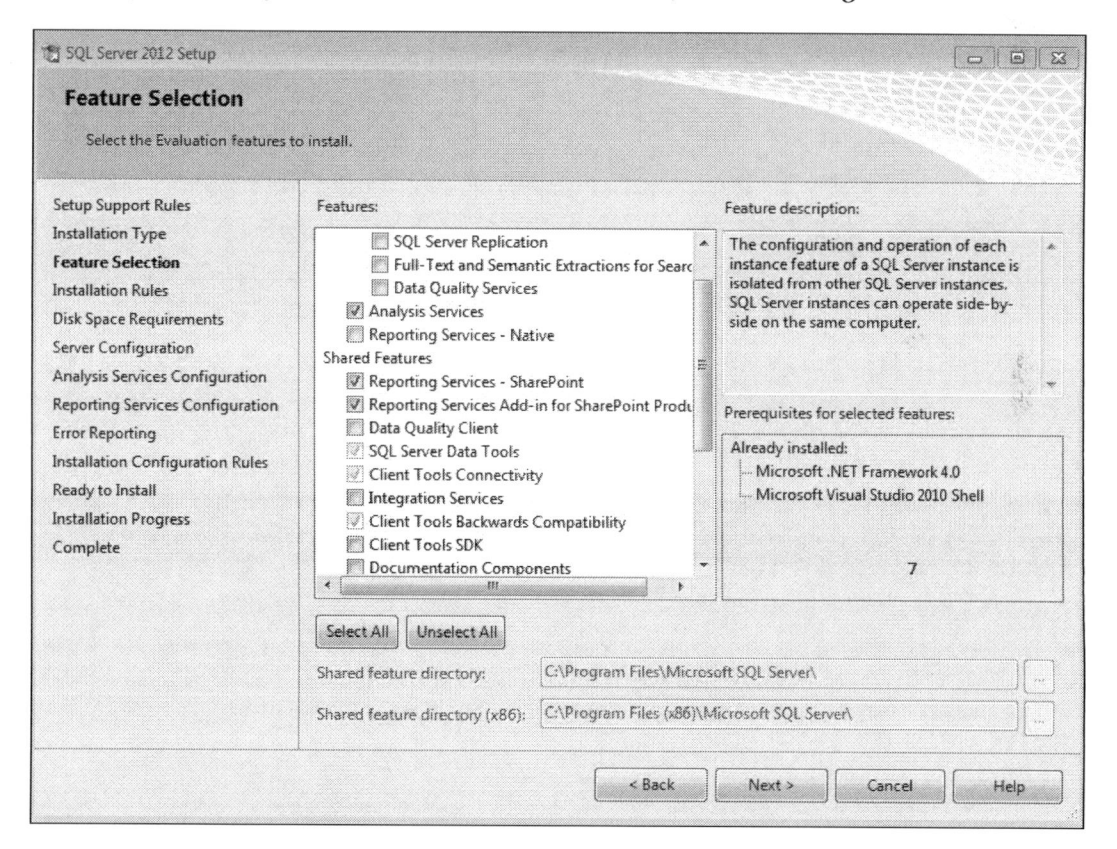

If you do not choose it at the time of installation, you can separately download (Web download) it from `http://www.microsoft.com/en-us/download/details.aspx?id=29068`.

This downloads an MSI named `ENU\x64\rsSharePoint.msi` (26.1 MB).

With the Reporting Services add-in installed, the following functionalities are available:

- The drag-and-drop ad-hoc reporting capability with Power View
- Calling up the Report Builder from SharePoint Library and saving reports to SharePoint
- Report Viewer Web Part for report viewing, page navigation, report export, print, and so on
- SharePoint Web pages, and the ability to create subscriptions and schedules, and manage reports and data sources
- Standard SharePoint Document management and deployment of report server content types
- Using SharePoint permission levels and roles to control access to the report server content
- Reporting Services Data Alerts, an alerting solution driven by data on the report that sends out e-mail notifications

Installing and starting the Reporting Services SharePoint Service

The type of SharePoint Server 2010 installation chosen was of standalone type. We need to install the Reporting Services SharePoint Service for this installation. Starting with SQL Server 2012, the configuration of RS Integrated with SharePoint is made by using PowerShell, whereas that of the Native mode operation is by using Configuration Manager. In this section, PowerShell is used to install the Reporting Services SharePoint Service.

> You will learn all about PowerShell and its use for working with Reporting Services in SharePoint Integrated mode and Reporting Services Native mode configuration in *Chapter 8, Reporting Services and Programming*.

Hands-on exercise 1.4 – installing the Reporting Services SharePoint Service

When SharePoint Server was installed, we had access to three of the shortcuts to SharePoint on **Start | All Programs**, one of which was SharePoint 2010 Management Shell.

1. Click on **Start** and then on **Microsoft SharePoint Products Group**.
2. Right-click on **SharePoint 2010 Management Shell** and select **Run as administrator**, as shown in the following screenshot:

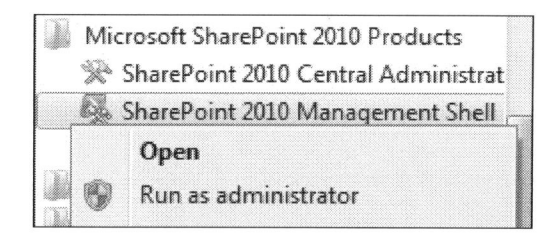

3. In the Power Shell command line, install the service and proxy, as shown, by using Power Shell cmdlets. First, install the service; if installed without any problem, you get no response. You just get a new line.
4. Run the second command in the new line to install the service proxy. You do not get a reply but a new line:

```
PS C:\Users\mysorian> Install-SPRSService
PS C:\Users\mysorian> Install-SPRSSERVICEProxy
PS C:\Users\mysorian>
```

5. You can start the service from the command line by using another PowerShell cmdlet, but it can be started from the SharePoint Server Central Administration, as shown.

> When you start the SharePoint Administration site on your browser, make sure you started the browser with elevated permissions by using the **Run as administrator** option. Some of the menu items may be displayed in a disabled condition if run without this elevated operation.

[63]

Starting the service

Although you can start and stop the SharePoint Administration site by using PowerShell, it can be started from the **SharePoint Central Administration** screens, as shown in this section.

1. Click on **Manage Services on server** in **Central Administration**:

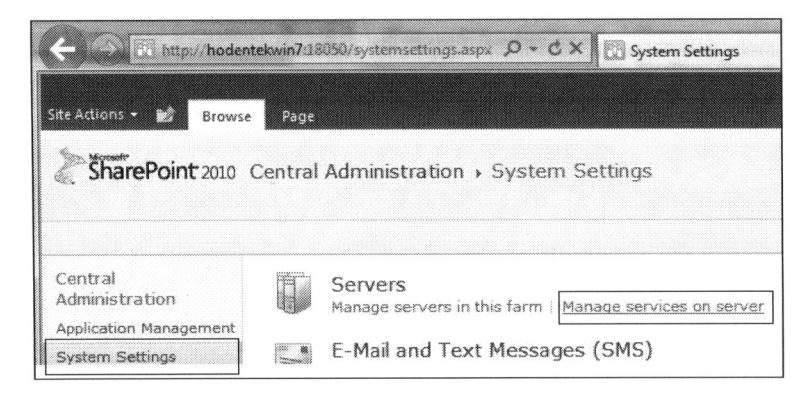

2. In the **Services on Server** page, Click on **Start** in the **Actions** column for **SQL Server Reporting Services**, as shown in the following screenshot:

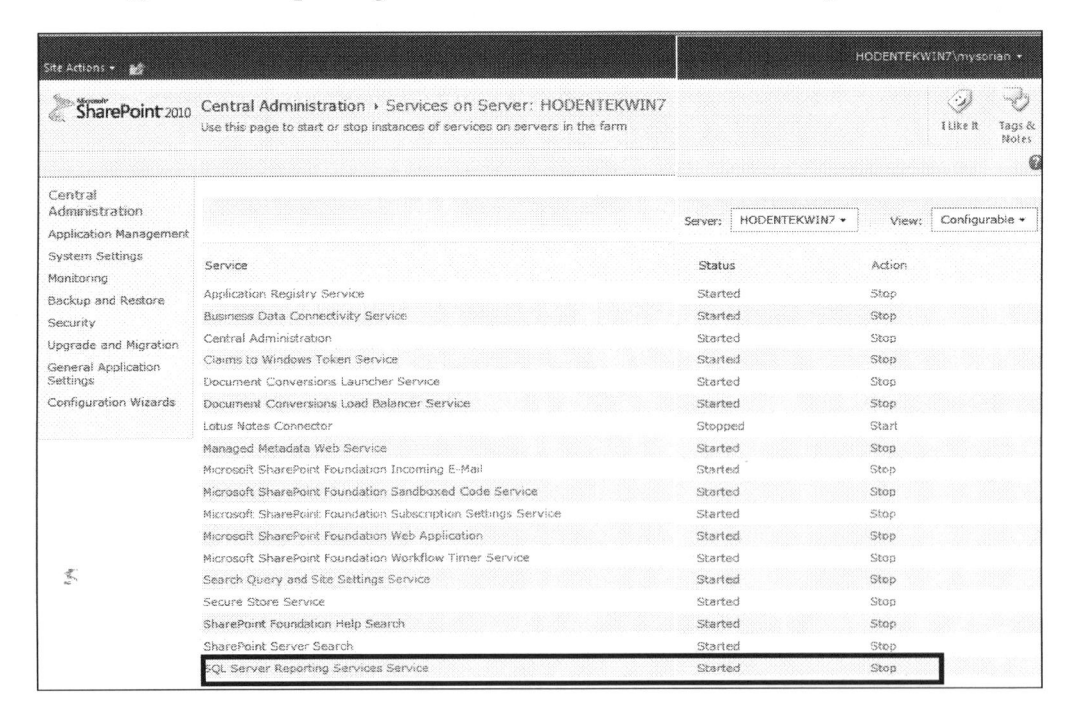

> Using this screen, you can start and stop the services. Note that you will not see the SQL Server Reporting Services if you skipped the installation in the previous screen using PowerShell.

Creating the Reporting Services Service application

In this section, we will install a Reporting Services Service application.

1. In **Central Administration**, click on the **Application** Management group, then click on **Manage service applications**, as shown in the following screenshot:

    The **Service Applications** tabbed page of the ribbon is displayed as shown in the next image.

2. Click on **New**.

Overview and Installation – SQL Server Reporting Services 2012

> If **SQL Server Reporting Services Application** is not present in the drop-down menu, the shared service is not installed. You have to go back and install it using Power Shell cmdlets, as described previously.

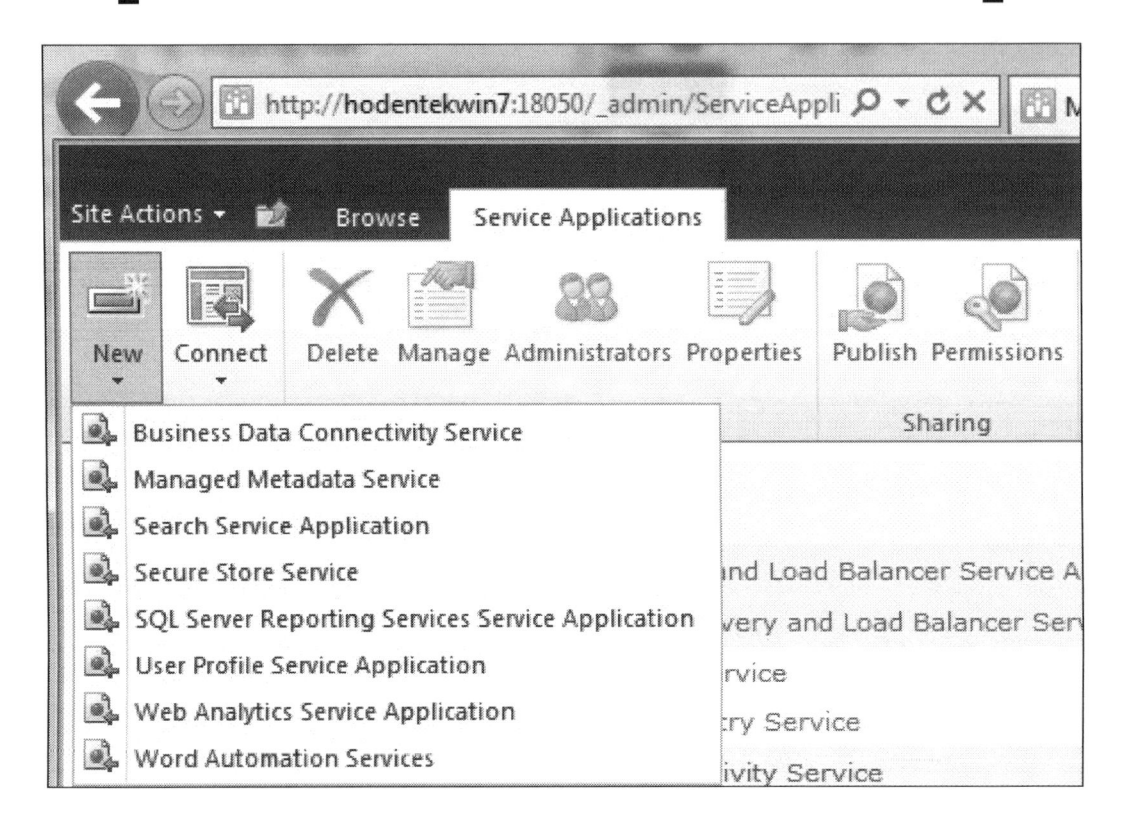

3. Click on **SQL Server Reporting Services Service Application** in the drop-down menu of **New**.

   The **Create SQL Server Reporting Services Service Application** page appears as shown in the following screenshot:

Chapter 1

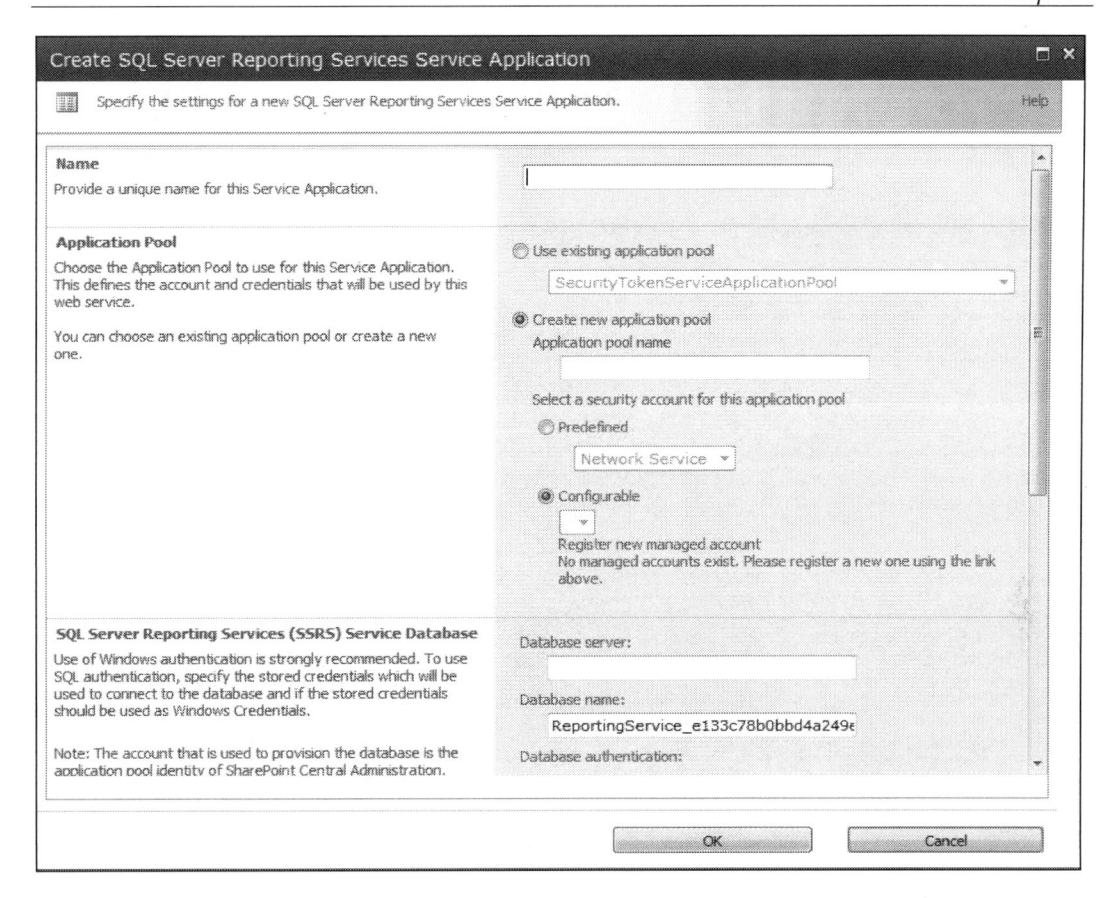

4. Provide a unique name for the service. Herein, SPYGLASS was used.

   For the the new service application, you need to choose **Application Pool** and **Security Account** for this application pool. This is an installation on a single computer that also hosts the Internet Information Server. Choose the option **Use existing Application Pool** set for SecurityTokenServiceApplicationPool with a predefined security account set for the domain account (in this case, HodentekWin7\mysorian) instead of the default NetworkService. You may follow this link to see how you can modify **Application Pool Identity**:

   http://hodentekhelp.blogspot.com/2013/04/how-do-you-make-changes-to-application.html

Overview and Installation – SQL Server Reporting Services 2012

5. Click on **OK**.

   The **Create SQL Server Reporting Services Service Application** page (bottom portion of the page) with these changes appears as shown in the following screenshot:

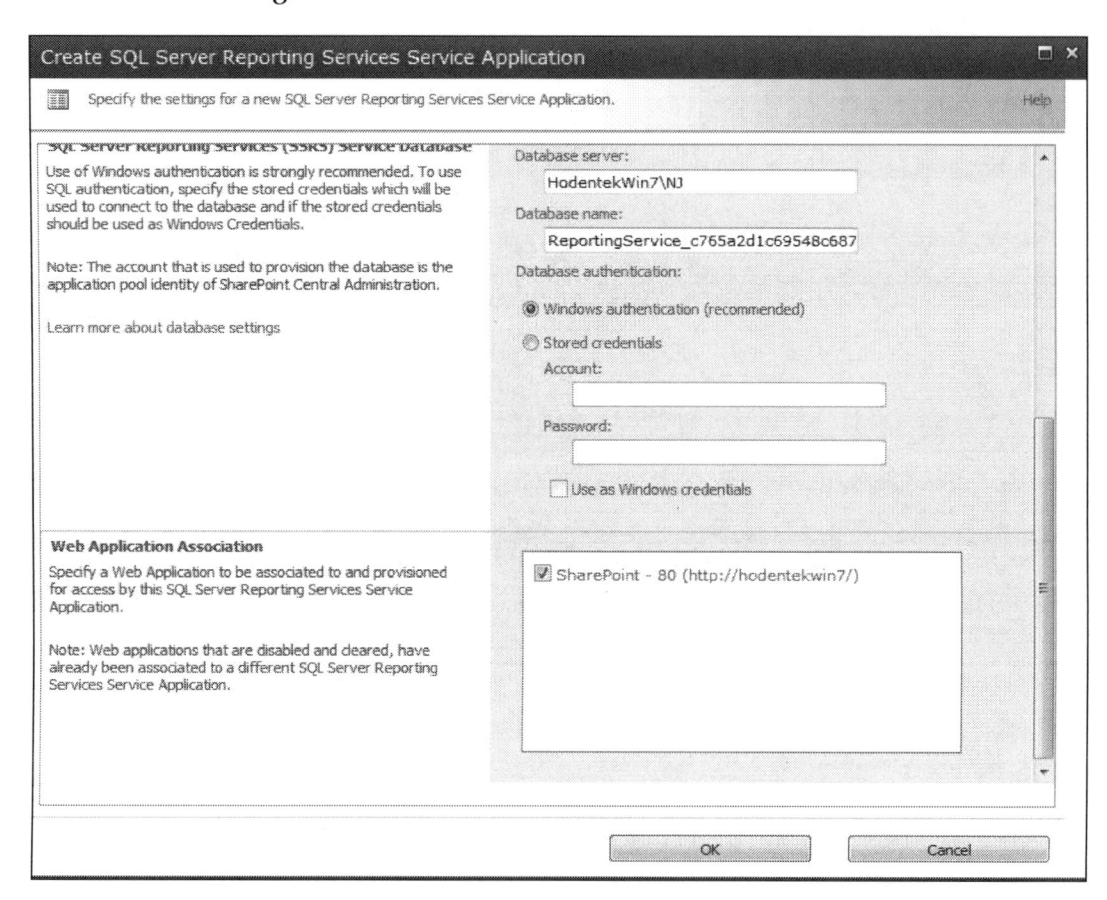

   Note that the database name is created for you. The value for the **Database Server** must be the one that was installed in the SharePoint Integrated mode.

6. The service application gets created, as shown in the following screenshot:

7. The databases used by the service are created, as shown on the SQL Server 2012 instance:

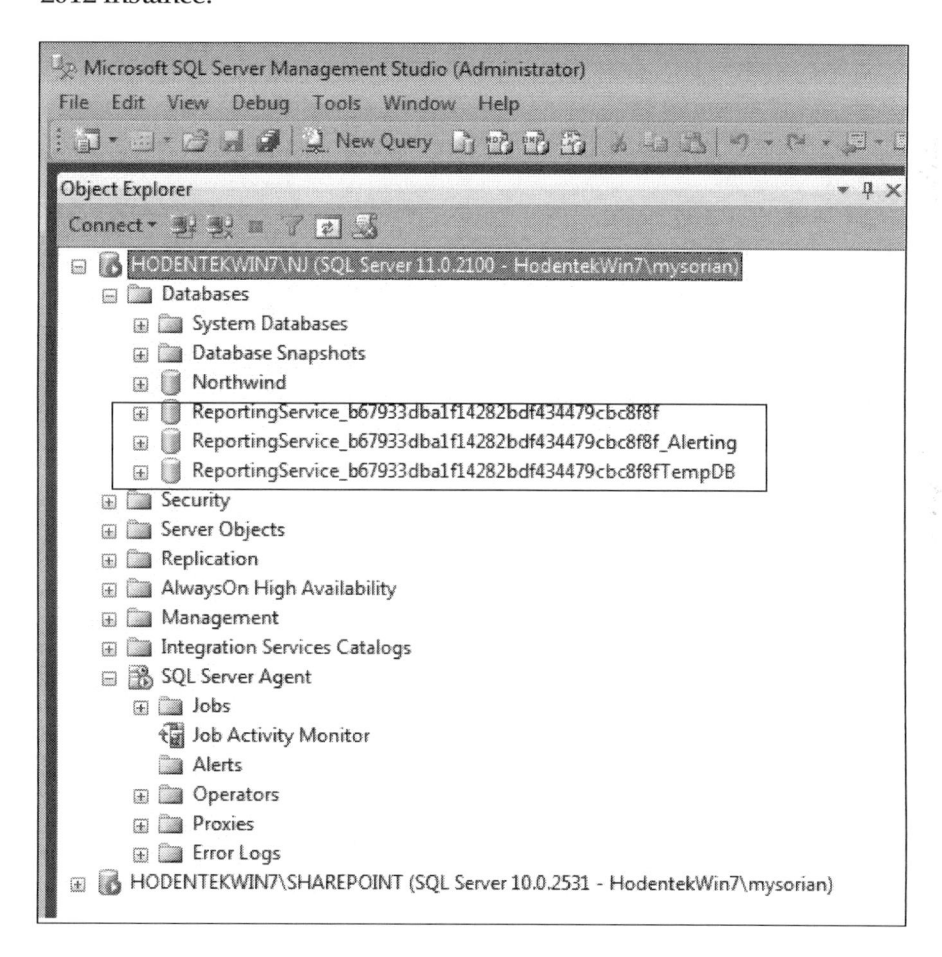

Overview and Installation – SQL Server Reporting Services 2012

8. The **Spyglass** service in the **Service Applications** page appears as follows:

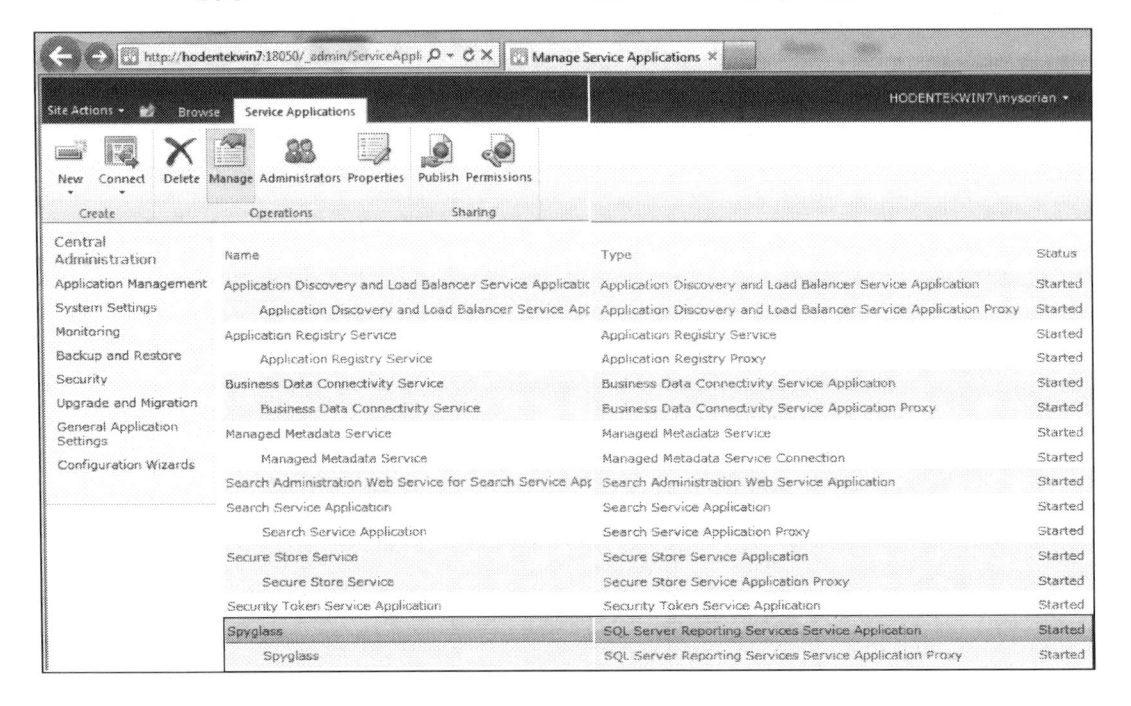

The **Service Applications** page can be used to manage this service from the preceding page.

9. Highlight **Spyglass** in the previous page and click on **Manage**.

    The **Manage Reporting Services Application** page will be displayed as follows:

[70]

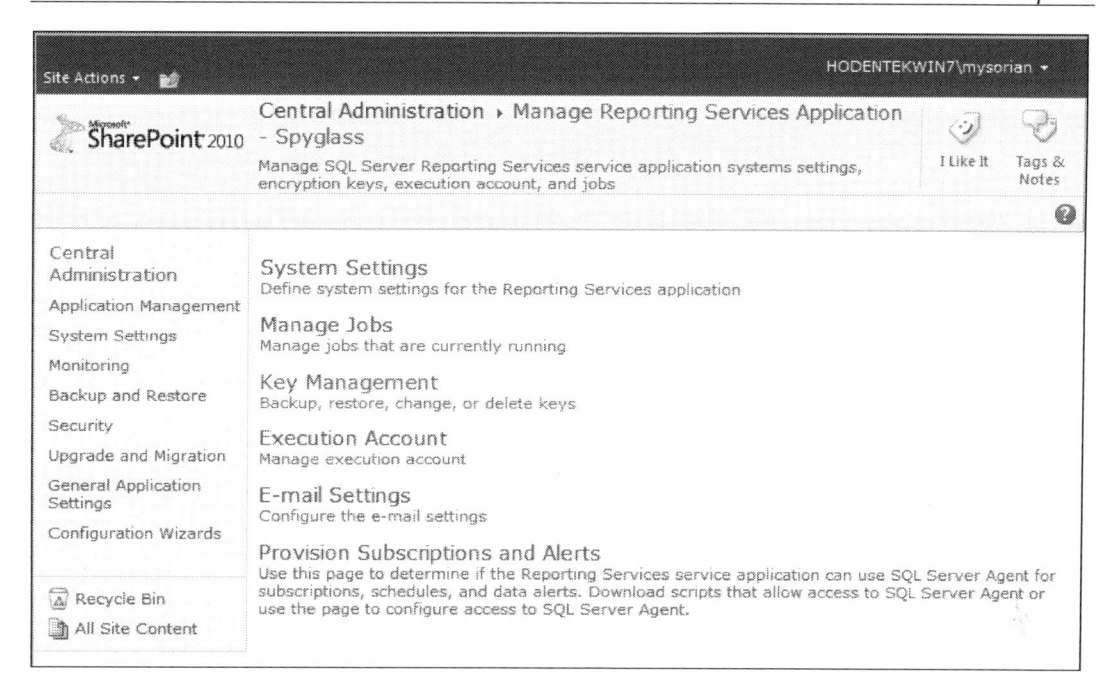

This screen functions somewhat like the configuration manager for the Native mode report server. Each of these settings open their detailed related pages, where you configure according to your needs and availability of resources.

In *Chapter 7, Self-Service Data Alerts in SSRS 2012*, on Data Alerts, the provision subscriptions, Data Alerts, and related information will be described.

Activating the Power View site collection feature

Power View is a site collection feature, which enables interactive data exploration possible for both PowerPivot workbooks (we are not concerned here) and Analysis Services Tabular databases. Make sure it is activated. If it is not, you may activate it in SharePoint Central Administration as follows:

1. Click on the menu item **Site Actions** (top-left), then click on **Site Settings** (at the bottom of the drop-down menu).

2. Look under the section named **Site Collection Administration**, and click on **Site Collection Features**.

3. Click on the **Power View Integration** feature, then click on **Activate**.

4. Verify that **Report Server Central Administration Feature** and **Report Server Integration Feature** are both activate. Activate them if they are not.

This completes the tasks that need to be done before you build Power View Reports and Data Alerts in SharePoint.

In *Chapter 6, Power View and Reporting Services*, creating a data source based on a BISM is described, which is the starting point for creating Power View Reports.

Summary

This chapter describes the key features of SQL Server Reporting Services 2012. All SQL server software components used in the preparation of this book as well as bringing in sample data to these servers are also described. Step-by-step instructions are provided for most of the installation related items in this book. One of the key features of this version of SQL Server Reporting Services is the tight integration with SharePoint Server, and therefore guided instructions are provided to install SharePoint Server 2010 on the same machine. The configurations of Reporting Services for the SQL Server Reporting Services 2012 installed in Native mode, as well as installing Reporting Services in SharePoint Integrated mode are described. This is a mandatory chapter to work with the rest of the book.

In the next chapter, which is also mandatory, we will be looking at what Visual Studio provides for authoring and deploying reports. We will be working with Visual Studio 2012 and **SQL Server Data Tools (SSDT)**.

2
SQL Server Reporting Services 2012 Projects with Visual Studio 2012

In the previous chapter, we prepared the ground for learning Reporting Services 2012 by installing the software environment on a single computer. In this chapter, we will look at one of the important tools, SQL Server Data Tools, used to create business intelligence projects in general and Reporting Services projects in particular.

What is business intelligence?

Business intelligence (BI) is the intelligent way of looking at raw business data, after processing the data with business intelligence tools. The motivation for using BI is to extract information contained in the data that would help the bottom line of the business; develop a new insight to branch out into new opportunities; set up business campaigns; extract information to determine problems, if any, in running the business in certain ways; predict the business trend by implementing calculated changes to business patterns; and so on.

The ability to crunch large amounts of data from many different sources of data and to wring out all the details necessary for such intelligent analysis is at the core of business intelligence. Reporting is a major part of the BI, to convey the result of data crunching in a format that can be easily grasped allowing us to take proactive measures.

In previous versions of SQL Servers, notably in SQL Server 2008, an installation of SQL Server installed a version of Visual Studio called **Business Intelligence Development Studio (BIDS)** containing only BI-related projects.

This has changed in SQL Server 2012 and a new Visual Studio Shell called **SQL Server Data Tools (SSDT)** dedicated to BI is installed with an installation of SQL Server 2012. Visual Studio 2012 continues to have projects of other types, not including those that are in SSDT. **Visual Studio 2012 (VS2012)** can be used for creating reports and viewing both local as well as (report) server-based reports. In this sense, if the Report Manager, the frontend tool for viewing reports on the Report Server, or the URL access is not available, then the report viewer controls in Visual Studio can be used. Report Viewer is also available as a redistributable runtime package.

In this chapter, we look at installing and using both SSDT and Visual Studio 2010. We also work with a number of hands-on exercises in acquiring the necessary skills to create and view reports with these tools.

In this chapter, we will learn about SQL Server Data Tools and carry out a number of tasks. The following list is an overview of the contents:

- Introduction to SSDT
- BI projects in SSDT
- Creating reports using SSDT
- Creating reports using VS2012

Introduction to SQL Server Data Tools

SSDT installs when you install SQL Server 2012 as a shared feature. Although it is not a complete replacement for SQL Server Management Studio, SSDT offers the user a similar canvas for working with the SQL Server except for a few specialized tasks (a quasi SSMS functionality). Follow this link to get the complete picture of what SSDT can do in terms of working with SQL Server 2012: `http://msdn.microsoft.com/en-us/library/hh272686(v=vs.103).aspx`

This quasi SSMS functionality is one part of SSDT. It is also the platform to work with BI projects and the latest BI semantic model, an all-inclusive model. The various pieces of the BI stack are woven together more tightly than before, and the model can be leveraged by all business users. In addition to SQL Server related tasks from inside Visual Studio Shell, SSDT also provides BI project types and tools for developing SQL Server 2012 Analysis Services, Reporting Services, and Integration Services BI solutions.

In the early days of SSDT, when it debuted, there was some confusion (`http://www.sqlservercentral.com/blogs/jamesserra/2012/04/13/ssdt-installation-confusion/print/`, also `http://blogs.msdn.com/b/ssdt/archive/2012/06/06/getting-started-with-localdb-debugging-using-ssdt.aspx?CommentPosted=true#commentmessage`) related to its installation. This seems to persist, as you can see that the SSDT installed with SQL Server 2012 Enterprise (Evaluation) still shows the Web install of SSDT as a project template, as shown in the next image. More information on SSDT and Visual Studio 2012 is available at `http://social.msdn.microsoft.com/Forums/en-US/sqlreportingservices/thread/1f005f31-82a6-4e1c-b221-cb2c798c4caa`. A few more ready-to-use details are at `http://hodentekmsss.blogspot.com/2012/12/december-update-to-ssdt.html`.
Also note that the Report Model of the BIDS project shown in the next image in column three is not supported in SSDT, as Microsoft enhanced the ad-hoc reporting capability with the new **Business Intelligence Semantic Model (BISM)**. The Report Model continues to be supported in the earlier version of SQL Server 2008 and SQL Server 2008 R2. In *Chapter 4*, *Visual Studio 2008 Business Intelligence Template* projects in *Learning SQL Server Reporting Services 2008*, *ISBN: 9781847916187*, a complete hands-on exercise steps you through creating a Report Model project and deploying to the Report Server.

In the first column, you see the project types available in Visual Studio Ultimate (notice the absence of BI projects) if you do not have SQL Server 2012 installed. In the middle column, what appears to be a project template is not a project but a link to a Web install of SSDT:

VS 2012 Ultimate (still the VS 2010 shell)	SQL Server 2012 Enterprise (Evaluation)	BIDS SQL Server 2008 R2
New Project ▷ Recent ▲ Installed 　▲ Templates 　　▷ Visual Basic 　　▷ Visual C# 　　▷ Visual C++ 　　▷ Visual F# 　　　SQL Server 　　　LightSwitch 　　▷ Other Project Types 　　　Modeling Projects 　▲ Samples 　　▷ Visual Basic ▷ Online	New Project Recent Templates **Installed Templates** ▲ Business Intelligence 　　Analysis Services 　　Integration Services 　　Reporting Services ▷ Visual Basic ▷ Visual C# 　SQL Server Web Install of SSDT from here ▷ Other Project Types Online Templates	Visual Studio installed templates Analysis Services Project Import Analysis Services Database Integration Services Connections Proje... Integration Services Project Report Server Project Wizard Report Model Project Report Server Project

SQL Server Reporting Services 2012 Projects with Visual Studio 2012

In December 2012, SSDT was updated and the readers do well to install SSDT from `http://msdn.microsoft.com/en-us/data/hh297027`. In here, there are two installs—one for Visual Studio 2010 and the other for Visual Studio 2012. For this book, the December update for VS 2012 has been used. These versions of programs are upgraded as follows:

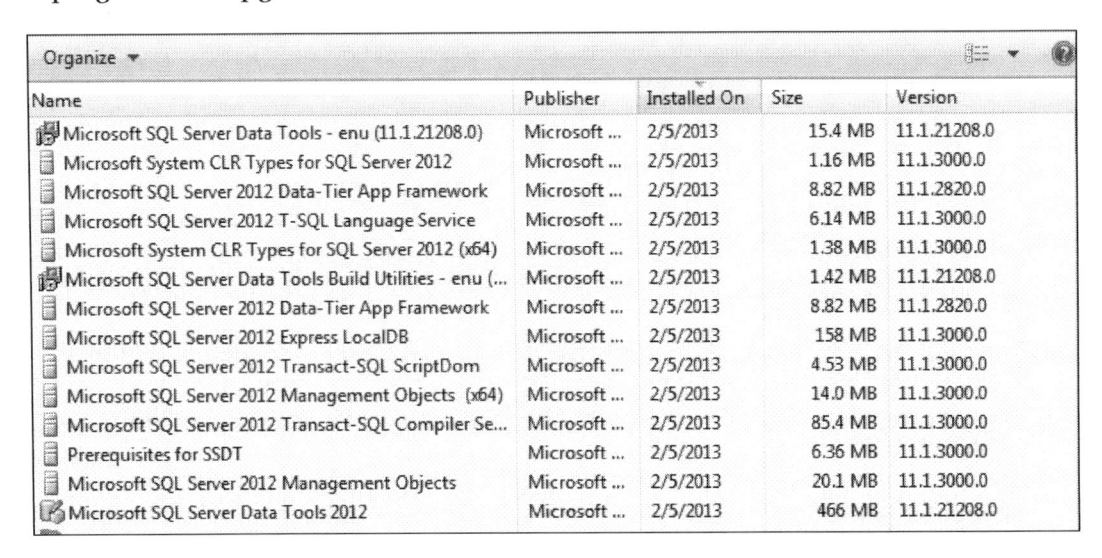

Name	Publisher	Installed On	Size	Version
Microsoft SQL Server Data Tools - enu (11.1.21208.0)	Microsoft ...	2/5/2013	15.4 MB	11.1.21208.0
Microsoft System CLR Types for SQL Server 2012	Microsoft ...	2/5/2013	1.16 MB	11.1.3000.0
Microsoft SQL Server 2012 Data-Tier App Framework	Microsoft ...	2/5/2013	8.82 MB	11.1.2820.0
Microsoft SQL Server 2012 T-SQL Language Service	Microsoft ...	2/5/2013	6.14 MB	11.1.3000.0
Microsoft System CLR Types for SQL Server 2012 (x64)	Microsoft ...	2/5/2013	1.38 MB	11.1.3000.0
Microsoft SQL Server Data Tools Build Utilities - enu (...	Microsoft ...	2/5/2013	1.42 MB	11.1.21208.0
Microsoft SQL Server 2012 Data-Tier App Framework	Microsoft ...	2/5/2013	8.82 MB	11.1.2820.0
Microsoft SQL Server 2012 Express LocalDB	Microsoft ...	2/5/2013	158 MB	11.1.3000.0
Microsoft SQL Server 2012 Transact-SQL ScriptDom	Microsoft ...	2/5/2013	4.53 MB	11.1.3000.0
Microsoft SQL Server 2012 Management Objects (x64)	Microsoft ...	2/5/2013	14.0 MB	11.1.3000.0
Microsoft SQL Server 2012 Transact-SQL Compiler Se...	Microsoft ...	2/5/2013	85.4 MB	11.1.3000.0
Prerequisites for SSDT	Microsoft ...	2/5/2013	6.36 MB	11.1.3000.0
Microsoft SQL Server 2012 Management Objects	Microsoft ...	2/5/2013	20.1 MB	11.1.3000.0
Microsoft SQL Server Data Tools 2012	Microsoft ...	2/5/2013	466 MB	11.1.21208.0

In general, the reason one may need to track versions is to have the ability to backtrack and see if something does not work. If any program is absent, for some reason or other, then you may be able to go back and install them. This is especially true when you install updates of programs. The earlier version of SSDT was `10.3.20116.0`, and was called **Microsoft SQL Server Data Tools-Database** projects.

The preceding installation seems to make these changes to the Visual Studio interfaces. The SSDT installed with SQL Server 2012 does not get altered, and continues to hold the BI project types. Visual Studio 2012 now has the new project type SQL Server, as shown here, when you launch the Visual Studio program from its shortcut:

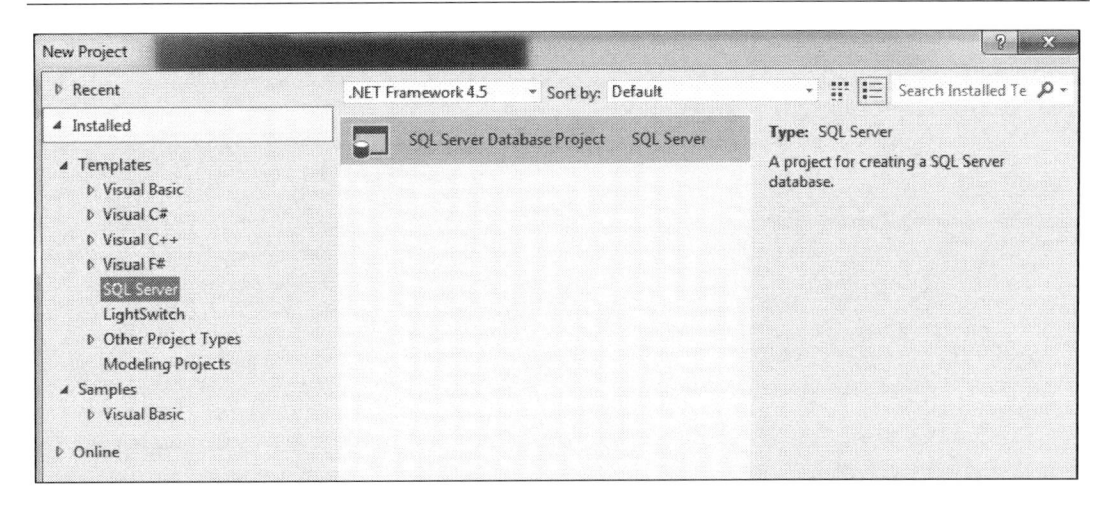

BI Projects on SSDT

The SSDT installed with SQL Server 2012 can be opened by launching the SSDT shortcut in the Microsoft SQL Server 2012 install folder, as shown, or `C:\ProgramData\Microsoft\Windows\Start Menu\Programs`:

This opens the Visual Studio 2010 shell. The **Reporting Services (RS)** projects that are available are as shown in the UI. The two types of RS projects available in SSDT are shown in the following screenshot:

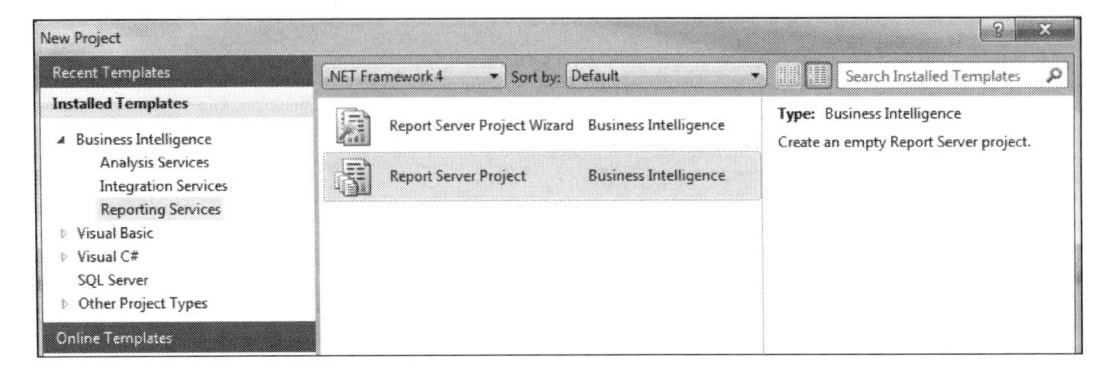

Here is a brief description of the two Report Server projects in the preceding image.

Report Server Project

When you choose **Report Server Project**, the **Report Designer** window will be displayed. The project properties apply to all the reports and all shared data sources. They can be seen by right-clicking on the project and choosing **Properties**.

Report Server Project Wizard

When you choose the **Report Server Project Wizard** option, the report creation is wizard driven. This automatically creates a report server project. The wizard guides you with instructions through the wizard pages to create a data source; a set of data source credentials; a query to extract data that you need for the report; add a table or matrix, specify report data, group and aggregate data; add themes and preview the data. You can make changes to the report by using the report designer and project properties.

Both the project types use the report designer. The report designer hosted in SSDT provides the means to carry out the following reporting services-related tasks:

- The **Report Data** pane to organize and modify data used in your report
- Tabbed views for design and preview of the interactive report design

- A query designer to specify which data to retrieve from data sources and how to filter it. There are two options for the query designer—one is text-based, which accepts a SQL statement, and the other is a graphic interface that you can use. Expression editor with IntelliSense builds Visual Basic expressions that customize the report content and appearance
- Allow custom report items and custom query designers

Due to space limitations, the preceding information is very brief; please follow this link for more details: http://technet.microsoft.com/en-us/library/ms173745.aspx.

In the next section, we will be creating reports, and to do so we will be using most of the preceding capabilities.

Creating reports using SSDT

In the following sections, we will look at creating reports using SSDT, deploying the report to the report server, and modifying a report in the SSDT user interface.

Hands-on exercise 2.1 – creating a report using the Report Server Project Wizard

We are now ready to try out and create a report using SSDT.

1. Click on **Report Server Project Wizard**. Change the default name from Report Project 1 to RSPW2012 and click on **OK**. This creates a folder for the project and the location of files at c:\users\<Username>documents\visual studio 2010\Projects.

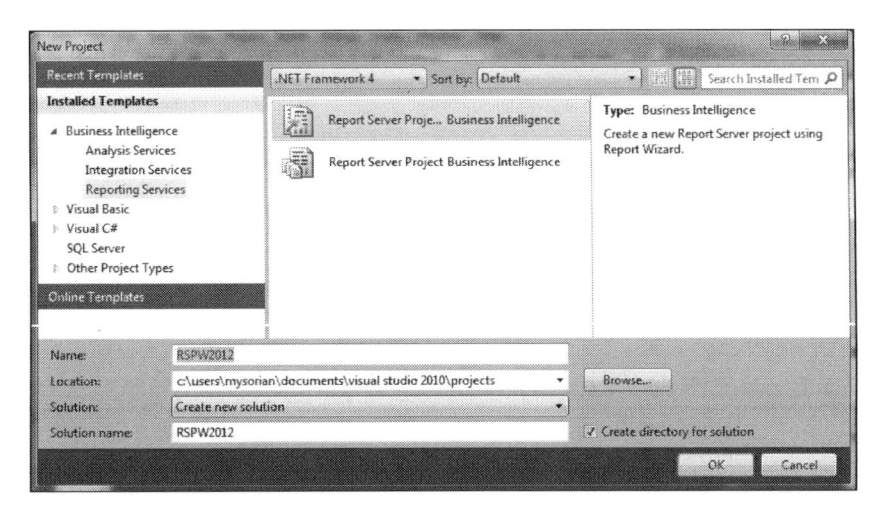

2. Click on **OK**. The RSPW2012 project-related folders will be displayed, and the report wizard's **Welcome** window will be displayed immediately. Read information on the **Welcome to Report Wizard** window.

   Notice that the project has folders for **Shared Data Sources** and **Shared Datasets**. There is a folder for the reports as well.

3. Click on **Next** on the **Welcome** screen.

   The wizard takes you to the **Select the Data Source** page of the **Report Wizard** window, as follows:

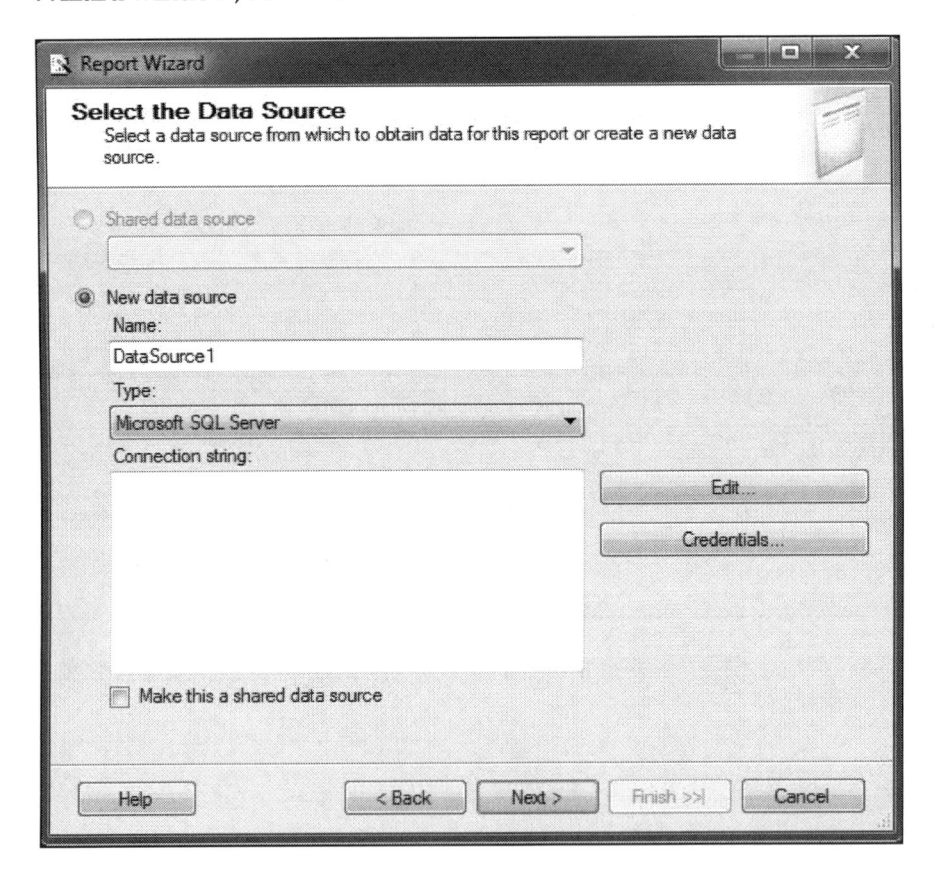

Chapter 2

The default name is `Data Source1`, and you may choose a different one. Here, it is DSNW. Click on the handle for **Type**. The drop-down list in the next image displays (only a part of the screen is shown) many other data sources from which you can fill a report:

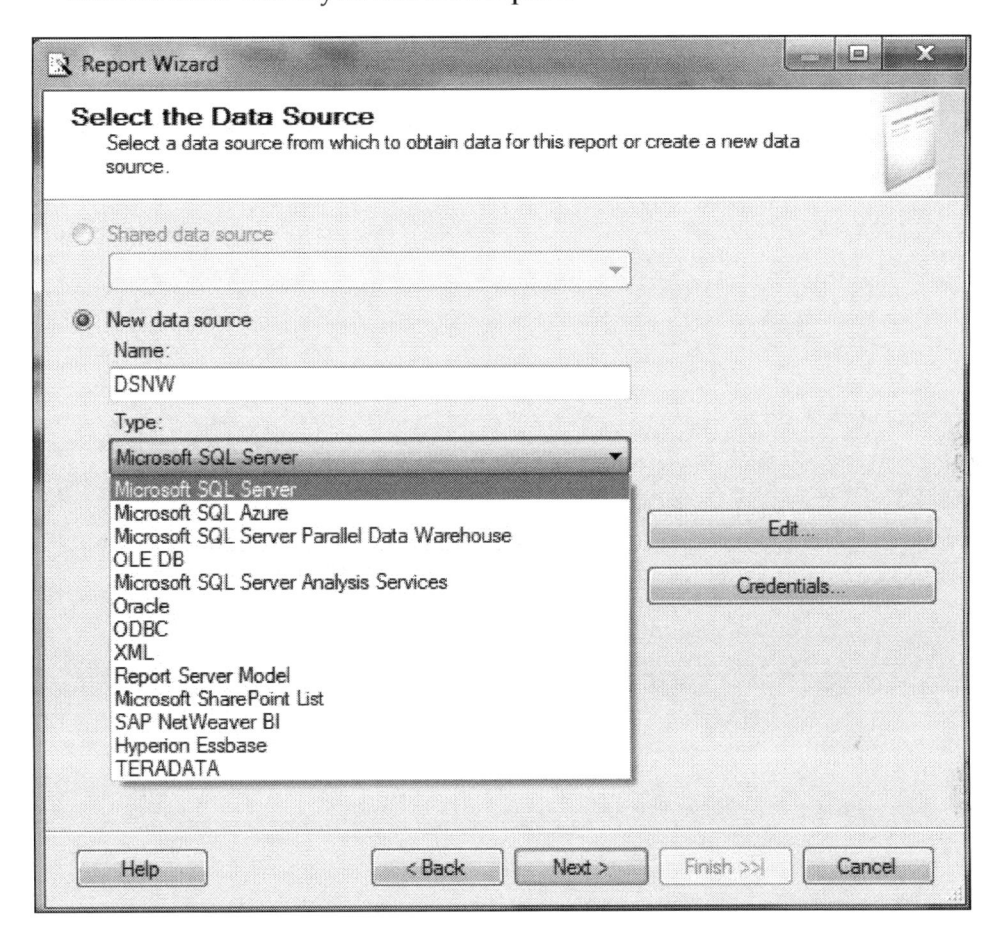

![Report Wizard - Select the Data Source dialog showing New data source named DSNW with Type dropdown listing: Microsoft SQL Server, Microsoft SQL Azure, Microsoft SQL Server Parallel Data Warehouse, OLE DB, Microsoft SQL Server Analysis Services, Oracle, ODBC, XML, Report Server Model, Microsoft SharePoint List, SAP NetWeaver BI, Hyperion Essbase, TERADATA]

You may notice that you can use a Report Server Model. Although you cannot create a Report Server Model using SSDT, you can still use report models from the earlier versions of SQL Server.

4. Click on Microsoft SQL Server. The connection string field is still empty. Click on the **Edit** button to the right of the empty field. The **Connection Properties** window will be displayed. Make suitable entries as shown; for the Server name, type of authentication, and picking a database from the drop-down list. You will see Northwind in the **Database** drop-down list because we downloaded the sample database and attached it to the SQL Server instance:

5. Click on **OK** after testing the connection. The **Connection string** field will be updated, as shown in the next screenshot.

Chapter 2

If you fail while testing, the reasons could be the Data Source client may be wrong, your server instance is wrong or not started, your credentials are wrong, or the database may not exist. However, after you enter your authentication information, the **Database** drop-down list itself will not display and you will get an error message. You have to correct all the errors and then try.

```
Connection string:
Data Source=HODENTEKWIN7\KAILUA;Initial
Catalog=Northwind
```

Now, we have an option to make this a shared source, which makes it available for other reports if needed.

6. Place a tick mark for the checkbox and click on **Next**.

    The **Query Builder** window will be displayed, which has an empty pane for the query string (a place for an SQL statement) and a **Query Builder...** button, which when clicked on, brings up a design area where a SQL statement can be built, starting from the tables/views.

    > In *Chapter 3, Report Integration with Report Viewer Controls*, in *Learning SQL Server Reporting Services 2008*, ISBN: 9781847916187, a complete hands-on exercise steps you through working with Query Designer.

    Here, we opt to use a SQL statement as follows:
    ```
    Select Customers.CustomerID, customers.CompanyName,customers.
    Address,
            Orders.EmployeeID, Orders.RequiredDate, Orders.
    ShippedDate,orders.Freight
    From Customers INNER JOIN Orders ON Customers.CustomerID=Orders.
    CustomerID
    ```

7. Type in the statement in the empty space for **Query String**.
8. Click on **Next**. The **Select the Report Type** window will be displayed.
9. Accept the default as **Tabular** and click on **Next**. The **Design the Table** window will be displayed with all the columns (in the query) in the **Available** fields' pane, with all others empty.

10. Click on an element in the **Available** field, then click on one of the buttons—**Page**, **Group**, or **Details**—to fill the displayed field's window. This arranges the report pages and groups the data on them with details selected. This should also empty the **Available** field's pane:

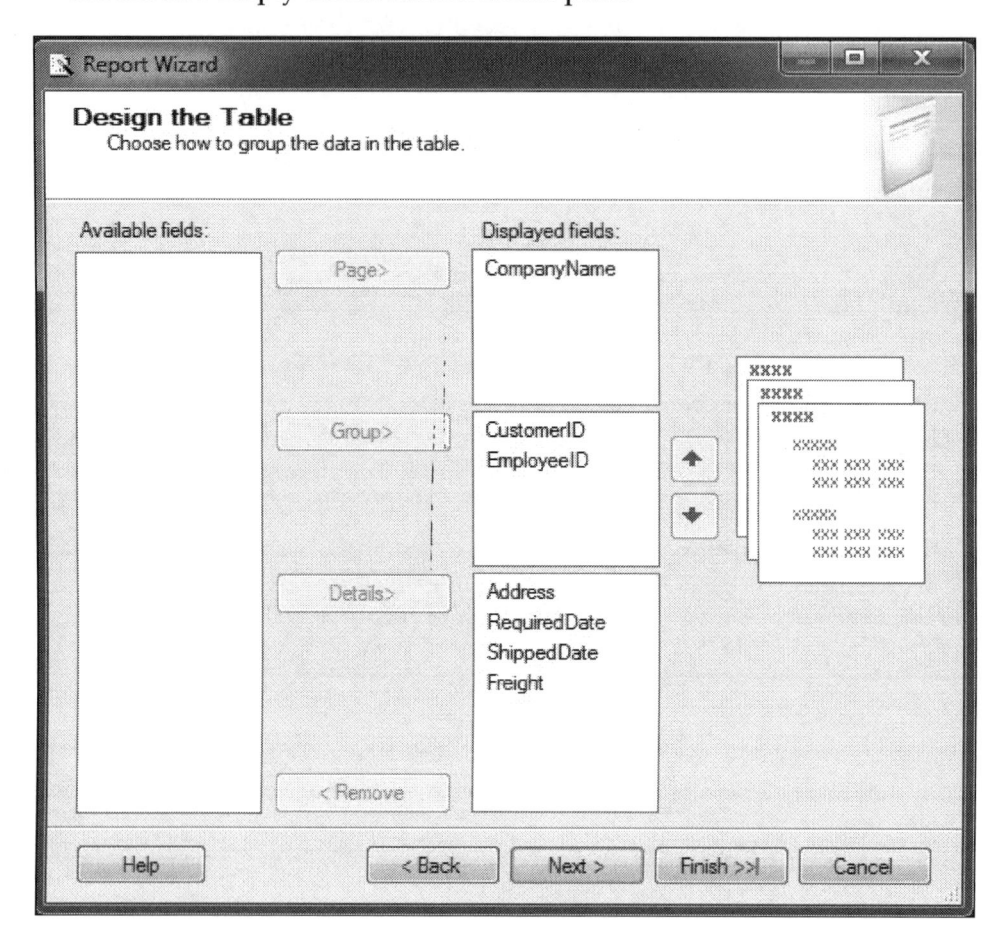

11. Click on **Next**. In the **Choose the Table Layout** page displayed, accept the default, **Stepped**. Place check marks for **Include Subtotals** and **Enable drilldown** checkboxes, and click on the **Next** button.
12. In the **Choose a Style** window, make a choice. Here, **Forest** was chosen. Each style is different from the other only in the theme; the one shown is **Mahogany** in the following screenshot:

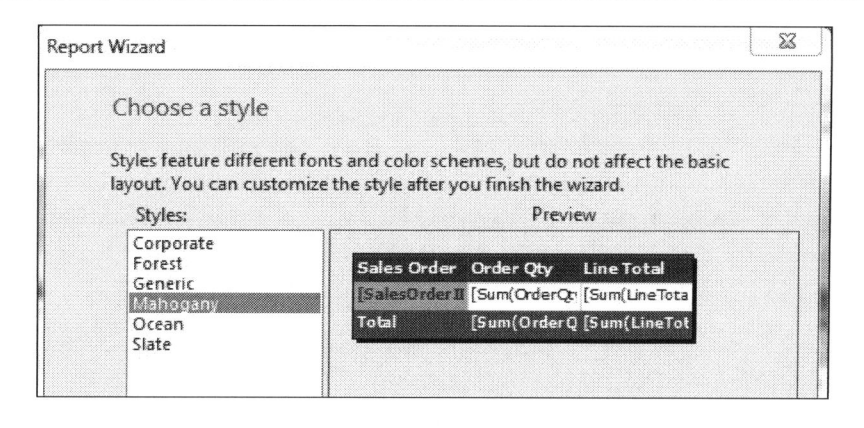

13. Click on **Next**.
14. The **Choose the Deployment Server Location** page will be displayed.
15. There are three important pieces of information you must provide in this window—a value for **Report Server Version**, which you can choose from a drop-down list; the default choice shown is **OK**, the other choice is SQL Server 2008. For the Report Server, we will use the Report Server configured for SQL Server 2012 in *Chapter 1, Overview and Installation – SQL Server Reporting Services 2012*. This is `http://HODENETKWIN7:80/Report_Server_KAILUA` and for the `Deployment` folder (also known as the `Path`) enter `/RSPW2012`. Make sure you read the specific instructions on this page. After making these changes, click on **Next**. The name of your Report Server would be different, and the path and report may be different as well.
16. The **Completing the Wizard** page will be displayed. Here, give a name for the report; the default is used for now. The window also shows the choices made. Place a check mark for **Preview report** and click on **Finish**.

    The following page shows up. The **Preview** control in the user interface is not working!

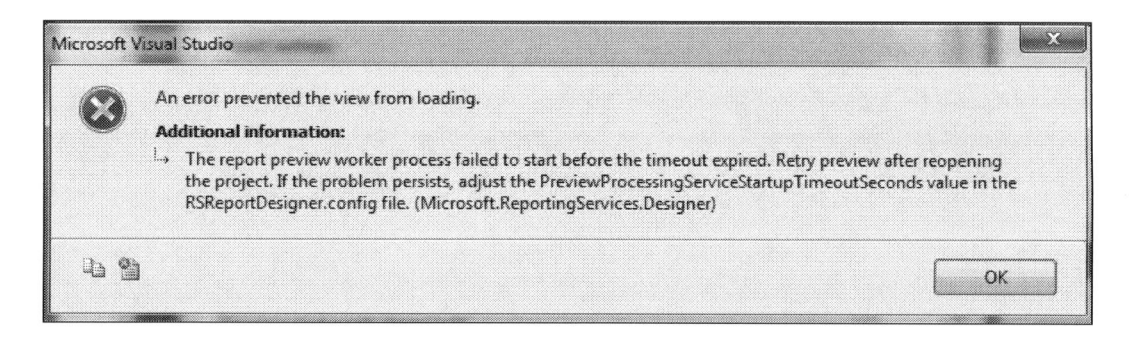

SQL Server Reporting Services 2012 Projects with Visual Studio 2012

17. Look for the preceding file in the computer in **Start | Search**. It will be found at `C:\Program Files (x86)\Microsoft Visual Studio 10.0\Common7\IDE\PrivateAssemblies`.

    Changing the default 15 seconds to 45 does not make any change. The Report Design will be displayed inside Visual Studio, as shown. Report Data is on the left. Only the data source is shared. Datasets contain `DataSet1` with all the fields on the report. The report design is in the **Design** tab of the designer window:

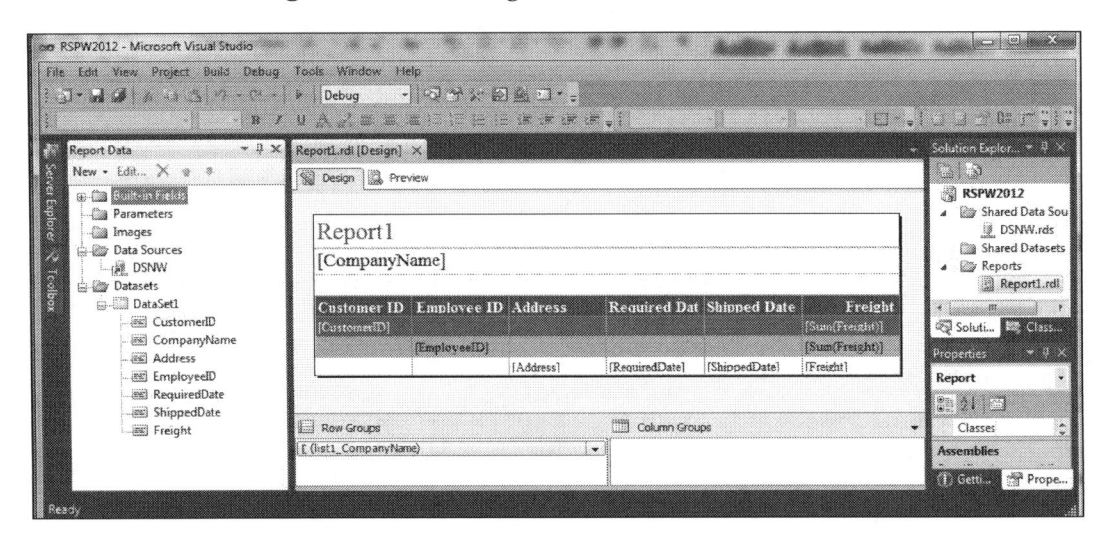

18. Click on the **Preview** tab; the previous error will show up again. A possible reason for this is that the **Service Principle Name** was not specified during the Reporting Services configuration. However, you can still display the report. Right-click on `Report1.rdl` in the solution explorer and select **Run**.

    `Report1` will be displayed after some processing. The error regarding preview will been posted to the forum at http://social.technet.microsoft.com/Forums/en-US/sqlreportingservices/thread/41d46c69-5a18-4915-8b5e-fc3c19da8db9 and http://social.technet.microsoft.com/Forums/en-US/sqlreportingservices/thread/38ff8d54-06aa-40c3-8916-378d5185320e:

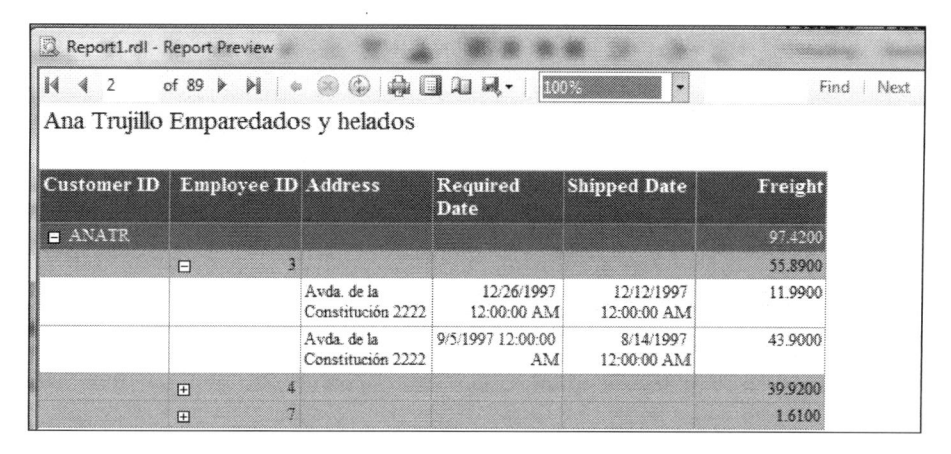

This concludes the hands-on exercise 2.1.

Hands-on exercise 2.2 – deploying the report to the Report Server

Now that the report is working and getting rendered, it is time to deploy the report to the Report Server.

You can view how and where the report is going to be deployed if you open the project's **Property Pages** window:

1. Click on Project | RSPW Properties... and open the property pages as shown.

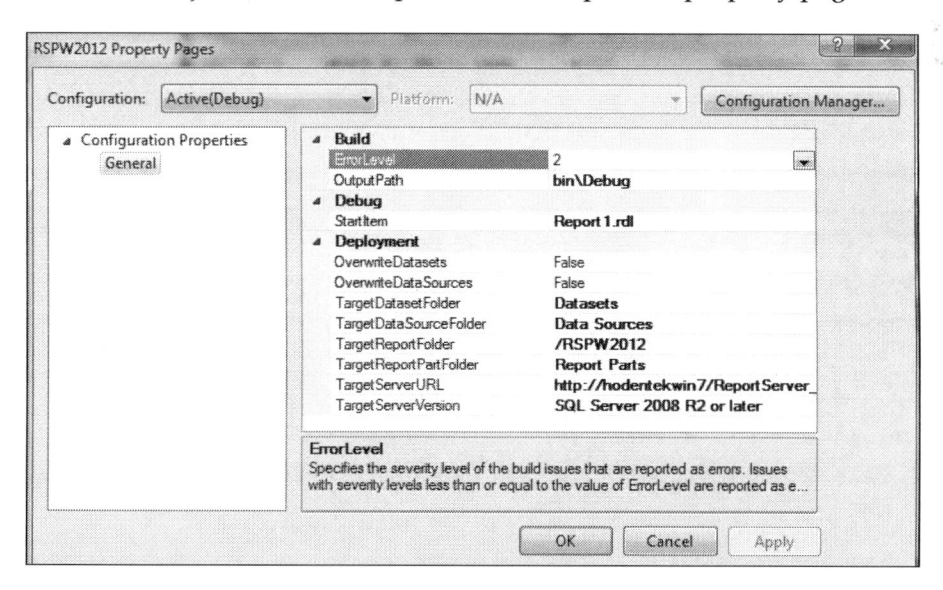

SQL Server Reporting Services 2012 Projects with Visual Studio 2012

2. Right-click on `Report1.rdl` and then on **Deploy**. The following error will be displayed:

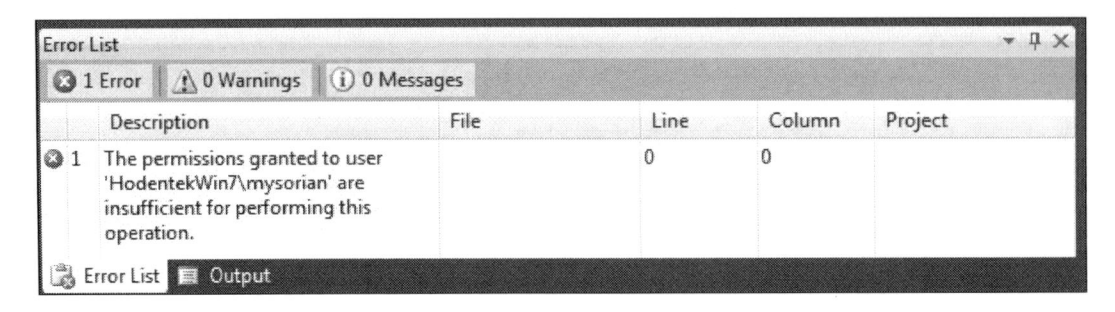

	Description	File	Line	Column	Project
1	The permissions granted to user 'HodentekWin7\mysorian' are insufficient for performing this operation.		0	0	

This appears to be a permissions related problem as we did not start the VS program as an administrator.

1. Open SSDT using administrator privileges (**Run as Administrator**). Open project `RSPW2012`.

   A new error message shows up:

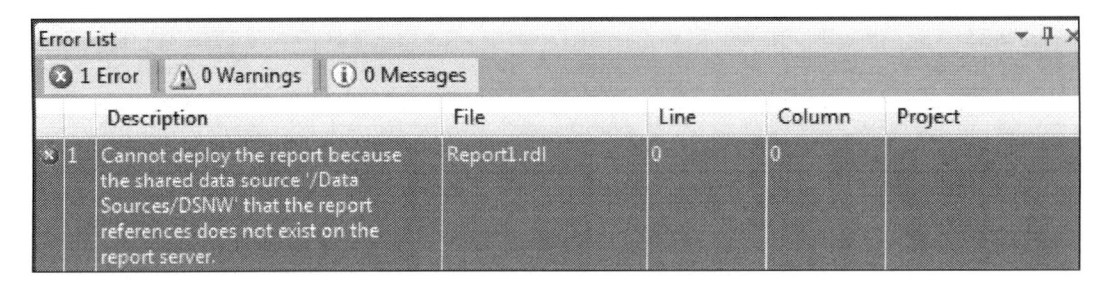

	Description	File	Line	Column	Project
1	Cannot deploy the report because the shared data source '/Data Sources/DSNW' that the report references does not exist on the report server.	Report1.rdl	0	0	

This error showed up because the report is based on a shared data source and the data source has not been deployed. Once that is done, this error goes away, as we will see in the following steps.

2. Right-click on `DSNW.rds` in the solution explorer and click on **Deploy** in the drop-down menu. The deployment succeeds. Clicking on the hyperlink (hold the *CTRL* key down) updates the designer, as follows:

[88]

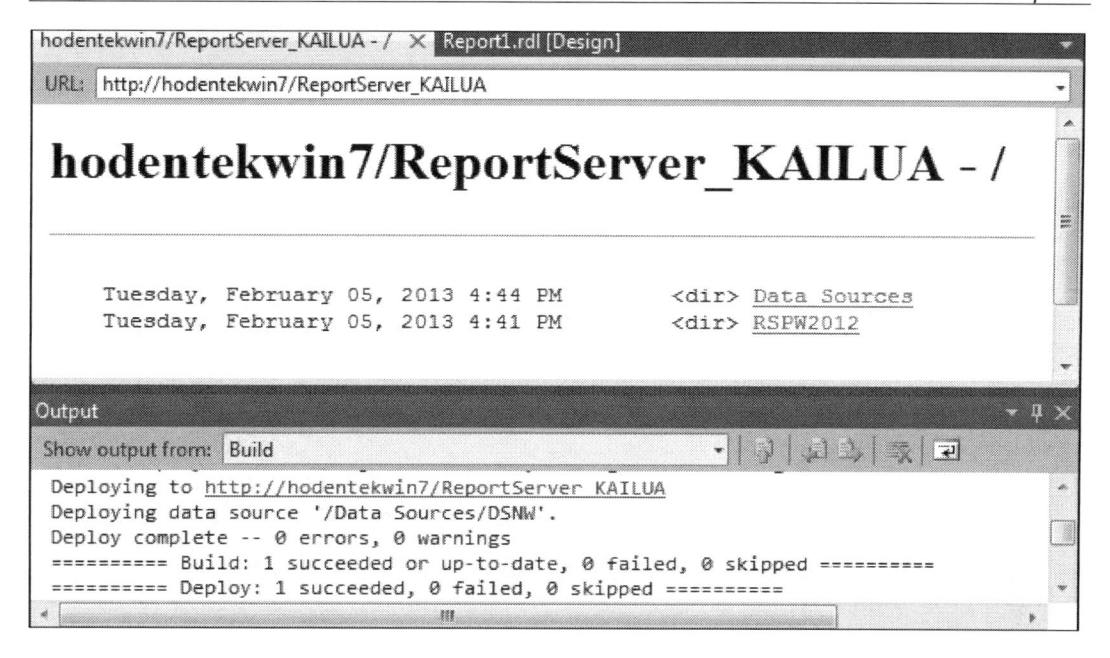

```
hodentekwin7/ReportServer_KAILUA - /

URL: http://hodentekwin7/ReportServer_KAILUA
```

hodentekwin7/ReportServer_KAILUA - /

```
   Tuesday, February 05, 2013 4:44 PM      <dir> Data Sources
   Tuesday, February 05, 2013 4:41 PM      <dir> RSPW2012
```

Output

Show output from: Build

```
Deploying to http://hodentekwin7/ReportServer_KAILUA
Deploying data source '/Data Sources/DSNW'.
Deploy complete -- 0 errors, 0 warnings
========== Build: 1 succeeded or up-to-date, 0 failed, 0 skipped ==========
========== Deploy: 1 succeeded, 0 failed, 0 skipped ==========
```

There are two directories on the Report Server—one for the project and the other for the data sources. In the **Data Sources** directory, you will find the DSNW.rds. You can click on the file to view the XML behind the file. The **Project** directory is empty.

3. Now right-click on Report1.rdl and then on **Deploy**. You get the message that the deployment succeeded.

4. Click on the hyperlink (with *CTRL* pressed) to see the Report Server in the top pane. Expand the project file to find Report1.rdl. Note that rs:Command = ListChildren is for listing subfolders:

URL: http://hodentekwin7/ReportServer_KAILUA?%2fRSPW2012&rs:Command=ListChildren

hodentekwin7/ReportServer_KAILUA - /RSPW2012

```
[To Parent Directory]
   Tuesday, February 05, 2013 4:51 PM          65035 Report1
```

The report will be displayed. Now, the command to display the report is `rs:Command = Render`. Note the changes in the URL as you make changes. `Report1` will be successfully deployed. This the first report on this Report Server.

The report and report-related information are stored in the catalog of the Report Server database, which you may recall is `ReportServer$Kailua`.

You can run a query against this database to get all the information related to the report, as shown in SQL Server Management Studio:

```
Use ReportServer$Kailua
go
Select * from dbo.catalog
```

Hands-on exercise 2.3 – creating a report using the Report wizard in SSDT

Report Server Project is the second template under **Reporting Services** in SSDT. In this section, we will be using this template to create a report.

1. Start SSDT from **All Programs | Microsoft SQL Server 2012 | SQL Server Data Tools**.
2. In the user interface, click on **File | New Project…**.
3. In the **New Project** window, click on **Report Server Project**. Change the default name of the project to `RP2012`. Accept the default location and click on **OK**. The `RP2012` project is created with the following folder structure:

Chapter 2

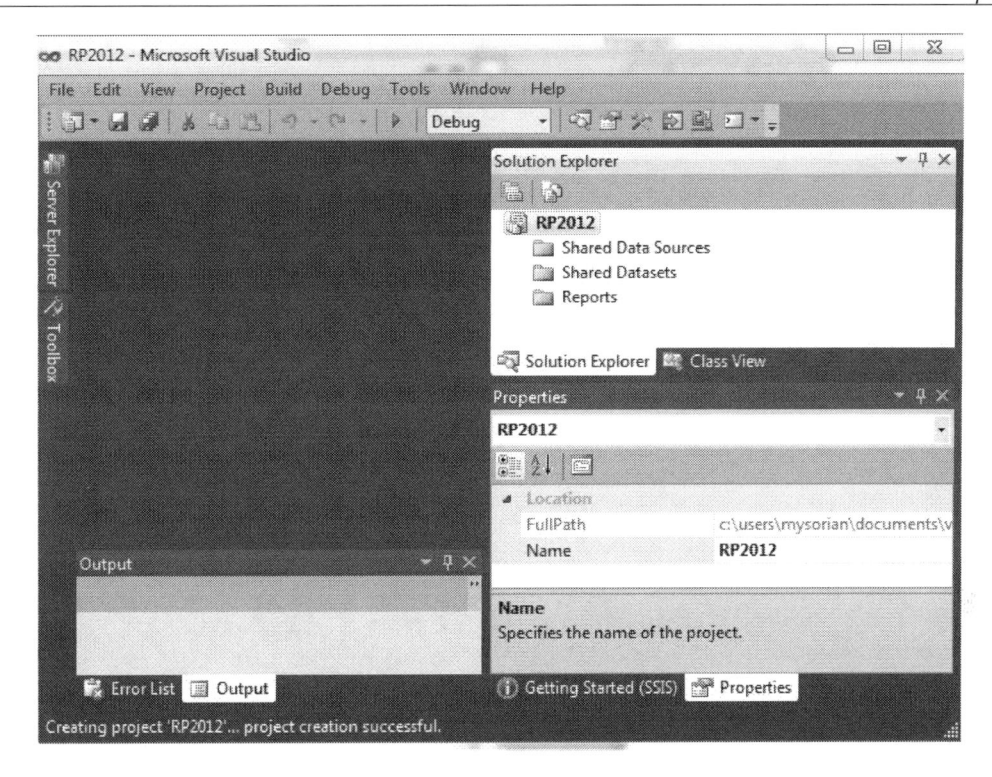

4. Right-click on the **Reports** folder and choose **Add Report** from the drop-down menu. The **Welcome to the Report Wizard** window will be displayed. Read the information on this window as it gives the steps you need to follow.

5. Click on **Next**. You get the same window you saw in *Hands-on exercise 2.1 – Creating a report using the Report Server Project Wizard*. Change the name of **New Data Source** to **DSSPL**. Click on the handle for the **Type** field to display a pick-list, as follows:

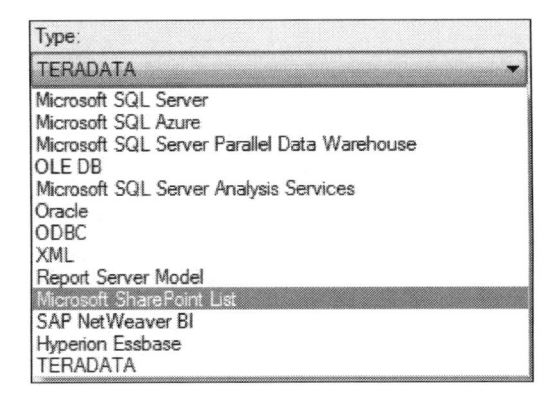

6. Click on **Microsoft SharePoint List**. For the connection string, provide the SharePoint site address as follows (this is the same as what you will see at the top of the **SharePoint 2010 Central Administration** window shown here):

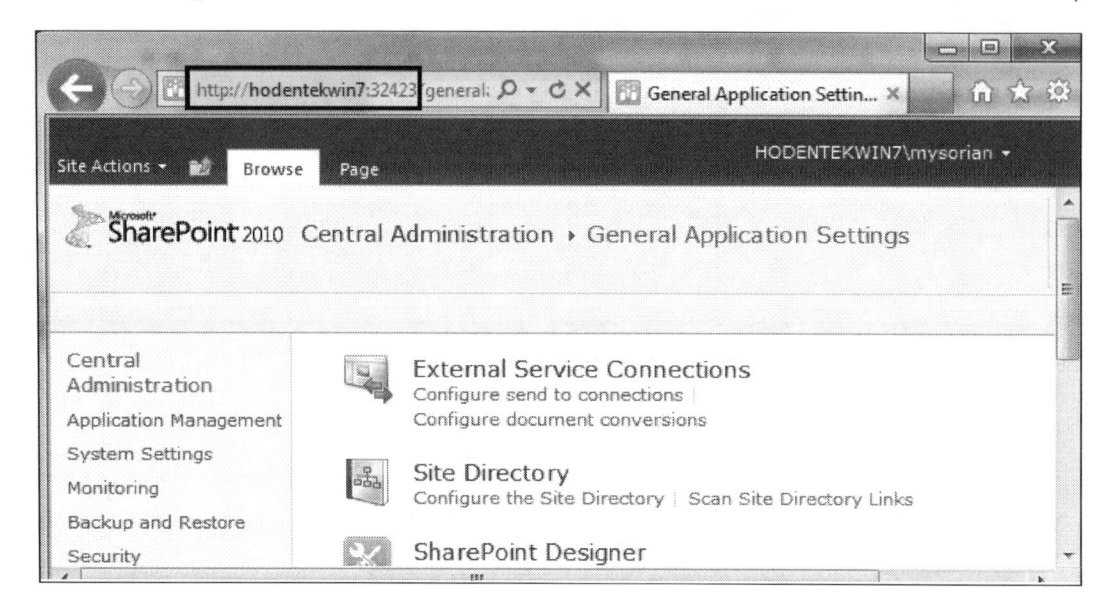

7. After entering the required information, choose the following for the **Select the Data Source** window of the Report Wizard:
    - **Name of Data Source**: DSSPL
    - **Type**: Microsoft SharePoint List
    - **Connection string**: http://hodentekwin7:32423

   Note that this address will be different in your case; use the address of the central administration site on your computer. Do not choose to make it a shared data source. Click **Next**.

8. In the **Design the Query** window displayed, click on on the **Query Builder** button. The program loads the needed items and displays the following Query Designer window:

Chapter 2

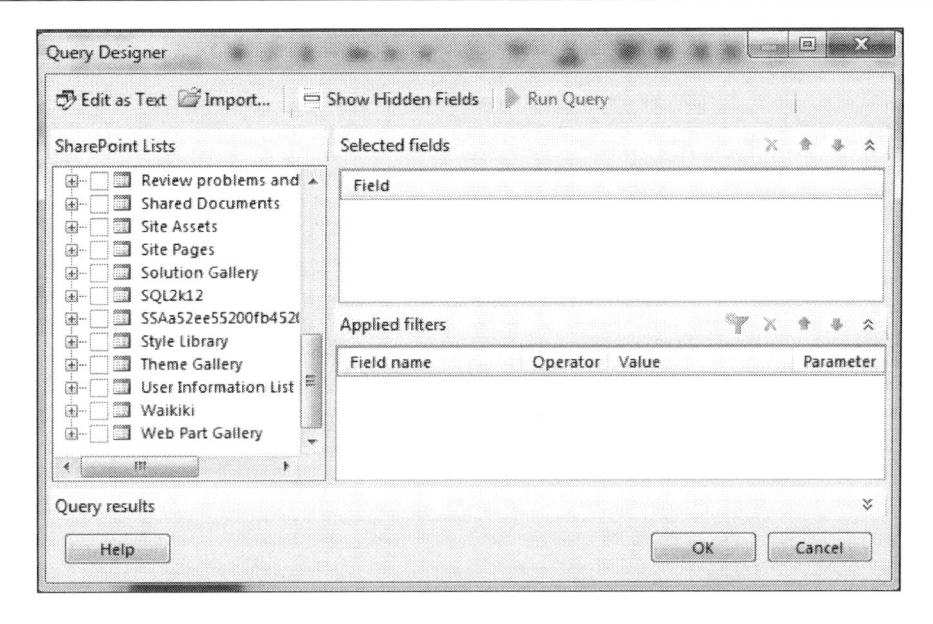

[Screenshot of Query Designer dialog with SharePoint Lists including Review problems and..., Shared Documents, Site Assets, Site Pages, Solution Gallery, SQL2k12, SSAa52ee55200fb452(, Style Library, Theme Gallery, User Information List, Waikiki, Web Part Gallery]

9. There are a couple of user created lists on this server. **Waikiki** is a simple list created by using the template for a custom list by the author. Place a check mark for **Waikiki** and the **Field** pane on the right is populated. Using the **Applied filters** pane (click on the downward pointed double carets), you can further filter the selected fields. Here, the selected fields are accepted:

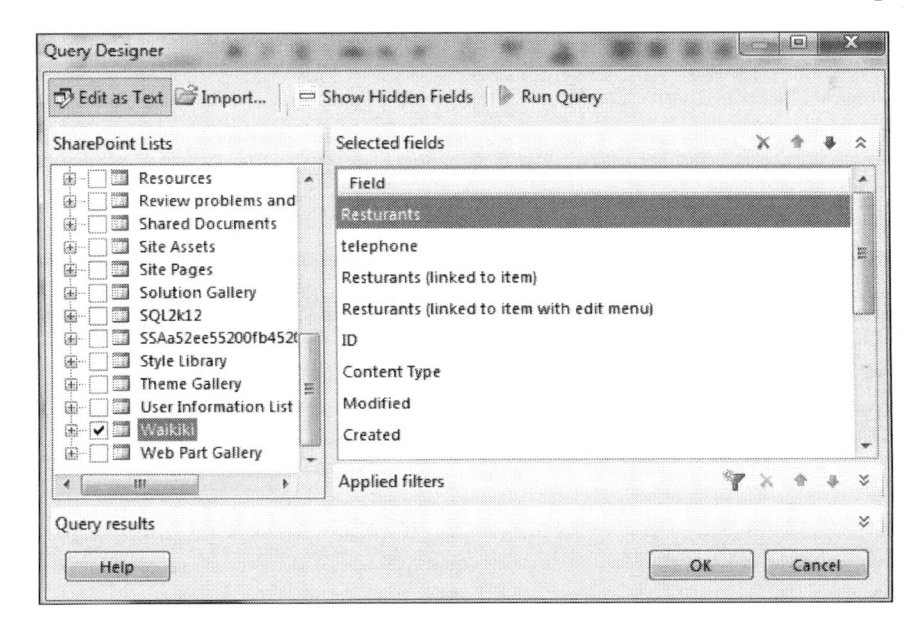

[Screenshot of Query Designer dialog with Waikiki checked, Selected fields showing: Resturants, telephone, Resturants (linked to item), Resturants (linked to item with edit menu), ID, Content Type, Modified, Created]

[93]

10. Click on **OK**. An XML code block is displayed in the **Query string** window as follows:

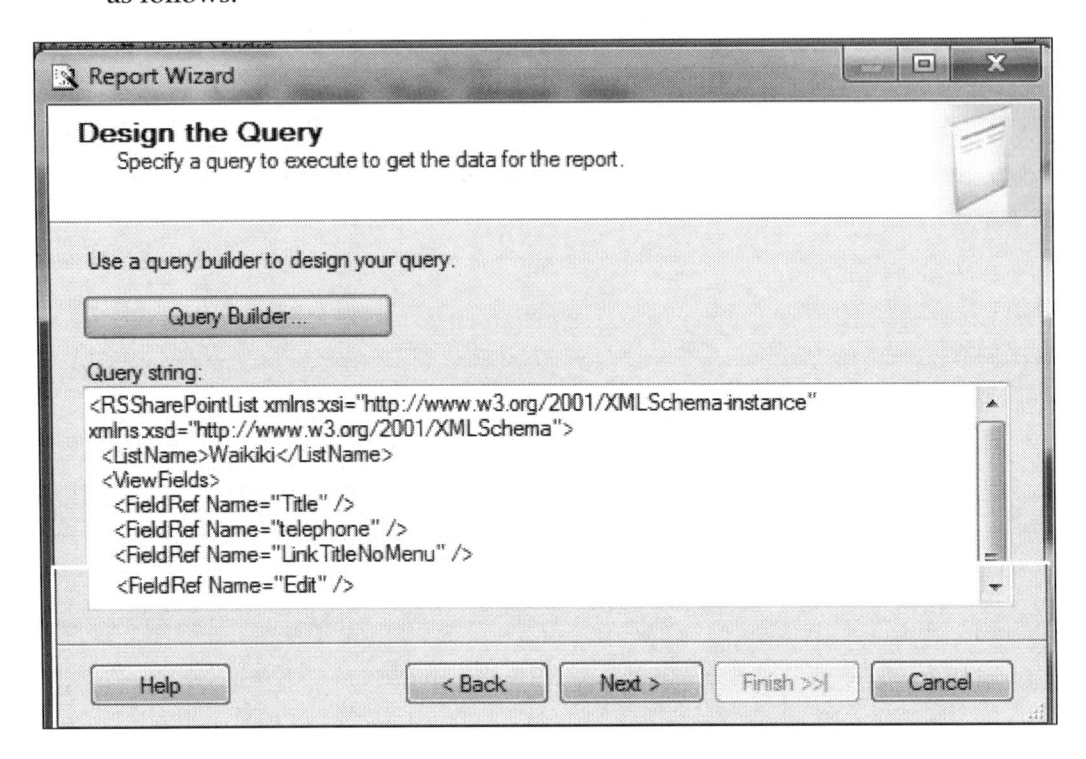

```
<RSSharePointList xmlns:xsi="http://www.w3.org/2001/XMLSchema-instance"
 xmlns:xsd="http://www.w3.org/2001/XMLSchema">
  <ListName>Waikiki</ListName>
  <ViewFields>
    <FieldRef Name="Title" />
    <FieldRef Name="telephone" />
    <FieldRef Name="LinkTitleNoMenu" />
    <FieldRef Name="Edit" />
```

11. Clicking on **Next** takes you to **Select the Report type** window. Accept **Tabular**.

12. Clicking on **Next** takes you to the **Design the Table** window. Follow the same procedure to transfer the details as in the previous exercise. After selecting what fields to show, click on **Next**.

13. In the **Choose the Table style** window, choose any. Here, **Ocean** was chosen.

14. Click on **Next**. In the **Completing the Wizard** window, change the report name to `Waikiki Restaurants`. Review the contents of this window. Select the **Preview** checkbox and click on **Finish**.

15. The **Report** will be rendered in Visual Studio's **Preview** pane.

16. Change to the **Design** view. Click on **Report** in the main menu and add footer to the report from the drop-down list. Expand **Built-in Fields** on the left, click on **Execution Time**, and drag it to the footer area as follows:

Chapter 2

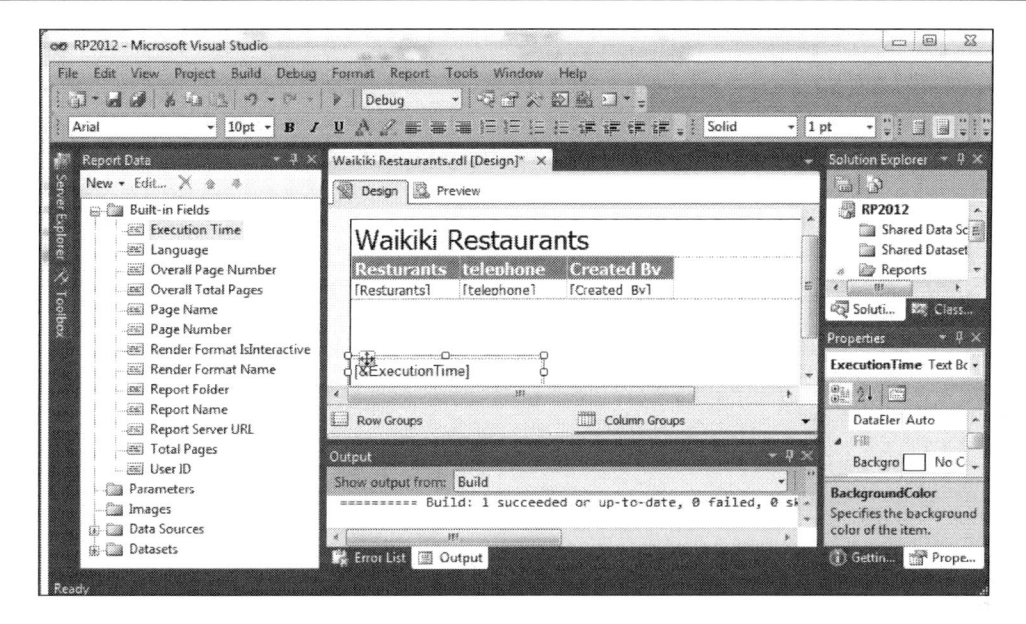

17. Click on **Project and Properties** in the drop-down menu. The **Project Property Pages** window appears as shown. Click on the handle for **Start Item** and pick the report shown, as follows:

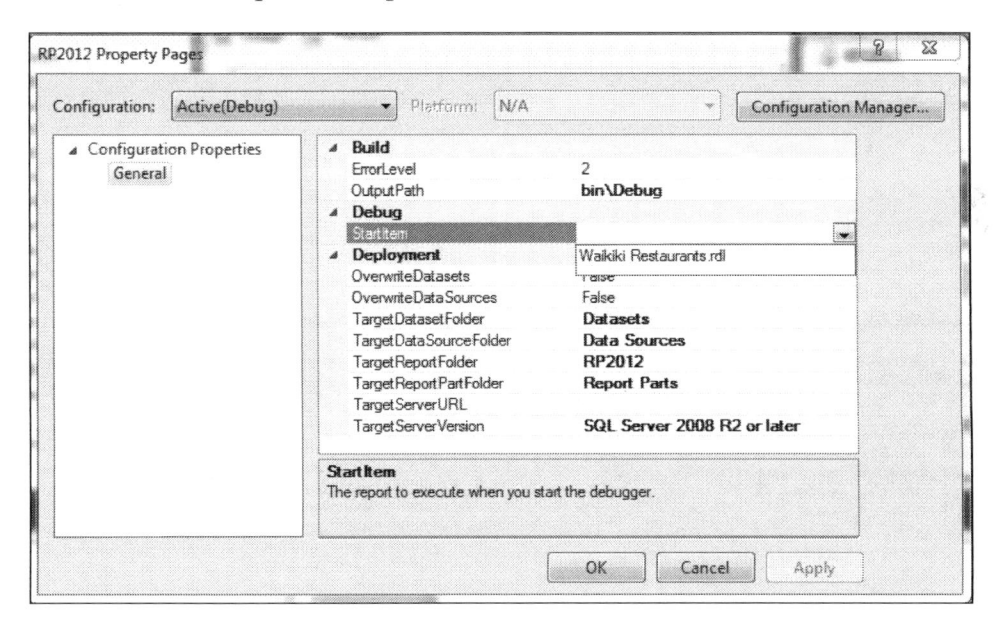

[95]

18. Click on **OK** and hit *F5*. The report will be processed and after a little while it will be rendered, as follows:

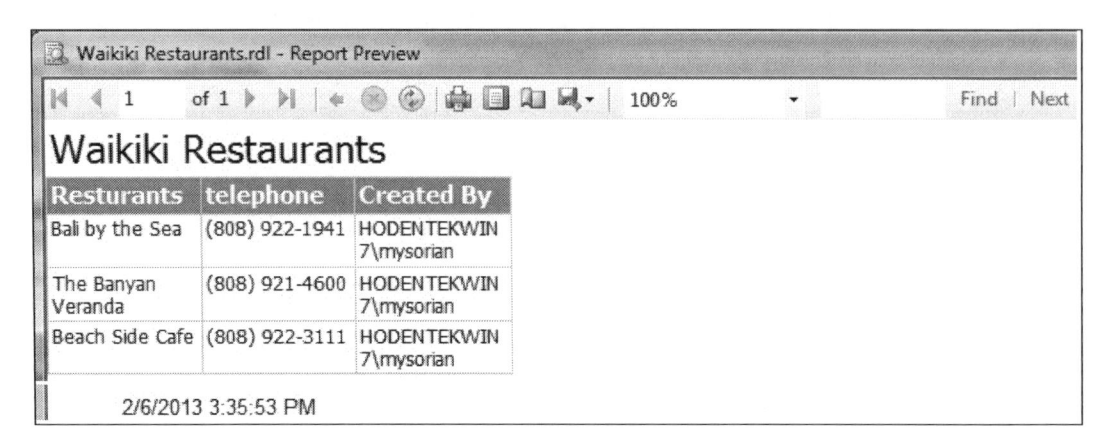

Resturants	telephone	Created By
Bali by the Sea	(808) 922-1941	HODENTEKWIN7\mysorian
The Banyan Veranda	(808) 921-4600	HODENTEKWIN7\mysorian
Beach Side Cafe	(808) 922-3111	HODENTEKWIN7\mysorian

2/6/2013 3:35:53 PM

This completes the hands-on exercise 2.3.

In *Learning SQL Server Reporting Services 2008*, ISBN: 9781847196187, you can find data sources from, Report Models, MS Access 2003, ODBC DSN, and XML DATA.

Hands-on exercise 2.4 – modifying the report in Project RSPW2012 using an expression

In the design window of the report, you can make many changes—add/remove columns, add columns with an expression, and so on. For example, in the RSPW2012 project, we have shipping information displaying the required and shipped date. You may like to see how many days it took for the shipment to be made. You can use an expression and display it in a column of the report:

1. Go to the design of the report in the RSPW2012 project.
2. Right-click on the **Shipped D**ate column and from the drop-down list, choose **Insert Column to the right** (click on the handle to get a drop-down list).
3. Right-click on the empty column you inserted next to **Shipped Date** and select **Text-box Properties...**, as follows:

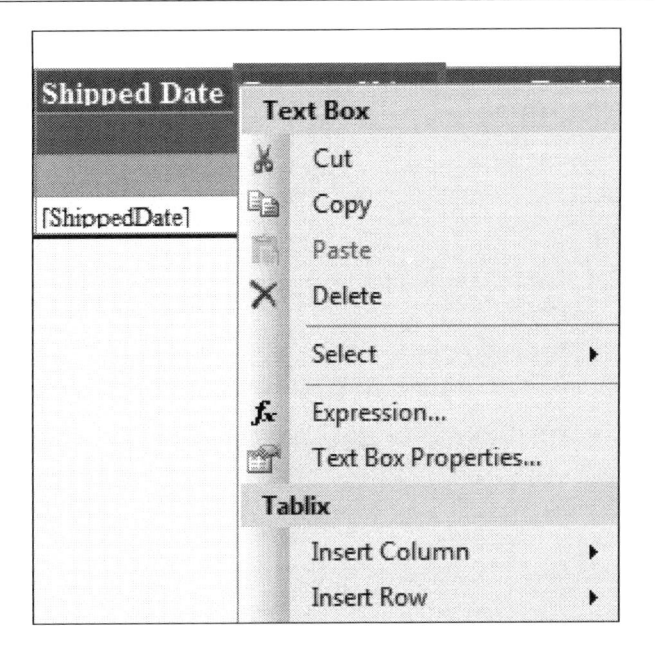

4. In the **Text-box properties** page in the **General** tabbed pane, change the value to **Days to Ship**.
5. In the details row of **Days to Ship**, right-click and select **Expression...**, as follows:

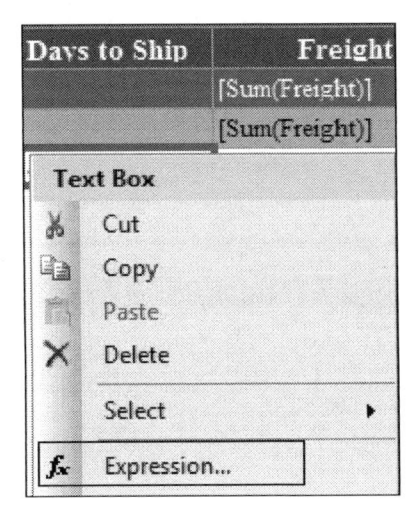

6. In the **Expression** window, using the items in the bottom pane, formulate the expression to embed in the value cell under **Days to Ship**, as shown. Make sure this expression is placed in the value cell:

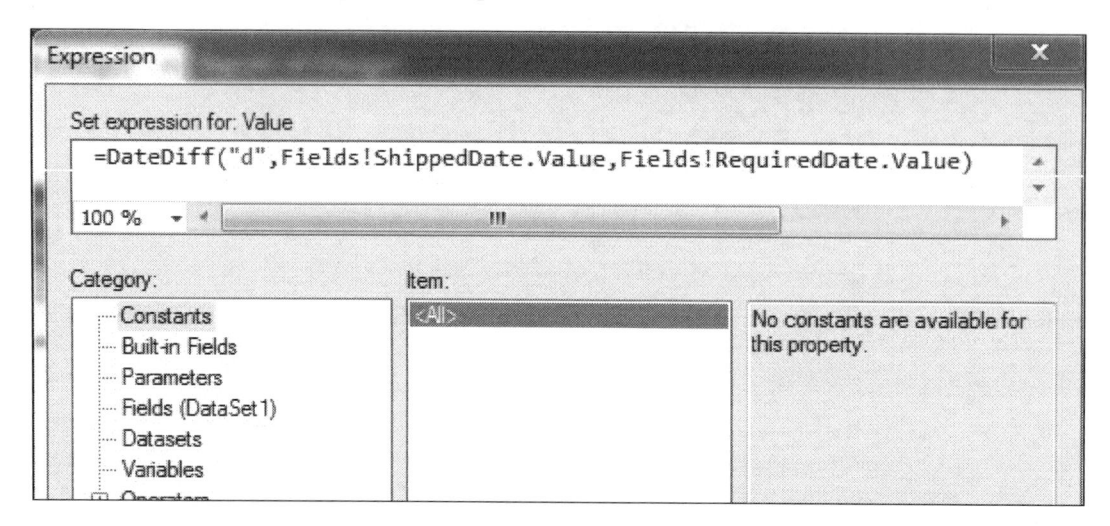

```
=DateDiff("d",Fields!ShippedDate.Value,Fields!RequiredDate.Value)
```

7. Click on **OK** on the **Expression** window. Build and run the report (F5). Click on **Preview** and the report will display the **Days to Ship** column, as follows:

Customer ID	Employee ID	Address	Required Date	Shipped Date	Days to Ship	Freight
ALFKI						225.5800
	1					109.9500
		Obere Str. 57	2/12/1998 12:00:00 AM	1/21/1998 12:00:00 AM	22	69.5300
		Obere Str. 57	4/27/1998 12:00:00 AM	3/24/1998 12:00:00 AM	34	40.4200

Report formats supported in Report Server Reports

The formats of reports using the Report Viewer controls were limited to the three—PDF, Excel, and Word. The server reports (RDL extension) support many other formats, as shown in the following screenshot. Click on the **Export** icon on the extreme right of the report's toolbar:

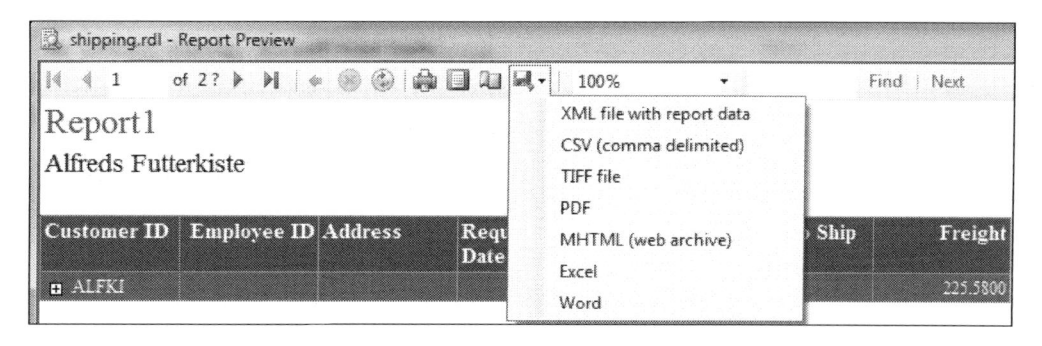

In SSDT, if you choose a **Report Server Project** to create a report, you have the option to import an MS Access database by right-clicking on the report and choosing **Import Reports** from MS Access, as shown in the following screenshot (also available under the **Project** menu):

At present, this is not working as there appears to be a missing assembly file from MS Office. This will be fixed in the future; see `http://connect.microsoft.com/SQLServer/feedback/details/735375/business-intelligence-bids-ssdt-missing-referenced-assembly`.

Report-related projects in Visual Studio 2012

In the installed templates in Visual Studio 2012, you can find a reports application, a project for creating an application with a Windows user interface, and a report (both VB and C#). You can also use the Report Viewer controls (version 11.0.0.0) for Windows, and the Web to use with Windows or Web applications. These can be configured for local or remote processing, and offer an alternative to Report Manager frontend or for URL access, for viewing reports on a Report Server.

Creating reports using Visual Studio 2012

Visual Studio 2012 Ultimate, used in the examples, was downloaded from `http://www.microsoft.com/visualstudio/eng/downloads`. There are three options—**Install**, **Program download**, and **ISO file**. Choose the appropriate option matching your resources. Here, the program was downloaded and saved to a directory.

Software and hardware requirements

The software requirements (for only the x64 architecture) are listed here for Windows Vista, Windows 7, Windows server 2003 and 2008 with Sp2, and Windows Server2008 R2.

The hardware requirements are as follows:

- **Processor**: 1 GHZ or faster
- **Memory**: 2 GB for 64-bit or more
- **Hard disk space**: 3 GB
- **Hard disk drive**: 5400 RPM
- DVD-ROM drive, monitor and mouse

Visual Studio 2012 provides Report Viewer controls that are of two types—one to use with Windows Forms applications and the other for the Web (version 11.0.0.0, a Microsoft .NET component), which can be embedded in a Web page but requires a ScriptManager control from AJAX extensions in the toolbox. ScriptManager is an AJAX Web Server control. A complete reference to Report Viewer Controls is found at `http://msdn.microsoft.com/en-us/library/ms251671.aspx`.

> There are two modes for which these controls can be configured, namely **Local Mode** and **Remote Mode**. The previously cited reference and my previous edition (*Learning SQL Server Reporting Services 2008, ISBN: 9781847196187*) completely explain the two modes. The book also describes the various programmatic approaches to the Reporting Services applications. These will not be described here.

The Report Viewer Controls you find in VS2012 (version 11.0.0.0) are similar to the ones available in VS2010 (version 10.0.0.0), and these controls are not upgraded. Instead of Visual Studio 2012, you can also use VS2010, which you may download from `http://www.microsoft.com/en-us/download/details.aspx?id=12187`.

In the following sections, the worked examples will show how these are used in creating reports. Local or remote is a property of the Report Viewer, or rather how and where the report is processed. You should familiarize yourself with the properties of this control, which is easily accomplished by a right-click on on the Report Viewer Control (they are found under the section *MISC* in the properties window in Visual Studio 2012 and as an independent node in the properties window in Visual Studio 2010).

Hands-on exercise 2.5 – creating a report for a Windows Form application using Report Viewer Control

Although viewing reports on the Web has become a norm, desktop applications are still used in businesses. Report Viewer Control comes in two forms, and the one for Windows Forms application is used in this exercise. Click **Start** | **All Programs** | **Microsoft Visual Studio 2012** | **Microsoft Visual Studio 2012**.

1. Click on **New Project** to open the **New Project** window, as follows:

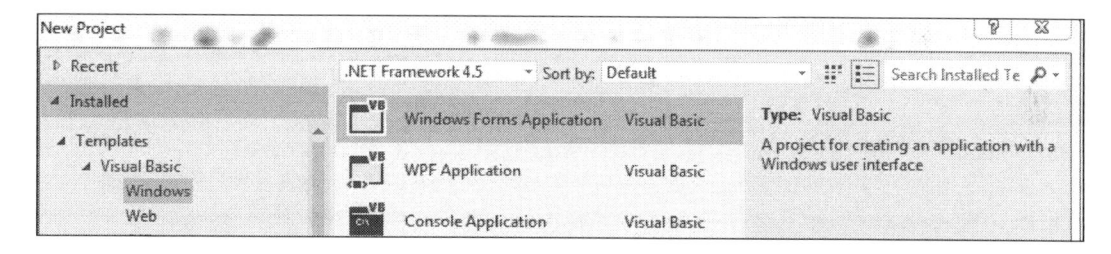

2. **Windows Forms Application** is the first option. Note that the target framework is **.Net Framework 4.5** and the default name of the project is `WindowsApplication1`. You can choose a name. Here, the name chosen is `Win7RV`. The location is the `Projects` folder of VS2012.

3. Click on **OK**. The application will be created after some processing, the **Form1** window will be displayed in the design pane, and the project **Win7RV** will appear in **Solution Explorer**, as follows:

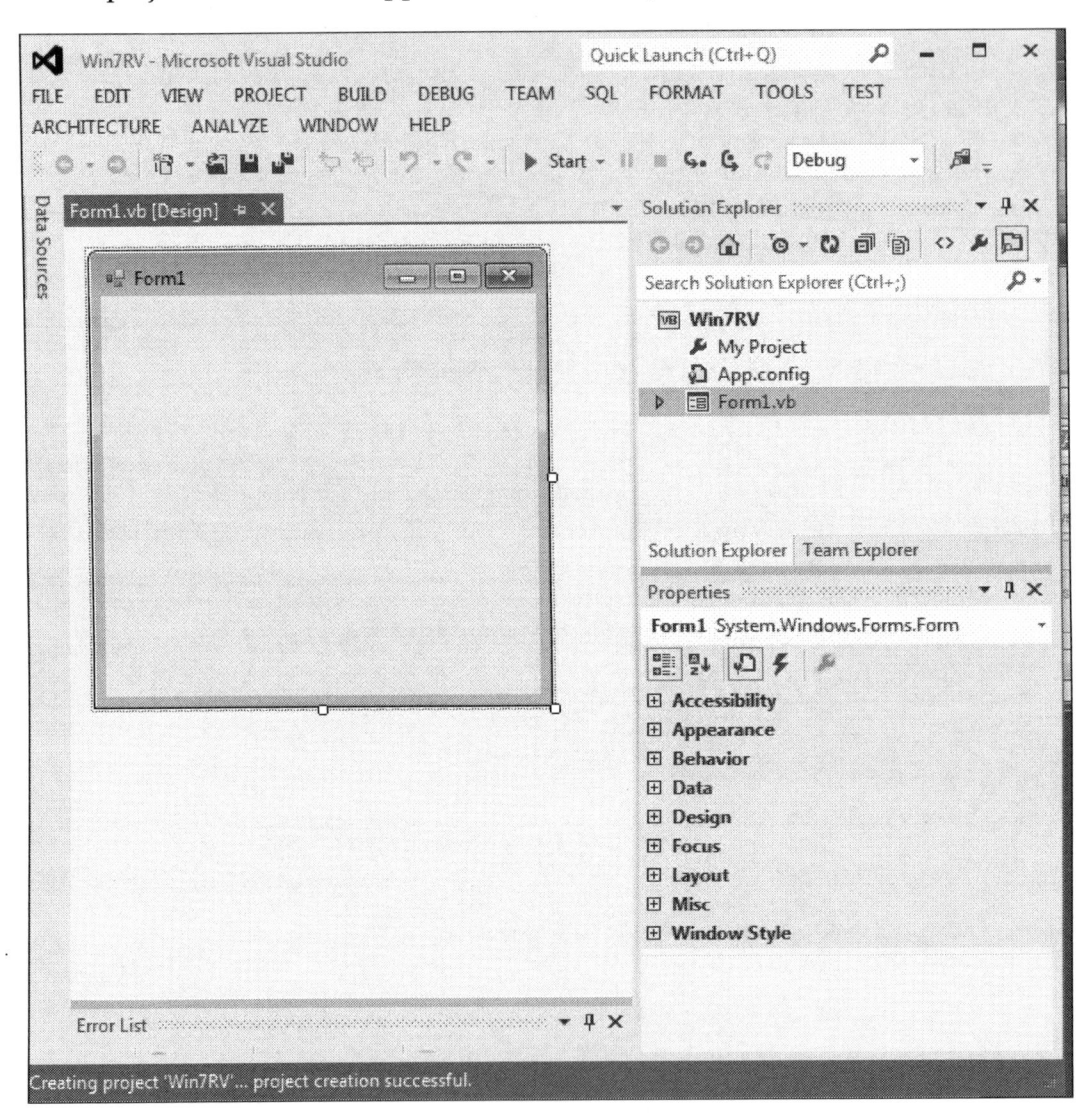

Chapter 2

4. Right-click on **Win7RV** in **Solution Explorer** and from the drop-down list, pick **Add | New Item...**.

   Add New Item window opens.

5. Click on **Report Wizard** in the center pane. The report writing will be guided by a wizard. Click on **Add**.

   The **Report Wizard** window will be displayed followed immediately by the **Data Source Configuration Wizard** window. Here, you can choose one of the four types of sources, as shown, with **Database** as default:

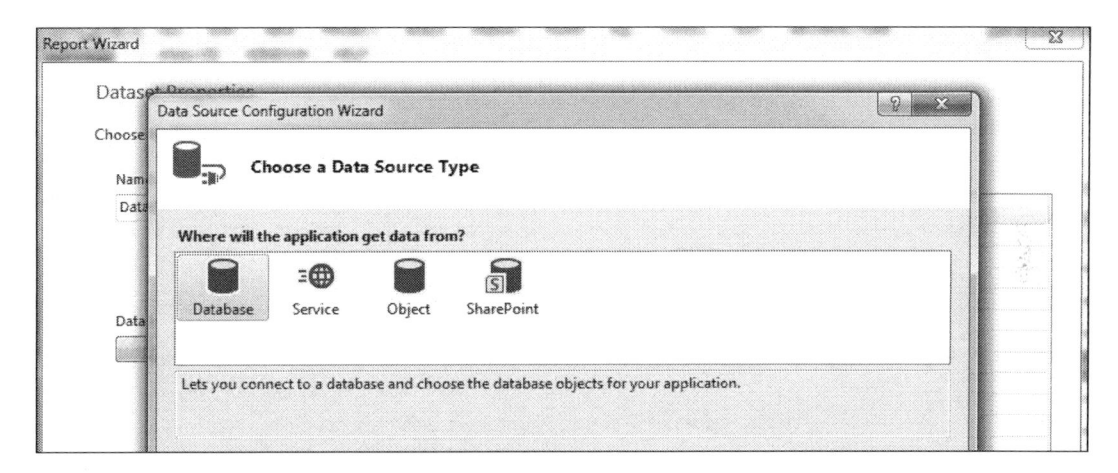

6. Click on **Next**.

   The **Choose a Data Source Type** page or window will be displayed, as shown, with **Database** as the default.

7. Accept the default (**Database**) and click on **Next**.

It connects to the `AdventureWorks2012` database on the `Kailua` server. Recall that the AdventureWorks2012 database was downloaded and attached to the SQL Server 2012 instance in *Chapter 1, Overview and Installation – SQL Server Reporting Services 2012*. This is perhaps due to an earlier connection made to the server. If it is a new connection that you want to establish, then you need to click on the **New Connection...** button and follow up the wizard to connect to `Kailua` and then to `Adventureworks2012`:

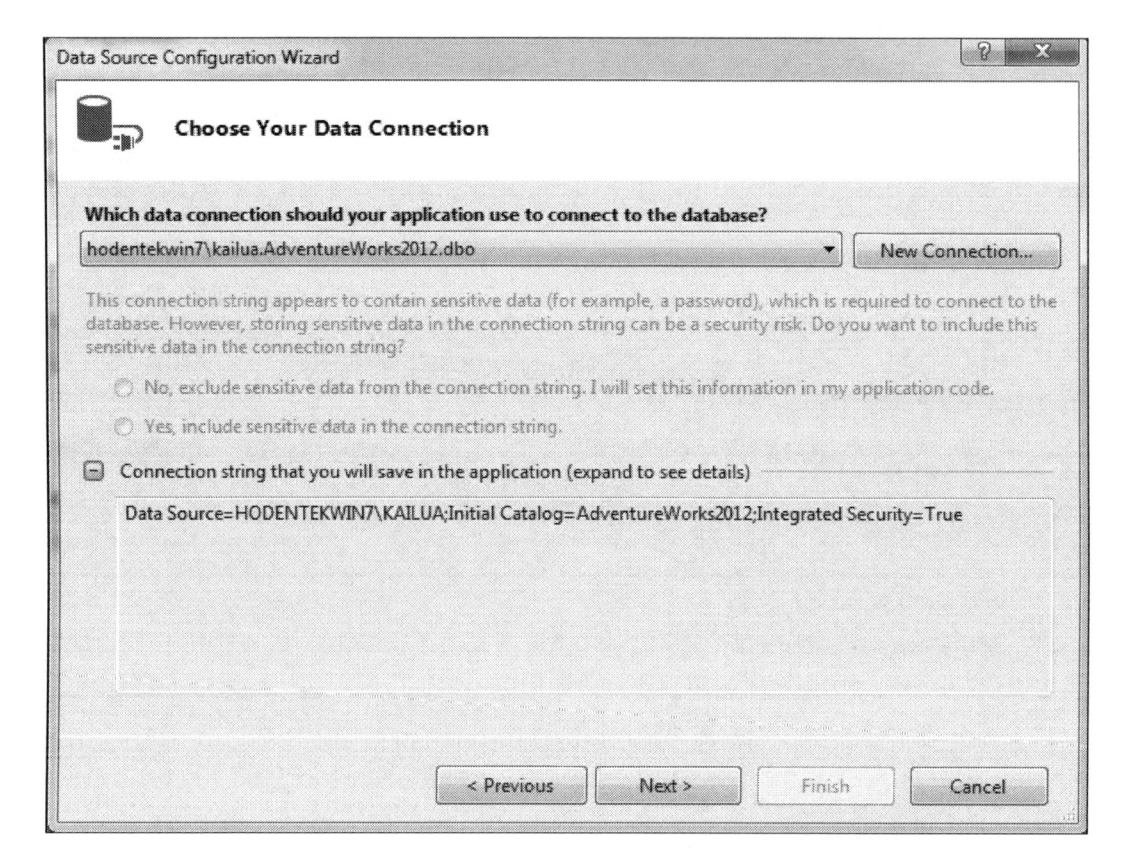

8. Click on **Next**. The **Save the Connection string to the application Configuration File** window will be displayed. Accept the default check mark to save as suggested.

    The connection string gets a name.

9. Click on **Next**.

The **Data Source Configuration Wizard** window with the **Choose Your Database Objects** page will be displayed. This displays all the usable objects in the database.

10. Expand the **Tables** node and select the `Sales.SalesOrderDetail` table. **Dataset** at the bottom will be set to `AdventureWorks2012Dataset`.

11. Click on **Finish**.

    The **Dataset Properties** page of **Report Wizard** gets updated. The **Fields** pane contains all the fields from **Dataset**.

12. Click on **Next**. The **Arrange Fields** window will be displayed. Drag-and-drop the items to the **Row groups** and **Values** boxes, as follows:

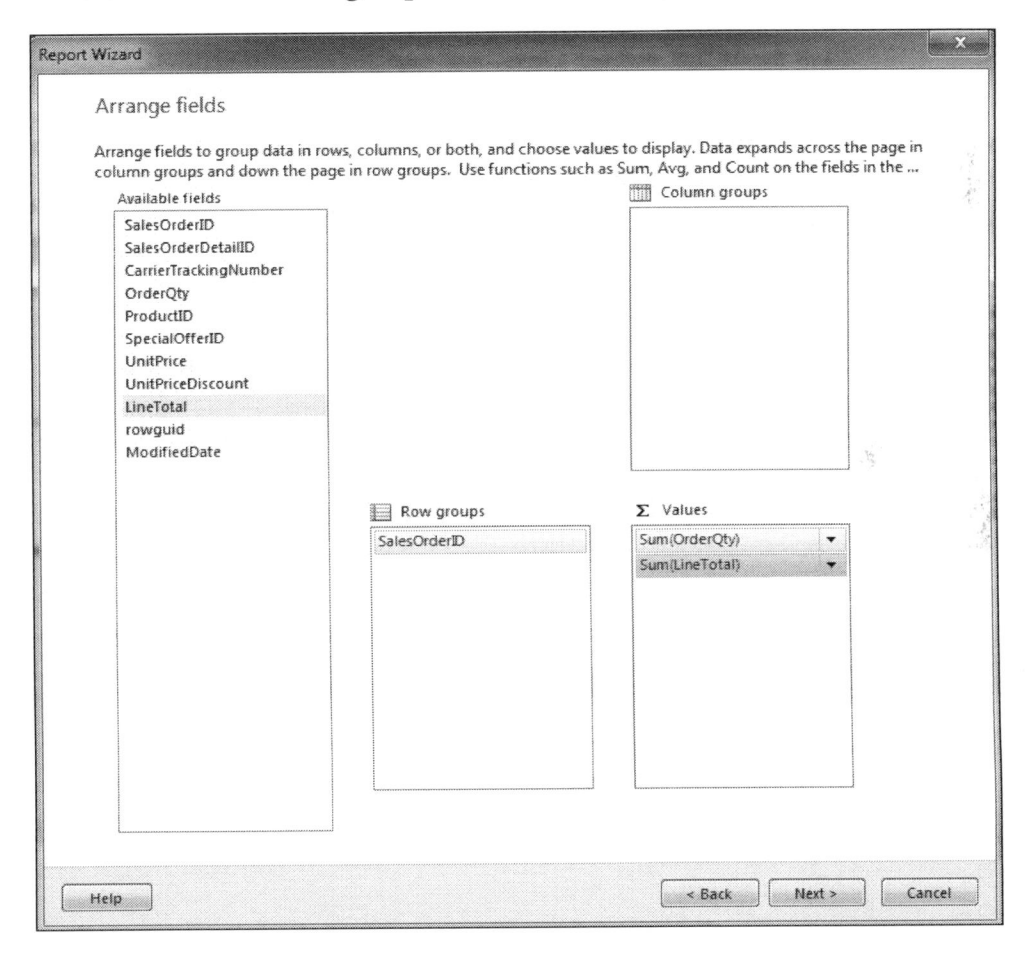

13. Click on **Next**. Note that we have chosen only a few items, as we are trying to fashion the following query to use in the report:

```
Select SalesOrderID, sum(orderqty) as Orders, Sum(LineTotal) as Total
from Sales.SalesOrderDetail
where Orderqty > 25
group by SalesOrderID
```

The **Choose the layout** page of **Report Wizard** will be displayed:

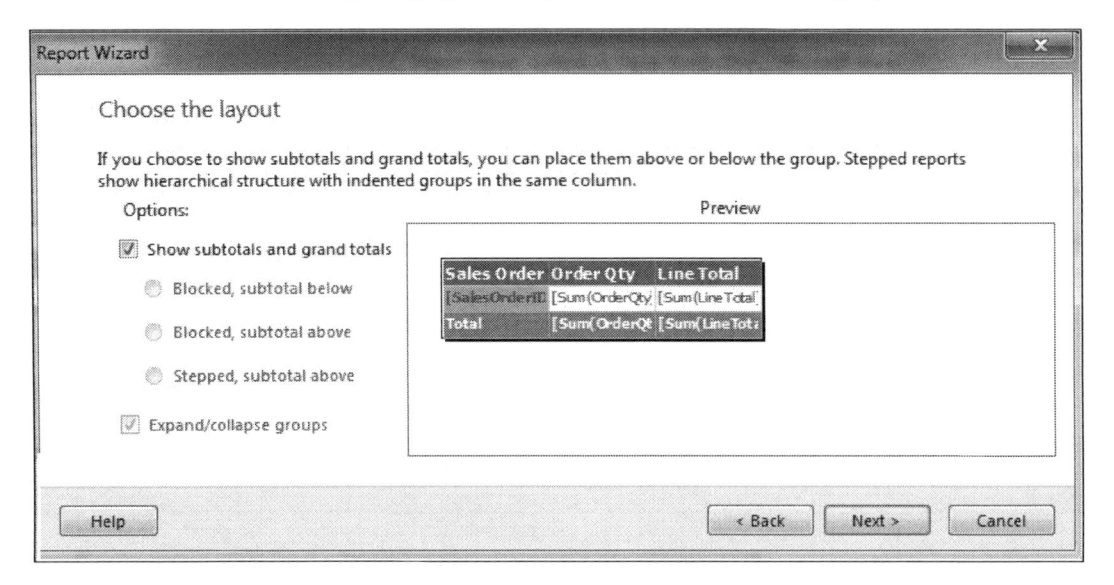

14. Accept the default arrangement and click on **Next**.

    The **Choose a Style** window will appear.

15. Choose **Mahogany**. Click on **Next**.

16. Click on **Finish**.

    The **Visual Studio** user interface will be displayed with the Windows Forms application we chose earlier, updated, as follows:

Chapter 2

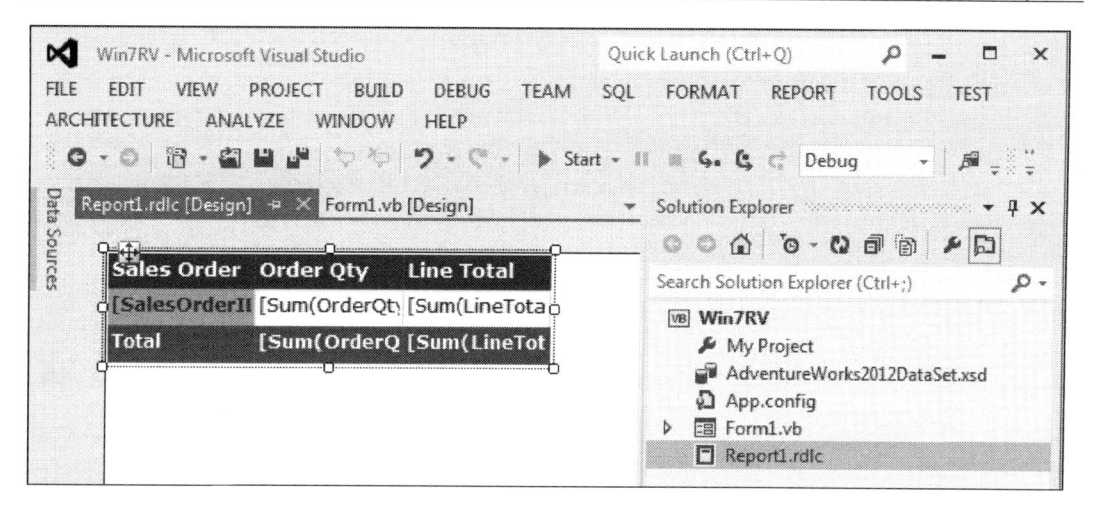

17. Notice that a report `Report1.rdlc` has been added to the project and its design shows a **Tablix** control with the report details we designed with the wizard. **Tablix1** (Tablix:=Table+Matrix) is the name of this control, and it takes data from `Dataset1`. Now we add a filter to this control.

18. Click on an empty region of **Filters**. An ellipsis button appears, as follows:

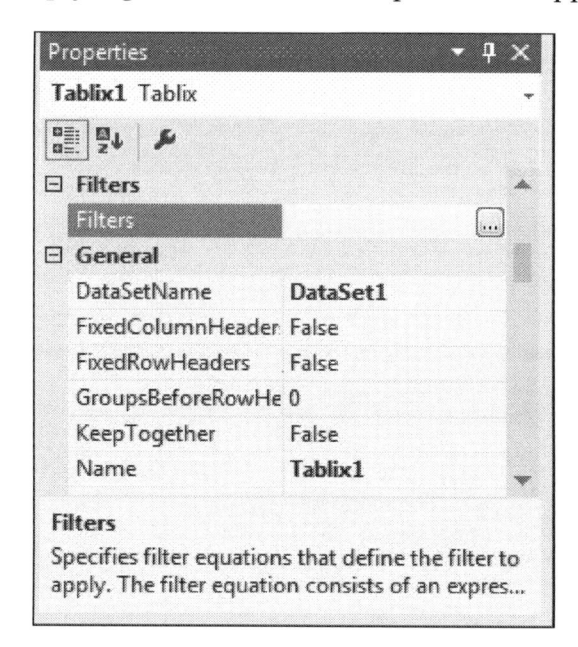

19. The **Tablix Properties** window, as shown in the previous screenshot, will appear with the default **Filters** section now empty.

20. The **Filters** section is provided so that you can apply an equivalent of "where" clause to the dataset. The **Expression** drop-down window lists the columns on which you may impose the "where" clause. The **Operator** drop-down list provides the various arithmetic/logic constraints that you can use, and the **Value** box is where you type a value, as described in the next two steps.

21. Click on **Add** in the **Change Filters** area and click on **OK**.

    The **Change Filters** window changes, as shown in the following screenshot:

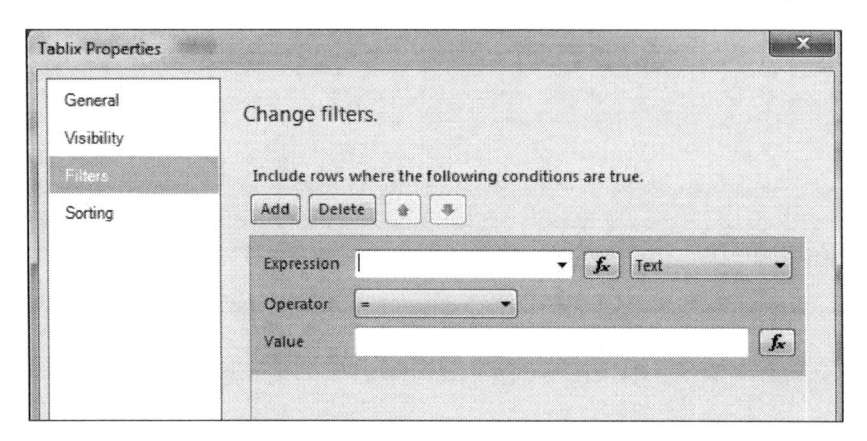

22. Use the handle for **Expression** and choose [OrderQty], as follows:

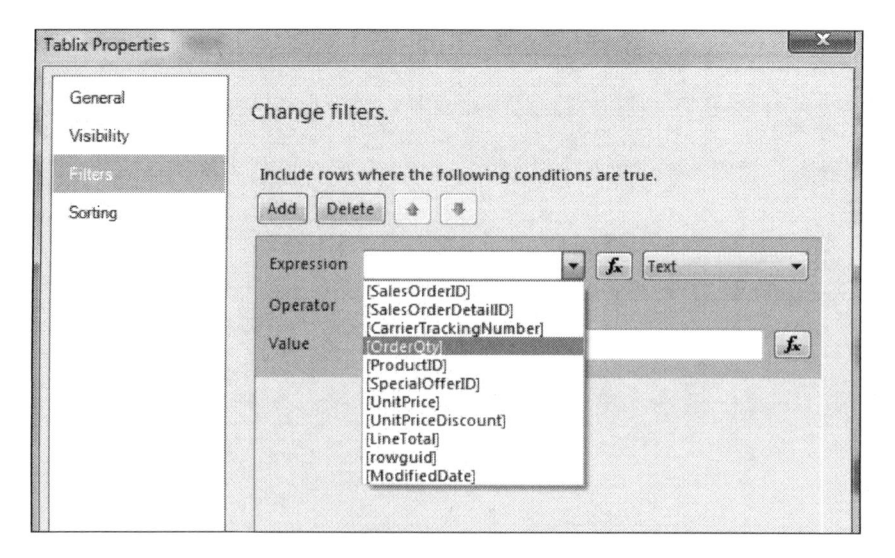

[108]

Chapter 2

23. For **Operator**, choose **>**, and for **Value** type in 25. The window should appear as shown in the following screenshot. Note that this choice will not add any more filtering than that already contained in the query used for producing the dataset. You can use the **Add** button to add more filtering, and **Delete** can remove an existing filtering. This filtering is over and above what is already present in the original query:

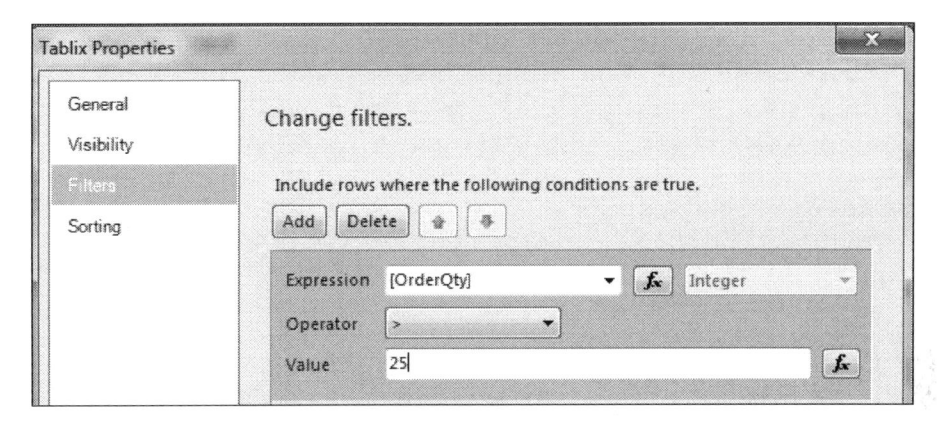

24. Click on **OK** or if you need to add sorting, click on on **Sorting** (we assume that sorting is needed):
25. The **Change sorting options** window shows up. In the **Sort by** column, use handle to choose [SalesOrderId].
26. Click on **Add**. In the **Sort by** column, use handle to choose [SalesOrderId], as follows:

27. Click on **OK**. Review **Tablix1** properties, and you can choose to change many of them. For example, under **Visibility**, you may use **ToggleItem** to show another part of the report item.

[109]

> At the bottom of the report, we only have a row group with **SalesOrderID** as the value to group by. At this point, you should be able to see the report.

28. Click on the **Start** menu item with the green arrow head.

    The processing starts, and an empty form will be displayed. The reason for this is that the wizard created the report according to your choices, but the form does not yet contain the Report Viewer control on it. Close the displayed **Form1** control. Click on **Form1** in the designer. Drag-and-drop a **ReportViewer** control for windows, as shown, from **Toolbox**:

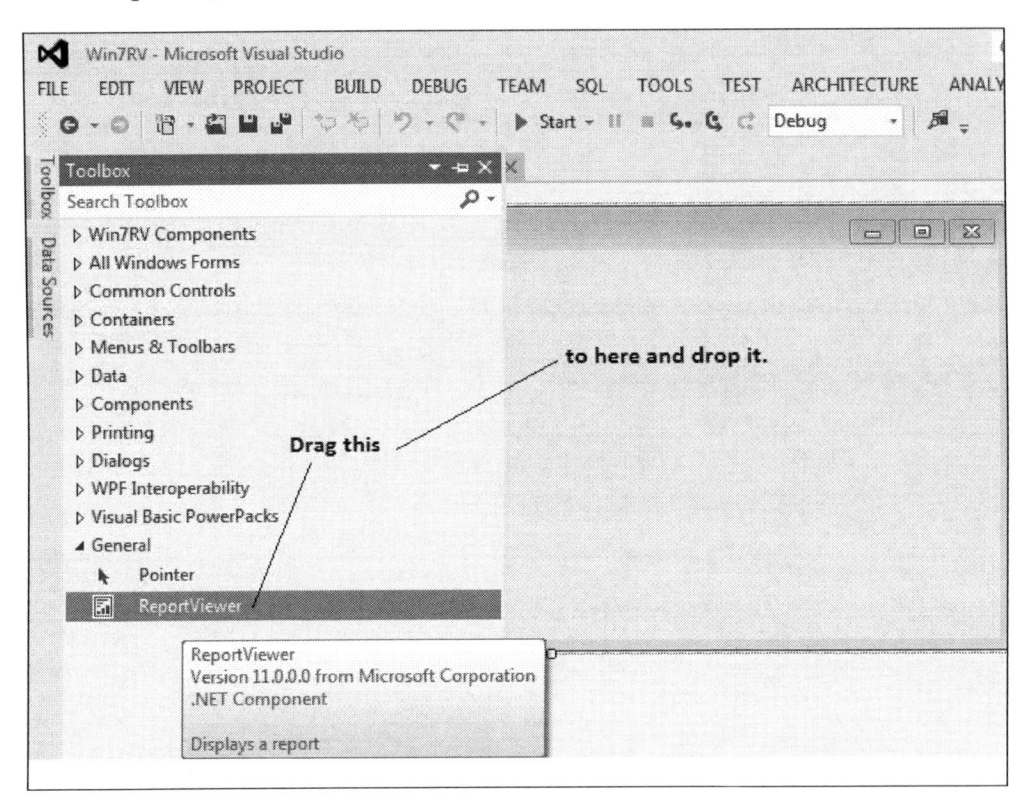

29. The **ReportViewer** control is now on the form, as shown. All you need to do is to carry out the tasks listed in **ReportViewer Tasks**, in order. You can dock/undock this list to the form:

[110]

Chapter 2

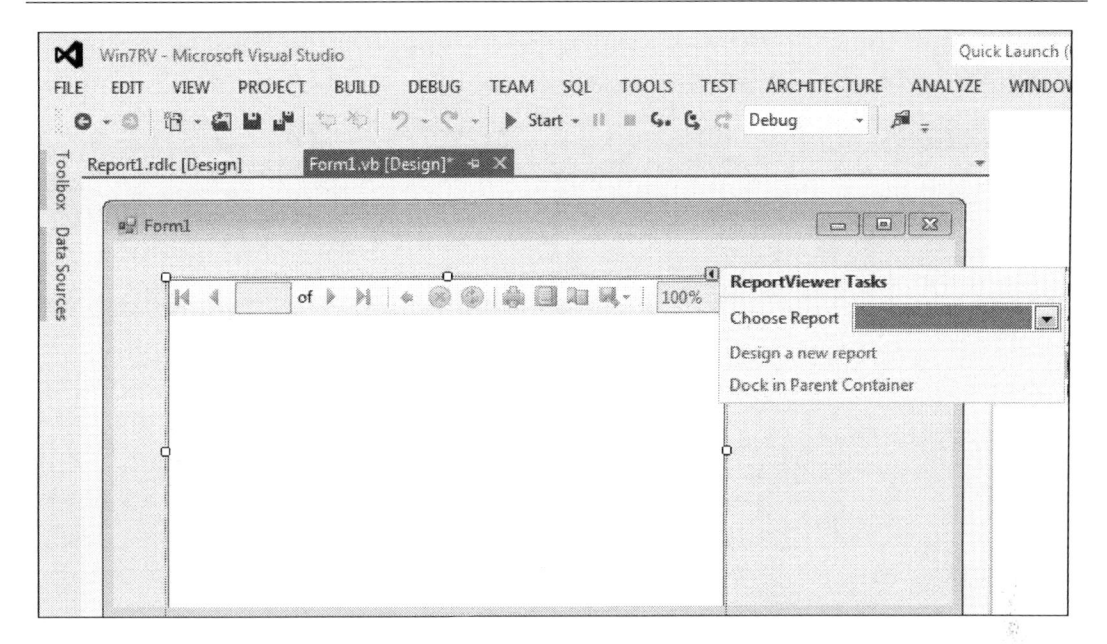

30. Click on the handle for **Choose Report** on **ReportViewer Tasks**, and pick **Win7RV.Report1.rdlc**:

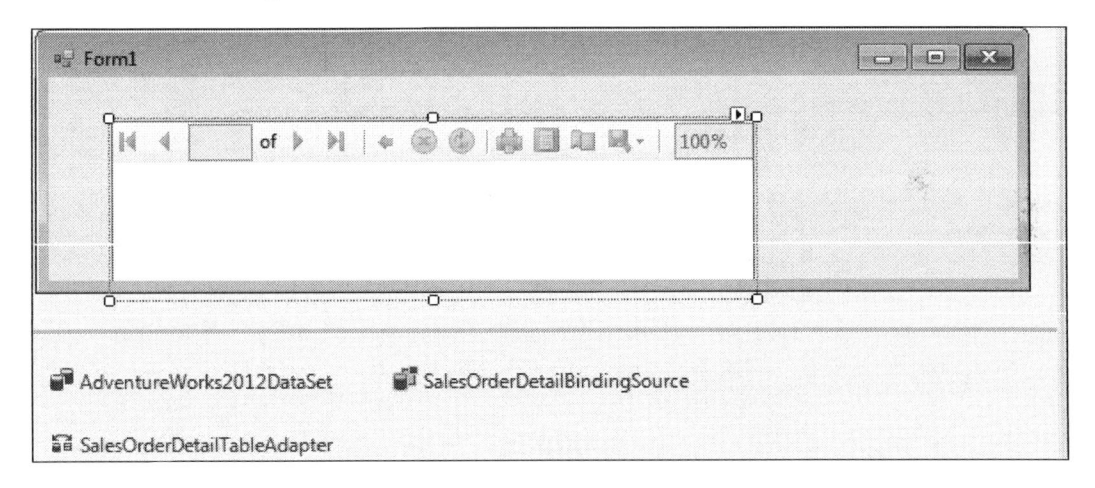

Notice **AdventureWorks2012DataSet**, **SalesOrderDetailBindingSource**, and **SalesOrderDetailTableAdapter** on the control tray of the form.

31. Now, click on the **Start** button (*F5*) and the processing begins, as shown in the following screenshot:

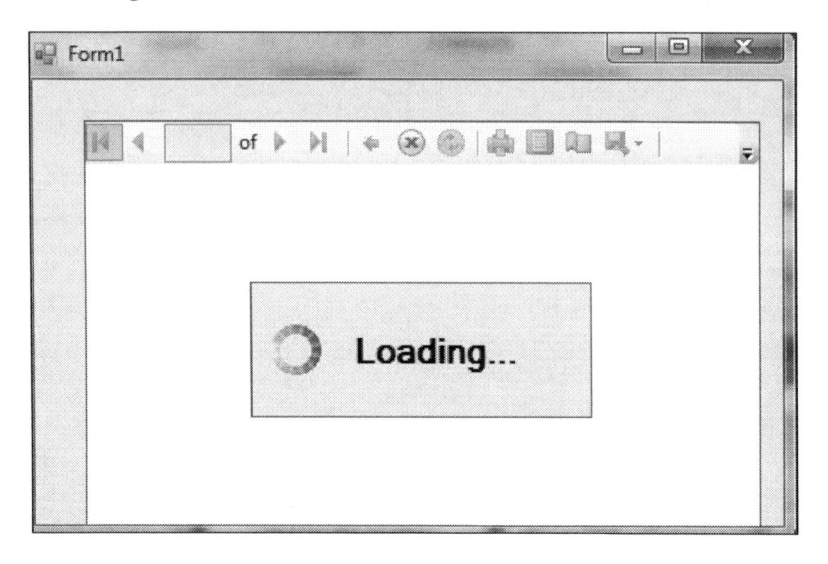

The Windows form will be displayed with the report, as follows:

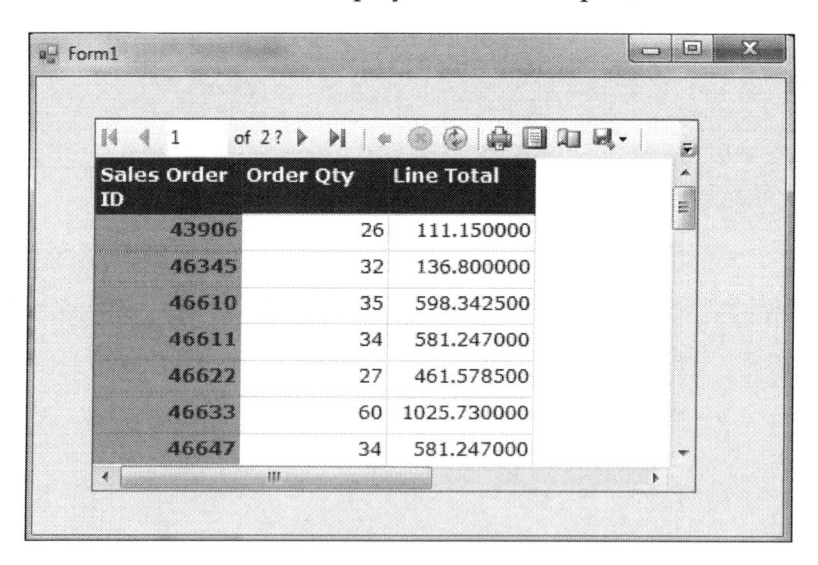

32. Close the previous form and return to the design. Review the properties of **ReportViewer1**, as shown. Each of the nodes can be expanded:

Chapter 2

33. Expand the toolbar and note that all tool bar items are active. Click on **Misc** and note the various items contained in it. Presently, it is processed in the local mode:

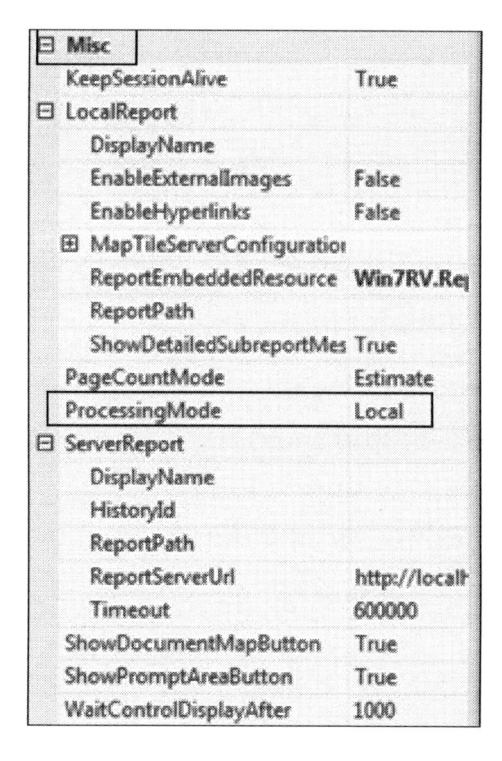

34. Now, it is time to review the **Project** components in **Solution Explorer**, as shown. Take some time, click and open various nodes and get familiarized with the structure:

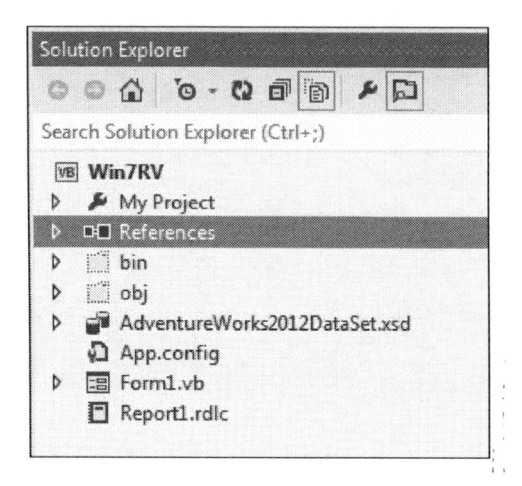

35. Click on to open the **Data Sources** list, as follows:

> We have only used a subset of the data. Although the report was designed by a wizard, we could have started with an empty report and added the report viewer and a control (such as **Tablix**) and then dragged-and-dropped items from **Data Sources** on to the report.

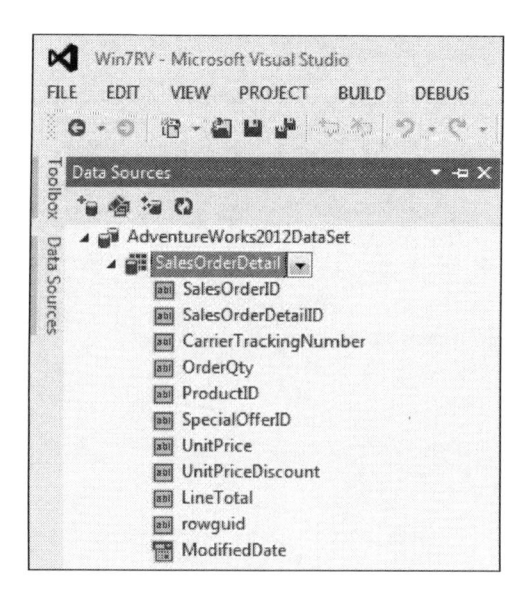

36. Run the application again using the **Start** button to bring up **Form1**, as follows:

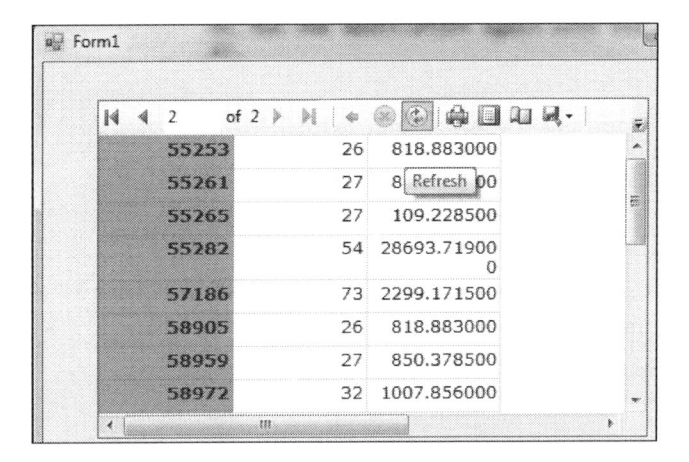

37. The **Refresh** button will be highlighted as shown, and to the right of it, in order are, **Print**, **Print Layout**, **Page Setup** (of the printer), and **Export** buttons. Click on the **Export** button to show the **Export** formats **Excel**, **PDF**, and **Word**.

38. Verify that you can export them to each of these formats, by choosing them in turn. Note that Adobe reader can convert PDF to Excel or Word quite easily with a click.

39. In **Solution Explorer**, click on **Form1.Designer.Vb** and you can see the coding necessary to achieve this display.

This concludes the hands-on exercise 2.5

Hands-on exercise 2.6 – creating a report using Report Viewer Control for the Web

We will be creating a Web project, which displays a report in one of its Web pages. A Report Viewer Control is used, which gets its data from the `Northwind` database on `Kailua` SQL Server 2012.

1. Start Visual Studio 2012 from its shortcut **All Programs | Microsoft Visual Studio 2012 | Visual Studio 2012** or the executable at `%ProgramFiles%\Microsoft Visual Studio 11.0\Common7\IDE\devenv.exe` from the command line.

2. Click on **File | New website....**
3. In the **New Website** window, click on **ASP.NET Empty website** and for **Web location**; use the handle to change it to **File System**. Accept the default location for the files. Change the name of the website to `RepView` and click on **OK**.
4. The project will be created with just the `Web.config` file with target as **Framework 4.5**.
5. Right-click on **RepView**, and from the drop-down list, choose **Add | Add New Item....**
6. In the **Add New Item - RepView** window, click on **Web Form**, accept the default name, `Default.aspx`, and click on **Add**. There is no master page in this Web. You always need a `Default.aspx` page.

    Default.aspx will be added to the Web.

7. From **Toolbox**, click on **ScriptManager** under **AJAX Extensions** and drag-and-drop on to the body of `Default.aspx` in the design view. Click on **ReportViewer** and drag-and-drop it below **ScriptManager**, you dropped earlier:

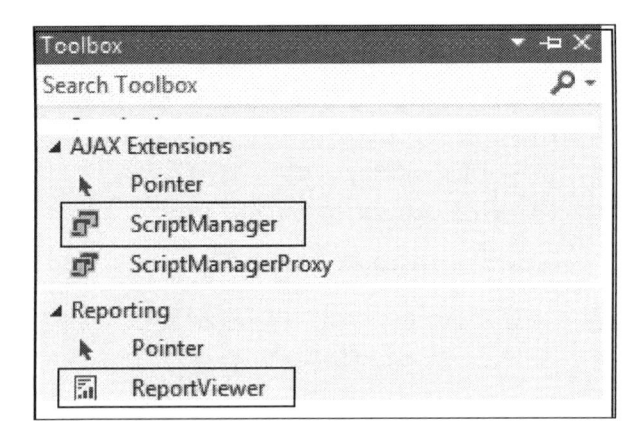

8. This adds the following code to the source page:
```
<body>
    <form id="form1" runat="server">
    <div>
```

[116]

```
            <asp:ScriptManager ID="ScriptManager1" runat="server">
            </asp:ScriptManager>
            <br />
            <rsweb:ReportViewer ID="ReportViewer1" runat="server"
Font-Names="Verdana" Font-Size="8pt" WaitMessageFont-
Names="Verdana" WaitMessageFont-Size="14pt" Width="729px">
                <LocalReport ReportPath="Report.rdlc">
                    <DataSources>
                        <rsweb:ReportDataSource DataSourceId="ObjectDa
taSource1" Name="DataSet1" />
                    </DataSources>
                </LocalReport>
            </rsweb:ReportViewer>
            <asp:ObjectDataSource ID="ObjectDataSource1"
runat="server" SelectMethod="GetData" TypeName="NorthwindDataSetTa
bleAdapters.OrdersTableAdapter"></asp:ObjectDataSource>

        </div>
        </form>
</body>
```

9. Right-click on **RepView**, and from the drop-down list, choose **Add | Add New Item...**.

You can choose to add a report or a report wizard to the Web. If you choose **Report**, it adds an empty report to the Web as shown. Here, it was named `Orders.rdlc`:

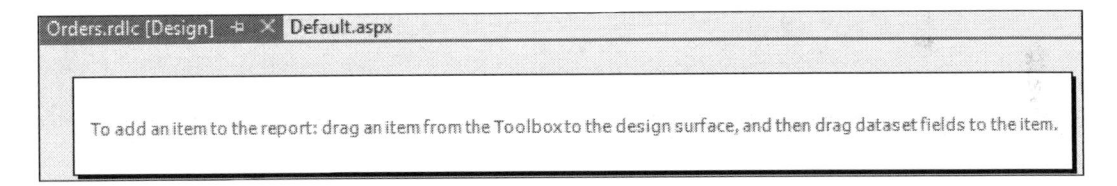

10. Click on the empty report and click on **Toolbox**. Drag-and-drop a **Table** control on to the report Orders.rdlc. Here, you find the new items such as **Maps**, **Sparkline**, and so on. These are also available in the Report Builder, and are described in *Chapter 5, Working with Report Builder 3.0*.

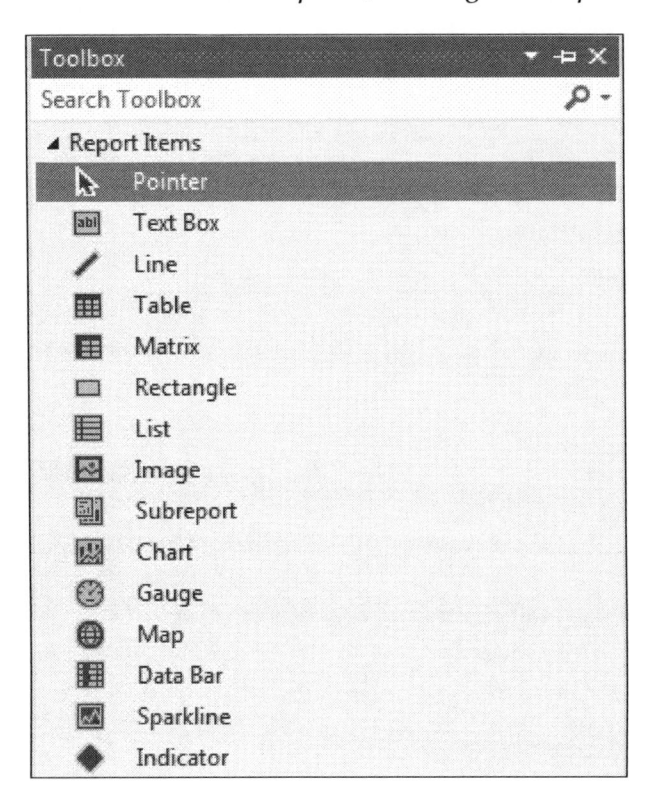

A three-column, two-row table will be added to the report with the middle column showing **Header** and **Data**:

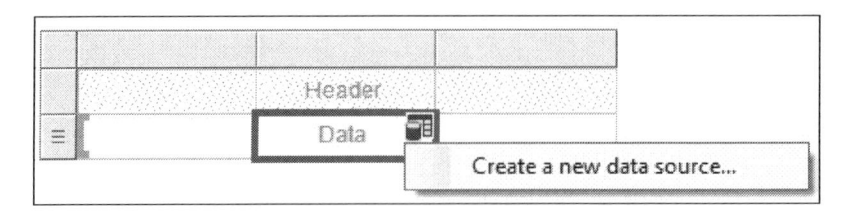

[118]

Chapter 2

11. Click on **Data** and then on the icon, and choose to create a new data source. The **Dataset Properties** window will be displayed.
12. In the **Dataset Properties** window, click on **New...** for the data source. The **Choose Your Data Connection** page of the wizard opens.
13. Click on **New Connection....**
14. In the **New Connection** window, establish a connection to **SQL Server 2012 Kailua,** and choose to use the Northwind database. This was already seen in the *Hands-on exercise 2.1 – creating a report using the Report Server Project Wizard* section. **Choose your Data Connection** gets updated with the following **Connection string**:

    ```
    Data Source=HODENTEKWIN7\KAILUA;Initial
    Catalog=Northwind;Integrated Security=True
    ```

15. Click on **Next**. The **Choose your Database Objects** page will be displayed, and after some processing, all the objects on the Northwind database will be displayed.
16. Choose the **Orders** table from this list. Change the name of **Dataset** to NDS.
17. Click on **Finish**. The **Dataset Properties** page gets updated, displaying all fields (with their type name) from the **Orders** table. Click on **OK**. Now, if you click on **Data** and then the icon in the 3 x 2 table you will see the column list from the **Orders** table.
18. Drag-and-drop items from the list on to the 3 x 2 table, as shown. If needed, you can insert as many more columns as you need:

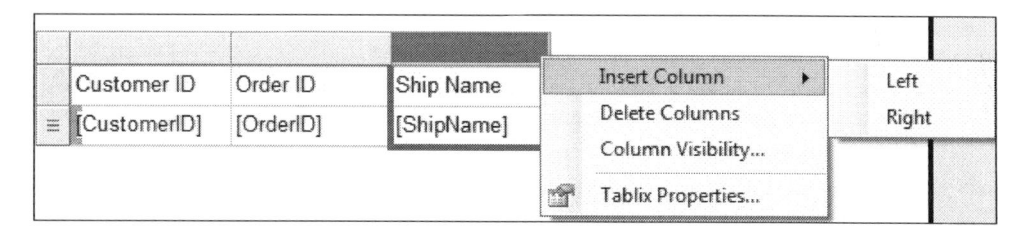

	Customer ID	Order ID	Ship Name	Insert Column ▶	Left
≡	[CustomerID]	[OrderID]	[ShipName]	Delete Columns	Right
				Column Visibility...	
				Tablix Properties...	

19. Now back to the Default.aspx page. Click on **ReportViewer Tasks**, and choose Orders.rdlc, as shown.

[119]

This adds an **ObjectDataSource** control to the report at the bottom of the report:

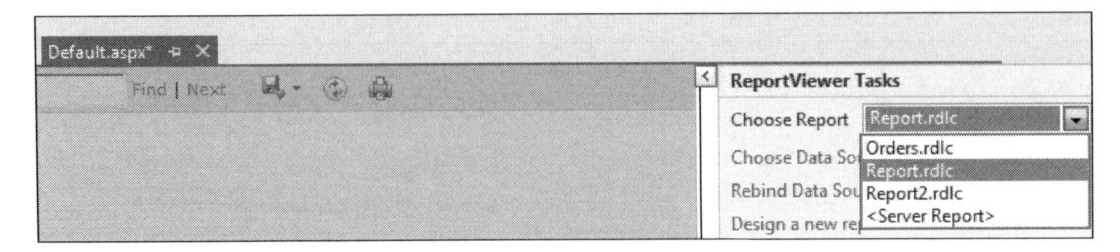

20. Build the website project from the main menu. Right-click on `Default.aspx` and click on **View in Browser**. The report gets displayed in the browser, as follows:

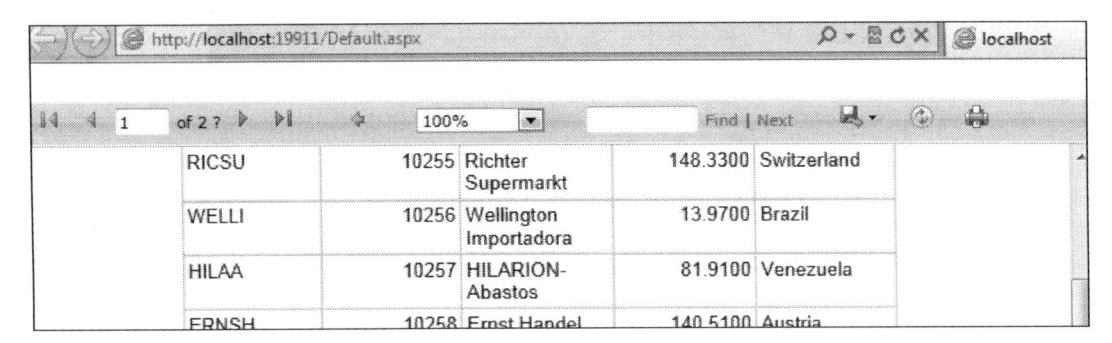

Since we chose an empty table, it has no formatting; just a bare bones report. There are two other reports on this site. The Report Viewer can be attached to any of the reports. If you want to format the report, you can do so by going to the report and changing either the table cell properties or the **Tablix** properties.

> An excellent post that shows how you can make changes to a report is available at http://dotnet.sys-con.com/node/982742. Also read *part 2* of this post at http://jayaramkrishnaswamy.sys-con.com/node/1227111. Although these posts are related to the Report Builder version 2, the design principles are the same.

Hands-on exercise 2.7 – using Report Viewer Control in the remote mode

Local processing is good for small reports and datasets. If they are big, you may take a performance hit. It is therefore less scalable.

In remote processing, report server retrieves the data and processes the report, whereas in the local mode only the report is processed. We use remote processing if there are many users accessing the report, or if the report has a large amount of data.

> For remote processing, you must have the report published to a report server and display in your application, say a Web page on a local server. This hands-on exercise shows how you can display a server report on a Web page. In *Chapter 10, Applications Accessing Report Servers*, you will see other types of applications for viewing reports.

1. Use SSDT and create a report using the Report Server project and deploy it to the Report Server. Here is an `Employees.rdl` report deployed to the folder `NwindEmployees` on the Report Server:

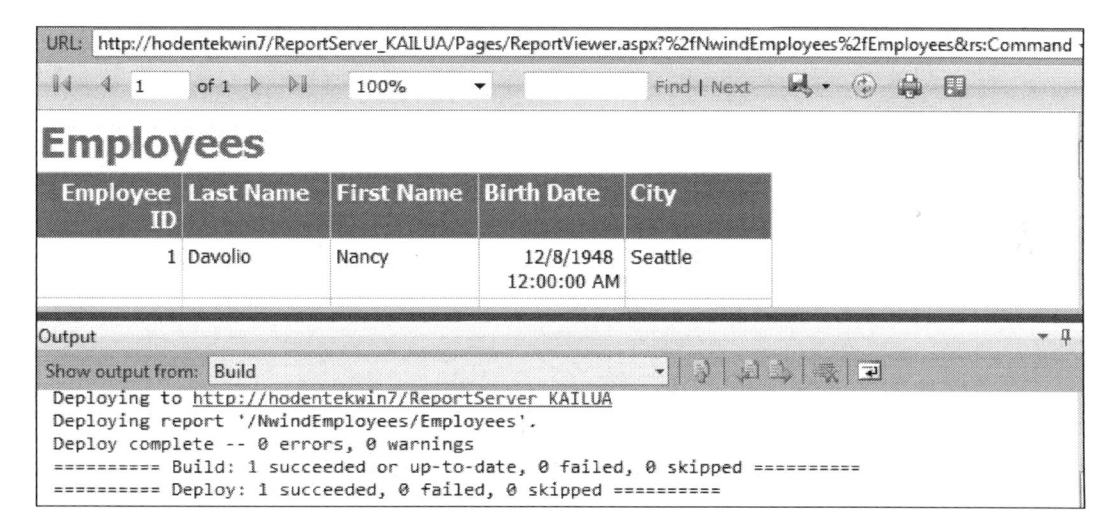

2. In Visual Studio 2012, create an empty ASP.NET Website project (`NorthwindEmployees`) and add a Web page named `Default.aspx`.

3. Drag-and-drop a **ScriptManager AJAX** control and a **ReportViewer** control on to this page.

4. Click on **ReportViewer Tasks** shown in the next image and configure it, as shown, using the handles. Use the handles for **Choose Report**, and you should fill in the details as shown. **Report Path** is the path on the Report Server where the report is deployed:

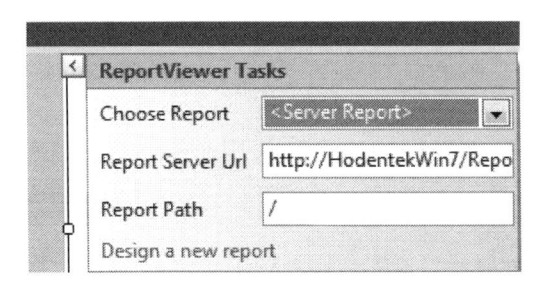

Enter the following values in the preceding screenshot:

- **Choose Report**: `<Server Report>`
- **Report Server URL**: `http://HodentekWin7/ReportServer_Kailua`
- **Report Path**: `/NwindEmployees/Employees`

5. Build the project and browse the `Default.aspx` page. The report will be displayed, as shown in the following screenshot:

You could have started with a Windows Forms application if you wanted to.

This concludes hands-on exercise 2.7

Hands-on exercise 2.8 – converting an RDLC to a RDL file

It is not very difficult to convert an RDLC file to a RDL file, especially when the report is based on data from an SQL Server. The schema for bare bones reports without any data in the report are as follows:

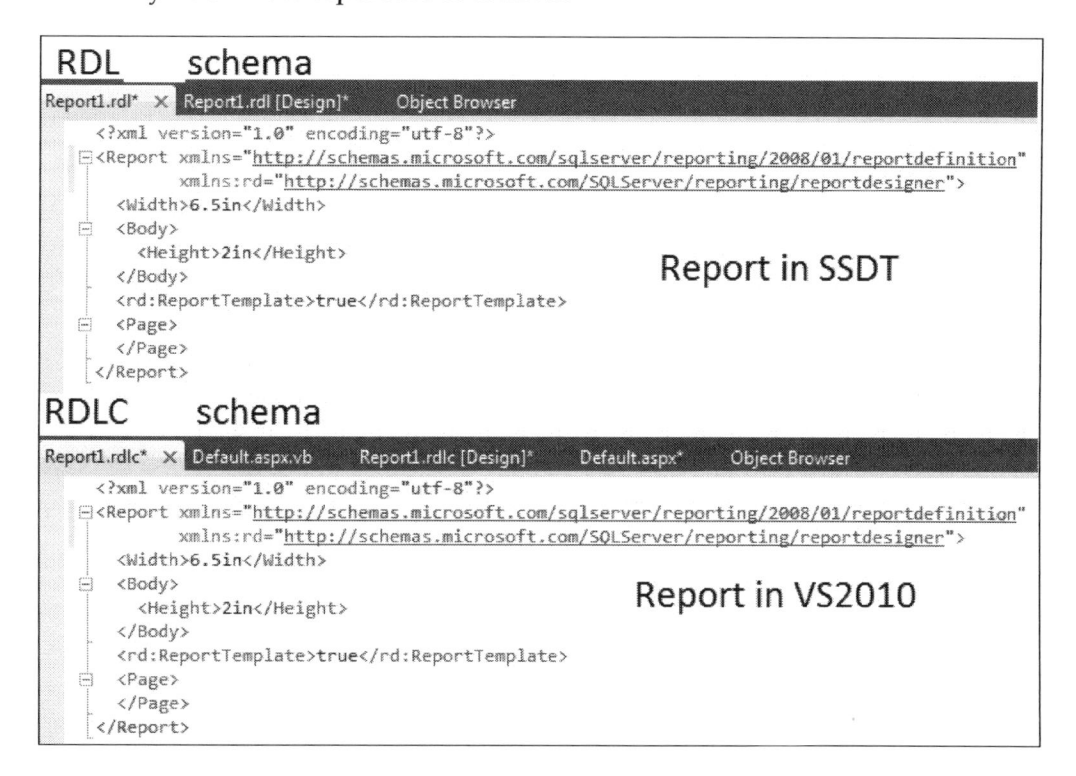

```xml
RDL    schema
<?xml version="1.0" encoding="utf-8"?>
<Report xmlns="http://schemas.microsoft.com/sqlserver/reporting/2008/01/reportdefinition"
        xmlns:rd="http://schemas.microsoft.com/SQLServer/reporting/reportdesigner">
    <Width>6.5in</Width>
    <Body>
        <Height>2in</Height>          Report in SSDT
    </Body>
    <rd:ReportTemplate>true</rd:ReportTemplate>
    <Page>
    </Page>
</Report>
```

```xml
RDLC    schema
<?xml version="1.0" encoding="utf-8"?>
<Report xmlns="http://schemas.microsoft.com/sqlserver/reporting/2008/01/reportdefinition"
        xmlns:rd="http://schemas.microsoft.com/SQLServer/reporting/reportdesigner">
    <Width>6.5in</Width>
    <Body>
        <Height>2in</Height>          Report in VS2010
    </Body>
    <rd:ReportTemplate>true</rd:ReportTemplate>
    <Page>
    </Page>
</Report>
```

For details regarding these two types of files and their latest schema, follow http://msdn.microsoft.com/en-us/library/ms252109.aspx.

In this hands-on exercise, we will be using the following:

- The `AdventureWorks2012` database on Kailua server
- The `ContactType` table on this database

Then we will follow this procedure:

1. First, we will create a report using Visual Studio and Report Viewer and create a report. This will be a report with RDLC extension (see the previous image).
2. We will then rename it using a different extension, RDL (right-click on the report and rename it; just change the extension).
3. Create a Report Server project and then bring report in step 2 into a Report Server project in SSDT.
4. We will then reconstruct the data source and the dataset to match the data used for creating the report with the RDLC extension. We build and test the report.

Here are the detailed steps:

1. Create a website project (`RDLCTest`) and create a Report. Use ReportViewer for the Web. While configuring the report, (`ContactType.rdlc`), use the `AdventureWorks2012` database on the Kailua server.
2. Build and test the report. The displayed report should appear as follows:

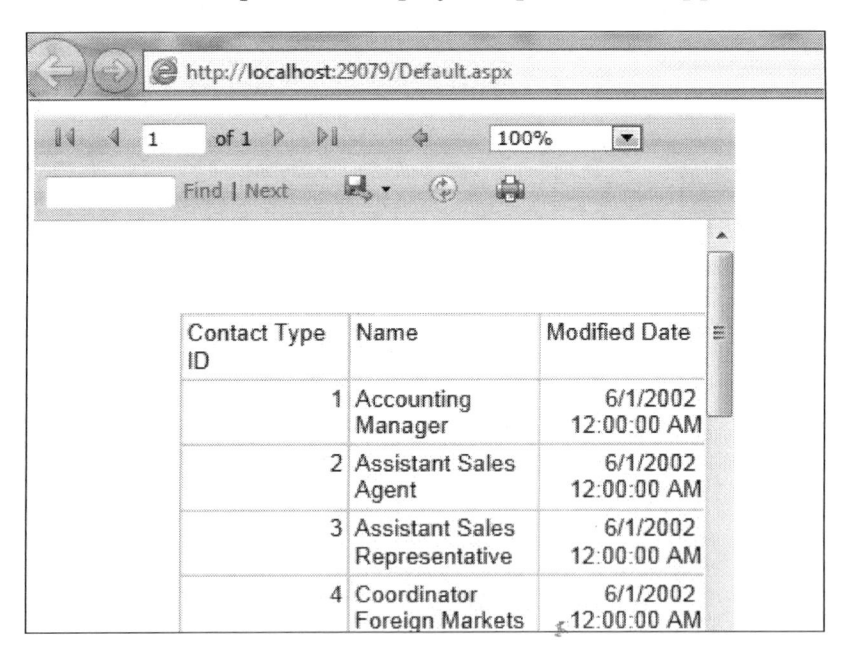

Contact Type ID	Name	Modified Date
1	Accounting Manager	6/1/2002 12:00:00 AM
2	Assistant Sales Agent	6/1/2002 12:00:00 AM
3	Assistant Sales Representative	6/1/2002 12:00:00 AM
4	Coordinator Foreign Markets	6/1/2002 12:00:00 AM

3. Create a copy of the report (right-click on **Copy**) in the same folder of the `RDLCTest` folder of the website (`C:\Users\mysorian\Documents\Visual Studio 2012\WebSites\RDLCTest`).

4. Rename the copy as `ContactTypeCopy.rdl` (you just renamed a RDLC file to have an extension RDL). You will get a **Rename** warning that the file may be unusable. Disregard the warning and click on **Yes**.

5. Use SSDT and create a Report Server project, `RDLCConvert`, as follows:

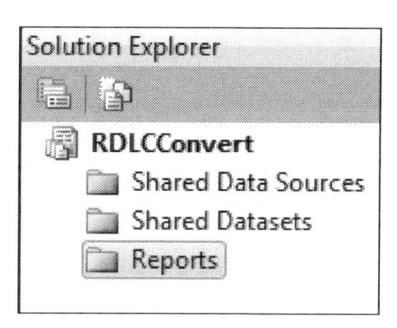

6. Right-click on the **Reports** folder and pick **Add Existing Item...**.Browse your folder system, pick the `ContactTypeCopy.rdl` file, and bring it into the project as follows:

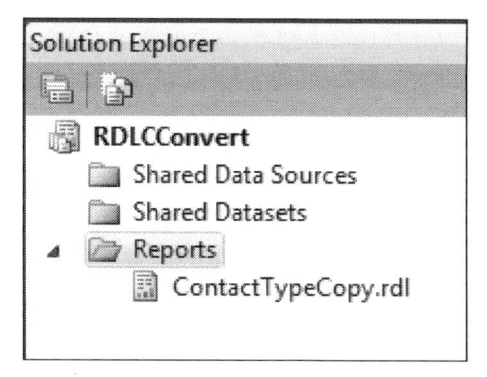

7. This opens the **Report Designer** and **Report Data** window, as follows:

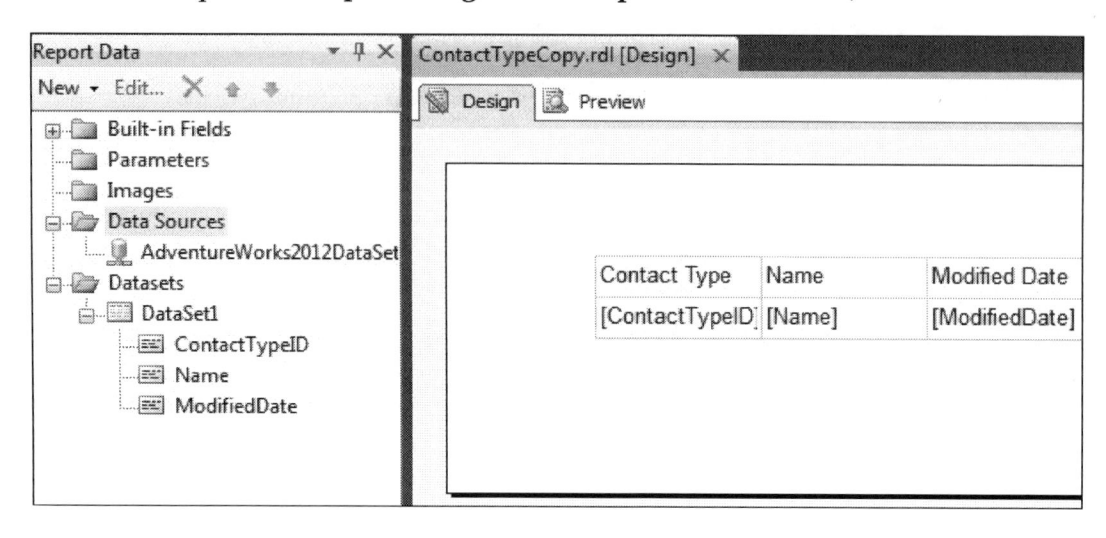

8. Double-click on `AdventureWorks2012DataSet`. The following window will be displayed:

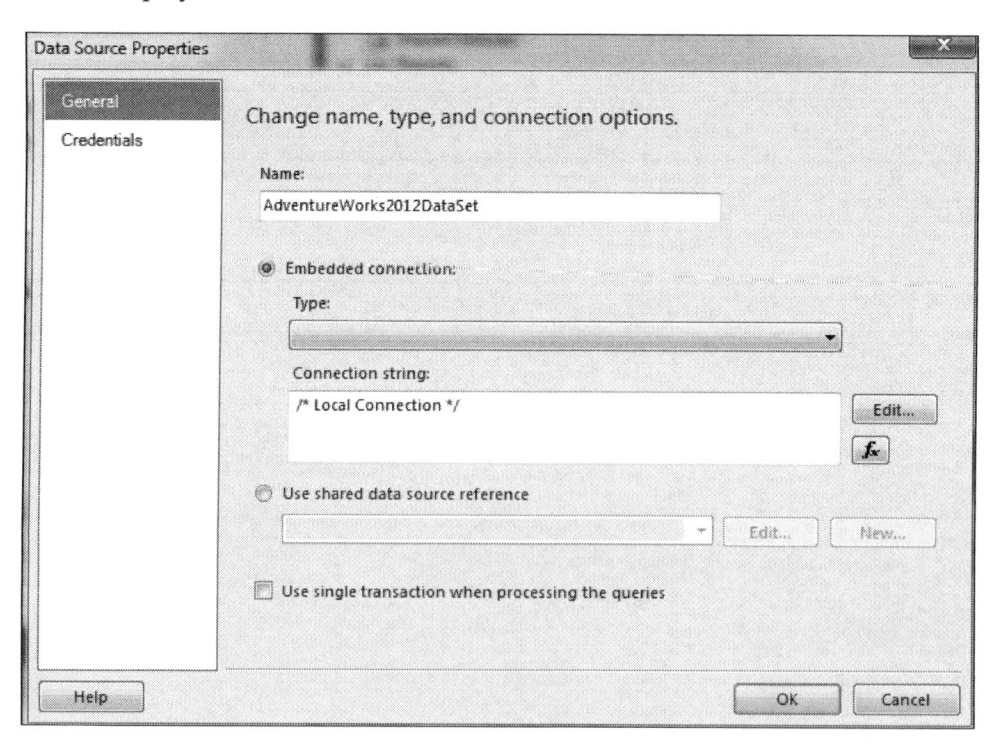

The connection is embedded in it is a local connection, since it came from an RDLC report.

9. Modify the preceding window to change the type to **Microsoft SQL Server**, and click on **Edit...** to obtain the proper connection from the Kailua server (you will work with the **New Connection** window we saw earlier). The **Data Source Properties** window now appears as follows:

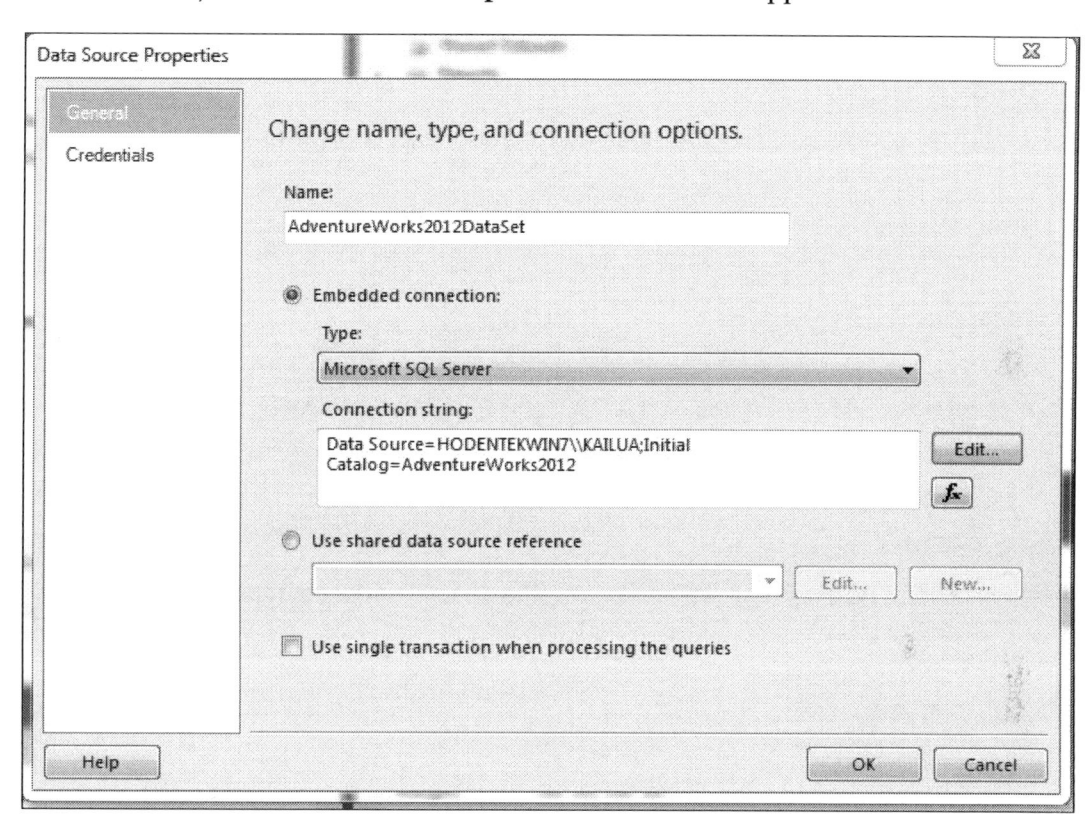

10. Double-click on **DataSet1** to open the following window:

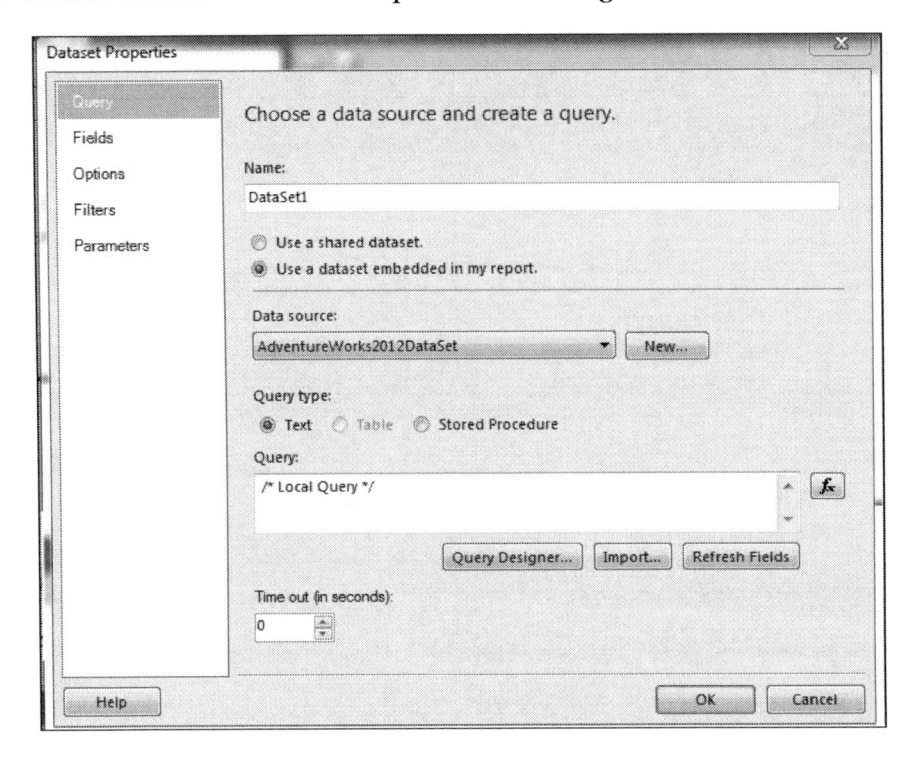

11. You can build the query by using **Query Designer...**, or type in the **Select** statement shown in the empty **Query** window:

    ```
    SELECT ContactTypeId, Name, ModifiedDate
    FROM Person.ContactType
    ```

12. Click on **OK**.

13. Build the project and click on **Preview**. You may get the following error:

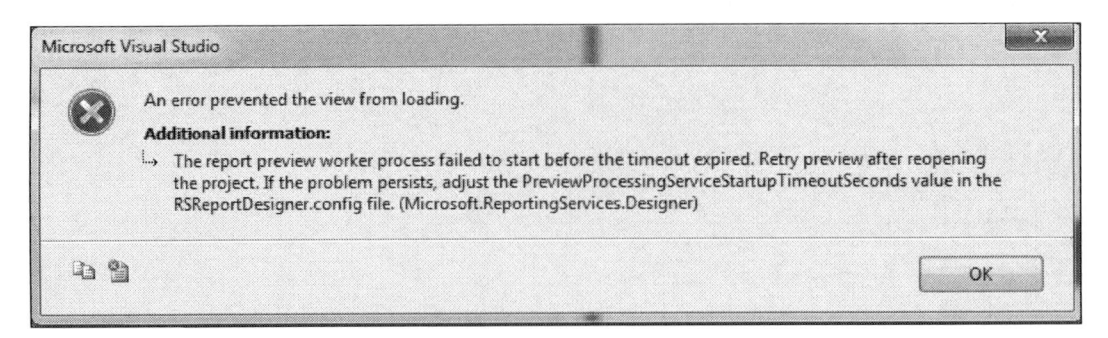

14. Right-click on `ContactTypeCopy.rdl` in the project and from the drop-down list, click on Run. The report gets displayed as follows:

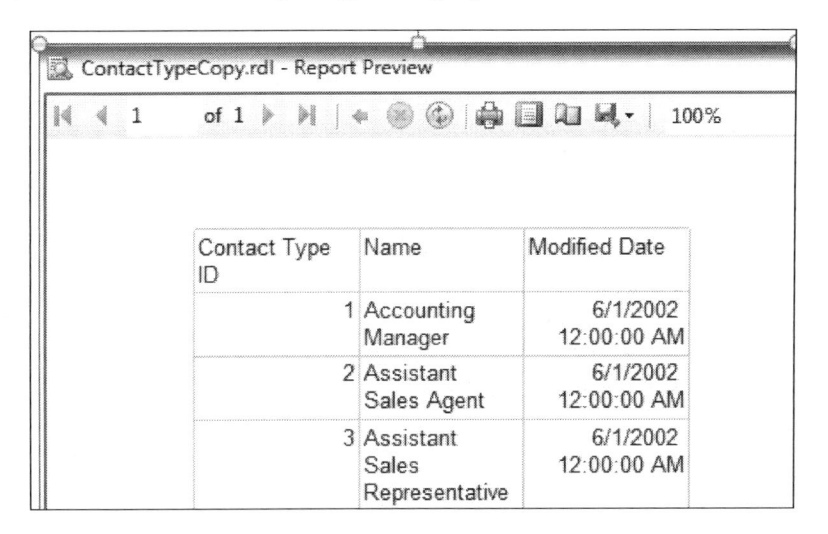

Microsoft Report Viewer Runtime

As Visual Studio gets updated from time-to-time, so do the controls used, and to keep up with this development, you may have to provide the control with the package, so that the end user can use to view the reports. You can redistribute this control with your applications for viewing reports. The download(s) contains controls for both Windows and the Web. It comes with all the necessary dynamic link libraries, but make sure you read about the requirements in each case. There are many versions of it that you can download:

- **Report Viewer Runtime 2008 version**:
  http://www.microsoft.com/en-us/download/details.aspx?id=6576

- **Report Viewer Runtime 2010 package**:
  http://www.microsoft.com/en-us/download/details.aspx?id=6442

- **Report Viewer Runtime 2010 SP1**:
  http://www.microsoft.com/en-us/download/details.aspx?id=6610

- **Report Viewer Runtime 2012**:
  http://www.microsoft.com/en-us/download/details.aspx?id=35747

Summary

In this chapter, Reporting Services' support provided by SQL Server Data Tools, a new feature in SQL Server, 2012 was described by way of examples. Creating or authoring reports is one of the main tasks in reporting services, and until now, creating reports for both Windows Desktop applications as well as Web applications was described. As for reports using Report Viewer Controls, both local and remote mode options were described. Deploying reports to Reporting Services Server and converting a report with the RDLC extension to RDL were also described.

In the next chapter, we will take a look at the overall infrastructure needed for Reporting Services, and the underlying architecture.

Overview of SQL Server Reporting Services 2012 Architecture, Features, and Tools

In the first two chapters, most of the components of Reporting Services were introduced, but how these are all wired together is still difficult to see from the previous two chapters alone. This chapter provides a summarized overview of SQL Server Reporting Services 2012 and the background information needed to work with the remaining chapters of the book. Most of the information is taken from Microsoft documentation.

In this chapter, we will have a look at the following topics:

- Structural design of environment and architecture of Native mode and SharePoint Integrated mode of Reporting Services
- Reporting Services configuration
- Features of Reporting Services 2012

In the first chapter, the following elements were installed and/or configured:

- SQL Server 2012
- Reporting Services 2012 configured in Native mode
- SQL Server with Reporting Services installed in SharePoint Integrated mode

- SharePoint Services 2010
- Creating a Reporting Services service in SharePoint

Each of the mentioned elements has its own individual architecture, topology of deployment, and features. It is important to see how users interact with them in doing the tasks assigned to them while working with Reporting Services as a whole. In order to interact with, author reports and manage them, tools are available and a good understanding of the tools and what support they provide is crucial in carrying out the tasks. The individual elements as well as the tools used in carrying out various tasks are described in the rest of the chapter.

Structural design of SQL servers and SharePoint environment

Depending on the business and the resources available, the various servers may be located in distributed locations and the Web applications may also be run from Web servers in a farm and the same can be true for SharePoint servers. In this book, by the word architecture we mean the way by which the preceding elements are put together to work on a single computer. However, it is important to know that this is just one topology (an arrangement of constituent elements) and in general it can be lot more complicated spanning networks and reaching across boundaries.

The Report Server is the centerpiece of the Reporting Services installation. This installation can be deployed in two modes, namely, Native mode or SharePoint Integrated mode. Each mode has a separate engine and an extensible architecture. It consists of a collection of special-purpose extensions that handle authentication, data processing, rendering, and delivery operations. Once deployed in one mode it cannot be changed to the other. It is possible to have two servers each installed in a different mode.

In *Chapter 1, Overview and Installation – SQL Server Reporting Services 2012*, we have installed all the necessary elements to explore the RS 2012 features, including Power View and Data Alerts. The next diagram briefly shows the structural design of the environment used in working with the book:

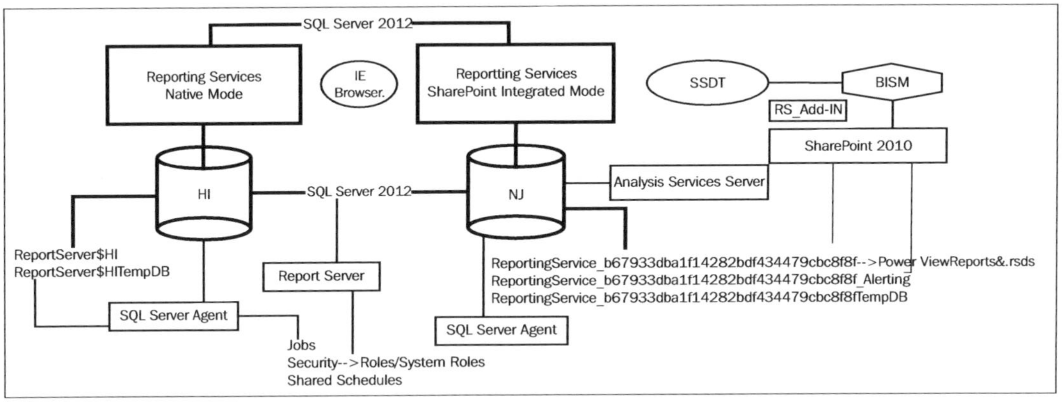

Primarily, SQL Server 2012 Enterprise Edition is used as described in *Chapter 1, Overview and Installation – SQL Server Reporting Services 2012*, for both Native mode as well as SharePoint Integrated mode. As we see in the previous diagram, Report Server Native mode is on a named instance `HI` (in some places another named instance `Kailua` is also used). This server has the Reporting Services databases `ReportServer$HI` and `ReportServer$HITempDB`. The associated Report Server handles Jobs, Security, and Shared Schedules. The Native mode architecture described in the next section is taken from the Microsoft documentation. The tools (SSDT, Report Builder, Report Server Configuration, and so on) connect to the Report Server. The associated SQL Server Agent takes care of the jobs such as subscriptions related to Native mode.

The SharePoint Server 2010 is a required element with which the Reporting Services add-in helps to create a Reporting Services Service. With the creation of the RS Service in SharePoint, three SQL Server 2012 databases (shown alongside in the diagram) are created in an instance with its Reporting Services installed in SharePoint Integrated mode. The SQL Server 2012 instance `NJ` is installed in this fashion. These databases are repositories for report content including those related to Power Views and Data Alerts.

The data sources (extension `.rsds`) used in creating Power View reports (extension `.rdlx`) are stored in the `ReportingService_b67933dba1f14282bdf434479cbc8f8f` database and the alerting related information is stored in the `ReportingService_b67933dba1f14282bdf434479cbc8f8f_Alerting` database. Not shown is an Express database that is used by the SharePoint Server for its content, administration, and so on. As described in *Chapter 1, Overview and Installation – SQL Server Reporting Services 2012*, `RS_ADD-IN` allows you to create the service. You will use the Power Shell tool to create and manage the service.

Overview of SQL Server Reporting Services 2012 Architecture, Features, and Tools

In order to create Power View reports, the new feature in SSRS 2012, you start off creating a data source in SharePoint library. Because of the RS Service, you can enable Reporting Services features such as Report Builder; and associate `BISM` file extensions to support connecting to tabular models created in `SSDT` deployed to Analysis Services Server. When Reporting Services is installed in SharePoint Integrated mode, SharePoint Web parts will be available to users that allow them to connect to RS Native mode servers to work with reports on the servers from within SharePoint Site.

Native mode

The following schematic taken from Microsoft documentation (`http://msdn.microsoft.com/en-us/library/ms157231.aspx`) shows the major components of a Native mode installation:

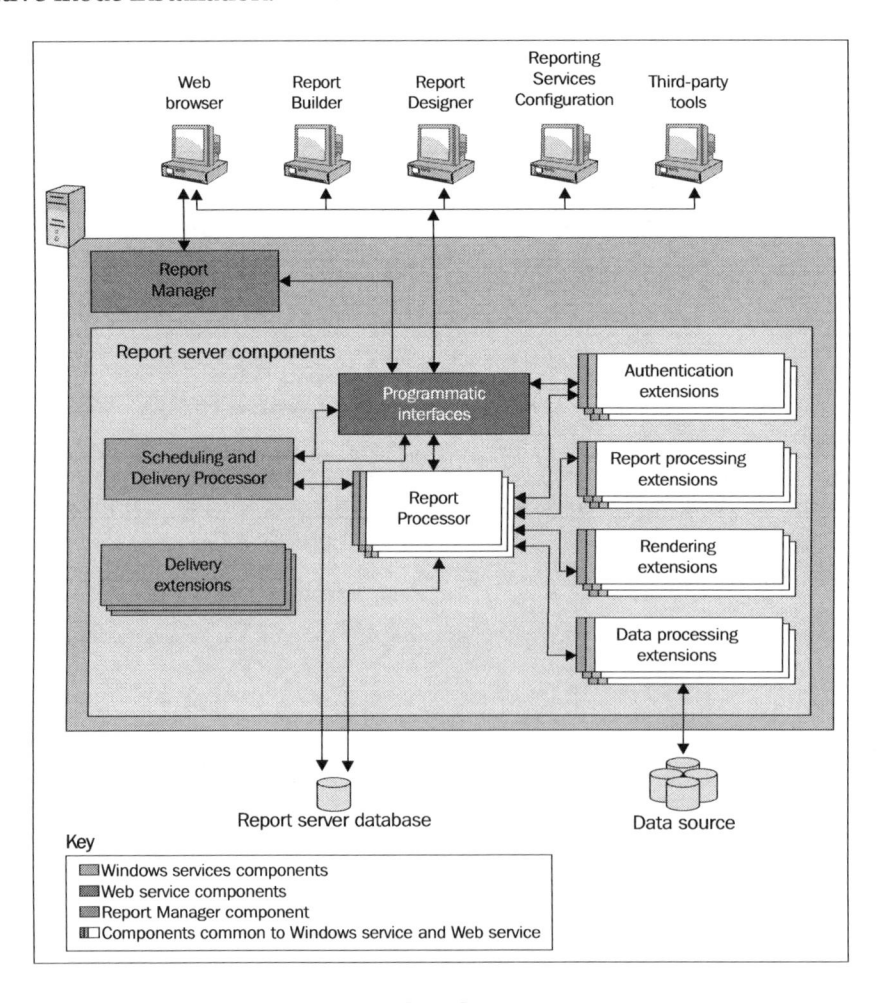

- Processing extensions (data, rendering, report processing, and authentication)
- Designing tools (Report Builder, Report Designer)
- Display devices (browsers)
- Windows components that do the scheduling and delivery through extensions (Report Server databases, a SQL Server 2012 database, which store everything connected with reports)

For the Reporting Services 2012 enabled in Native mode for this book, the following image shows the ReportServer databases and the Reporting Services Server installed in *Chapter 1, Overview and Installation – SQL Server Reporting Services 2012*. A similar server HI was also installed after a malware attack. The Report Server is implemented as a Microsoft Windows service called Report Server Service.

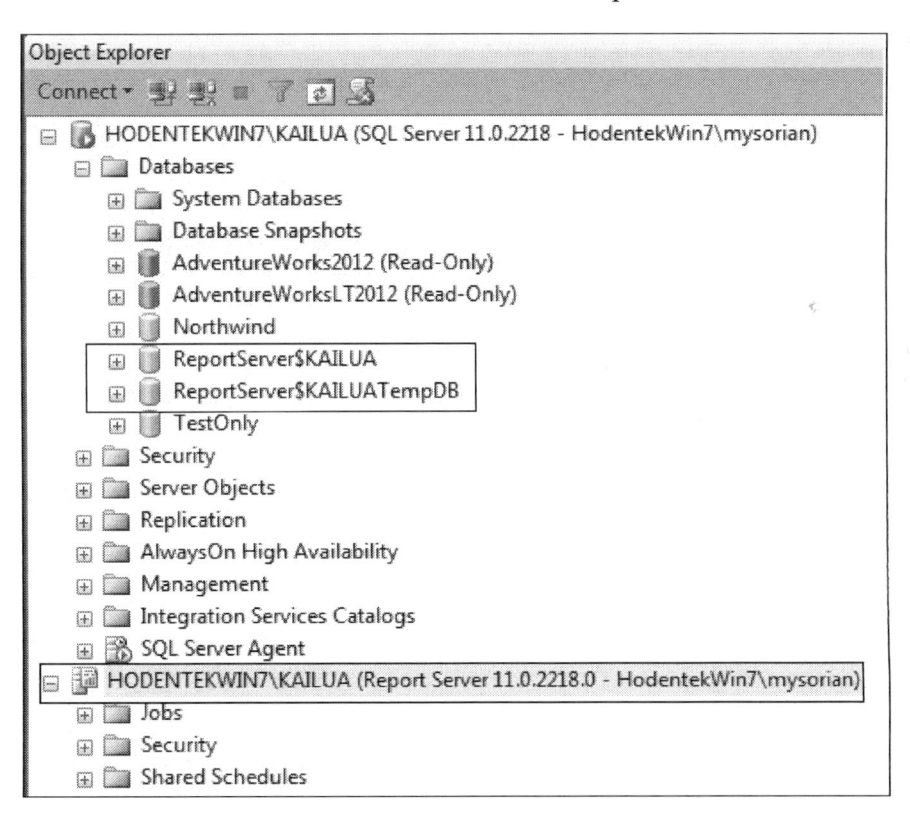

SharePoint Integrated mode

In SharePoint mode, a Report Server must run within a SharePoint Server (even in a standalone implementation). The Report Server processing, rendering, and management are all from SharePoint application server running the Reporting Services SharePoint shared service. For this to happen, at SQL Server installation time, the SharePoint Integrated mode has to be chosen. The access to reports and related operations in this case are from a SharePoint frontend.

The following elements are required for SharePoint mode:

- SharePoint Foundation 2010 or SharePoint Server 2010
- An appropriate version of the Reporting Services add-in for SharePoint products
- A SharePoint application server with a Reporting Services shared service instance and at least one Reporting Services service application

The following diagram taken from Microsoft documentation illustrates the various parts of a SharePoint Integrated environment of Reporting Services. Note that the alerting Web service and Power View need SharePoint Integration.

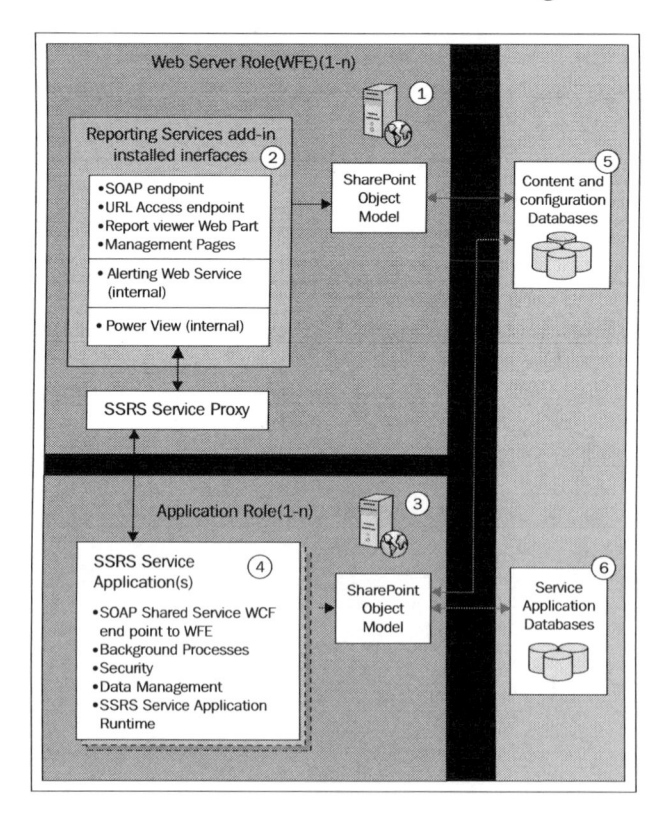

The numbered items and their description shown next are also from the same Microsoft document. Follow the link at the beginning of this section.

The architectural details presented previously were taken from Microsoft documentation.

Item number in the diagram	Description
1	Web servers or Web Frontends (WFE). The Reporting Services add-in must be installed on each Web server from which you want to utilize the Web application feature such as viewing reports or a Reporting Services management page for tasks such as managing data sources and subscriptions.
2	The add-in installs URL and SOAP endpoints for clients to communicate with application servers through the Reporting Services Proxy.
3	Application servers running a shared service. Scale-out of report processing is managed as part of the SharePoint farm and by adding the service to additional application servers.
4	You can create more than one Reporting Services service application with different configurations, including permissions, e-mail, proxy, and subscriptions.
5	Reports, data sources, and other items are stored in SharePoint content databases.
6	Reporting Services service applications create three databases for the Report Server, temp, and data alerting features. Configuration settings that apply to all SSRS service applications are stored in `RSReportserver.config` file.

When you install Reporting Services in SharePoint Integrated mode, several features that you are used to in Native mode will not be available. Some of them are summarized here from the MSDN site:

- URL access will work but you will have to access SharePoint URL and not Native mode URL. The Native mode folder hierarchy will not work.
- Custom Security extensions can be used but you need to use the special purpose security extension meant to be used for SharePoint Integration.
- You cannot use the Reporting Services Configuration Manager (of the Native mode installation).You should use the SharePoint Central Administration shown in this section (for Reporting Services 2008 and 2008 R2).

- Report Manager is not the frontend; in this case, you should use SharePoint Application pages.
- You cannot use Linked Reports, My Reports, and My Subscriptions in SharePoint mode.
- In SharePoint Integrated mode, you can work with Data Alerts and this is not possible in a Native mode installation.
- Power View is another thing you can do with SharePoint that is not available for Native mode. To access Power View the browser needs Silverlight installed.
- While reports with RDL extension are supported in both modes, reports with RDLX are only supported in SharePoint mode.
- SharePoint user token credentials, AAM Zones for internet facing deployments, SharePoint back and recovery, and ULS log support are only available for SharePoint mode.

For the purposes of discussion and exercises in this book, a standalone server deployment is used as shown in the next diagram. It must be remembered that there are various other topologies of deployment possible using more than one computer. For a detailed description please follow the link http://msdn.microsoft.com/en-us/library/bb510781(v=sql.105).aspx.

The standalone deployment is the simplest, in that all the components are installed on a single computer representative of the installation used for this book. The following diagram taken from the preceding link illustrates the elements of the standalone deployment:

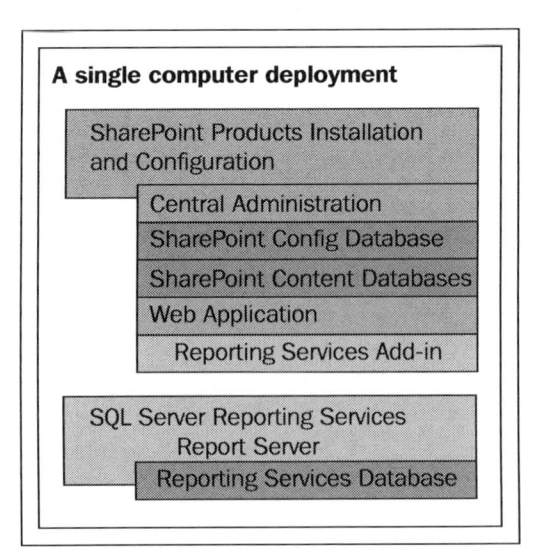

A single computer deployment

- SharePoint Products Installation and Configuration
  - Central Administration
  - SharePoint Config Database
  - SharePoint Content Databases
  - Web Application
  - Reporting Services Add-in
- SQL Server Reporting Services Report Server
  - Reporting Services Database

Reporting Services configuration

For both modes of installation, information for Reporting Services components is stored in configuration files and the registry. During setup the configuration files are copied to the following locations:

- Native mode

    `C:\Program Files\Microsoft SQL Server\MSRS11.MSSQLSERVER`

- SharePoint Integrated mode

    `C:\Program Files\Common Files\Microsoft Shared\Web Server Extensions\15\WebServices\Reporting`

    Follow the link `http://msdn.microsoft.com/en-us/library/ms155866.aspx` for details.

Native mode

The Report Server Windows Service is an orchestrated set of applications that run in a single process using a single account with access to a single Report Server database with a set of configuration files listed here:

Stored in	Description	Location
`RSReportServer.config`	Stores configuration settings for feature areas of the Report Server Service: Report Manager, the Report Server Web Service, and background processing.	`<Installation directory> \ Reporting Services \ReportServer`
`RSSrvPolicy.config`	Stores the code access security policies for the server extensions.	`<Installation directory> \ Reporting Services \ReportServer`
`RSMgrPolicy.config`	Stores the code access security policies for Report Manager.	`<Installation directory> \ Reporting Services \ReportManager`
`Web.config` for the Report Server Web Service	Includes only those settings that are required for ASP.NET.	`<Installation directory> \ Reporting Services \ReportServer`

Stored in	Description	Location
`Web.config` for Report Manager	Includes only those settings that are required for ASP.NET.	`<Installation directory> \ Reporting Services \ReportManager`
`ReportingServicesService.exe.config`	Stores configuration settings that specify the trace levels and logging options for the Report Server Service.	`<Installation directory> \ Reporting Services \ReportServer \Bin`
Registry settings	Stores configuration state and other settings used to uninstall Reporting Services. If you are troubleshooting an installation or configuration problem, you can view these settings to get information about how the Report Server is configured. Do not modify these settings directly as this can invalidate your installation.	`HKEY_LOCAL_MACHINE \SOFTWARE \ Microsoft \ Microsoft SQL Server \<InstanceID> \ Setup` and `HKEY_LOCAL_MACHINE\ SOFTWARE\ Microsoft\ Microsoft SQL Server\Services\ ReportServer`
`RSReportDesigner.config`	Stores configuration settings for Report Designer. For more information follow the link `http://msdn.microsoft.com/en-us/library/ms160346.aspx`.	`<drive>:\Program Files \Microsoft Visual Studio 10 \Common7 \IDE \ PrivateAssemblies`
`RSPreviewPolicy.config`	Stores the code access security policies for the server extensions used during report preview.	`C:\Program Files\ Microsoft Visual Studio 10.0\ Common7\IDE\ PrivateAssembliesr`

Chapter 3

First is the RSReportServer configuration file which can be found in the installation directory under Reporting Services. The entries in this file control the feature areas of the three components in the previous image, namely, Report Server Web Service, Report Server Service, Report Manager, and background processing.

The ReportServer Configuration file has several sections with which you can modify the following features:

- General configuration settings
- URL reservations
- Authentication
- Service
- UI
- Extensions
- MapTileServerConfiguration (Microsoft Bing Maps SOAP Services that provides a tile background for map report items in the report)
- Default configuration file for a Native mode Report Server
- Default configuration file for a SharePoint mode Report Server

The three areas previously mentioned (Report Server Web Service, Report Server Service, and Report Manager) all run in separate application domains and you can turn on/off elements that you may or may not need so as to improve security by reducing the surface area for attacks. Some functionality works for all the three components such as memory management and process health.

Overview of SQL Server Reporting Services 2012 Architecture, Features, and Tools

For example, in the reporting server `Kailua` in this book, the service name is `ReportServer$KAILUA`. This service has no other dependencies. In fact, you can access the help file for this service when you look at Windows Services in the Control Panels shown. In three of the tabbed pages of this window you can access contextual help.

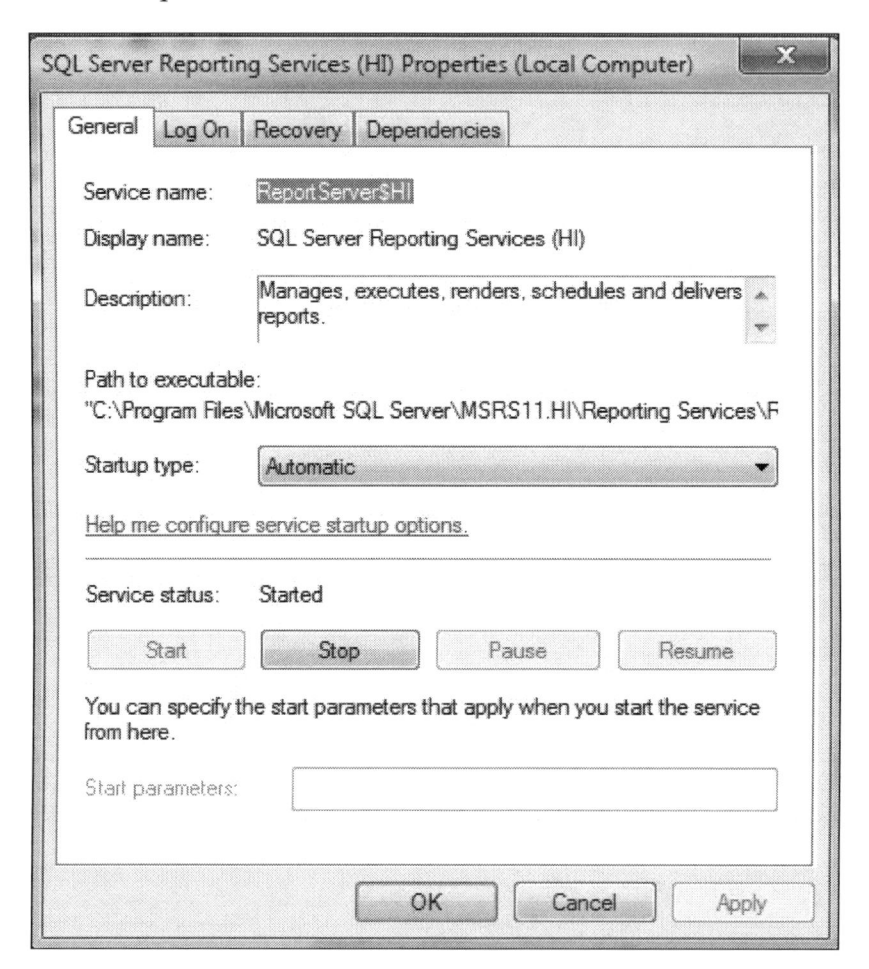

SharePoint Integrated mode

The following table taken from Microsoft documentation describes the configuration files used in the SharePoint mode Report Server. Configuration settings are stored in SharePoint Service application databases.

Stored in	Description	Location
RSReportServer.config	Stores configuration settings for feature areas of the Report Server Service: Report Manager, the Report Server Web Service, and background processing.	`<Installation directory> \Reporting Services \ ReportServer`
RSSrvPolicy.config	Stores the code access security policies for the server extensions.	`<Installation directory> \Reporting Services \ ReportServer`
Web.config for the Report Server Web Service	Includes only those settings that are required for ASP.NET.	`<Installation directory> \Reporting Services \ ReportServer`
Registry settings	Stores configuration state and other settings used to uninstall Reporting Services. Also stores information about each Reporting Services service application. Do not modify these settings directly as this can invalidate your installation.	`HKEY_LOCAL_MACHINE \ SOFTWARE \Microsoft \ Microsoft SQL Server \<InstanceID> \Setup` For example instance ID: `MSSQL11.MSSQLSERVER` and `HKEY_LOCAL_MACHINE\ SOFTWARE\Microsoft\ Microsoft SQL Server\ Reporting Services\ Service Applications`
RSReportDesigner.config	Stores configuration settings for Report Designer.	`<drive>:\Program Files \ Microsoft Visual Studio 10 \Common7 \IDE \ PrivateAssemblies`

Hands-on exercise 3.1 – modifying the configuration file in Native mode

We can make changes to the `rsreportserver.config` file if changes are required or some tuning has to be done. For example, you may need to change, to accommodate a different e-mail, change authentication, and so on. This is an XML file that can be edited in Notepad.exe (you can also use an XML Editor or Visual Studio). You need to start Notepad with administrator privileges.

Turn on/off the Report Server Web Service

In this exercise, we will modify the configuration file to turn on/off the Report Server Web Service. Perform the following steps:

1. Start Notepad using Run as Administrator.

2. Open the file at this location (you may use **Start | Search** for `rsreportserver.config`) which is located at `C:\Program Files\Microsoft SQL Server\MSRS11.KAILUA\Reporting Services\ReportServer\rsreportserver.config`.

3. In **Edit | Find** type in `IsWebServiceEnabled`. There are two values **True/False**. If you want to turn off, change **TRUE** to **FALSE**. The default is **TRUE**. Here is a section of the file reproduced:

```
<Service>
  <IsSchedulingService>True</IsSchedulingService>
  <IsNotificationService>True</IsNotificationService>
  <IsEventService>True</IsEventService>
  <PollingInterval>10</PollingInterval>
  <WindowsServiceUseFileShareStorage>False
    </WindowsServiceUseFileShareStorage>
  <MemorySafetyMargin>80</MemorySafetyMargin>
  <MemoryThreshold>90</MemoryThreshold>
  <RecycleTime>720</RecycleTime>
  <MaxAppDomainUnloadTime>30</MaxAppDomainUnloadTime>
  <MaxQueueThreads>0</MaxQueueThreads>
  <UrlRoot>
  </UrlRoot>
  <UnattendedExecutionAccount>
     <UserName></UserName>
     <Password></Password>
     <Domain></Domain>
  </UnattendedExecutionAccount>
  <PolicyLevel>rssrvpolicy.config</PolicyLevel>
  <IsWebServiceEnabled>True</IsWebServiceEnabled>
  <IsReportManagerEnabled>True</IsReportManagerEnabled>
  <FileShareStorageLocation>
     <Path>
```

```
      </Path>
    </FileShareStorageLocation>
  </Service>
```

4. Save the file to apply changes.

Turn on/off the scheduled events and delivery

This changes the report processing and delivery. Make changes in the `rsreportserver.config` file in the following section of `<Service/>`:

```
<IsSchedulingService>True</IsSchedulingService>
<IsNotificationService>True</IsNotificationService>
<IsEventService>True</IsEventService>
```

The default value for all of the three is TRUE. You can make it FALSE and save the file to apply changes. This can be carried out modifying FACET in **SQL Server Management Studio (SSMS)**, but presently this is not available.

Turn on/off the Report Manager

Report Manager can be turned off or on by making changes to the configuration file.

Make a change to the following section in the `<Service/>`:

```
<IsReportManagerEnabled>True</IsReportManagerEnabled>
```

Again, this change can be made using the Reporting Services Server in its FACET. To change this make sure you launch SQL Server Management Studio as Administrator. In the following sections use of SSMS via Facets is described.

Overview of SQL Server Reporting Services 2012 Architecture, Features, and Tools

Hands-on exercise 3.2 – turn the Reporting Service on/off in SSMS

The following are the steps to turn the Reporting Service on/off in SSMS:

1. Connect to `Reporting Services_KAILUA` in SQL Server Management Studio as the Administrator. Choose **HODENTEKWIN7\KAILUA** under **Reporting Services**. Click on **OK**.

2. Right-click on **HODENTEKWIN7\KAILUA (Report Server 11.0.22180 – HodentekWin7\mysorian)**.

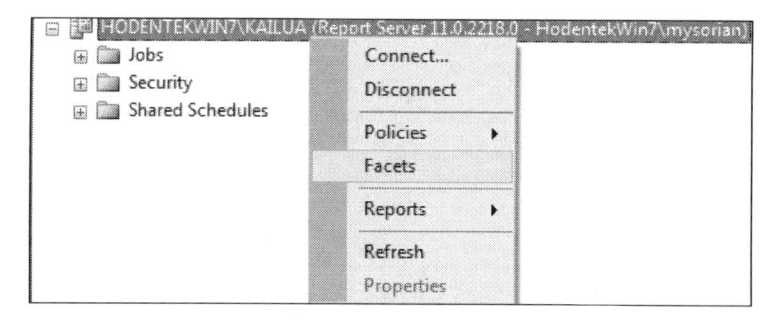

[146]

3. Click on **Facets** to open the following properties page.

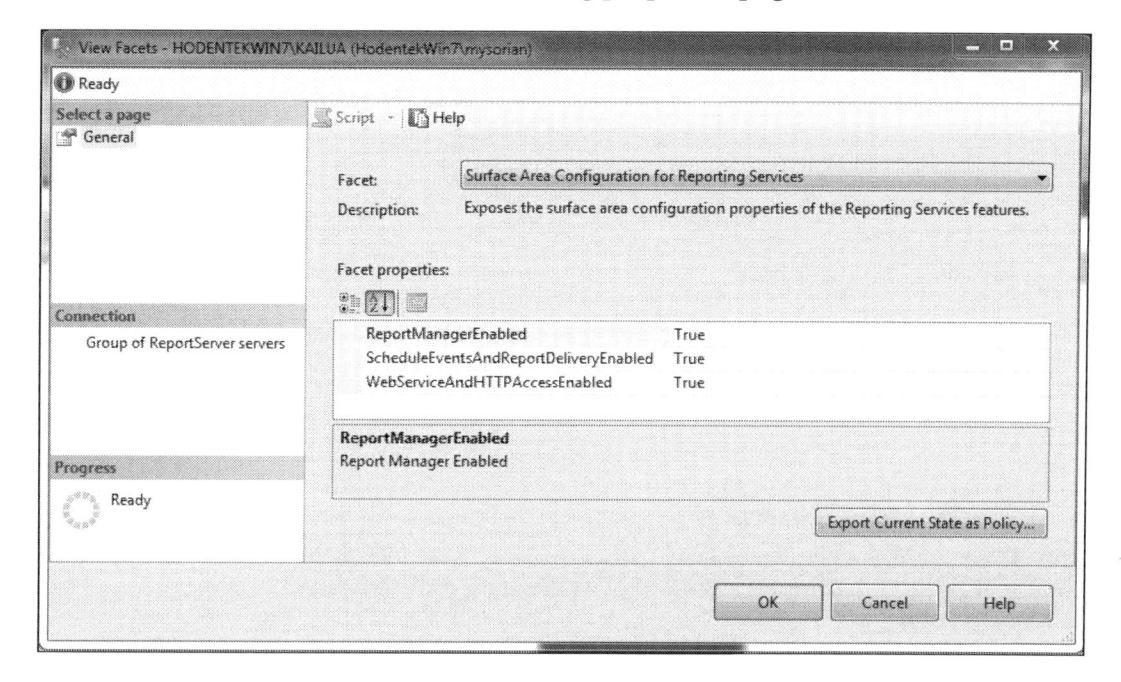

4. Click on the handle and set it to **True** or **False** and click on **OK**. The default is **True**. It should be possible to turn Windows Integrated security on or off by using SQL Server Management Studio. However, the Reporting Services Server properties are disabled.

Salient features of Reporting Services 2012

In the previous sections we described the environment created for working through the examples in this book and the details of the engines that work with the two modes of installation and the configuration files (or Registry settings) that are associated with them.

In this section we will look at the features of Reporting Services in the following sequence:

- Report definition
- Report processing stages
- Creating reports

Overview of SQL Server Reporting Services 2012 Architecture, Features, and Tools

- Report parts and reusability
- Customizing reports
- Saving and deploying reports
- Report validation
- Viewing reports
- Managing reports
- New features in RS2012 SharePoint Integrated
- Implementing security – authentication and authorization
- URL access
- Reporting Services extensions
- Reporting Services tools

The RS reports follow XML based report definitions that include report data and report layout elements. On the file system they have the extension RDL. A report item is published to a Report Server or SharePoint Site. It is accessed from a Report Manager, SharePoint Site, or even on an IIS server after some modification. As mentioned previously, reports on a Report Server installed in Native mode can be accessed using Web parts on a SharePoint server.

Report definition

Report definition is XML based and complete in all details. This means it is portable and can be recreated easily. However, one may have to implement the details in the report definition especially those related to data and the layout details in the XML file.

XML-based report definition (the .rdl file)

Here is the XML code of a typical report data's shared data source connection information in XML:

```
<?xml version="1.0" encoding="utf-8"?>
<RptDataSource
  xmlns:xsi="http://www.w3.org/2001/XMLSchema-instance"
  xmlns:xsd="http://www.w3.org/2001/XMLSchema" Name="DataSource1">
    <ConnectionProperties>
      <Extension>SQL</Extension>
      <ConnectString>Data Source=HODENTEKWIN7\KAILUA;Initial
        Catalog=Northwind</ConnectString>
      <IntegratedSecurity>true</IntegratedSecurity>
```

```
      </ConnectionProperties>
    <DataSourceID>893b9e01-8a18-4abe-bb89-61c804b3aabb
      </DataSourceID>
</RptDataSource>
```

This defines a `DataSourceID` for obtaining data in the `Northwind` database tables on the SQL Server 2012. The access method is via Windows Authentication. The DataSource name is `DataSource1`. The `<IntegratedSecurity/>` tag with value `true` is for Windows Authentication.

With this as the connection, a dataset is derived from one of the tables as shown in the next XML document for the dataset:

```
<?xml version="1.0" encoding="utf-8"?>
<SharedDataSet
  xmlns:rd="http://schemas.microsoft.com/SQLServer/reporting/
  reportdesigner" xmlns="http://schemas.microsoft.com/sqlserver/
  reporting/2010/01/shareddatasetdefinition">
  <DataSet Name="">
    <Query>
      <DataSourceReference>DataSource1</DataSourceReference>
      <CommandText>SELECT        LastName, FirstName
        FROM           Employees</CommandText>
    </Query>
    <Fields>
      <Field Name="LastName">
        <DataField>LastName</DataField>
        <rd:TypeName>System.String</rd:TypeName>
      </Field>
      <Field Name="FirstName">
        <DataField>FirstName</DataField>
        <rd:TypeName>System.String</rd:TypeName>
      </Field>
    </Fields>
  </DataSet>
</SharedDataSet>
```

Here the following query is used to just extract `FirstName` and `LastName` from the `Employees` table in the `Northwind` database. This is a shared dataset that can be used in more than one report, if needed. Have a look at the following query:

```
SELECT LastName, FirstName
  FROM Employees
```

This dataset populates the layout elements that you choose from the Toolbox completing the report design. The report with RDL extension has all the XML elements of data and the layout information.

> The layout information even for a single field takes up a couple of pages on Notepad and it is not reproduced here. Readers are urged to take a look at the XML of a RDL report. If you are authoring a report in SQL Server Data Tools (SSDT), right-click on a report and click on **View Code** to review the XML of the report.

Power View report contents

Power View reports have the extension .rdlx. These files are ZIP files containing the report definition file, a reportState file (XML), and a folder.

Using the same query as the one used for Native mode, a report with .rdlx extension was created. The report definition file is very large and cannot be shown here but the download of the report file is provided for the readers so that they can open and take a look at how the report is structured.

After a report is authored it goes through a number of processing steps shown here before it is displayed:

- **Compilation**: Report definition evaluation, store compiled intermediate format for server
- **Processing**: Run queries and combine with layout
- **Rendering**: Format page using a rendering extension

The rendered report can be exported if required through another processing step, Export. Reports are authored using authoring tools such as Report Builder and SSDT and they are processed by the Report Servers. We have already seen how reports are authored using SSDT where the compiled files are processed and displayed. In the next chapter we will look at authoring reports using Report Builder.

Creating reports

Creating reports, including how reports are deployed, processed, rendered, and scheduled were discussed in *Chapter 6, Working with the Report Builder* and *Chapter 7, Report Authoring with Report Builder2.0* of the of the first edition (*Learning SQL Server Reporting Services 2008, ISB:9781847196187*) using Report Builder 2.0. Report Builder 3.0 that started with SQL Server 2008 introduced enhancements to the toolset. With Visual Analytics gaining a lot of traction, new tools were added to support creating stunning Visual Analytics.

Report data

In order to create a report you must first create data sources and then extract datasets that are present in the underlying data source and bind them to the report. In order to get to the data source you need a data connection. Both Report Builder and SSDT provide Graphic User Interfaces to connect to data sources.

Report data may come from multiple sources of data. The following image shows the different sources of data that can be used in a report. The inclusion of ODBC, OLE DB, and XML provides a vast source of data as many other data sources can be accessed if drivers are available. Search on the Internet for 64-bit ODBC drivers for the third-party data source you are interested in (for example, Microsoft Access and Microsoft Excel can be accessed via these types of sources).

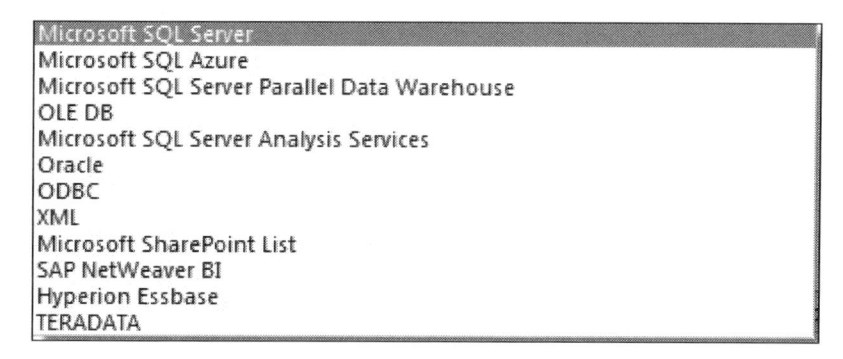

```
Microsoft SQL Server
Microsoft SQL Azure
Microsoft SQL Server Parallel Data Warehouse
OLE DB
Microsoft SQL Server Analysis Services
Oracle
ODBC
XML
Microsoft SharePoint List
SAP NetWeaver BI
Hyperion Essbase
TERADATA
```

> In principle you can get an idea of the type of OLE DB sources that can be accessed by reviewing the Linked Sources providers in SQL Server Management Studio as shown in the next screenshot:

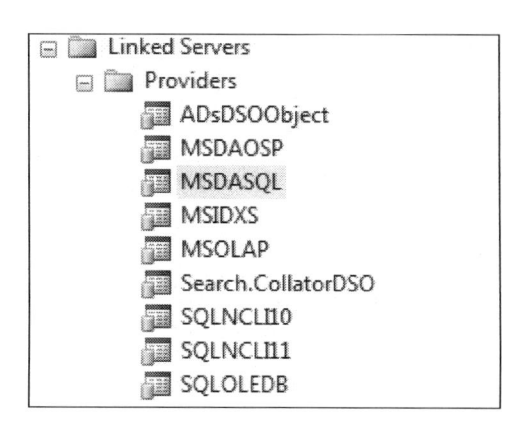

```
□ 📁 Linked Servers
  □ 📁 Providers
       📄 ADsDSOObject
       📄 MSDAOSP
       📄 MSDASQL
       📄 MSIDXS
       📄 MSOLAP
       📄 Search.CollatorDSO
       📄 SQLNCLI10
       📄 SQLNCLI11
       📄 SQLOLEDB
```

[151]

The ODBC drivers available to you on the computer can be obtained from the Drivers' tabbed page of the ODBC Data Source Administrator in the Control Panel. If a certain driver is not available you may need to install from its source.

After getting connected to the data source you need to run queries to define datasets, the data that gets into your report. Both SSDT and Report Builder provide graphic as well as text-based interfaces to run queries against the data. The dataset contains fields that are the selected columns of the data. These fields in the dataset are then bound to the table, matrix, chart, map, and so on in the Report Designer canvas. Both data sources and datasets can be embedded (specific to the report) or shared. In case of shared, the data source or dataset can be bound to other reports as well.

Report data may be filtered in the query or attached to reports. Parameters are part of the query that fetch data for the reports and can be used for parameterized reports. When the reporting services is installed in SharePoint Integrated mode, Data Alerts, new in SQL Server 2012, help you to receive a message from the server to the effect that some data on the report you were interested in got changed. It is an alert based on change of data, when the change meets certain preestablished rules. The notification comes in the form of an e-mail using a local or remote SMTP Server.

Grouping and aggregating of data can be carried out in the query as well as in the report. Similarly, sorting of data can be carried out in a query or in a report. You can embellish sorting to be interactive by installing a button that sorts the data.

Use of expressions helps in controlling data and reports as it can use data fields, logical, mathematical expressions, and report parameters. This tool is similar to what users of Microsoft Access have been using for a long time.

Subreports display data from multiple datasets and expressions can be used with one set of data referencing another set of data.

Power View reports, new in SQL Server 2012, are authored making use of data extracted from Analysis Services Tabular models (this requires you to install Analysis Services installed to support Tabular Model). Power View also requires installing SQL Server Reporting Services in SharePoint Integrated mode.

Although there are so many details involved in authoring reports, *Chapter 5, Working with Report Builder 3.0*, provides step-by-step guidance in authoring reports using Report Builder. In *Chapter 4, Working with Report Manager*, all aspects of Report Management are detailed. In *Chapter 6, Power View and Reporting Services*, step-by-step guidance is provided for authoring Power View reports. *Chapter 7, Self-Service Data Alerts in SSRS 2012*, describes self-service Data Alerts in detail.

New toolbox items in Report Builder 3

The following new items have been added to the report writing tool since the previous edition of this book mentioned earlier:

- Spark lines
- Data Bars
- Indicators
- Maps

The use of new items as well as some of the items from the previous edition will be demonstrated by way of examples in *Chapter 5, Working with Report Builder 3.0*. These items are available in both SSDT and Report Builder 3.0. The rest of the items in the toolset will also be used in the Hands-on examples of *Chapter 5, Working with Report Builder 3.0*.

Report parts and their reusability

Report parts, which are new in SSRS 2008 R2 and continue in SSRS 2012, add to productivity through reuse of objects. Object reuse is supported in Report Builder 3.0. Follow the link http://msdn.microsoft.com/en-us/library/ee635721.aspx to read more about report parts and their usage. The report parts that can be reused are the following:

- Charts
- Gauges
- Images and embedded images
- Maps
- Parameters
- Rectangles
- Tables
- Matrices
- Lists

Overview of SQL Server Reporting Services 2012 Architecture, Features, and Tools

You can publish report parts from Visual Studio (SSDT) Report Designer as shown here:

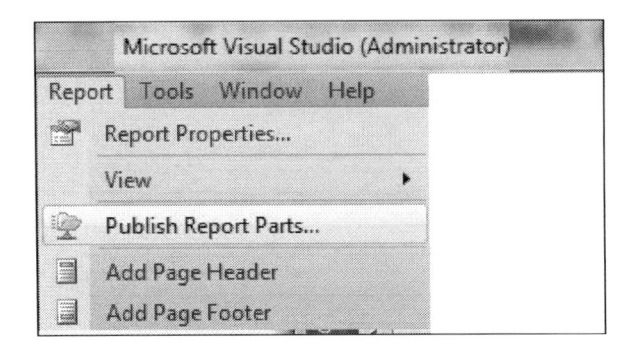

In Report Builder 3.0 you publish report parts from the `File` menu and can access **Report Parts** here as shown in the following screenshot:

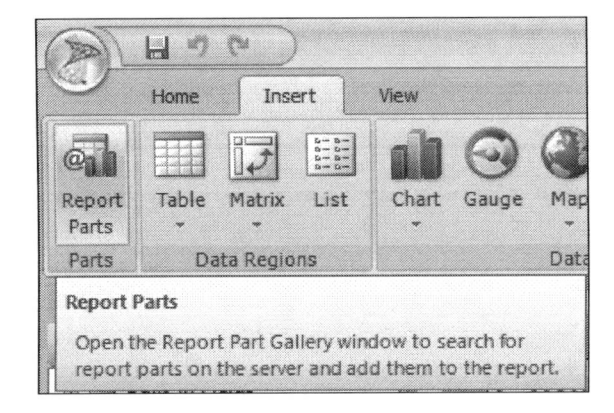

Customizing reports

The primary report authoring tools are Report Builder 3.0 and SSDT. Authoring reports with SSDT has been discussed with examples in *Chapter 2, SQL Server Reporting Services 2012 Projects with Visual Studio 2012*. Creating reports using Report Builder3.0 will be considered in *Chapter 5, Working with Report Builder 3.0*, to include examples of customizing reports using the following:

- Filter, group, and sort data
- Report parameters
- Expressions

- Formatting report items
- Images, text boxes, rectangles, and lines
- Page layout and rendering

Most of them were described with examples in the first edition of this book. These can be carried out in SSDT as well. Interactive features such as links, interactive sort, and document maps are fully supported. The reports before being published can be previewed as seen in *Chapter 2, SQL Server Reporting Services 2012 Projects with Visual Studio 2012*. Previews are also supported in Report Builder 3.0. Preview features help you to flush out problematic areas in report layout, blank pages in reports, page breaks, and many other troublesome problems.

Most of the report types are also described in *Chapter 5, Working with Report Builder 3.0*. The hands-on exercises guide you to work with all aspects of authoring different types of reports in *Chapter 5, Working with Report Builder 3.0*.

Saving and deploying reports

In Report Designer you can save reports locally, deploy them to the Report Server or SharePoint Site. Deploying to the Native mode Report Server was described in *Chapter 2, SQL Server Reporting Services 2012 Projects with Visual Studio 2012*. Unless the Reporting Services with SharePoint Integration is properly configured, it will not be possible to deploy it to a SharePoint Site. You need not only the Server URL but also the following items:

- Target dataset folder
- Target data source folder
- Target report folder
- Target report parts folder
- Target server URL
- Target server version, SQL Server 2008 R2 or later

The target dataset folder and report parts folder are optional and the other items must be fully qualified URLs. In the case of target server URL, you should use the site name.

Overview of SQL Server Reporting Services 2012 Architecture, Features, and Tools

Deploying (which amounts to saving) a report developed using Report Builder to SharePoint Server is a lot easier as the process is interactive as shown in the next image that displays the server and folders while saving a report to a SharePoint Server.

Report validation

Reports created in SSDT are validated before preview and during deployment. If there are several elements some of them may get skipped because they are up to date and need no verification. Error level property is used to manage build warnings and errors and they run from 0 to 4. The default **Build ErrorLevel** is set to **2**, which means it is less severe, but may change layout drastically. Build errors may crop up due to several reasons and are written to the output window. The following screenshot is taken from the project's property pages shows the error levels.

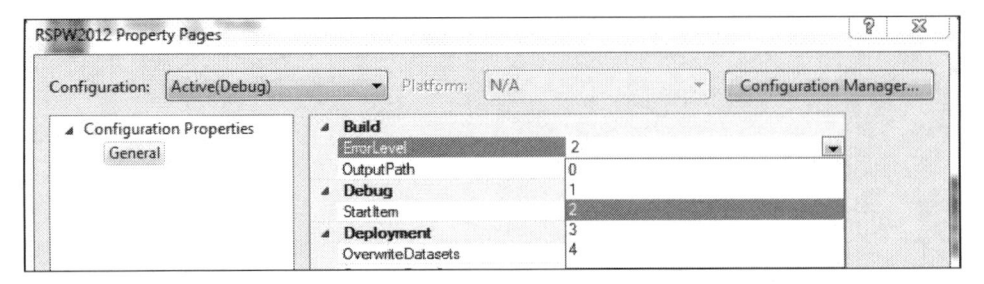

You can change this error level in the property pages of a SSDT project. This is to allow you to take a look at what changes you can make and avoid errors. This is not intended for a novice developer. **ErrorLevel** property is used to test the sensitivity of build to errors as shown in the next table:

ErrorLevel	Description
0	Most severe and unavoidable build issues that prevent preview and deployment of reports
1	Severe build issues that change the report layout drastically
2	Less severe build issues that change report layout insignificantly
3	Minor build issues that change the report layout in minor ways that might not be noticeable
4	Minor build issues that change the report layout in minor ways that might not be noticeable

Viewing reports

There are a variety of viewing options to view reports, local as well as published. Some of the following are already covered in *Chapter 2, SQL Server Reporting Services 2012 Projects with Visual Studio 2012*:

- Using a browser to view reports on Reporting Services Web Service or SharePoint Site, including viewing Power View
- Report delivery by subscription by e-mail or shared folder to be viewed by a report reader
- Export of report via Report Viewer toolbar to different formats (configured on the Report Server)
- Hardcopy of a report
- Reports for Web or Windows Forms Application and the Report Viewer can point to content on the Report Server

Managing reports

Report Management in Native mode is described comprehensively in *Chapter 4, Working with Report Manager*. In *Chapter 6, Power View and Reporting Services*, report management in Reporting Services installed in SharePoint Integrated mode is described. The following aspects of a published report can be managed independently from report definition:

- Shared and embedded data sources
- Shared datasets
- Parameters, if changed on the server, authoring clients cannot change
- Image and ESRI* Shape files can be published and managed

> * ESRI is the leading worldwide supplier of **Geographic Information System (GIS)** software and geo-database management applications. Review this link, http://www.esri.com/library/whitepapers/pdfs/shapefile.pdf

The following aspects of published reports can also be managed:

- Use of report cache to schedule large reports to off-peak periods
- Report snapshot for realistic comparisons
- Create report archival history using report snapshots to build a picture of report data change over time

Report scheduling

Report scheduling can be created and managed from the following modes:

- Report Manager in Native mode
- SharePoint Site Administration pages in SharePoint Integrated mode

However, scheduling is only supported in SQL Server Version Professional or higher. Review the link, http://go.microsoft.com/fwlink/?linkid=232473 for details.

In both modes, report delivery can be scheduled in the following ways:

- In a standard subscription, or a data-driven subscription
- To schedule report history so that new snapshots are added to report history at regular intervals

- To schedule refreshes of report snapshot
- To schedule expiration of report cache or shared dataset to occur at predefined times

You can create shared schedules for the use of many reports or subscriptions. Schedule information is stored in the following databases:

- Native mode: Report Server database
- SharePoint Integrated mode: Service Application database

Schedules are triggered by SQL Agent Jobs and processing is based on local server time. For details about how to create, modify, and delete schedules review the link `http://msdn.microsoft.com/en-us/library/ms155897.aspx`.

There are differences between shared schedules and report-specific schedules. Shared schedules are system-level items and you require system-level permissions to create them. Usually, these are carried out by Report Server administrator. Report-specific schedules are defined on a per report basis (that is in the context of an individual report, subscription, or report execution). System Administrators and Content Managers can create and manage any schedule, but if you are planning a custom role, then for the custom role to create and manage scheduling, the schedule related tasks must be correctly defined.

To do this	Include this task	Native mode predefined roles	SharePoint Integrated mode groups
Create, modify, or delete shared schedule	Manage shared schedules	System Administrator	Owners
Select shared schedules	View shared schedules	System user	Members
Create, modify, or delete report-specific schedules in a user-defined subscription	Manage individual subscriptions	Browse, Report Builder, my reports, Content manager	Visitors, members
Create, modify, or delete report-specific schedules for all other scheduled operations	Manage report history, manage all subscriptions, manage reports	Content manager	Owners

Subscriptions and delivery

In order for a report to be delivered to you by some means you should arrange for a subscription, a standing request to get a report at a specific time, in a specific format. If you are not scheduling you could also view a report on demand, by actively selecting the report from the server.

Subscriptions allow you automate scheduled report deliveries. Subscriptions are processed on the Report Server and are distributed using delivery extensions deployed on the server. By default, you can get reports to a shared folder, or to an e-mail address. In case of a Report Server installed in SharePoint Integrated mode, you can get delivery of the report to a SharePoint library.

Out of the box, the following subscription and delivery options are supported but extensions can be used to create custom subscriptions as well:

Scenario	Description
E-mail reports	E-mail reports to individual users and groups. Create a subscription and specify a group alias or e-mail alias to receive a report that you want to distribute. You can have Reporting Services determine the subscription data at run time. If you want to send the same report to a group that has a changing list of members, you can use a query to derive the subscription list at run time.
View reports offline	Users can select PDF, Microsoft Excel, or Web archive formats in a subscription. These formats are recommended for viewing reports offline. Reports that you want to archive can be sent directly to a shared folder that you backup on a nightly schedule. Large reports that take too long to load in a browser can be sent to a shared folder in a format that can be viewed in a desktop application.
Preload cache	If you have multiple instances of a parameterized report or a large number of report viewers, you can preload reports in the cache to reduce processing time used to display the report.
Data-driven reports	Use data-driven subscriptions to customize report output, delivery options, and report parameter settings at run time. The subscription uses a query to get input values from a data source at run time. You can use data-driven subscriptions to perform a mail-merge operation that sends a report to a list of subscribers that is determined at the time the subscription is processed.

There are two kinds of subscriptions, standard and data-driven. Standard subscriptions are created and managed by users. In a standard subscription, only one kind of report presentation option and delivery option is supported as this kind of subscription has static subscription related values. Data-driven subscriptions, on the other hand, obtain the delivery options at run time by querying an external data source that provides the specifics of the subscription, such as recipient, report parameters, or application format. Data-driven subscriptions are used for a larger client base. Examples of standard and data-driven subscriptions were given in the first edition of this book.

There are certain prerequisites to be met before subscription can be created. These are listed in the following table:

Requirement	Description
Permissions	You must have access to the report. Before you can subscribe to a report, you must have permission to view it. Your role assignment must include the "Manage individual subscriptions" task.
Stored credentials	The report must use stored credentials or no credentials to retrieve data at runtime. You cannot subscribe to a report that is configured to use the impersonated or delegated credentials of the current user to connect to an external data source. The stored credentials can be a Windows account or a database user account.
User dependent values in a report	For standard subscriptions only, you can create subscriptions to reports that incorporate user account information in a filter or as text that appears on the report. In the report, the user account name is specified through a `User!UserID` expression that resolves to the current user. When you create a subscription, the user who creates the subscription is the considered the current user.
No model item security	You cannot subscribe to a Report Builder report that uses a model as a data source if the model contains model item security settings. Only reports that use model item security are included in this restriction.
Parameter values	If the report uses parameters, a parameter value must be specified with the report itself or in the subscription you define. If default values have been defined in the report, you can set the parameter value to use the default.

The following are the formats and delivery methods, and the user can choose them when a subscription is created. There are custom delivery types that can be created using extensions; the ones shown are available out-of-the box.

Delivery Extension	Description
Windows file share	Delivers a report as a static application file to a shared folder that is accessible on the network.
E-mail	Delivers a notification or a report as an e-mail attachment or URL link.
SharePoint library	Delivers a report as a static application file to a SharePoint library that is accessible from a SharePoint Site. The site must be integrated with a Report Server that runs in SharePoint Integrated mode.
Null	The null delivery provider is a highly specialized delivery extension that is used to preload a cache with ready-to-view parameterized reports. This method is not available to users in individual subscriptions. Null delivery is used by administrators in data-driven subscriptions to improve Report Server performance by preloading the cache.

Features new in RS2012 SharePoint Integrated

The combination of Silverlight application together with the reporting services installed in SharePoint Integrated development made it possible to create highly interactive reports that feed off live data, called Power Views. Presently there are two ways they are created, using Excel with PowerPivot add-in or SQL Analysis Services with Tabular Model and Reporting Services add-in for SharePoint.

In this section we will take a brief look at Power View features as well as Data Alerts, a self-service technique to send out messages automatically via e-mail whenever data in a report gets changed.

Power View

If you are looking to work with Visual Analytics, Power View is the way to go. Power View provides for ad-hoc reporting. Ad-hoc reporting in Reporting Services 2012 enables data analysts, business decision makers, and information workers to make interactive data exploration possible even if they do not understand where the data is or how it is structured. The users can easily create and interact with views of data from data models based on PowerPivot workbooks published to PowerPivot Gallery or, tabular models deployed to SQL Server 2012 Analysis Services instances. Power View is a browser-based Silverlight application and requires SharePoint 2010 to launch. Power View is a great replacement for the Report Model Project template used in SQL Server Reporting Services 2008. This model project template is absent in SSDT as it is deprecated, however, for backward compatibility SSDT can work with legacy report models.

Power View has some great features summarized from the Microsoft documentation (`http://office.microsoft.com/en-us/excel-help/power-view-explore-visualize-and-present-your-data-HA102835634.aspx`):

- Power View report is always ready to be presented as it works off live data. No need for a preview.
- Power View can be in reading mode and full-screen (such as videos), made possible by taking away items not needed from screen area.
- It has the same look and feel of Microsoft Office for its menus.
- Power View reports are interactive with filtering and highlighting supported.
- The data for Power View comes from Tabular Model running in SQL Server 2012 Analysis Services Server (in this book).
- Creating reports is a breeze. You can create a variety of visualization of data very rapidly. All you need to know is dragging data fields to design area and create tables/matrices; and with a click change them to charts.
- Reports can have a variety of chart types such as bar, line, and so on.
- Filtering can be for the entire view of visualization or can be for a section of a visualization.
- Filtered data can be sorted as well. You can sort tables, matrices, charts, and so on.

- Reports can have multiple views all based on the same underlying data model.
- Performance-wise Power View does a great job retrieving only data needed for the visualization.
- Power View reports can be exported to Power Point with each view becoming a Power Point slide and each slide interacting with Power View. Power View reports can be published to SharePoint Server 2010.

Power View should be considered as an ad hoc reporting tool that complements Report Builder and Report Designer and not a replacement.

Data Alerts

Data alerts, as the name implies, are alerts driven by data, that is, when the data on a report changes. For example, if a change in the report data takes place, you get an alert by an e-mail. There can be multiple recipients to this alert. The frequency of these alerts is customizable.

> This proactive feature is new in SQL Server 2012 but is only possible when integrated with SharePoint.

Data Alerts are created by users.

Data Alert creator owns the Data Alert and no one else does.

Data Alert owners can view data alerts, modify, or delete them if necessary. After you create a report, you identify the data of interest that you may want to monitor. You also define a recurrence pattern for sending the Data Alert when the monitored data changes to the recipients you designate. Once the definition of data to be alerted is defined, alert service processing takes over and at scheduled times retrieves data to compare with the definition, and based on pre-established rules an alert instance is created that sends an alert message to e-mail recipients. The rules for sending out alert check the data in the reports and send out alerts unlike alerts that are generated when a document changes takes place.

Data Alert creation and alert functionality is clearly explained in this diagram from Microsoft's documentation:

Chapter 3

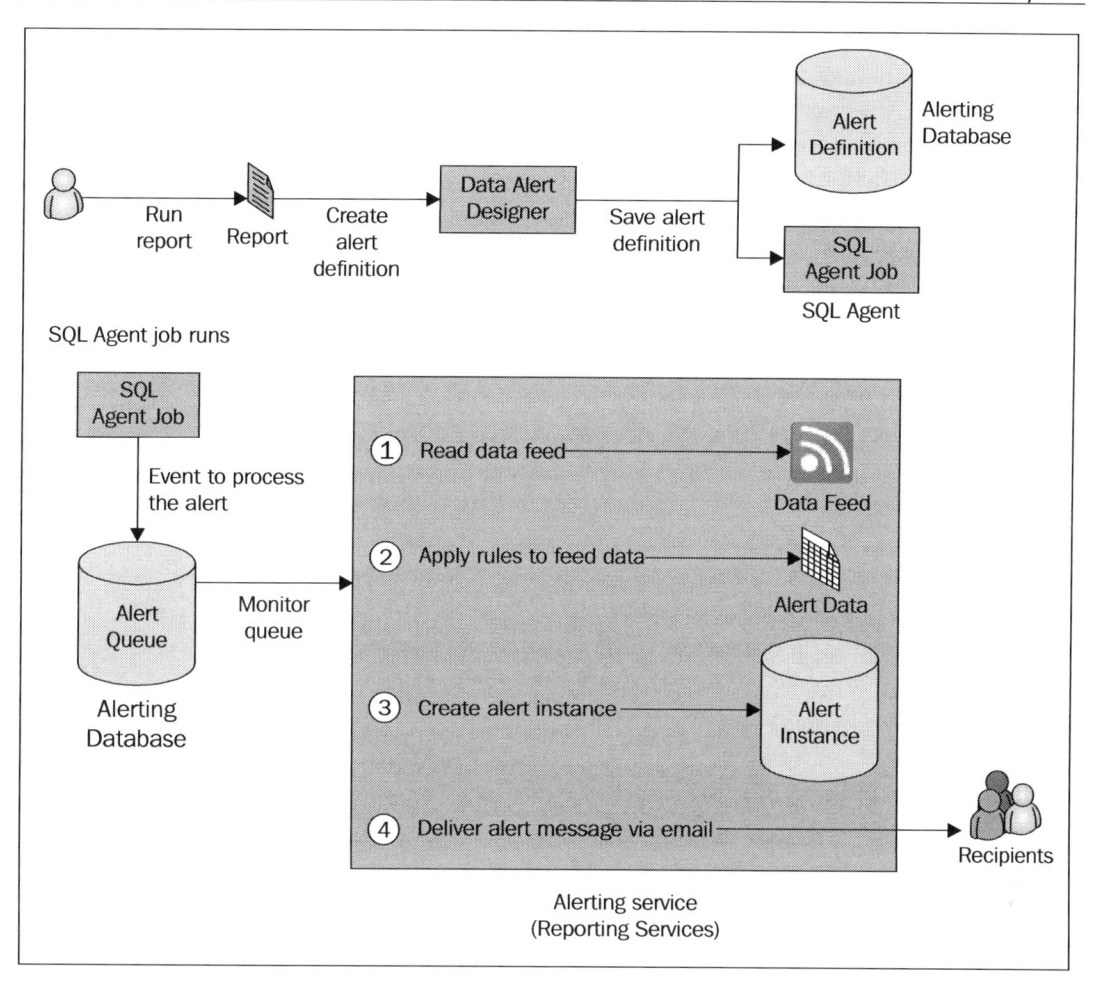

```
[Diagram: Data Alert processing workflow]

User → Run report → Report → Create alert definition → Data Alert Designer → Save alert definition → Alert Definition (Alerting Database) / SQL Agent Job (SQL Agent)

SQL Agent job runs:
SQL Agent Job → Event to process the alert → Alert Queue (Alerting Database) → Monitor queue → Alerting service (Reporting Services):
  (1) Read data feed → Data Feed
  (2) Apply rules to feed data → Alert Data
  (3) Create alert instance → Alert Instance
  (4) Deliver alert message via email → Recipients
```

Data Alerts can be created for reports (RDL extension) using either Report Designer in SSDT or with Report Builder. Data Alerts can be created even for very complex reports but the report must have at least one data region of any type and the report data source configured to use stored credentials, or no credentials. Another restriction regarding Data Alert creation is that you cannot create data alerts for Power View reports. One other requirement for Data Alerts is that the report for which Data Alert is created should be saved (or uploaded) to a SharePoint Library, which means it is set up inside SharePoint. This implies that if your computer is installed in Native mode you cannot create Data Alerts (data driven subscriptions are not the same as Data Alerts). Data Alerts do not use integrated security credentials or will not prompt for credentials. The report processing and alert processing happen together and if credentials are not present the Data Alert will not be processed.

As a first step, you run the report containing data in a SharePoint library. It goes without saying that without data you cannot create Data Alerts. If the report is parameterized, the parameter values will be saved in the Data Alert. The values are used when alert processing takes place. Any changes you want to make to parameters must be made and the report is run to use the change value after which you create a Data Alert. The Data Alert Designer, which is available on the SharePoint Site's Actions menu item can be used to design a Data Alert. You can save Data Alert definitions in the SQL Server Alerting Database created when you install Reporting Services in SharePoint Integrated mode. Data Alerts are discussed in more detail in *Chapter 7, Self-Service Data Alerts in SSRS 2012*.

Implementing security – authentication and authorization

Authentication is the first step in security clearance before you start working with reports. Authentication is based on built-in Windows authentication or a custom authentication module. For the purposes of this book Windows authentication is assumed.

Authentication

Reporting Services provides different authentication types for users and client applications to authenticate with the Report Server.

Since SQL Server 2008 R2, Extended Protection for authentication is available; this feature provides extra protection of authentication using channel binding and service binding. This is not available by default and the operating system (as well as the client application) must support Extended Protection. This is not considered in this book. Further details on this topic can be reviewed at http://msdn.microsoft.com/en-us/library/bb283249.aspx.

Authentication types

All users who want to access Report Server need authentication. The following table from Microsoft shows the authentication types available:

Authentication type name	HTTP authentication layer value	Used by default	Description
RSWindowsNegotiate	Negotiate	Yes	RSWindowsNegotiate directs the Report Server to handle authentication requests that specify Negotiate. Negotiate attempts Kerberos authentication first, but falls back to NTLM if Active Directory cannot grant a ticket for the client request to the Report Server. Negotiate will only fall back to NTLM if the ticket is not available. If the first attempt results in an error rather than a missing ticket, the Report Server does not make a second.
RSWindowsNTLM	NTLM	Yes	NTLM authenticates a user through an exchange of private data described as challenge-response.
			The credentials will not be delegated or impersonated on other requests. Subsequent requests will follow a new challenge-response sequence. Depending on network security settings, a user might be prompted for credentials or the authentication request will be handled transparently.

RSWindowsKerberos	Kerberos	No	For requests that specify Kerberos authentication, the Report Server reads permissions on the security token of the user who issued the request. If delegation is enabled in the domain, the token of the user who is requesting a report can also be used on an additional connection to the external data sources that provide data to reports.
			Before you specify RSWindowsKerberos, be sure that the browser type you are using actually supports it. If you are using Internet Explorer, Kerberos authentication is only supported through Negotiate. Internet Explorer will not formulate an authentication request that specifies Kerberos directly.
RSWindowsBasic	Basic	No	Basic authentication is defined in the HTTP protocol and can only be used to authenticate HTTP requests to the Report Server.
			Credentials are passed in the HTTP request in base 64 encoding. If you use Basic authentication, use Secure Sockets Layer (SSL) to encrypt user account information before it is sent across the network. SSL provides an encrypted channel for sending a connection request from the client to the Report Server over an HTTP TCP/IP connection.

Custom	(Anonymous)	No	Anonymous authentication directs the Report Server to ignore the authentication header in an HTTP request. The Report Server accepts all requests, but call on, a custom ASP.NET Forms authentication that you provide to authenticate the user.
			Specify custom only if you are deploying a custom authentication module that handles all authentication requests on the Report Server. You cannot use the custom authentication type with the default Windows Authentication extension.

For the Report Server `Kailua` used in this book, the authentication is as shown in the following XML block in the `rsreportserver.config` file described earlier.

> Please review this in the configuration files in the <Authentication/> node.

Authentication types such as Anonymous, Passport, Digest, and so on are not supported.

Basically, the Report Server uses the authentication provider and permissions defined in the SharePoint Web Application to control access to Report Server items. SharePoint authentication can be Windows authentication or Forms authentication. The assignment of roles follows a similar pattern to Native mode but the number of tasks a role can perform is lot more fine-grained than a Native mode installation.

In the present case where the computer administrator installed the SharePoint Server and configured the portal site, he is the site owner. The administrator in this case set permissions to the SharePoint Web Application as we shall see later.

Authorization

For authorization, Reporting Services adopts roles and permissions to control user access to content in the Report Server catalogue.

Reporting Services installs with a set of predefined roles. Roles are authorized to carry out specific tasks. Report Server operations are carried out by authenticated users or groups assigned to the roles. Here is the complete list of roles taken from Microsoft documentation that are available and their scope:

Predefined Role	Scope	Description
Content Manager Role	Item	Includes all item-level tasks. Users who are assigned to this role have full permission to manage Report Server content, including the ability to grant permissions to other users, and to define the folder structure for storing reports and other items.
Publisher Role	Item	Users who are assigned to this role can add items to a Report Server, including the ability to create and manage folders that contain those items.
Browser Role	Item	Users who are assigned to this role can run reports, subscribe to reports, and navigate through the folder structure.
Report Builder Role	Item	Users who are assigned to this role can create and edit reports in Report Builder.
My Reports Role	Item	Users who are assigned to this role can manage a personal workspace for storing and using reports and other items.
System Administrator Role	System	Users who are assigned to this role can enable features and set defaults, set site-wide security, create role definitions in Management Studio, and manage jobs.
System User Role	System	Users who are assigned to this role can view basic information about the Report Server such as the schedule information in a shared schedule.

URL access

URL access in SQL Server Reporting Services enables you to send commands to the Report Server through a URL request. Using this you can customize the rendering of a report on a Native mode server or in a SharePoint library by sending a request to the Report Server. The request command can encapsulate report parameter values, page related values, and a lot of others. There are predefined URL access parameters that you need to use. You can e-mail the URL with parameters so that others can access your reports (assumes email recipients have access to report server.)

These are some of the other actions you can perform via URL:

- Send commands to the HTML viewer, such as adjusting its look and feel
- List the children of a folder
- Retrieve the XML definition of an item on the server
- Render a specific report history snapshot
- Manage report sessions

The syntax for addressing an URL is as follows:

```
rswebserviceurl?reportpath [&prefix:param=value]...n]
```

Here is an example we saw earlier in *Chapter 2, SQL Server Reporting Services 2012 Projects with Visual Studio 2012*, where `rs:command=ListChildren` displayed the folder contents on the Report Server `Kailua`.

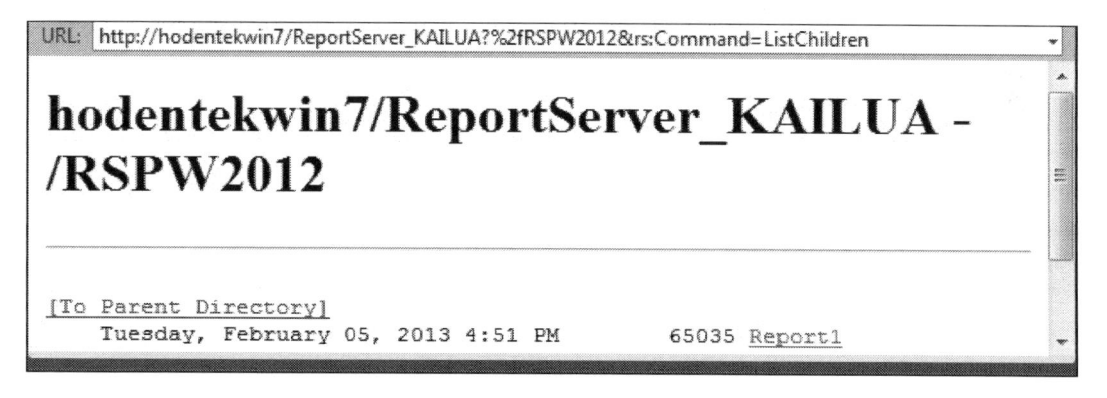

```
URL: http://hodentekwin7/ReportServer_KAILUA?%2fRSPW2012&rs:Command=ListChildren
```

**hodentekwin7/ReportServer_KAILUA -
/RSPW2012**

[To Parent Directory]
    Tuesday, February 05, 2013 4:51 PM   65035 Report1

A complete list of URL access parameters is available at http://msdn.microsoft.com/en-us/library/1c3e680a-83ea-4979-8e79-fa2337ae12a3. We will revisit this topic in *Chapter 8, Reporting Services and Programming*, section on *URL Access*, and *Chapter 10, Applications Accessing Report Servers*, Hands-on exercise 10.2.

Here is an example of listing folder contents with `rs:Command= ListChildren` command to a SharePoint Report Server.

hodentekwin7/ - http://hodentekwin7/Documents/FirstFolder

```
[To Parent Directory]
    Wednesday, March 27, 2013 12:51 PM      <dir> InsideFolder
    Wednesday, April 03, 2013 3:03 PM       <dir> April13_2
    Wednesday, April 03, 2013 2:40 PM       <dir> April3
```

Microsoft SQL Server Reporting Services Version 11.0.2218.0

The syntax used for URL addressing for this example is `http://hodentekwin7/_vti_bin/ReportServer/?http%3a%2f%2fhodentekwin7%2fDocuments%2fFirstFolder&rs:Command=ListChildren`.

Reporting Services extensions

SQL Server Reporting Services uses extensions to modularize the types of input/output it accepts for the following tasks:

- Authentication
- Data processing
- Report processing
- Rendering
- Delivery
- Custom report processing

A Report Server requires at least one extension from authentication, data processing, and rendering.

However there are default extensions that can be used without the necessity to create custom extensions. Here are details of the defaults taken from the `Microsoft.com` link `http://msdn.microsoft.com/en-us/library/ms157231.aspx`.

Type	Default
Authentication	A default Report Server instance supports Windows authentication, including impersonation and delegation features if they are enabled in your domain.

Type	Default
Data processing	A default Report Server instance includes data processing extensions for SQL Server, Analysis Services, Oracle, Hyperion Essbase, SAPBW, OLE DB, Parallel Data Warehouse, and ODBC data sources.
Rendering	A default Report Server instance includes rendering extensions for HTML, Excel, CSV, XML, Image, Word, SharePoint list, and PDF.
Delivery	A default Report Server instance includes an e-mail delivery extension and a file share delivery extension. If the Report Server is configured for SharePoint integration, you can use a delivery extension that saves reports to a SharePoint library.

The available extensions that are configurable are shown in the `rsreportserver.config` file. Please open the `rsreportserver.config` file in Notepad with administrator privileges (or Visual Studio) to review the extensions configured in a default install.

> Please review the `<Extension/>` section in the configuration file.

For more detailed information, follow the link `http://msdn.microsoft.com/en-us/library/hh213576.aspx`.

Reporting Services tools

There are a number of tools available in Reporting Services some of which have already been described. Here we catalog the items under three categories. *Chapter 8, Reporting Services and Programming,* describes URL Access, Rskeymgmt Utility, Power Shell, and so on.

Tools for Report Server administration

The following are the tools used in administering a Report Server in Native mode installed when SQL Server is installed with Reporting Services in Native mode. We have seen some of them already and some we will review in the remaining chapters. Here is the list of the tools:

- Reporting Services Configuration Manager
- SQL Server Management Studio

- SQL Server Configuration Manager
- RSConfig Command line Utility
- Rskeymgmt Utility
- Windows Management Instrumentation (WMI) Classes

The following two are installed when SharePoint 2010 is installed and used for Reporting Services in SharePoint mode:

- SharePoint Central Administration
- PowerShell Cmdlets

Tools for report authoring

Report Designer in SSDT and Report Builder are full service developer tools whereas Power View is mostly for ad-hoc report authoring by non-developer type. These are the tools for report authoring:

- Report Designer
- Report Builder
- SharePoint Site for Power View – New in SSRS 2012

Tools for report content management

These are used in working with the hands-on exercises in the book. Tools depend on deployment mode of the Report Server. The following are the tools used for report content management:

- Report Server Web Service
- Report Manager
- RS Utility-RS Server Command Prompt

Summary

A whole range of topics related to SQL Server Reporting Services were covered in this chapter beginning with the installation of all programs needed for exploring RS 2012 and summarized in a diagram the set up used for developing this book. This chapter provides an extremely brief review of SSRS describing both modes of Report Server installation, the Native mode as well as the SharePoint Integrated mode. There are some major differences, for example Reporting Services in Native mode is a Windows Service whereas Reporting Services in SharePoint Integrated mode is a SharePoint Shared Service. SharePoint Integration brings in many more components that are absent if one were to focus on Native mode only. However, SharePoint Integrated mode widens the usage of Reporting Services to non-programmer types with the new features of Power View and self-service Data Alerts and adds to business agility.

Many features of RS 2012 were described for both modes of installation and they are described again in more detail in the rest of the book. The reader is encouraged to work through the hands-on exercises in the rest of the chapters to acquire the skill to work with many features.

In the next chapter, Report Manager, the Web frontend for the Report Server, will be described. All aspects of Report Management for the Report Server in Native mode will be discussed and illustrated with many guided examples. Report Management in SharePoint Integrated mode is described in *Chapter 6, Power View and Reporting Services*.

4
Working with Report Manager

In the previous chapter we looked comprehensively at the features of SQL Server Reporting Services 2012, both old and new. Authoring, viewing and administering are some of the important features. Report Manager for Native mode installation and SharePoint Site for SharePoint Integrated site are the Web-based frontend for viewing and administering reports. Even reports on Native mode can be viewed and managed using SharePoint Web parts.

Report Manager is a Web facing, frontend application for administering a single Report Server instance installed in Native mode from a remote location over HTTP. It is a Soap Client for the Reporting Services Web Service. Report Manager can also be used for viewing reports with its Report Viewer and navigational features. You need Internet Explorer 7.0 or higher with scripting enabled. Examples illustrated in the book use IE 9.0.

> Report Manager works in Quirks mode (more for backward compatibility) and not standard mode (W3C and IETF standard). You may run into view window problems if you use standard mode.

Reports can be viewed on Report Manager as well as by accessing the URL. While URL access is supported on surface devices such as iPad, accessing Report Manager from an iPad is not supported. Also, Report Manager is not supported on a reporting services server installed with SharePoint Server integration, you need to use SharePoint Server tools.

Most of the reporting services tasks can be accomplished if you are using Enterprise or Business Intelligence editions of SQL Server 2012. Standard edition may also be used but without support for some of the features.

> Standard edition does not support Data Driven subscriptions, Power View, and Data Alerts.

All others versions do not support SSRS adequately and the Express editions provide no support.

The reader is urged to review *Chapter 2, SQL Server Reporting Services 2012 Projects with Visual Studio 2012*, and create a couple of reports and deploy them to the Report Server before digging into this chapter.

Tasks performed using Report Manager

The following are the tasks that you can perform with **Report Manager (RM)**:

- Create, secure, and maintain the folder hierarchy to organize items on the server
- Configure role-based security that determines access to items and operations
- View, search, print, and subscribe to reports
- Configure report execution properties, report history, and report parameters
- Create report models that connect to and retrieve data from a Microsoft SQL Server Analysis Services data source or from a SQL Server relational data source
- Set model item security to allow access to specific entities in the model, or map entities to predefined `clickthrough` reports that you create in advance
- Create shared schedules and shared data sources to make schedules and data source connections more manageable
- Create data-driven subscriptions that roll out reports to a large recipient list
- Create linked reports to reuse and repurpose an existing report in different ways

We will be doing some of these in this chapter. Report Manager and the tasks one can undertake were also described in the 1st edition of this book, *Learning SQL Server Reporting Services 2008*, ISBN: 9781847196187, *Chapter 5, Working with Report Manager*. For details regarding Report Manager review the link `http://msdn.microsoft.com/en-us/library/ms157147.aspx`.

Starting Report Manager

In the RS Configuration Manager (as shown in *Chapter 1, Overview and Installation – SQL Server Reporting Services 2012*) you can access the URL of the Report Manager as shown in the following screenshot:

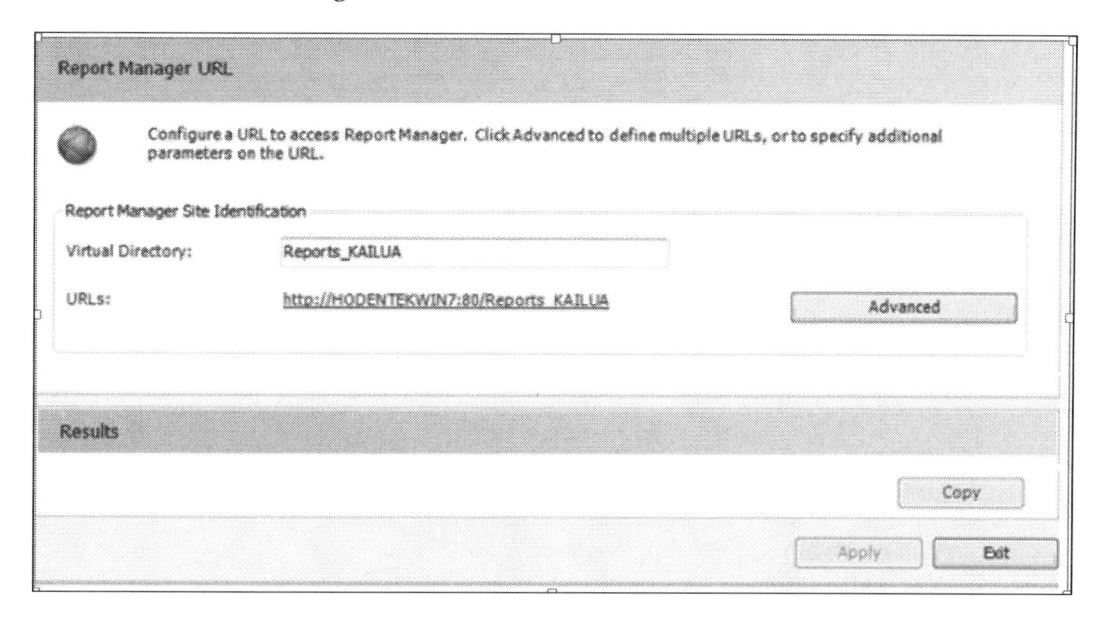

Clicking on the link `http://HodentekWin7/Reports_KAILUA` will take you to the **Home** page of Report Manager (RM) as shown in the following screenshot:

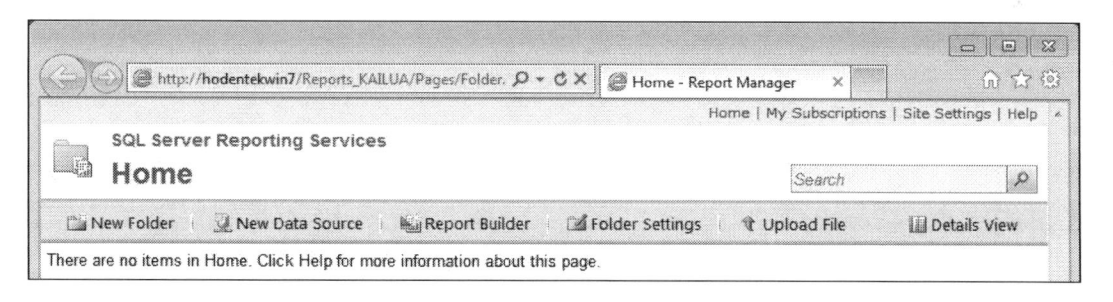

If you are accessing from Windows Vista or Windows Server follow the link `http://msdn.microsoft.com/en-us/library/bb630430.aspx`.

Starting Report Manager for the URL

Open the IE Browser 7.0 or higher and type in the URL of the RM previously described or type `http://Hodentekwin7/Reports_KAILUA`

User access to Report Server (Report Manager)

As seen in *Chapter 3, Overview of SQL Server Reporting Services 2012 Architecture, Features, and Tools*, Reporting Services uses role-based security to grant access to Report Server. Only users in the group of Local Administrators group have permissions to objects on the Report Server. Report Manager assigns roles to users in a Native mode installation.

Basically there are two types of roles:

- **System-level roles**: System-level roles grant access to items on the site and are not bound to anything specific. In order to add a user to an item-level role, you should also add him to a system-level role. While adding a user to a role you choose from among the existing roles. Role management (create, modify, or delete) is carried out on SSMS.
- **Item-level roles**: Item-level roles can manage reports on the Report Server, subscriptions, report processing, and report history. You assign item-level roles in Report Manager Home, or to specific folders containing the item.

For Report Servers installed for **SharePoint Integration,** access permissions are configured from a SharePoint Site using **SharePoint Permissions**. For details review this link, `http://msdn.microsoft.com/en-us/library/ms159840.aspx`

Considerations for giving user access to the Report Server

If you are planning to allow users to carry out activities on the Report Server, review the following:

- Users must be members of the Local Administrators group on the computer hosting the Report Server
- Users who have Content Manager and System Administrator permissions can add users to a Report Server

- For custom roles you may want to create and include collections of tasks that is appropriate

First step – deploying reports

In order to work with reports you must first deploy the reports to the Report Server. Once it is deployed, the detailed information will be recorded in the Catalog as shown here. This was obtained by running the query `SELECT * FROM dbo.Catalog` (Catalog table in the `ReportServer$KAILUA's Northwind` database in the Database Engine). There are lot more rows and lot more columns not shown in the screenshot.

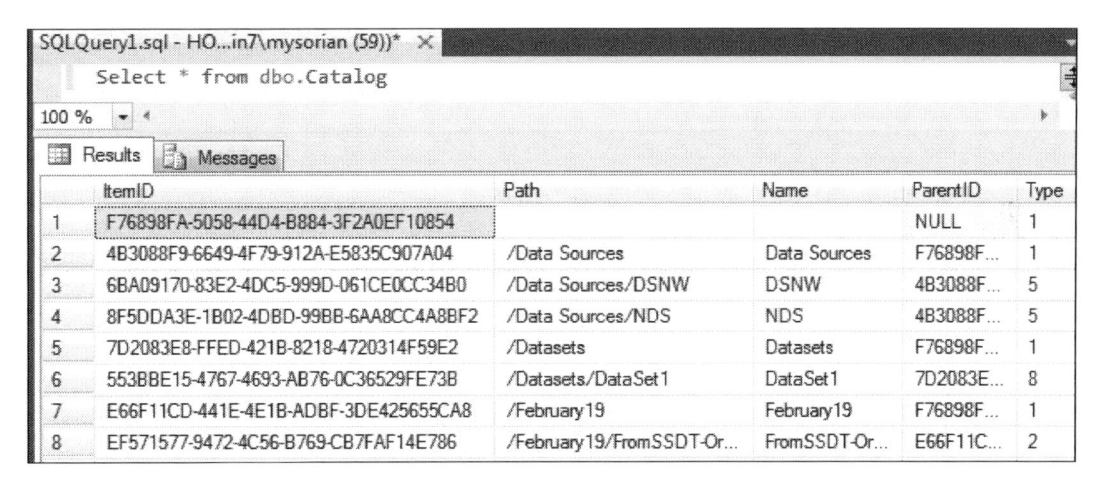

#	ItemID	Path	Name	ParentID	Type
1	F76898FA-5058-44D4-B884-3F2A0EF10854			NULL	1
2	4B3088F9-6649-4F79-912A-E5835C907A04	/Data Sources	Data Sources	F76898F...	1
3	6BA09170-83E2-4DC5-999D-061CE0CC34B0	/Data Sources/DSNW	DSNW	4B3088F...	5
4	8F5DDA3E-1B02-4DBD-99BB-6AA8CC4A8BF2	/Data Sources/NDS	NDS	4B3088F...	5
5	7D2083E8-FFED-421B-8218-4720314F59E2	/Datasets	Datasets	F76898F...	1
6	553BBE15-4767-4693-AB76-0C36529FE73B	/Datasets/DataSet1	DataSet1	7D2083E...	8
7	E66F11CD-441E-4E1B-ADBF-3DE425655CA8	/February19	February19	F76898F...	1
8	EF571577-9472-4C56-B769-CB7FAF14E786	/February19/FromSSDT-Or...	FromSSDT-Or...	E66F11C...	2

Most of the objects were deployed by SSDT, an example of which was given in *Chapter 2, SQL Server Reporting Services 2012 Projects with Visual Studio 2012*. Once the report is deployed to the Report Server, Report Manager takes over to assign roles to the users cleared by the Report Server's security features. Report Manager can help in many report related tasks mentioned earlier in this chapter.

The following hands-on exercise in this chapter gives you the flavor of things you can do in the Report Manager UI. Before moving on to the hands-on exercise, it is advisable to look at the Report Manager UI.

Report Manager user interface

When the Report Manager is accessed for the first time from the Reporting Services Configuration Manager or using its URL, you will not see any user-created objects except for the Report Manager's features. It is assumed that the current user is the Administrator of the computer who installed SQL Server 2012 and configured the Report Server (this is so as mentioned in *Chapter 1, Overview and Installation – SQL Server Reporting Services 2012*). We have seen an image of the Report Manager UI without any user-created objects earlier in this chapter.

As you start deploying report projects or uploading them to the server, user created objects start appearing on the Report Manager as shown here. Note that although you type in http://hodentekwin7/Reports_KAILUA, it will take you to **Home** whose URL is fully displayed as http://hodentekwin7/Reports_KAILUA/Pages/Folders.aspx.

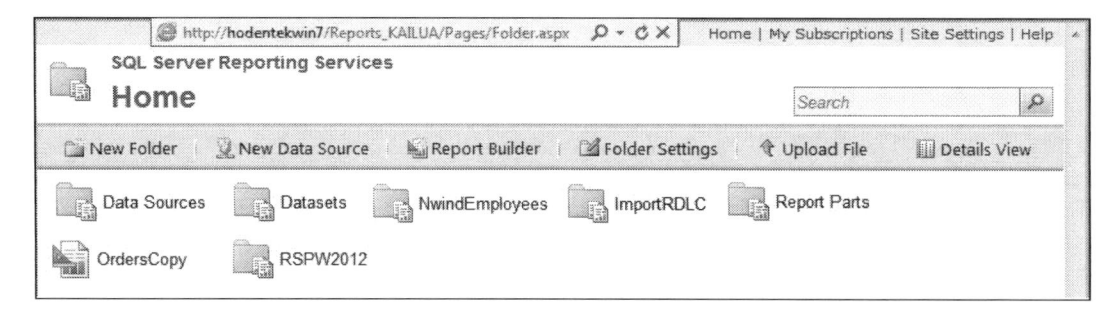

As you can see, you will be able to create **New Folder**, **New Data Source**, launch **Report Builder**, access **Folder Settings**, and **Upload File**. **Details View** is a toggle switch that shows the user created objects as Tiles. When you click on the toggle switch, you will see details of the user created (uploaded or deployed) objects and the switch changes its title to **Tile View**.

Presently there is some problem launching the Report Builder and if you try, it would throw an error. The link for the launch item is http://hodentekwin7/ReportServer_KAILUA/ReportBuilder/ReportBuilder_3_0_0_0.application, but there is no such folder on the Report Server. A question has been submitted to the forum regarding this issue at http://social.msdn.microsoft.com/Forums/en-US/sqlreportingservices/thread/ec0a6b15-1816-4d6c-87c0-b2f1f28f3d04.

Chapter 4

> This problem was solved by removing the folder `C:\Documents and Settings\username\Local Settings\Apps` especially if you had an earlier version installed. After removing this folder, access RM and click on Rebuilder. A launch window is displayed as shown in the next image after which the Report Builder gets displayed.

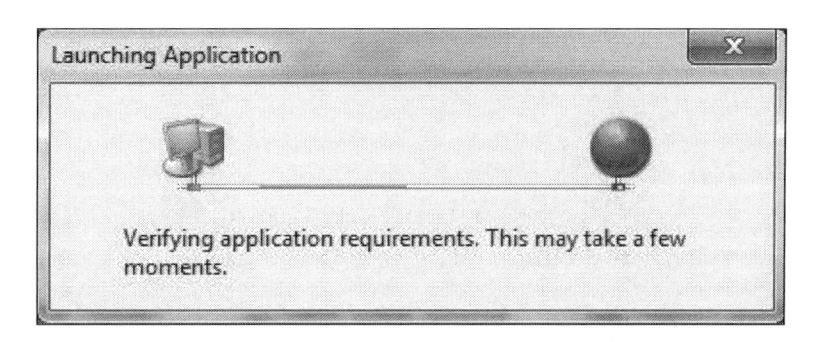

In the previous screenshot of Report Manager, on the right, there are a few more items (readers are urged to click on the items to review using the following information):

- **Home**: Link back to **Home**
- **My Subscriptions**: There will not be any subscriptions to start with
- **Site Settings**:
    - **(General)** You can change the default SQL Server Reporting Services to something different, and choose how many snapshots you want to keep in report history.
    - **(General)** Choose how many snapshots you want to keep in report history.
    - **(General)** Set a timeout for report processing (the default is 1800 seconds).
    - **(General)** Designate a custom Report Builder Launch URL.
    - **(Security)** There is one system wide role, System Administrator, who belongs to the BUILTIN\Administrators group. Use the New Role Assignment control to confer a role to an user.
    - **(Schedule)** You can create a New Schedule using the control; to start with it will be empty.
    - Help: http://msdn.microsoft.com/en-us/library/ms181194.aspx.
- **Help**: http://msdn.microsoft.com/en-us/library/ms189690.aspx

[183]

Working with Report Manager

This is what you will find from the toolbar items of the user interfaces:

- **New Folder**: Create a new folder on **Home** by giving a name and some description.
- **New Data Source**: Opens the Web page where you provide the information as shown in the following screenshot:

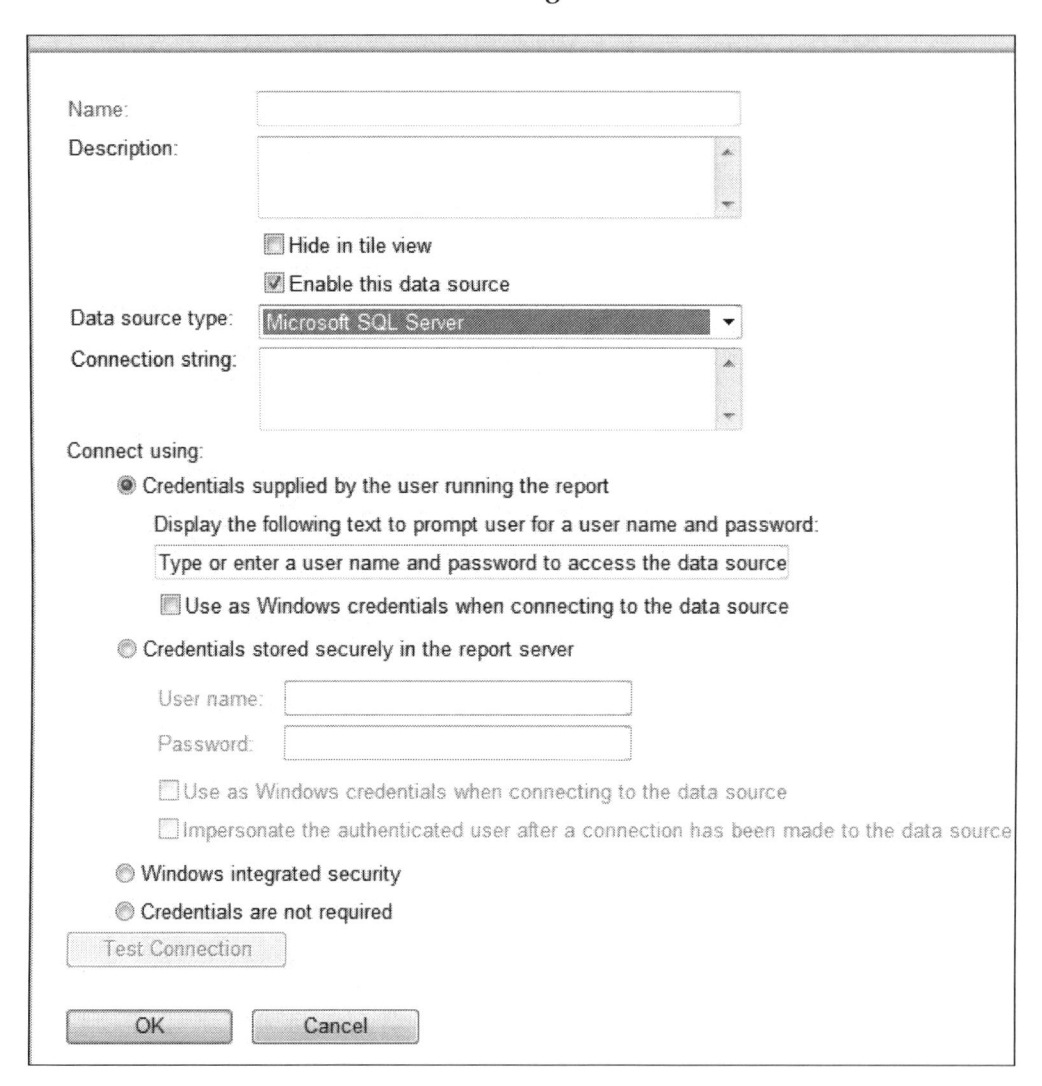

- **Folder Settings**: Set folder security by using/creating a role using **New Role Assignment** control.

- **Upload File**: You upload from browsed location files of type report (.rdl), model (.smdl), shared dataset (.rsd), report part (.rsc), or other resource to **Home**. If it exists, you may choose to over write or give a name to it.

> Each object on the Report Manager UI may have a menu of its own as shown in this figure. Any action that you may want to take is best done by choosing items from the drop-down menus.

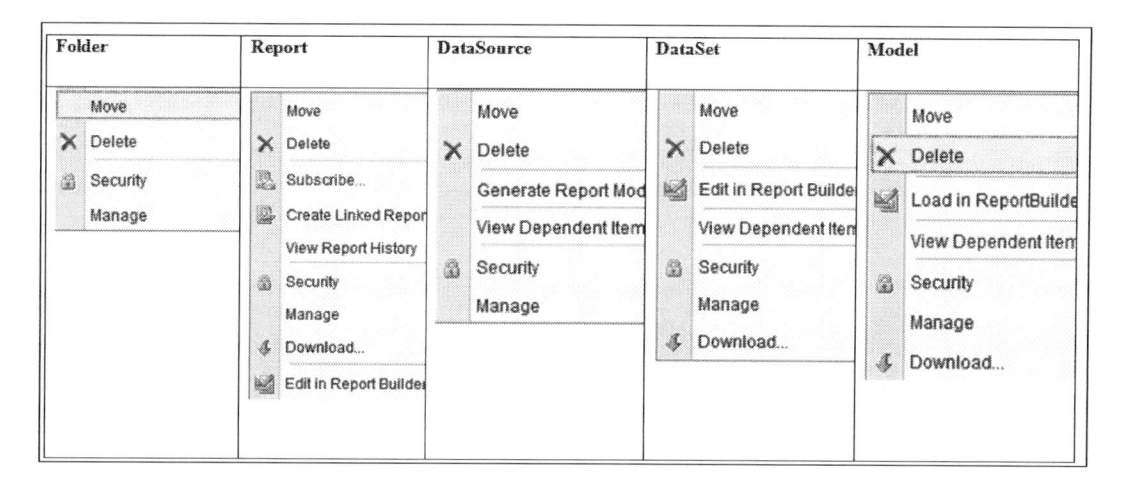

Folder	Report	DataSource	DataSet	Model
Move	Move	Move	Move	Move
Delete	Delete	Delete	Delete	Delete
Security	Subscribe...	Generate Report Model	Edit in Report Builder	Load in ReportBuilder
Manage	Create Linked Report	View Dependent Items	View Dependent Items	View Dependent Items
	View Report History	Security	Security	Security
	Security	Manage	Manage	Manage
	Manage		Download...	Download...
	Download...			
	Edit in Report Builder			

Customizing Report Manager

Some customization is possible but very limited. You can change the look and feel slightly by making changes to the stylesheet of the page. The stylesheet of the Reporting Services is available at C:\Program Files\Microsoft SQL Server\<Native InstanceName>\Reporting Services\ReportManager\Styles and requires a knowledge of **Cascading Style Sheets (CSS)**.

Hands-on exercise 4.1 – creating, modifying, moving, and deleting folders

Report Manager is folder based with subfolders that in turn may contain reports, DataSources, models, and other deployed/uploaded objects. The Report Manager folder structure mimics the Windows folders/files structure. The Report Manager folders/files are found in the Report Server database. When you deploy a project from Visual Studio it is deployed as a folder in the Report Manager with the name of the project for the folder.

Working with Report Manager

Navigating through the folders

Using the **Details View / Tile View** toggle button you can get to the two different views of the folders. You can click on a folder or an item in any of the views to open the subfolder as follows:

1. Type in `http://Hodentekwin7/Reports_KAILUA` in the URL address of browser.

   The page you land in when you access Report Manager is the **Folders.aspx** page we saw earlier, with several folders deployed or uploaded to the Report Manager (reproduced here).

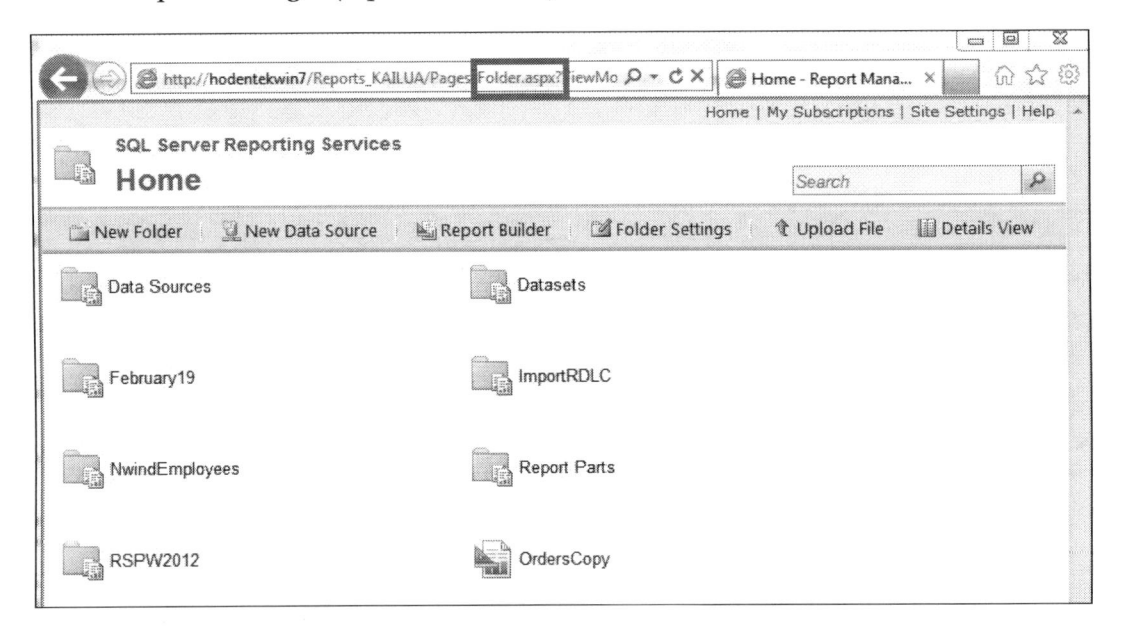

   This is a view where folders are tiled.

2. Click on the **Details View** on the top right to display the detailed folder structure. **Details View** changes to **Tiles View**.

[186]

Chapter 4

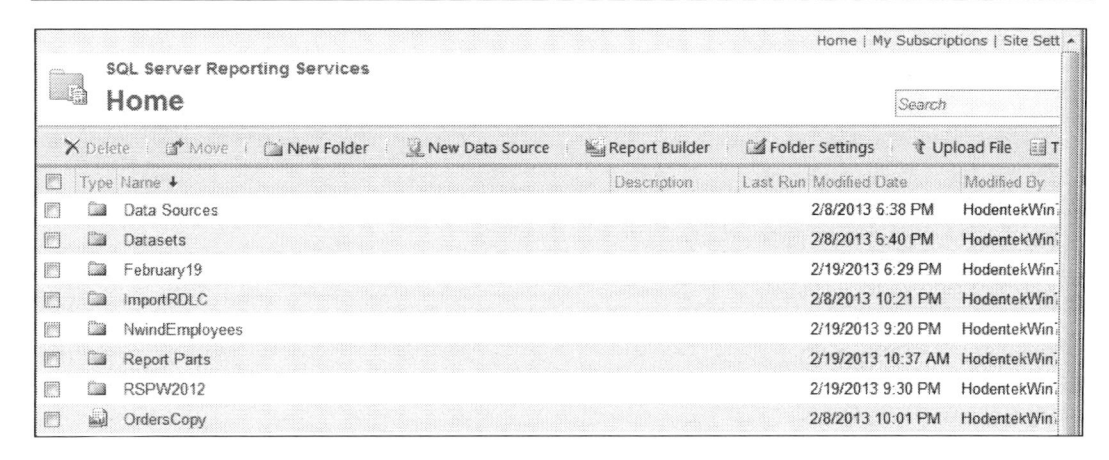

	Type	Name ↓	Description	Last Run	Modified Date	Modified By
☐	📁	Data Sources			2/8/2013 6:38 PM	HodentekWin
☐	📁	Datasets			2/8/2013 6:40 PM	HodentekWin
☐	📁	February19			2/19/2013 6:29 PM	HodentekWin
☐	📁	ImportRDLC			2/8/2013 10:21 PM	HodentekWin
☐	📁	NwindEmployees			2/19/2013 9:20 PM	HodentekWin
☐	📁	Report Parts			2/19/2013 10:37 AM	HodentekWin
☐	📁	RSPW2012			2/19/2013 9:30 PM	HodentekWin
☐	📄	OrdersCopy			2/8/2013 10:01 PM	HodentekWin

3. Click on **RSPW2012**.

   The **HOME** changes to **RSPW2012** and you will see the contents of **RSPW2012** as shown in the following screenshot. It has two reports and a data source all in one folder.

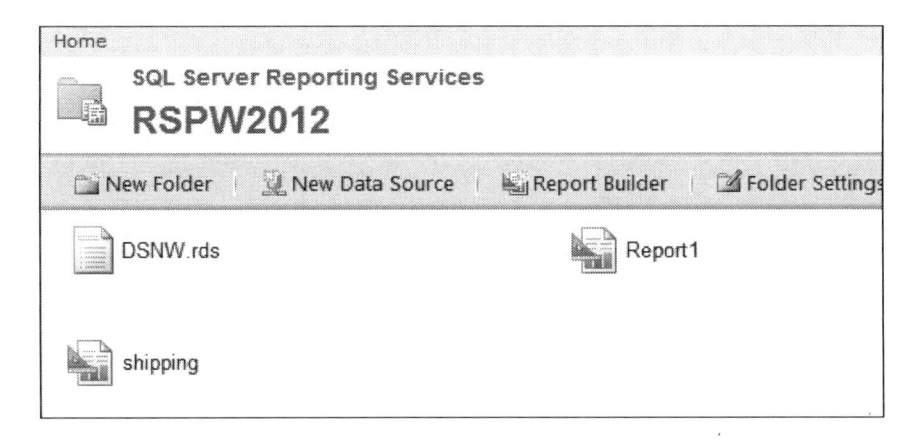

   It is also possible to have a folder within a folder.

Creating a folder and a subfolder

In this exercise we will create a folder and a subfolder in Report Manager as follows:

1. Click on **HOME** at the top right wherever you are.

   You will be brought back to **HOME**, in either **Details View** or **Tiles View**.

[187]

Working with Report Manager

2. Click on **New Folder** on the toolbar in the centre.

   The **New Folder** page opens as the following:

3. Provide a name for the folder, herein `Main_Feb19`. For the description you provide an appropriate description. In our case, we can write **Creating a new folder under Home**. If you want, you can hide it in the **Tiles view** by placing a check mark.

4. Choose not to hide for now and click on **OK**.

   A new folder will be created under **Home** as follows:

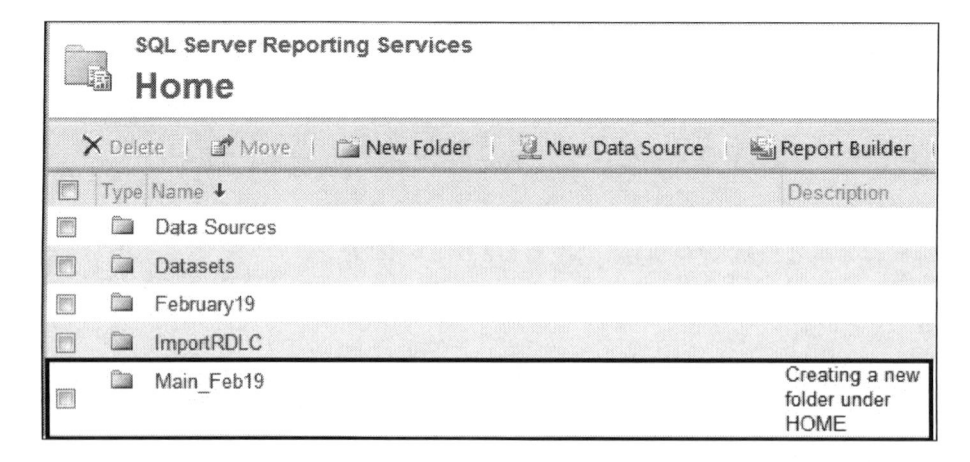

Chapter 4

Now we will create a subfolder named `Sub_Feb19` in the folder `Main_Feb19`.

5. Click on `Main_Feb19` in **Home**.

   The `Main_19 folder` opens as shown here. There are no objects and it is empty.

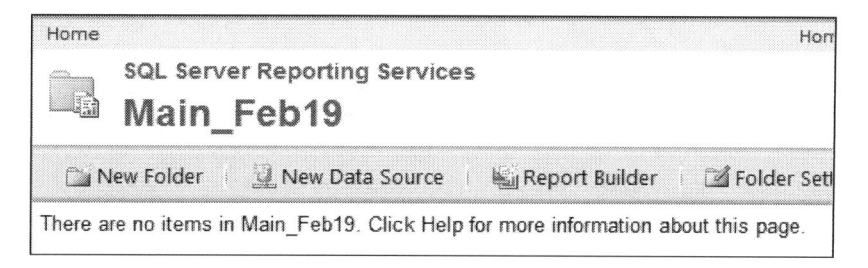

6. Click on **New Folder** in the previous window.

   The **New Folder** window opens in a new page, but it will create a subfolder for the `Main_Feb19`. Review highlighted regions of the image:

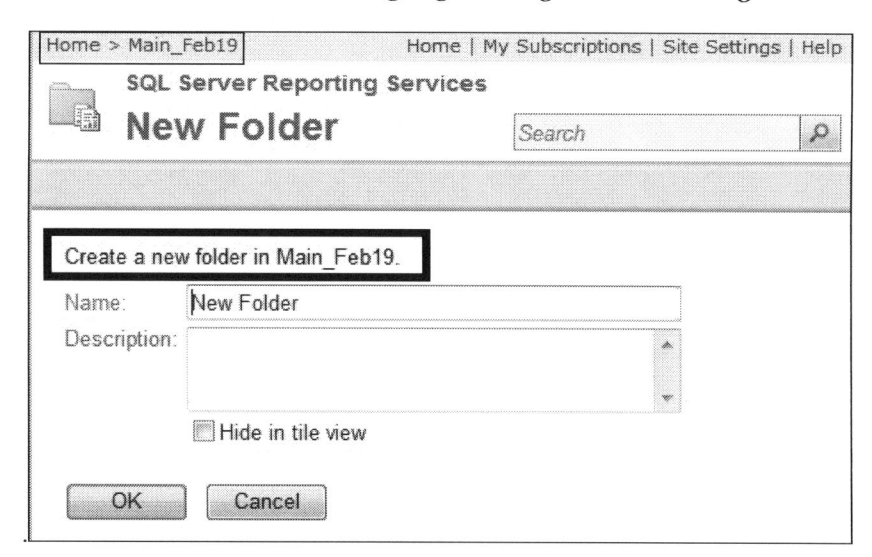

7. Provide a name for the folder (which is going to be the subfolder) and a description. Herein the name is `Sub_Feb19` and the description is **This is a sub-folder for Main_Feb19** and click on **OK**. The subfolder will be created.

[189]

Working with Report Manager

Moving an item into a folder

Report Manager allows for movement of items in and out of folders. In this exercise we will move a folder `February19` into the `Sub_Feb19` folder we created earlier as follows:

1. Click near the `February19` folder in any of the views to display the dropdown as shown in the following screenshot:

2. Click on **Move**. The page with **Move February19** form shows up. Expand the `Main_Feb19` node.

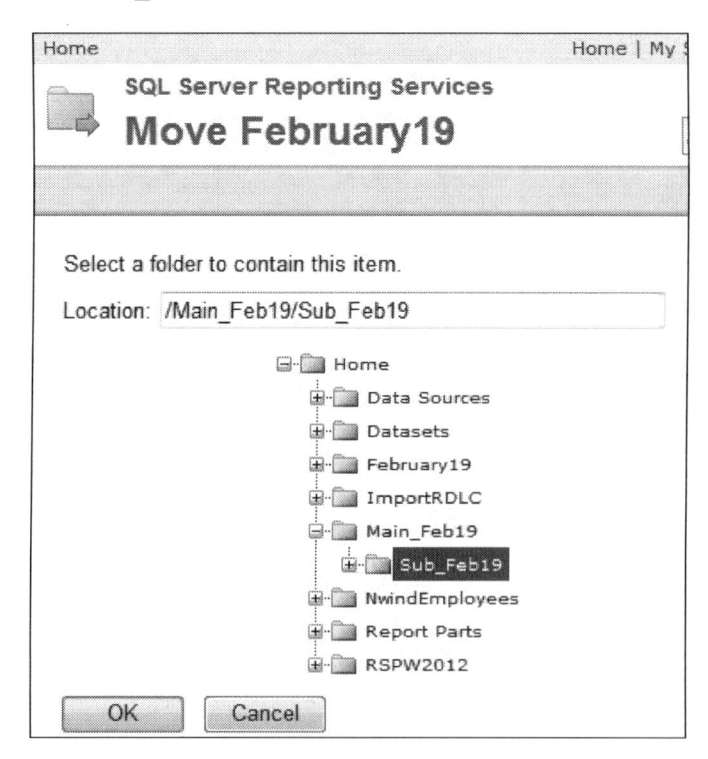

— [190] —

Chapter 4

3. Review the Location. It is /Main_Feb19/Sub_Feb19. The symbol / stands for **Home**. Click on **OK**. You don't get a message but will be returned to **Home**.
4. Click on Main_Feb19 and on the page that displays click on Sub_Feb19. The contents of Sub_Feb19 will be displayed as shown in the following screenshot:

You will notice that February19 folder has moved into Sub_Feb19.

5. Click on February19 and you will see the following:

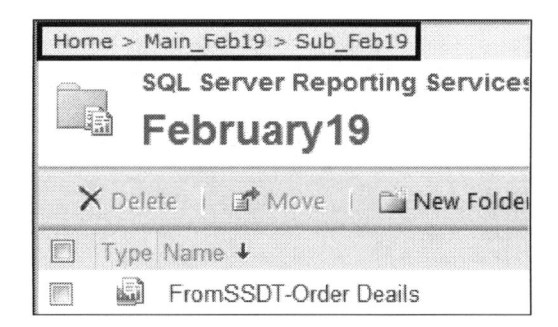

This is a project named February19 deployed to the Report Server containing a report with an embedded data source. Deleting or modifying can be carried out using the drop-down menu.

Configuring permissions from Report Manager

While it is just some properties and security that you can manage on a folder in Report Manager, you can manage data sources, subscriptions, processing options, cache refresh options, report history, snapshot options, and security for reports deployed to or uploaded to the Report Server. Additionally you can also create linked reports, edit the report on Report Builder (there is a missing file that prevents the Report Builder showing up from Report Manager), and render the report. However, for all of this to happen, permissions must be in place to satisfy the security requirements.

Reporting Services, as we have seen in previous chapters, is a Windows service and so it depends on Windows user authentication and does not store its own usernames and passwords. However, Windows users must have permissions to access objects on the Report Server. These permissions are set up on the Reporting Services and managed by the Report Manager in the Security tab of most objects. The next section deals with permissions and only a few of the many scenarios possible are explored with the hands-on. However, these basic hands-on could be used for most of the usual cases. Permissions in Reporting Services can be very fine grained and permissions can be set for individual report if needed.

The available permissions were shown in *Chapter 3, Overview of SQL Server Reporting Services 2012 Architecture, Features, and Tools*, and you can find them on the Report Server database in the Security node.

An administrator can set up new `Item Roles`, new `System Roles` and customize them as in the link `http://msdn.microsoft.com/en-us/library/ms186541.aspx`.

For example, in SSMS, by right-clicking on the `Roles` folder in the `Security` node, you can bring up a **New Role...** or **Delete Roles** (shown in the following screenshot) window. By clicking on the drop-down item **New Role...** you begin creating a new role.

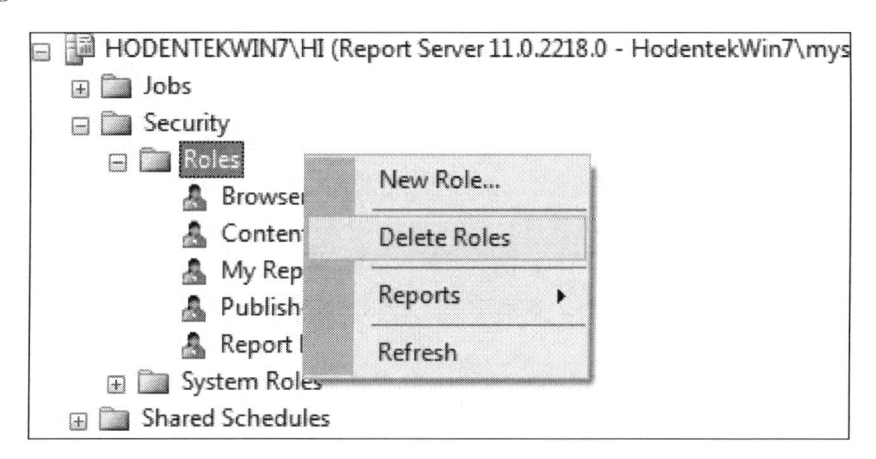

Configuring role-based security

In the following you will be creating a few Windows users and assign them to Item and System roles. We will use the ideas discussed earlier in assigning roles. We will also create permissions to a specific item on the Report Manager.

It is assumed that you are ready with the following:

- You are the administrator of the computer and know how to work with administrative tools on the computer and Reporting Services is installed in Native mode
- You can create reports using SSDT or Report Builder and deploy them to the Report Server
- You have working knowledge of SSMS

> A number of users will be added with different usernames but use the same password (SSRS2012) that never expires. This is not the best practice. In a production system you should use separate passwords for each user or place users in a group.

Hands-on exercise 4.2 – assigning a Windows user to the System Administrator role

In order to be a Windows user, that user must be created by the computer administrator.

Creating a Windows user

Follow these steps to create a Windows user:

1. Go to **Start** | **Control Panel** | **System and Security** | **Administrative Tools** | **Computer Management** and expand **Local Users and Groups** as shown and click on **Users**.

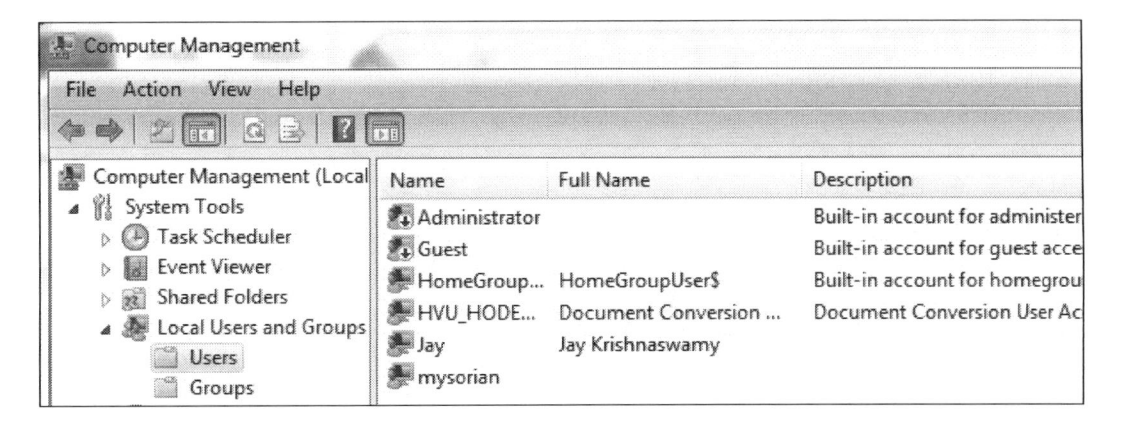

Working with Report Manager

2. There are a number of users created during installation of the **Operating System (OS)** and some created by the administrator.
3. Right-click on **Users** and click on **New User...** Fill in the details as shown in the following screenshot:

New User	
User name:	RSMax
Full name:	
Description:	Report Services Expert.
Password:	••••••••
Confirm password:	••••••••

- ☐ User must change password at next logon
- ☐ User cannot change password
- ☑ Password never expires
- ☐ Account is disabled

[Help]   [Create]   [Close]

4. Click on **Create**.
5. User `RSMax` will be added as a Windows user whose **Password never expires** is created as shown in the following screenshot:

Jay	Jay Krishnaswamy	
mysorian		
RSMax	RSMax	Report Services Expert.

Assigning RSMax to the RS System Administrator role

Open the Report Manager Web page by typing in the URL as discussed previously (if needed you may have to open the IE browser with administrative privileges).

On the Report Manager's page, click on **Site Settings** at the top-right of the page and perform the following steps:

1. Click on the **Security** link on the left-hand side.

    The Security related tabbed page of **Site Settings** is displayed as shown in the following screenshot:

    > **BUILTIN\Administrators** are assigned to **System Administrator**.

2. Click on **New Role Assignment**. The **New System Role Assignment** page is displayed. Fill it out as shown in the next screenshot and read information on this page:

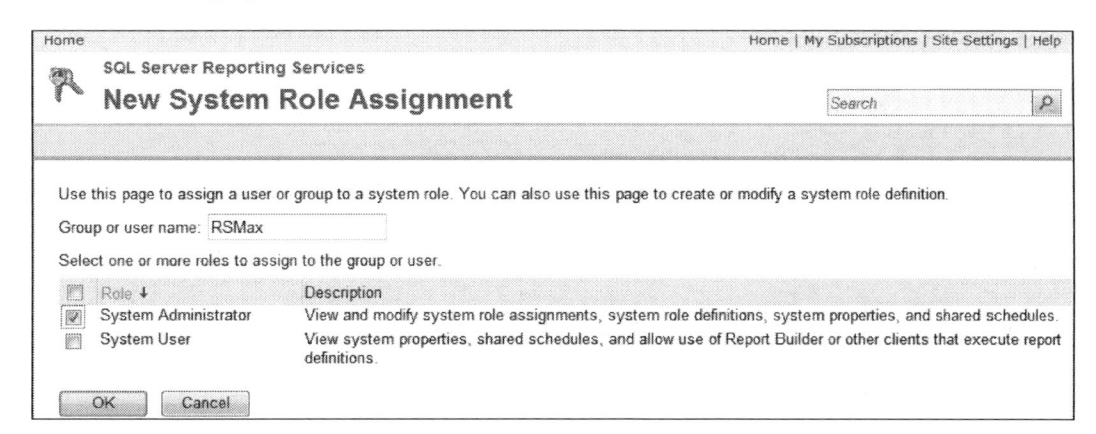

Working with Report Manager

3. Click on **OK** and **RSMax** will be assigned the role of System Administrator. The Security page is modified as shown in the following screenshot. You can **Edit** as well as **Delete** roles from this page.

```
SQL Server Reporting Services
Site Settings

            X Delete      New Role Assignment
General           Group or User ↓         Role(s)
            Edit  BUILTIN\Administrators  System Administrator
Security    Edit  HodentekWin7\RSMax      System Administrator
```

In the next section of hands-on we look at assigning users to Item-Level roles.

Assigning users to item-level roles

The role `Browser` is a lower privileged role than `Content Manager`. We create a Windows user `RsBrowse` and assign him to the role of `Browser`. Perform the following steps:

1. Create a Windows user **RsBrowse** on the same lines as you created **RsMax**. **RsBrowse** will be added to the Local Users group in much the same way **RSMax** was added.

```
RSBrowse    RSBrowse    User with Browser role
RSMax       RSMax       Report Services Expert.
```

2. Open Report Manager in an IE browser. Click on **Folder settings** (do not click on any folder).

3. The **Security** page for **Home** is displayed.

```
SQL Server Reporting Services
Home                                        Search

            X Delete      New Role Assignment
Security          Group or User ↓         Role(s)
            Edit  BUILTIN\Administrators  Content Manager
```

[196]

Chapter 4

4. Click on **New Role Assignment**. The **New Role Assignment** page opens. Fill in the details as shown in the following screenshot:

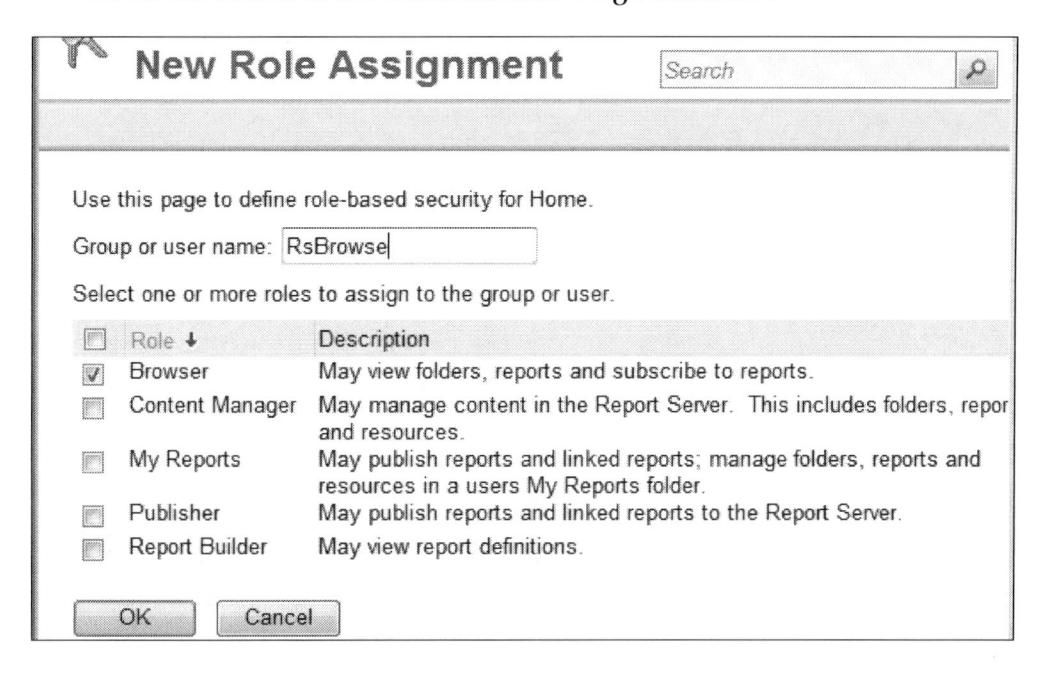

5. Click on **OK** and the **RsBrowse** user will be assigned to the role of **Browser**. Note the tasks he can carry out. The **Security** page of **HOME** gets updated as shown in the following screenshot:

Working with Report Manager

Review users on a Reporting Services database

The Reporting Services users are stored in the Reporting Services database. We will review them now:

1. Open SSMS and connect to the SQL Server 2012 named instance KAILUA. You may need administrative rights.

2. Run the query shown in the next screenshot (with results shown) against the ReportServer$KAILUA database. You will notice that the two users created previously are added to the user's table (items 4 and 5).

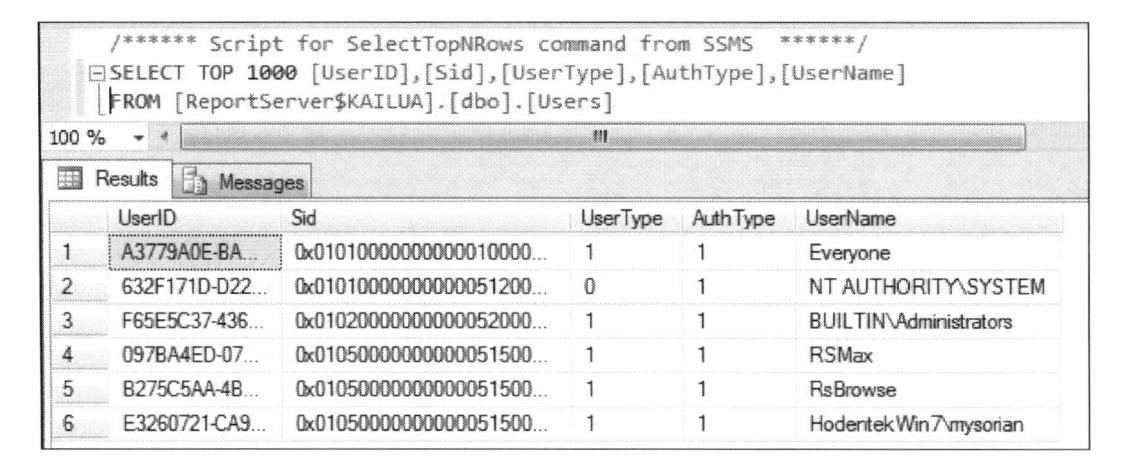

```
/****** Script for SelectTopNRows command from SSMS ******/
SELECT TOP 1000 [UserID],[Sid],[UserType],[AuthType],[UserName]
FROM [ReportServer$KAILUA].[dbo].[Users]
```

	UserID	Sid	UserType	AuthType	UserName
1	A3779A0E-BA...	0x010100000000000010000...	1	1	Everyone
2	632F171D-D22...	0x010100000000000051200...	0	1	NT AUTHORITY\SYSTEM
3	F65E5C37-436...	0x010200000000000052000...	1	1	BUILTIN\Administrators
4	097BA4ED-07...	0x010500000000000051500...	1	1	RSMax
5	B275C5AA-4B...	0x010500000000000051500...	1	1	RsBrowse
6	E3260721-CA9...	0x010500000000000051500...	1	1	HodentekWin7\mysorian

In the next section of the hands-on exercise we will look at assigning a user to a Custom role

Hands-on exercise 4.3 – assigning a user to a Custom role

We will create a username **Navigator** (like the other Windows users we created earlier) and assign him to a Custom role.

1. Create a Windows user with the name **Navigator** along similar lines to **RSBrowse**. **Navigator** will be added to the Windows users as shown in the following screenshot:

Navigator	HodentekWin7\Navigator	He has a custom role
RSBrowse	HodentekWin7\RSBrowse	User with Browser role
RSMax	HodentekWin7\RSMax	Report Services Expert.

2. Log on to Reporting Services Server in SSMS.
3. Under **Security** node right-click on the **Roles** node and click on **New Role...**.
4. The user role properties appears as shown in the following screenshot. Fill in the details as shown here. The user with the role **Navigate** can only view reports.

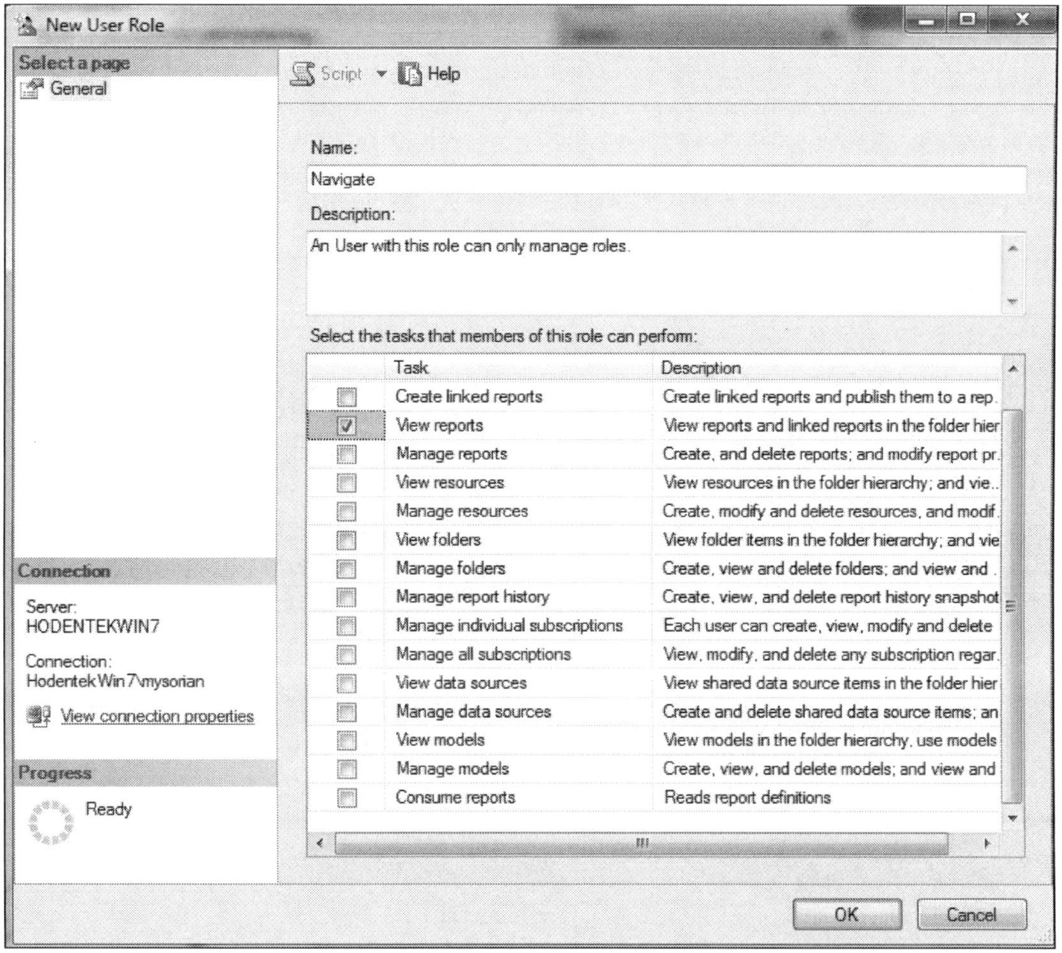
New User Role
Select a page
General
Script
Help
Name:
Navigate
Description:
An User with this role can only manage roles.
Select the tasks that members of this role can perform:
Task
Description
Create linked reports
Create linked reports and publish them to a rep.
View reports
View reports and linked reports in the folder hier
Manage reports
Create, and delete reports; and modify report pr.
View resources
View resources in the folder hierarchy; and vie..
Manage resources
Create, modify and delete resources, and modif.
View folders
View folder items in the folder hierarchy; and vie
Manage folders
Create, view and delete folders; and view and .
Manage report history
Create, view, and delete report history snapshot
Manage individual subscriptions
Each user can create, view, modify and delete
Manage all subscriptions
View, modify, and delete any subscription regar.
View data sources
View shared data source items in the folder hier
Manage data sources
Create and delete shared data source items; an
View models
View models in the folder hierarchy, use models
Manage models
Create, view, and delete models; and view and
Consume reports
Reads report definitions
Connection
Server:
HODENTEKWIN7
Connection:
HodentekWin7\mysorian
View connection properties
Progress
Ready
OK
Cancel

5. Click on **OK**. The role gets into the RS Server database shown earlier.
6. Open Report Manager (you may need to open IE with **Run as Administrator**) and assign the role **Navigate to the Windows User, Navigator**. (Click on **Folder Settings** in **HOME**.)

Hands-on exercise 4.4 – creating a permission to a specific report

The Home folder is at the root and the rest of the folders come under it. Folders may have subfolders and they in turn can have subfolders. That's the hierarchy. Permissions are inheritance based. A folder directly under Home inherits the permission from Home. However, the security of the folder can be edited. You may be warned at that time that you are changing the security from the default. This way we can set the permission to a folder/file.

In an earlier hands-on exercise, we created a subfolder to which we moved a folder containing a report. The report FromSSDT_OrderDetails is in the hierarchy Home | Main_Feb19 | Sub_Feb19 | Feb19 | FromSSDT_OrderDetails.rdl.

1. Presently the folders Main_Feb19, Sub_Feb19, February19, and FromSSDT_OrderDetails all have the **Content Manager** permission.

```
SQL Server Reporting Services
Main_Feb19

              X Delete    New Role Assignment    Revert to Parent Security
Properties          Group or User ↓         Role(s)
               Edit  BUILTIN\Administrators   Content Manager
Security
```

2. We now change the permissions to the Main_Feb19 folder and because of inheritance it will be conferred to the report.
3. Click on **Edit** in the Main_Feb19 folder's **Security** page. The **Edit Role Assignment** page is displayed.

[200]

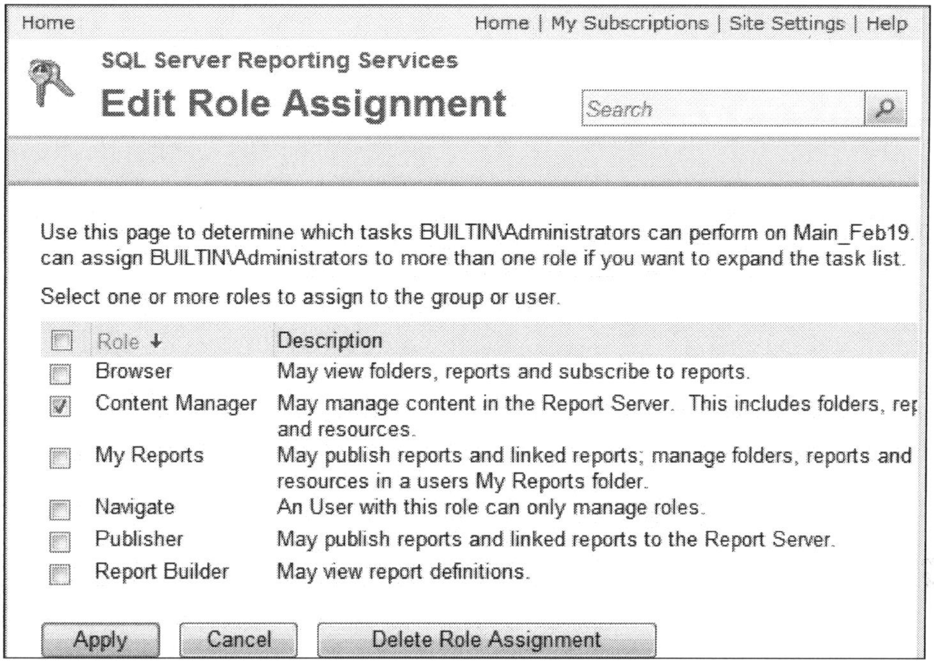

4. Remove the check mark from **Content Manager** and place a check mark for **Navigate**. Click on **Apply**.
5. The folder permission is now **Navigate**.

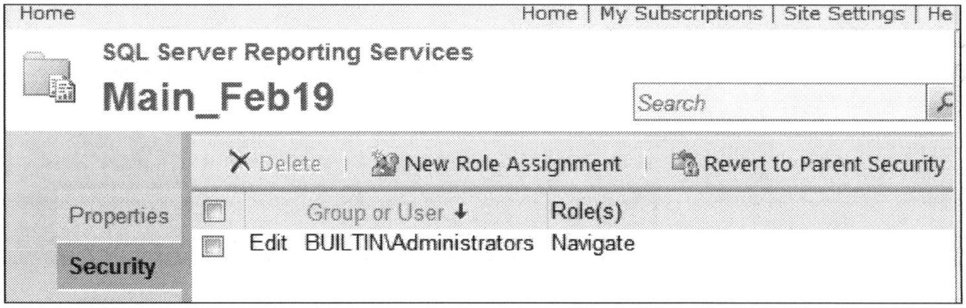

6. Verify that the folder permissions of `Sub_Feb19`, `February19`, and `FromSSDT_OrderDetails` have the same permission **Navigate**.

Working with Report Manager

Report data sources

In the previous chapter we have seen how data sources are created and bound to reports. There are basically two types of data sources that you come across in reporting services. The data that stays and travels with the data that only that particular report will use is called the embedded data source and the other is called a shared data source. Shared data sources can be used by one or more other reports.

An embedded data source

In the next chapter, *Chapter 5, Working with Report Builder 3.0*, we create a report called ReportEmbed.rdl that uses an embedded data source with the data being sourced from a SQL Server 2012 database. This report is saved on the Report Server and is therefore available on the Report Manager.

The data source properties of this report accessed on the Report Manager are shown in the next screenshot:

Report Manager calls it a custom data source. The data source type, the connection string, and the authentication are all present at design time. If you were to display the report from Home there would be no problem. When the creator owner tried to save it as folder Main_Feb19, the program generated an error as the folder did not have the right permission.

A shared data source

Report Builder cannot create a shared data source, although it can create a report based on a shared data source on the Report Server. Report Manager can create a shared data source. In the following hands-on exercise you will be creating a shared data source.

Hands-on exercise 4.5 – creating a shared data source on Report Manager

1. Connect to the Report Manager using its URL (http://Hodentekwin7/Reports_Kailua).

   You may need to open with administrator's permission (**Run as Administrator**).

2. Click on the **New Data Source** icon on Report Manager as shown in the following screenshot:

The **New Data Source** page opens as shown in the following screenshot:

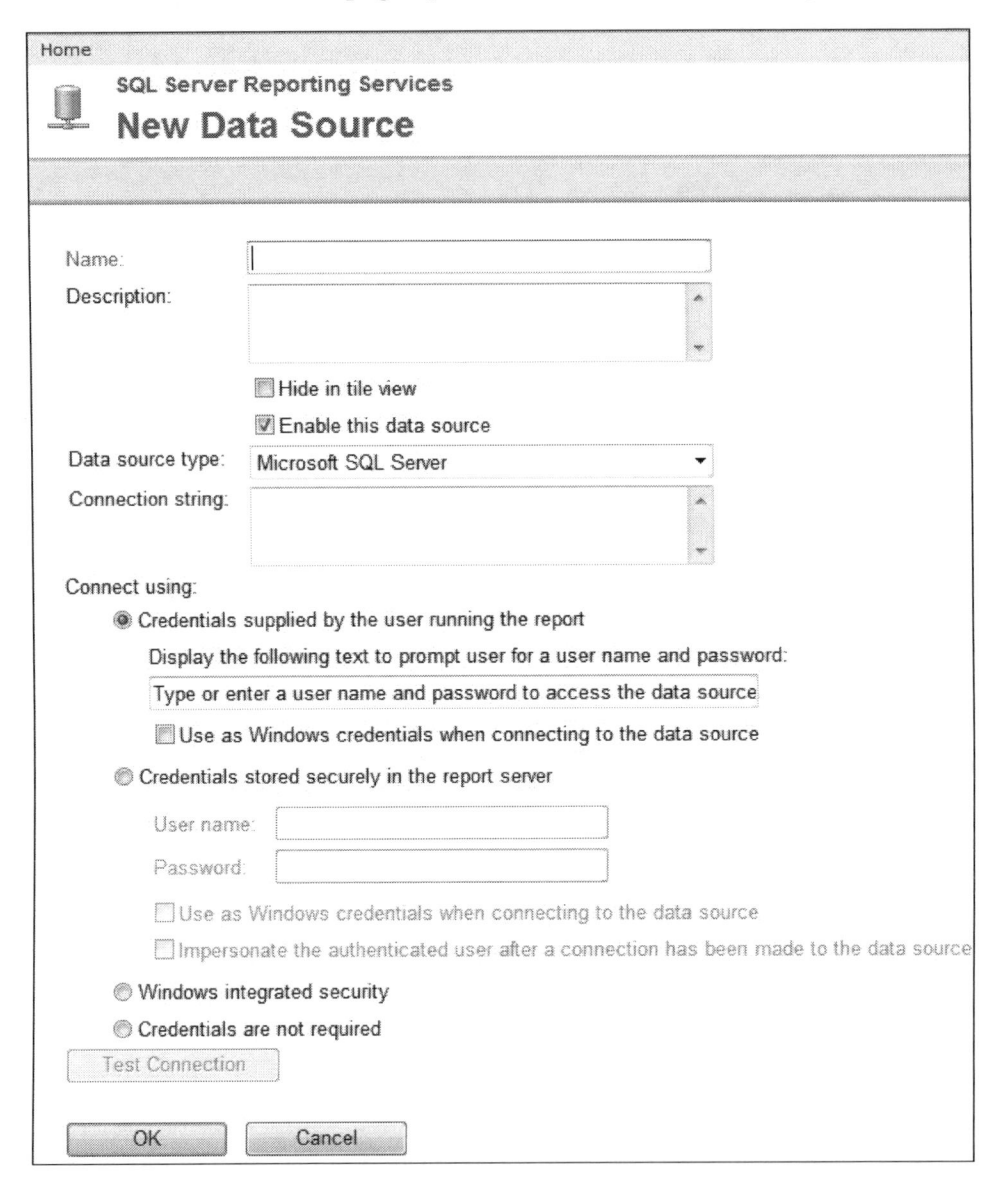

3. We use the following information to create the data source:

   Name: DS_Shared, **Data Source type:** Microsoft SQL Server, **Connection string:** Data Source=Hodentekwin7\Kailua, **Initial Catalog** = Northwind; **Credentials:** supplied by the user running the report.

4. After filling the details in the page click on **OK**.

    The data source is saved to the Report Manager and using its **Manage** drop-down menu it is moved to the Data sources folder on Report Manager. The shared data source is in the Data Sources folder on the Report Server (Report Manager).

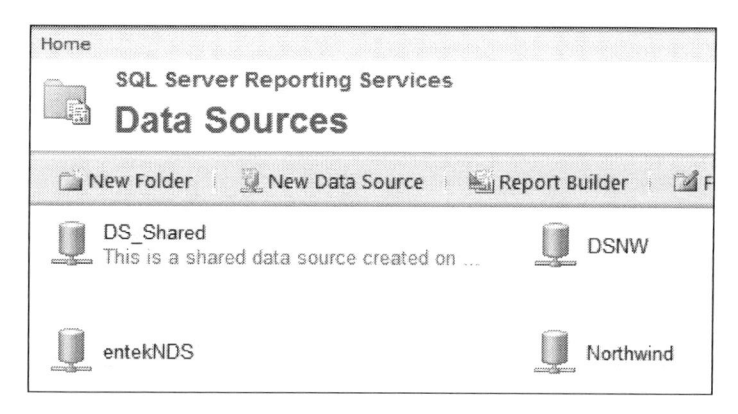

```
Home
      SQL Server Reporting Services
      Data Sources

   New Folder    New Data Source    Report Builder

   DS_Shared
   This is a shared data source created on ...        DSNW


   entekNDS                                           Northwind
```

5. On the Report Server also it will be in the Data Sources folder as shown in the following screenshot:

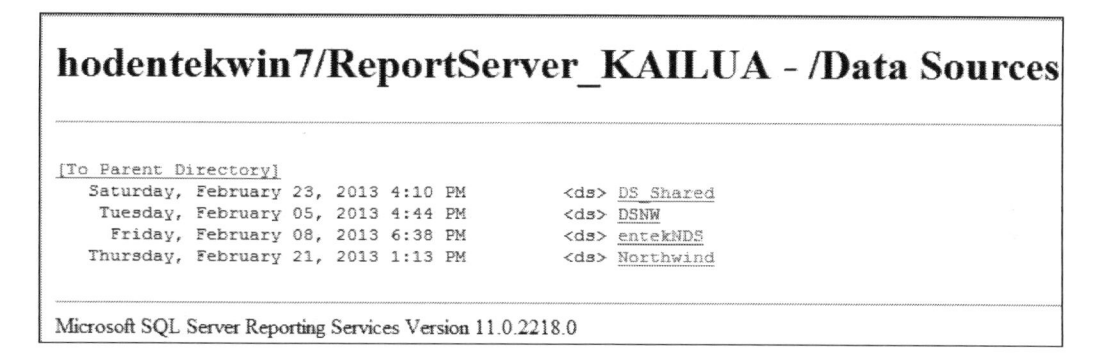

```
hodentekwin7/ReportServer_KAILUA - /Data Sources


[To Parent Directory]
    Saturday, February 23, 2013 4:10 PM     <ds> DS_Shared
    Tuesday, February 05, 2013 4:44 PM      <ds> DSNW
     Friday, February 08, 2013 6:38 PM      <ds> entekNDS
   Thursday, February 21, 2013 1:13 PM      <ds> Northwind

Microsoft SQL Server Reporting Services Version 11.0.2218.0
```

Hands-on exercise 4.6 – creating a data model from a data source

> SSDT does not have the Report Model project template. This is deprecated. However, it is possible to create a report model in Report Manager from a data source on the Report server.

Working with Report Manager

In the previous hands-on exercise we created a shared data source `DS_Shared`. We will use `DS_Shared` to create a data model.

1. Open Report Manager and open the `Data Sources` folder and right-click on the `DS_Shared` data source as shown in the following screenshot:

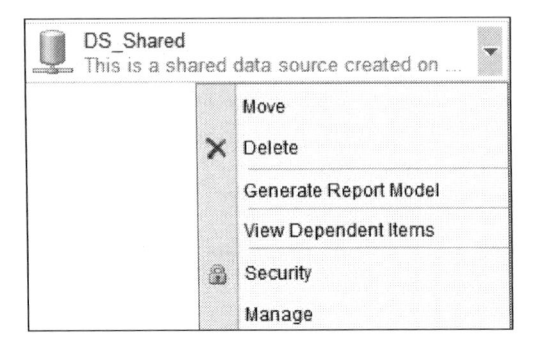

2. Click on **Generate Report Model**.
3. The **DS_Shared** page opens as shown in the following screenshot:

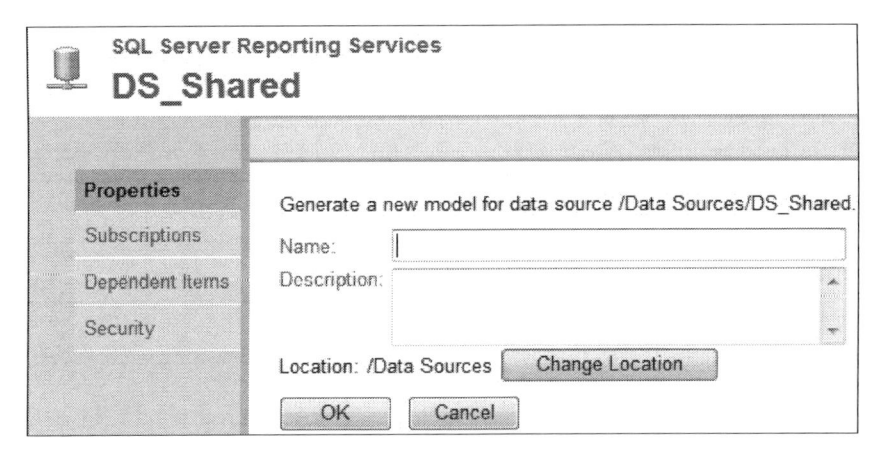

4. Provide **Name** and **Description**. Accept the default location and click on **OK**.

    If you try to create a data model you will get a message saying the following:

    "The current action cannot be completed. The user data source credentials do not meet the requirements to run this report or shared dataset. Either the user data source credentials are not stored in the Report Server database, or the user data source is configured not to require credentials but the unattended execution account is not specified. (`rsInvalidDataSourceCredentialSetting`)"

5. A look at the security page shows that the permission is that of a `Content Manager` for the Group **BUILTIN\Administrator**.
6. Add the current user to have the role of `Content Manager` for this source as shown in the following screenshot:

DS_Shared			
	X Delete	New Role Assignment	Revert to Parent Security
Properties	☐	Group or User ↓	Role(s)
Subscriptions	☐ Edit	BUILTIN\Administrators	Content Manager
	☐ Edit	HodentekWin7\mysorian	Content Manager

7. Now try to save the Report Model as in the earlier step.
8. You will get a similar message regarding the data source credentials.
9. Change the Connection properties as shown here:

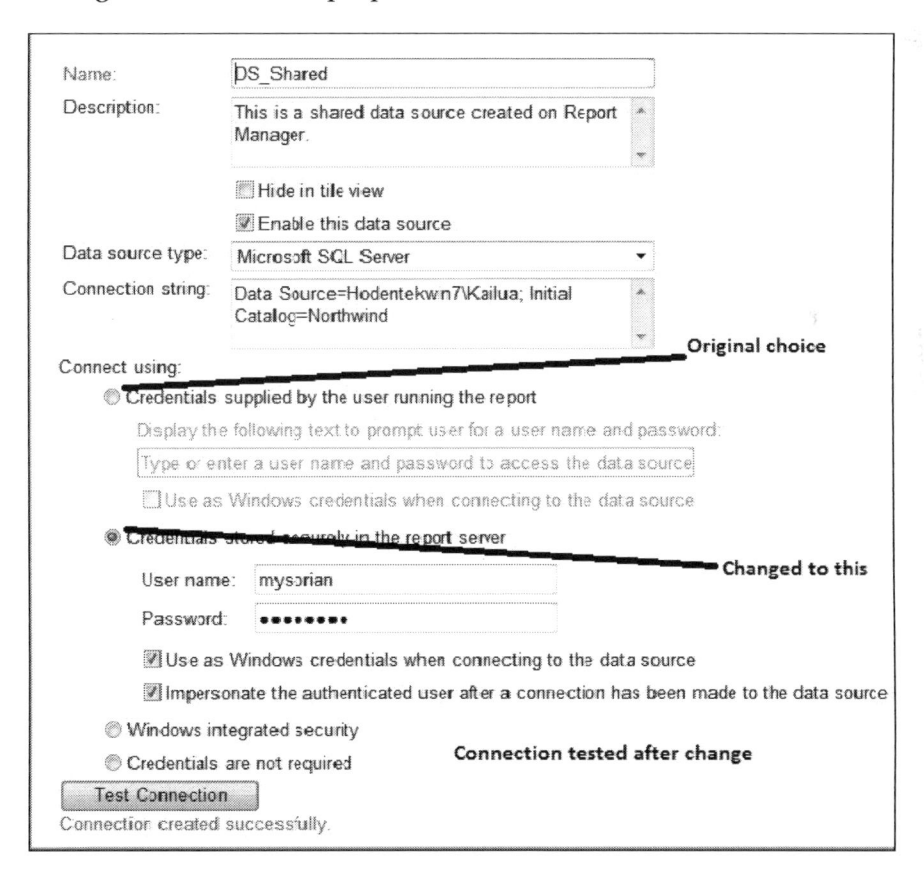

[207]

10. Click on **Apply**.
11. Go back to **Step 3** enter name and description and click on **OK**.
12. The data model **DsSharedModel** is created as shown in the following screenshot:

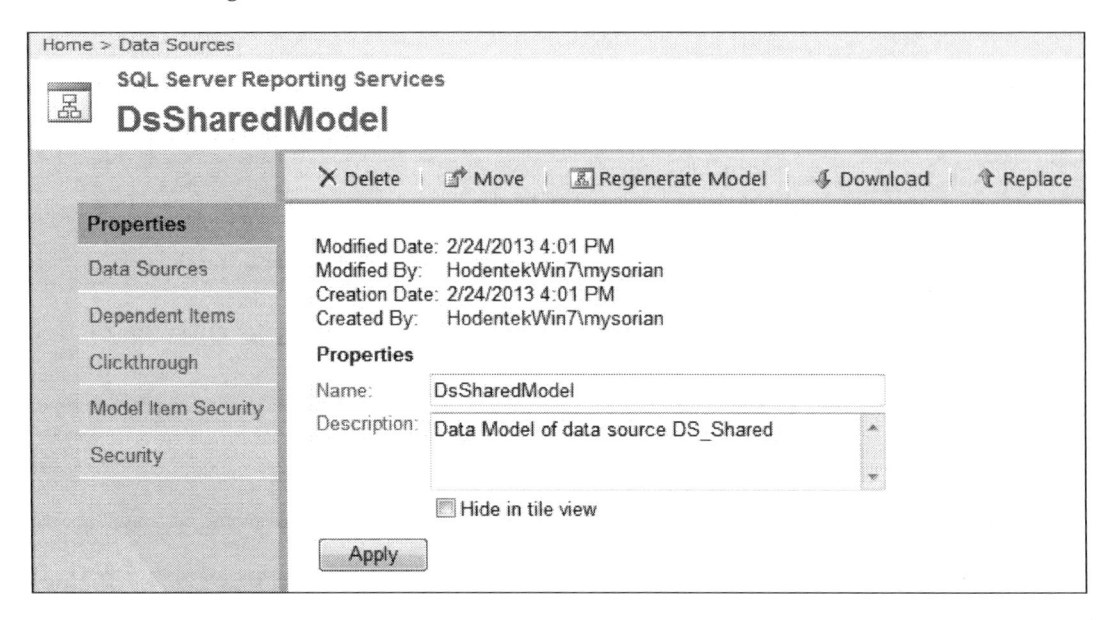

Home > Data Sources

SQL Server Reporting Services
DsSharedModel

| × Delete | Move | Regenerate Model | Download | Replace |

Properties
Data Sources
Dependent Items
Clickthrough
Model Item Security
Security

Modified Date: 2/24/2013 4:01 PM
Modified By: HodentekWin7\mysorian
Creation Date: 2/24/2013 4:01 PM
Created By: HodentekWin7\mysorian

Properties
Name: DsSharedModel
Description: Data Model of data source DS_Shared

☐ Hide in tile view

[Apply]

Go through the various items on the left starting from **Properties** and get yourself familiarized with the items.

13. Here is the **Model Item security** showing the contents:

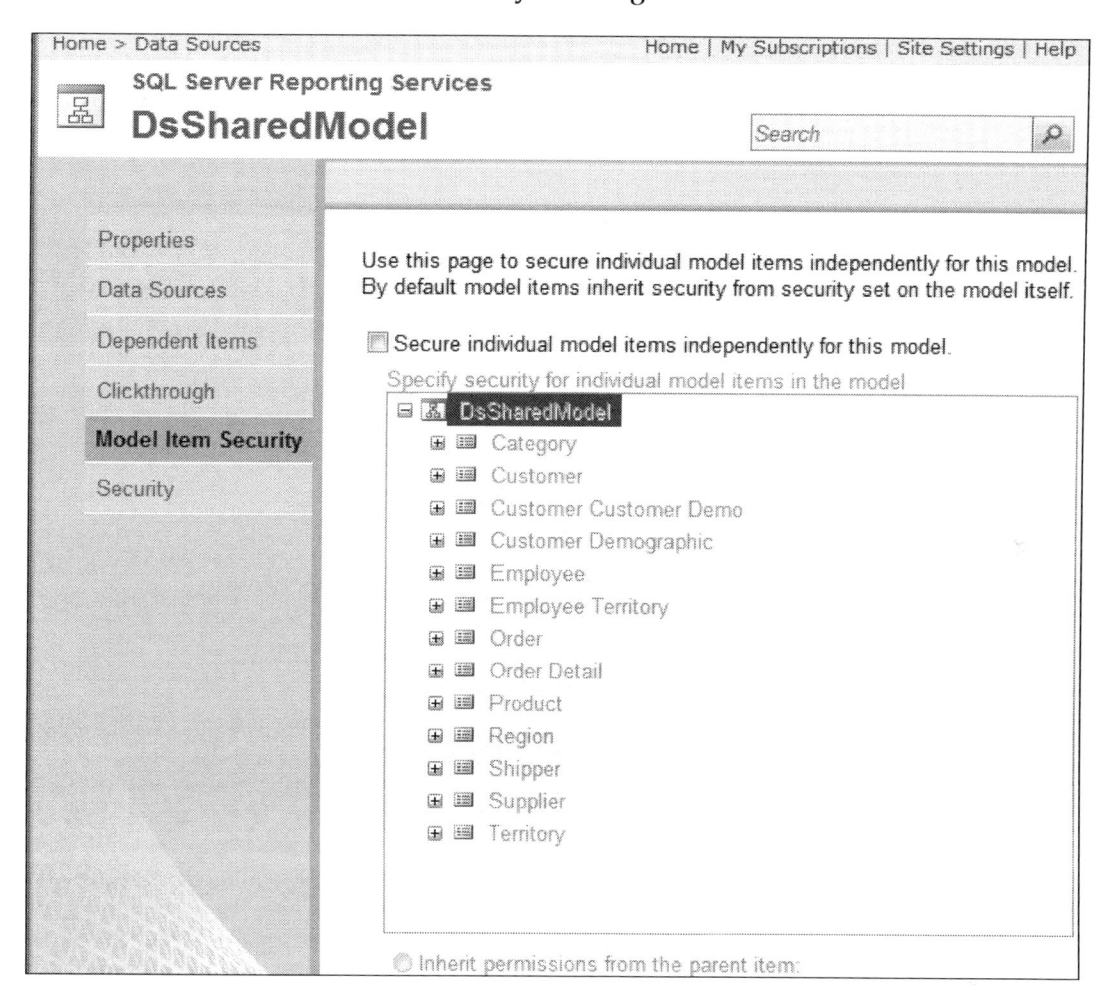

14. Here is the content of **Clickthrough**:

> Home > Data Sources   Home | My Subscriptions | Site Settings | Help
>
> **SQL Server Reporting Services**
>
> # DsSharedModel   Search
>
> Properties
>
> Data Sources   Use this page to set custom clickthrough reports for entities in this model.
>   Each entity can have one report which returns a single instance of the entity
> Dependent Items   and one report which lists multiple instances for the entity.
>
> **Clickthrough**   Select the model item for which to set custom clickthrough reports:
>
> Model Item Security   ⊟ DsSharedModel
>   Category
> Security   Customer
>   Customer Customer Demo
>   Customer Demographic
>   Employee
>   Employee Territory
>   Order
>   Order Detail
>   Product
>   Region
>   Shipper
>   Supplier
>   Territory
>
>   Single instance report:
>   [   ] Browse
>   Multiple instances report:
>   [   ] Browse

> Make sure you read the information provided at the top of the page. We will revisit this topic in the next chapter. Follow the link http://technet.microsoft.com/en-us/library/ms345252.aspx and get yourself familiar with the details of clickthrough reports in SSRS 2012.

Chapter 4

Viewing, searching, and printing reports

Viewing reports and printing the reports are some of the major activities that businesses do on a daily or scheduled basis. Reports are generated electronically. During printing they must be transformed into user required specific formats. The reports generated by the Reporting Services accommodate several different formats both for print and for Web. Reports on demand as well as reports for which subscription is provisioned support several print format options. For example, a user can subscribe to a report to be sent to him/her by e-mail in a Word format for printing and HTML format for easy browsing.

In a business environment the number of reports created can be very large and overwhelming. Searching for reports in a large archive is a must. In addition to report search, there must also be a tool for searching within reports for some specific information and this is accomplished by the **Find** tool.

Viewing of reports is tightly bound to security as to who can and who cannot. The following hands-on exercise enables the administrator to see reports and other objects that he finds on a report server. The administrator needs to set up roles to users so that their access is limited by their role. These roles also have to comply with accessing data on the server on which the report is based.

When you open a report in Report Manager you will notice some common features shown in the next figure of a report toolbar that aggregates many of the activities you carry out with reports such as viewing, searching, printing, and so on.

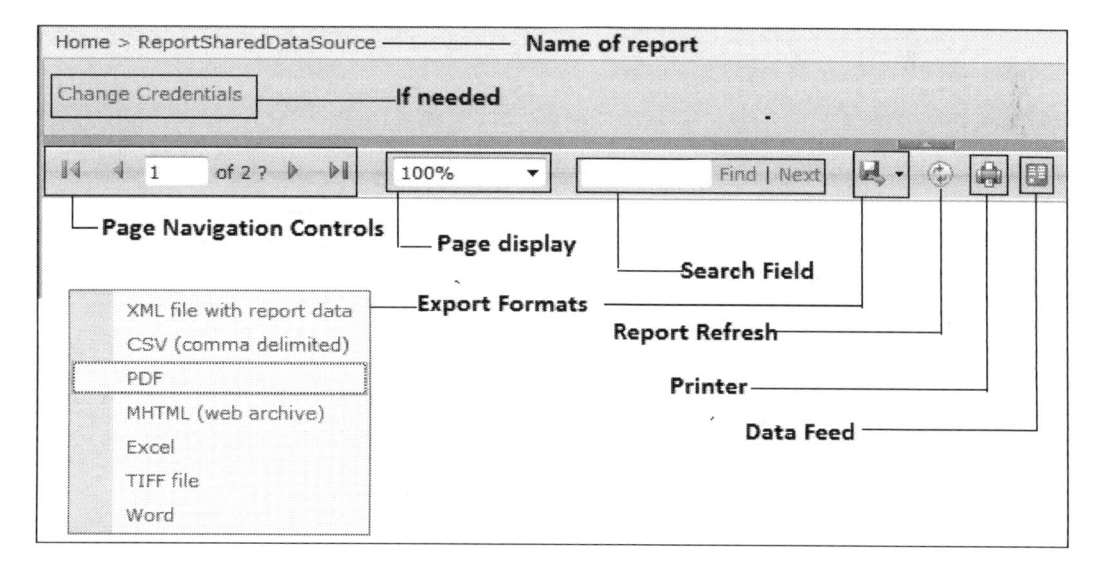

[211]

Hand-on exercise 4.7 – view, print, and search on Report Manager

We will be using objects on Report Manager to explore the main tasks of this exercise.

Viewing reports

Viewing a report as it is authored is possible in SSDT and Report Builder. Once it is deployed to the Report Server, you may want to take a look at it. Once you are sure that you are able to view it without problems and check the details you may want to carry out other activities such as printing, scheduling, and so on.

1. Open Report Manager by typing its URL address in a browser (Using **Run as Administrator**).

2. Click on any report deployed to the Report Server, such as **ReportEmbed**.

    ReportEmbed on the Report Server was created using Report Builder.

    The Report opens as shown in the following screenshot:

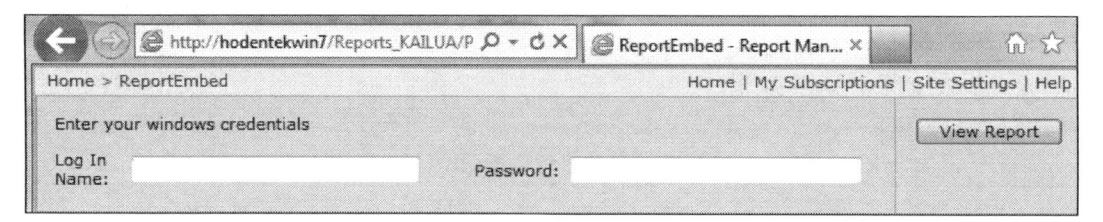

3. You are required to provide the credentials as the data source credentials were set so that the user will be asked to provide credentials. Enter credentials and click on the **View Report** button on the right.

Chapter 4

There is some report loading activity after which the report is displayed as shown in the following screenshot:

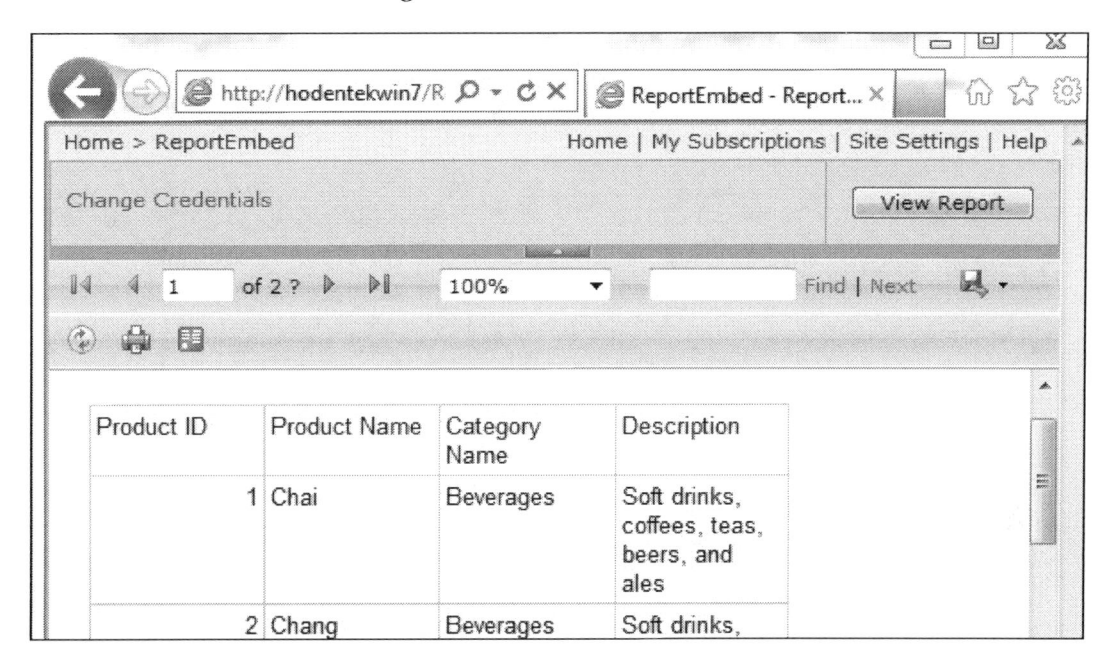

Printing reports

In many cases printed reports (hardcopy) are needed. This is especially true since the online reports could undergo changes sometimes unintentionally. Some businesses have a longstanding practice to archive hardcopies of reports.

The previous screenshot is an HTML page and can be printed. Depending on the printer and how it is set up you should be able to print it without any problem. The print icon should be clicked to begin printing assuming all other printer requirements are met.

Click on the **Print** toolbar item on the report.

Working with Report Manager

You may get the message "According to Microsoft you may need to install an ActiveX Component to print".

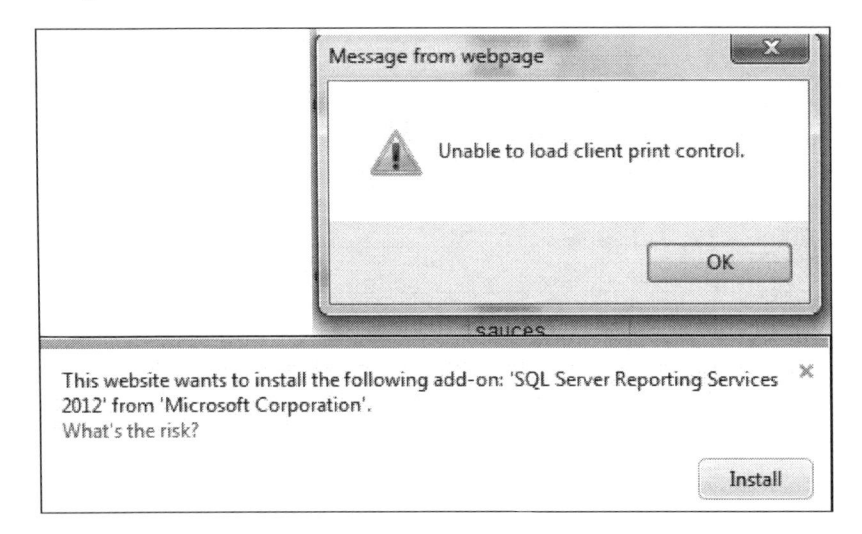

1. Click on **OK** and click on **Install**.

   The report page gets reloaded and you may need to enter the credentials one more time. After some time the **Print** window will be displayed.

   The computer already had this XPS Document Writer and it is hard to understand why the program did not recognize it! Besides this printer, there is also a Canon MX430 networked printer.

2. Make no changes and click on **Preview**.
3. The Printer dialog changes to the other option, namely, `\\<ComputerName>\<PrinterName>`.

   The Preview works and the Report Embed report is displayed in the preview.

   You may print using the **Print** button.

4. Make sure your printer correctly printed the page.

Change the report format

Many would like to have the report formatted in Word. Other formats such as PDF and Excel are also popular. In this exercise we change the format to Word. You will find more details about report formats at `http://msdn.microsoft.com/en-us/library/dd239307.aspx`. The following are the steps for changing the format of the report:

1. With the report open in Report Manager, click on the **Export Format** button and from the dropdown list click on **WORD**.

   You will get a browser message as to what you want to do with the downloaded document ReportEmbed.docx. Choose your option.

2. Click on **Open** or **Save**.
3. You can save it to a location of your choice.

   If you click on **Open**, several pages of a Word document, Reportembed.docx, will be displayed (WORD 2013 opened the application in the present case).

> Report Manager opened and displayed correctly in Mozilla 13.0.1 but Google Chrome Version 26.0.1410.64 m could access the Report Manager but did not display the report.

Data feed format

Businesses sometimes need to exchange information in yet more modern formats such as data feeds. The icon for data feed when clicked generates an atom-compliant data feed from the report. The data feed can be read on an application such as SQL Server 2012 PowerPivot Client. Perform the following steps:

1. With the report open in Report Manager click on data feed icon.
2. Click on **Open** or **Save** to save the document (with .atomsvc extension) to a folder of your choice. If your choice is **Open**, then the computer may offer choices to open the document or direct you to the Internet to search for programs.

> Excel 2013 with PowerPivot add-in enabled can view this report with extension .atomsvc if the credentials are correctly set.

Search

Search is a very important feature if the number of reports is large and the report database contains extensive information. The Report Server may have hundreds of objects, folders, reports, report models, data sources, report parts, and so on.

Working with Report Manager

Searching the Report Manager site

In the **Search** box at top-right of the Report Manager's **Home** page you begin your search.

Type-in `FromSSDT` in the search box.

Search will immediately bring up the `FromSSDT_OrderDetails.rdl` report item in the Report Manager.

It is not necessary to search for the exact name; even a substring should locate the object. Try `DS_` and you will see the `DS_Shared` data source we created earlier on.

Search within a report

After searching for the object you may be required to search for information within the report. This is a very common scenario in a business. For this purpose you must first bring up the report and use the **Find** button and the **Find** field to search. Multiple occurrences can be found by clicking on the **Next** button by the side of **Find**.

Open the previous report and in the search field type `Hokk` and click on **Find**.

The Search routine finds the record that contains the substring `Hokk` as shown in the following screenshot:

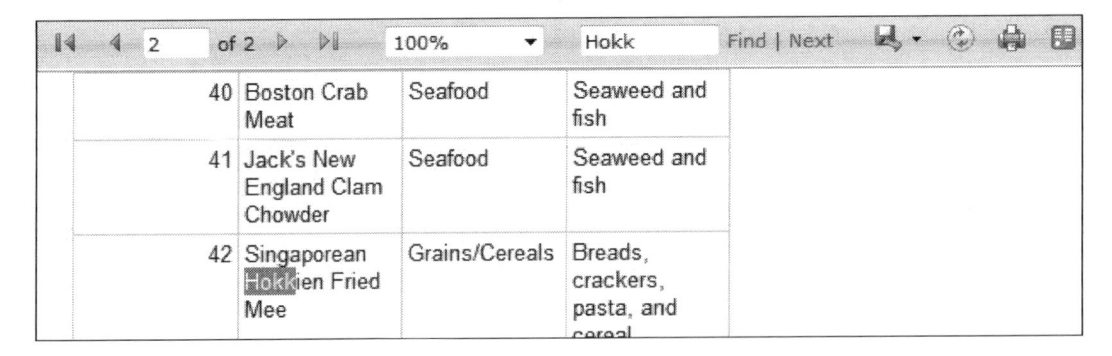

	2	of 2	100%	Hokk	Find | Next
	40	Boston Crab Meat	Seafood	Seaweed and fish	
	41	Jack's New England Clam Chowder	Seafood	Seaweed and fish	
	42	Singaporean Hokkien Fried Mee	Grains/Cereals	Breads, crackers, pasta, and cereal	

[216]

Uploading and downloading files from the Report Server to the filesystem

Having the flexibility to move resources from the Report Server to file system and from the file system to the Report Server is desirable. It makes the working with reports and modifications to reports on the Report Server at the file system level easier. With Report Builder as an intermediary you can move reports from Native mode to SharePoint mode report servers and vice versa.

Uploading a report on the computer to the Report Server

If the report is not created by a Report Server administrator, the report can be saved to the file system by the author and then uploaded by the Report Manager to the Report Server. There is a file `CustomersNw.rdl` saved to the file system (`C:\Users\mysorian\skydrive`) that will be used in the hands-on exercise. You may use one of your own.

`Skydrive` is Microsoft Cloud storage location for users of `Live.com` and `Hotmail.com` (presently changed to `Outlook.com`). Users can also have a desktop folder by the same name that can be synchronized with the folder in the Cloud (Microsoft Data Center). This makes desktop items to be shared across the Internet via Cloud.

Hands-on exercise 4.8 – uploading a report to the Report Server

We begin by accessing the report saved on the desktop as follows:

1. Open Report Manager using the URL.
2. Click on the icon Upload Files.
3. On the **Upload** page displayed click on the **Browse** button and locate the report using the information provided earlier as shown in the following screenshot:

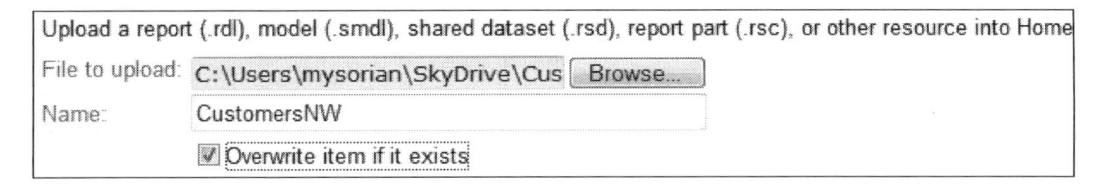

Upload a report (.rdl), model (.smdl), shared dataset (.rsd), report part (.rsc), or other resource into Home
File to upload: C:\Users\mysorian\SkyDrive\Cus Browse...
Name: CustomersNW
☑ Overwrite item if it exists

Working with Report Manager

> You can upload not only objects whose extensions are shown but also other resources.

4. Click on **OK**.

   The report `CustomersNw.rdl` appears in the Report Manager (that is, it is uploaded to the Report Server).

5. Click on the report in the Report Manager (if the Report Manager throws an error), change the security for this report with permission set to `Content Manager` for the data source.

   The report will be displayed.

Hands-on exercise 4.9 – downloading and reviewing a report definition file from the Report Server

We will download a file from the Report Server as follows:

1. Bring up the Report Manager using its URL in the IE Browser.
2. Click on the **FromSSDT-OrderDetails** report as shown in the following screenshot:

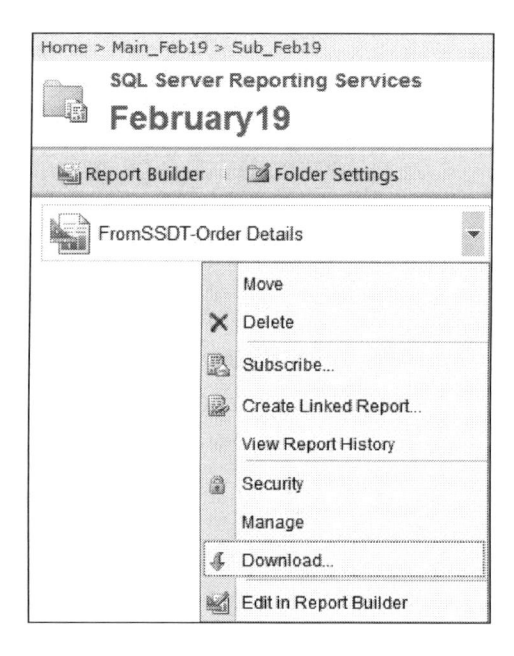

[218]

Chapter 4

3. Click on **Download**. You may get the **Error** page displayed with the error **rsAccessDenied**.
4. Use the browser back button and this time click on **Security** in the drop-down list.

   The **Security** page is displayed as shown in the following screenshot:

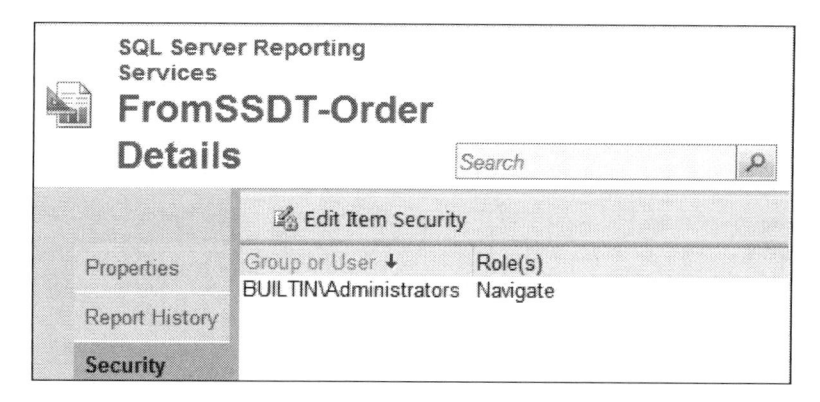

5. Click on **Edit Item Security**. You have no permission since the permission is only to the role `Navigate`. We temporarily over-ride this permission.

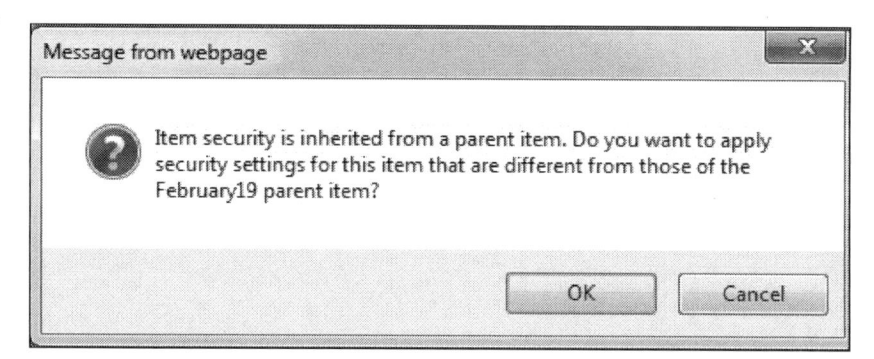

6. Click on **OK**. This gives us the opportunity to create a **New Role Assignment**, which we can later delete.
7. Click on **New Role Assignment** and add `HodentekWin7\mysorian` as the user with the role of `Content Manager` as described in an earlier hands-on exercise.

Working with Report Manager

8. Now try the download again. This time you will see the following page displayed:

9. Click on **Save** and save it to the `Skydrive` folder or any other folder.

Report subscription and delivery

You make a delivery request by creating a subscription. The delivery takes place at a certain time (by an event or a timer) in a format (Word, PDF, Excel, and so on.) in which you have requested a delivery. The delivery may reach the recipient in a number of ways. Some of these have already been discussed in *Chapter 3, Overview of SQL Server Reporting Services 2012 Architecture, Features, and Tools*. Subscriptions are created so that the reports are sent to the destination e-mail or to a shared folder. It is important to note that subscription is not available for all versions of SQL Server 2012. The version used for this book, the Enterprise Edition does support subscriptions.

A subscription needs to be defined and these are the items to be defined:

- A pointer to the location of the report that can run unattended (report to use stored credentials and use no credentials)
- If delivery by e-mail, the e-mail address
- Delivery format (PDF, Word, and so on)
- Event that starts the subscription processing (timer and a schedule)
- If the report runs as a snapshot, you can specify that the subscription runs whenever the snapshot is refreshed
- Parameters used when running the report (only if the report requires parameters, otherwise it is optional)

There are two kinds of subscriptions:

- **Standard**: Managed by individuals and has only one set of presentation, parameter, and delivery options.
- **Data Driven**: This kind of subscription is query based and requires knowledge of parameters. Report Server administrators create and manage these subscriptions. This is normally used when there are a large number of recipients.

There are two ways report can be delivered:

- **By e-mail**: There are several ways by which the reports are delivered by e-mail.

    Through a hyperlink to the generated report, send a notification in the subject line containing report name (@ReportName) and Executiontime (@ExecutionTime) embedding or attaching a report.

- **Send report file to a shared folder**: In order to create a subscription, a report must have stored credentials. The user must have permission to view the report and create individual subscriptions. Scheduled events and report delivery must be enabled on the Report Server.

> E-mail addresses are not checked and users must correctly enter e-mail addresses.

Hands-on exercise 4.10 – creating an event-driven report subscription for delivery by an e-mail

1. Open Report Manager and change the **Data Sources** of **EmployeeMarch28** to the one shown in the screenshot. Make sure you click on the **Apply** button after testing the connection.

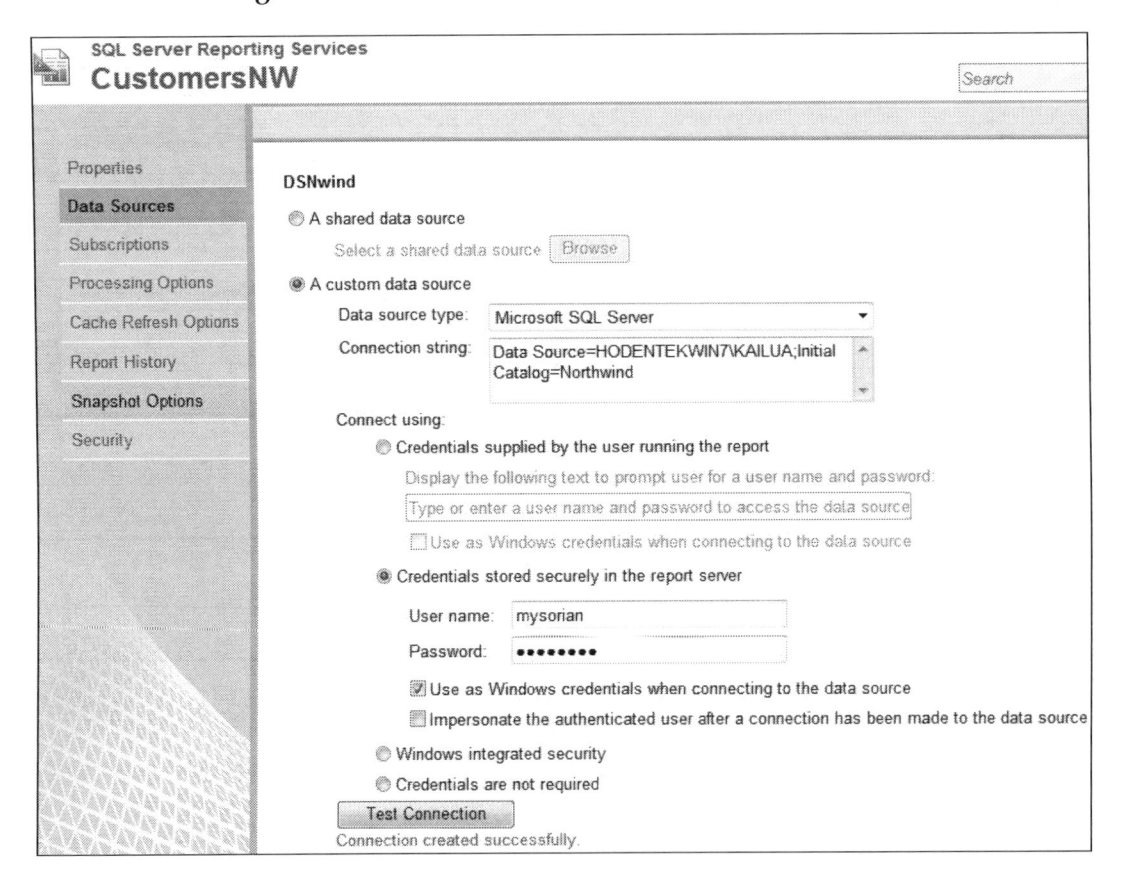

2. Click on **Subscriptions**. The **Subscriptions** page opens and presently there are no subscriptions as shown in the following screenshot:

From here you can create a **New Subscription** or a **New Data-driven Subscription**.

3. Click on **New Subscription**.
4. The **Subscriptions** page opens as shown here:

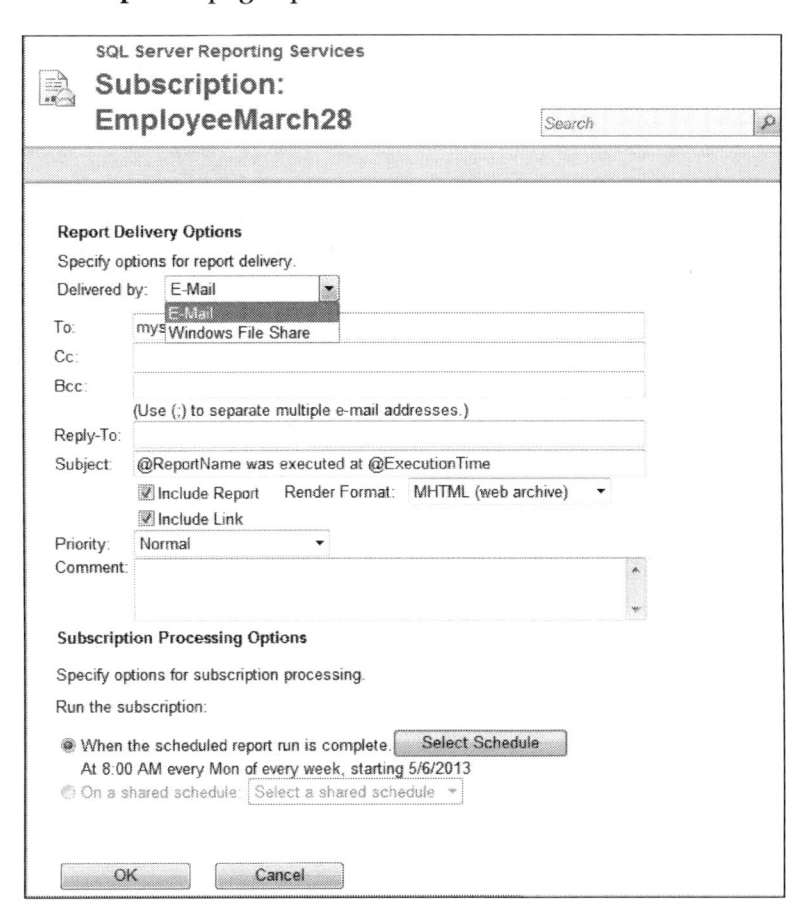

Working with Report Manager

5. Note that there are two delivery means, **Windows File Share** or **E-mail**. Let us assume it is by e-mail as in the previous screenshot.

6. Fill out the e-mail address. Choose a render format from the drop-down list shown in the following screenshot:

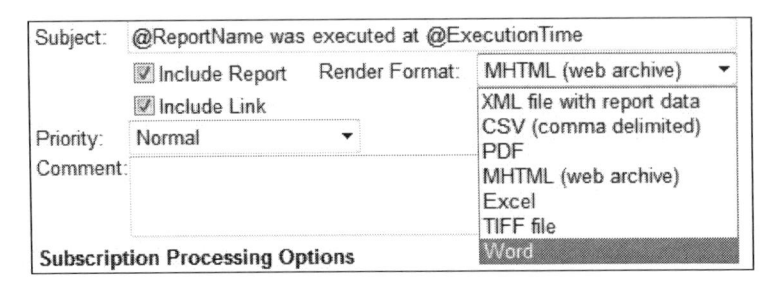

Subject:	@ReportName was executed at @ExecutionTime	
	☑ Include Report Render Format:	MHTML (web archive) ▼
	☑ Include Link	XML file with report data
Priority:	Normal ▼	CSV (comma delimited)
Comment:		PDF
		MHTML (web archive)
		Excel
		TIFF file
Subscription Processing Options		**Word**

7. For the present subscription a **PDF** format is chosen. **Normal priority** is chosen, the other options are low and high.

8. Click on **Select Schedule** to set up the schedule. (Herein, to test the program the option **Once** was chosen to run at a predetermined time.)

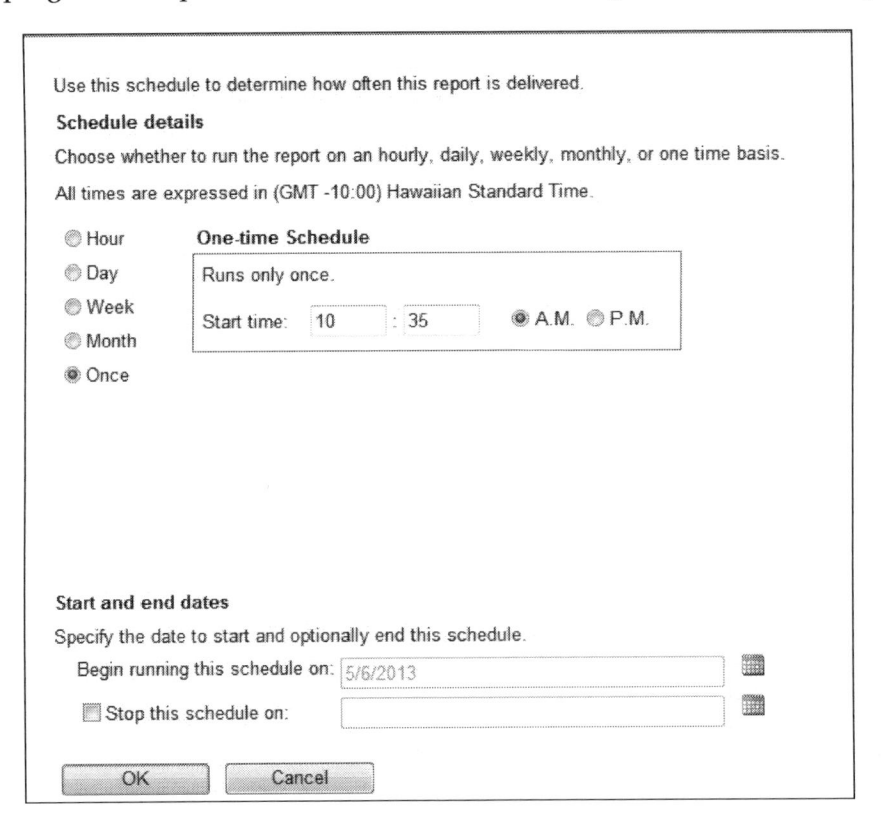

Use this schedule to determine how often this report is delivered.

Schedule details

Choose whether to run the report on an hourly, daily, weekly, monthly, or one time basis.

All times are expressed in (GMT -10:00) Hawaiian Standard Time.

- ○ Hour   **One-time Schedule**
- ○ Day   Runs only once.
- ○ Week   Start time: 10 : 35   ● A.M. ○ P.M.
- ○ Month
- ● Once

Start and end dates

Specify the date to start and optionally end this schedule.

Begin running this schedule on: 5/6/2013

☐ Stop this schedule on:

[OK]   [Cancel]

[224]

Chapter 4

9. You can also create **Start and end dates** for the report. As you can see there is a lot of flexibility in setting up the subscription.

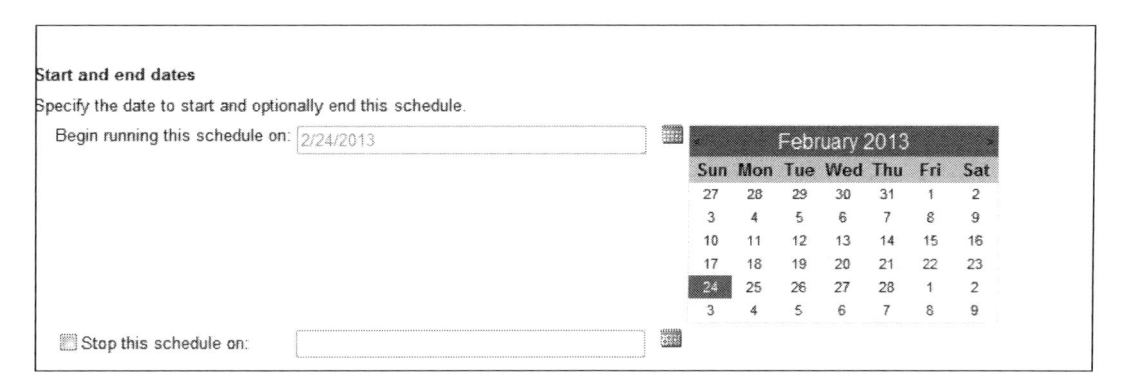

10. Click on **OK** for scheduling as well as the subscription.

    A subscription is created that will be delivered to the e-mail at the specified time in the specified format (make sure the SQL Server Agent service is running otherwise you get a **rsScheduleNotResponding** error).

11. After the specified time you can check the status of the subscription as shown here:

[225]

Working with Report Manager

When you refresh the Report Manager you may get a message that it was successfully sent or if there were some errors it will show up in the **Status** column. You may also edit subscriptions in this page. If it is still not sent you get a **Pending** message in **Status** column.

12. Check the e-mail to verify that the report was delivered.

    The report has been delivered as shown in the following screenshot:

This completes the event driven subscription related exercise.

Hands-on exercise 4.11 – creating an event-driven report subscription for delivery to a file share

This is the other option for creating a subscription. Most of the steps are the same except for a few, which will be described:

1. Open the Report Manager **Home** by using its URL address.
2. Click on Manage to manage the report used earlier, CustomersNW.
3. Click on Subscription and click to create a New Subscription.
4. The Subscription page opens; only a small portion is shown here.

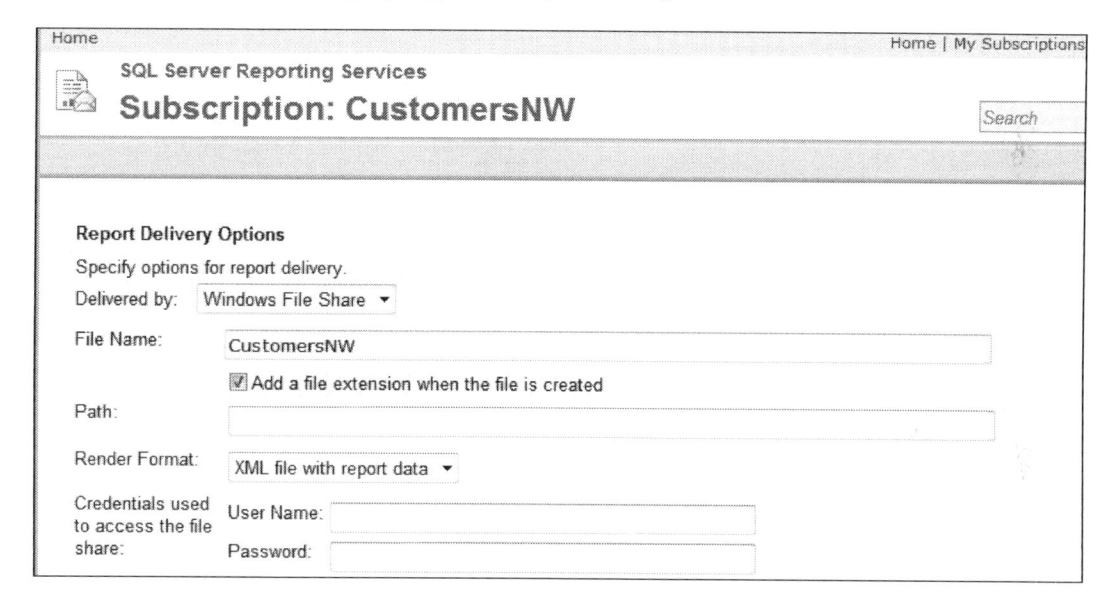

> The delivery method has been changed to Windows File Share.

5. For the Path field type \\ALOHAONE\Users (UNC format, \\<ComputerName>\<Shared folder_name>).

    Aloha is another computer on this network and it is in the Windows 7 Home Network.

Working with Report Manager

6. Enter the **User Name** and **Password** to access this location on the computer. You may also modify or verify the security aspects of this file share location.

   The completed subscription appears as shown in the following screenshot:

   Report Delivery Options

   Specify options for report delivery.

Delivered by:	Windows File Share
File Name:	CustomersNW
	☑ Add a file extension when the file is created
Path:	\\ALOHAONE\Users
Render Format:	PDF
Credentials used to access the file share:	User Name: mysorian
	Password: xxxxxxxxx

   Overwrite options:
   - ⦿ Overwrite an existing file with a newer version
   - ○ Do not overwrite the file if a previous version exists
   - ○ Increment file names as newer versions are added

   Subscription Processing Options

   Specify options for subscription processing.

   Run the subscription:
   - ⦿ When the scheduled report run is complete. [Select Schedule]
     At 6:10 AM on 2/25/2013
   - ○ On a shared schedule: Select a shared schedule

   [OK] [Cancel]

7. Click on **OK**.

8. The subscription is ready to run as shown in the following screenshot:

[228]

If the scheduler has no permission to the file share there will be a delivery error as shown in the following screenshot:

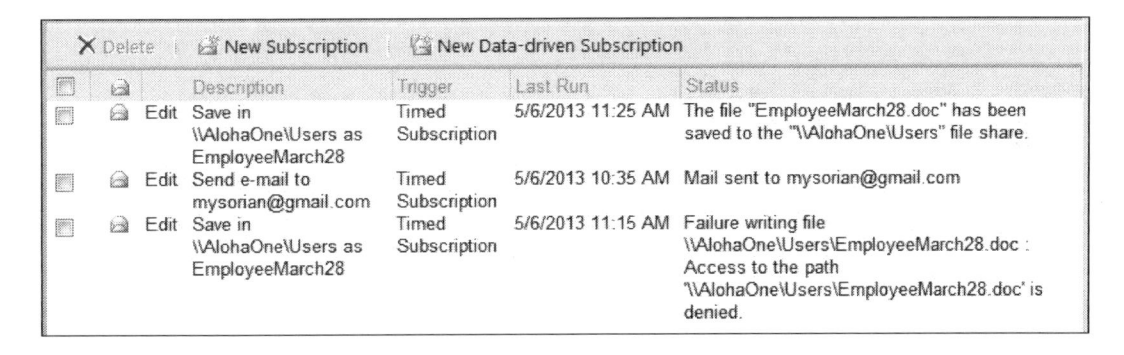

Using the **Edit** button it is possible to edit the subscription. In the previous screenshot, after obtaining the permission to file share the subscription was edited and it was run again. It was successfully delivered to the file share as shown in the previous screenshot.

Hands-on exercise 4.12 – creating data-driven report subscription for delivery to a file share

Data-driven subscriptions send out reports not just to one individual or two but to a large number of recipients whose desired format among other details are maintained in a database on the server. This is report delivery targeted at mass distribution. In order to work with this hands-on exercise, you need to keep a database of recipients ready. When the subscription is processed the Report Server customizes the output for each of the recipients maintained on the database. The example shown sends out reports to multiple recipients by e-mail.

Create a Subscribers database in SQL Server

You must first create a database called Subscribers using the SQL Server Database Engine to hold the address and e-mails of the people you want to send the report as follows:

1. Connect to the Database engine (HodentekWin7\KAILUA in this case) in the SQL Server Management Studio).

2. Right-click on the **Databases** node and select **New Database**.

3. In the **New Database** window type in Subscribers for the database name and click on the **OK** button (accept all other defaults).

The database gets created.

Populate a table in the Subscribers database

Now we need to add a table to the Subscribers database that holds the recipient information. You can do this by running a transact SQL query:

1. Write a SQL statement as shown to create a table RecipientInfo in the Subscribers database:

```
Use Subscribers
CREATE TABLE [dbo].[RecipientInfo] (
  [SubscriptionID] [int] NOT NULL PRIMARY KEY,
  [RecipientID] [int] ,
  [Email] [nvarchar] (50) NOT NULL,
  [FileType] [bit],
  [Format] [nvarchar] (20) NOT NULL ,
) ON [PRIMARY]
GO
INSERT INTO [dbo].[RecipientInfo] (SubscriptionID,
  RecipientID, Email, FileType, Format) VALUES (1, 289,
  'John@ixy.net', '1', 'IMAGE')
INSERT INTO [dbo].[RecipientInfo] (SubscriptionID,
  RecipientID, Email, FileType, Format) VALUES (2, 284,
  'dona@pix.com', '1', 'MHTML')
INSERT INTO [dbo].[RecipientInfo] (SubscriptionID,
  RecipientID, Email, FileType, Format) VALUES (3, 275,
  'mysorian@gmail.com', '1', 'PDF')
GO
```

Chapter 4

2. Run the query in SSMS. Make sure you are targeting the query to `Subscribers` database.
3. Verify that three rows of data are created in the table.

Creating the data-driven Subscription and testing it

After creating and populating the table you can now create a data-driven subscription along the same lines to send a standard subscription:

1. Access Report Manager by providing the URL.
2. Click on the report (herein `CustomersNw.rdl`) you want to subscribe to and open it (the report runs).
3. Click on the **Subscriptions** tab, and then click on **New Data-Driven Subscription**.

   The **Subscription** page **Step1-Create a data-driven subscription: CustomersNW** gets displayed.

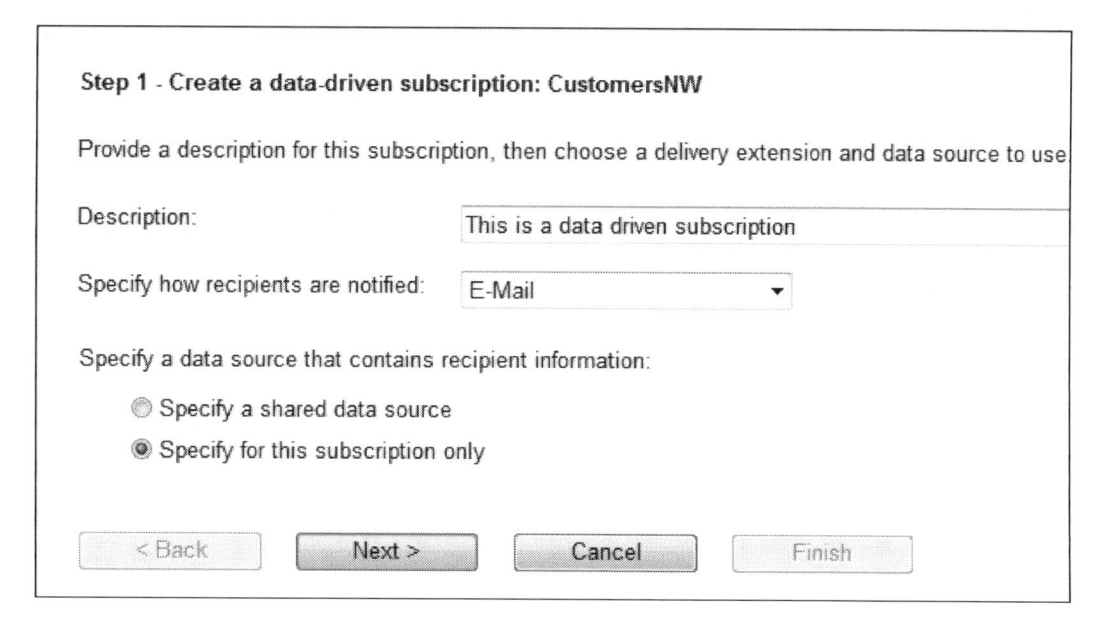

Step 1 - Create a data-driven subscription: CustomersNW

Provide a description for this subscription, then choose a delivery extension and data source to use

Description: This is a data driven subscription

Specify how recipients are notified: E-Mail

Specify a data source that contains recipient information:
  ○ Specify a shared data source
  ● Specify for this subscription only

[< Back] [Next >] [Cancel] [Finish]

---

[231]

Working with Report Manager

4. Provide a **Description** and accept the default **Specify for this subscription only**. Choose **E-Mail** from the drop-down list for **Specify how recipients are notified** and click on the **Next** button.

   The other options in the drop-down list are **Windows File Share** and **Null Delivery**. **Null Delivery** will not deliver but if Report Cache is enabled then the result of executing the subscription with this setting will end up here. This may be useful in cases where you may want to keep copies of a report that depend on various parameter settings.

5. Fill it out as shown in the following screenshot:

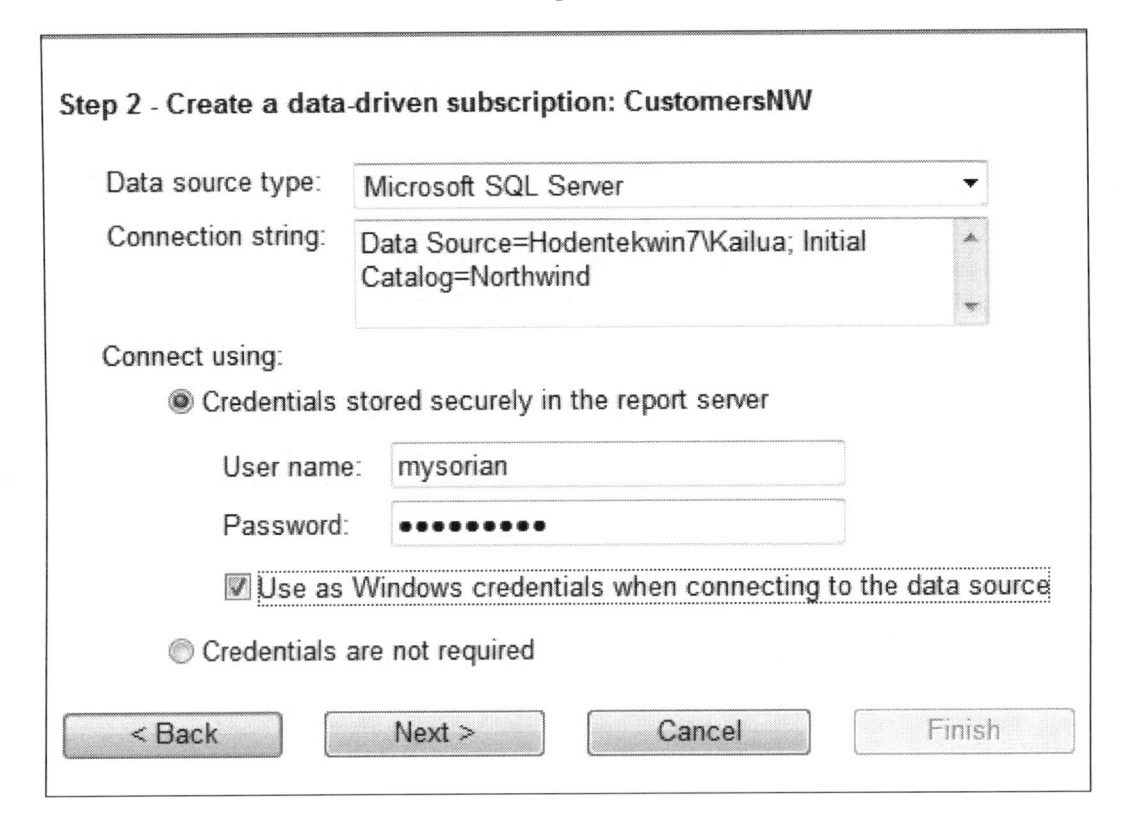

Step 2 - Create a data-driven subscription: CustomersNW

- Data source type: Microsoft SQL Server
- Connection string: Data Source=Hodentekwin7\Kailua; Initial Catalog=Northwind
- Connect using:
  - ◉ Credentials stored securely in the report server
    - User name: mysorian
    - Password: •••••••••
    - ☑ Use as Windows credentials when connecting to the data source
  - ○ Credentials are not required

[< Back] [Next >] [Cancel] [Finish]

6. Click on **Next**.

Chapter 4

Step 2 is displayed as shown in the next screenshot. The connection string will be empty. The connection string is not that something you can build here. You will have to know beforehand. It is also assumed that the **User name** and **Password** are stored in the Report Server.

Step 2 - Create a data-driven subscription: CustomersNW

- Data source type: Microsoft SQL Server
- Connection string: Data Source=Hodentekwin7\Kailua; Initial Catalog=Northwind
- Connect using:
  - ◉ Credentials stored securely in the report server
    - User name: mysorian
    - Password:
    - ☑ Use as Windows credentials when connecting to the data source
  - ○ Credentials are not required

[< Back] [Next >] [Cancel] [Finish]

7. Enter **Password** and place a check mark as shown in the previous screenshot:
8. Click on **Next**.

Working with Report Manager

In **Step 3** that gets displayed enter the query `SELECT * from RecipientInfo`. The delivery extension settings are the ones that the program will pull out from the `RecipientInfo` table in the `Subscribers` database.

Step 3 - Create a data-driven subscription: CustomersNW

Specify a command or query that returns a list of recipients and optionally returns fields used to vary delivery settings and report parameter values for each recipient:

```
Select * from RecipientInfo
```

The delivery extension settings and report parameter values can use field values returned by the command or query. If there are field values that map to these settings, include the fields in your command or query.

    The delivery extension has the following settings: TO, CC, BCC, ReplyTo, IncludeReport, RenderFormat, Priority, Subject, Comment, IncludeLink, SendEmailToUserAlias

    The report takes the following parameters: The "CustomersNW" report has no parameters.

Specify a time-out for this command: `30` seconds

Verify that the command is correct for the selected data source: [Validate]

[< Back] [Next >] [Cancel] [Finish]

---

9. Click on the **Validate** button to verify if the query can be run.

    The page returns an error.

10. Modify the query in the previous window as shown:

    `SELECT * FROM [Subscribers].dbo.[RecipientInfo]`

11. Click on **Validate**.

    You get a **Query validated successfully** message just above the buttons at the bottom of the previous page.

12. Click on **Next**.

    Step 4 is displayed as shown in the following screenshot:

13. Use the following information to fill in the fields. For others, accept the default.

    To: hodentek@live.com

    Include Report: TRUE

    Render Format: Word 2003

14. Click on **Next**.

    Step 5 gets displayed.

    ```
    Step 5 - Create a data-driven subscription: CustomersNW

    Specify report parameter values for CustomersNW

        The "CustomersNW" report has no parameters.

        [ < Back ]   [ Next > ]   [ Cancel ]   [ Finish ]
    ```

15. Click on **Next**.

    Step 6 will be displayed.

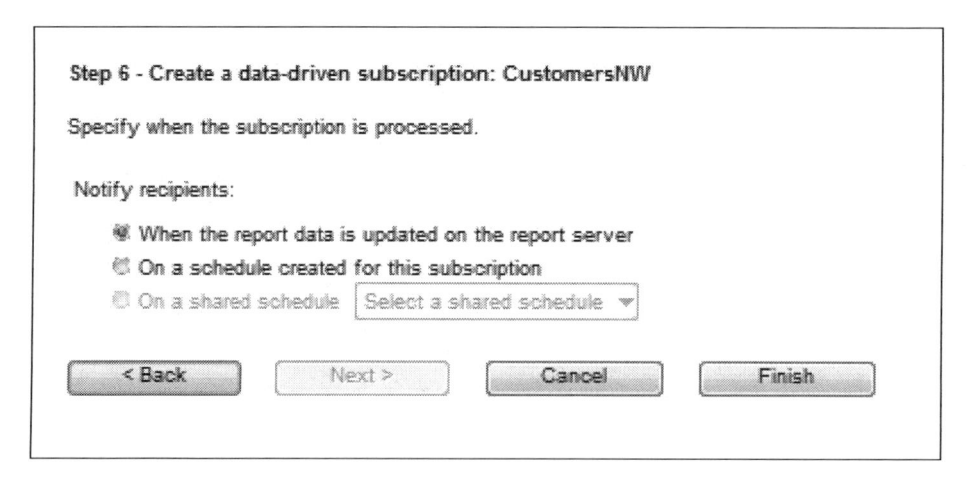

    ```
    Step 6 - Create a data-driven subscription: CustomersNW

    Specify when the subscription is processed.

    Notify recipients:
        ● When the report data is updated on the report server
        ○ On a schedule created for this subscription
        ○ On a shared schedule  [ Select a shared schedule ▼ ]

        [ < Back ]   [ Next > ]   [ Cancel ]   [ Finish ]
    ```

16. Click on **Finish**.

    This creates a new subscription that is data-driven. The **Status** changes when the report data changes.

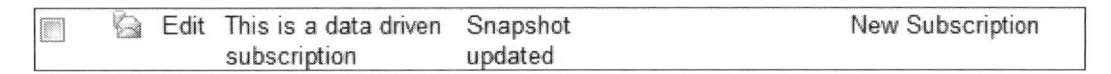

		Edit	This is a data driven subscription	Snapshot updated		New Subscription

You can also schedule the subscription by using the other two options in **Step.6**.

This will, however, make an event (timer) driven subscription.

The previous subscription was edited to a timed one and ran once. The subscription status changed as shown in the following screenshot. However, the GMAIL has not yet (last checked at 09:17 A.M.) delivered the report in PDF.

		Report ↓	Description	Folder	Trigger	Last Run	Status
		Edit CustomersNW	This is a data driven subscription	Home	Timed Subscription	2/25/2013 9:10 AM	Done: 3 processed of 3 total; 0 errors.

> Data-driven Subscriptions are only supported in Enterprise and Business Intelligence Editions of SQL Server 2012.

In the next section Report caching will be described.

Report caching

You can cache a copy of a processed report on the Report Server and serve a cached copy from the server. Since the cached information is retrieved from the temporary location where it was stored the first time it was requested, the turn-around is very fast as no data is queried again. The idea of report caching is very much analogous to Web page caching.

This can be turned on for individual reports by the user. There is a cache lifetime that can be specified as you do not need the same report forever. In addition, it can affect resources. The report cache can also bring in problems of security breaches and to mitigate this, the report should only be available to the user or group that created the cache in the first place. Hence, the user who creates the cache must have the report data source configured to store his credentials.

The Report cache is a step before the final rendering and therefore it is in an intermediate format internal to reporting services and can be rendered in a chosen format at the time of printing or using a cached copy. The cached report has a finite lifetime after which it is removed. It may also be removed if the underlying report is updated to reflect new information.

Working with Report Manager

While access to a cached report has been taken care off by storing the credentials of the user creating the cache, the permissions to change the cache properties must also be covered by security. These are secured by permissions that are only given to the some of the roles such as `Content Manager`, `Publishers`, and so on. Follow the link http://msdn.microsoft.com/en-us/library/ms155927.aspx to learn more.

The Report cache is created by the user but it can be created automatically by Execution Snapshot. Execution Snapshot can be used to create a cache on a scheduled basis. This feature needs to be turned on for each report. Execution Snapshot lends itself for handling cache expiry by proper scheduling.

How does a user know that he has got a cached report? Well, the time of execution is the clue. If the date and time of execution is not current and it is not a snapshot, then it is a cached copy.

Report processing options

Here is an image of the **Processing Options** available on Report Manager in SQL Server 2012.

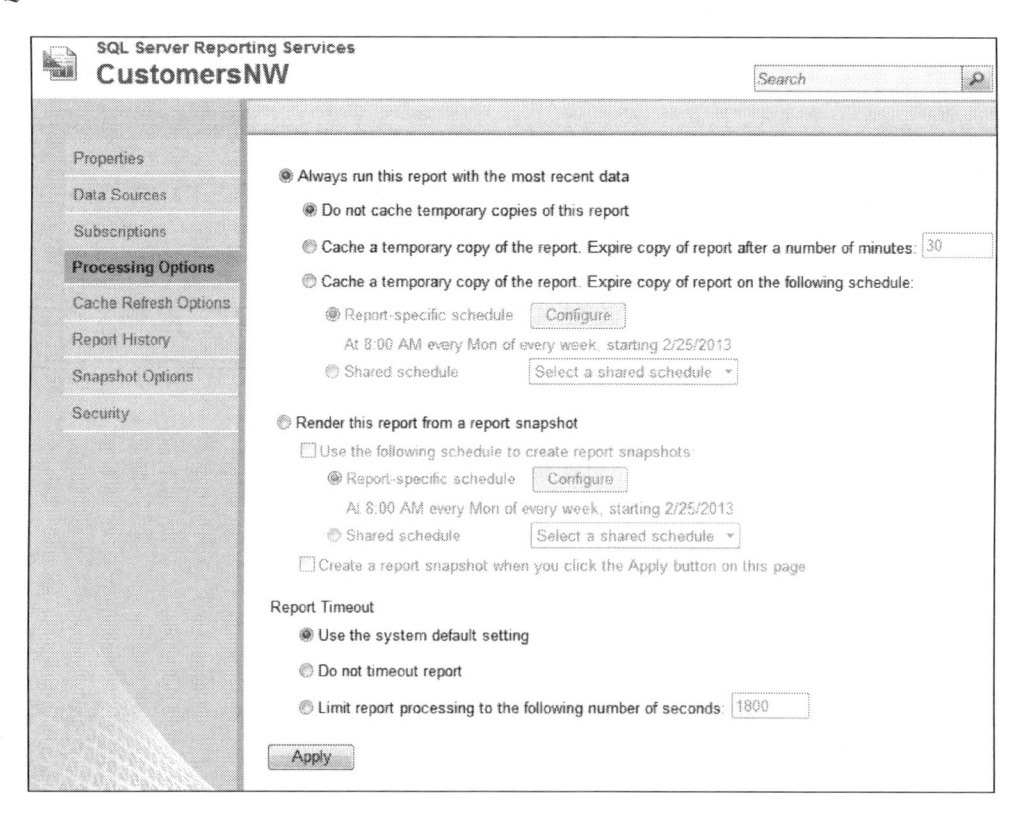

There are two major choices, **Always run this report with the most recent data** or **Render this report from a report snapshot**.

You may decide not to cache it, cache a temporary copy and remove (expire) the copy of report after a specified number of minutes, or set up a schedule to expire the copy.

When you choose the second option, the items to configure are shown in the next screenshot:

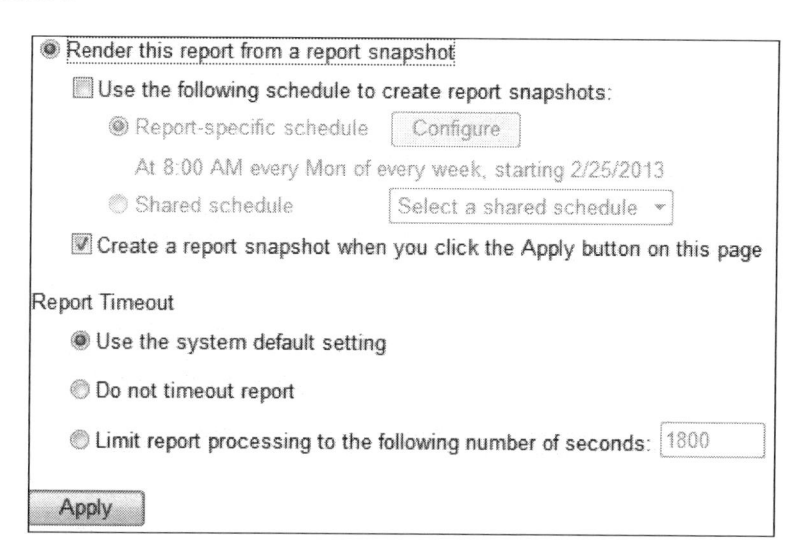

In this case you can also choose whether or not to time out or specify number of seconds to process.

Cache refresh options

The cache can be preloaded using Report Manager. You can preload the cache for a shared dataset by creating a cache refresh plan for the cached report. Alternatively, a data-driven subscription can be used to preload the cache. The former is the best recommended practice.

The following requirements are to be met before creating a plan:

- The shared dataset or the report must have caching enabled
- The shared data sources for the shared dataset or the report must be configured to use stored credentials or no credentials
- The SQL Server Agent service must be running

Working with Report Manager

For the report we used earlier, we do know that the report uses stored credentials. You can verify if SQL Server Agent is running in SSMS. If not, you can start it from there or in the Control Panel by accessing Windows Services.

Hands-on exercise 4.13 – creating a cache refresh plan by preloading the cache

We will create a cache refresh plan for the `CustomersNW` report (you may use one of your report) we used in creating subscriptions as follows:

1. Open the **Home** page of Report Manager using its URL.
2. Click on the report `CustomersNW` report on the contents of **HOME**.
3. Click on **Manage** from the dropdown for this report.
4. Click on the **Cache Refresh Options** tab on the left.

    Presently there are no plans as shown here:

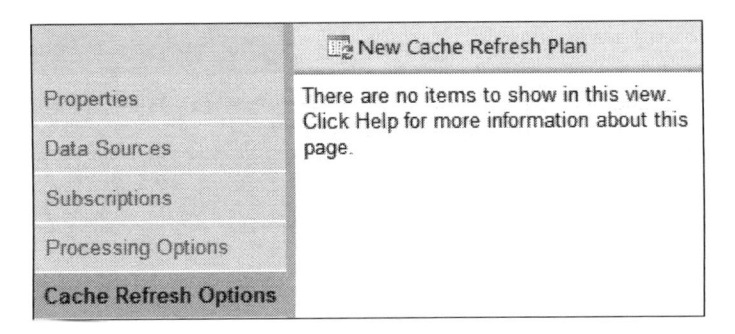

	New Cache Refresh Plan
Properties	There are no items to show in this view. Click Help for more information about this page.
Data Sources	
Subscriptions	
Processing Options	
Cache Refresh Options	

5. Click on **New Cache Refresh Plan'**
6. You will get a message as caching is not enabled for the report. If the item does not have caching enabled, you will be prompted to enable caching.

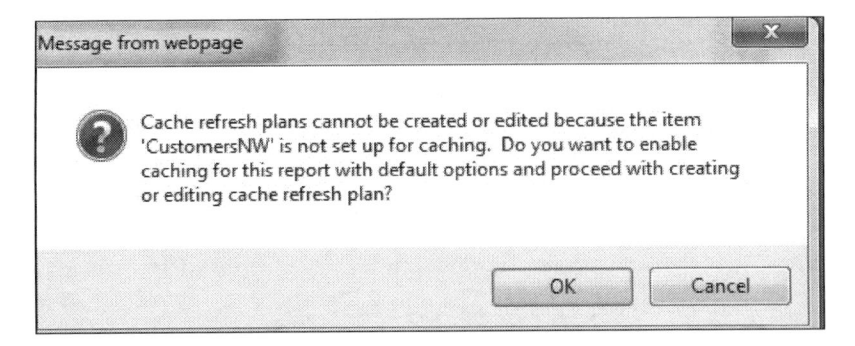

    Message from webpage

    Cache refresh plans cannot be created or edited because the item 'CustomersNW' is not set up for caching. Do you want to enable caching for this report with default options and proceed with creating or editing cache refresh plan?

    OK   Cancel

[240]

7. Click on **OK** to enable caching for the report.
8. The **Cache Refresh Plan: CustomersNW** window is displayed as shown in the following screenshot:

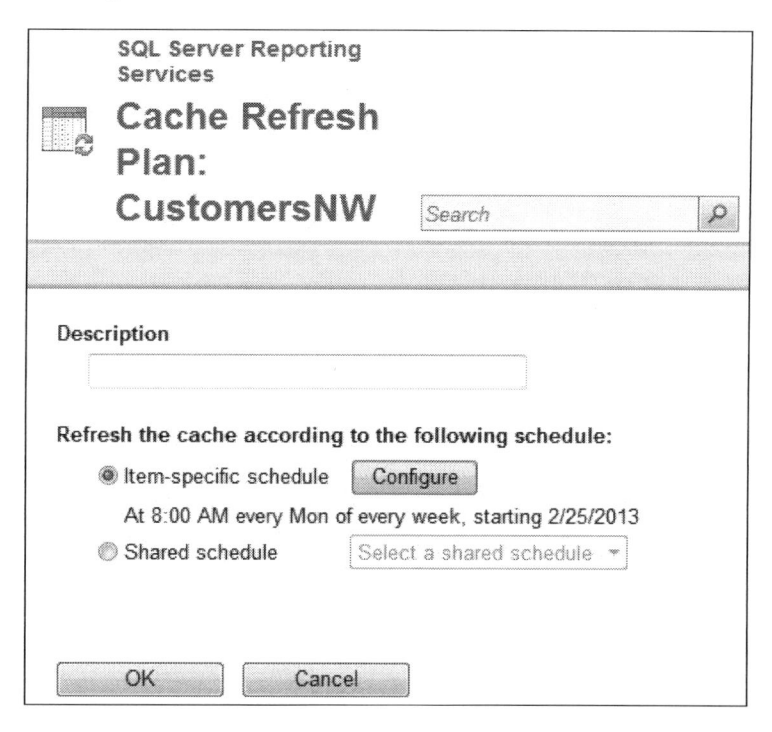

9. You can give a description to the plan (optional).
10. You choose the type of schedule.

    In the following, we have chosen the item-specific schedule.
11. If you click on **Configure**, the scheduling window opens that allows you correctly schedule.
12. Accept the default 8:00 AM every Monday.
13. Click on **OK**.
14. The cache refresh plan is created as shown here:

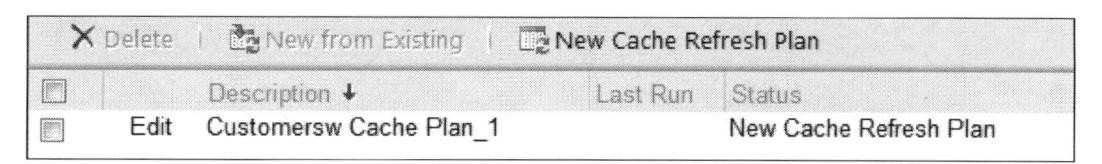

Working with Report Manager

Snapshot and snapshot history

Report history is an archive of report snapshots. These can be created manually or on a schedule. The archive is report history archive and is managed by adding and removing report snapshots. You should have the role that can carry out the task **Manage Report History**. This means this role should also be able to carry out View reports task. If you are permitted to view reports, you are also permitted to view report history. A Snapshot includes data and the time when the query was executed.

Hands-on exercise 4.14 – creating a snapshot and snapshot history

For the report `CustomersNW`, we create a snapshot as follows:

1. For the report `CustomersNW`, access the **View Report History** menu item using the dropdown.

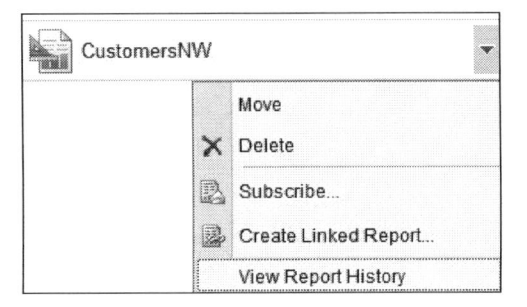

2. Click on **View Report History** and as there are no snapshots, there is no history as shown in the following screenshot:

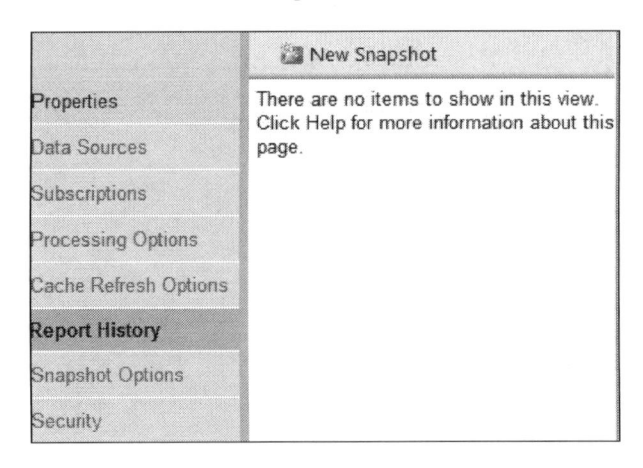

[242]

3. Click on **New Snapshot**. A new snapshot will be created as shown in the following screenshot:

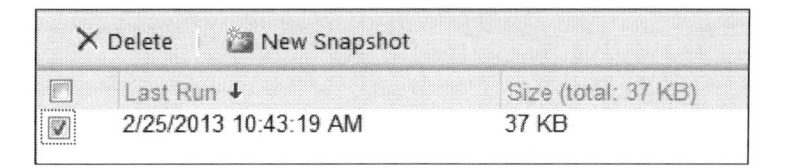

	Last Run ↓	Size (total: 37 KB)
✓	2/25/2013 10:43:19 AM	37 KB

(✗ Delete   New Snapshot)

In this way, you can manually create snapshots and they are added to **Report History**, and using **Delete** you can take them out of Report History. If they are added according to a schedule, they all end up in the **Report History**.

4. Click on **Snapshot Options** in the previous window. The window opens as shown in the following screenshot:

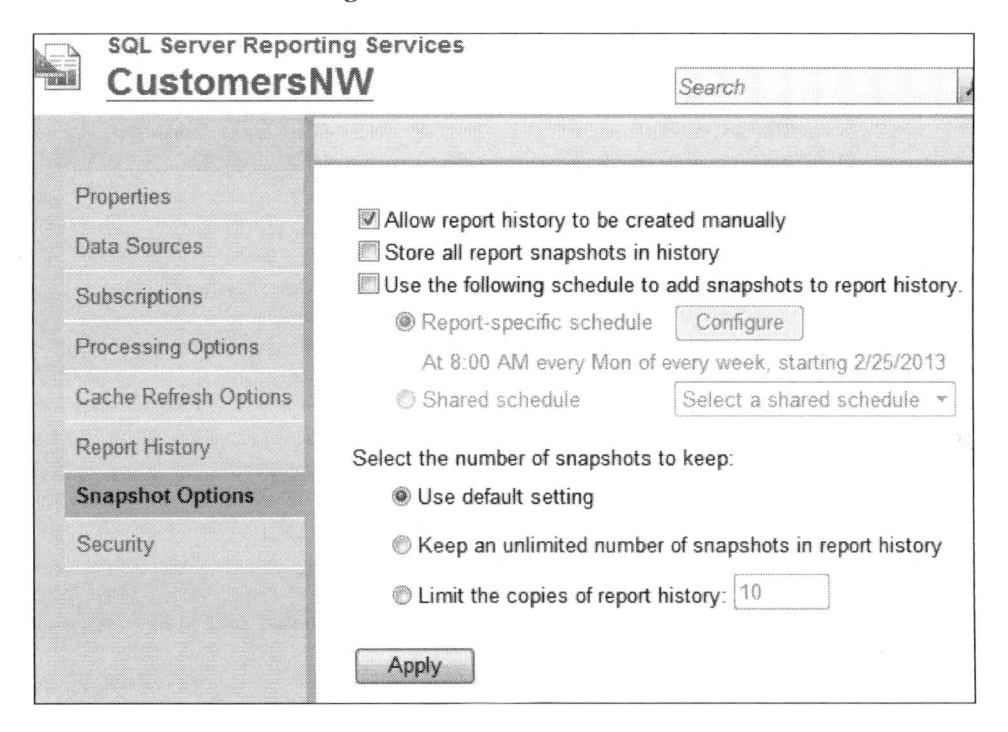

SQL Server Reporting Services
CustomersNW

Properties
Data Sources
Subscriptions
Processing Options
Cache Refresh Options
Report History
Snapshot Options
Security

☑ Allow report history to be created manually
☐ Store all report snapshots in history
☐ Use the following schedule to add snapshots to report history.
   ● Report-specific schedule [Configure]
      At 8:00 AM every Mon of every week, starting 2/25/2013
   ○ Shared schedule [Select a shared schedule ▼]

Select the number of snapshots to keep:
   ● Use default setting
   ○ Keep an unlimited number of snapshots in report history
   ○ Limit the copies of report history: 10

[Apply]

Here you can choose the options and then click on **Apply**.

Summary

Report Manager, the one-stop user interface to interact with the reporting services installed in the Native mode, is described in great detail by highlighting many of the tasks it is designed to help carry out. The hands-on exercises would help a user in finding his way around with this important tool in Microsoft SQL Server Reporting Services 2012. Individual hands-on exercises deal with many tasks this Web client has been designed to carry out on the Report Server such as managing folders, assigning roles to users, viewing and printing of reports, uploading and downloading reports, manage scheduling of reports, managing delivery of reports in several ways, creating data sources, creating models, and many others. The readers will find it useful to create a couple of reports that are embedded as well as shared data sources using SSDT and deploy them to the Report Server before beginning with this chapter.

In the next chapter we will work with Report Builder 3.0, also a one-stop tool to create reports rapidly from a variety of data sources, embellish them with interactive features, and get them ready with cutting edge graphic support with a variety of tools to make a visual and analytic presentation of your data. Report Builder can create reports for both Native as well SharePoint Integrated reporting and save/deploy them to Native Report Servers and SharePoint Document libraries.

5
Working with Report Builder 3.0

Report Builder 3.0 is feature-rich reporting tool with the latest Microsoft Office look and feel (the ribbon). Report Builder 3.0 supersedes its predecessors (Version 1.0 and 2.0) and it was launched with SQL Server 2008 R2. It provides an extremely flexible GUI with user-friendly wizards, a versatile construct for creating the tablix (table + matrix) data regions, tables, matrices, charts, gauges, data bars, sparklines, maps, and so on.

Report Builder is an authoring tool for creating reports that can be deployed to native mode report servers as well as SharePoint integrated mode report servers. As it can be used for both modes of the server, reports can be easily accessed on one, modified, and deployed to the other, offering a high degree of flexibility. While Report Builder can create embedded data sources from a variety of vendor products, shared data sources can be created only by using the Report Manager, SharePoint sites, or the SQL Server Data Tools.

Report Builder 3.0 supports server resources such as shared data sources, works with SQL Server data sources, XML data, and many third-party products, and can directly open and edit server-hosted reports. Report Builder together with Report Manager provides powerful support for building and managing a bewildering array of report types with stunning graphic and interactive support. The ad-hoc reporting capabilities are moved over to SharePoint with SQL Server 2012.

Report Builder cannot be used for authoring Power View Reports, a new feature of SQL Server Reporting Services 2012 in SharePoint Integrated mode.

Report authoring with Report Builder

This chapter is all about Report authoring using Report Builder 3.0. In this chapter, you will be doing most of the Report authoring yourself. Most of the time, you will start from a blank report and then author it, but sometimes you will use a wizard. The snapshot and cached reports were described in *Chapter 4*, *Working with Report Manager*, but you will be working with the rest of the report types in this chapter.

In the hands-on exercises, you will be specifically working with the following points:

- Embedded and share data sources
- Parameterized reports
- Column grouping and document map
- Subreports
- Drill down and drill through reports
- Linked reports
- Report with an XML data document source
- Using more recent gadgets for Visual Analytics

As far as ad hoc reporting is concerned, it is the type of report a business user (decision maker) would like to see in order to make some decisions. This has been shifted over to SharePoint Server via Reporting Services Integration and Power View. Authoring Power View Reports using a Tabular Model in SQL Server Analysis Services is described in *Chapter 6*, *Power View and Reporting Services*.

Downloading and installing Report Builder

The Report Builder .msi file can be downloaded from http://www.microsoft.com/en-us/download/details.aspx?id=29072

The version of the file used in the preparation of this book is 11.0.2100.60 (24.8 MB). This is the standalone version. Details of the file are as follows:

- **File name**: ENU\x86\ReportBuilder3.msi
- **Version number**: 11.0.2100.60 (3/6/2012)
- **Size**: 24.8 MB

Some of the basic requirements are:

- Access to SQL Server 2012 Database Engine
- Microsoft .NET Framework 4.0 installed
- 80 MB of hard disk space and 512 MB of RAM

While it can be installed in attended or unattended modes, for the preparation of material for this book it was installed in the attended mode.

In the attended mode, you are guided by a wizard. During installation, you need to point to the report server as shown.

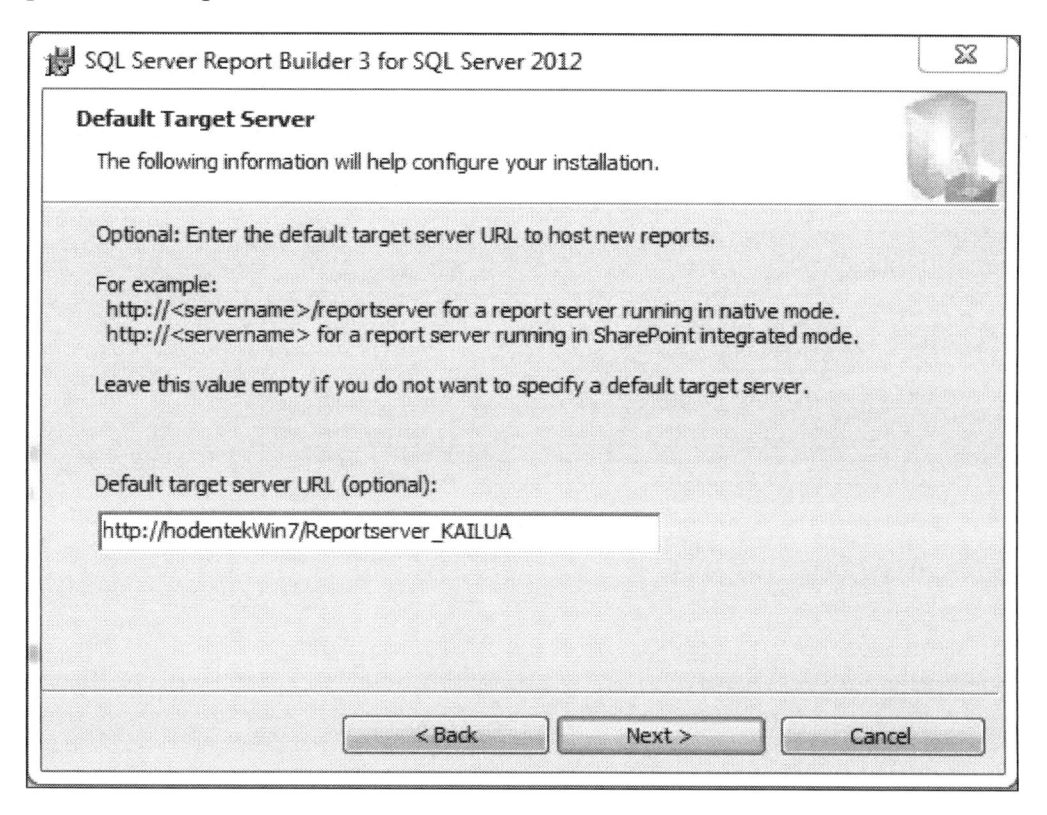

In case you decide to use the command-line installation, use the `msiexec.exe` from command line and accept the license terms, and point to the report server.

Report Builder 3.0 user interface

Report Builder 3.0 interface has not gone through much of a change from Report Builder 2.0 except perhaps how the wizard pages are sequenced with some additional wizard pages added. The readers are urged to review the following book, which describes the Report Builder 2.0 User Interface in great detail (*Learning SQL Server 2008 Reporting Services*, *Jayaram Krishnaswamy* by *Packt Publishing*):

However, as we go through the various hands-on exercises, we will be using the UI more frequently so that by the time you finish this chapter, you would have acquired sufficient skills.

The enhancements to Report Builder 3.0 after the release of SQL Server 2012 are Excel and Word rendering extensions, which support rendering Word and Excel documents that are compatible with Microsoft Office 2007 and Microsoft Office 2010, as well as Microsoft Office 2003 Word and Excel documents. However, they require the installation of Microsoft Office Compatibility pack for Word, Excel, and PowerPoint. The format of these documents is **Office Open XML** with file extensions .xlsx and .docx.

Report authoring

Report writing starts with planning like most of the other activities. Some of the key considerations are:

- Audience
- Report structure
- Look and feel of report
- Report visibility related to security
- Report delivery format
- Canned or AD_HOC
- Web or desktop
- Internet, Intranet, or hard copy

Although these considerations are separately listed, they are interconnected. Once some of these requirements are defined then one begins to come up with a more detailed plan that needs the source of data (local, SQL Server, cloud, or third party), the connectivity issues, the delivery type (desktop, Intranet, download, Internet, cloud application, and so on), the delivery format for hard copies, Web access via Intranet IIS or through SharePoint, and a multitude of others that are too numerous to enumerate.

This chapter is not about planning but about using the Report Builder 3.0 tool to author reports of different kinds that are normally encountered. Of course, there are others that require custom treatment. SSDT and Report Builder 3.0 have the same set of tools and most of what you do in one can be done with the other. SSDT is capable of creating both server- and client-based reports (as related to reporting activity) and Report Builder creates server (hosted) reports. In addition, SSDT has the full backing of Microsoft .NET classes that provide programmatic support, which Report Builder does not provide. This translates to SSDT being used by developers well versed in Microsoft Visual Studio environment whereas Report Builder aligns more with report developers and content managers. In *Chapter 2*, *SQL Server Reporting Services 2012 Projects with Visual Studio 2012*, report authoring with SSDT was covered.

Hands-on exercise 5.1 – creating a report with an embedded data source

In the following steps, it is assumed that you have installed a standalone version of Report Builder 3.0 and as the administrator of the computer, you have the permissions to author reports and in fact, you are a *Content Manager*. Installing Report Builder 3.0 also adds a folder shortcut to **All Programs** as shown here:

1. The Report Builder 3.0 has essentially the same features as Report Builder 2.0, which have been thoroughly described in the article at `http://dotnet.sys-con.com/node/982742`.

Working with Report Builder 3.0

2. Launch Report Builder 3.0 shown in the preceding screenshot with administrator's privileges.

   After configuring Reporting Services in *Chapter 1, Overview and Installation – SQL Server Reporting Services 2012,* you could also launch Report Builder (ClickOnce) from the Report Manager or SharePoint site.

   > ClickOnce Report Builder is launched from Report Manager using the Report Builder Toolbar item in Report Manager's Home page. If you get an error while launching from Report Manager the reason is you must have had an earlier version of Report Builder. To rectify, remove the contents of the `C:\Users\<user>\AppData\Local\Apps\2.0` folder.
   >
   > Similarly, it can be launched in a SharePoint site configured for Reporting Services 2012 Integration by creating a new document of the type Report Builder report

3. Right-click on the **Data Sources** node in the left side as shown:

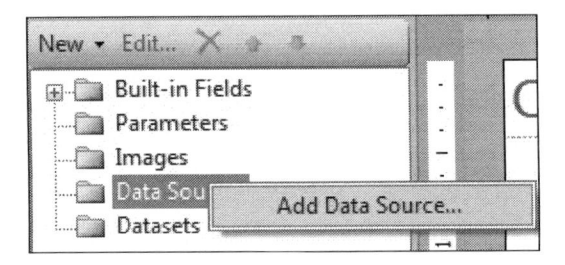

4. Click on **Add Data Source**. The **Data Sources properties** page is displayed.

5. Make changes in the window as described. We will use an embedded data source created using a table on Microsoft SQL Server.
   - In the **Name** field, enter `DS_Embed`
   - Choose the option **Use a Connection embedded in my report**
   - Select **Microsoft SQL Server** as **Connection type**

[250]

```
Name:
DS_Embed

○ Use a shared connection or report model
⦿ Use a connection embedded in my report

Select connection type:
Microsoft SQL Server                    ▼
Connection string:
Data Source=HODENTEKWIN7\\KAILUA;Initial     [ Build... ]
Catalog=Northwind
```

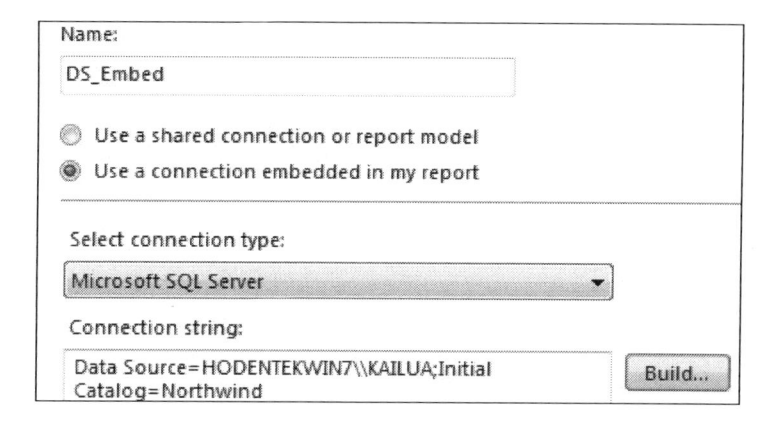

6. Click on **Build...** to create a connection string. The **Connection Properties** page is displayed.

7. Make changes to the window as described. We use the SQL Server 2012 named `KAILUA` and the `Northwind` database. You may verify that the connection is successful. Set the following values in the fields:
    - **Data source: Microsoft SQL Server (SqlClient)**
    - **Server name** (choose from drop-down): **HodentekWin7\KAILUA**
    - **Log on to the server: Use Windows authentication**
    - **Connect to a database** (Choose from drop-down): **Northwind**

8. Click on **Test Connection** to test your connection.

9. Click on **OK** and it is updated in the **Data Source Properties** page as shown:

10. Click on the **Credentials** page on the left side on the **Data Source Properties** window. The **Credentials** page is displayed with a single option, namely, **Use current Windows user, Kerberos delegation may be required**.

> Note the couple of options and the message "**This information is only stored when the report is saved to the report server**". The details of this window are well documented here,
> http://msdn.microsoft.com/en-us/library/ms178308.aspx

Working with Report Builder 3.0

11. Choose the **Prompt for credentials** option, place a check mark for **Use as Windows credentials** and for prompt text, **Enter your windows credentials** as shown in the following screenshot:

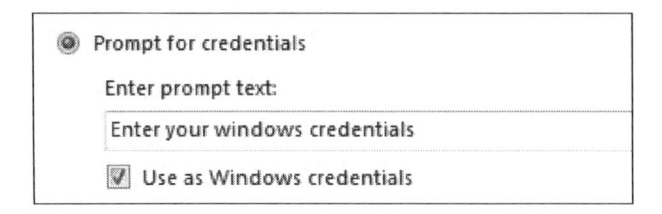

12. Click on **OK**.

13. Right-click on **Datasets** on the left side and click on **Add Dataset...** as shown on the following screenshot:

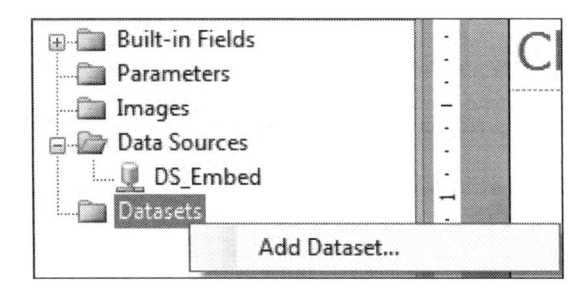

> Note that the dataset can also be shared among reports. We choose to do otherwise.

14. Change the dataset name to `DatasetEmbed`, choose the option to use a dataset embedded with the report, and for the data source choice that gets enabled choose the one created earlier (`DS_embed`) using the drop-down list. We use **Query type** to be **text**.

    Now we need to choose the table and create a query. The dataset from the query will be used in the report. There are options to create a dataset. We will choose to use a query as shown:

    ```
    SELECT          Products.ProductID, Products.ProductName,
    Categories.CategoryName, Categories.Description
    FROM            Products INNER JOIN
                            Categories ON Products.CategoryID =
    Categories.CategoryID
    ```

[252]

15. Type this into the **Query** field in the previous window and click on **OK**. The following authentication window is displayed (the modal window shown in the front):

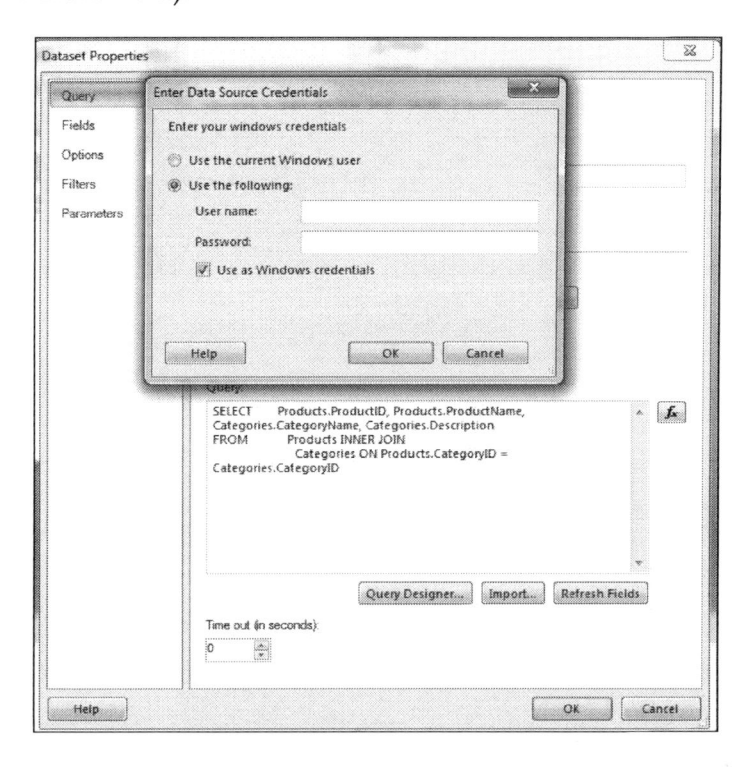

16. Click on **Use the current Window user** (the administrator) of the computer and click on **OK**. The **Report Data** bar is updated as shown:

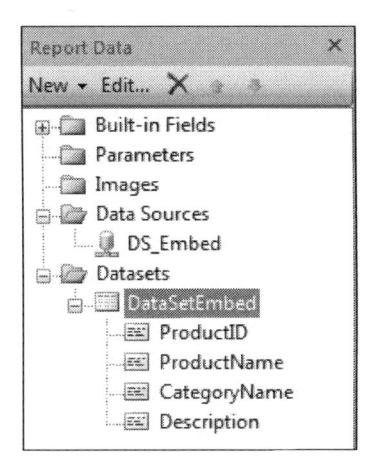

17. On the ribbon, go to **Insert | Table | Insert Table** and click in the report design area under **Click to add title**.

A 3 x 2 table design appears in the design area as shown:

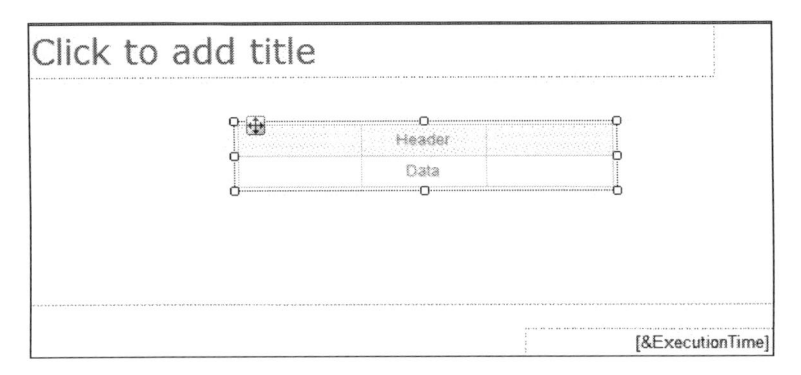

The column name from the database table will occupy the **Header** and in the cell marked **Data,** the data of that column will appear. Notice that when you place your cursor in any cell in the data row a small icon representing the data appears. The table can be extended in all directions by right-clicking the cell and making the right choice. Since we have chosen four columns from the database, we will add another column to the table.

18. Right-click the last column on the right side and choose to add another column to its right as shown in the following screenshot:

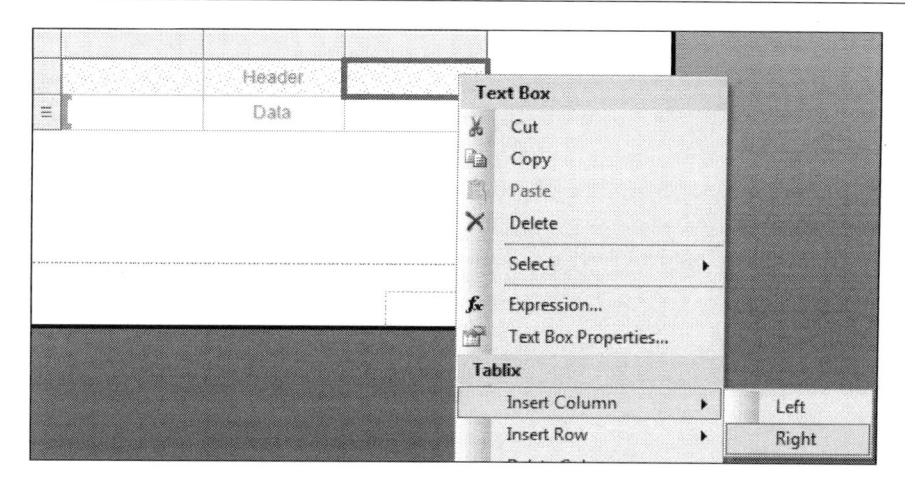

Now we have a 4 x 2 table.

19. Pick the first column and click on the data icon that appears, a pick-list of columns appear as shown in the following screenshot:

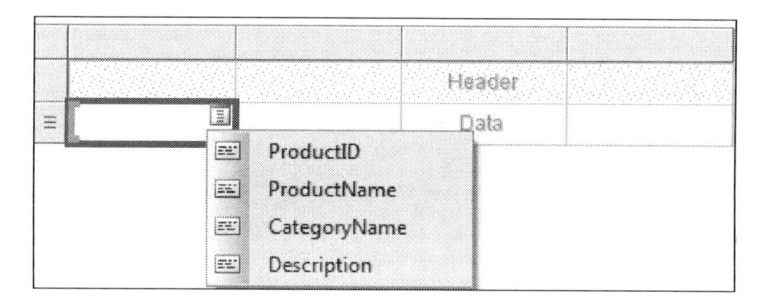

20. You can pick one from this list. Click on **ProductID**. The column header and data appears with **ProductID** in the `Header` and **[ProductID]** in the `Data` cells of the first column.

21. In a similar manner, place the rest of the data from the dataset into the table cells. Notice that the data details are in the row group shown here:

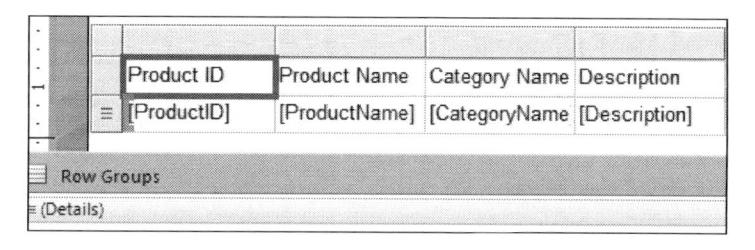

Working with Report Builder 3.0

22. The report is practically done. Click on **Run** from menu or hit *F5*. The **Credentials** page will be displayed asking you to enter your Windows credentials. Enter your credentials.

23. Click on **OK**. The report is displayed after some processing as shown in the following screenshot:

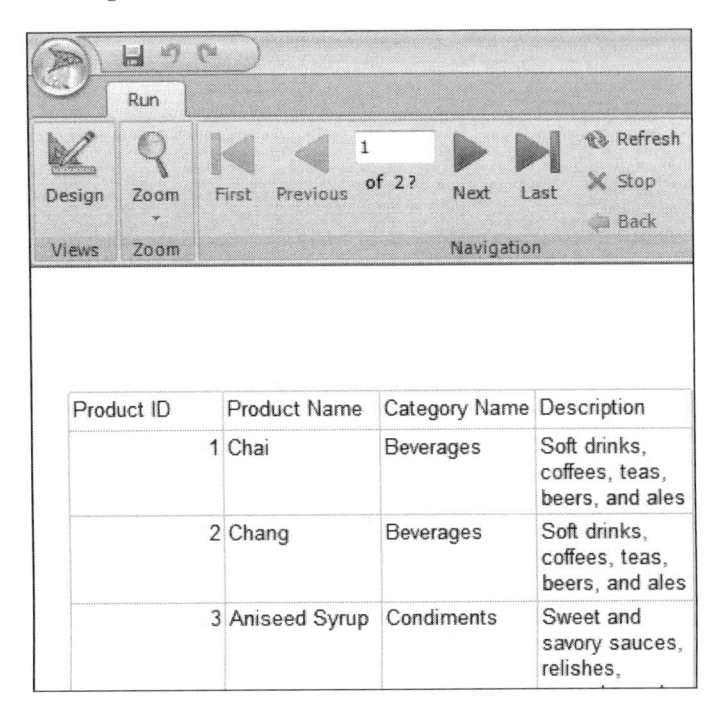

Product ID	Product Name	Category Name	Description
1	Chai	Beverages	Soft drinks, coffees, teas, beers, and ales
2	Chang	Beverages	Soft drinks, coffees, teas, beers, and ales
3	Aniseed Syrup	Condiments	Sweet and savory sauces, relishes,

24. Click on the button shown to open the drop-down menu and choose **Save As**:

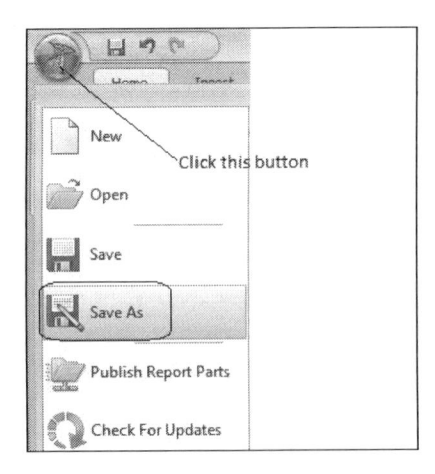

[256]

Chapter 5

In the **Save as Report** window, you can browse and save to a location of your choice on the report server. Here it is saved to a folder called `Sub_Feb19`.

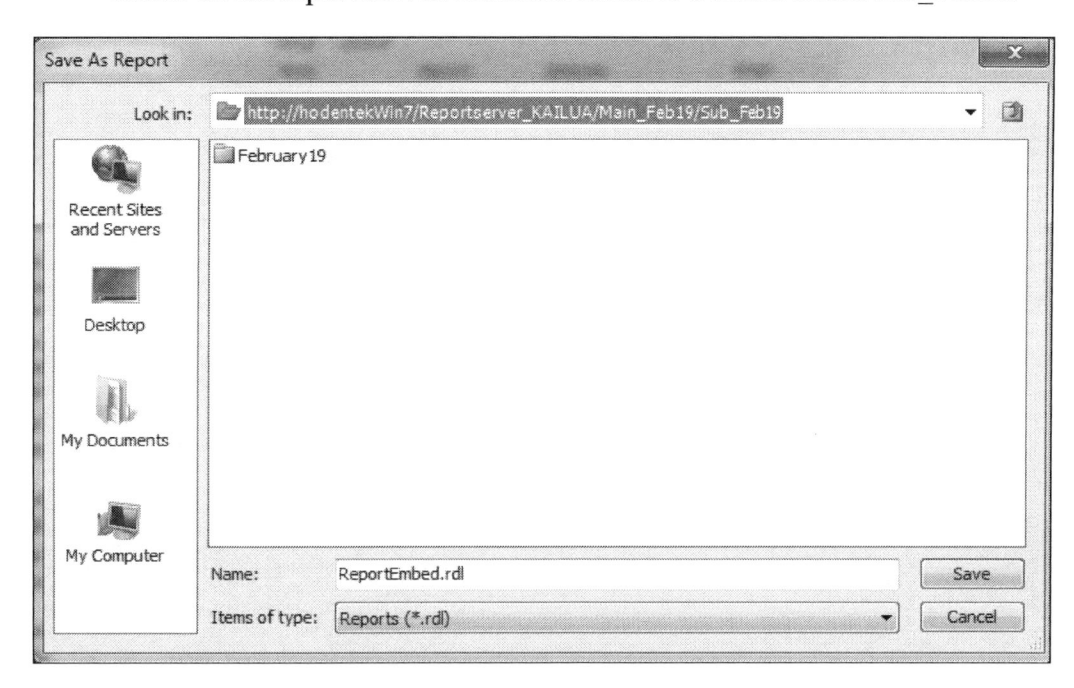

25. Click on **Save** and the report is now saved to the report server. There was an error while saving as shown in the following screenshot:

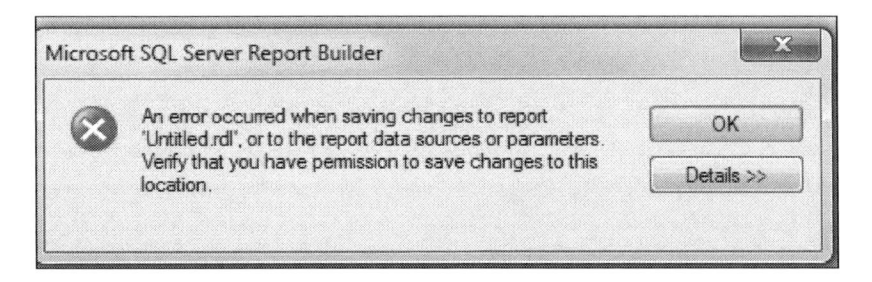

The reason for this was that `Sub_Feb19` did not have the correct permission (its permission at this point was Navigate with very limited capability).

> Any permission issue that needs to be modified is to be carried out on Report Manager as described in *Chapter 4, Working with Report Manager*.

Working with Report Builder 3.0

26. Click on **OK** and save it to the report server (move up from folders) as shown in the following screenshot:

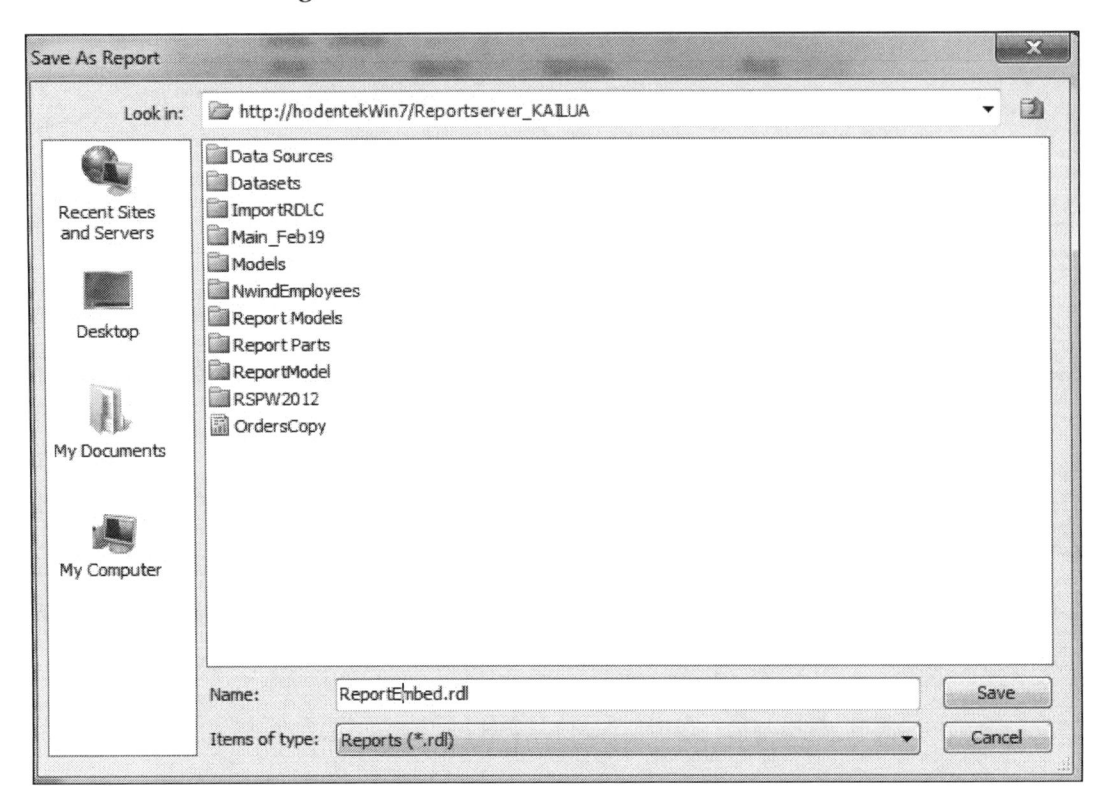

27. Click on **Save**. It is saved to the report server as shown:

Chapter 5

This completes the process of creating a report with an embedded data source and publishing it to the server.

Hands-on exercise 5.2 – creating a report from a shared data source

In *Chapter 4, Working with Report Manager*, we created a data source, a shared data source named `DS_Shared`. In this hands-on exercise, we will create a report using the shared data source on the report server.

> You cannot create a shared data source in Repot Builder and you will have to create one using Report Manager or SSDT.

1. Start Report Builder with **Run As Administrator** permissions.
2. Right-click **Data Sources** under **Report Data**.
3. Click on **Add Data Source...**.
4. The **Data Source Properties** page opens as shown in the following screenshot:

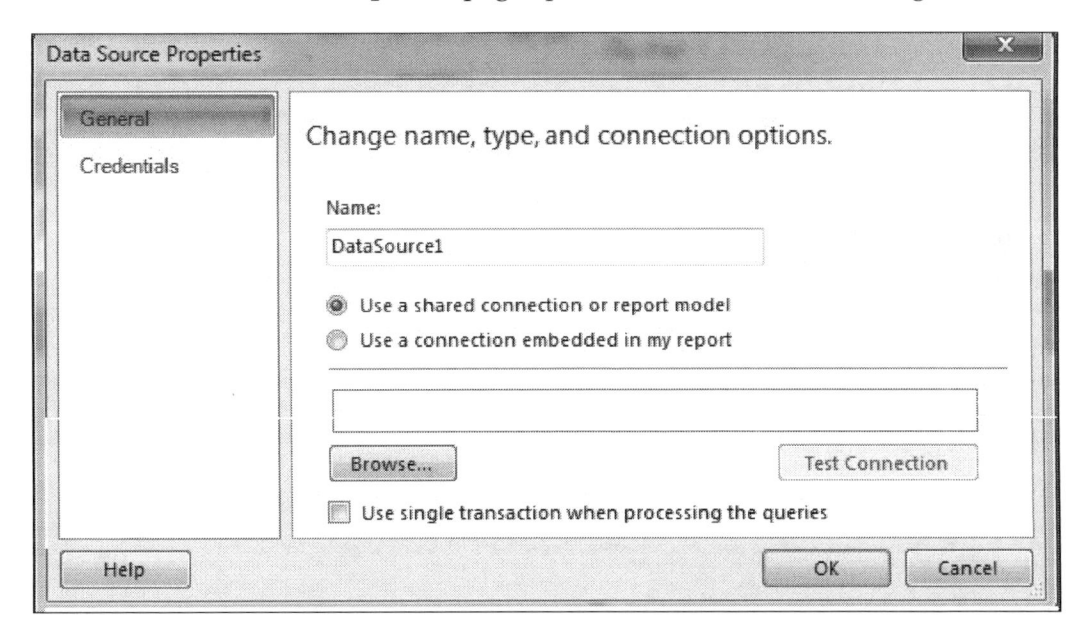

Working with Report Builder 3.0

5. Change `DataSource1` to one of your choice, herein `MSS_Shared`. Click on **Browse...** and choose **DS_Shared** in the `Data Sources` folder on the server. The **Data Source Properties** page gets updated as shown in the following screenshot:

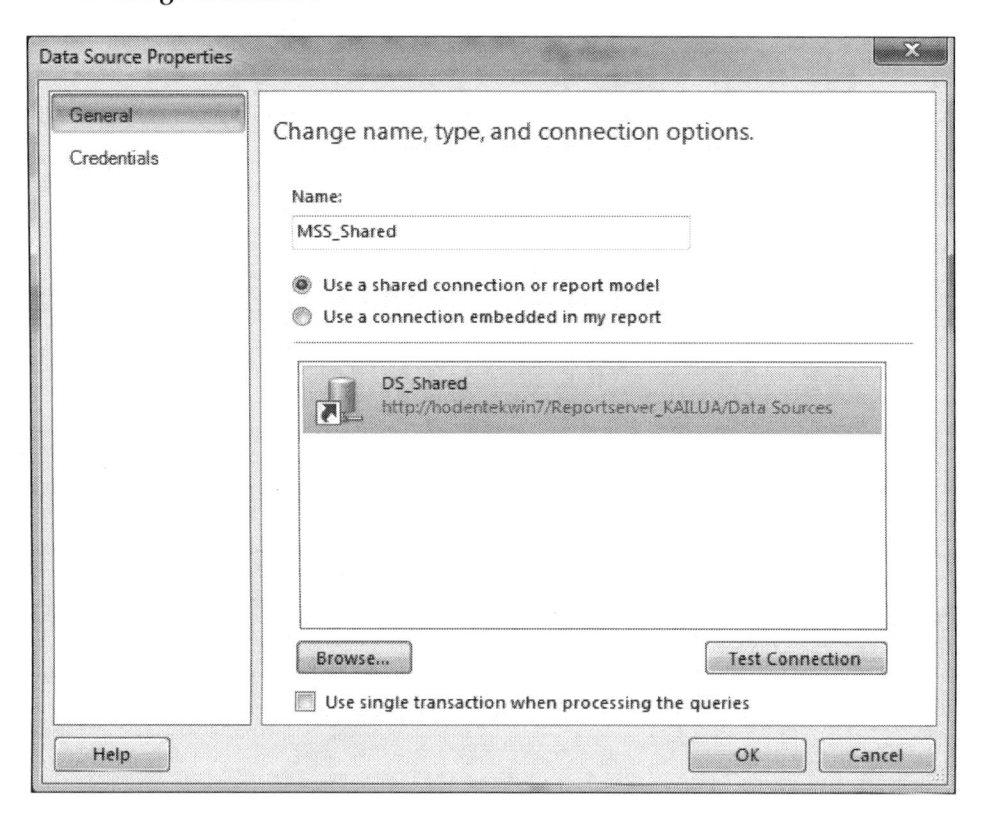

6. Test the connection by hitting the **Test Connection** button. The **Enter Data Source Credentials** window is displayed.
7. Enter the **Data Source Credentials** and click on **OK**.

> When you create a shared data source on Report Manager the permissions are those of the built-in administrator. If there is a problem you can go to Report Manager, and check. If needed, you can modify the security.

You should get a response. If you like, you may place a check mark for remember my password. This is going to appear repeatedly.

Chapter 5

8. Click on **OK** in the **Data Source Properties** page as well. The data source is added to the **Data Sources** node as shown. The icon shows that it is shared:

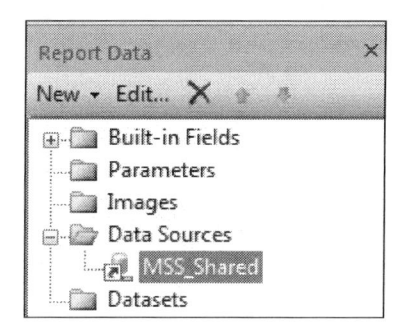

9. Right-click on the **Datasets** node and click on **Add Dataset...**

   The **Dataset Properties** page is displayed with default name `DataSet1` (as a shared dataset).

10. Change the name to one of your choice, herein `Dataset_embed`. Click on **Use a dataset embedded in my report**.

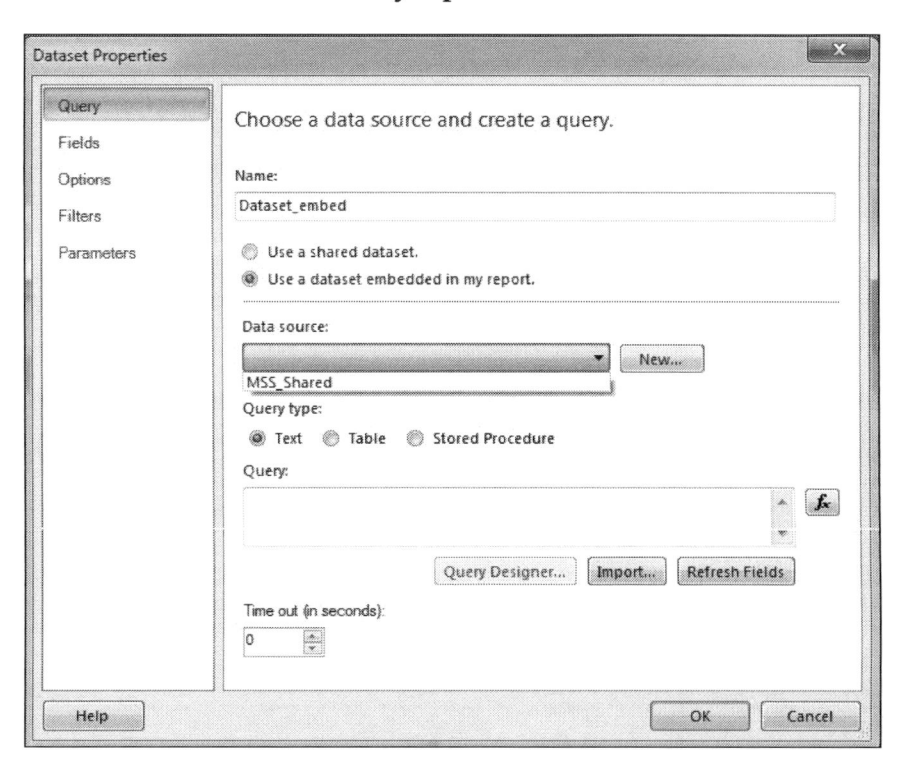

[261]

Working with Report Builder 3.0

11. For the query, you could enter an SQL SELECT statement shown when **Query type** is **Text**.

    ```
    SELECT         Categories.CategoryName, Categories.Description,
    Products.ProductName, Products.ProductID, Products.CategoryID,
    Orders.OrderID, Orders.OrderDate,
                             Orders.RequiredDate, Orders.ShippedDate,
    [Order Details].UnitPrice, [Order Details].ProductID AS Expr1,
    [Order Details].Quantity
    FROM           Products INNER JOIN
                             [Order Details] ON Products.ProductID =
    [Order Details].ProductID INNER JOIN
                             Orders ON [Order Details].OrderID =
    Orders.OrderID INNER JOIN
                             Categories ON Products.CategoryID =
    Categories.CategoryID
    ```

    Alternatively, you could create the query by using the following tables in the Query Designer when you click on the **Query Designer...** button: Order, Order_Details, Products, and Categories. Here the SQL statement will be used.

12. Type in the SQL statement (copy and paste), as shown in the following screenshot:

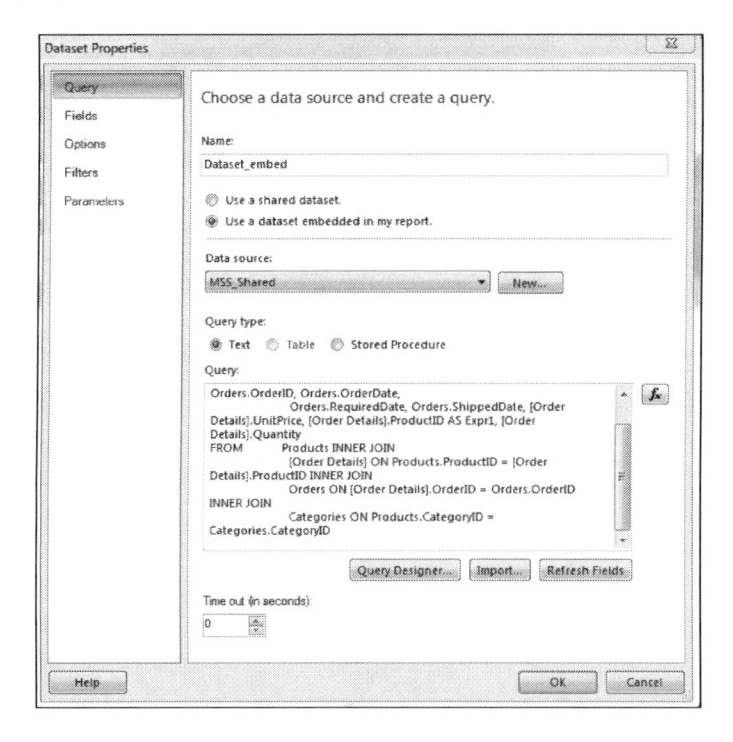

[262]

13. Click on **OK**.
14. The Report Data's `Datasets` folder is updated as shown in the following screenshot:

- Data Sources
  - MSS_Shared
- Datasets
  - Dataset_embed
    - CategoryName
    - Description
    - ProductName
    - ProductID
    - CategoryID
    - OrderID
    - OrderDate
    - RequiredDate
    - ShippedDate
    - UnitPrice
    - Expr1
    - Quantity

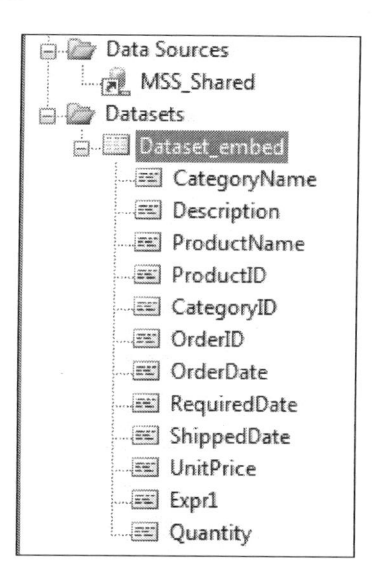

You may choose to create a report of the type you like from this dataset. You need not use all the fields in the dataset; you can pick and choose.

In the next part, we will create report of the `List` type, which is a free form report that allows you to place your report data in any suitable way you like.

Creating a List report

A `List` report is a free-form report that does not adhere to the column and row confines of a table or matrix report.

1. On the ribbon, click on **Insert** and double-click on **List**.
2. A list is added to the report as shown in the following screenshot:

Click to add title

[&ExecutionTime]

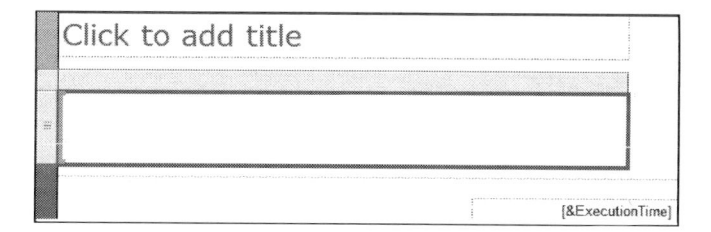

3. Now you can drag and drop items from the dataset on to the list at locations of your choice:

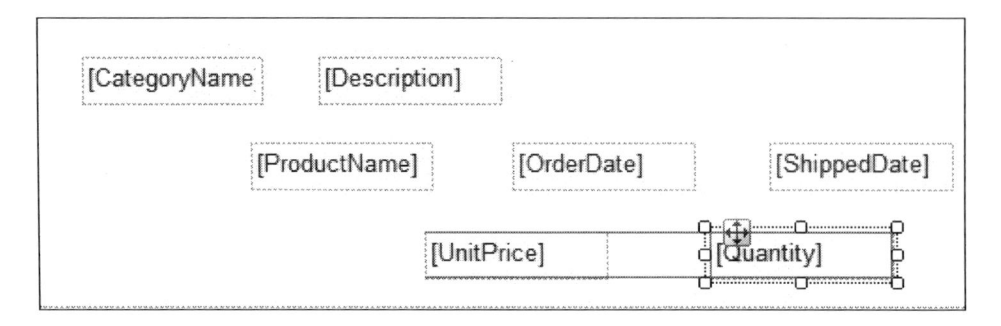

[CategoryName] [Description]

  [ProductName]   [OrderDate]   [ShippedDate]

      [UnitPrice]   [Quantity]

Use the guide lines (horizontal and vertical) to align them as shown in the preceding screenshot. You see only horizontal guides and if the cells are near alignment vertically you will see the vertical guides as well.

4. Right-click any item and you can change **Text Box Properties...** as well as inserting an **Expression** as shown for the **[Description]** item in the following screenshot:

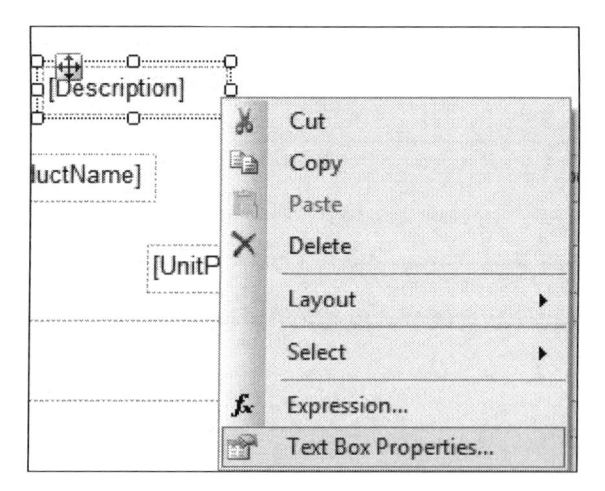

5. Click on **Text Box Properties...** and the **Text Box Properties** window is displayed as shown in the following screenshot:

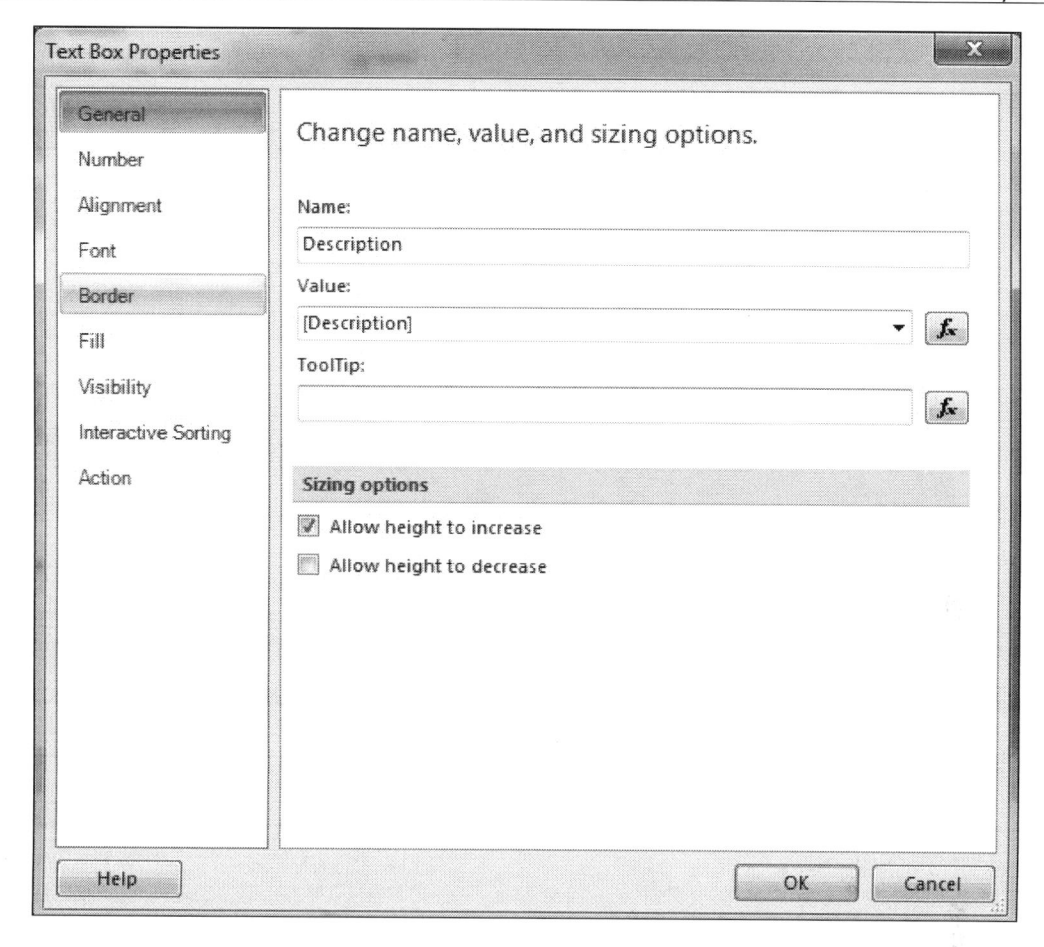

Lot of features can be changed. The properties that can be changed are in the left navigable pane such as **General**, **Number**, and so on, and clicking any item provides the page for the item, which you can modify. These were described in *Chapter 7, Report Authoring with Report Builder 2.0*, of the first edition of the book where the **Interactive Sorting** and **Visibility** properties were modified. You will see few more in *Hands-on exercise 5.5*.

6. Click on **Cancel**.
7. Run the report from the menu or hit *F5* with focus on the report.

Working with Report Builder 3.0

8. The report is displayed as shown in the following screenshot:

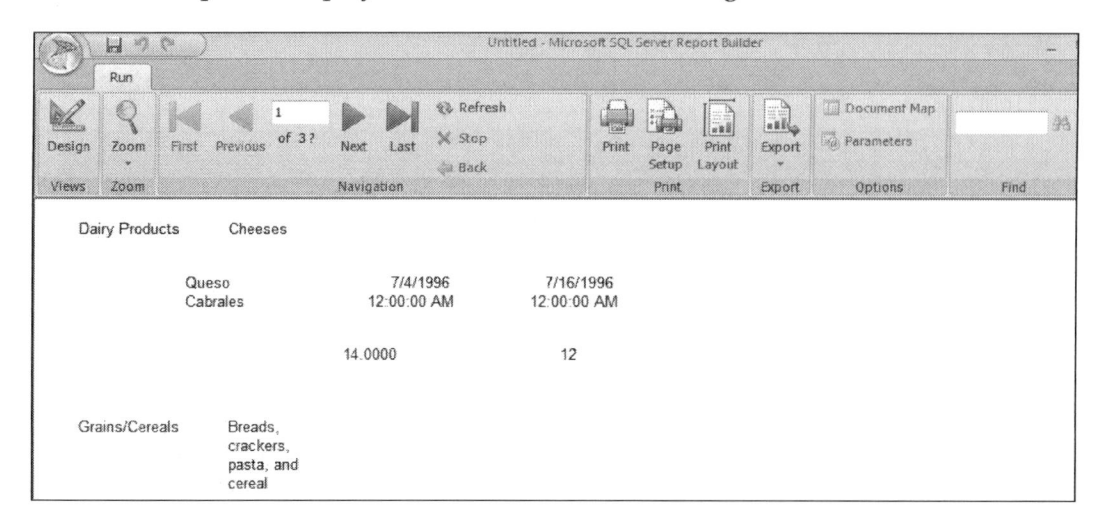

This is pretty bland and can be improved using many other possible things you can do using Report Builder.

9. Now save the report using the **Save As** menu item.
10. Save as `ReportSharedDataSource` to the server.

```
Tuesday,   February 19, 2013 10:26 AM       <dir> Report Parts
Saturday,  February 23, 2013  2:03 PM       18333 ReportEmbed
Thursday,  February 21, 2013  1:23 PM       <dir> ReportModel
Saturday,  February 23, 2013  6:01 PM       19386 ReportSharedDataSource
Tuesday,   February 05, 2013  4:41 PM       <dir> RSPW2012
```

11. Open Report Manager and review the preceding report:

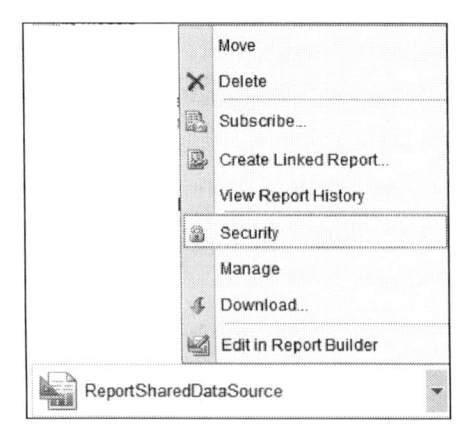

12. Click on **Security** and verify the properties of the report.

Parameterized reports

Filtering the data is an essential part of effectively retrieving relevant data in a short time.

A parameterized report depends on the report reader typing in the specific parameter to complete the processing of the report. The output of a parameterized report would depend on the parameter(s). Parameterized reports are frequently used in creating drill-through reports, linked reports, and subreports.

There are two kinds of parameters used in Report Builder 3.0: report parameters and query parameters. Query parameters are used at the source of data during data retrieval. For the query parameter, a value must be specified by the user (or a default value provided) to complete the processing of the SELECT statement or the stored procedure in the query. The usage of query parameters requires you to make trips to the server for processing the query as the data is first processed before it is used in the report.

Report parameters are used during report processing with most data available at hand where the filtering is made. Hence, report parameters work on a larger dataset and they are processed in the report.

Parameterized report authoring was described in a detailed hands-on exercise 7.1 in the 1st edition of the book in *Chapter 7, Report Authoring with Report Builder 2.0*, in the book *Learning SQL Server 2008 Reporting Services, Jayaram Krishnaswamy* by *Packt Publishing*. The next section uses a parameterized report as well.

Subreports

Using subreports is an excellent method to merge several reports and produce a consolidated report. Subreports can be linked or unlinked. In the case of a linked report, there is a synchronization of information between the main report and the subreports. There is no such synchronization in an unlinked subreport. Subreports are invaluable in displaying details in parent/child tables. There is no limit on the number of subreports a main report can have. Since the subreport is going to occupy a certain physical region on the main report, its layout may have to be properly sized. Creating a main report that uses a subreport was also described with an example in the first edition of the book mentioned previously.

Working with Report Builder 3.0

Hands-on exercise 5.3 – creating a report that has a subreport

We will be using the same data source, the `Northwind` database on SQL Server 2012 KAILUA for both the main report as well as the subreport. The subreport is embedded (placed inside) in the main report.

In the following section we will create a subreport, which will later be inserted into the main report.

Creating the subreport

1. Create a data source `DataSource1` (default name) from the `Northwind` database. Use the following connection string and test it:

   `Data Source=HODENTEKWIN7\\KAILUA; Initial Catalog=Northwind`

2. Create a dataset with the following properties (items that you use in the wizard):
   - Name: `QryProducts`
   - Query type: **text**
   - Dataset is embedded in the report;
   - Query:

   ```
   SELECT
   Products.ProductName, Products.CategoryID AS [Products CategoryID]
   ,Products.ProductID ,Products.UnitPrice ,Products.UnitsInStock
   ,Categories.CategoryID AS [Categories CategoryID]
           FROM
   Categories
   INNER JOIN Products ON Categories.CategoryID = Products.
   CategoryIDWHERE Categories.CategoryID = @CategoriesCategoryID
   ```

3. Drop a table from the **Insert** menu and populate the cells of the table with the values. The `ExecutionTime` variable is normally in the footer. Herein, it has been shifted to a blank row of the table and centered. If the main report has an execution time, it may not be even necessary.

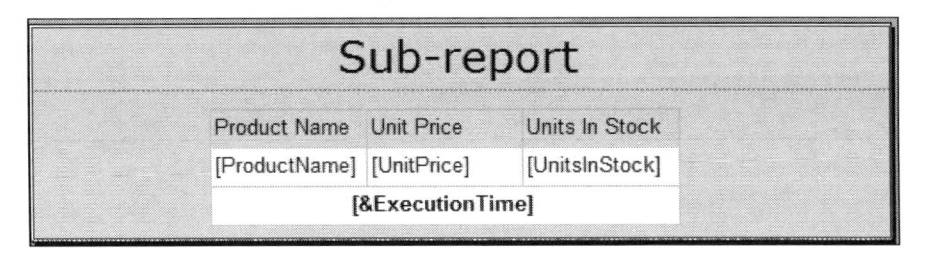

> Note that the preceding report has a **@CategoriesCategoryID** parameter (review the query earlier), which takes integer values. When you run the report (hit *F5*) you can change the parameter and see what is displayed for those values. The first time it shows a value for the parameter=1.

Making background-color of alternate rows different

When a report consists of a large number of rows of data close together, it will be nice to have alternate rows highlighted in some way. This is usually achieved by making the background color of alternate rows gray. This can be implemented by conditionally formatting the background color of data rows.

1. Click on **View** and place a check mark for **Properties**. This is needed so that we can set the properties for the table rows.
2. Choose the entire row of data whose background color needs to be changed as shown in the following screenshot:

3. In the properties of rows, type the following expression in the background color's **Fill** field as shown or you can invoke the **Expression** builder to build this statement.

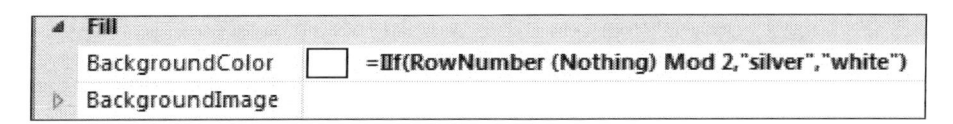

4. Run the report (hit *F5*) and you will see the following screenshot:

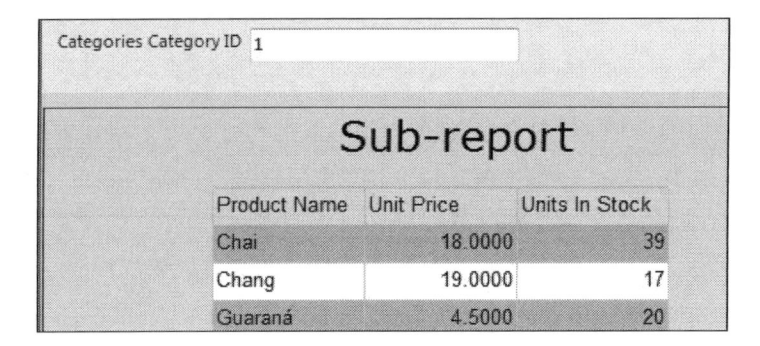

Product Name	Unit Price	Units In Stock
Chai	18.0000	39
Chang	19.0000	17
Guaraná	4.5000	20

Categories Category ID 1 — Sub-report

5. Save the report to a local folder or to the report server. Herein, the name `ProductsSubReport` was used.

Creating the main report

The main report can be of any type, a table, a list, and few more. In this example we will use a list (you have seen this in an earlier hands-on exercise):

1. Create a new blank report from the **Getting Started** screen when you launch the Report Builder.

2. Create a data source `DataSourceMain`, the same exact data source used for the `ProductsSubReport` in the previous step. This is also an embedded source.

3. Create a dataset, `QryCTG`, the query type is text and the dataset is embedded. Use the following query statement:

   ```
   SELECT Categories.CategoryName, Categories.Description,
   Categories.Picture,
   Products.ProductID, Products.ProductName, Products.
   QuantityPerUnit, Products.UnitPrice,Categories.CategoryID
   FROM Categories INNER JOIN Products ON Categories.CategoryID =
   Products.CategoryID WHERE Products.CategoryID=@Parameter1
   ```

Adding a freeform report (List)

A List control that you can drop on the report design interface is used for a freeform report:

1. From the **Insert** main menu, click on **List** and place it on the design surface.

2. From the QryCTG dataset, drag the following fields to the **List** that you placed earlier: **CategoryName, Description**.
3. In the same **List**, right-click an empty region to display a list of objects that you can insert as shown in the following screenshot:

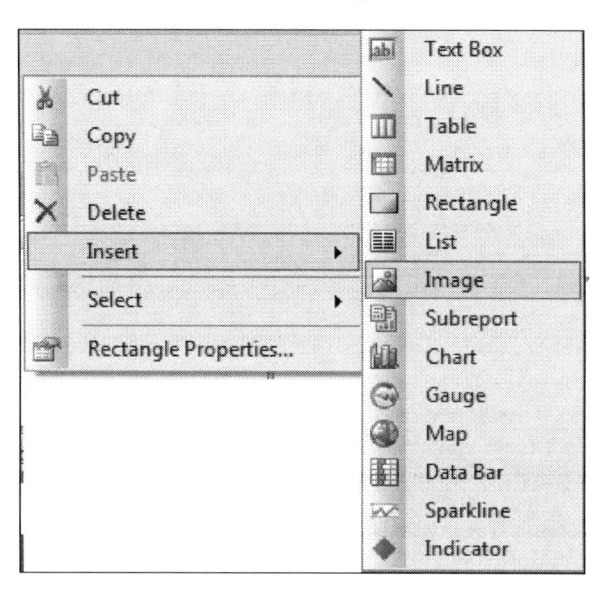

4. Click on **Image** and this places an image control on the list. The **Image Properties** page is displayed.
5. In the **General** tab of this window, change the **Select the image source** from **Embedded** to **database**; two more controls are displayed with handles. For **Use this field**, select **[Picture]** from the drop-down list; for the **Use this MIME type** field, use **image/bmp** from the drop-down list.

    Click on the symbol to invoke the **Expression** builder for the field marked; use this field where we placed the picture. The expression value is as shown here:

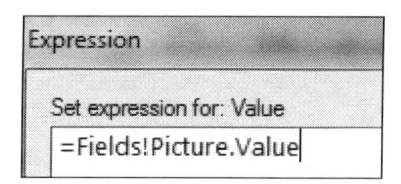

6. Replace the preceding expression by the following code. This is needed for the BMP files to display without an error:

    =System.Convert.FromBase64String(Mid(System.Convert.
    ToBase64String(Fields!Picture.Value),105))

7. Click on **OK** in the **Expression** builder tool and **OK** on the **Image Properties** page.

8. The report now appears as shown. The other changes are cosmetic, that you can do from report properties or using the ribbon.

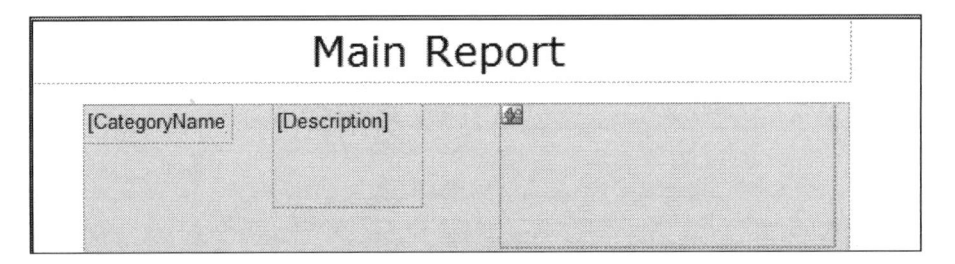

	Main Report	
[CategoryName]	[Description]	

9. Remember, in QryCTG we used a **Parameter1** parameter (you will see this when you click the **Parameters** node under **Report Data** of this report). If we run the report it would run, but then we would have to supply the parameter each time. What we need is a drop-down pick-list.

10. For this purpose we create another dataset, named **Dataset1**, which uses the same data source DataSourceMain as the main report, but the embedded query uses the following statement and returns just one field:

    Select CategoryID FROM Categories;

11. Run the report and verify that it works and displays the images as well.

12. Save the report as Subrep.

Embedding the subreport in the main report

Now we have two reports: the ProductsSubReport and the Subrep report. We will embed ProductsSubReport in the Subrep report. There are different ways you can place the subreport in a report as described in *Chapter 6, Working with the Report Builder*, of the first edition of this book. Briefly, the subreport can be a part of the main report designed to be of List type; the subreport can occupy one of the cells in a table type report, or it can be placed apart from the main report.

Chapter 5

The business scenarios that would require a subreport usually involve parent-child relationships where the parent will be main report and the children's report forms the subreport.

1. Open the Subrep report in the design view.
2. Right-click an empty region inside the List that you added, to display the same drop-down list you displayed when you added the image control previously.
3. Click on **Subreport** in the drop-down menu displayed. A gray-colored rectangle gets into the main report. This will be occupied by the ProductsSubReport.
4. Right-click the **Subreport** to display its properties as shown in the following screenshot (**Use this report as a subreport will be empty**):

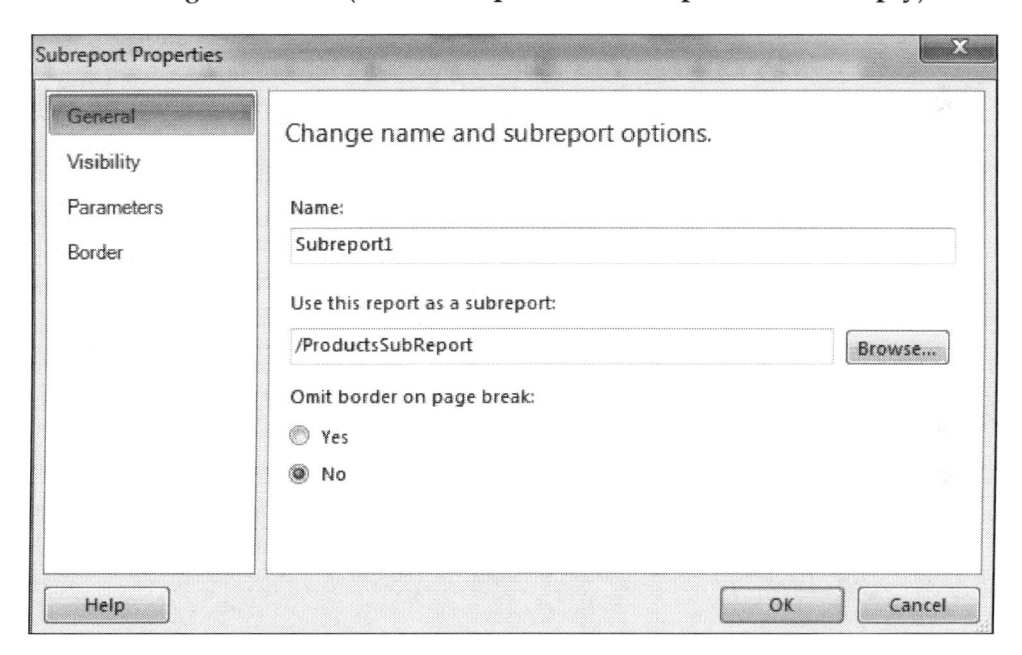

5. Use the **Browse...** button to insert ProductsSubReport (either from your local file system or from the report server). It is added as shown (/ProductsSubReport).

Working with Report Builder 3.0

6. Click on the **Parameters** tab and use the handles to point the parameter to point as shown in the following screenshot:

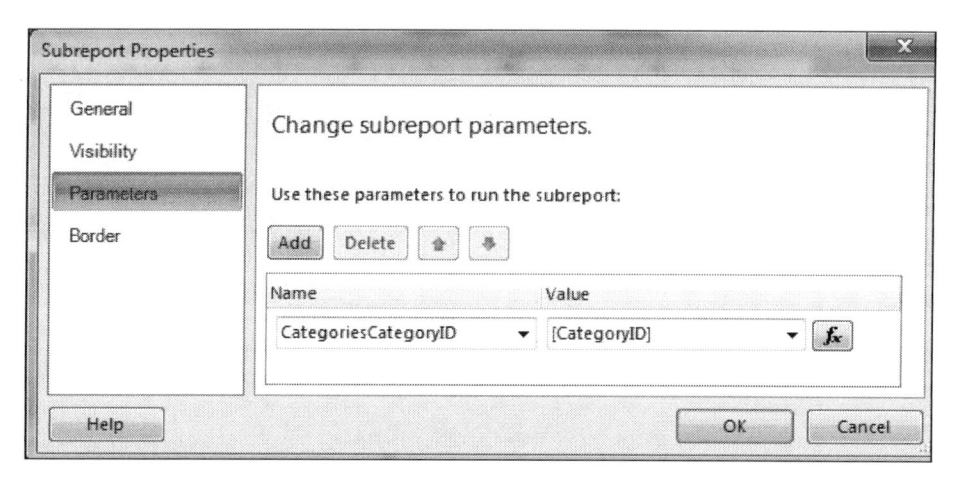

7. Click on **OK**. `ProductsSubReport` is now configured correctly.
8. The main report appears as shown:

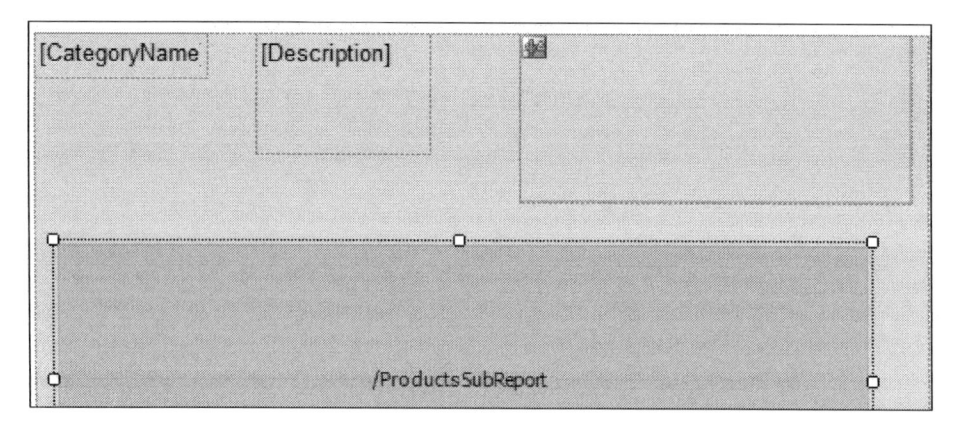

9. Run the main report (named `Subreport`). The report will be displayed as shown in the following screenshot:

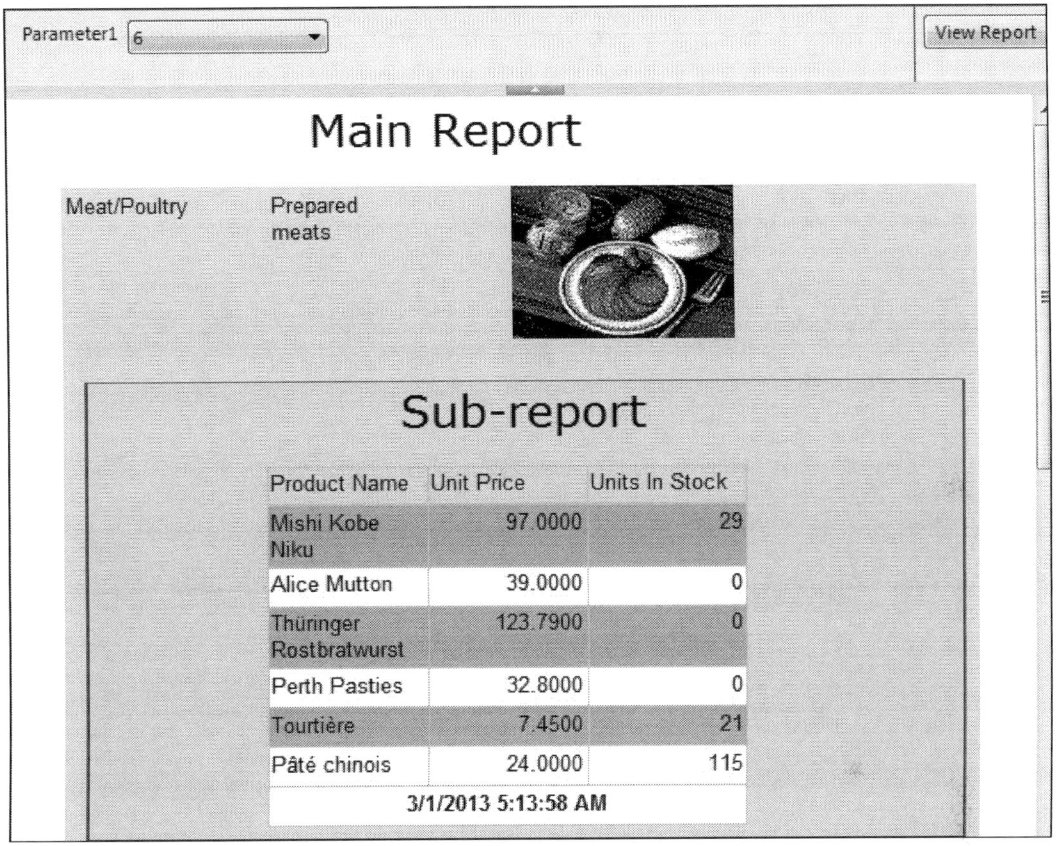
Parameter1
6
View Report
Main Report
Meat/Poultry
Prepared meats
Sub-report
Product Name
Unit Price
Units In Stock
Mishi Kobe Niku
97.0000
29
Alice Mutton
39.0000
0
Thüringer Rostbratwurst
123.7900
0
Perth Pasties
32.8000
0
Tourtière
7.4500
21
Pâté chinois
24.0000
115
3/1/2013 5:13:58 AM

10. Save the main report.

Report with groups

A group in a report is a named set of data from the report dataset that you bind to a data region. You will use a simple example of this in this hands-on. There could be many other groups as well. The layout designer in Report Builder 3.0 assigns this intuitively. You could have groupings by rows or columns. We will be using groups in most of the hands-on exercises without explicitly mentioning it.

Working with Report Builder 3.0

Hands-on exercise 5.4 – setting up a group and creating a document map

Demographic data provides a good example of the idea of groups. The global data of country is first broken up into information pertaining to states and information related to the states in turn comes from the various counties. Grouping of information helps in providing global pictures of the state of things of importance such as education, health, welfare programs, and so on.

Report Builder's GUI provides a great deal of support for groupings of data in a database.

In the previous hands-on exercise, you created a query that had a parameter in it. You later associated this with the report. As we are going to use the same report, at first, you will modify the query to drop the parameter. Once the parameter is dropped, you have no filtering and you will get all the rows.

To work with groups, you will start with this set from a single data source. Using this source, you will group your data based on `City`.

Bring up the report from the previous hands-on exercise and remove a parameter

You need to bring up the report either from the report server, if you saved it there, or from the file system. You should look for the report file, `ParametricReport.rdl`.

We are doing this because we want to use the report we created earlier. We could start from scratch as well. However, by doing this we also learn how to undo things.

1. From the button at top-left side of Report Builder 3.0, click on **Open** and browse. Most likely, you will find it in the adjoining list of **Recent Documents**.
2. Double-click on **Dataset1**. This brings up the **Dataset Properties** page, click on the **Parameters** tab as shown in the following screenshot:

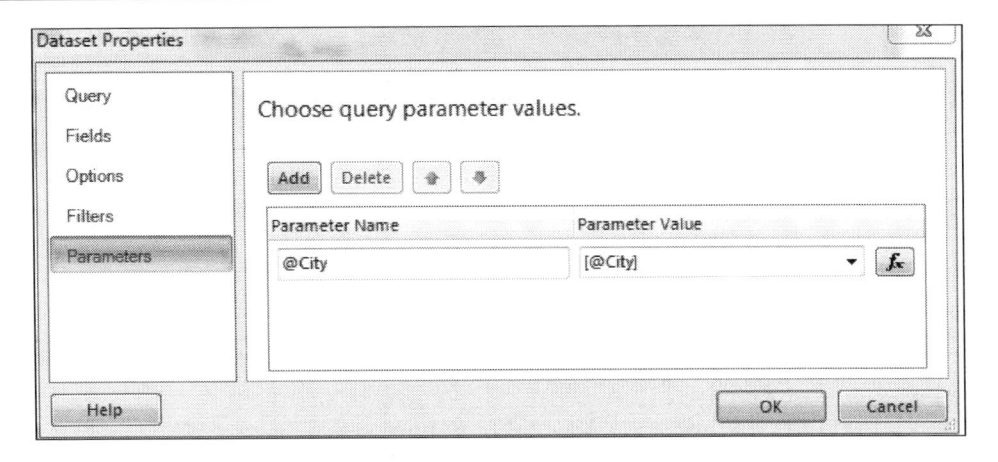

3. Click next to **Parameter Name** to display value **@City**. Both the boxes get a gray border and the **Delete** button is enabled. However, it appears this will not modify the query.

4. Click on **Delete** and click on **OK** to the **Dataset Properties** screen and in the **Query** tabbed page remove the where clause:

   `"WHERE Customers.City LIKE @City"`

5. Then, delete **@City** from the **Parameters** node under **Report Data**. Run the report (hit *F5*) and verify that the parameter for searching is removed.

6. Delete the **Total** row as well. Verify the third row has been removed.

Adding a group to the data

Right now, there is no column grouping. We have seen earlier that the data can be grouped by **City** or **Country** and we will now create a column group.

1. Delete the **Country** column as shown in the following screenshot:

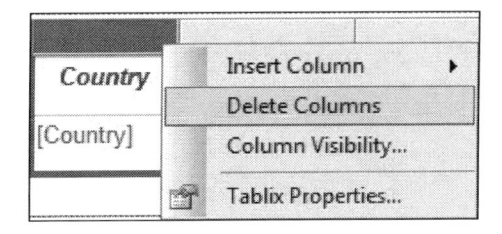

Working with Report Builder 3.0

2. Right-click on the first column as shown in the next screenshot:

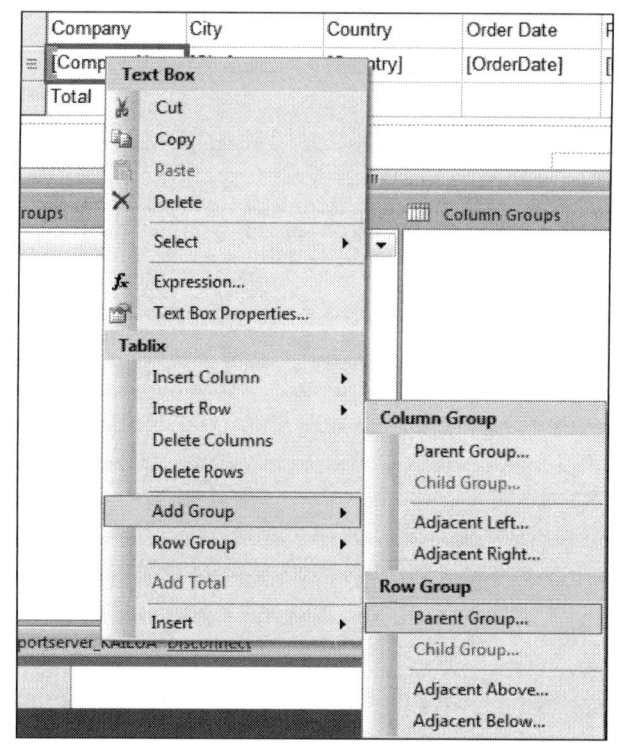

As mentioned earlier, the parent-child relationship should exist to realize the creation of groups. By choosing the **Parent Group** we will choose an item in the data, which is used for the group. In the following steps we create a group, Country; and all data will be grouped on the basis of **Country**.

3. Then, click on **Parent Group...** under **Row Group**. The **Tablix group** window is displayed as shown in the following screenshot:

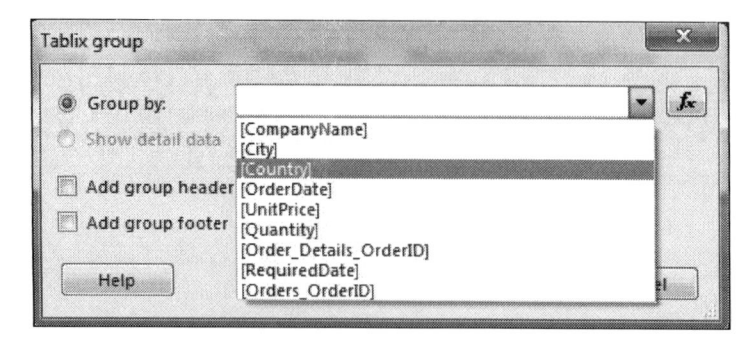

[278]

4. Click on **Country** in the drop-down list, place check marks for **Add group header** and **Add group footer** and click on **OK**. The table layout changes as shown in the following screenshot:

Country	Company Name	City	Country	Order Date	Required Date	Unit Price
[Country]						
	[CompanyName]	[City]	[Country]	[OrderDate]	[RequiredDate]	[UnitPrice]

5. Run the report (hit *F5*) and verify that you have groups of data under **Country**.

6. Here is an image of the parts of group under **France** and **Germany**. By adjusting the page, we can make the report to show only the country chosen by page breaks.

France	Bon app'	Marseille	France	5/6/1998 12:00:00 AM	6/3/1998 12:00:00 AM	9.2000
Germany						
	Toms Spezialitäten	Münster	Germany	7/5/1996 12:00:00 AM	8/16/1996 12:00:00 AM	18.6000
	Toms Spezialitäten	Münster	Germany	7/5/1996 12:00:00 AM	8/16/1996 12:00:00 AM	42.4000

Working with Report Builder 3.0

Adding a Document Map to the report

Document Map is a navigational feature that, when implemented, allows the user to navigate through the document and its hierarchies. When a document map is added, an extra side panel is added to the report much like the "List of Chapters" in a book. You can jump to a directed location from the navigation list.

1. Click on the **Country** row group as shown in the following screenshot:

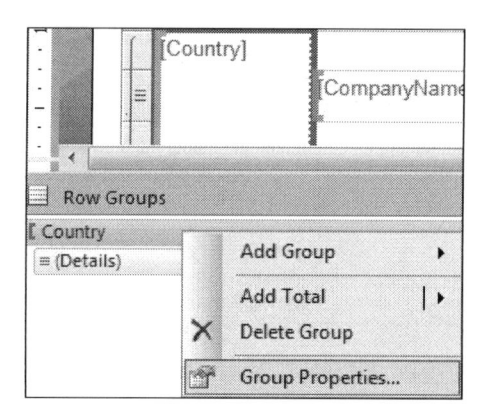

2. Then, click on **Group Properties...**.
3. In the **Group Properties** window displayed, click on **Advanced**.

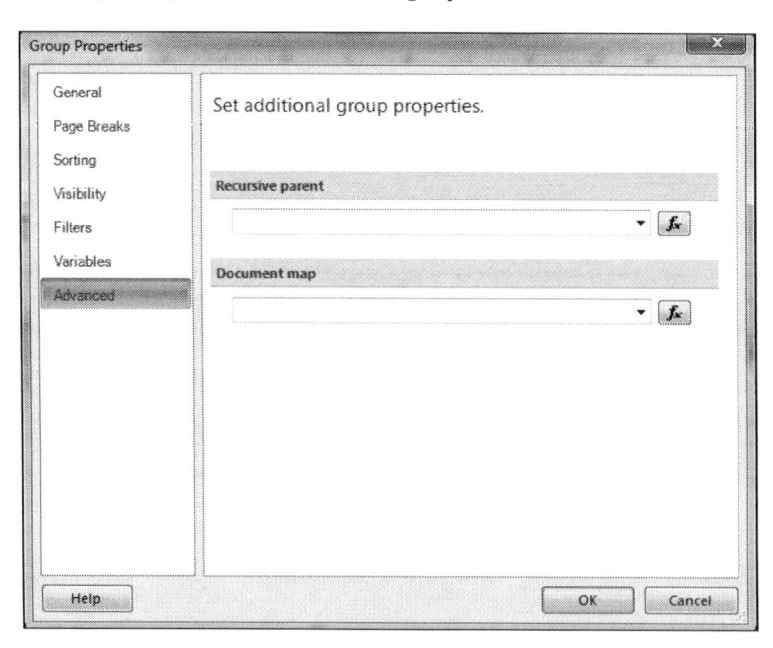

4. Click on the handle under **Document Map** and choose **Country**. Click on **OK**.

5. Run the report (by pressing *F5*), and the report is displayed as shown. The document map is on the left-hand side and **Country** is linked to the data on the details side.

Configuring page breaks

Sometimes you want page breaks in a report, either for improving the performance (you don't need to load all the rows) or to control amount of information on a page. The **Group Properties** window can also help you set this up.

1. Bring up the **Group Properties** window as before and click on **Page Breaks** tab.

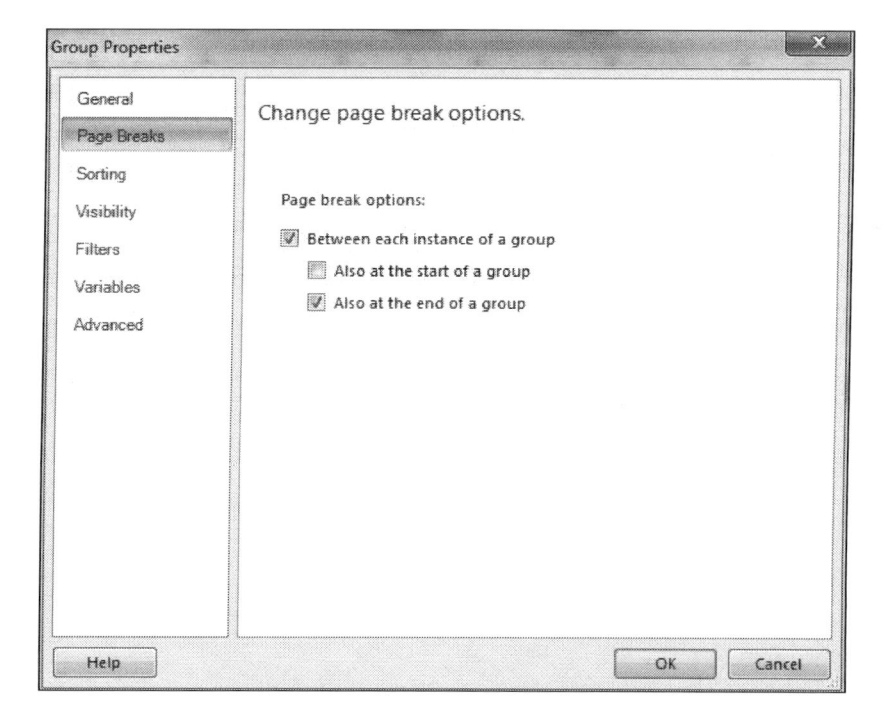

[281]

2. Place check marks as shown and click on **OK**.
3. Review the displayed report and experiment with this property.
4. Save the report, either to the local folder or to the report server.

Adding interactive sorting

Interactive sort is one of the sort methods available. With interactive sort, the user can sort the results of the column(s) by just clicking on the column heading (usually the textbox that holds the column heading). Windows Explorer also has this property and you can sort on any column. You must implement the interactive sorting for reports in the design.

The methods available for sorting are:

- Sort data in a dataset query (use ORDER BY clause)
- Define a sort expression for a data region or a group
- Provide interactive sort buttons to tables and matrices

We now look at adding interactive sorting to one of the columns in the report.

1. Click on **CompanyName** in the table as shown in the following screenshot. Initially this textbox will be empty.

2. This brings up its properties page as shown in the following screenshot:

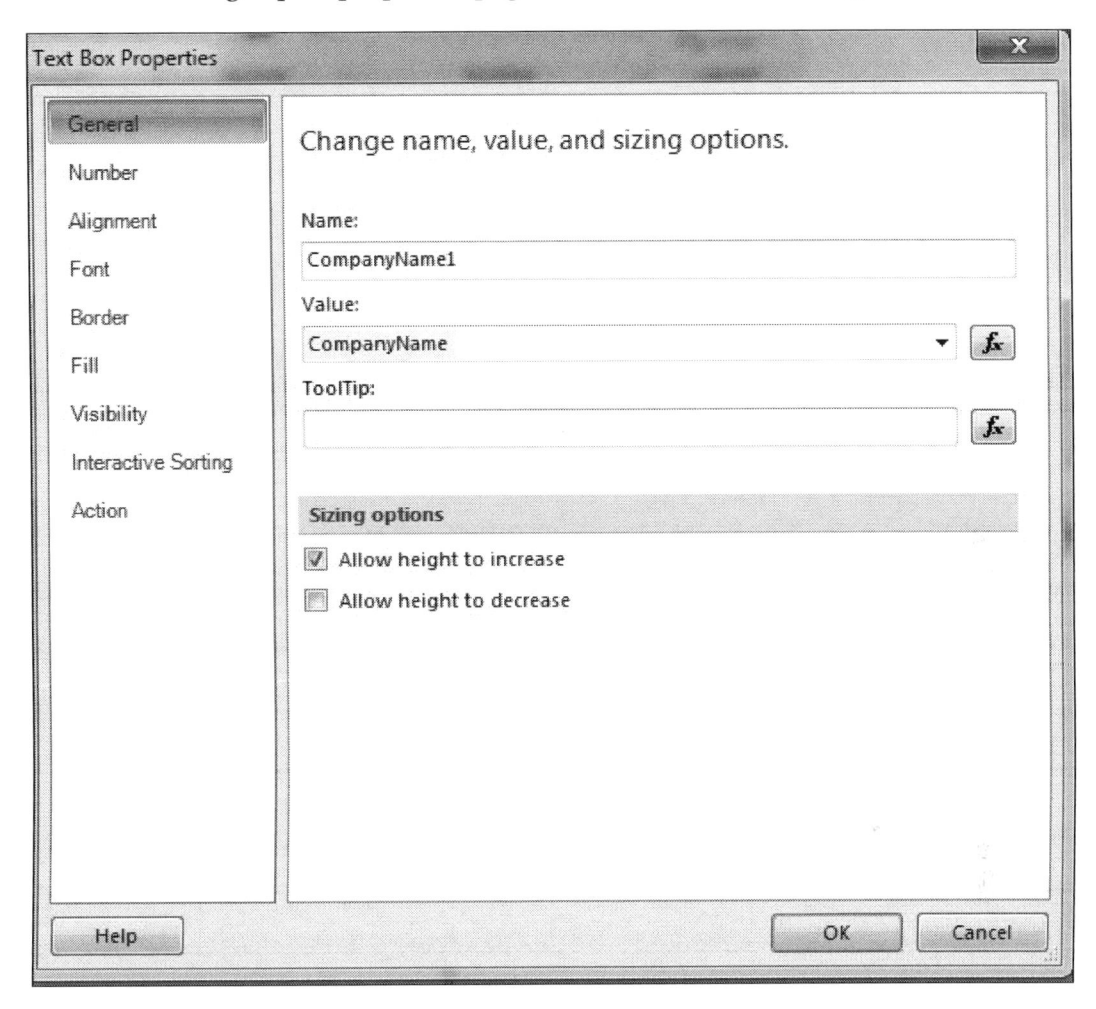

3. Type `CompanyName` in the **Value** field as shown in the preceding screenshot.

4. Click on **Interactive Sorting** and fill in details as shown using drop-down boxes.

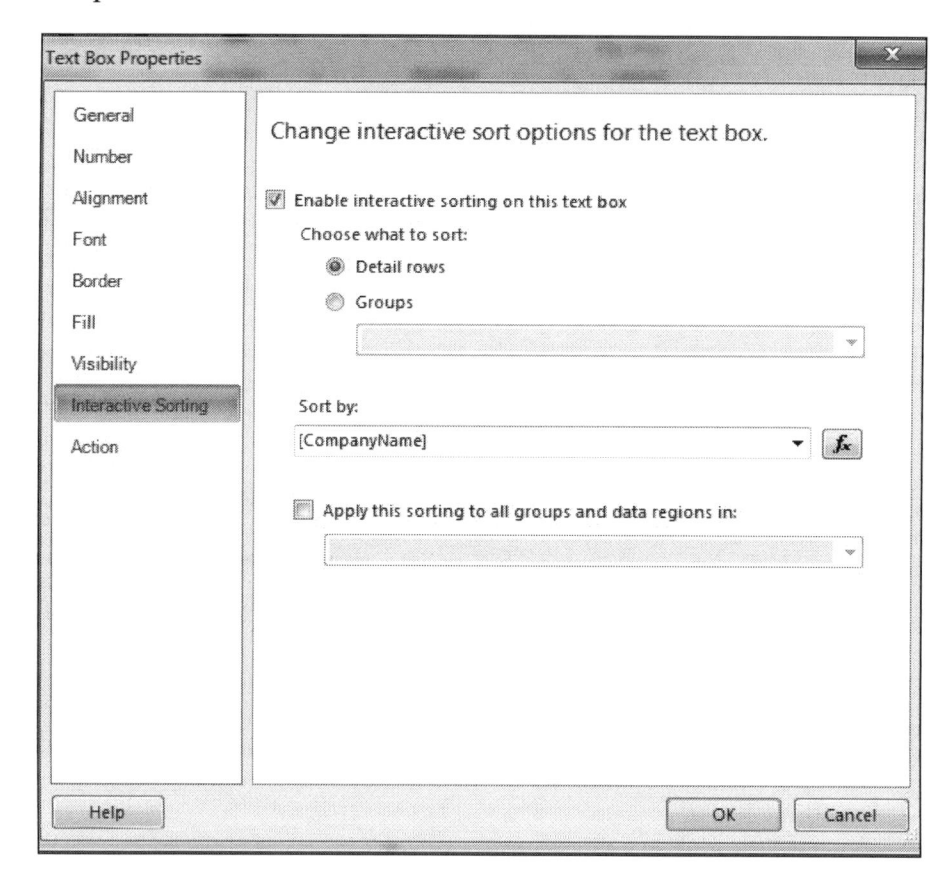

5. Click on **OK**. Run the report (hit *F5*). The report gets displayed as shown. You can click the little arrow and sort the **CompanyName** column for all **Country** in the Document Map.
6. Save it as `DocMapInteractiveSort`.

Drill-through and drill-down reports

If you are working with information, especially lots of it, it is overwhelming to confront all of the data in one shot. The drill-through and drill-down reports make your life relatively easy by introducing features that help you to wade through data easily. Drill-through and drill-down reports are some of the features originating from data analytics.

Drill-through reports

A drill-through report passes a parameter to a target (destination report) report via a link in the report. When you click the link, you get more information related to what you clicked. The drill-through report is called the source report. The destination report is a parametric report that receives the parameter from the source report. The drill-through links can only be textboxes or images (look up the property boxes of textboxes and images).

For example, the Orders table and the Order Details table have a 1-to-n relationship. For each order, there are many details. If you had to look up something about the details of an order, if you know the OrderID, you can look up the details.

Hands-on exercise 5.5 – Creating a drill-through report

We create two reports: a source report that uses the Orders table and a destination report that uses the Order Details table. For both sources, we use the same Northwind database on the Kailua server as in the other hands-on exercises.

Source report

We will create a simple source report using the Orders table in Northwind database:

1. Use a blank report.
2. Add a data source embedded in the report called DataSource1 (Default name) using Northwind database on the SQL Server 2012 KAILUA server.
3. Add a dataset using the following:
    - DataSource1 (embedded dataset)
    - Query type : **text**
    - Query:

   SELECT OrderId, CustomerId FROM Orders

4. Drop a table on the design surface from **Insert** menu item

Working with Report Builder 3.0

5. In the 3 x 2 table, populate the first and second column using the `OrderId` and `CustomerID` fields from the dataset as shown in the following screenshot:

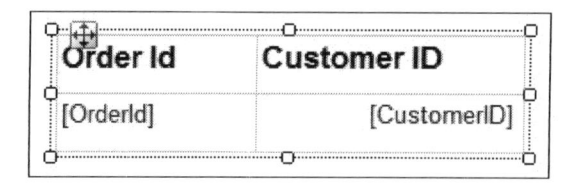

Order Id	Customer ID
[OrderId]	[CustomerID]

6. When you run this report, you will see several pages of this table. Saves this table as `OrdersOnly`.

Destination report

We create the destination report using the `Order_Details` table.

1. Create an embedded data source using the same type of connection to `Northwind` database on SQL Server 2012 KAILUA.

2. Create an embedded dataset with query type as **text** with the following query:

   `SELECT * FROM [Order Details] where OrderID=@OrdID`

   `@OrdID` is a parameter.

3. Drop a table element from the **Insert** menu. Assign the fields in the dataset to the table cells as shown:

Product ID	Unit Price	Quantity	Discount
[ProductID]	[UnitPrice]	[Quantity]	[Discount]

4. Run the report and provide a value for `OrderID` (such as 10248, 10257, and so on). You may have to know these `OrderID` values just for testing.

5. Save the report as `OrderDetails`.

[286]

Set up the drill-through action

We need to associate using a link in the source that sends out a parameter to the destination.

1. Bring up the source report and right-click in the `OrderID` data cell to display the properties for that cell as shown:

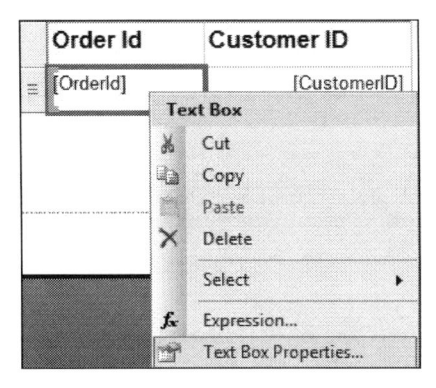

2. Click on **Text Box Properties....** Click on the **Action** tab to display the properties.

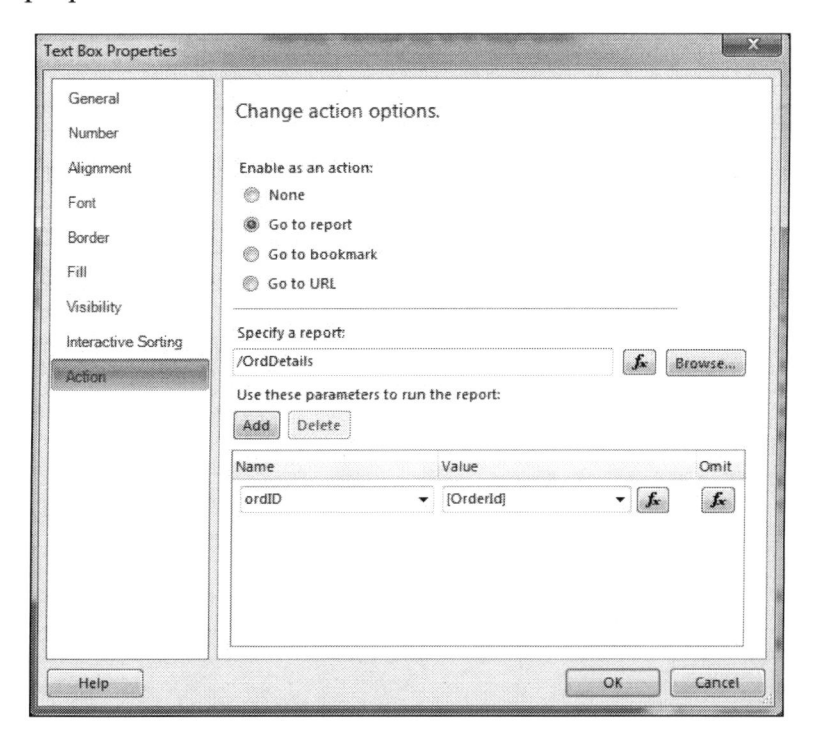

Working with Report Builder 3.0

3. Click on the radio button marked **Go to report | Browse** and find the `OrderDetails` report (destination report); click on **Add** and a **Name & Value select list** controls will be enabled.

4. Use the handles to assign the name to the **Parameter** column and value to the `OrderID` column in which you are displaying the properties (review the **General** tab). Click on **OK**. Optionally color the font for `OrderId` (in the source table) and underline the text in the cell.

5. Run the source report and click on any `OrderID` and you will display a corresponding target report.

Drill-down report

You want to avoid looking through a whole lot of data about an entity (person, for example). You are not interested in hundreds of items related to a person, but if you knew the social security number of a person, you could just click on that number; hey presto you get all the details! In a drill-down report, all information is in the same report, but you can choose how much you want to display with just a click. It is just a matter of hiding/revealing information. You can also drill-down in stages, like the first drill-down shows the full name, address, and so on and a further drill-down reveals other details such as his financial information and so on.

Here is a basic idea of drill-down but it can be implemented in many other scenarios as well. In the `Order Details` table whose META data is shown in the next image, `OrderID` by itself is not a **primary key**.

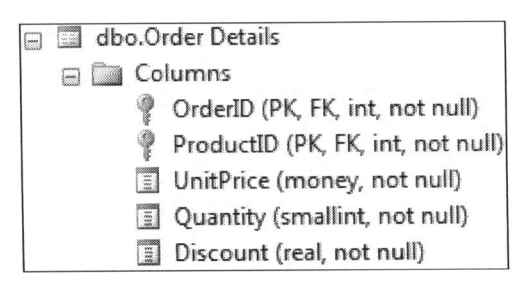

By itself, it is a **foreign key**. This means there are a number of identical `OrderID` in the `Order Details` table. Each `OrderID` and `ProductID` produces a unique record as shown in the next image for the `OrderID=10248`:

Product ID	Unit Price	Quantity	Discount	Order ID
11	14.0000	12	0	10248
42	9.8000	10	0	10248
72	34.8000	5	0	10248

In the drill-down report what you are going to show is just the OrderID and when you click on the OrderID, the rest of it is revealed.

Hands-on exercise 5.6 – Creating a drill-down report

Now, we will create a main report containing just OrderID from the Order Details table and containing a subreport that contains the details of the Order Details table.

1. Create a main report using the Order Details table, which uses the following query:

    ```
    Select OrderID from [Order Details] group by OrderID
    ```

2. Create a report based on this query as shown in the following screenshot:

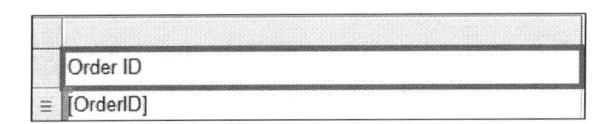

Order ID
[OrderID]

3. Run the report. You will see all OrderID in the Order Details table. Save the report as DrillDown.

4. Create a new report OrdDetails with the following query:

    ```
    SELECT * FROM [Order Details] where OrderID=@ordID
    ```

5. Use a table control to display the fields from the preceding query as shown in the following screenshot:

Product ID	Unit Price	Quantity	Discount	Order ID
[ProductID]	[UnitPrice]	[Quantity]	[Discount]	[OrderID]

Working with Report Builder 3.0

6. Bring up the `DrillDown` report in design view and place the `OrdDetails` report as a subreport as shown in the following screenshot. (You know how to do this from a previous hands-on exercise).

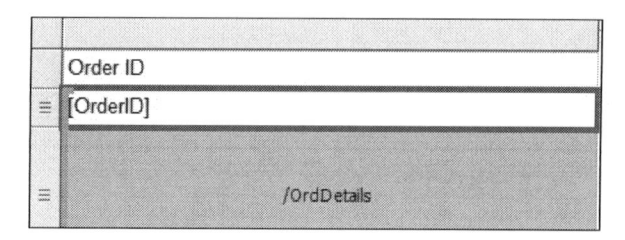

7. Focus on the properties of the subreport in the Report Builder and set the **Visibility** property as shown. The subreport is visible or not by toggling the `OrderID`.

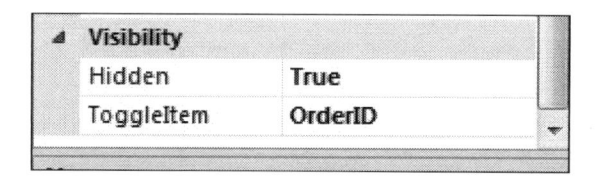

8. Save the report and run it, and you will see rows of `OrderID` with a plus (+) to the left side as shown and if you click any `OrderID` you will see the details (image on the right side); and if you click again it will be hidden as shown in the following screenshot:

This completes the procedure to create a drill-down report and in the following we will look at linked reports.

Linked reports

This particular topic really belongs to *Chapter 4, Working with Report Manager*, but is placed here because report authoring except through SSDT was not described earlier.

A report to be linked must be kept on a server and the users can access the report on the server. The linked report is a parametric report. When you create a linked report from it, it can be viewed by the user who provides the parameter. In Report Manager, it is very easy to customize the linked report depending on the folder in which it is placed. The layout and data source properties are kept the same, but other properties such as security, location, subscription, and so on, can be managed from Report Manager.

Hands-on exercise 5.7 – creating linked reports

Following are the steps to create linked reports:

1. Create three folders on Report Manager: Global, France, and Germany.

2. Using Report Builder, create a parametric report named qryCountry using the following query:
   ```
   SELECT TOP 1000 [CustomerID],[CompanyName],[City],[Country],[Phone]
   FROM [Northwind].[dbo].[Customers]
   WHERE Country=@country
   ```

3. Save this report to the Global folder on the Report Server.

4. Return to Report Manager, open Global and click on the report to manage the report saved in the folder in the previous step, as shown in the following screenshot:

Working with Report Builder 3.0

5. Click on **Create Linked Report....** In the open window, provide a name and description as shown in the following screenshot:

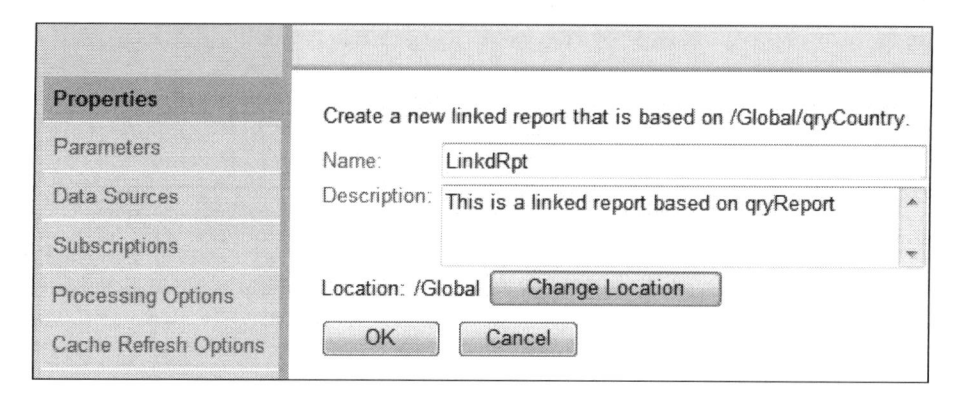

Properties	Create a new linked report that is based on /Global/qryCountry.
Parameters	Name: LinkdRpt
Data Sources	Description: This is a linked report based on qryReport
Subscriptions	
Processing Options	Location: /Global [Change Location]
Cache Refresh Options	[OK] [Cancel]

6. Click on **Change Location** and move it to the France folder. This will take you to the tree view of the Report Manager's **HOME** and back.
7. Click on **OK**. The report gets into the France folder.
8. Create and move a linked report to the Germany folder.
9. Verify you have the linked report in both folders as shown in the following screenshot:

France	Germany
New Folder New Data Source	New Folder New Data Source
LinkdRpt — This is a linked report based on qryReport	LinkdRpt — This one is for Germany

Customizing the linked report in the France folder

When users access the France folder, they should see the customer information related to France only. This customization is very simple.

1. Open the France folder in Report Manager, right-click on the **LinkdRpt** and click on **Manage**.
2. Click on the **Parameters** tab to display the details about the parameter as shown in the following screenshot:

Chapter 5

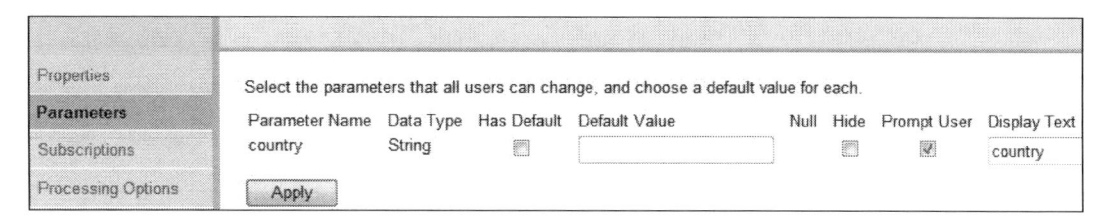

3. Place a check mark for **Has Default**, type in France in the **Default Value** textbox and place check mark for **Hide**. The check mark is removed from **Prompt User** and the **Display Text** field will be disabled.
4. Click on **Apply**. It immediately takes effect.
5. Return to **HOME | France** and display the report and you should see the France related customer information only.
6. Repeat the same for Germany.
7. Now, when you click on **France** or **Germany** you will see only data related to those countries in the report.

Creating a report with XML data sources

XML is text based and well suited for data exchange and XML data can be easily parsed. Most browsers can directly deal with XML data as it is an Internet-standard format. XML data can come from many sources such as data from Web services, data from Excel documents, and many others.

XML data is being used extensively between businesses and there are times you may need to create reports using XML-formatted data. This hands-on exercise shows a simple example of creating a report based on data in an XML file. This file can be on your desktop/laptop or on the server.

To understand how we create a report using XML data, we should have XML data to start with. If not, we need to create XML data. You could write an XML file with Notepad with some data in which you are interested, such as contact details. In the following, we create an XML source from a table in the Northwind database.

Working with Report Builder 3.0

Creating well-formed XML data

In this step, we will create XML data from a SQL Server 2012 table.

1. In SSMS, run the following query against the `Northwind` database:

    ```
    SELECT TOP 6 [CustomerID],[CompanyName],[Address],[City],[Country]
    ,[Phone]
    FROM [Northwind].[dbo].[Customers]
    For XML RAW
    ```

2. In the **Results** pane, click on the only hyperlink.

    > When you retrieve data from a SQL Server using the `For XML` clause, the result is usually in the form of a link to an XML document.

3. Then, copy the data to Notepad. The data should appear as shown in the following query:

    ```
    <row CustomerID="ALFKI" CompanyName="Alfreds Futterkiste" Address="Obere Str. 57" City="Berlin" Country="Germany" Phone="030-0074321" />
    <row CustomerID="ANATR" CompanyName="Ana Trujillo Emparedados y helados" Address="Avda. de la Constitución 2222" City="México D.F." Country="Mexico" Phone="(5) 555-4729" />
    <row CustomerID="ANTON" CompanyName="Antonio Moreno Taquería" Address="Mataderos  2312" City="México D.F." Country="Mexico" Phone="(5) 555-3932" />
    <row CustomerID="AROUT" CompanyName="Around the Horn" Address="120 Hanover Sq." City="London" Country="UK" Phone="(171) 555-7788" />
    <row CustomerID="BERGS" CompanyName="Berglunds snabbköp" Address="Berguvsvägen  8" City="Luleå" Country="Sweden" Phone="0921-12 34 65" />
    <row CustomerID="BLAUS" CompanyName="Blauer See Delikatessen" Address="Forsterstr. 57" City="Mannheim" Country="Germany" Phone="0621-08460" />
    ```

    We will use the above data when we create a data source in Report Builder. The query we use in creating the data source is shown in the next step.

4. Embed this block of XML data between the tags shown here:

    ```
    <Query>
    <XmlData>
    <rows>
    ```

```
<!-- start first row of your data below this line -->
```
Your data from Step 3 gets in here

```
<!--last row of your data is above this line-->
</rows>
</XmlData>
<ElementPath>rows/row</ElementPath>
</Query>
```

5. Launch Report Builder to create a blank report.
6. Add a data source; connection type is **xml**. Connection string is `<empty>`. Connection is embedded.
7. Add a dataset. The **Dataset Properties** window appears as shown in the following screenshot. Paste the XML data created in Step 4 as shown:

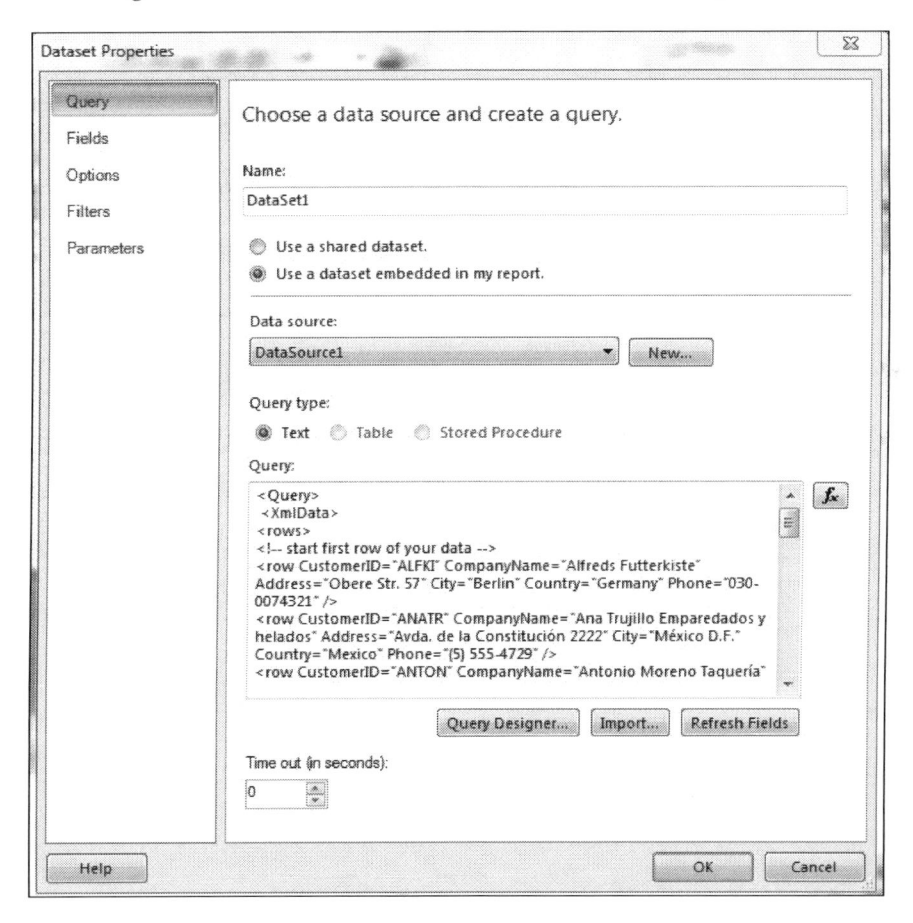

Working with Report Builder 3.0

8. Click on **Query Designer**. In the designer, click the ! symbol This executes the query.

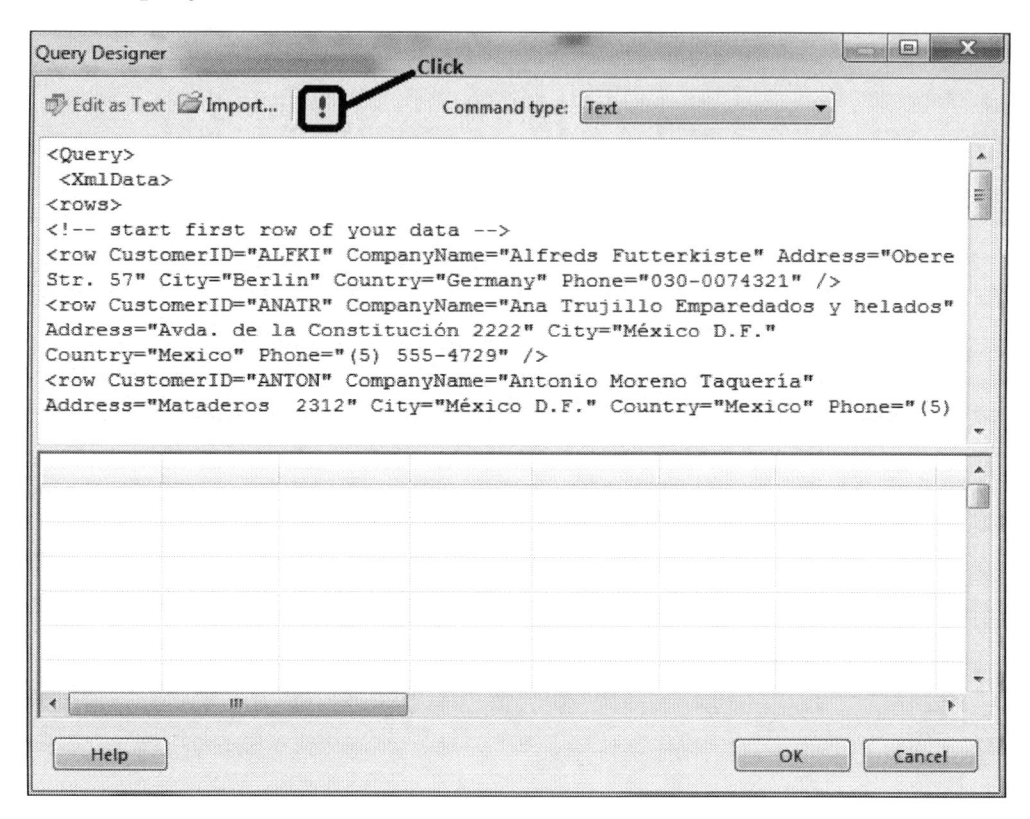

```
Query Designer
                                Click
Edit as Text   Import...   !        Command type:  Text

<Query>
 <XmlData>
 <rows>
 <!-- start first row of your data -->
 <row CustomerID="ALFKI" CompanyName="Alfreds Futterkiste" Address="Obere
 Str. 57" City="Berlin" Country="Germany" Phone="030-0074321" />
 <row CustomerID="ANATR" CompanyName="Ana Trujillo Emparedados y helados"
 Address="Avda. de la Constitución 2222" City="México D.F."
 Country="Mexico" Phone="(5) 555-4729" />
 <row CustomerID="ANTON" CompanyName="Antonio Moreno Taquería"
 Address="Mataderos  2312" City="México D.F." Country="Mexico" Phone="(5)
```

The empty panel below the query is now populated with the fields in the XML data.

9. Click on **OK** in the **Query Designer** window as well as the **Dataset Properties** window.

    The `DataSet1` in the `Datasets` folder under **Report Data** displays the fields.

10. Complete the report by adding a table and embedding the fields.
11. Run the report and verify it functions. Save the report as `XMLDATA`.

Displaying data with sparklines, maps, data bars, and indicators

Using dashboards to display data so that decision makers can easily get a good picture of what is happening very quickly has become very popular. For example, during election time most of the television networks come up with a dashboard, a map of a state or states to display how a particular party is doing.

The various gadgets, some of them in this chapter and the others in the previous edition, serves the purpose of highlighting information so that you can very quickly review the status of a particular entity.

Data bars are graphical elements you add to display data that makes it more attractive and appealing. You can use them very effectively in tables; they can represent multiple data points but in the hands-on exercise you will be implementing only one.

Hands-on exercise 5.8 – creating a report and highlighting data with data bars

Following are the steps to highlight data with data bars:

1. Launch Report Builder to create a blank report.
2. Add a data source connecting to the SQL Server 2012 Northwind database making an embedded connection.
3. Create an embedded dataset by running the following SQL statement in the **Query** window:

    ```
    SELECT OrderID, Sum (UnitPrice*Quantity) as 'Total amount'
    FROM [Order Details]
    WHERE OrderID <= '10262'
    GROUP BY OrderID
    ```

    The Dataset1 (default name) will be added with two fields: OrderID and Total_amount.

4. Insert a table on to the design pane. A 3 x 2 table will be inserted.
5. Drag fields from Dataset1 and place them in the first two cells.

Working with Report Builder 3.0

6. Right-click in the data cell of the third column to display the drop-down menu as shown in the following screenshot (you could also click this item under the Insert menu in the ribbon):

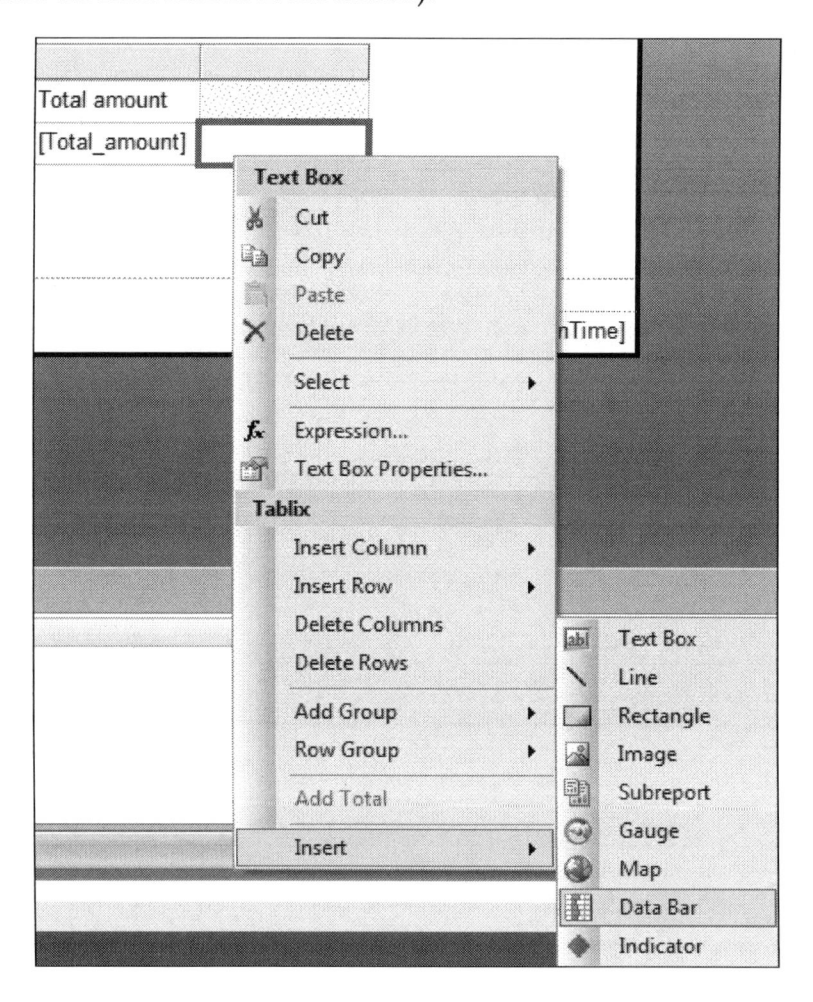

7. Click on the **Data Bar** option. In the **Select the Data Bar Type** window, click on **Data Bar**. Click on **OK**.
8. The third cell gets a data bar control with background color blue.
9. Right-click inside the data bar control to display the **Chart Data** menu as shown in the following screenshot:

[298]

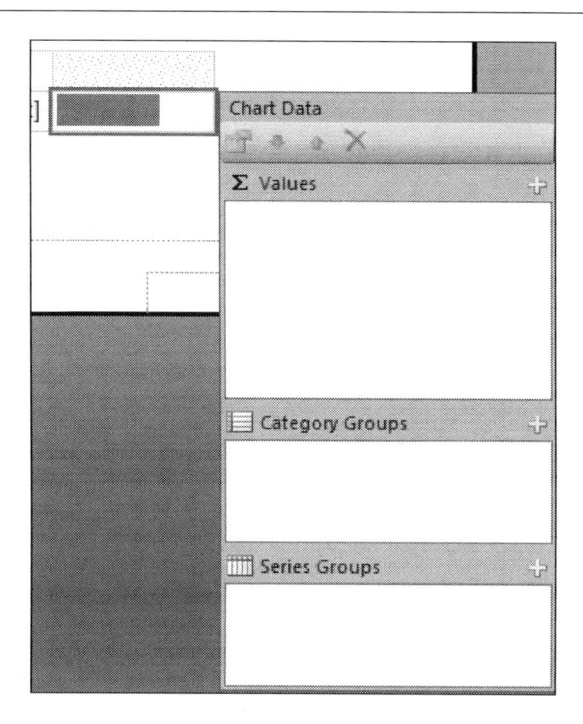

10. Click on the **+** symbol on the first panel under **Chart Data** on the right side to reveal the options you can choose as shown in the following screenshot:

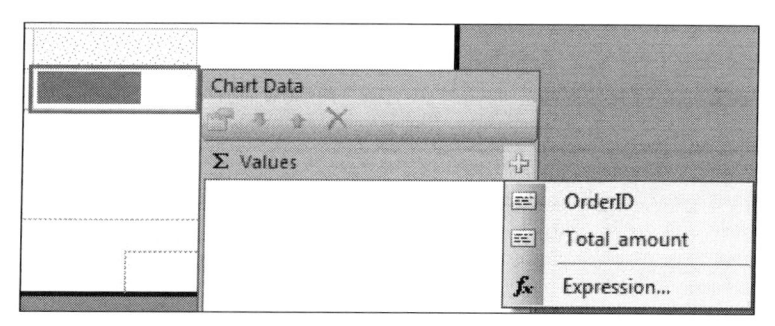

11. Click on `Total_amount`. This is the value that the data bars will represent. In the properties of the data bar, you can make many more choices. However, for a basic data bar implementation, this is sufficient.

12. The table design changes as shown in the following screenshot:

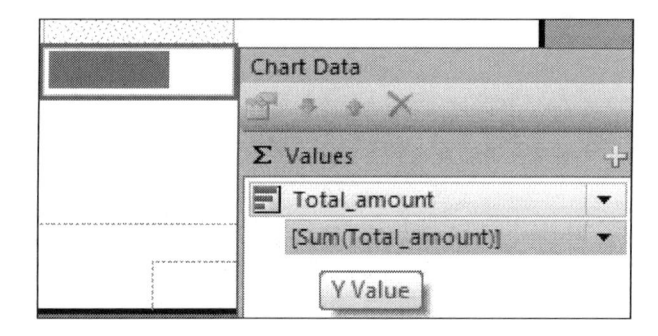

13. The width of the data bar would represent the value of `Total_amount`.
14. Run the report (press F5). The report gets displayed as shown in the following screenshot (the background color has been added):

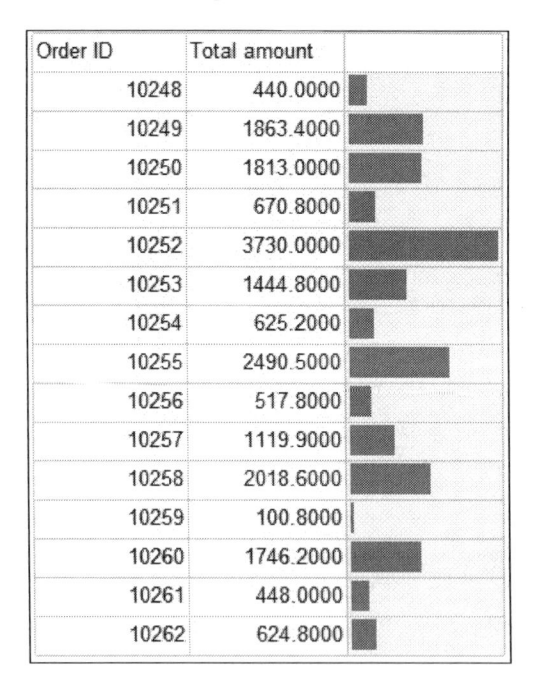

Order ID	Total amount
10248	440.0000
10249	1863.4000
10250	1813.0000
10251	670.8000
10252	3730.0000
10253	1444.8000
10254	625.2000
10255	2490.5000
10256	517.8000
10257	1119.9000
10258	2018.6000
10259	100.8000
10260	1746.2000
10261	448.0000
10262	624.8000

Displaying data with sparklines

Sparklines are small charts (usually line chart) shown along a group of data to show at a glance how the data of a group of entities varied over a period.

You can create sparklines using Report Builder as well as Report Designer in SSDT. In SSDT, you can drag and drop it on the report into one of the cells. In Report Builder, you right-click the data cell and insert the sparkline or click on **Insert | Sparkline**.

Hands-on exercise 5.9 – creating reports with sparklines

We first create a table with data and then create a report using the table. We implement the sparklines for the data on the report.

Creating a table

Before we create sparklines, we need to have the data in place. The following query when run on SQL Server 2012 provides the data for this exercise. We create a table and populate it with data.

1. Start SSMS with administrator's permissions.
2. Right-click on the `Northwind` database node and click on **New Query**.
3. In the query window run the following script:

   ```
   CREATE TABLE [dbo].[PrincetonTemp](
       [Id] [int] NOT NULL,
       [Mnth] [nchar](10) NULL,
       [AvgTemp] [float] NULL,
       [HighTemp] [float] NULL,
    CONSTRAINT [PK_PrincetonTemp] PRIMARY KEY CLUSTERED
   (
      [Id] ASC
   )WITH (PAD_INDEX = OFF, STATISTICS_NORECOMPUTE = OFF, IGNORE_DUP_KEY = OFF, ALLOW_ROW_LOCKS = ON, ALLOW_PAGE_LOCKS = ON) ON [PRIMARY]
   ) ON [PRIMARY]
   GO
   INSERT INTO PrincetonTemp (Id, Mnth, AvgTemp,HighTemp)
    VALUES (1, 'January', 40, 60), (2,'February',32,50),(3,'March',43,65),
     (4,'April',50,70),(5,'May',53,74),(6,'June',60,78),(7,'July',68,70),
     (8,'August',71,70),(9,'September',60,82),(10,'October',55,67),(11,'November',45,55),
     (12,'December',40,62)
   ```

4. After running the script, refresh the `Northwind` database and verify the table is created. Run a `SELECT` statement shown here:

   `SELECT * FROM PrincetonTemp`

Creating a report and inserting sparklines

Here, we will go through the steps to insert sparklines in our report.

1. Launch Report Builder to create a blank report.
2. Create a data source to connect to `Northwind` database on SQL Server 2012 KAILUA; use an embedded data connection, query type: **text**, Connection string: `Data Source=HODENTEKWIN7\\KAILUA`, Initial Catalog=`Northwind`.
3. Create a dataset using the preceding data source and the following query in the **Query** window:

   `Select * FROM PrincetonTemp`

4. Create a report as shown in the following screenshot:

Month	Average Temperature	High Temperature
[Mnth]	[AvgTemp]	[HighTemp]

5. Insert a row below the second row called **Outside Group - Below**.
6. In the third row, third column place the cursor and from the **Insert** menu item, click on the sparklines and click in the third row, third column.
7. In the **Select Sparkline Type** window displayed, choose **Line | Stepped Line**.
8. Similarly for the second column, third row insert a sparkline. Now the report looks like the following screenshot:

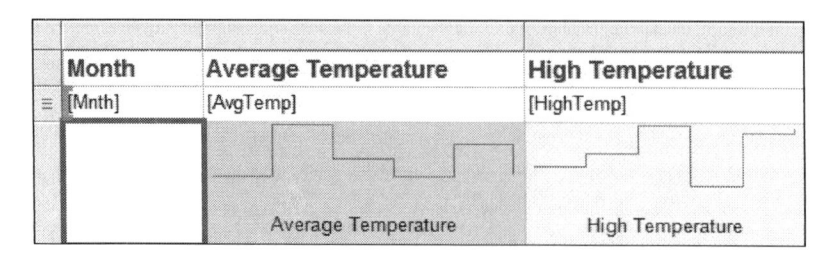

The annotations and the background color were later added from the **Properties** window.

Chapter 5

9. Click on the sparkline and review the pop-up drop-down as shown in the following screenshot:

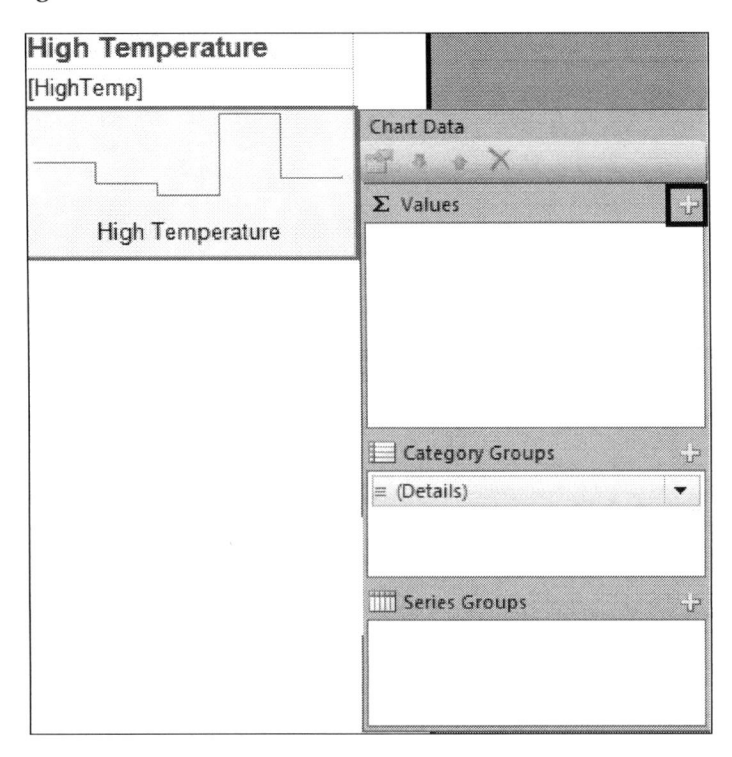

10. Click on the cross (+) along (Sigma) **Values** tab below **Chart Data**.

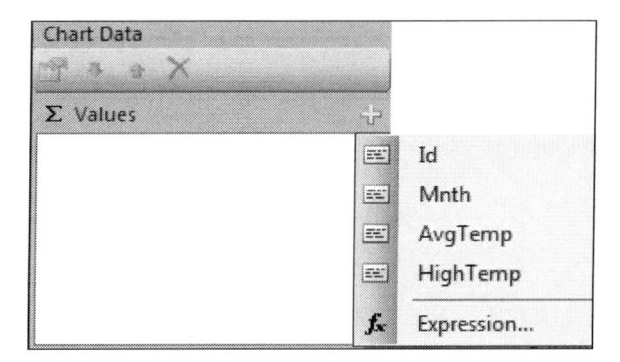

11. The drop-down list is displayed, click on **HighTemp**.

[303]

Working with Report Builder 3.0

12. Similarly add a sparkline to the **Average Temperature** column and choose `AvgTemp` for this sparkline.
13. Run the report (press *F5*) and verify the sparklines' appearance as shown in the following screenshot:

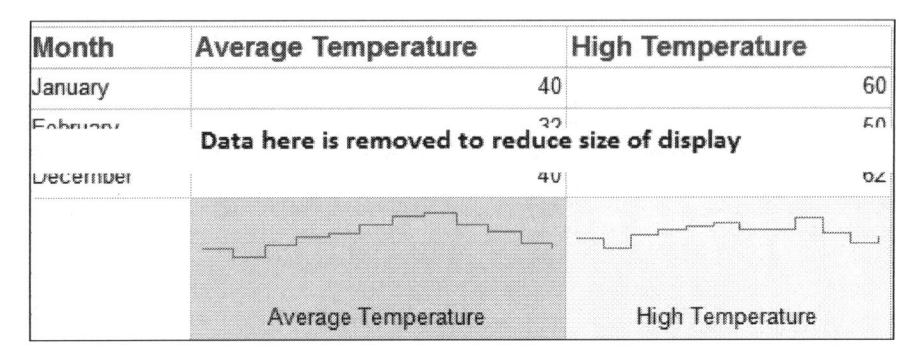

Month	Average Temperature	High Temperature
January	40	60
February	32	50

Data here is removed to reduce size of display

| December | 40 | 62 |

You can format the sparklines and enrich them with lot more details than shown in this exercise, but the general idea is to show how the fields vary over the duration using sparklines. You could also turn sparklines into charts.

Indicators

Indicators are small icons added to the report displaying the range of data in the report such as high, low, too low and so on. It is very similar to conditional formatting, such as Red for small numbers, Green for large ones, and so on.

Hands-on exercise 5.10 – creating reports using indicators

We will use the same data source and dataset as in the previous hands-on.

1. Create a report with `Northwind` database and the `PrincetonTemp` table.
2. Create the report as shown. Click and add an empty column to the right side of **AvgTemp** and **HighTemp** columns. Into each of these columns, insert an indictor control (right-click and go to the bottom of the drop-down list to insert, you have seen how to do this earlier. These can also be inserted from the main menu in the ribbon.)

Mnth	Avg Temp	Header	High Temp	
[Mnth]	[AvgTemp]	○	[HighTemp]	⇨

When you insert an indicator, you get a window to choose the type of indicator as shown in the following screenshot:

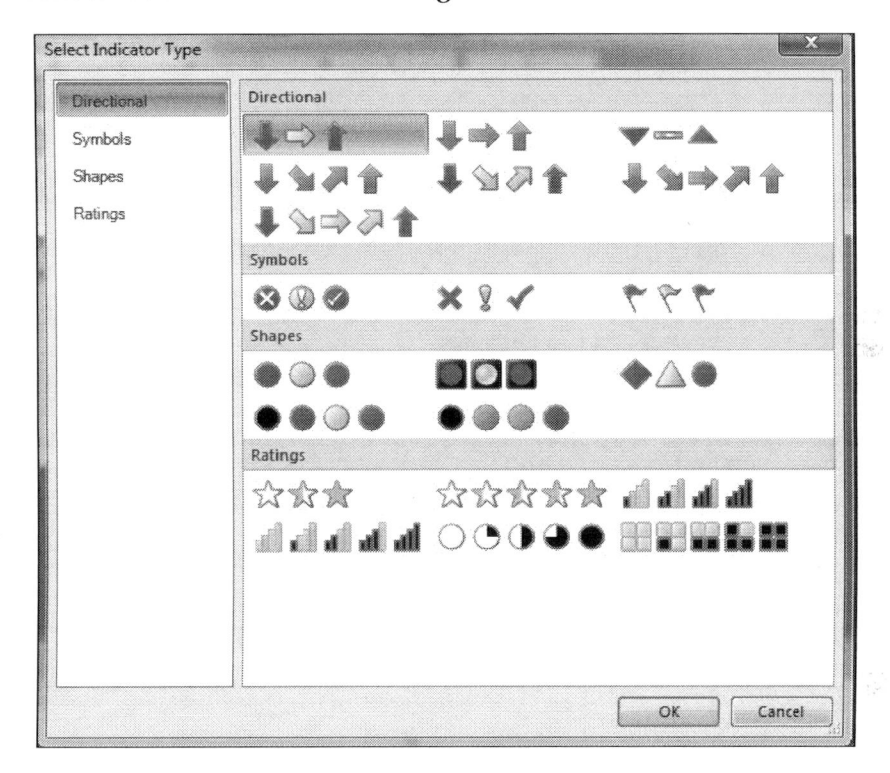

3. Click on the indicator by the side of **HighTemp**. A drop-down list is displayed as shown in the following screenshot:

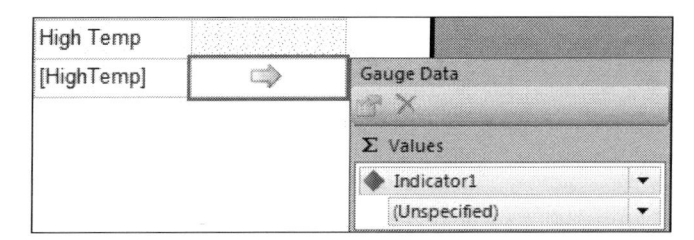

Working with Report Builder 3.0

4. Click on the **(Unspecified)** item to bring up another drop-down list that shows the data to which the indicator is mapped as shown in the following screenshot:

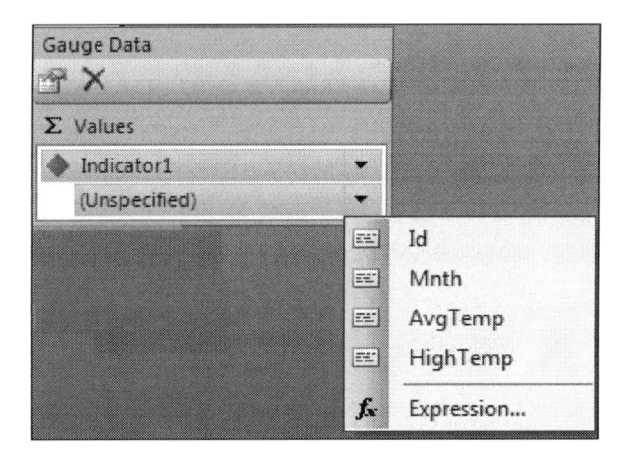

5. Click on **HighTemp** in the list.
6. Similarly configure the indicator for the **AvgTemp** column.
7. Run the report (press *F5*) and verify the data as shown (the title was changed) in the following screenshot:

The next image shows the **HighTemp** indicators properties and you can change them to set up the conditions for showing the range:

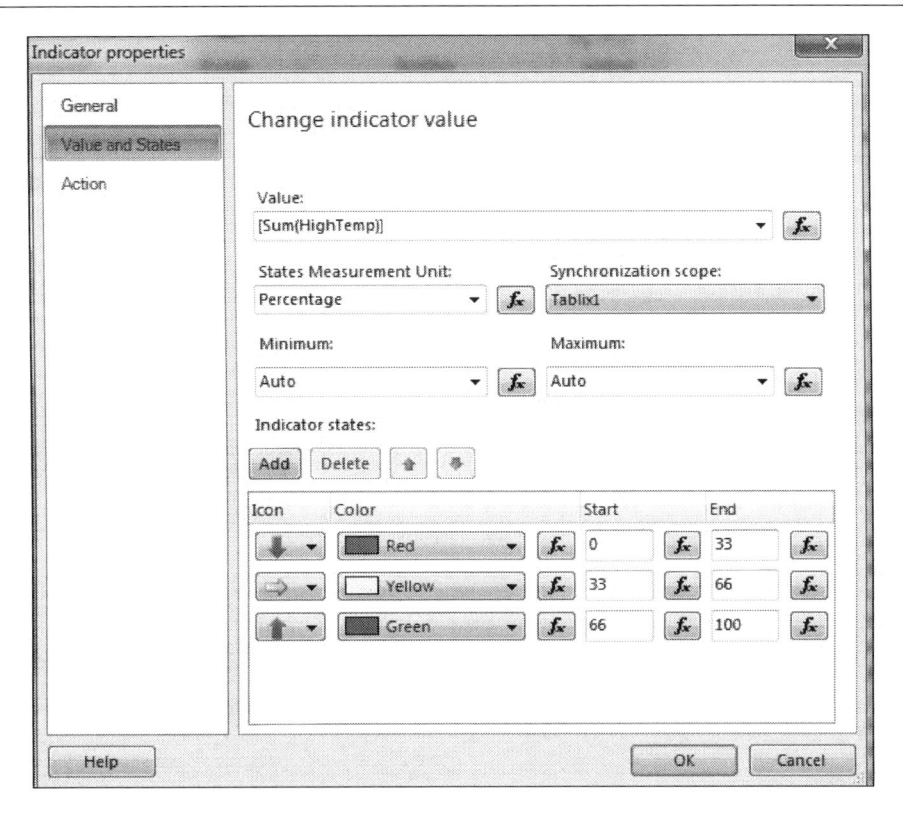

Reports with maps

Reports showing demographic maps, store sales with maps, crime rate with maps, and so on have become all too common. In creating reports, with embedded map displaying data became possible with spatial data types in SQL servers. These next hands-on just shows the basic steps for creating a report with embedded map.

Hands-on exercise 5.11 – creating reports with embedded maps

In doing this, you should have a database that contains business data stored in relation to the geographical data. Adventure Works 2012 has such data and it will be used. Only some basic steps will be shown due to space limitations.

1. Launch Report Builder with administrative privileges.

2. In the **Getting Started** page, click on **Map Wizard**.
3. In the **New Map** page displayed, click on **Map gallery**.
4. Expand **States by County** and choose **California**. You get to see a preview of the map of California.
5. Click on **Next**. The **Choose spatial data and map view** options page is displayed.
6. Use the slider bar on the left side to expand/contract map area visible in the window.
7. You can place your cursor on the map and move it to a position you desire.
8. Expand and move till you see **Los Angeles** (it's third up on the left side from bottom) adequately positioned.
9. Click on **Next**.
10. In the **Choose map visualization** page, click on **Color Analytical Map | Next**.
11. Click on **Next**.
12. In the **Choose color theme and data visualization** page, choose **Theme** from the drop-down list and click on **Display labels**, and choose county name from drop-down list.
13. Click on **Finish**.
14. Your report now appears as shown in the following screenshot:

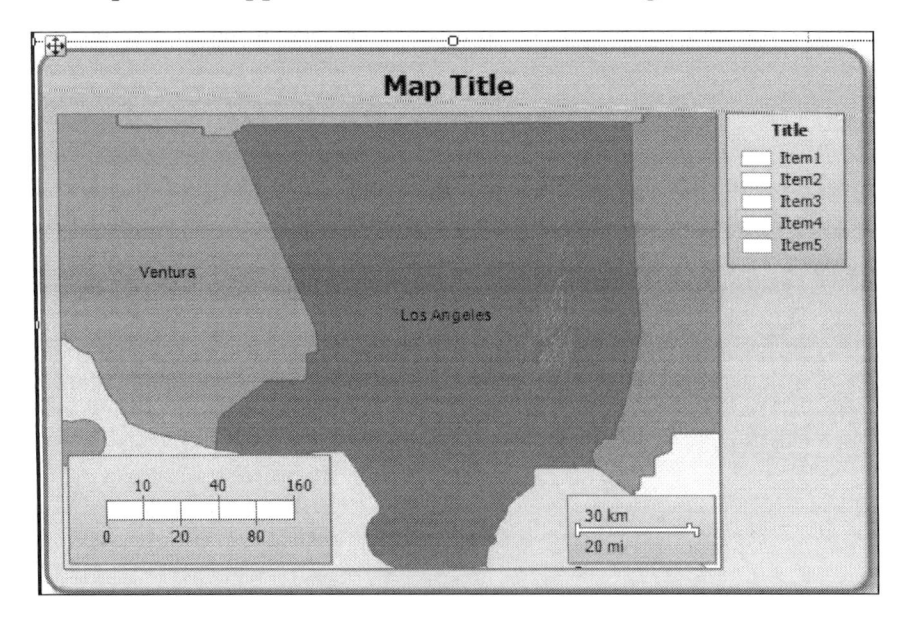

15. Double-click the map to display the **Map Layers** menu as shown in the following screenshot:

16. Click on the **New Layer Wizard**. **The New Map Layer** page is displayed.
17. Click on **SQL Server Spatial Gallery** and then click on **Next**.

> The other way to get data into your report is via ESRI Shapefile. Follow the link on the **New Map Layer** page for more info.

18. The **New Map Layer** wizard's **Choose a dataset with SQL Server spatial data** page appears. At the very bottom, click on **Add a new dataset with SQL Server Spatial data**.
19. Click on **Next**.
20. The **New Map Layer** wizard's **Choose a connection to a SQL Server spatial data source** page appears. Click on **New**.
21. The **Data Source Properties** page is displayed. Create a connection with the following information:
    - embedded or shared: **embedded**
    - Connection type: **MS SQL Server**
    - Connection string: `Data Source=HODENTEKWIN7\\KAILUA;Initial Catalog=AdventureWorks2012`
22. Test the connection using the button and click on **OK**.
23. You are back in the **New Map Layer** wizard's connection page.

Note that the name of connection embedded is `DataSource1` (default)

1. Click on **Next**. The **Design a query** page of the **New Map Layer** wizard appears.

[309]

2. Click on **Edit as Text**. The page opens with a top and bottom pane and a link for importing as well as an icon (!) to execute the query.

3. Paste the following SQL statement in the top box:
```
SELECT top 10 Person.Address.SpatialLocation, Person.Address.City,
Sales.SalesTerritory.SalesYTD,Sales.SalesTerritory.CostYTD
FROM         Sales.SalesTerritory INNER JOIN
                    Person.StateProvince ON Sales.
SalesTerritory.TerritoryID= Person.StateProvince.TerritoryID INNER
JOIN
                    Person.Address ON Person.StateProvince.
StateProvinceID = Person.Address.StateProvinceID AND
                    Person.StateProvince.StateProvinceID =
Person.Address.StateProvinceID
         where Person.Address.city  ='Los Angeles'
```

4. Click on the execute icon (!).

5. The bottom pane should show some 10 rows of data like the portion shown in the following screenshot:

SpatialLocation	City	SalesYTD
POINT (-118.28415305028 3...	Los Angeles	10510853.8739
POINT (-118.402389908587 ...	Los Angeles	10510853.8739

6. Click on **Next**. You will be back in the report design page. It is showing the whole of California with a little filled circle in Los Angeles.

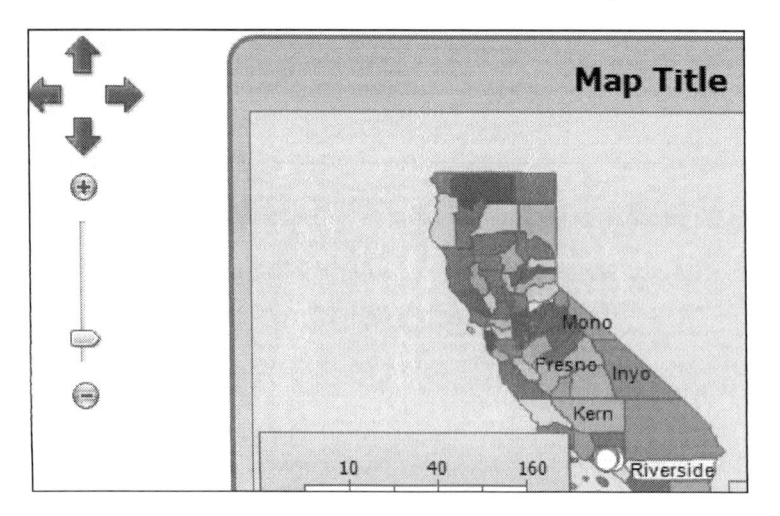

Chapter 5

7. Adjust the map with slider bar and by moving to bring **Los Angeles** into view window as shown in the following screenshot:

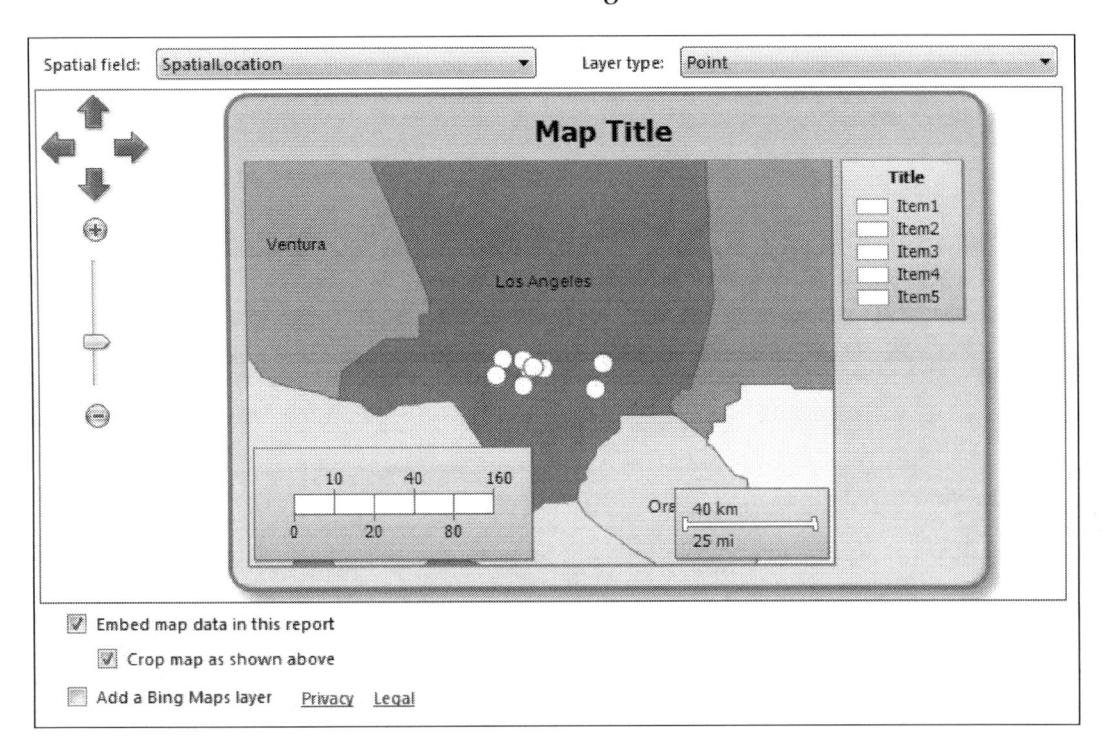

8. Check **Embed map data in this report** and **Crop map as shown above**.
9. Click on **Next**.
10. In the **Choose Map Visualization** page, click on **Bubble Map**. Click on **Next**.
11. The **Choose the analytical dataset** page is displayed.

12. Click on **DataSet1 in this report** at the top and click on **Next**. The **Specify the match fields for spatial and analytical data** page of the **New Map Layer** wizard appears as shown in the following screenshot:

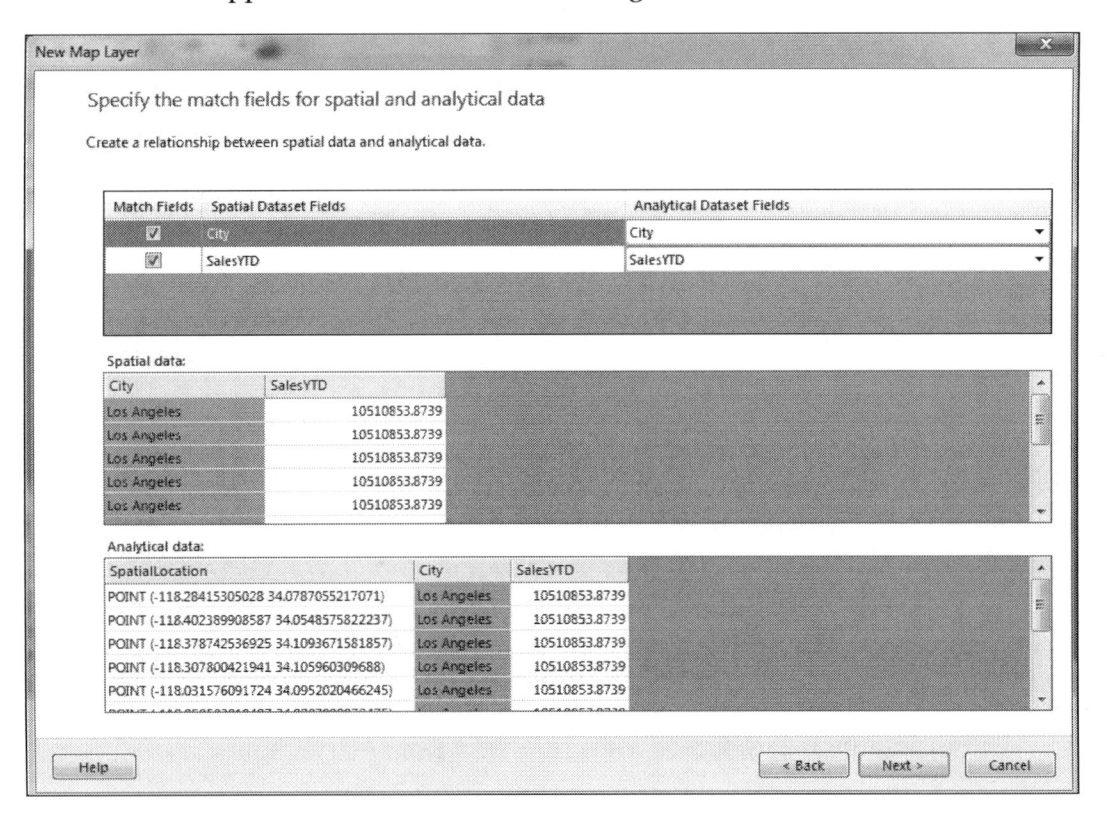

13. Click on **Next**.
14. In the **Choose color themes and data visualization** page choose the items you would like to show. The map changes are shown in the following screenshot:

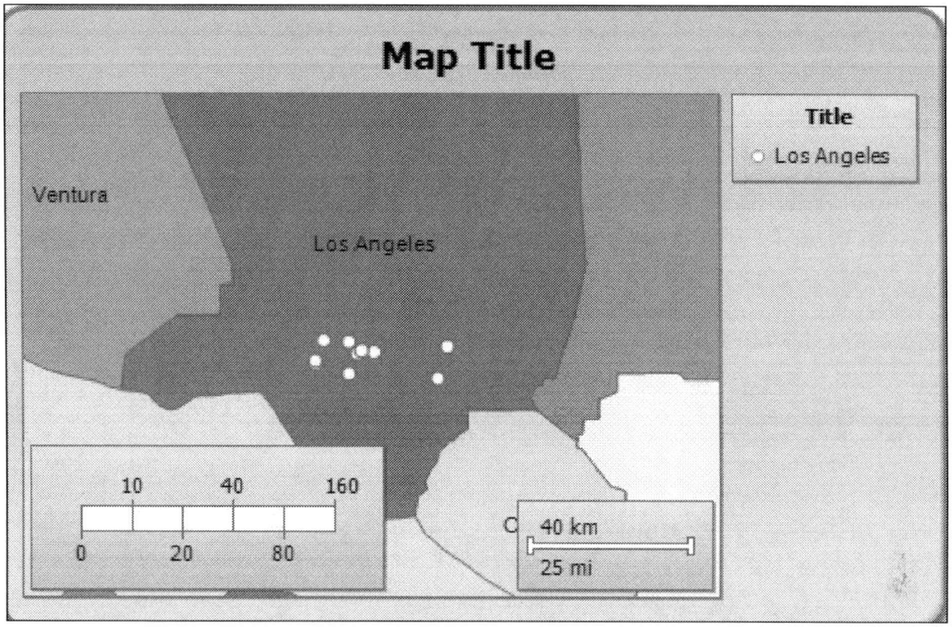
Map Title
Title
Los Angeles
Ventura
Los Angeles
10
40
160
0
20
80
40 km
25 mi

The map is showing the ten data points from our query on the `Adventure Works` database.

15. Click on **Finish**.
16. Run the report and save as `LosAngelesData`.

The data selected is not that great. It is very essential that you know your data very well before you embark on creating a report.

```
SELECT        SUM([Order Details].UnitPrice * [Order Details].
Quantity) AS 'Total sales', Categories.CategoryName
FROM             [Order Details] INNER JOIN
                            Orders ON [Order Details].OrderID = Orders.
OrderID INNER JOIN
                            Products ON [Order Details].ProductID =
Products.ProductID INNER JOIN
                            Categories ON Products.CategoryID =
Categories.CategoryID
GROUP BY  Categories.CategoryName
```

Report parts

Barring small Microsoft .NET-based shops, larger establishments will have more than one developer and in fact reports are created to be authored and managed in collaboration with other developers, or report authors. Starting in SQL Server 2008 R2 Reporting Services, the idea of **report parts** emerged. The idea behind report parts is to support reuse of parts of the developed reports for improved productivity. Microsoft developed this by adding the functionality to publish report items to the Report Servers as report parts to both Native mode and SharePoint Integrated mode Report Servers. For details follow this link: http://technet.microsoft.com/en-us/library/ee635721.aspx.

Both Report Designer in SSDT and Report Builder can publish report items as report parts. In the case of Report Designer, it is one way only. You can publish as report parts, but you cannot reuse an existing item in report part. In Report Builder, however, one can work in the collaboration mode suited for more than one report developer working with report parts. Since data sources depend on the credentials to facilitate reuse in a collaborative scenario, it is best to use shared data sources with the credentials stored in the server. When the original report is updated, the reused report part in another report also gets updated.

Hands-on exercise 5.12 – creating report parts and reusing an item

The report shown in the next screenshot was created in Report Builder 3.0 using the Northwind database and a shared data source with the dataset created using the query after the screenshot:

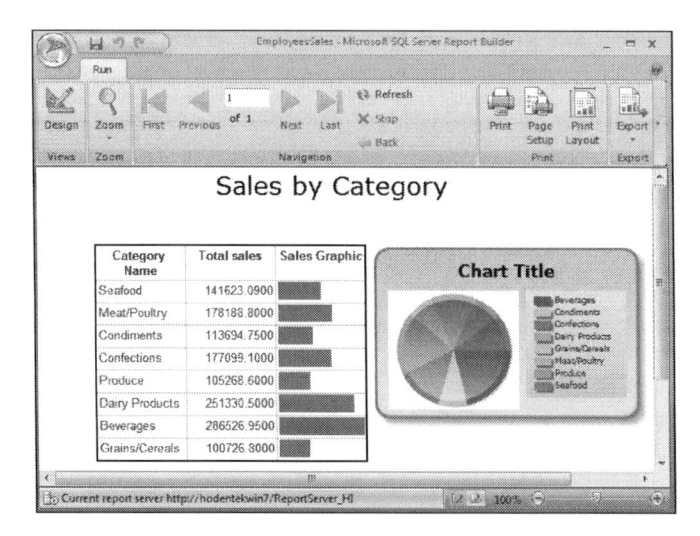

Chapter 5

```
SELECT        SUM([Order Details].UnitPrice * [Order Details].
Quantity) AS 'Total sales', Categories.CategoryName
FROM          [Order Details] INNER JOIN
                     Orders ON [Order Details].OrderID = Orders.
OrderID INNER JOIN
                     Products ON [Order Details].ProductID =
Products.ProductID INNER JOIN
                     Categories ON Products.CategoryID =
Categories.CategoryID
GROUP BY      Categories.CategoryName
```

The steps for creating the report are not described as it has been covered in earlier hands-on. In the next section, we will save the report to the server as report parts.

Saving a report as report parts

This section details the steps on how to save a report as report parts:

1. Click on the top button on the left side to display the following drop-down list:

Working with Report Builder 3.0

2. Click on **Publish Report Parts** and the **Publish Report Parts** window is displayed as shown in the following screenshot:

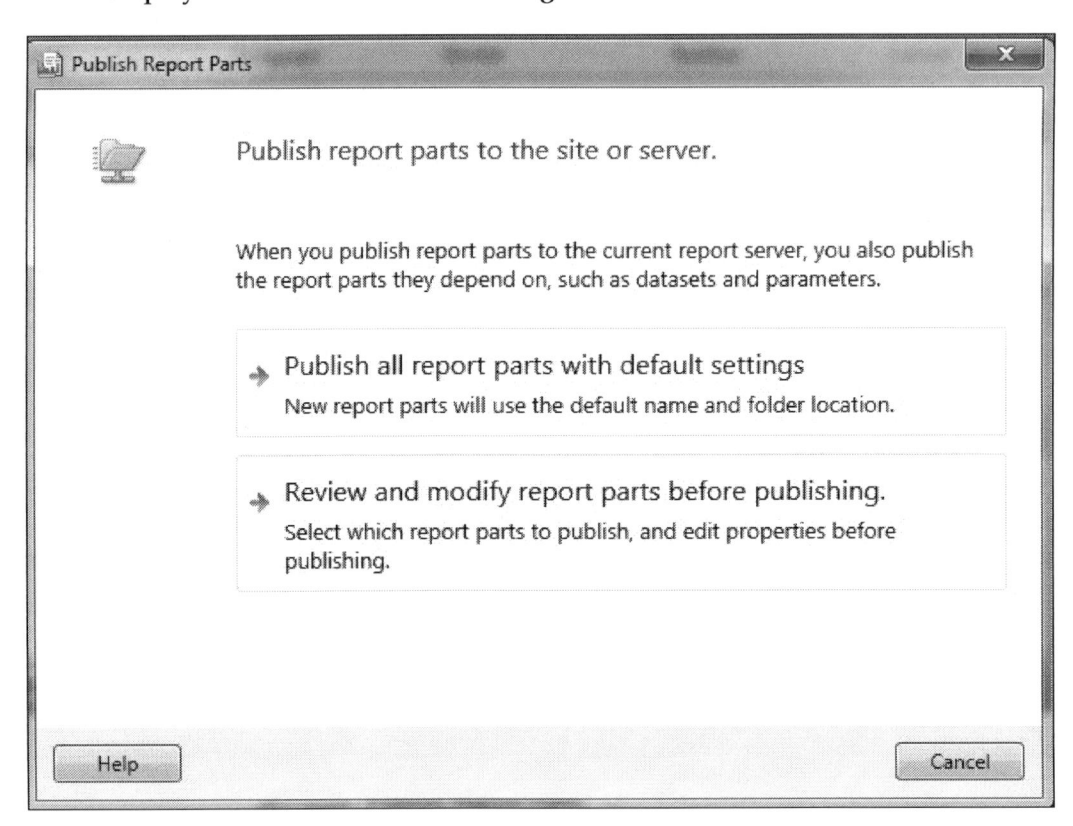

> Publish Report Parts
>
> Publish report parts to the site or server.
>
> When you publish report parts to the current report server, you also publish the report parts they depend on, such as datasets and parameters.
>
> → **Publish all report parts with default settings**
> New report parts will use the default name and folder location.
>
> → **Review and modify report parts before publishing.**
> Select which report parts to publish, and edit properties before publishing.
>
> [Help]   [Cancel]

You can review and modify report parts before publishing. You may also look up help by clicking on **Help** at bottom left. **Help** brings up the Report Builder 3.0 Help window.

3. Click on the second option **Review and modify report parts before publishing**. This brings up a window where you can make some changes as shown in the following screenshot:

Chapter 5

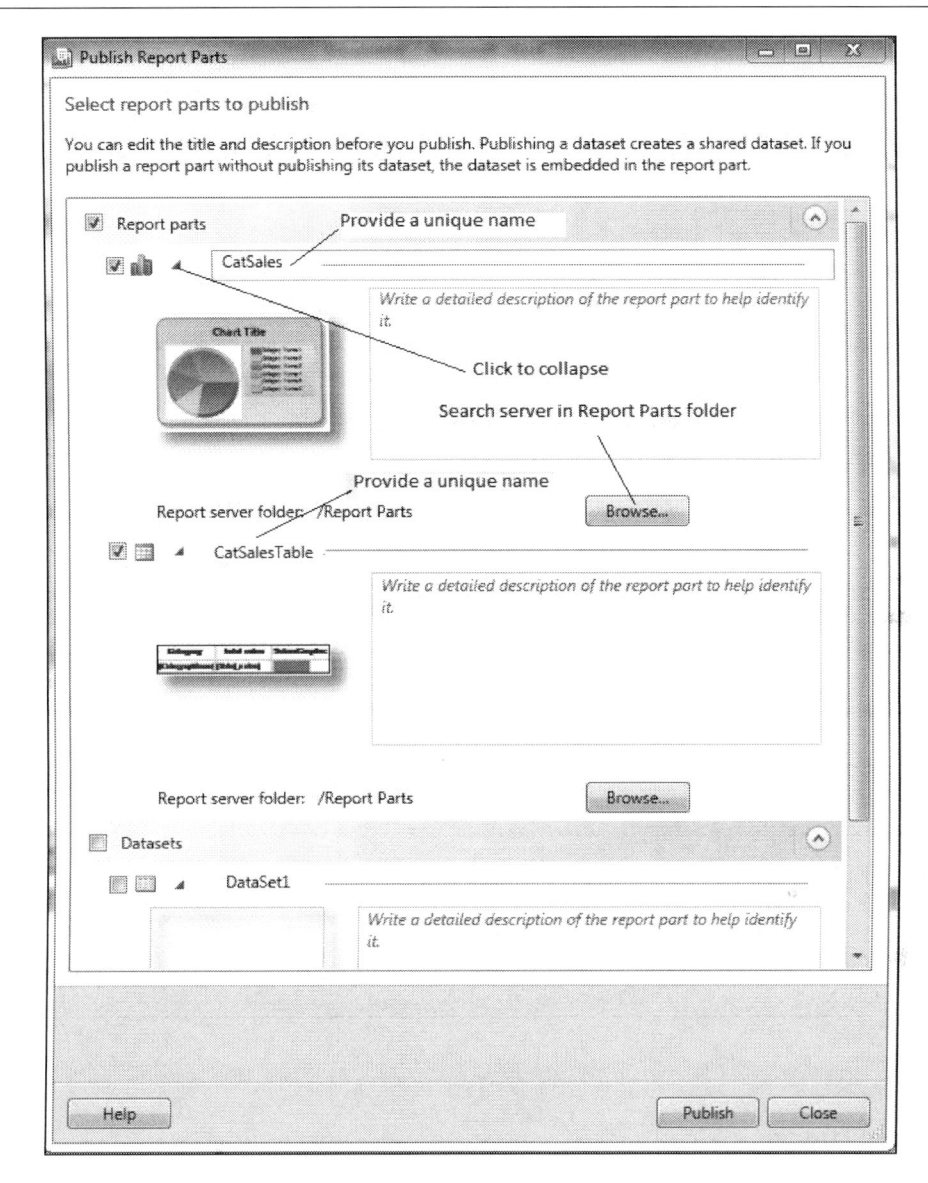

You can change the default name of items by overwriting; add a description and choose items to be saved by placing checkmarks.

4. Click on **Publish**. The items are published to the server as shown in the Report Manager.

Working with Report Builder 3.0

> You can also use the **Browse** button for a location to publish as well for each item. In case there is a problem, it will be flagged as such and you may modify the option and try again.

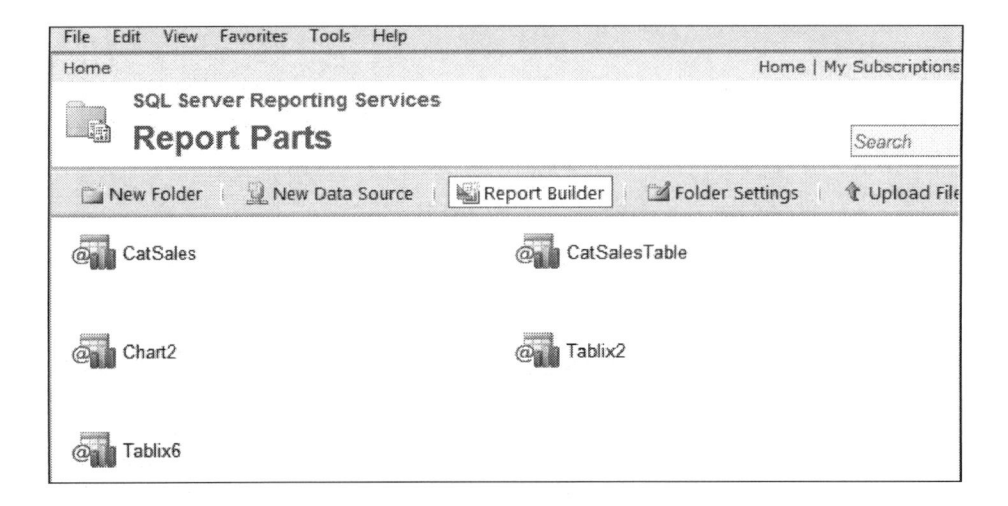

We can review the published items to Report Server in the Report Manager.

5. Click on **CatSales** (or any other item in the `Report Parts` folder). The screen related to the item opens as shown in the following screenshot:

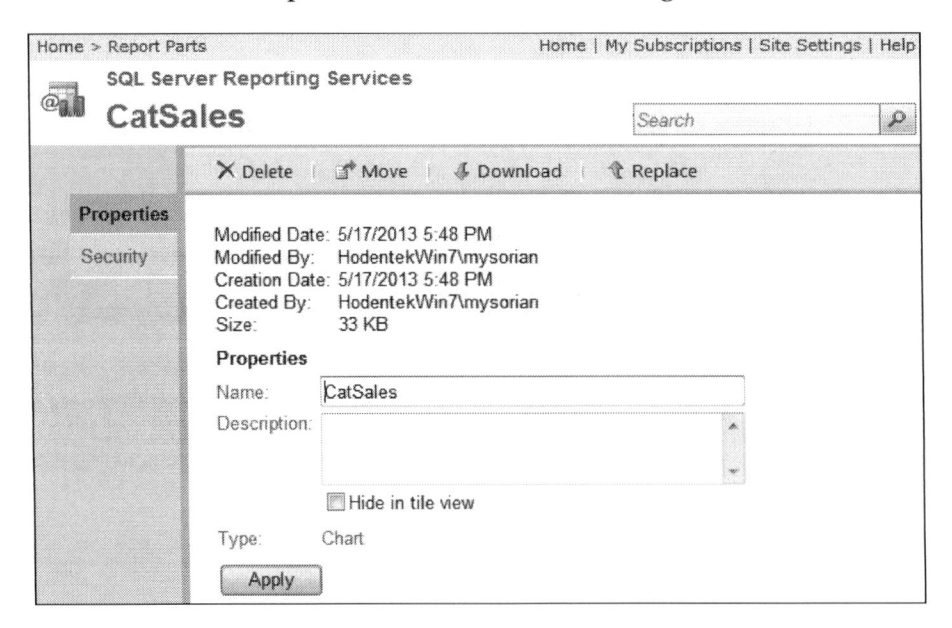

All items have the same features, including the tool bar items. A downloaded report parts item such as the preceding one can be saved to a chosen location on the computer with the `.rsc` extension. This is XML formatted containing the information of the item. Its size depends on the complexity of the item and even for simple item such as the one before, it is quite large.

The basic idea of report parts is that they are reusable by another developer/author. In the next section, we will use one of the report part items in another report.

Reusing the report parts items

In this section we will create a blank report and bring in (to a blank report) the `CatSales` report part from the previous section. Since the Permissions can be managed on the Report Manager, another developer can be given permission to this report part as described in *Chapter 4, Working with Report Manager*.

1. Launch Report Builder 3.0. Report Builder opens as shown in the following screenshot for creating a blank report. Note that it is not connected yet.

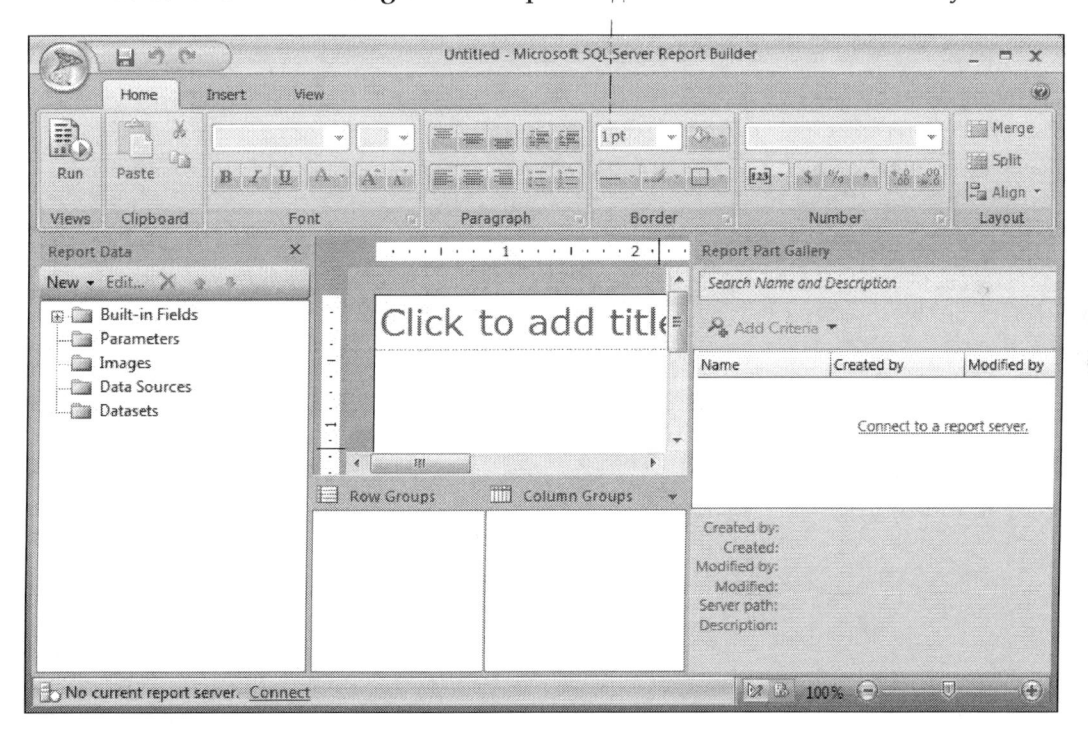

Notice **Report Part Gallery** on the right-hand side, which has all the report part items.

Working with Report Builder 3.0

2. Click on **Connect** at the bottom of the screen or the link in the **Report Part Gallery** area on the right side.

3. In the **Connect to Report Server** window displayed use the drop-down handle to choose the Report Server and click on **Connect**.

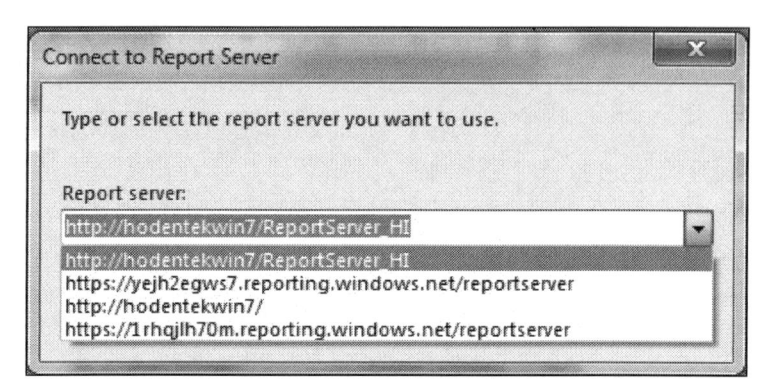

4. Click on **Insert | Repot Parts** at the extreme left of the ribbon. You may not see any report part items yet in the gallery.

5. Click on the **Search** icon under the gallery and the items are displayed as shown in the following screenshot:

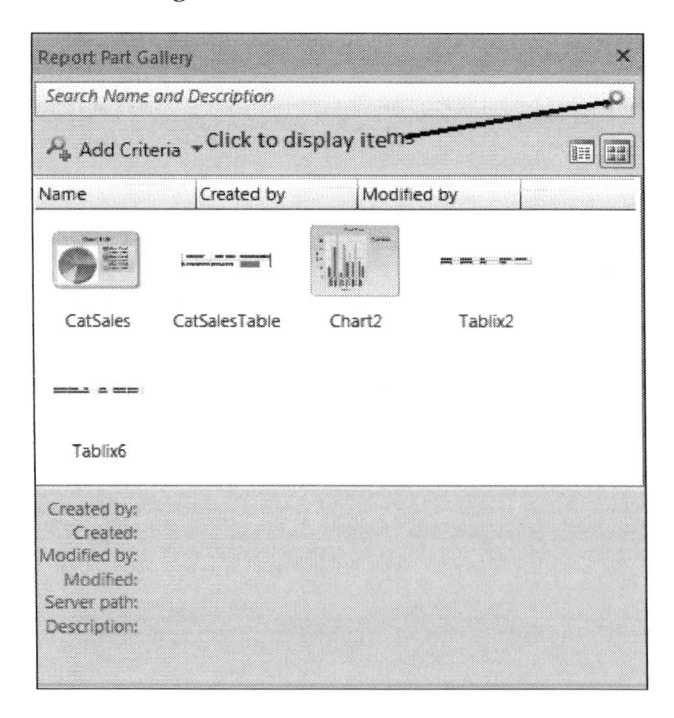

You can also find the items in the Report Manager and search for an item in **Report Part Gallery** by explicitly searching for the item, which is needed if the gallery has many items,

6. Just drag and drop **CatSales** from **Report Part Gallery** to the design area of the blank report.

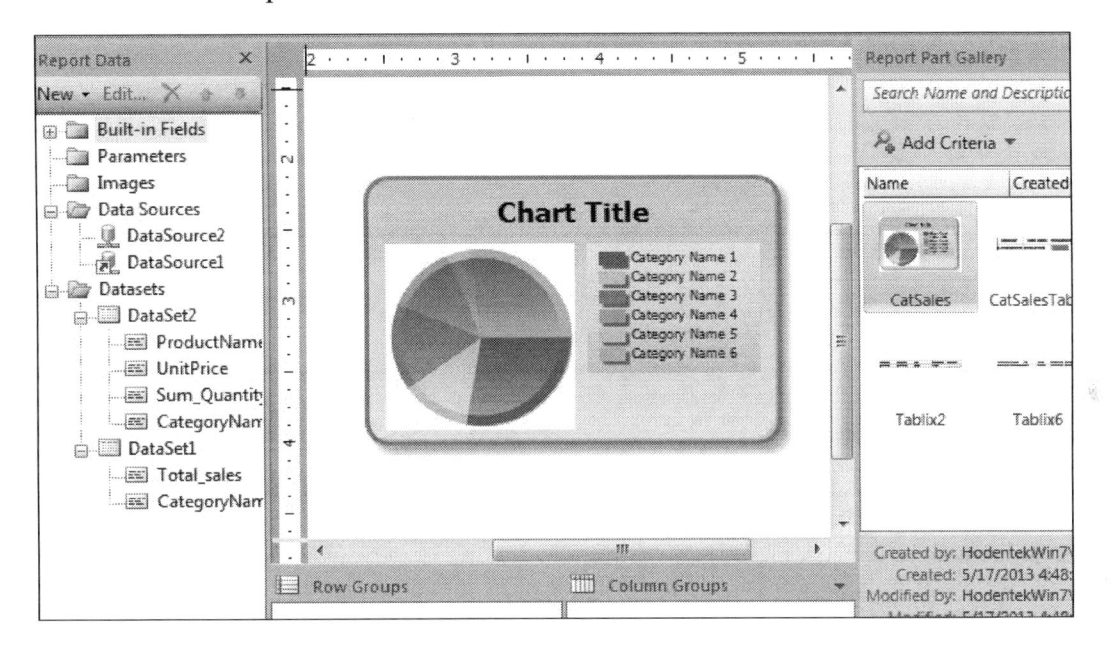

> Note that everything related to `CatSales` such as data sources as well as datasets were also brought into the blank report.

7. Run the report.

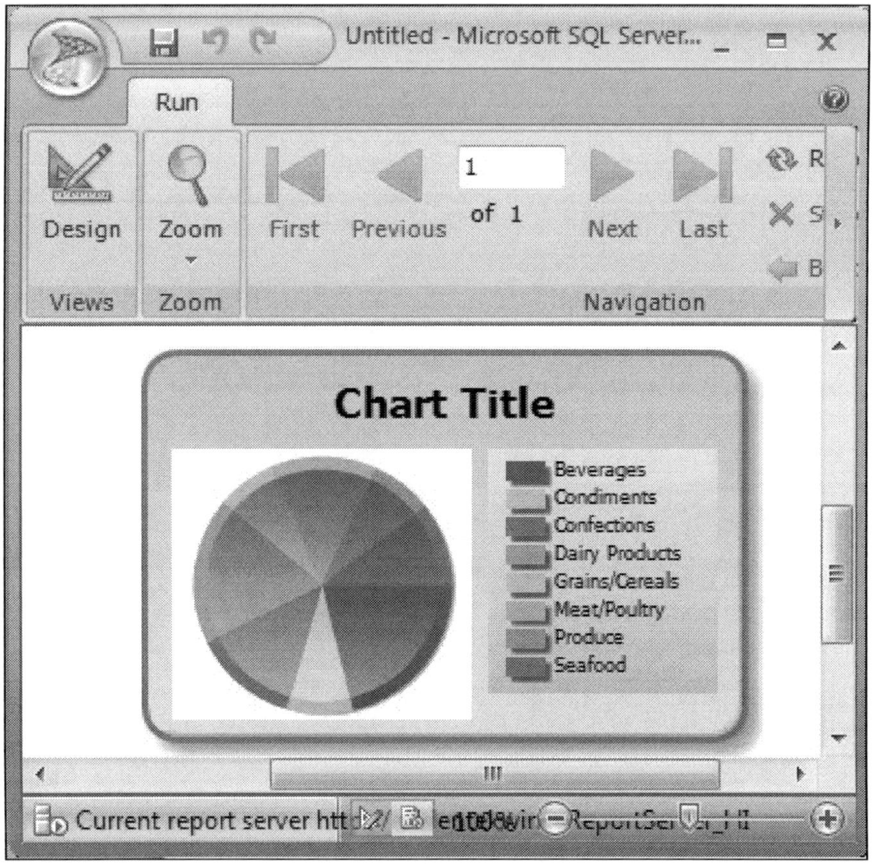
Untitled - Microsoft SQL Server...
Run
Design
Zoom
First
Previous
1
of 1
Next
Last
Views
Zoom
Navigation
Chart Title
Beverages
Condiments
Confections
Dairy Products
Grains/Cereals
Meat/Poultry
Produce
Seafood

8. Save it to the server or folder location.

> Although you can download a report parts item from Report Manager or save it to a folder, you cannot bring in a `.rsc` file from a saved location on the computer's folder into the Report Builder 3.0. You get the following error:

> **Microsoft SQL Server Report Builder**
>
> ⚠ Failed to open report 'Tablix6.rsc'.
>
> [OK] [<< Details]
>
> The report definition has an invalid target namespace 'http://schemas.microsoft.com/sqlserver/reporting/2010/01/componentdefinition' which cannot be upgraded.

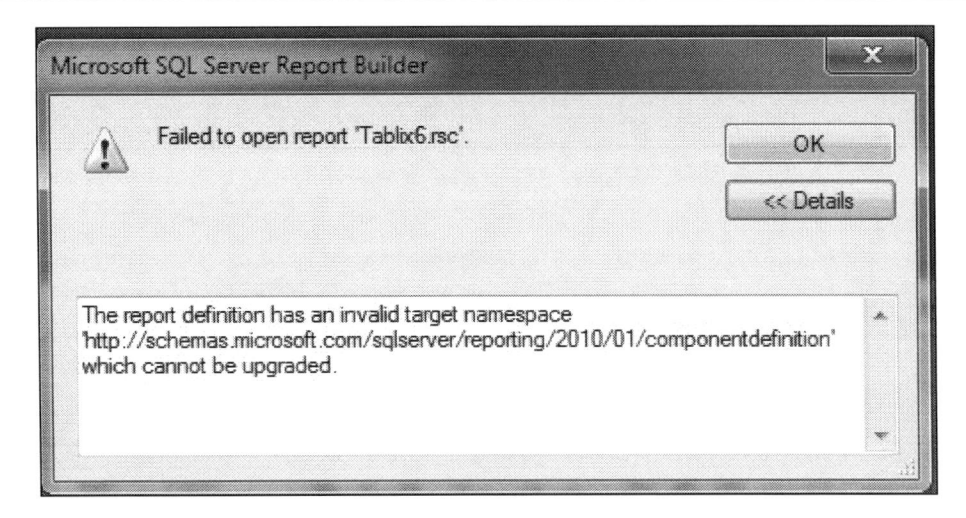

Summary

This chapter described the different kinds of reports you can author with Report Builder 3.0 such as parameterized reports, free form list reports, drill-down and drill-through reports, subreports, and so on. It also provides hands-on examples of getting data from SQL Server and XML data documents. Many of the interactive features such as document maps, interactive sort, and alternate row highlighting are also described and included in the exercises. There are also hands-on exercises for the new gauges/gadgets such as maps, sparklines, data bars, and indicators. Creating report parts and reusing report part items are also described.

Report Builder 3.0 can also be used for authoring reports that can be published to SharePoint site and the authoring works the same way as it is used to author for native mode. This will be covered in *Chapter 7, Self-Service Data Alerts in SSRS 2012*.

SQL Server 2012 integration with SharePoint 2010 provides a means to author more engaging, highly interactive reports known as Power View reports with live data making previewing totally redundant. In the next chapter, creating Power View reports from scratch is described with complete details.

6
Power View and Reporting Services

This chapter describes how Power View reports are created using SQL Server Reporting Services 2012 in conjunction with SharePoint Server 2010. The upgrade to this set will be SQL Server 2012 SP1 and SharePoint 2013. The Power View examples of this chapter are compatible with SharePoint 2013 (backward compatibility); readers should access Microsoft SharePoint site for details. As Power View reports are based on a **tabular data model** (**TDM**), creating a tabular model using SQL Server Analysis Services is described together with creating a data source for the Power View report using SharePoint Server 2010. Also described is a flavor of the rich visualization experience that you can get working with Power View reports.

What is Power View?

Power View is a Silverlight browser application launched from SharePoint Server 2010, although there are many voices asking to make it independent of SharePoint Server. In SQL Server Reporting Services 2008, Microsoft had dealt with an earlier form of ad hoc reporting capability based on report model using multidimensional data but with Power View it has made the earlier attempt look primitive.

> Power View is not exclusive to SharePoint but can be created using Excel as well, more easily in Excel 2013. Power View using Power Pivot in Excel is considered sometimes as a junior version of the enterprise grade Power View in SharePoint. All of these can change in days to come. With SQL Server 2014 due this year, Excel may not even need the add-in, and the in-memory business intelligence capability will be that much more enhanced.

Power View does ad hoc reporting accessible to all levels of expertise in the business, from data analysts to business decision makers and everyone else in between. However, it is model dependent; this time around, it depends on what is called a tabular data model, which is based on Microsoft's all inclusive **Business Intelligence Semantic Model (BISM)**. This model is different from the report model used in the earlier 2008 ad hoc reporting. This is data in-memory and works superfast at turbo speeds using xVelocity/Vertipaq technology (http://blogs.msdn.com/b/analysisservices/archive/2012/03/09/xvelocity-and-analysis-services.aspx).

In Power View, data visualization takes center stage and does it so well that is truly remarkable. The Power View report is interactive, and the visualization and presentation of data are truly exceptional. Power View can be compared to live TV whereas the previous report varieties were mere taped programs.

The technology is evolving as this line is written. Follow this link to read more about the future of Power View: http://office.microsoft.com/en-us/excel-help/whats-new-in-power-view-in-excel-2013-and-in-sharepoint-server-HA102901475.aspx. Look forward to new formatting possibilities, such as adding background images, formatting the background, choosing themes, and formatting text and numbers.

Querying and access is fast in Power View as a consequence of having data in memory using the xVelocity/Vertipaq technologies, since no disk input/output is involved. For fast data access and querying, tabular model does much better than multidimensional; but multidimensional model handle complexities in data querying much better. Follow this link for detailed models comparison: http://www.jamesserra.com/archive/2012/04/sql-server-2012-multidimensional-vs tabular/. However, Power View reports have been extended to even a multidimensional model (still in CTP stage) so that a range of capabilities are envisioned for Power Viewing. All in all, the realm of Power View is extending in all directions in providing greater productivity and a better user experience. Power View that you will learn in this chapter is still in its early stages.

Helpful resources

There are lots of videos and articles on the Internet. In fact, it is somewhat overwhelming. These are two of the links that will take you to most of others:

- TechNet Wiki (http://social.technet.microsoft.com/wiki/contents/articles/3726.power-view-overview.aspx#Useful_links_for_Project_Crescent_and_SQL_Server_Denali)

- Power View Office link (`http://office.microsoft.com/en-us/excel-help/power-view-explore-visualize-and-present-your-data-HA102835634.aspx`)

If for some reason you do not have access to the software needed, then there are sites that host SharePoint server serving the reports linked to data that you can practice with. I recommend that you visit the following site: `http://blogs.msdn.com/b/oneclickbi/archive/2011/12/27/more-demos-of-power-view-available.aspx`.

What do you need to author a Power View report?

This is the first question that you ask yourselves. As Power View report is based on data it finds on a tabular data model, you need **SQL Server Analysis Services (SSAS)** server, which can host a tabular model. This means that you must have configured the SQL Server Analysis Server to support tabular model. You create the tabular model using SSDT, which installs when you install SQL Server 2012. Installing SSAS to support tabular model was covered in *Chapter 1, Overview and Installation – SQL Server Reporting Services 2012*.

Also, as the Power View is launched from SharePoint Server 2010, you want the SQL Server Reporting Services 2012 configured to operate in integrated mode with SharePoint Services. Installing RS2012 in SharePoint Integrated mode was described in *Chapter 1, Overview and Installation – SQL Server Reporting Services 2012*. The Power View reports in this chapter are based on these premises. Power Views are only possible for enterprise-grade servers for both SharePoint Server 2010 and SQL Server 2012.

The environment for developing Power View described in this book is based on the following:

- Possibility of installing SharePoint 2010 Server on Windows 7 (x64) computer
- Installing SQL Server 2012 Reporting Services in SharePoint Integrated mode
- Configuring SQL Server 2012 Analysis Services to support tabular data model
- Availability of a Silverlight-enabled browser

Creating a tabular model

In order to create tabular data models, you need a SQL Server Analysis Services server installed to support Tabular Data Model (TDM) because a default installation can only work with multidimensional models (which work with much larger datasets).

For the purposes of this book, the SQL Server 2012 server NJ—a named instance—has been installed to support TDM. In this section, we are only describing what steps are needed to create the model and deploy it to an analysis server suitable for creating Power View reports.

In the following exercise we create a tabular model using SQL Server Analysis Services with SQL Server Data Tools.

Hands-on exercise 6.1 – creating a tabular model

This can be created using SQL Server Data Tools(SSDT). SSDT installs when you install SQL Server 2012.

1. Start SSDT with administrator privileges.
2. In the **Start** page, click **File | New Project...**.
3. The **New Project** window is displayed.
4. Click on **Analysis Services Tabular Project**. Change the name at the bottom for the project to TabularNW. Place a check mark for **Create directory for solution**. Click on **OK**.
5. The **Workspace and Deployment Server Configuration** window is displayed when you create the project for the first time. Use handles in the default server box to point to localhost/NJ.
6. Verify that the default server is correct using the **Test Connection** button. Click on **OK**.
7. The Model.bim file gets added to the project as shown in the following screenshot:

Chapter 6

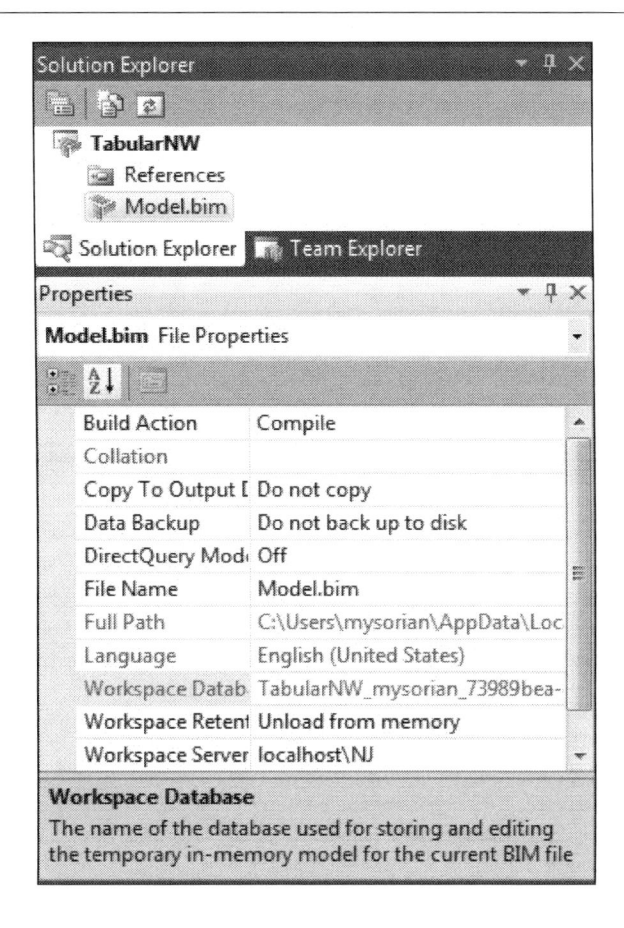

Build Action	Compile
Collation	
Copy To Output D	Do not copy
Data Backup	Do not back up to disk
DirectQuery Mod	Off
File Name	Model.bim
Full Path	C:\Users\mysorian\AppData\Loc
Language	English (United States)
Workspace Datab	TabularNW_mysorian_73989bea-
Workspace Retent	Unload from memory
Workspace Server	localhost\NJ

Workspace Database
The name of the database used for storing and editing the temporary in-memory model for the current BIM file

> The tabular data model's Workspace server is the local instance of analysis server and the databases are created for the model as shown in the next screenshot:

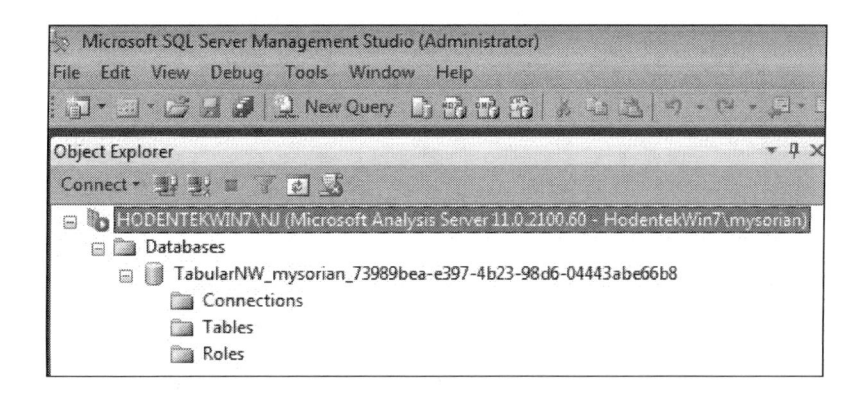

HODENTEKWIN7\NJ (Microsoft Analysis Server 11.0.2100.60 – HodentekWin7\mysorian)
- Databases
  - TabularNW_mysorian_73989bea-e397-4b23-98d6-04443abe66b8
    - Connections
    - Tables
    - Roles

[329]

Brief review of an SSDT ribbon

The SSDT menu items that you will be working will have the following features:

- Using the **File** menu, you can save the `Model.bim` as is or, with a different name
- The project's drop-down menu brings up the **TabularNW Property pages**, displaying the **server**, the **database name**, the **query mode** (in-memory by default), and the **impersonation** settings.
- The **Model** menu has the following choices: **Import From a Data source...**, **Process ->**, **Existing Connections**, **Model View->**, **Show Hidden**, and **Calculate Options.....**
- The **Table and Columns** menu become enabled after you are connected to the database.
- The **Tools** menu displays the following choices:

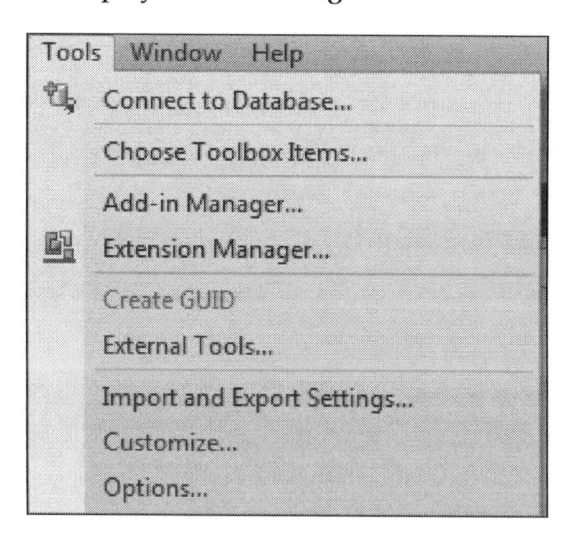

Tools	Window	Help
Connect to Database...
Choose Toolbox Items...
Add-in Manager...
Extension Manager...
Create GUID
External Tools...
Import and Export Settings...
Customize...
Options...

Creating a connection to the Northwind database

We have attached a `Northwind` database to `SQL server 2012 NJ` following the steps in *Chapter 1, Overview and Installation – SQL Server Reporting Services 2012*, or we ran a script to create the database. We will be connecting to that database.

1. In the **Model** menu drop-down list, click on **Import From Data Source**. The **Connect to a Data Source** page of **Table Import Wizard** is displayed. You can connect to a great many data sources such as the ones listed here:
    - Microsoft SQL Server
    - Microsoft SQL Azure
    - Microsoft SQL Server Parallel Data Warehouse
    - Microsoft Access
    - Oracle
    - Teradata
    - Sybase
    - Informix
    - IBM DB2
    - OLEDB/ODBC
    - Microsoft Analysis Services
    - Azure DataMarket dataset
    - Other feeds
    - Excel file
    - Text file

> It may be noted that Microsoft recently made a major move in its push to encompass big data by releasing **Windows Azure HDInsight** as one of its cloud services. This enables enterprise to crunch huge data volumes of both structured and unstructured data using Microsoft SQL Server and the Hadoop files. Of course, the Microsoft BI stack can leverage this new offering and Power View and PowerPivots have a great role to play. Read more at http://redmondmag.com/blogs/the-schwartz-report/2013/03/big-data-fray.aspx.

2. For now, accept **Microsoft SQL Server** and click on **Next** on **Table Import Wizard**. The **Connect to a Microsoft SQL Server Database** page is displayed. The following settings are appropriate for our model:

    - **Friendly connection name**: SqlServer HODENTEKWIN7NJ NorthwindNorthwind

        Server name: HodentekWin7\NJ

        Authentication: Use Windows authentication

        Database name: Northwind

    You use the handle to get the Server name HodentekWin7\NJ; the text in the Friendly connection name box has changed from **SqlServer** to **SqlServer HODENTEKWIN7NJ**. Click the handle for **Database name** to display a drop-down list to select Northwind.

3. Fill in the details as before. You may test the connection and click on **Next**. The **Impersonation Information** page of **Table Import Wizard** is displayed.

    Herein, choose the **Specific Windows user name and password** option. For the **User Name** field, provide HodentekWin7\mysorian and the associated password that you chose at installation time. The current username and password has been used.

4. Click on **Next**.

In the next section, we will choose the data that we want to bring into our report. This data resides in the tables.

Getting tables from the database

We will use the tables and views in the database to get the data for the model.

1. The **Choose How to Import Data** page of the wizard is displayed.
2. Accept default (**Select from a list of tables and views to choose the data to import**) and click on **Next**. The **Select tables and Views** window is displayed with all tables and views on the Northwind Database.

3. Select the tables and views you want in your model and click on **Select Related Tables**.

   Some of the selections made for this hands-on exercise are shown. The details will come later.

4. Click on **Preview & Filter** after highlighting one of the source table (`Employees`) or view. The next image shows the information, for the `Employees` table from which you can delete columns (filter columns), and so on.

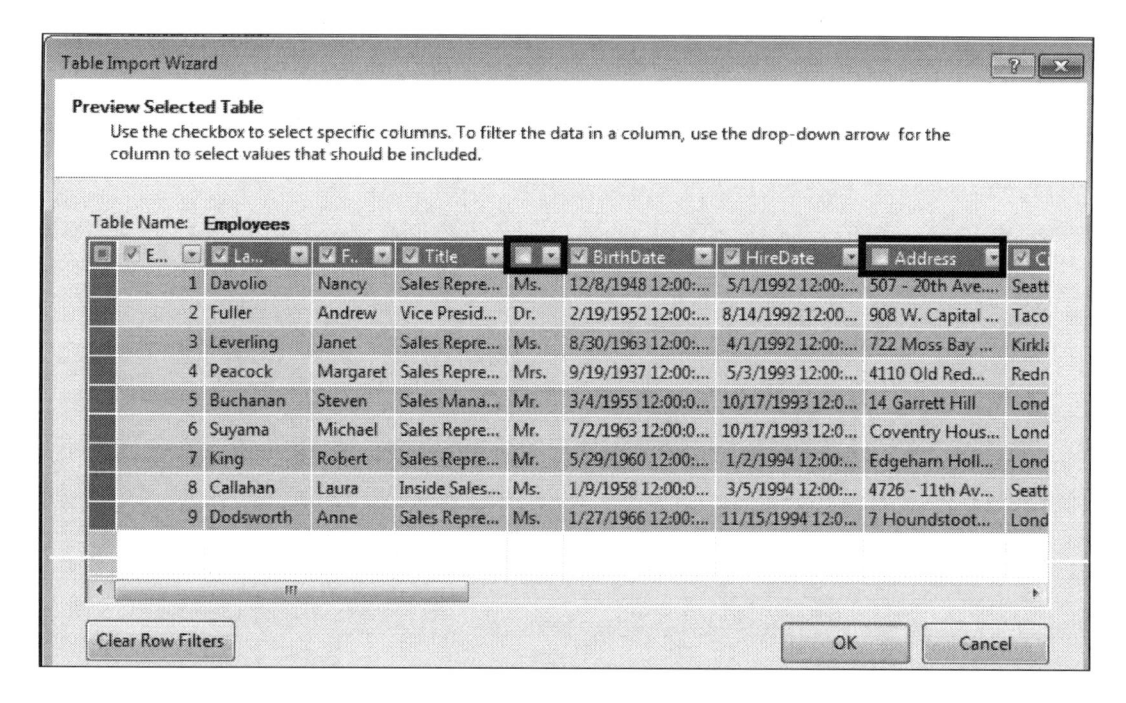

It is easy to see that this is where the model developer/business analyst will spend time to filter as much as they need (to get the information). You do not want to overwhelm the end user of the model with too many tables (this also consumes resources). You have to go through all the tables and do the filtering. The more information you need to include, the more resources you would need. The UI clearly shows which of them were filtered and which were discarded (`TitleOfCourtsey` and `Address` were deleted. Hint: Right-click on column).

5. Click on **Finish**.
6. **Table Import Wizard** gets cranking to bring in data into the project.

Chapter 6

This process may take some time depending on your choices and resources. When the importing is finished, a window displaying success and the number that succeeded is shown.

7. Click on **Close** on **Table Import Wizard**.

   Immediately the tables are shown in **Grid view**. The tables/views are imported into the model and are as shown in the next image. This rendering is called **Diagram view**.

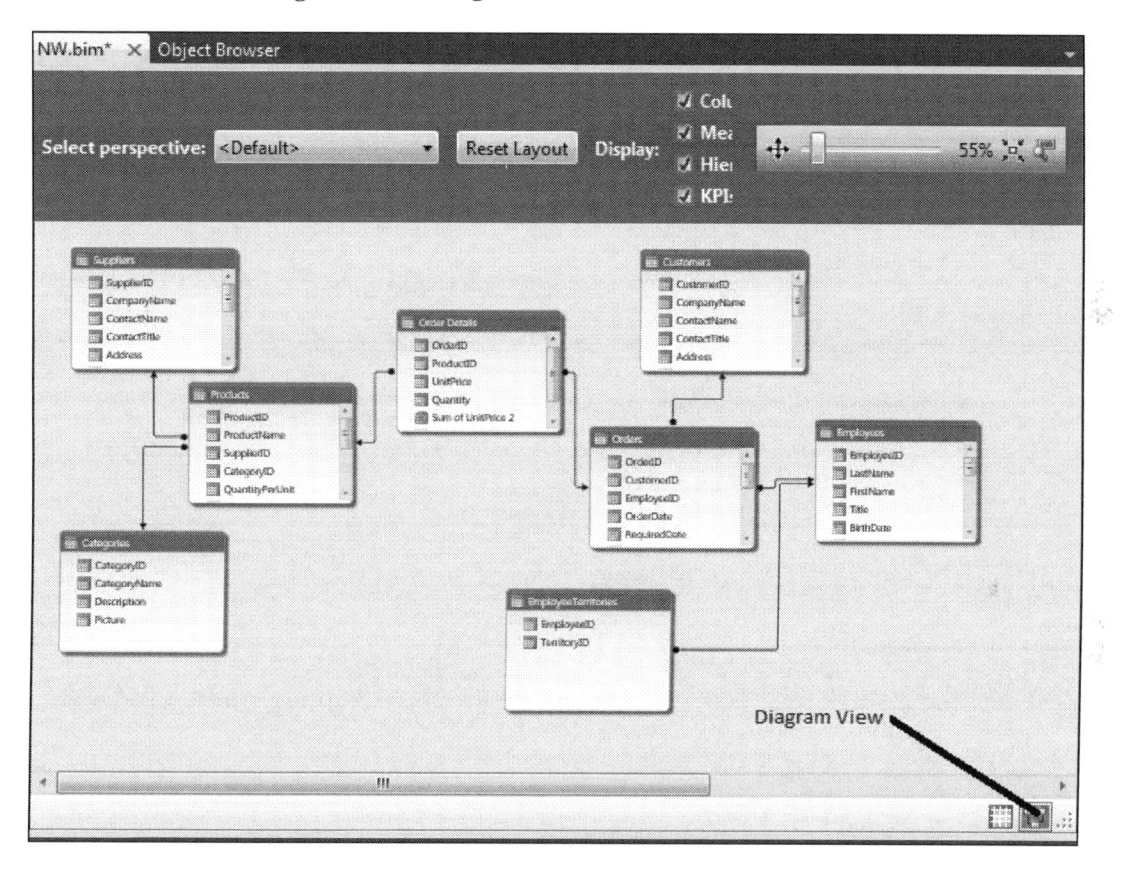

Power View and Reporting Services

When rendered in Grid view, the tables appear in Excel sheet format as shown in the following screenshot:

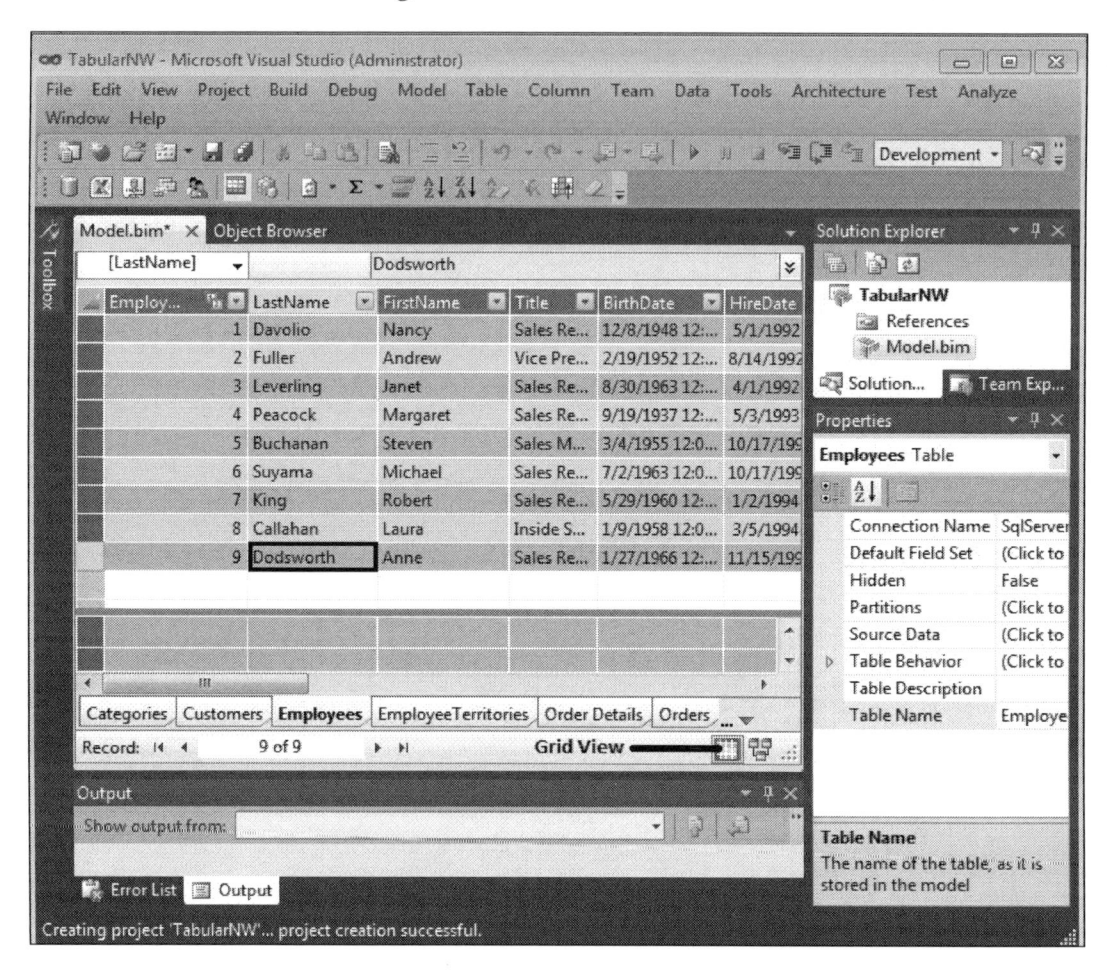

The `Table` and `Column` menu items now have their menu items enabled. The tables imported are shown at the bottom of the imported rows (in Grid view) just like the worksheets in an Excel file. You can tab and review the various tables and you can add/remove columns. The properties of the tables are shown when you highlight a table, such as the one shown for **Employees**.

We added a new column to the `Employees` table, `Full Name` and for the values, we used a **Data Analysis Expression (DAX)** language for the PowerPivot function as shown, which formats the `Full Name` as `LastName, FirstName`.

```
=Concatenate ([LastName], Concatenate (", ",[FirstName]))
```

You can click on a column and see everything connected on the properties directly below **Solution Explorer**.

Every time you make changes to the underlying table some processing takes place, which you can see, taking place below the table.

We delete columns we think are not necessary by removing the check mark to the left of column.

Default field set and table behavior

There are two properties of special significance while planning for Power Views. They are the **default field set** and **table behavior**. With the default field set, you will be creating a set of fields (such as a custom property) that are brought into the Power View as a group. This group is a kind of a template group that typifies the data in the table that you plan to display. Of course, you can bring them one by one manually to Power View as in the hands-on exercise (in the *Creating the first view of the Power View Report* section) for fields that are not marked for default field set. The table behavior is also visually oriented; what is chosen (such as default label and default photo) is shown prominently in some views. Both these properties can be modified by clicking in the indicated position in the property window of the table and making choices.

1. Click on the items related to the default field set of the `Employees` table. The following window is displayed. Initially the **Default fields** pane is empty; you pick and choose from the **Fields in the table** pane and using **Add/Remove** buttons as well as the Move Up/**Move Down** buttons arrange them as shown. Learn more about the default field set by following this link: http://msdn.microsoft.com/en-us/library/hh479569.aspx.

Power View and Reporting Services

2. Move fields from the left pane (**Fields in the table**) to the right pane (**Default fields, in order**) by highlighting each in the left side and using the **Add/Remove** and Up/Down buttons as shown in the following screenshot:

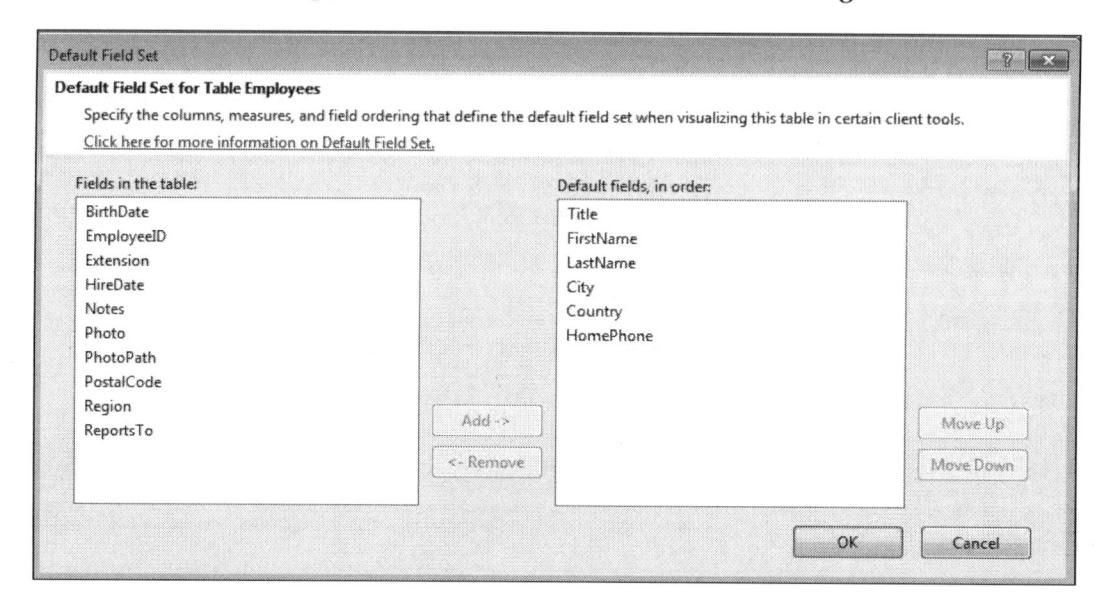

3. Click on **OK**.
4. Similarly, click to edit the table behavior, which opens a window and you enable the following using the handles:

    - **Row Identifier**: `EmployeeID`
    - **Default Label**: `LastName`
    - **Keep Unique Rows**: `EmployeeID`
    - **Default Image**: `Photo`

These are by no means the optimum or the best. Only after running Power View a few times, you will get the intuitive feeling for these choices. Of course, you can modify the model. These two choices affect the way the field list in Power Views is presented and make it easier in authoring ad hoc reports.

Adding measures

In tabular models, **measures** are calculations created using DAX formula. Measures are different from calculated values, which are on a per row basis. Measures are related to taking slices of data or filtering of data. The **Key Performance Indicator (KPI)**, although not described in this chapter, is related to measure and you can create a KPI using measure by creating it in Grid view.

1. Click a column (the UnitPrice column) in the Order Details table and add a measure by clicking **AutoSum (Column | AutoSum | Sum)** as shown in the next image. Review this link to learn more about measures here: http://msdn.microsoft.com/en-us/library/hh230824.aspx. Make sure you understand the difference between calculated value and measure, and the relationship between KPI and measure.

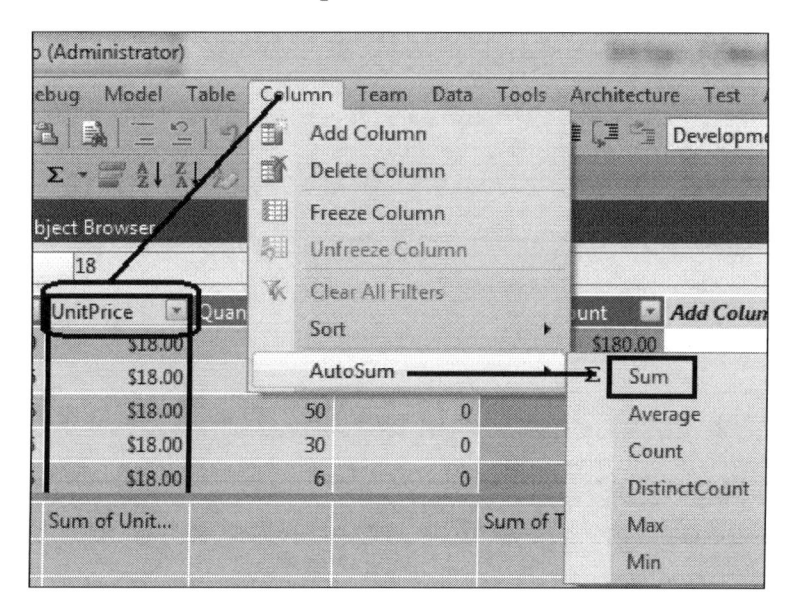

2. In a similar fashion, add an **AutoSum** to **Product Sales for 1997**.
3. Click on **File | Save** to save the model. It is recommended to save the project. It is saved to C:\Users\mysorian\AppData\Local\Temporary Projects\TabularNW\NW.bim (default Model.bim changed to NW.bim using **Save As**).
4. Click on **Build**. Verify that the build succeeds as seen in the **Output** pane.

The workspace database gets updated with the changes in the analysis server.

You do minimum changes to the preceding database except for detaching or deleting the database (these should be done while the model is not open in the designer).

Deploying the model

For client access, the model needs to be deployed. There are several ways this can be done. Herein, the deployment of the model from SSDT will be used. Default deployment options shown in the following list will be used:

- **Processing Option** (default): Analysis service determining the type of processing; faster than `full`
- **Transactional Deployment**: `False`
- **Query Mode In-Memory**: Queries are answered by cache only
- **Server**: `localhost\NJ`
- **Edition**: `Developer`
- **Database**: `TabularNW`
- **Cube Name**: `Model`
- **Impersonation Settings**: `Default`
- **Server: Deployment Server**

Hands-on exercise 6.2 – deploying the model

1. Right-click on the `TabularNW` project in **Solution Explorer** and choose **Deploy**. Deployment begins immediately. After some processing, the deployment success will be displayed.
2. Click on **Close** to close the deployment window.

The deployment is shown in the following screenshot:

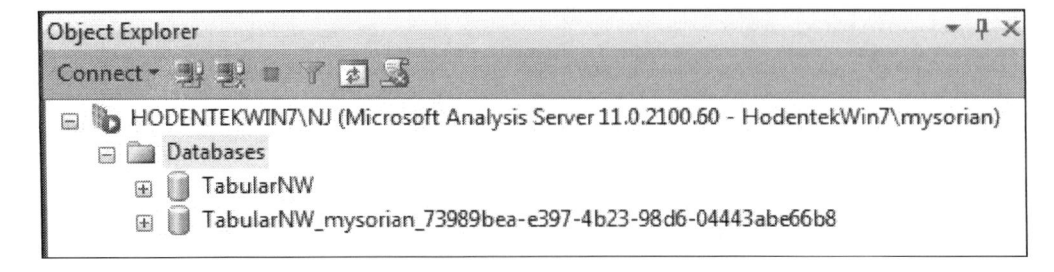

```
Object Explorer
Connect ▼
└─ HODENTEKWIN7\NJ (Microsoft Analysis Server 11.0.2100.60 - HodentekWin7\mysorian)
   └─ Databases
      ├─ TabularNW
      └─ TabularNW_mysorian_73989bea-e397-4b23-98d6-04443abe66b8
```

The model can be changed. After making changes to the model build, process, and deploy. This process can be repeated till you are comfortable with the results that you are looking for. The model can be built with many tables or even a single table.

Tabular model permissions

Permissions are role-based. Permissions for model are created in tabular model roles. Roles for model projects are defined using **Role Manager** dialogue in SSDT. When a model is deployed, roles are managed by database administrators in SQL Server Management Studio. The following are the roles that are available:

Administrator: Can make changes to schema and query data

Process: Only process operations

Read and Process: Query data and process operations but cannot make changes to model schema

Read: can query data but cannot make changes to model schema

None: not permitted to make changes to model schema and cannot query data hands-on

Hands-on exercise 6.3 – creating a role in SQL Server Data Tools

You define a role in SSDT as described here:

1. Click on **Model** to display the drop-down menu.
2. Click on **Roles...**.

    The **Role Manager** window appears displaying a top and a bottom pane. In the top pane, you click the **New** button and create a role and in the bottom pane add members to that role.

3. Click on **New**.

Power View and Reporting Services

4. Add a name for the role and using handles assign the role as shown in the following screenshot:

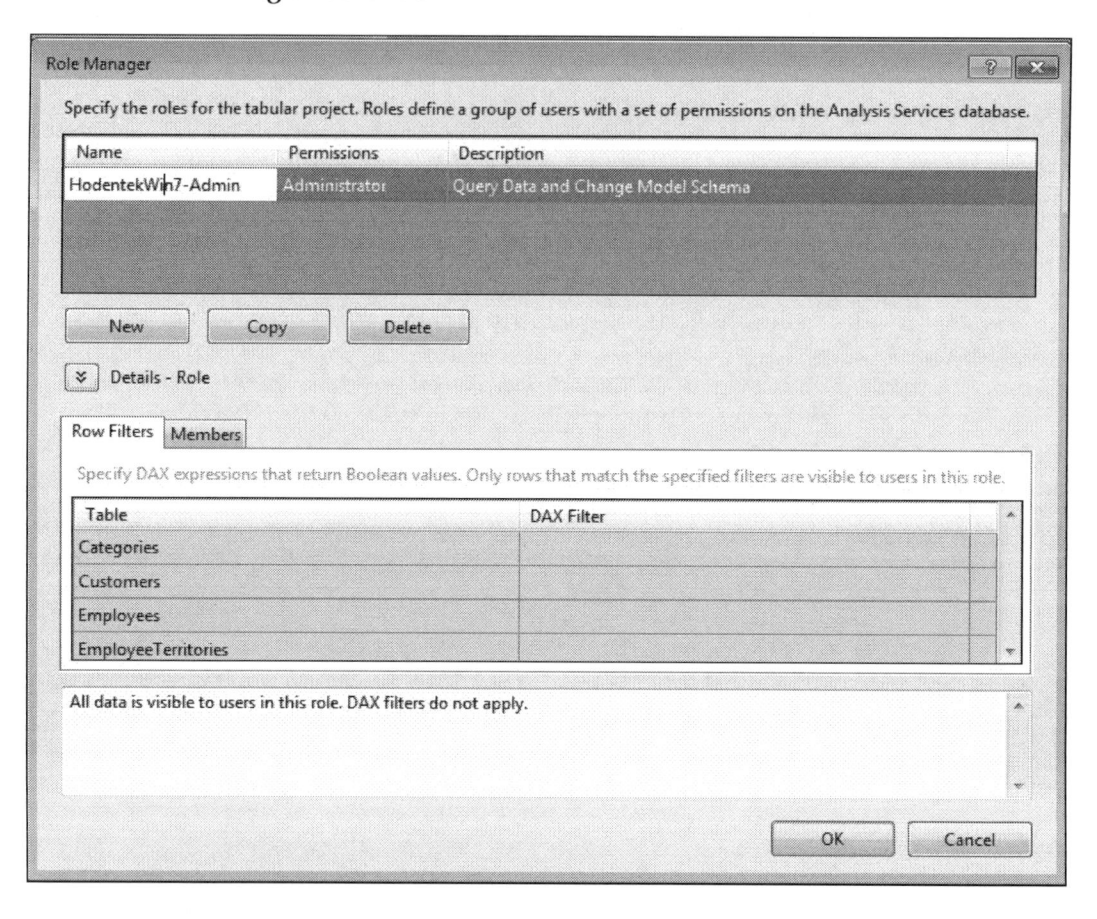

![Role Manager dialog showing HodentekWin7-Admin role with Administrator permissions and Row Filters tab displaying Categories, Customers, Employees, and EmployeeTerritories tables]

5. Add another role `Hodentekwin7\User`. In the row filters in the bottom for `Orders` table, use **Orders [OrderID]>10600** for DAX filter and for `Products` use **Products [UnitPrice]>30** for DAX filter.

   With his permission, the `HodentekWin7-User` has access to only the filtered rows of data from the two tables.

6. Highlight the `Hodentekwin7-Admin` (the first role you added) and click on **Members** in the bottom pane.

   Now you can add members to this role in the window that gets displayed as shown in the following screenshot:

[342]

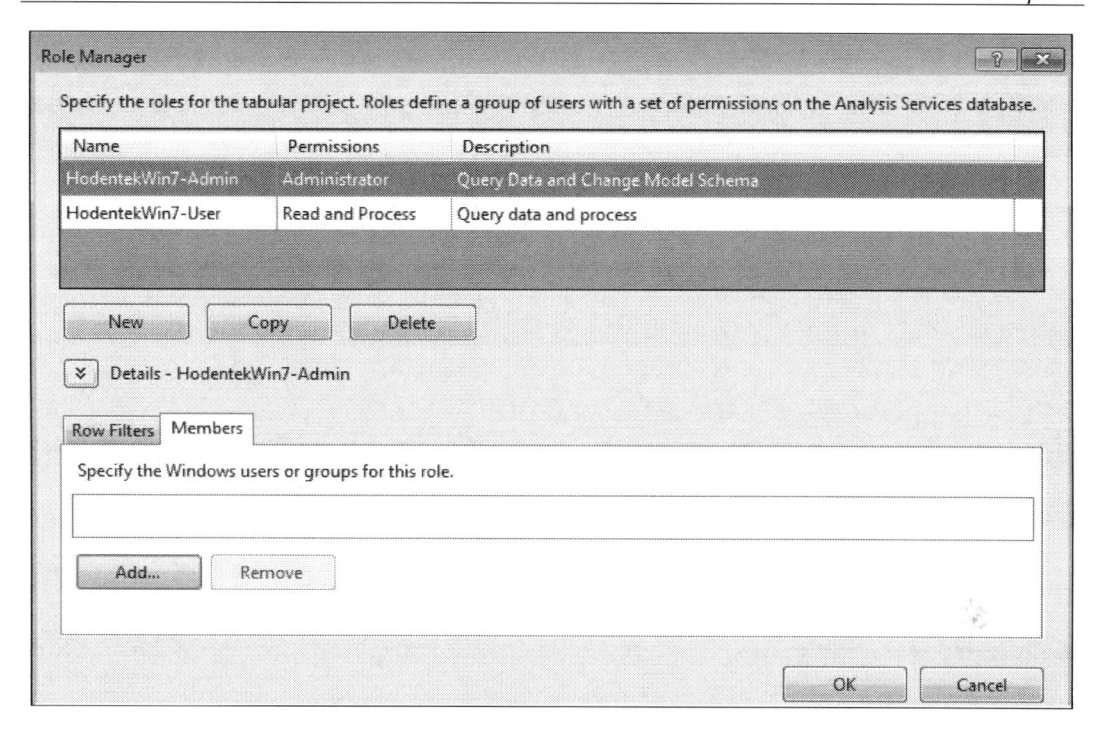

Role Manager

Specify the roles for the tabular project. Roles define a group of users with a set of permissions on the Analysis Services database.

Name	Permissions	Description
HodentekWin7-Admin	Administrator	Query Data and Change Model Schema
HodentekWin7-User	Read and Process	Query data and process

[New] [Copy] [Delete]

Details - HodentekWin7-Admin

Row Filters | **Members**

Specify the Windows users or groups for this role.

[Add...] [Remove]

[OK] [Cancel]

7. Click on **Add...**. The Windows' **Select Users and Groups** dialog is displayed.
8. Type in the name of the administrator and click on **OK**.

After some processing, this role is created. There is no message displayed after this processing. The roles are entered into the database as shown in SSMS.

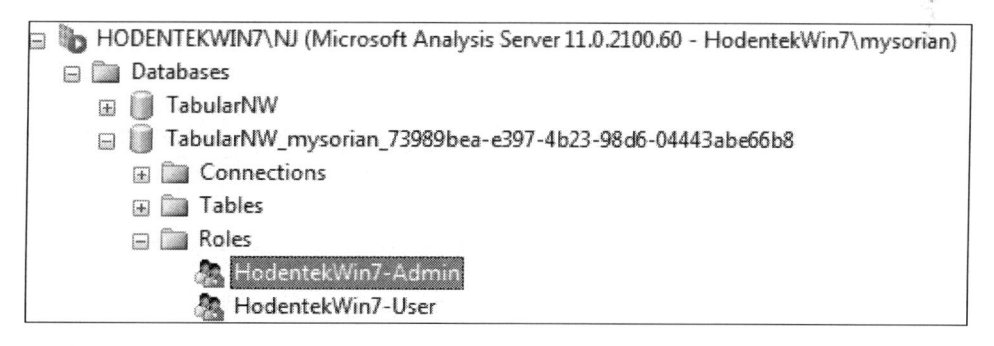

- HODENTEKWIN7\NJ (Microsoft Analysis Server 11.0.2100.60 - HodentekWin7\mysorian)
  - Databases
    - TabularNW
    - TabularNW_mysorian_73989bea-e397-4b23-98d6-04443abe66b8
      - Connections
      - Tables
      - Roles
        - HodentekWin7-Admin
        - HodentekWin7-User

[343]

Creating a Power View

In the previous section, we have seen how we can create a tabular model using SSAS 2012 based on a `Northwind` database in SQL Server 2012 using SQL Server Data Tools. In the following we will connect to this model from SharePoint Server 2010 and then create a Power View report.

In this section a number of features are described that the reader should be able to carry out using the steps as a guide. It is possible that the reader may be using a different BISM data source but the concept is the same. The different features described here are:

- Multiple views and view navigation
- Interactive highlighting
- Interactive filtering and sorting
- Visualization as a card
- Tiles visualization
- Slicers
- Filtering and advanced filtering
- Scatter and bubble charts
- View navigation
- Save, do, undo, and refresh

Hands-on exercise 6.4 – connecting to the model from SharePoint Server 2010

There are a couple of ways of connecting to the data on the analysis services server and here we look at one of them:

1. Bring up IE 9.0 with administrative rights and connect to the `HodentekWin7` site (not the administrative site) as shown in the following screenshot:

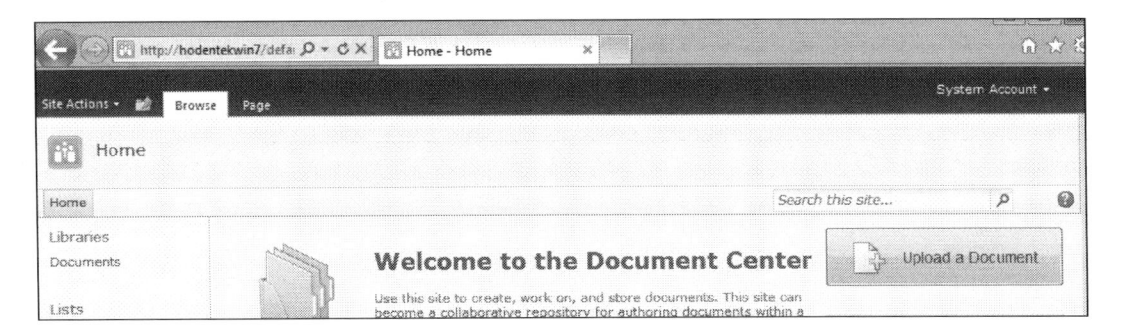

Chapter 6

[screenshot of SharePoint Document Center home page]

We now create SharePoint permissions on the BI Semantic Model Connection

2. Open the **Permissions Tools** section of the site as shown in the following screenshot:

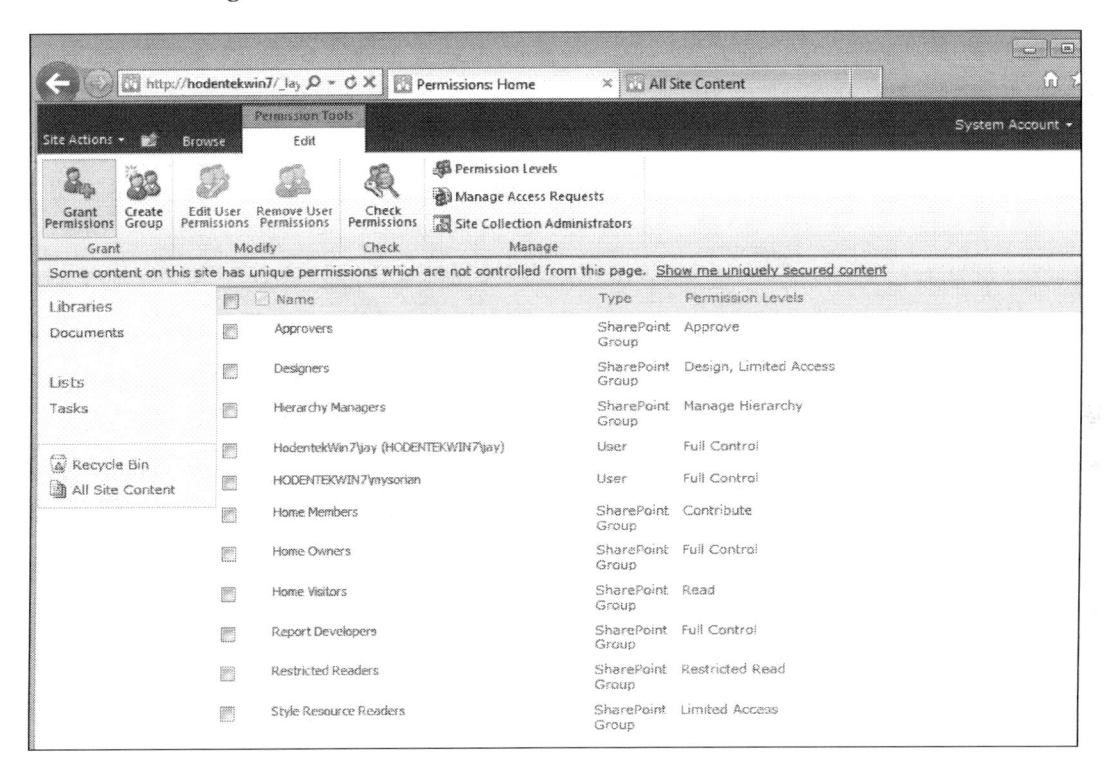

[screenshot of SharePoint Permissions Tools page showing list of groups and users with their permission levels]

Power View and Reporting Services

3. Click on **Create Group** and name the new group BISM USERS.

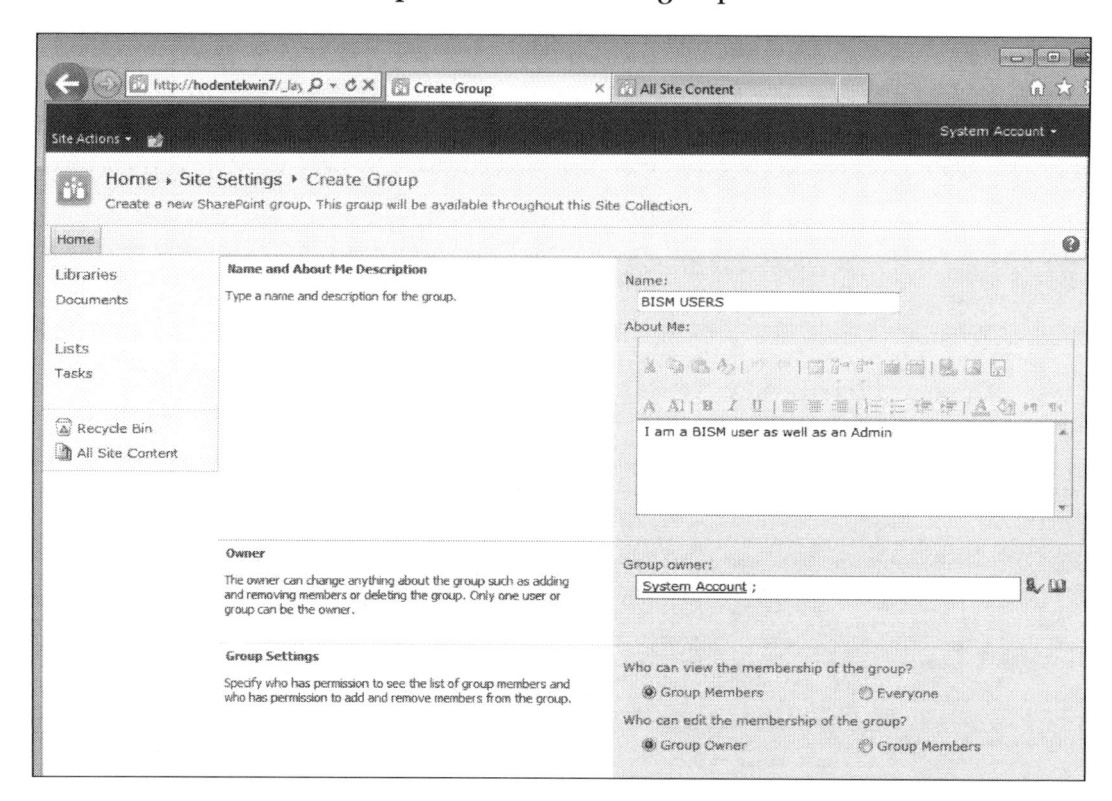

Only top half of the screen is shown. In the bottom half, place a check mark for **Full Control** in the **Give Group Permission to this site** section. If needed, you can view site permission assignments with the link on this half of the screen.

Normally read permission is all that is needed. By default there are no permissions checked. Herein **Full Control** was checked.

4. Click on **Create** on the bottom half of screen. The **BISM USERS** group is selected as shown in the following screenshot:

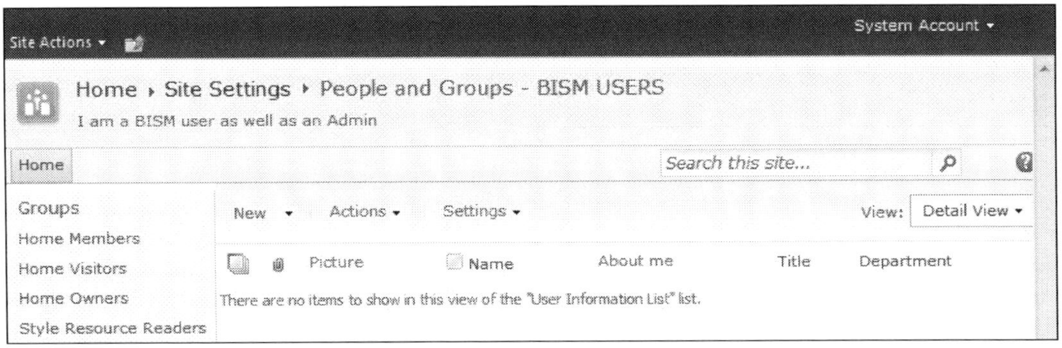

5. Click on **New** to add a user or group accounts and they will have read permission. In the same screen, you can delete users as well.

Connecting to the model

You need to connect to the model from SharePoint server. This is carried out by creating a data source in SharePoint server's document library that hooks up to the model on the SQL Server Analysis Server.

Creating a data source using the model as the source

Here, we create a data source using the model as the source:

1. Create a data source in the Documents library of type **Report Data Source**.
2. Change **Data Source Type** to **Microsoft BI Semantic Model for Power View** as shown in the following screenshot:

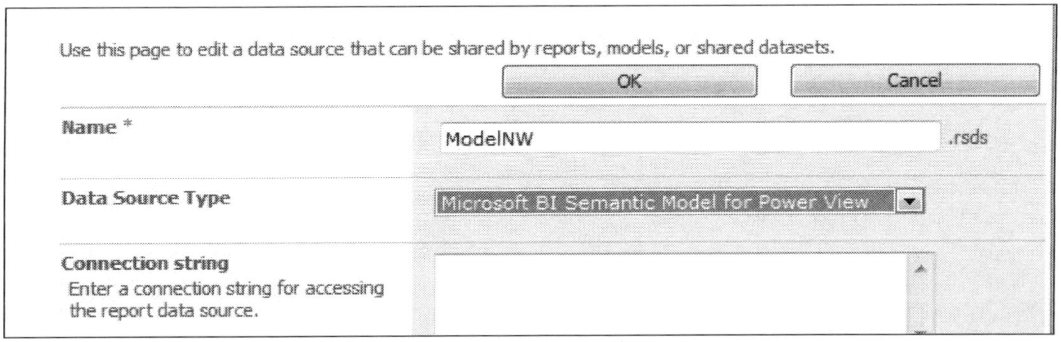

Power View and Reporting Services

3. The full view of data source is as shown here in the following screenshot:

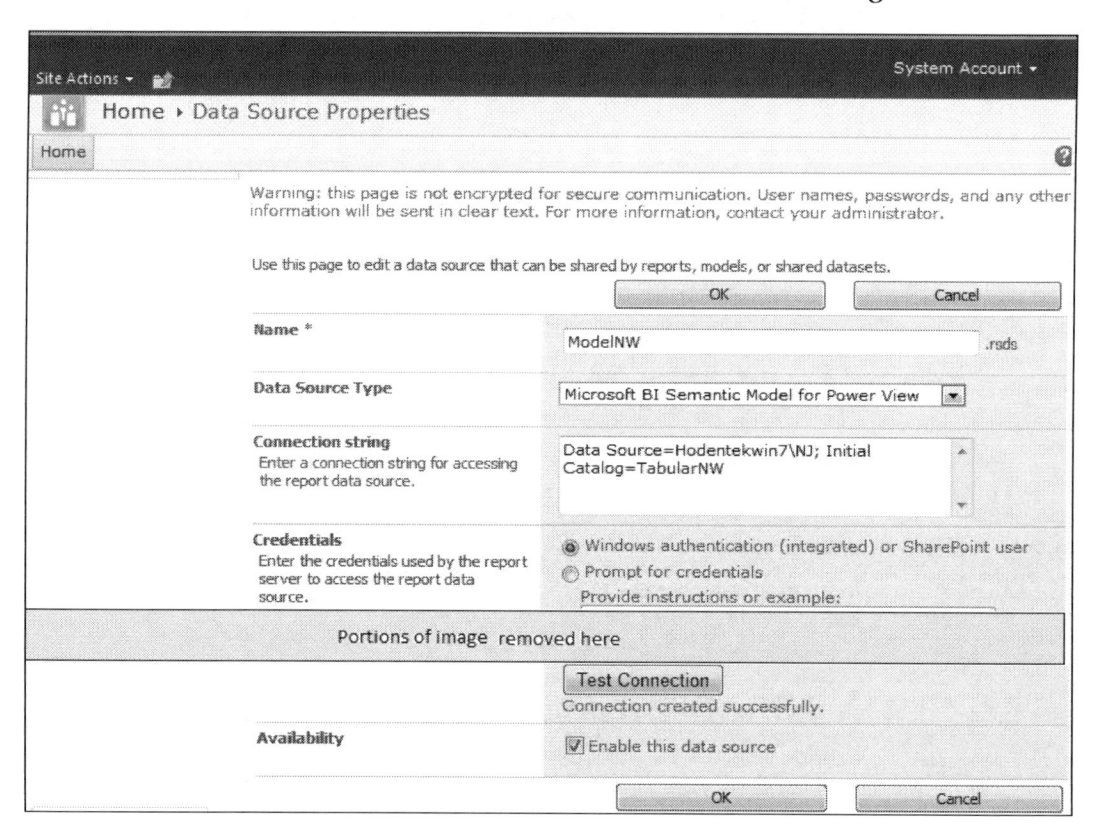

> You need to know the connection string to enter here. You will know this when you create a tabular model in SSDT. You can also expand the database node in the workspace database in your analysis services server where you deployed the model. It is as shown:
> - Data source=<name of SQL Server 2012 which has the database>
> - Catalog = <Name of database>

4. Click on **OK**. The data source is created as shown in the following screenshot:

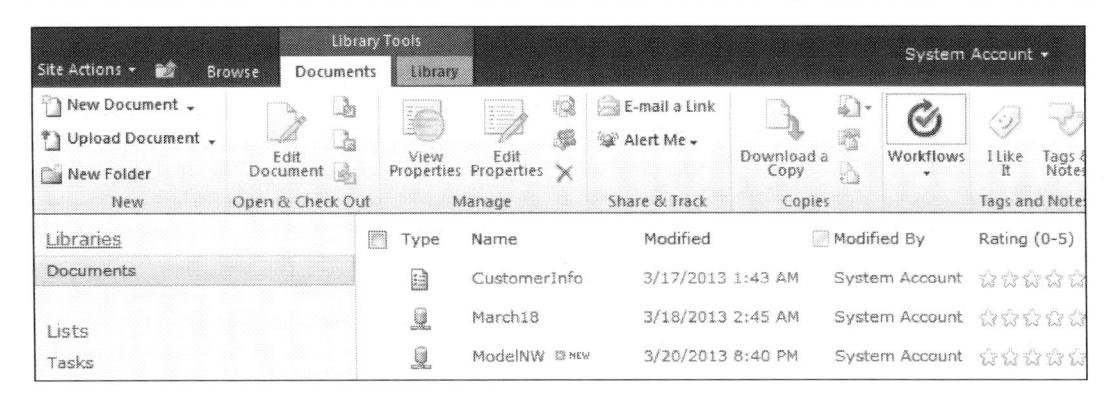

When you want to modify the data in the data source you check it out of SharePoint and modify the META data of the model in SSDT and deploy it to SSAS. When you check in again, assuming the connections are all in place you will have the modified data in the data source. This is schematically shown in the next image:

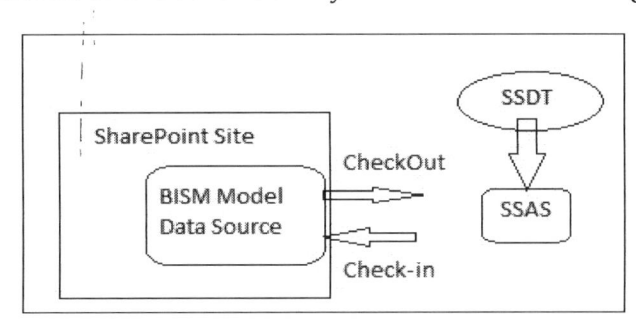

Creating a Power View report using the data source

Power View reports can be created in Excel as well, but we will be using the data source created previously based on a tabular model.

> Power View could be created with a tabular model only, but Microsoft has released a CTP version, which works with multidimensional models as well; follow this link for details:
> http://blogs.msdn.com/b/analysisservices/archive/2012/11/29/power-view-for-multidimensional-models-preview.aspx

Power View and Reporting Services

In the following hands-on exercise we will create our first Power View report using the data source we created in the previous section.

Hands-on exercise 6.5 – exploring a Power View report

We start off using the `ModelNW` data source we created earlier:

1. Click on the handle for `ModelNW` data source created earlier to display the drop-down menu.

2. Click on **Create Power View Report**.

   `Report1.rdlx` with **View 1/1** is displayed as shown in the following screenshot. The tables we selected in creating the tabular model are all on the right side. **View 1/1** is the first of the many views that can be created using **New View** in the menu.

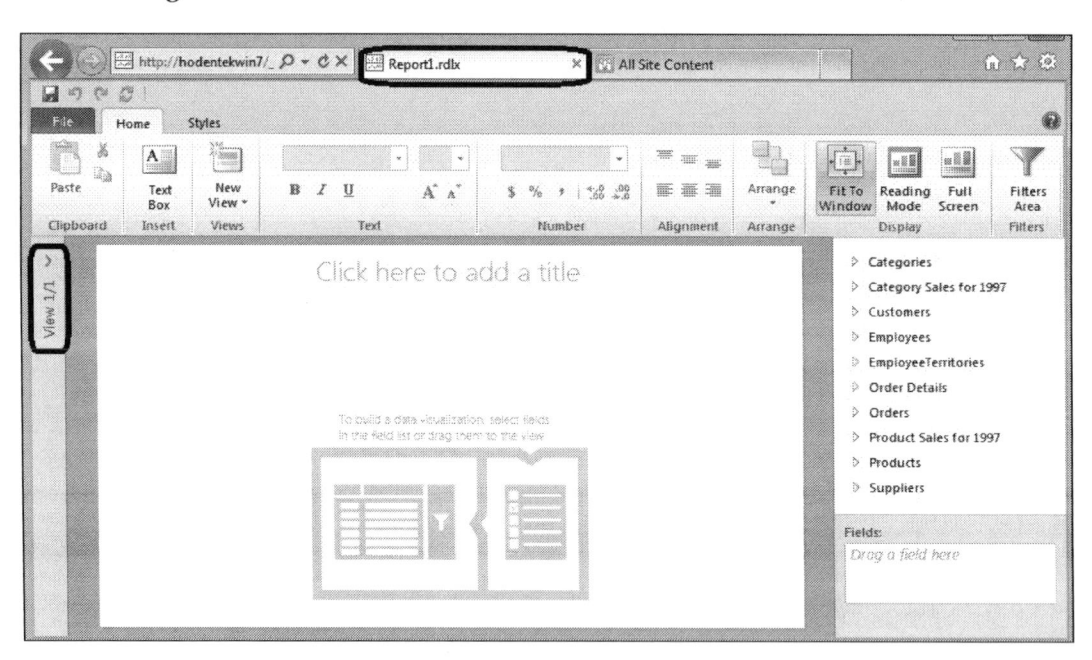

3. Click on **File** to display the following:

[350]

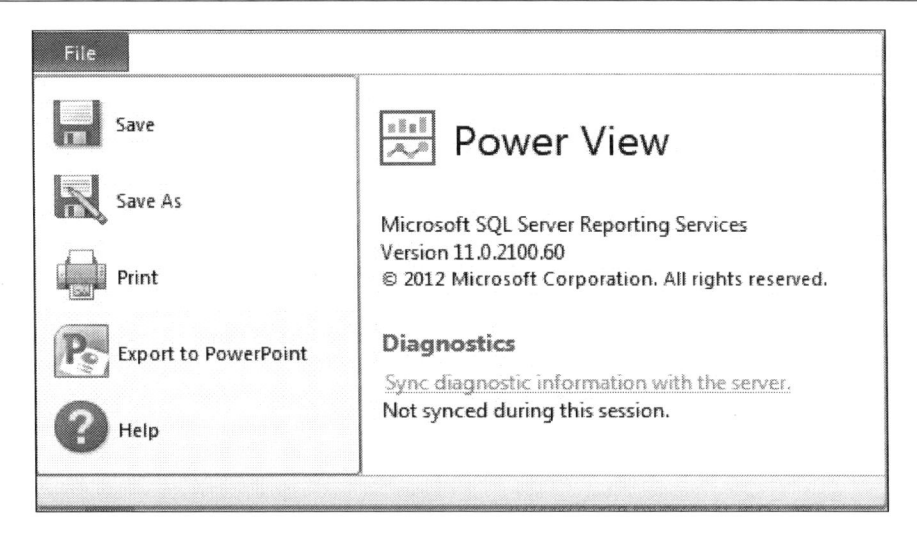

4. Click on **Styles** to display the themes you can choose from as shown in the following screenshot:

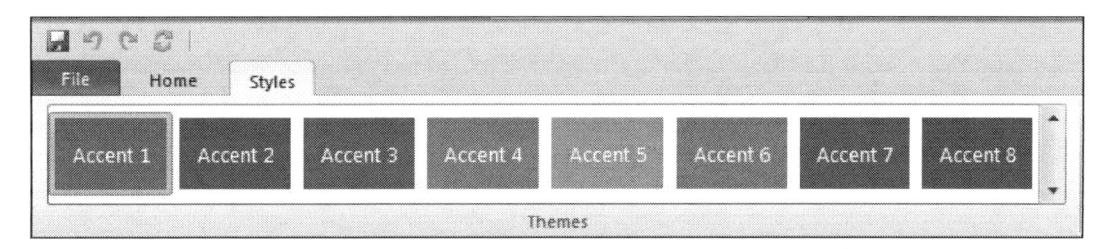

Creating the first view of the Power View report

A Power View report consists of a number of views of the data contained in the tables selected while building the models. In creating a view, we choose a number of columns from related tables and bring them to the area of the view named **Fields** which is directly below the list of tables.

1. Create the title `Orders by NW Employees` by overwriting the text in the indicated area **click here to add a title**.
2. Expand the table nodes and choose the following by placing a check mark for the following:
    - **CategoryName** from the **Categories** table
    - **Full Name** from the **Employees** table

- ∑**TotalAmount** from the **Order-Details** table
- **ShipCity** from the **Orders** table

This fills up the **Fields** area as shown in the following screenshot:

Tile by:
Drag a field here

Fields:
- CategoryName
- ShipCity
- Full Name
- ∑ TotalAmount

This also adds the table shown here in the view on the left side:

Orders by NW Employees

CategoryName	ShipCity	Full Name	TotalAmount
Beverages	Aachen	Peacock, Margaret	$247.20
Beverages	Albuquerque	Buchanan, Steven	$679.50
Beverages	Albuquerque	Callahan, Laura	$285.00
Beverages	Albuquerque	Davolio, Nancy	$523.00
Beverages	Albuquerque	Dodsworth, Anne	$10,540.00
Beverages	Albuquerque	Fuller, Andrew	$135.00
Beverages	Albuquerque	Leverling, Janet	$6,324.00
Beverages	Albuquerque	Peacock, Margaret	$848.40

From this information alone, we are not sure how much data is being accessed and we could filter using the filter icon, which becomes visible when you hover on the top-right edge of the table as shown in the following screenshot:

Pop-Out

Show Filters

> Some of the controls such as **Show Filters**, **Pop-out**, **Sorting Asc / Desc**, and controls on columns to sort are small and sometimes seen only when you hover over them. The contrast of text is very poor as well.

3. Click on the **Show Filters** icon.

   The filters area is displayed on a side pane (**>filters**) as shown. The image shows the employee **FullName** that we can filter. Similarly, we can filter the other columns in this table as well.

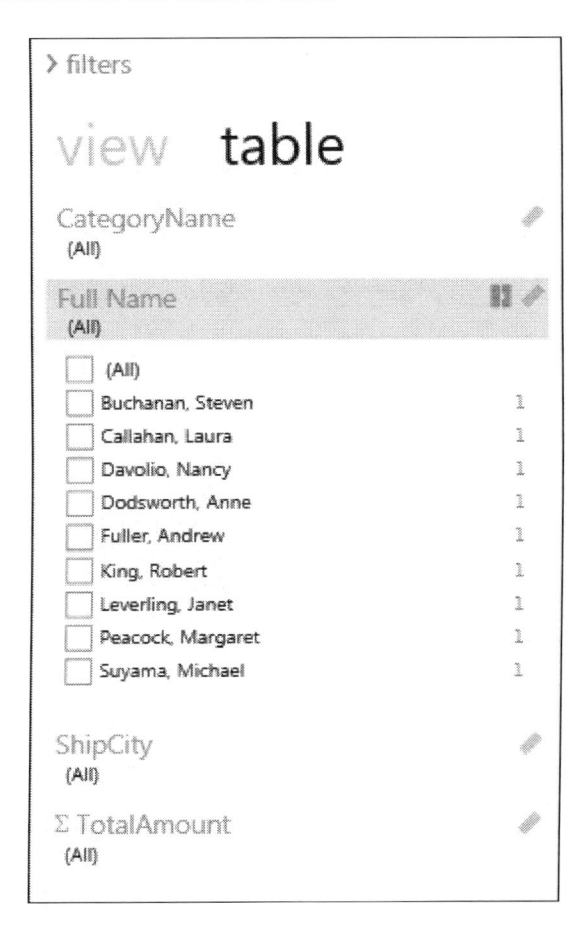

   > filters

   view **table**

   CategoryName
   (All)

   Full Name
   (All)
   - (All)
   - Buchanan, Steven — 1
   - Callahan, Laura — 1
   - Davolio, Nancy — 1
   - Dodsworth, Anne — 1
   - Fuller, Andrew — 1
   - King, Robert — 1
   - Leverling, Janet — 1
   - Peacock, Margaret — 1
   - Suyama, Michael — 1

   ShipCity
   (All)

   Σ TotalAmount
   (All)

4. In the filters area, expand **ShipCity** and choose the following cities: **Kirkland**, **Elgin**, **Madrid**, and **Torino**.

The filters area now appears as shown. Notice **ShipCity is Kirkland, Elgin, Madrid or Torino**. You may also use an **Advanced Filter** if you need to. It is skipped here but described later.

Deleting the columns from the table is also easy. We can clear the check mark in the tables or, click on the handle for the corresponding field in the **Fields** area as shown and choose **Remove Field**:

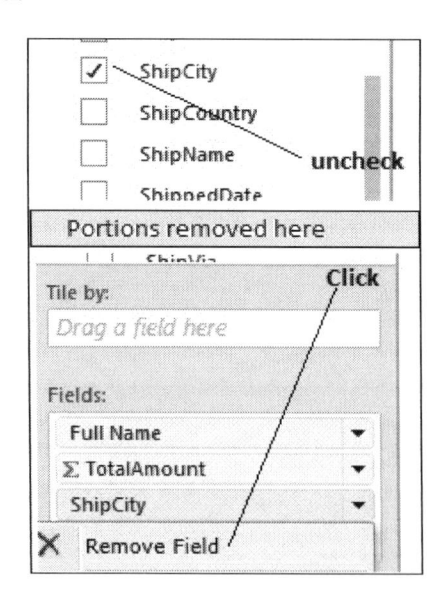

In what follows, however, **ShipCity** is not removed.

Creating a chart showing sales orders from NW Employees shipped from cities

Here, we'll be creating a chart showing the sales order shipped from cities:

1. Keep the first table and create another table with the fields: `FirstName` from `Employees`, `ShipCity` from `Orders`, and `∑TotalAmount` from `Order Details`.
2. With this table in focus, click on the `Column` icon in **Tables Tools** shown in the following screenshot:

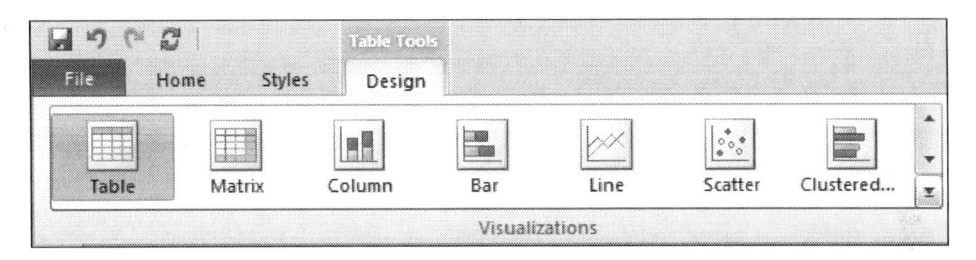

A column chart is generated as shown, which replaces the table:

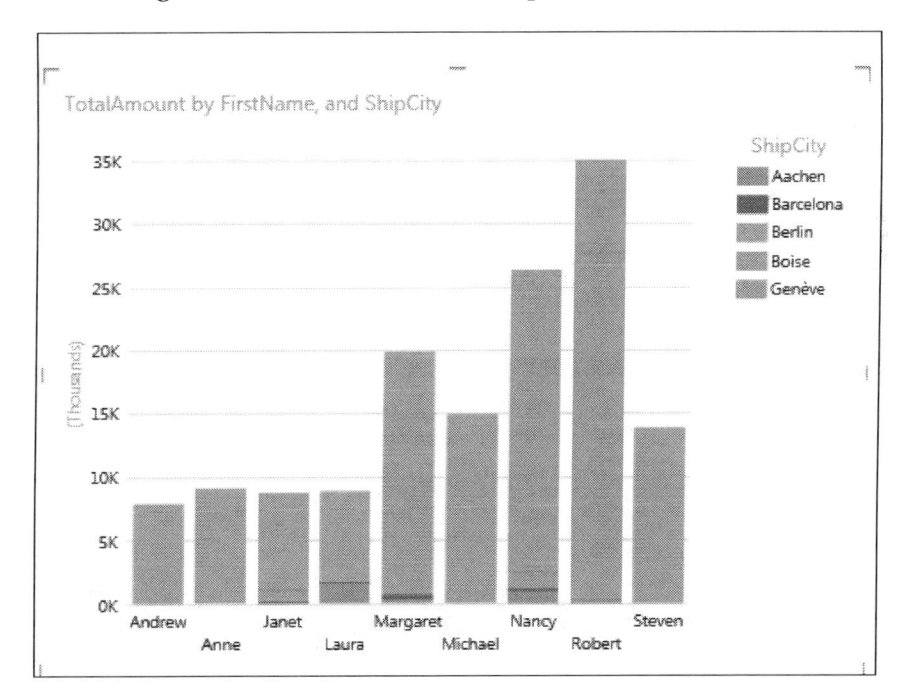

Power View and Reporting Services

This chart is very interactive; you can pick and choose (filter) the items such as **ShipCity** and **FirstName** from **Employee** and immediately render the chart. This next one shows a different choice of filter where only the sales handled by female employees for chosen cities are displayed:

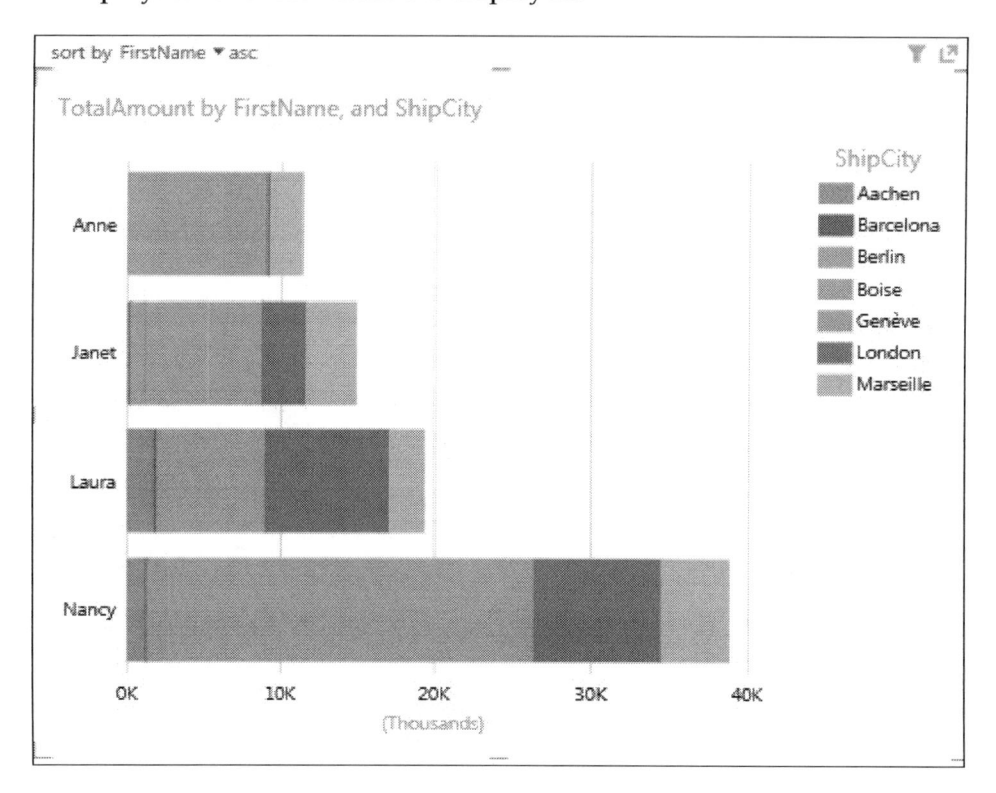

The **Chart Tools** option from the ribbon allows you to display the type of chart design you want to display as shown in the following screenshot:

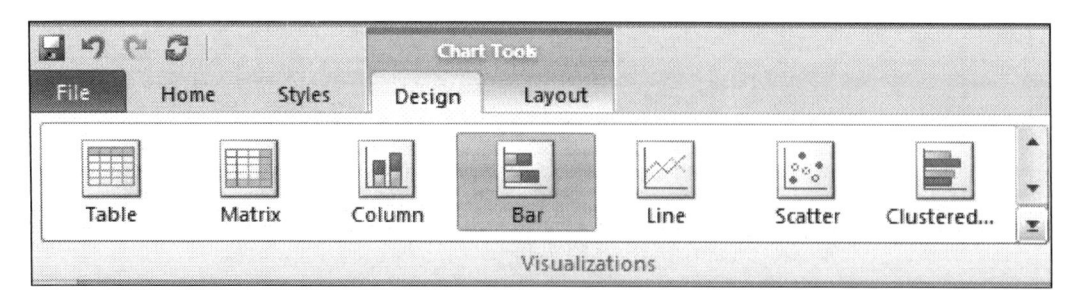

The **Layout** tab of **Chart Tools** allows you to make changes to the layout as shown in the following screenshot:

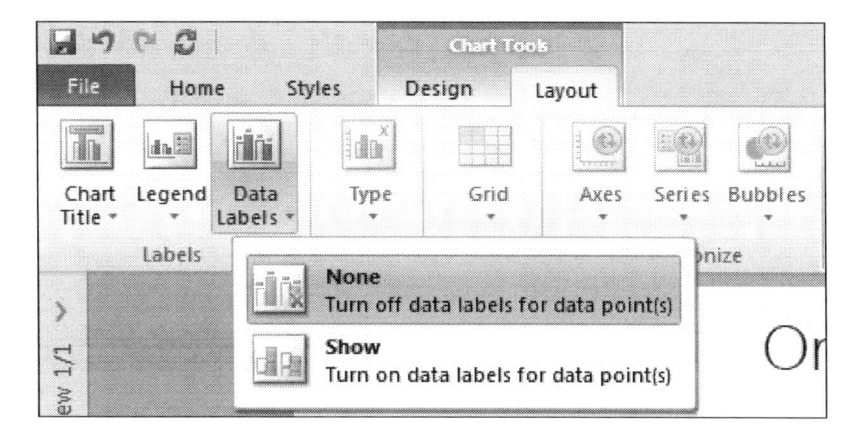

Reports generally have just one view, the one you see, which translates to one view per report. The possibility of creating multiple views per report in Power View is a brand new feature of SSRS 2012 when RS is installed in SharePoint Integrated mode. We explore this in the next section.

Adding a second view to the Power View report

The Power View report can consist of a number of views of data made available simultaneously although you will be viewing a single view at a time. We add another view to this report to understand how multiple views are created.

1. Click on **Home** in the ribbon and click on **New View** and choose to add a new one or a duplicate of the existing. You may want to show a duplicate with different filtering or a different kind of chart.

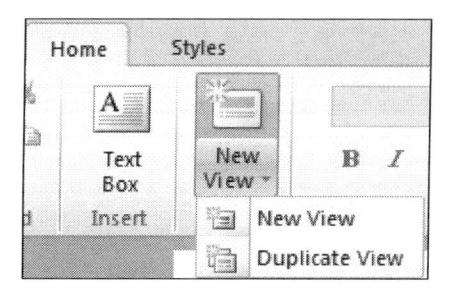

Power View and Reporting Services

2. Click on **New View**.

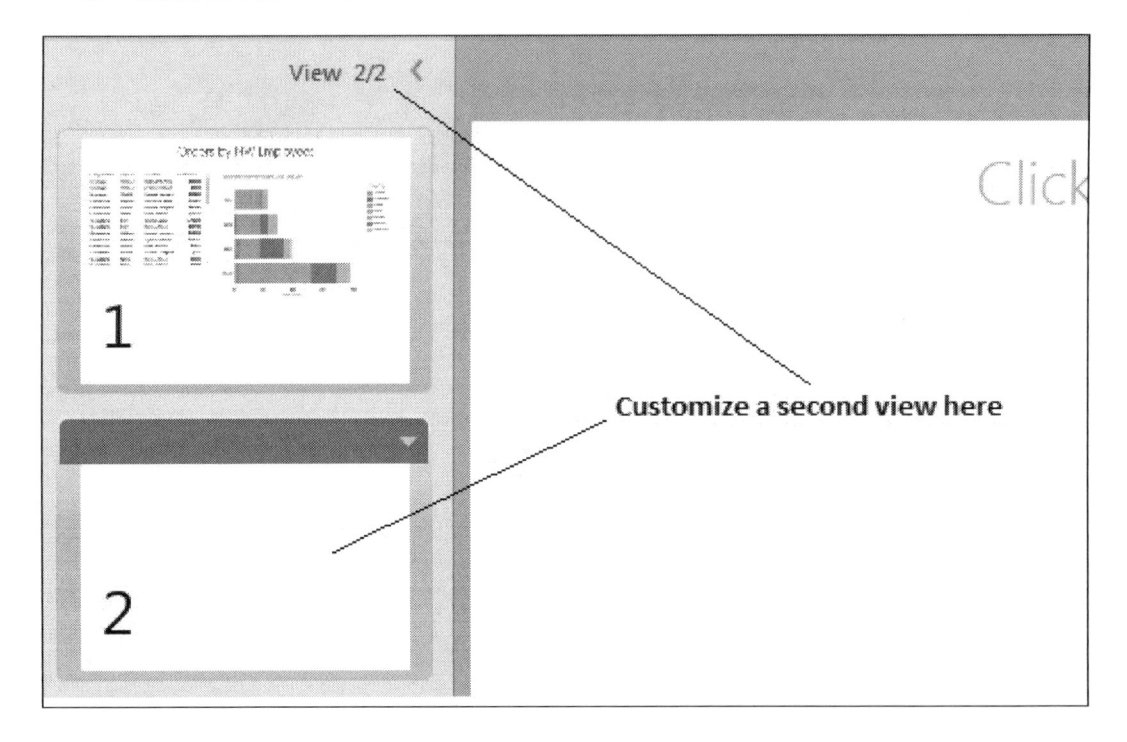

A second view, which is presently empty, will be added as shown in the preceding screenshot and it will be fed from the same tables as before. The first view is present and you can immediately bring it into view by clicking on the first view in the preceding screenshot.

3. In this view choose the following: **ProductName** from Products, **CategoryName** from Categories, and show ∑**TotalAmount** as related to before (Hint: you will be adding these to the fields).
4. Click to change this to **Column chart** of type **100% Column**.

The following chart will be displayed:

[358]

Chapter 6

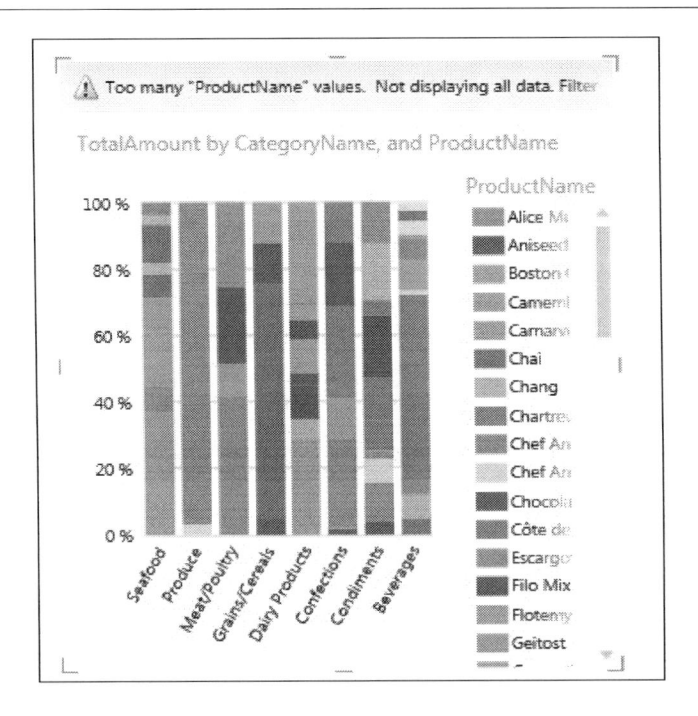

[Chart: TotalAmount by CategoryName, and ProductName — warning "Too many 'ProductName' values. Not displaying all data. Filter"]

This shows that there is a need for filtering (actually, it needs a great deal of filtering).

5. Filter both **CategoryName** (only three categories now) as well as **ProductName** to arrive at something that your ad hoc reporting needs dictate, such as the one shown in the following screenshot:

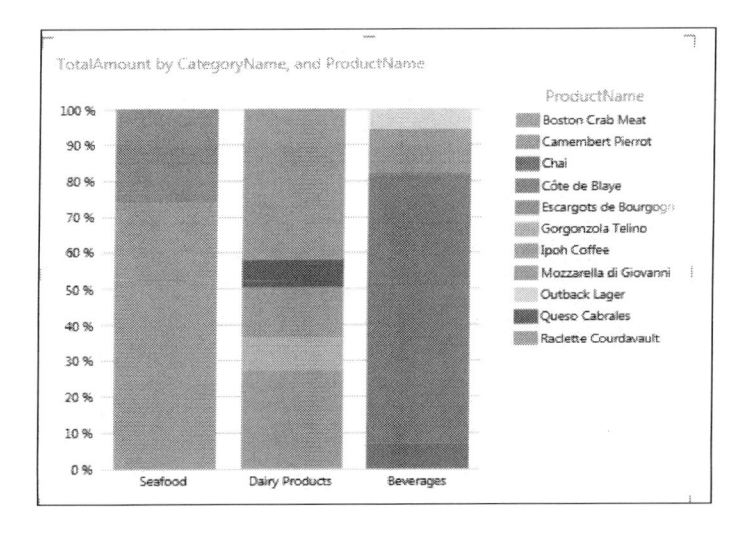

[Chart: TotalAmount by CategoryName, and ProductName — filtered to Seafood, Dairy Products, Beverages. ProductName legend: Boston Crab Meat, Camembert Pierrot, Chai, Côte de Blaye, Escargots de Bourgogne, Gorgonzola Telino, Ipoh Coffee, Mozzarella di Giovanni, Outback Lager, Queso Cabrales, Raclette Courdavault]

[359]

Power View and Reporting Services

Power View has lots of interactive features, highlighting is one such feature. In the next section we see how highlighting works.

Highlighting of data

The chart created in the preceding section is interactive and allows you to look at any of the products' performance.

1. Click on any **ProductName** in the second view you created.

   The **Total Amount by ProductName and Category Name** option only shows that product.

   For example, if you click on **Chai** in the previous image you will see that **Beverages** gets highlighted in **Total Amount by ProductName and Category Name**.

2. Hold *Ctrl* key and click on any product and you are back into the unselected view you started with.

Another visualization of table is the `Card` format. When integrated into a dashboard they become powerful. In the next section, we look at creating cards.

Displaying data as a card

Card is another popular display format and `Table Behavior`, which we configured (during tabular model building process in SSDT) earlier should help in visualizing the `Card` type display. Each row in the table is converted to a card with **Table Behavior** influencing the display.

1. Add a third view to the report using the following: **FullName, City, Country, HomePhone** from the `Employees` table and ∑**TotalAmount** (**Autosum of [UnitPrice*Quantity]**) from the **Order_Details** table.

2. Open **Table Tools** to access **Card**.

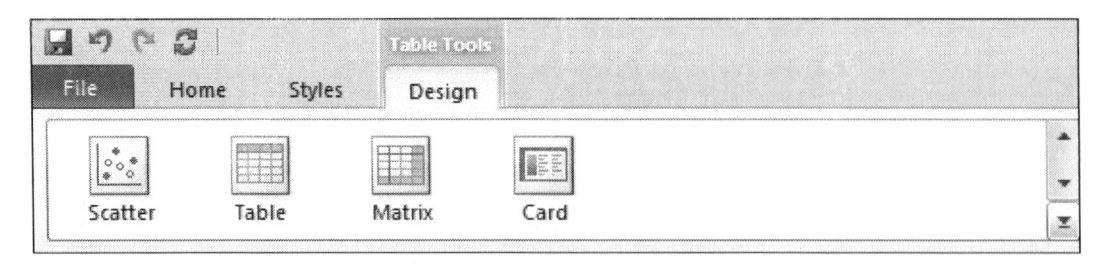

[360]

Chapter 6

3. Click on **Card**. The table changes to Card type as shown in the following screenshot:

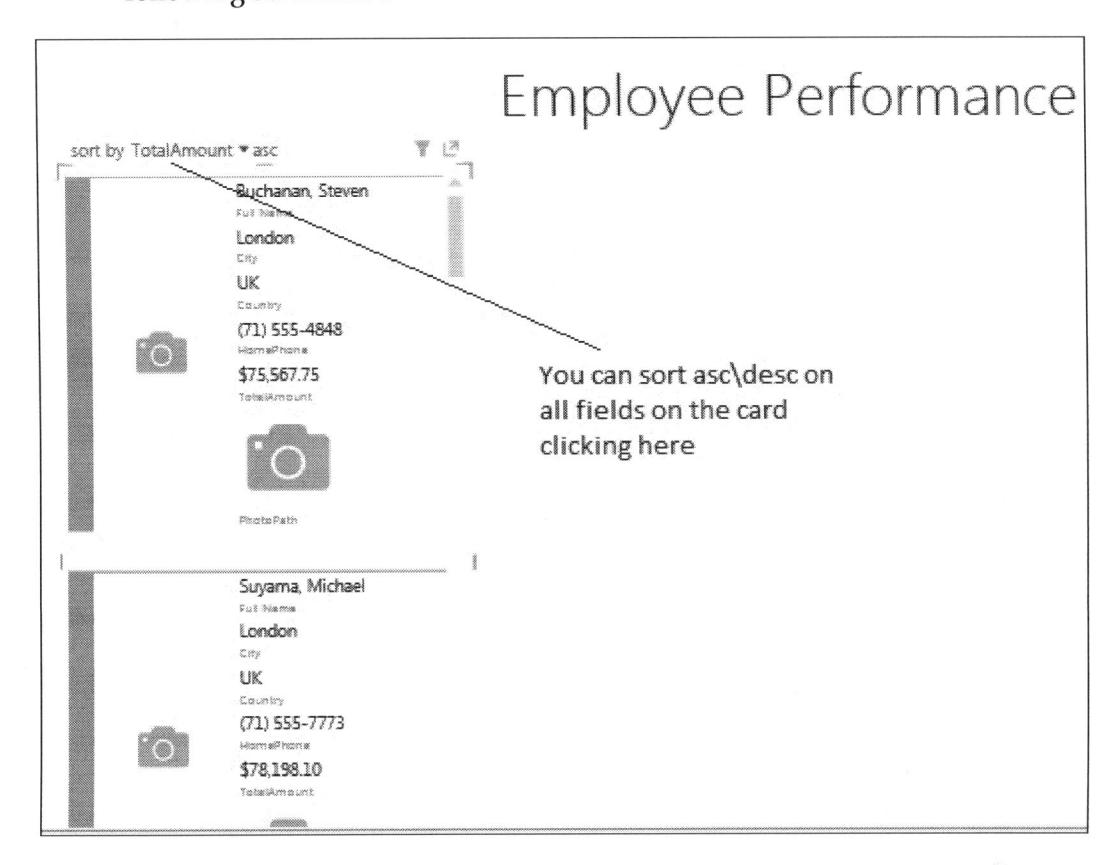

![Employee Performance card view screenshot showing cards for Buchanan, Steven and Suyama, Michael with sort by TotalAmount asc, and annotation "You can sort asc\desc on all fields on the card clicking here"]

Note that the graphics in the data are not shown, and the model needs fixing, or some formats may not be easily displayed. The `Northwind` database we attached to the server came from an old Access database and the picture links are not what they should be for displaying here.

> The work around for this is too involved and is provided in a word document separately. The next image shows the result of changing the image data to display the graphics. The way the image and the full name formatted are a consequence of the default field set and table behavior we used in the model.

Power View and Reporting Services

Another type of visualization that you can use to transform a table is a tiled view. We visualize the table as tiles in the following section.

Using tiles

Tiles contain a navigational strip that can be used to navigate between the rows of the table. When you click on **Tiles** in the ribbon one of the columns become the dominant feature of the view with the rest of the table displayed by a filter that uses the dominant feature. By default, the first column of the table becomes the dominant feature.

1. Create a table with the following: **EmployeeID**, **FullName**, **HomePhone**, **Photo**, **City**, and **Country**.
2. Click on **Tiles**.

3. The tiled view gets displayed as shown in the following screenshot:

Slicer is yet another kind of filter in Power View. You use an attribute to filter the data and the attribute column (say the `City` field) is first set as a separate table from the data to be sliced (say the main table). You click the single column table and click on **Slice** to convert it into a slicer. In the next section, you create a slicer and experiment with it.

Slicing the data

This is another visualization/filtering aid that very much implements the WHERE clause in SQL queries.

1. Create another table by the side of the card in the preceding section using just `City` from the `Employees` table as shown in the following screenshot:

[363]

Power View and Reporting Services

2. After clicking on the **City** table, click on **Slicer** as shown in the next screenshot:

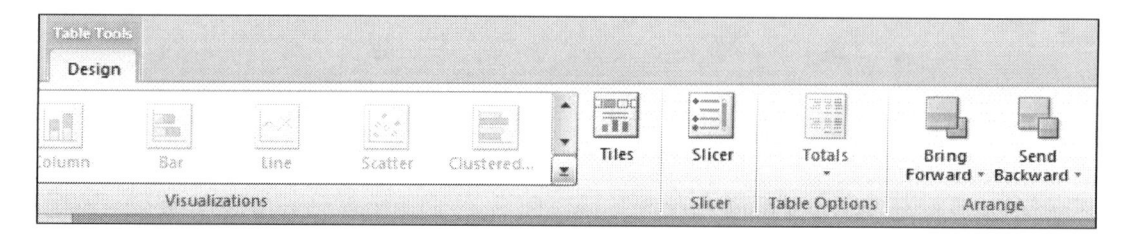

The **City** table changes with a blue square button for each of the cities in the list.

3. Click on any city in the **City** list.

   You will see that both the cards and the table are filtered for the city you chose as shown. Slicer works like a global filter for all items in the view.

When your filtering requirements are not satisfied by the filters described above, you can use advanced filtering, another great GUI driven interface where you can easily set up the filtering criterion (you can filter more than one column). In the next section, you will work with this interface.

[364]

Advanced filtering

In this section, we will discuss advanced filtering techniques:

1. Create a table in any of the views consisting of: **Sum of UnitPrice 2**, **TotalAmount**, **EmployeeID**, and **Ship Country**.
2. Filter the table where **Sum of UnitPrice2** is greater than or equal to 300 as shown using the Advance Filter control.

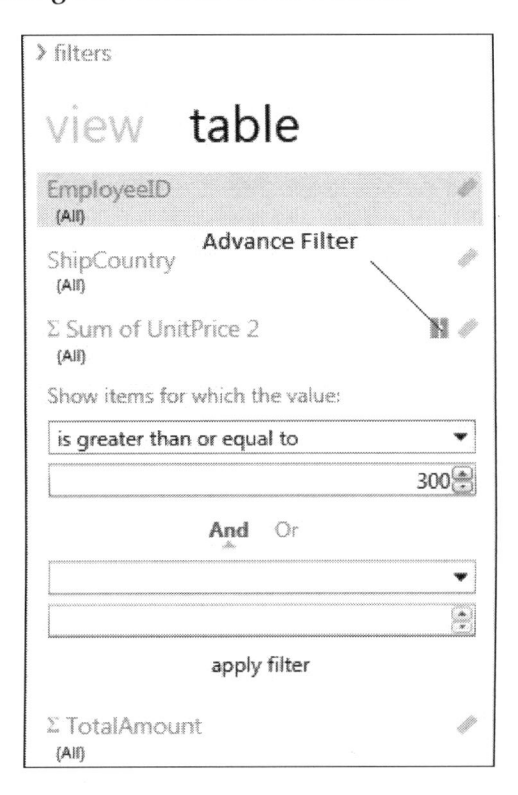

```
> filters

view   table

EmployeeID
(All)
                    Advance Filter
ShipCountry
(All)

Σ Sum of UnitPrice 2
(All)

Show items for which the value:

is greater than or equal to          ▼

                                 300 ⬍

            And   Or

                                     ▼

                                     ⬍

            apply filter

Σ TotalAmount
(All)
```

3. Click on **apply filter**.
4. The table you added gets filtered to satisfy this condition.

Scatter and **bubble** charts adds extra visualization of the nature of data. This is especially useful when you are comparing data from two different series. Scatter charts provide the data as points in a chart with each point representing data. In a bubble chart, a second series adds the comparison information to each of the data points as related to the second series with which it is compared.

Power View and Reporting Services

Scatter and bubble charts

Using scatter and bubble charts is a great way to show the variability of the data when you are dealing with a large set of data. Even in this small data set of `Northwind` we can see some of the features. In a scatter chart, both axes show measures.

1. Create a table in a new view with the following columns: `ProductName` from the `Products` table, ∑`UnitPrice` from the `Products` table, `Sum of UnitPrice2` from the `Order Details` table.
2. In the **Chart Tools** menu, click on **Scatter**.

   The table gets changed to a scatter chart as shown in the following screenshot:

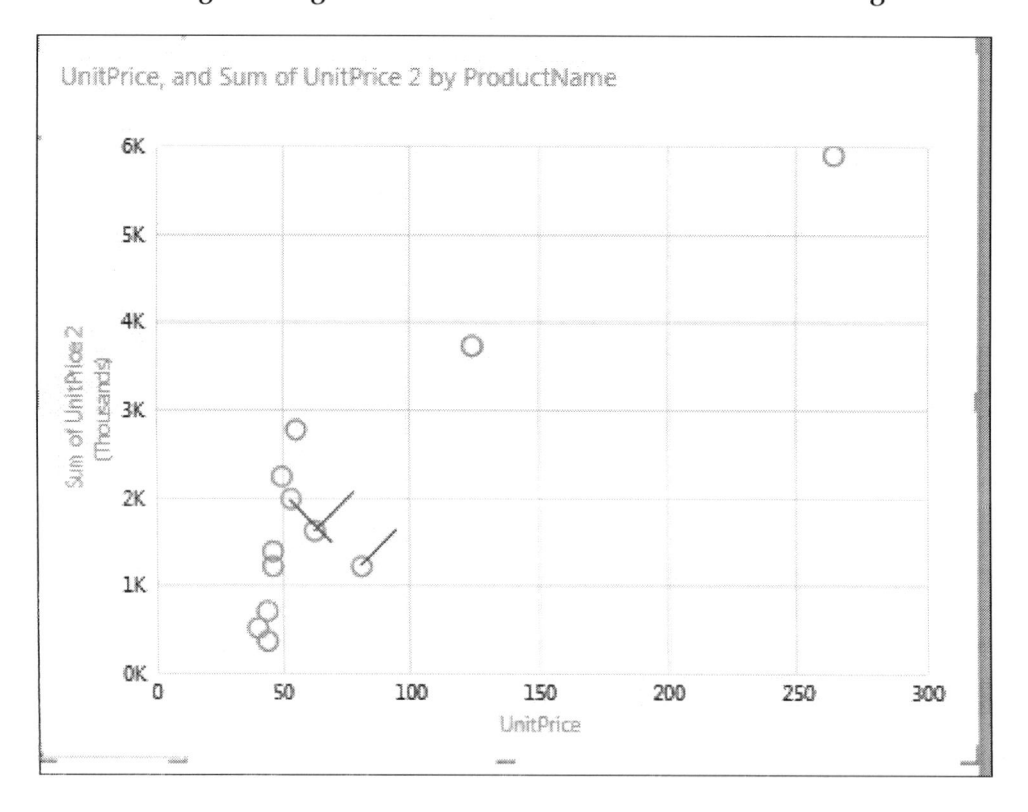

The field list for the preceding chart should appear as shown here:

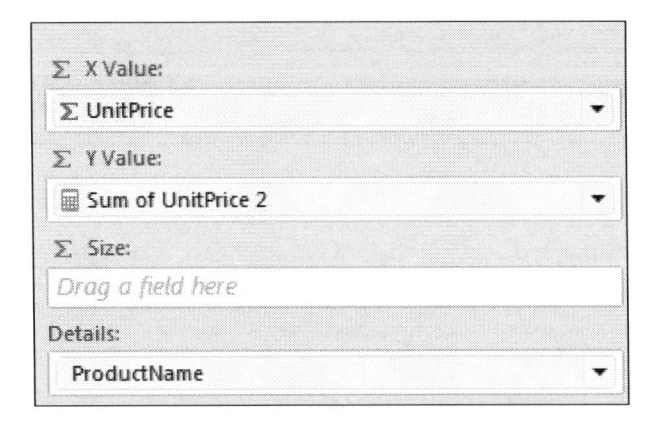

The sizes of data points in the Scatter chart are all the same, but if we add another variable to the chart we could see how big or small each point is (like modulating with a third variable).

3. Click on ∑**TotalAmount** in the table in order to provide a size to the data points as shown in the following screenshot:

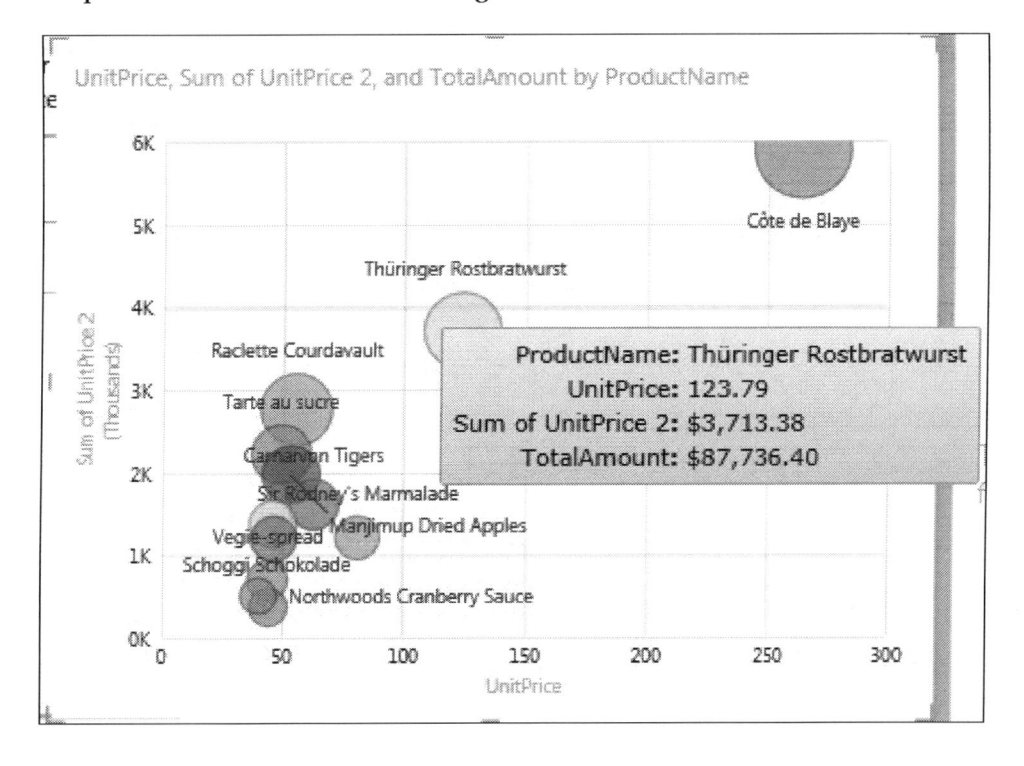

The field list now appears as shown in the following screenshot:

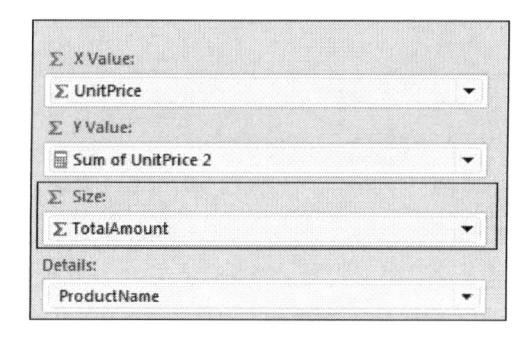

Another interesting interactive feature is animation. You can add another axis to the data called the `Play` axis, which is usually a date (year, month, quarter etc.) type data but can be other data types as well. In the next section you will add 'City' to play axis and as the animation scans through cities you will see related information as an animation.

Animation with Power View

In this section, we are going to add animations to Power View.

1. Into **Play Axis** in the field list area drag and drop **City** from **Suppliers** as shown in the following screenshot:

This adds a video interface to the previous chart as shown:

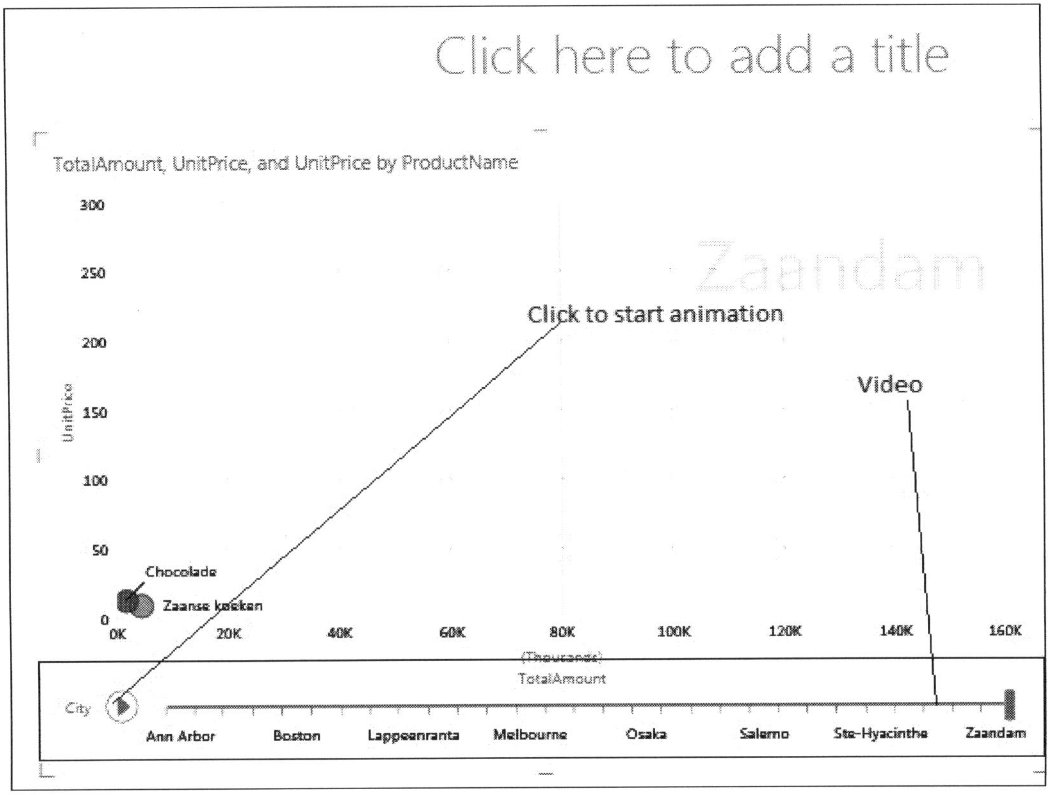

2. Click on the indicated position and enjoy the animation.

You have created multiple views and you can easily navigate from one view to another as shown in the following section.

Power View and Reporting Services

Navigating through the views of the Power View report

While designing the report you can switch between views by clicking the view you want to design on the left-hand side of the report. We have seen this while creating the second view. When you click on **Reading Mode** in the ribbon, you will get the following display:

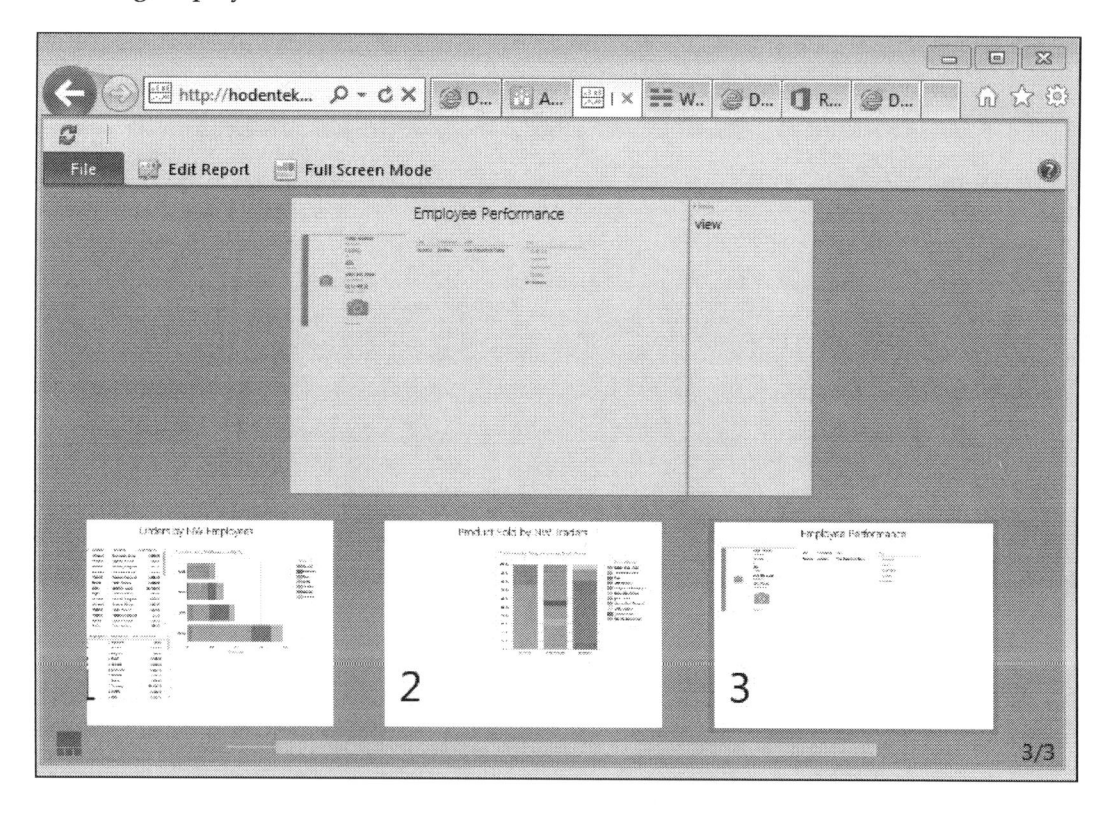

In here, you can navigate to the view you want in the main area by clicking on the image in the bottom of the screen. When you want to return to the editing mode, you may click on **Edit Report** at the top of the screen. The other mode of viewing is the **Full Screen** mode when the report fills the screen (you press *Esc* to return).

Save, do, undo, and refresh

All these buttons are at the top-left corner of a report. When you first create a report it gets a default name `Report1.rdlx`. When you save, you can save it with a different name. It usually gets saved to the `Documents` folder, but you can save it to a different location.

Saving to PowerPoint

PowerPoint got a shot in the arm by this new approach. The PowerPoint files created by saving Power View to PowerPoint are interactive as well. This is a very interesting feature if you want to show your portfolio to your clients. You do so by picking the **Export to PowerPoint** option in the **File** menu's drop-down shown earlier. When you click on the drop-down menu item, your report gets exported to PowerPoint, which can be saved to a location of your choice. You can export to both 32-bit and 64-bit PowerPoint.

Each view in Power View becomes a PowerPoint slide and each view is fully interactive just as in SharePoint server. You can even make changes and save the PowerPoint file. In order to get to see the views with which you can interact, you should switch over to the **Reading Mode** as shown here.

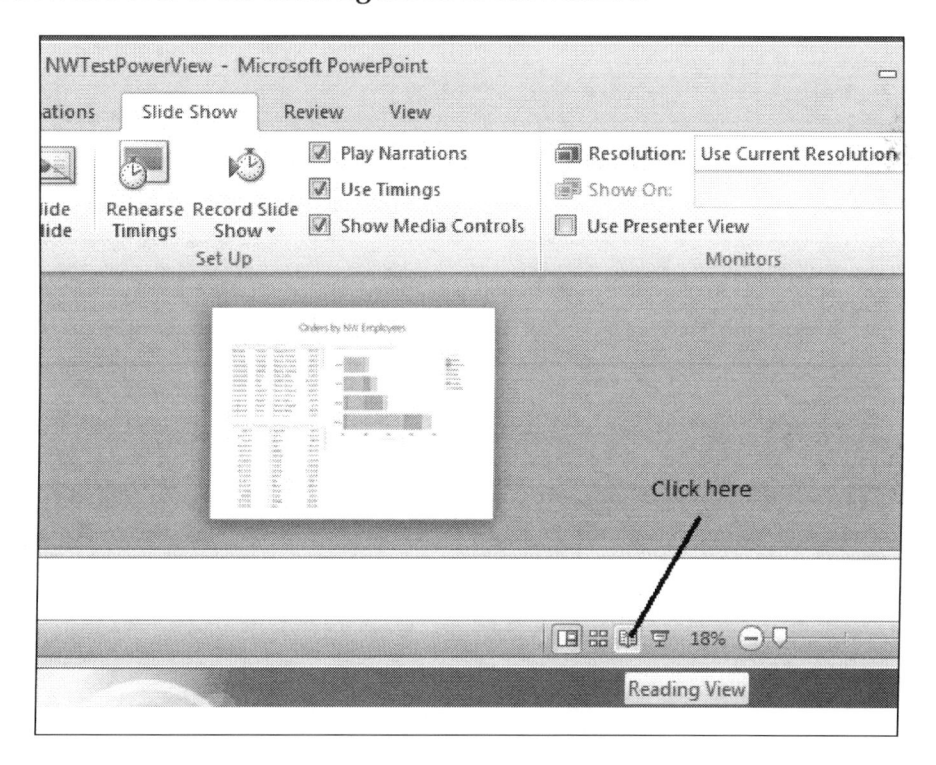

This creates a region marked **click to interact** at the bottom of each view and clicking that region enables the interactivity. You can filter, sort, and perform a few more actions. PowerPoint files' interactivity is possible as long as they can access the SharePoint Server but once they are denied this access, the slides become just static images of the views.

Summary

After describing some general features of Power View in SQL Server 2012 Reporting Services in SharePoint Integrated mode, creating a tabular data model deploying it to the SQL Server Analysis Server is described. Connecting the SharePoint server to the deployed model to create a data source was then described. This data source was used to create the Power View report. The following features were described: interactive highlighting, interactive filtering and sorting, visualization as a card, tiles visualization, slicers, filtering and advanced filtering, scatter and bubble charts, view navigation, animation, save, do, undo and refresh, and saving to PowerPoint.

In the next chapter, we look at the new feature in SQL Server 2012, which is Data Alerts generated in a SQL Server Reporting Server's service application in SharePoint Server 2010.

7
Self-service Data Alerts in SSRS 2012

Self-service alerts or **Data Alerts** are a new feature of SQL Server Reporting Services 2012. These alerts help you monitor data of interest to you or your organization. For example, many companies are alerting their customers when their payments are due (which is perhaps by setting up time-triggered schedule). But Data Alerts are triggered automatically when some data in the report changes and an e-mail is sent. These Data Alerts are different from data-driven subscriptions in Native Mode Reporting Services.

This feature could be very useful in monitoring inventories, monitoring stock prices, last name changes, personnel information changes, and in many other scenarios. Make sure you review this link from MSDN regarding Data Alerts:

`http://msdn.microsoft.com/en-us/library/gg492252.aspx`

In order to use this feature, you need to satisfy the following requirements:

- You must have installed SQL Server 2012 Reporting Services in the SharePoint Integrated mode (SharePoint Server 2010).

    SQL Server 2012 Reporting Services is set up as a shared service in SharePoint Sever 2010, which means you need to configure a SQL Server Reporting Services service, to leverage this feature. In *Chapter 1, Overview and Installation – SQL Server Reporting Services 2012*, installing SQL Server Reporting Services in SharePoint integrated mode was covered.

- The report for which you want to set up the data alert feature must first be saved to a SharePoint library.

    In fact you need to run the report in SharePoint to set up a data alert.

- The data source of the report must have its access credentials stored in the database or should require no credentials. Windows credentials does not work.
- A data alert requires at least one data region; *no data, no data alert.*
- A report should change over time due to changes in the underlying data for the data alert features to alert changes despite report parameter changes.

The Data Alerts are set up in SharePoint Central Administration, which also provides you with the necessary user interfaces in the form of Data Alerts Designer and Data Alerts Manager for alerting administrators and users to work with Data Alerts.

Getting ready for Data Alerts

As mentioned earlier, we need to set up a SQL Server Reporting Services service in **SharePoint (SP)** to use this feature. In *Chapter 1, Overview and Installation – SQL Server Reporting Services 2012*, the installation of SharePoint Server 2010 was described. This installation is not on the usual platform (Windows server) on which it is installed and therefore the installation on Windows 7 (x64) desktop/laptop may be one of the difficulties users may face. After installing the SP server, you will have to set up a service to run on this server that integrates with a SQL Server 2012. The SQL Server 2012's instance must have been set up to run in SP integrated mode. This was not described in detail but when you come to the installation set up of **Reporting Services (RS)**, make sure that it follows the settings in this screen.

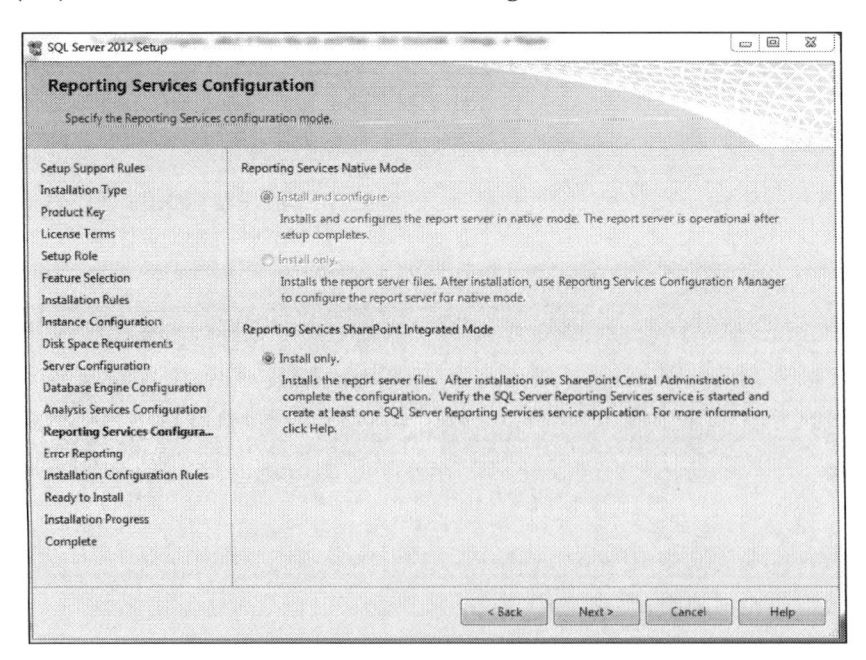

The starting point for the chapter is after the setting up of the SQL Server Reporting Services service in SP's Central Administration (CA) shown in the next screenshot. For the purposes of this chapter, a SQL Server 2012 instance NJ has been set up with its Reporting Services set up in SP integrated mode.

The SharePoint Server 2010 (Evaluation edition) was installed and configured on Windows 7 as described in *Chapter 1, Overview and Installation – SQL Server Reporting Services 2012*. In order to use this server for Reporting Services, you need to configure a SQL Server Reporting Services service. Additionally, you may install a site you use for your report documents, and so on.

In the SP server used for this book, a site was created using the template as shown in the next screenshot, which you may create immediately after configuring the SP server. Since reports are documents a Document Center template was adopted. It could have been a Records Center as well.

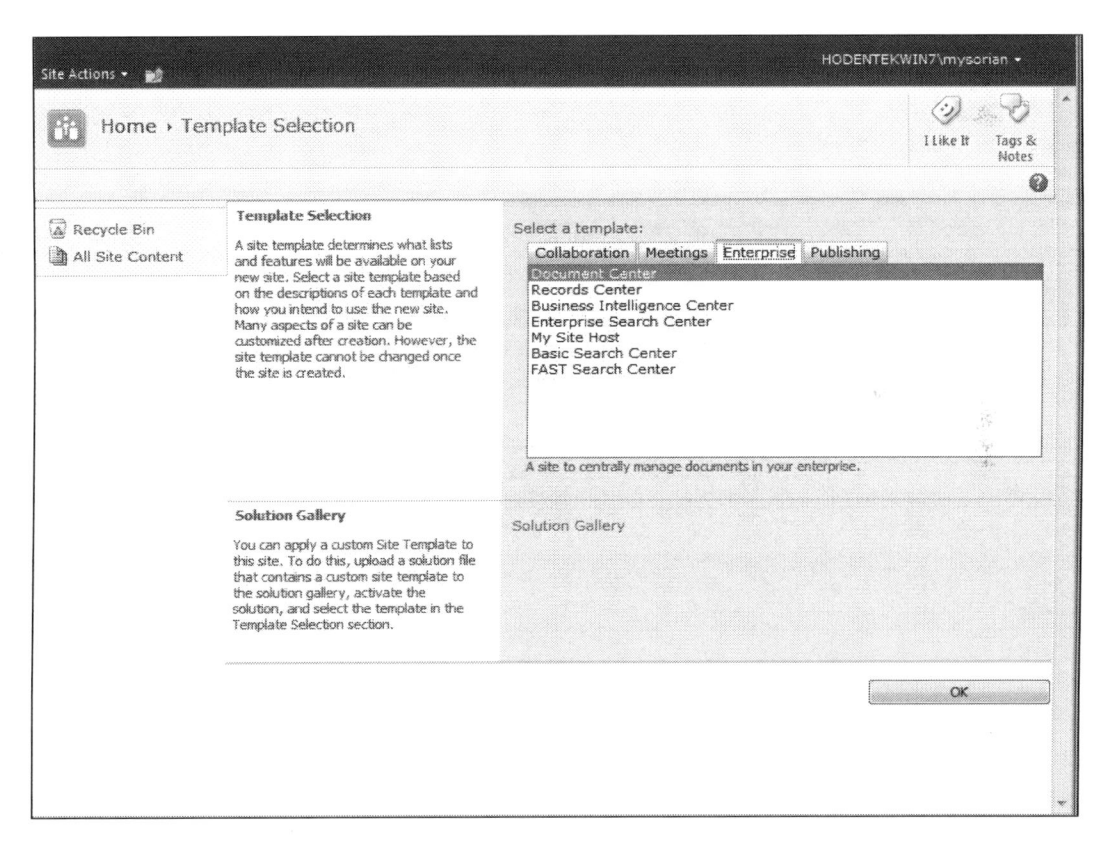

Self-service Data Alerts in SSRS 2012

The name of the RS service application created in SP (review the *Creating Reporting Services service application* section in *Chapter 1, Overview and Installation – SQL Server Reporting Services 2012*), `Spyglass`, is shown in the following screenshot:

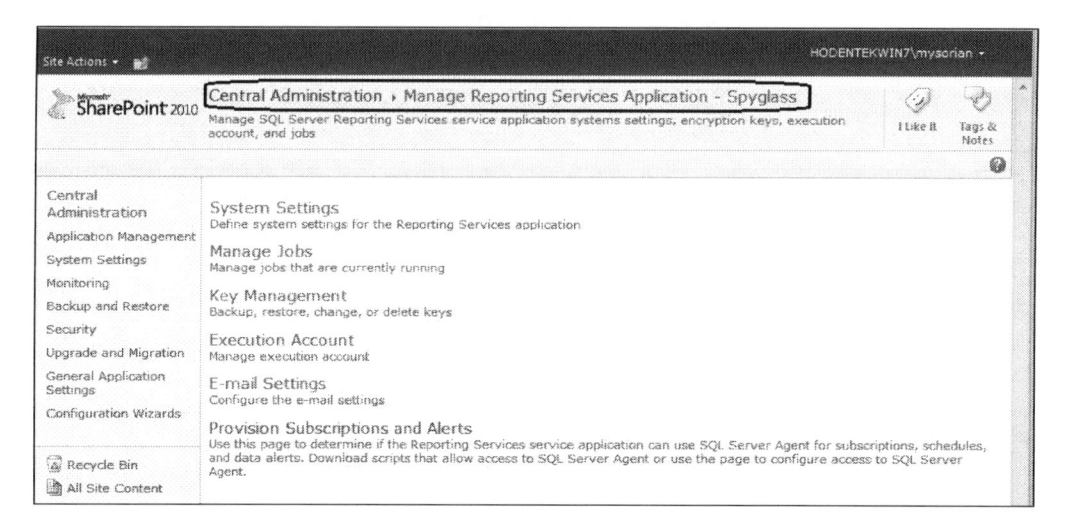

The last item (**Provision Subscriptions and Alerts**) in the preceding screenshot is where you start your activities in order to set up the Data Alerts.

The RS service's subscriptions, scheduling, and Data Alerts require that you configure the SQL server agent who does the alerting. It may be useful to review the next screenshot, which contains the elements essential for data alerting. The SQL Server Agent is the middleman between the application and the various databases, reporting and others.

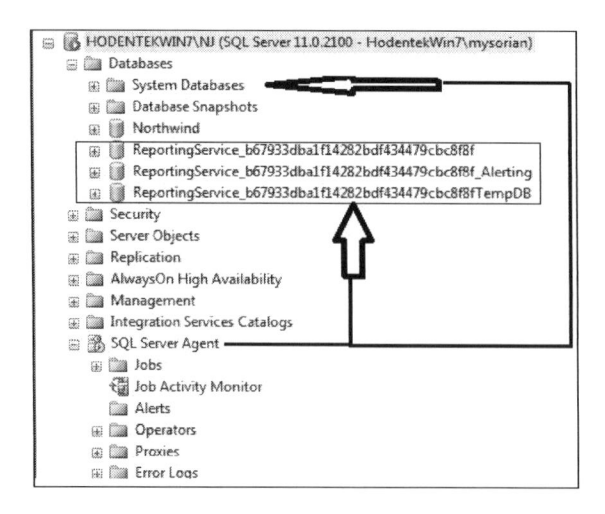

Granting permissions to work with Data Alerts

Data Alerts use SQL Server Agent and therefore need permissions. The credentials you type in for Data Alerts should have sufficient permissions to run them. If the SQL Server Agent is running and your credentials are not sufficient you may get an error and you need to update permissions.

There are three ways to update permissions. One of them is from the **Provision Subscriptions and Alerts** section of the Reporting Services service `Spyglass` application, which can be reached by following this breadcrumb on the SharePoint Central Administration: `Central Administration > Managing Reporting Services Application > Spyglass`

This breadcrumb displays the following page on the SharePoint Central Administration site:

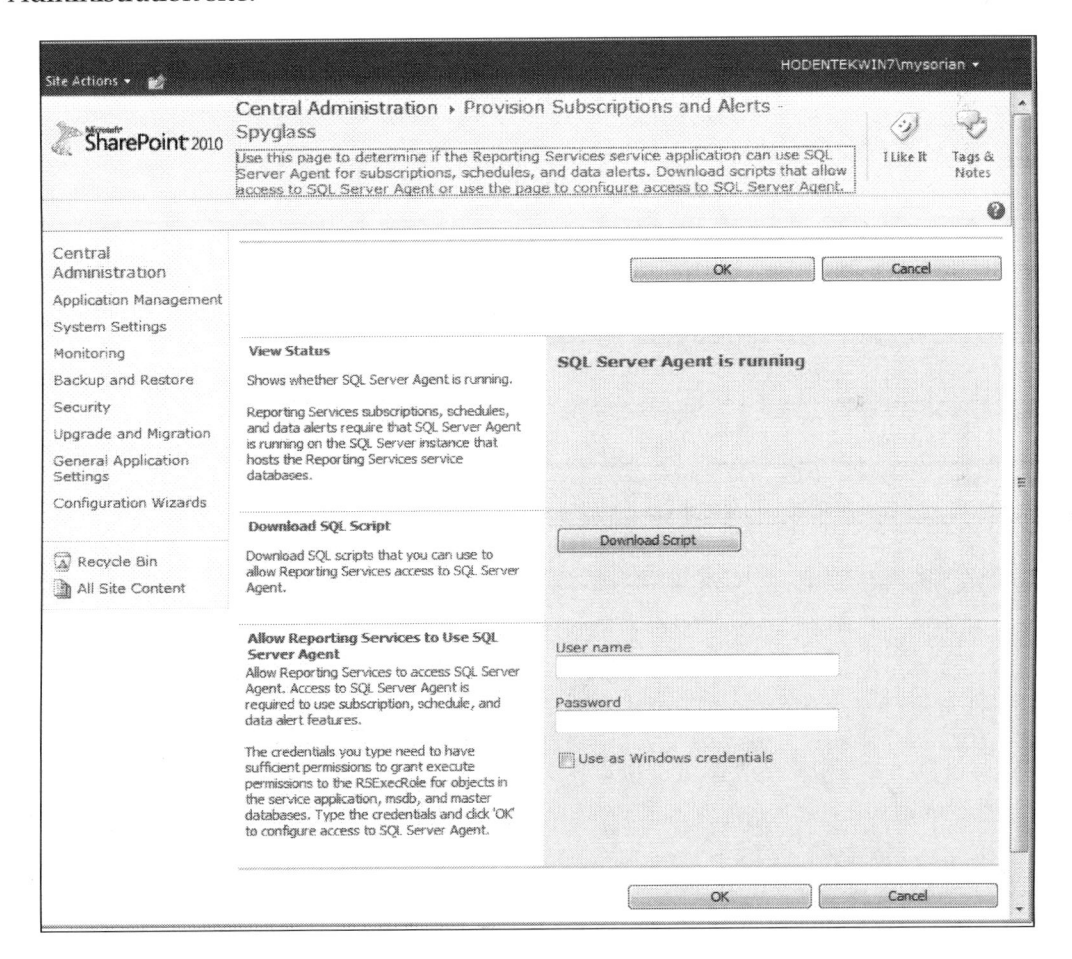

When you click on **OK** on the **Spyglass** page (preceding page) and if the SharePoint administrator has enough permissions to the **master** database of the service application then the permissions are updated. In the present case, the computer administrator administers both SharePoint and the SQL Server 2012 databases, and therefore the permissions are updated for the SharePoint administrator who is accessing the Data Alerts feature.

The other two ways are the following:

- From the **Spyglass** page you can download a script by clicking on the **Download Script** button shown (after making sure the SQL Server Agent is running), and run it on the server which has the three databases previously mentioned. The download button creates the `Spyglass-GrantRights.sql` file shown at the end of this section.

- You can generate the preceding T-SQL script using the two PowerShell cmdlets shown here:

```
Get-SPRSDatabaseRightsScript –DatabaseName <ReportingServices
database name> -UserName <app pool account> -IsWindowsUser | Out-
File <path of statement>

Get-SPRSDatabaseRightsScript –DatabaseName ReportingService_46
fd00359f894b828907b254e3f6257c –UserName "NT AUTHORITY\NETWORK
SERVICE" -IsWindowsUser | Out-File c:\SQLServerAgentrights.sql
```

Again, you need to run this script on the SQL Server 2012 databases as in the previous method.

Here is the `Spyglass-GrantRights.sql` file:

```
/************************************************************/
/* Copyright (c) Microsoft.  All rights reserved. */
/************************************************************/
USE master
GO

if not exists (select * from sysusers where issqlrole = 1 and name =
'RSExecRole')
BEGIN
 EXEC sp_addrole 'RSExecRole'
END
GO
```

Chapter 7

```
DECLARE @AccountName nvarchar(260)
SET @AccountName = SUSER_SNAME(0x010500000000000515000000b243564b496c6
d2a8c486941e8030000)

if not exists (select name from syslogins where name = @AccountName
and hasaccess = 1 and isntname = 1)
BEGIN
EXEC sp_grantlogin @AccountName
END
GO


USE [ReportingService_b67933dba1f14282bdf434479cbc8f8f]
GO

if not exists (select * from sysusers where issqlrole = 1 and name =
'RSExecRole')
BEGIN
 EXEC sp_addrole 'RSExecRole'
END
GO


DECLARE @AccountName nvarchar(260)
SET @AccountName = SUSER_SNAME(0x010500000000000515000000b243564b496c6
d2a8c486941e8030000)

DECLARE @name_in_db nvarchar(260)
select @name_in_db = sysusers.name from sysusers inner join master.
dbo.syslogins logins on logins.sid = sysusers.sid where logins.name =
@AccountName and logins.isntname = 1
if @name_in_db IS NULL
BEGIN
EXEC sp_grantdbaccess @AccountName, @name_in_db OUTPUT
END
IF @name_in_db IS NOT NULL AND @name_in_db != 'dbo' AND @name_in_db !=
'sys'
BEGIN
EXEC sp_addrolemember 'RSExecRole', @name_in_db
END
GO

USE [ReportingService_b67933dba1f14282bdf434479cbc8f8f_Alerting]
GO
```

```sql
if not exists (select * from sysusers where issqlrole = 1 and name = 
'RSExecRole')
BEGIN
 EXEC sp_addrole 'RSExecRole'
END
GO


DECLARE @AccountName nvarchar(260)
SET @AccountName = SUSER_SNAME(0x010500000000000515000000b243564b496c6
d2a8c486941e8030000)


DECLARE @name_in_db nvarchar(260)
select @name_in_db = sysusers.name from sysusers inner join master.
dbo.syslogins logins on logins.sid = sysusers.sid where logins.name = 
@AccountName and logins.isntname = 1
if @name_in_db IS NULL
BEGIN
EXEC sp_grantdbaccess @AccountName, @name_in_db OUTPUT
END
IF @name_in_db IS NOT NULL AND @name_in_db != 'dbo' AND @name_in_db != 
'sys'
BEGIN
EXEC sp_addrolemember 'RSExecRole', @name_in_db
END
GO


USE [ReportingService_b67933dba1f14282bdf434479cbc8f8fTempDB]
GO


if not exists (select * from sysusers where issqlrole = 1 and name = 
'RSExecRole')
BEGIN
 EXEC sp_addrole 'RSExecRole'
END
GO


DECLARE @AccountName nvarchar(260)
SET @AccountName = SUSER_SNAME(0x010500000000000515000000b243564b496c6
d2a8c486941e8030000)

DECLARE @name_in_db nvarchar(260)
```

Chapter 7

```sql
select @name_in_db = sysusers.name from sysusers inner join master.
dbo.syslogins logins on logins.sid = sysusers.sid where logins.name =
@AccountName and logins.isntname = 1
if @name_in_db IS NULL
BEGIN
EXEC sp_grantdbaccess @AccountName, @name_in_db OUTPUT
END
IF @name_in_db IS NOT NULL AND @name_in_db != 'dbo' AND @name_in_db !=
'sys'
BEGIN
EXEC sp_addrolemember 'RSExecRole', @name_in_db
END
GO


USE msdb
GO


if not exists (select * from sysusers where issqlrole = 1 and name =
'RSExecRole')
BEGIN
  EXEC sp_addrole 'RSExecRole'
END
GO


DECLARE @AccountName nvarchar(260)
SET @AccountName = SUSER_SNAME(0x010500000000000515000000b243564b496c6
d2a8c486941e8030000)

DECLARE @name_in_db nvarchar(260)
select @name_in_db = sysusers.name from sysusers inner join master.
dbo.syslogins logins on logins.sid = sysusers.sid where logins.name =
@AccountName and logins.isntname = 1
if @name_in_db IS NULL
BEGIN
EXEC sp_grantdbaccess @AccountName, @name_in_db OUTPUT
END
IF @name_in_db IS NOT NULL AND @name_in_db != 'dbo' AND @name_in_db !=
'sys'
BEGIN
EXEC sp_addrolemember 'RSExecRole', @name_in_db
END
GO
```

Self-service Data Alerts in SSRS 2012

```
USE master
GO


DECLARE @AccountName nvarchar(260)
SET @AccountName = SUSER_SNAME(0x010500000000000515000000b243564b496c6
d2a8c486941e8030000)


DECLARE @name_in_db nvarchar(260)
select @name_in_db = sysusers.name from sysusers inner join master.
dbo.syslogins logins on logins.sid = sysusers.sid where logins.name =
@AccountName and logins.isntname = 1
if @name_in_db IS NULL
BEGIN
EXEC sp_grantdbaccess @AccountName, @name_in_db OUTPUT
END
IF @name_in_db IS NOT NULL AND @name_in_db != 'dbo' AND @name_in_db !=
'sys'
BEGIN
EXEC sp_addrolemember 'RSExecRole', @name_in_db
END
GO


USE [ReportingService_b67933dba1f14282bdf434479cbc8f8f]
if exists (select 1 from [dbo].[sysobjects] where id = object_
id(N'[dbo].[schedule]') and OBJECTPROPERTY(id, N'IsUserTable') = 1)
BEGIN
   declare id_cursor cursor for select scheduleId from schedule s join
msdb.dbo.sysjobs j  on (convert(sysname, s.scheduleid) = j.name) open
id_cursor
   declare @next_id uniqueidentifier, @account nvarchar(260)
   select @account = SUSER_SNAME(0x010500000000000515000000b243564b496c
6d2a8c486941e8030000)
   fetch NEXT from id_cursor INTO @next_id
   while (@@fetch_status <> -1)
   BEGIN
     if (@@fetch_status <> -2)
     BEGIN
       exec msdb.dbo.sp_update_job @job_name = @next_id, @owner_login_
name=@account
     END
   fetch NEXT FROM id_cursor INTO @next_id
   END
```

```
    close id_cursor
    deallocate id_cursor
END
GO




-------------------------------------------------
------------- Master and MSDB rights
------------ Same as in RSGrantRightsSqlAccount
-------------------------------------------------


USE master
GO
GRANT EXECUTE ON master.dbo.xp_sqlagent_notify TO RSExecRole
GO

GRANT EXECUTE ON master.dbo.xp_sqlagent_enum_jobs TO RSExecRole
GO

GRANT EXECUTE ON master.dbo.xp_sqlagent_is_starting TO RSExecRole
GO

USE msdb
GO

-- Permissions for SQL Agent SP's
GRANT EXECUTE ON msdb.dbo.sp_help_category TO RSExecRole
GO
GRANT EXECUTE ON msdb.dbo.sp_add_category TO RSExecRole
GO
GRANT EXECUTE ON msdb.dbo.sp_add_job TO RSExecRole
GO
GRANT EXECUTE ON msdb.dbo.sp_add_jobserver TO RSExecRole
GO
GRANT EXECUTE ON msdb.dbo.sp_add_jobstep TO RSExecRole
GO
GRANT EXECUTE ON msdb.dbo.sp_add_jobschedule TO RSExecRole
GO
GRANT EXECUTE ON msdb.dbo.sp_help_job TO RSExecRole
GO
GRANT EXECUTE ON msdb.dbo.sp_delete_job TO RSExecRole
GO
```

```
GRANT EXECUTE ON msdb.dbo.sp_help_jobschedule TO RSExecRole
GO
GRANT EXECUTE ON msdb.dbo.sp_verify_job_identifiers TO RSExecRole
GO
GRANT SELECT ON msdb.dbo.sysjobs TO RSExecRole
GO
GRANT SELECT ON msdb.dbo.syscategories TO RSExecRole
GO

-- Yukon Requires that the user is in the SQLAgentUserRole
if exists (select * from sysusers where issqlrole = 1 and name =
N'SQLAgentUserRole')
BEGIN
EXEC msdb.dbo.sp_addrolemember N'SQLAgentUserRole', N'RSExecRole'
END
```

The generated Data Alerts are sent by e-mail to the party defined in the alert. The next required step is to configure outgoing e-mail for the Reporting Services service. In the first image, there is a **E-mail Settings** link to configure e-mail. You can also use CA as shown here by clicking on **Manage** after highlighting the service.

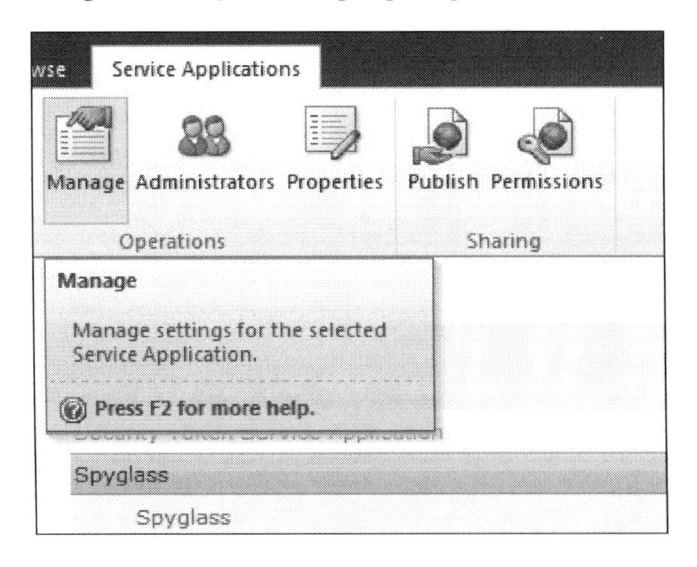

The first page is displayed again, click on **E-mail Settings**. This brings up the **E-mail Settings - SpyGlass** page shown here:

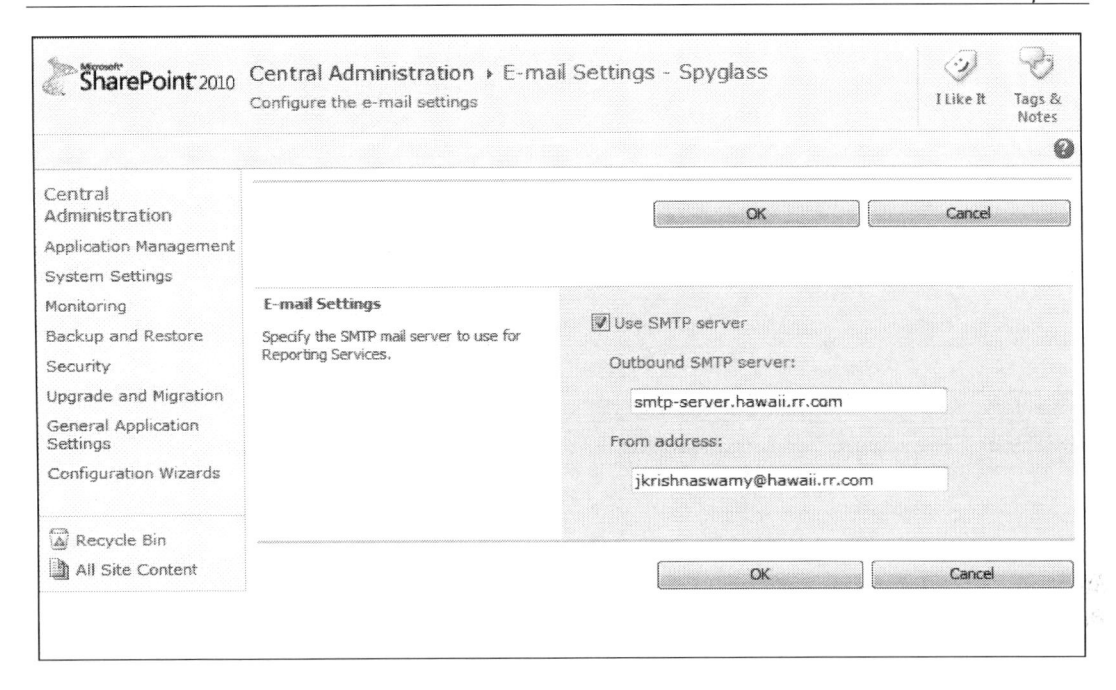

You enter the following information:

- Checkmark for **Use SMTP server**
- In **Outbound SMTP Server**, enter the SMTP server name of service provider. Herein, smtp-server.hawaii.rr.com.
- In the **From address** field, enter your e-mail address with ISP provider. Herein, jkrishnaswamy@hawaii.rr.com.

Click on **OK**. You will be returned to the page in first screenshot. Note that the same e-mail settings were used in Native Mode installation as well.

Creating a report and saving to the Report Server

You begin by creating a library called Documents, then using the **Library Settings** page in the ribbon you set up such that the reports library has the SQL Server Reporting Services content types. Review the following to set up the content types (refer to the next screenshot for the content types):

http://msdn.microsoft.com/en-us/library/bb326289.aspx

With this accomplished, you can now have documents of the Reporting Services content type in Documents as shown for **New Document**. You can also have documents of the type shown to this library. When you save a report created using SSDT or, Report Builder, you will save it to the Reports library in SharePoint site.

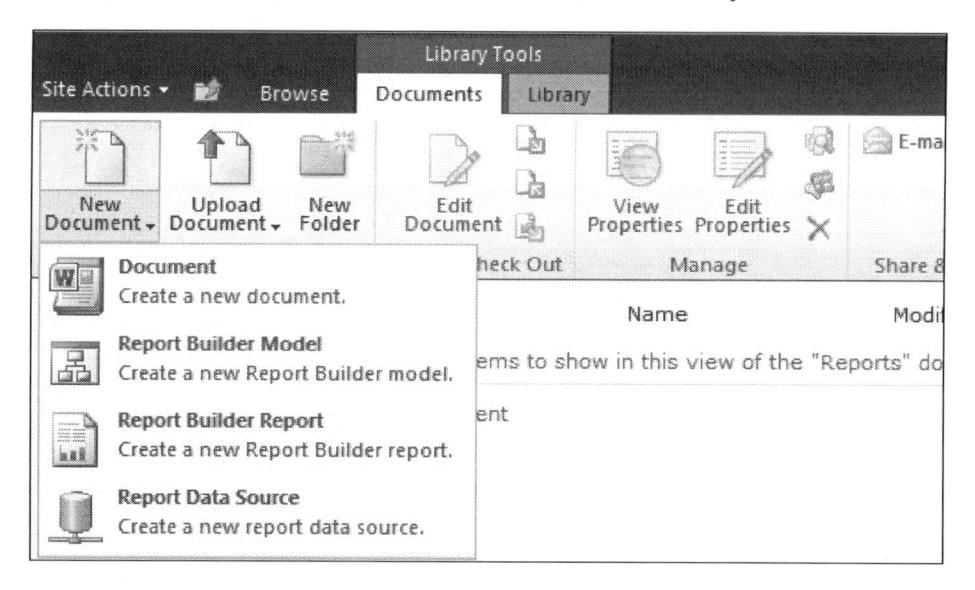

There are a few more steps before you start creating reports and work with them in SharePoint. The SQL Server Reporting Services service has a proxy that you need to associate with the web application for your reports. This was shown in *Chapter 1, Overview and Installation – SQL Server Reporting Services 2012*. Follow this link to create the association: http://msdn.microsoft.com/en-us/library/gg492284.aspx.

This can be carried out in Central Administration.

Creating a report in Report Builder and saving it to the Documents library

We keep the SharePoint server running. You can bring a report into SharePoint server in three ways:

- Author a report using SSDT, or Report Builder and deploy/save to the Documents folder
- You can upload a report on your file system using the Upload option

- You can bring up the Report Builder from inside SharePoint site (clicking the Report Builder Report in the drop-down list of the previous image).

Hands-on exercise 7.1 – creating a report in Report Builder and saving it to the SharePoint site

The process of creating reports has been described with many hands-on exercises in *Chapter 5, Working with Report Builder 3.0*. The process is exactly the same.

1. Launch Report Builder. Create a report `Customer info` using the `Northwind` database on the SQL Server 2012 instance (herein an instance named `NJ` has been used).

   The Report Builder is disconnected and you need to connect to the Report Server, in this case the site where the proxy has been associated with SQL Server Reporting Services.

   > You can also launch Report Builder as mentioned in the previous section in the third point).

2. Click on **Connect** and in the **Connect to Report Server** window, enter the site name as shown and click on **Connect**.

3. Verify that you are connected to the server at the bottom of Report Builder.

4. Create a report that resembles the following using the `Northwind` database's `Customers` table (use embedded data source which requires login information). Alter its credentials such that the authentication information is saved in the database.

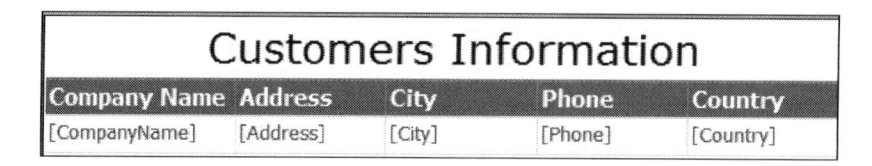

Customers Information				
Company Name	**Address**	**City**	**Phone**	**Country**
[CompanyName]	[Address]	[City]	[Phone]	[Country]

5. Run the report and verify that it works.
6. Use the top-left button and click on **Save As**.
7. Save the report as `CustomerInfo.rdl` to the Documents as shown.

    You can also create folders for reports, report data sources, and so on, and save related items. For the purposes of this book all of the reporting services contents were saved to `Documents` except some images.

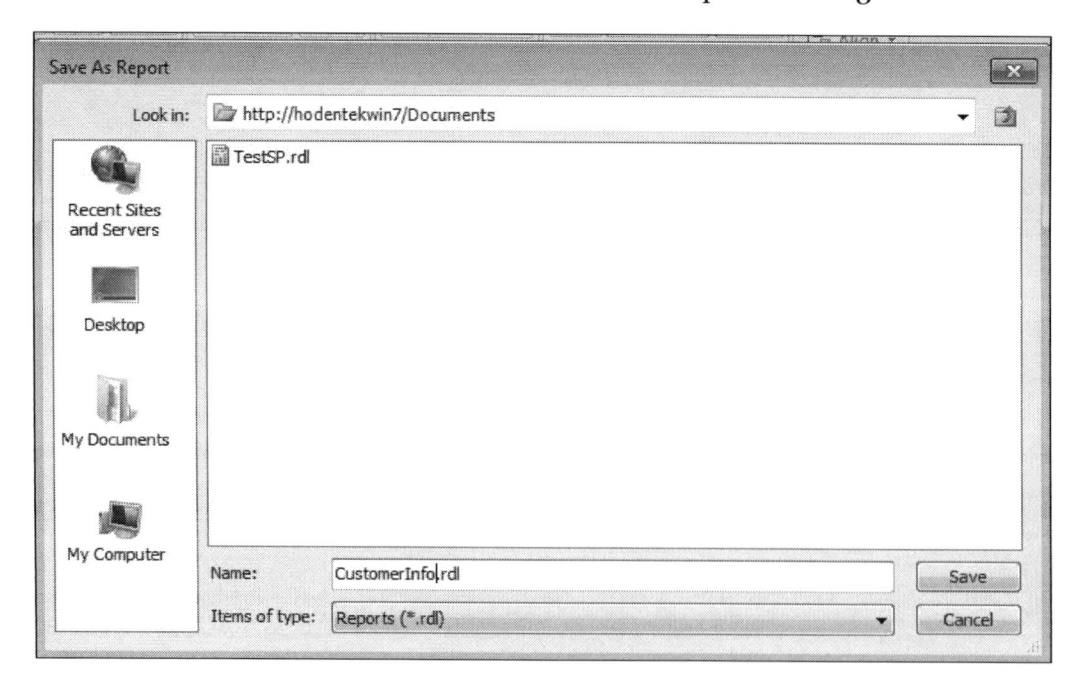

8. Open an IE browser as administrator and type in the server name (`http://hodentekWin7`) in the browser.

   Notice that the report has appeared in your site as shown in the following screenshot:

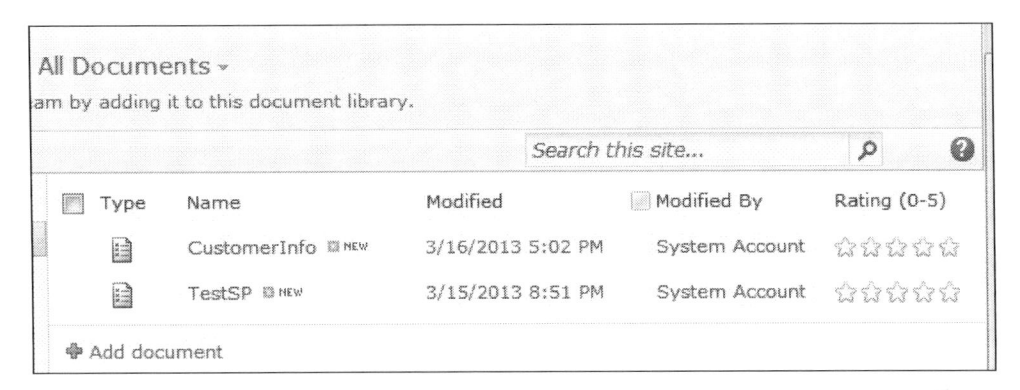

Type	Name	Modified	Modified By	Rating (0-5)
	CustomerInfo NEW	3/16/2013 5:02 PM	System Account	☆☆☆☆☆
	TestSP NEW	3/15/2013 8:51 PM	System Account	☆☆☆☆☆

9. Click on **CustomerInfo** in the preceding page and verify that the report displays. You may get a warning about encryption. Disregard for the time being, provide credentials, and click on **OK**.

> As an alternative to the preceding steps, you can launch Report Builder and create a report or you could upload a saved report from your file system.

Giving permission to a report

Permissions govern which task one can carry out. Permissions in SP are like roles in native mode reporting services. SharePoint has some 33 predefined permissions that can be bundled into a permission level.

The built-in security features of SharePoint Foundation 2010 can be used to grant access to Report Server items on SharePoint sites and libraries. Users already permitted to the sites and libraries can access these items unless their permissions are modified. But regarding the permissions for users added after SharePoint integration there are recommendations for granting permissions to securable items on the site such as libraries, documents, lists, and so on.

Users belong to SharePoint groups that you can create to manage permissions. These users can be Windows users/groups or those who have logins via Forms Authentication. The administrator who installs SharePoint 2010 and creates the portal site is the default portal owner. The portal owner sets permissions in Central Administration. Herein login via Forms is not considered.

Recommendation is to use standard SharePoint groups (Owners, Members, and Visitors) and assign permissions at site level. As a site owner (you are permitted), it is possible to create permission for a user for the preceding report.

Hands-on exercise 7.2 – giving full control of a report to a user

In the following, full control to the preceding report is granted to the user Jay.

1. Click on the handle for the report open in Documents as shown in the following screenshot:

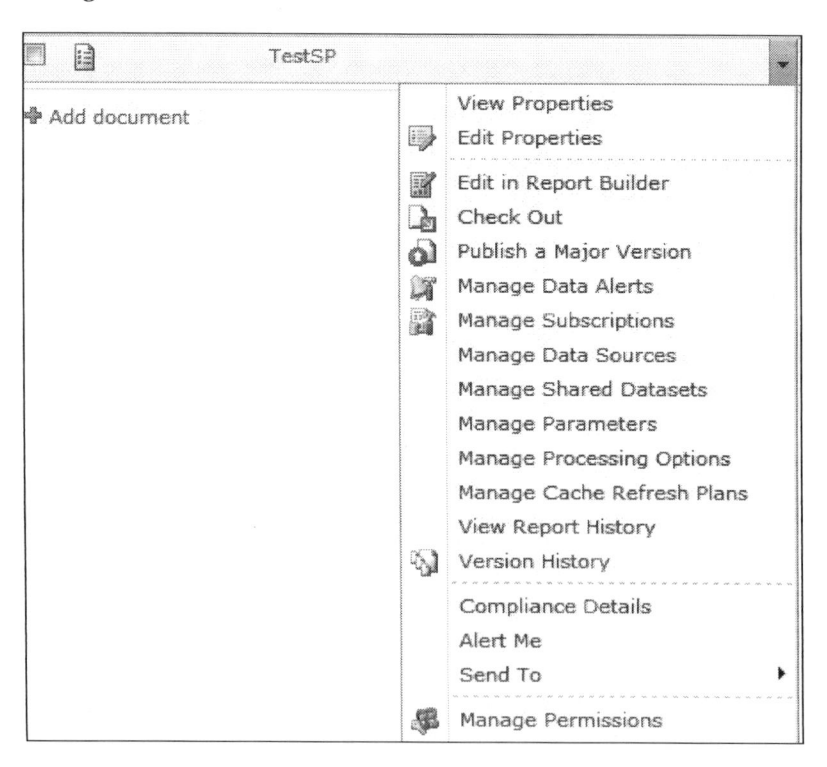

2. Click on **Manage Permissions**. The **Permission Tools** section of the ribbon is displayed as shown in the following screenshot:

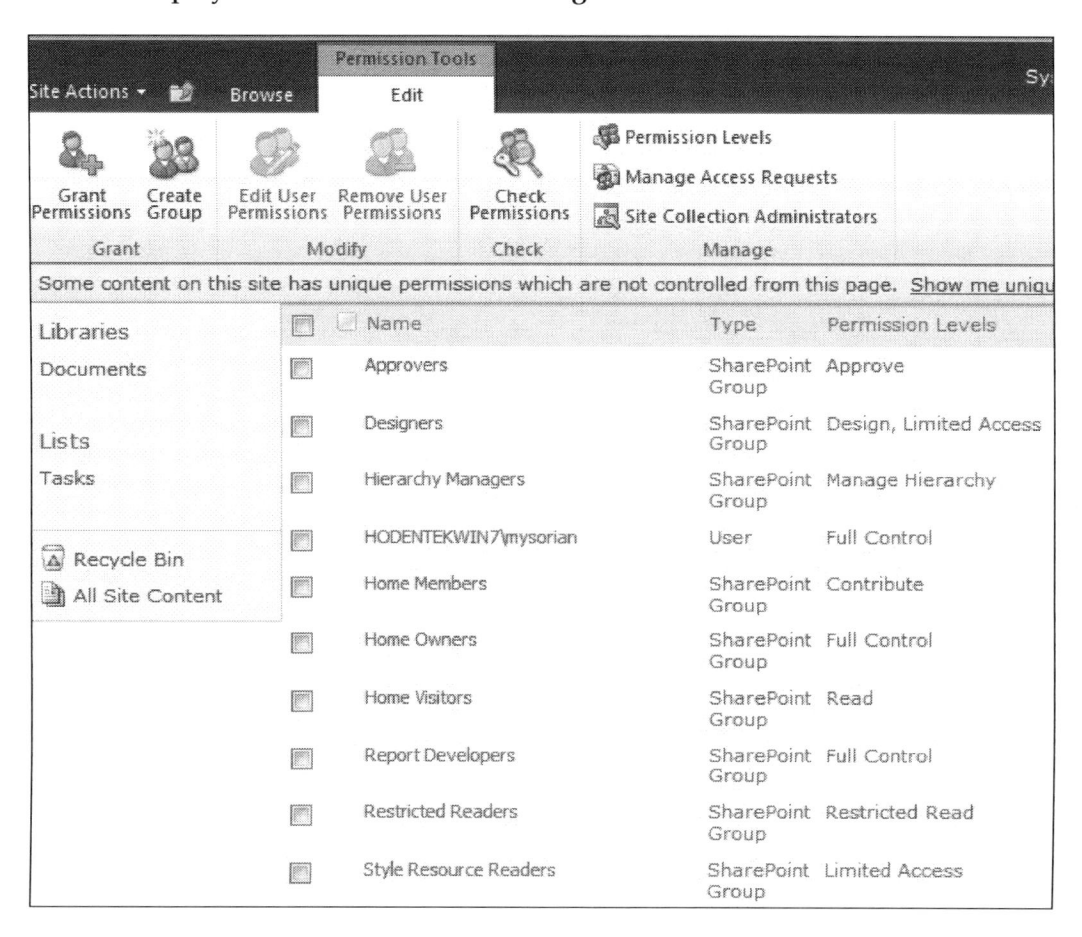

Name	Type	Permission Levels
Approvers	SharePoint Group	Approve
Designers	SharePoint Group	Design, Limited Access
Hierarchy Managers	SharePoint Group	Manage Hierarchy
HODENTEKWIN7\mysorian	User	Full Control
Home Members	SharePoint Group	Contribute
Home Owners	SharePoint Group	Full Control
Home Visitors	SharePoint Group	Read
Report Developers	SharePoint Group	Full Control
Restricted Readers	SharePoint Group	Restricted Read
Style Resource Readers	SharePoint Group	Limited Access

3. Click on **Grant Permissions** and the following page will be displayed:

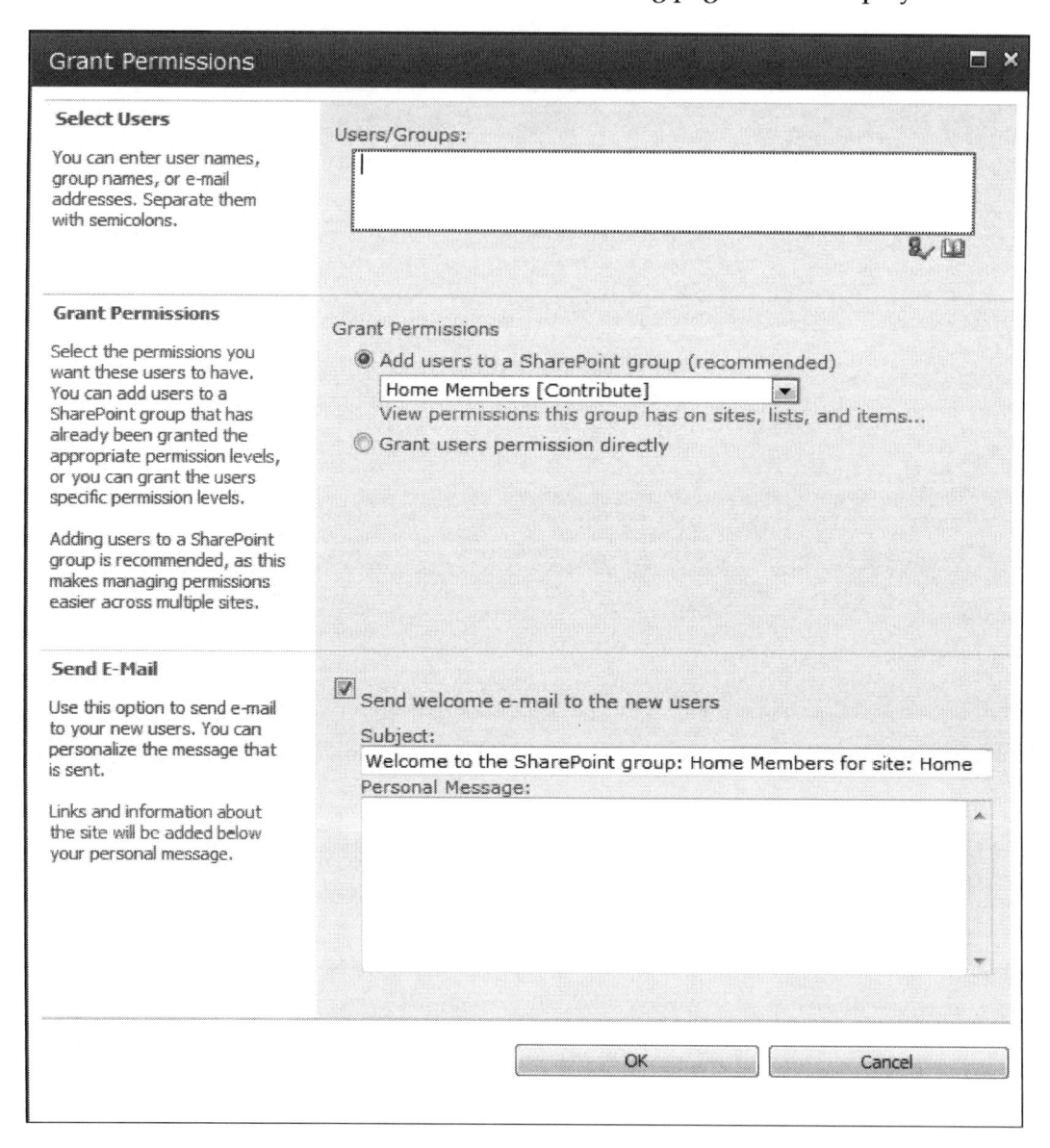

Grant Permissions

Select Users

You can enter user names, group names, or e-mail addresses. Separate them with semicolons.

Users/Groups:

Grant Permissions

Select the permissions you want these users to have. You can add users to a SharePoint group that has already been granted the appropriate permission levels, or you can grant the users specific permission levels.

Adding users to a SharePoint group is recommended, as this makes managing permissions easier across multiple sites.

Grant Permissions
- ◉ Add users to a SharePoint group (recommended)
  - Home Members [Contribute]
  - View permissions this group has on sites, lists, and items...
- ○ Grant users permission directly

Send E-Mail

Use this option to send e-mail to your new users. You can personalize the message that is sent.

Links and information about the site will be added below your personal message.

☑ Send welcome e-mail to the new users

Subject:
Welcome to the SharePoint group: Home Members for site: Home

Personal Message:

[OK] [Cancel]

4. Type in the name in the **User/Group** field, in this Jay is a user; type his name and you can click the small icon with a tick mark. Click on the icon to verify the user as shown in the following screenshot:

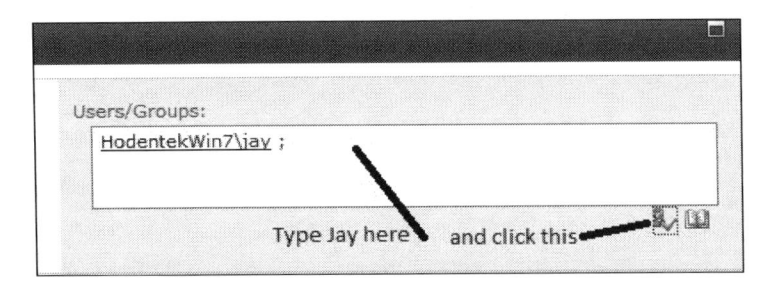

5. Choose **Grant Users permission directly**. In the expanded node, place a check mark for **Full Control**. Enter a personal message and click on **OK**.

   User Hodentekwin7\Jay gets full control for the selected report as shown in the following screenshot:

6. You as the site owner can easily remove the permission using **Permission Tools**.

Creating a Data Alert

A data alert is created by the report author and he is the sole owner. An administrator may be able to see the Data Alerts. The SharePoint server provides a graphic user interface to create Data Alerts.

Self-service Data Alerts in SSRS 2012

Hands-on exercise 7.3 – creating Data Alert in Data Alert Designer

You start with a report to create a data alert.

1. Click on the `TestSP` report to display the report as shown in the following screenshot:

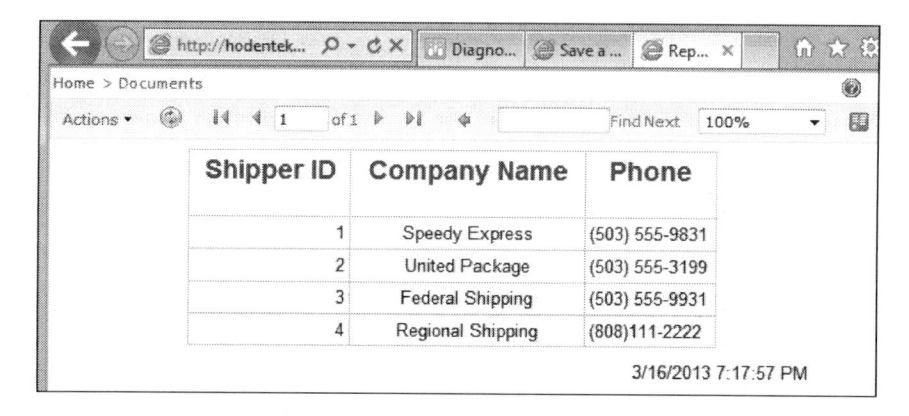

   This report displays all the columns in the `Shippers` table in the `Northwind` database. It originally had only the first three columns and a fourth was added later.

2. Click on **Actions** at the top-left corner on the preceding report to display a drop-down menu as shown in the following screenshot:

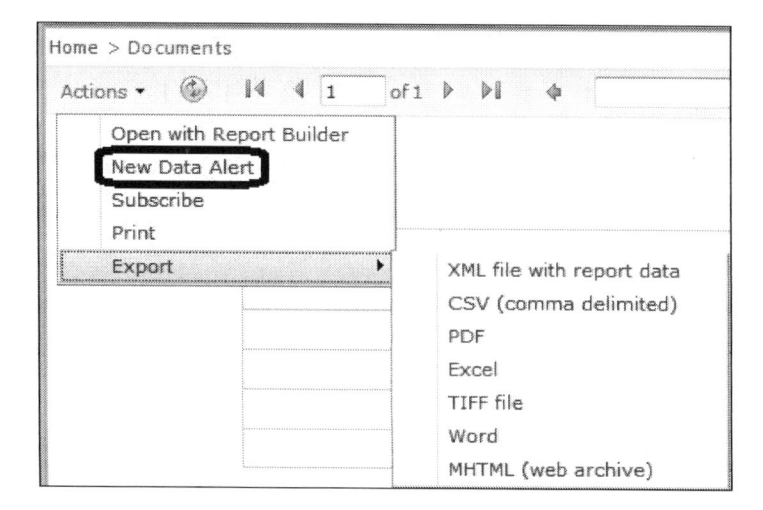

[394]

Chapter 7

3. Click on **New Data Alert** to display the Data Alert Designer's **New Data Alert – TestSP** as shown in the following screenshot:

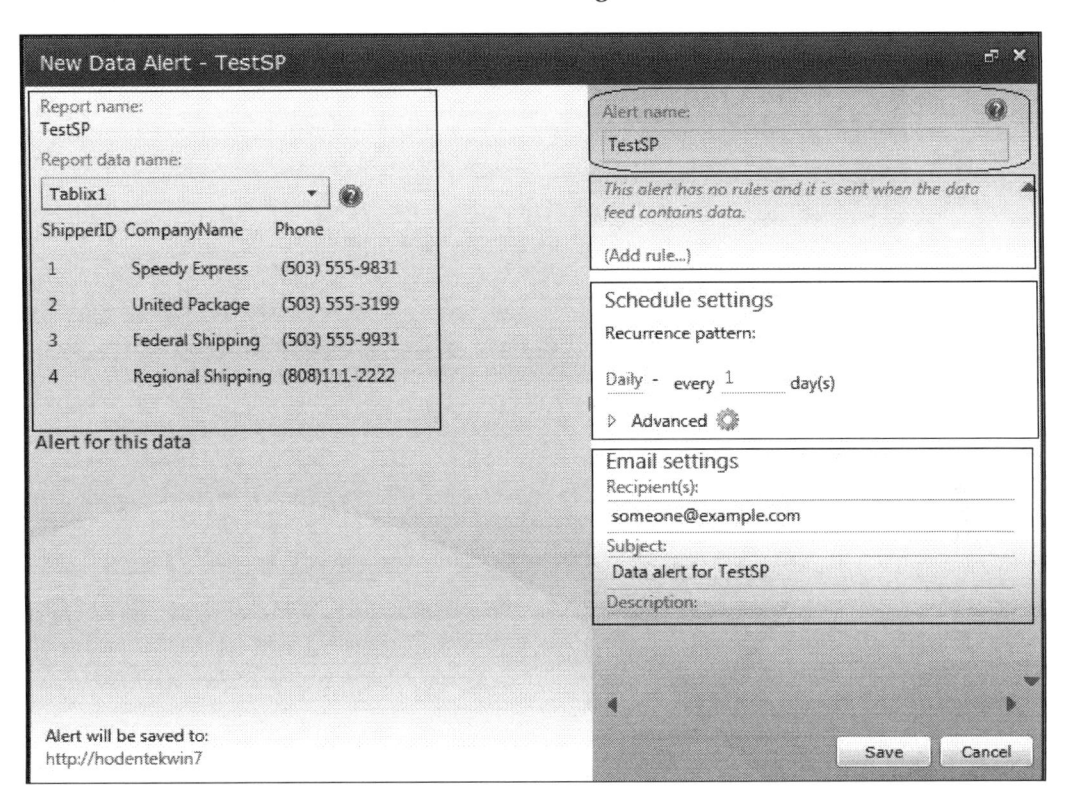

It shows the report details on the left side under **Report name** for alerted data with all the fields in the report; the alert and its schedule are on the right side with **Schedule settings**, the area where you can create alert rules and the details of e-mail settings.

You can set up a more detailed schedule by clicking on the **Advanced** node in the preceding step to display the following screenshot:

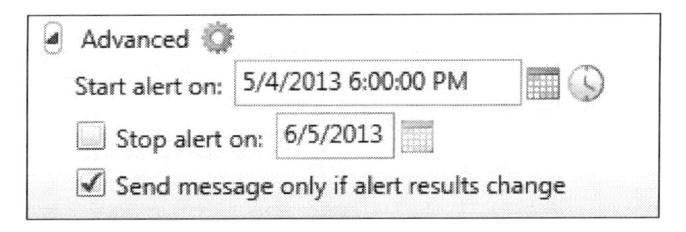

[395]

In the present case, there is only one tablix but in general a tablix may contain many more tablix, charts, and other widgets. However, for describing the principle involved, the one chosen is sufficient.

The data chosen is cached data feed and it is preferable you run the report before setting up a rule.

> Rules that you set up are very similar to the filtering you do on data. You can set up rules based on Values as well as Fields. The fields in the left are automatically displayed while customizing the rule.

Rules are stored in the alerting database in XML format. Here is a sample of rules in the database.

```
<data-condition xmlns="http://schemas.microsoft.com/
rsalerting/2011/03/alertdefinition">
  <scope>Any</scope>
  <clause>
    <is-or-clause>False</is-or-clause>
    <expression-type>String</expression-type>
    <left-operand>CompanyName</left-operand>
    <operator>Equal</operator>
    <right-operand>
      <operand-type>Value</operand-type>
      <value><![CDATA[Jet Shipping]]></value>
    </right-operand>
  </clause>
</data-condition>
```

Here is a simple rule to alert the receiver of an e-mail when there is an entry in the CompanyName field of a company that has the **Jet Shipping** string in it. From the drop-down on the right side of **CompanyName** in the rule there are other comparisons (**is, is not**) possible. The name of the alert is different from its default name (name of the report). Since you can create multiple alerts to the same report, a named alert is highly recommended to do a follow up.

The scheduling of the report is very similar to the scheduling in Report Manager you have seen in *Chapter 4, Working with Report Manager*. The e-mail recipient and description are choices that you make to deliver your data alert. Follow this link to learn more about alert rules and alert schedules:
http://technet.microsoft.com/en-us/library/gg492254.aspx

Chapter 7

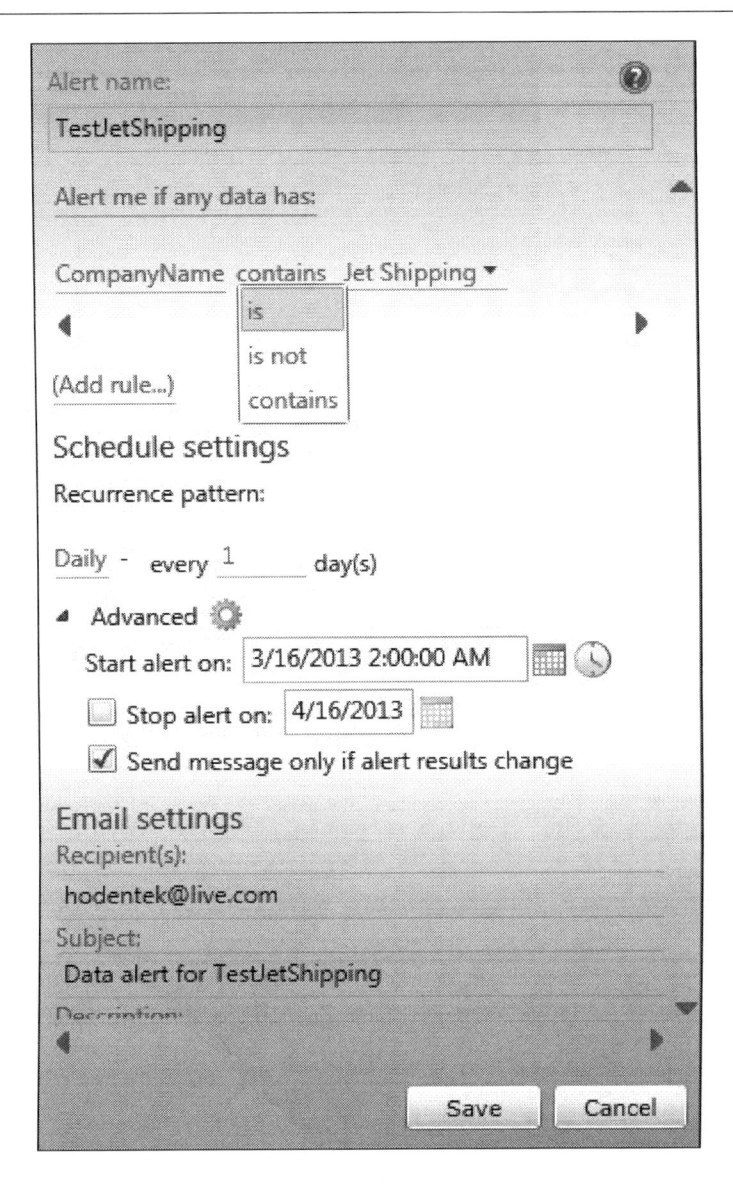

![Alert configuration dialog showing Alert name: TestJetShipping, CompanyName contains Jet Shipping, Schedule settings with Daily recurrence, Start alert on 3/16/2013 2:00:00 AM, Stop alert on 4/16/2013, Send message only if alert results change checked, Email settings with Recipient hodentek@live.com, Subject: Data alert for TestJetShipping, Save and Cancel buttons]

4. After satisfying yourself about the alert rule, the schedule, and the recipient's e-mail address, click on **Save**.

5. Close the report.

[397]

Self-service Data Alerts in SSRS 2012

6. Right-click the report in `Documents` and click on **Manage Data Alerts** in the drop-down list. The **Data Manager** window opens as shown in the following screenshot:

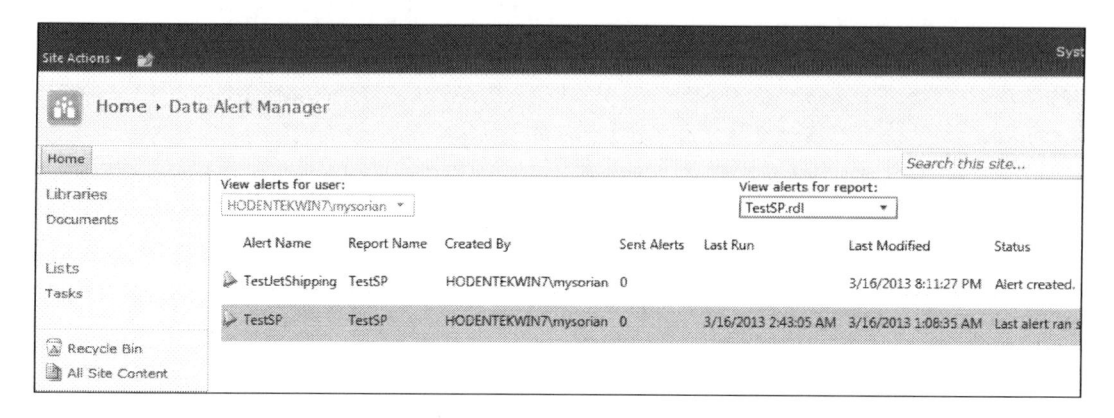

Notice that the `TestJetShipping` alert created earlier has appeared in the list of Data Alerts in **Data Alert Manager**. It shows the creator of the alert (the owner) and the name of the report in the drop-down list (**View alerts for report:**). The listing also shows **Sent Alerts**, **Last Run**, **Last Modified**, and **Status**. Notice an earlier data alert named `TestSP`, which ran successfully but no alert was sent (some text truncated in the image).

The Data Alerts you send end up in the SQL Server Agent on the Report Server as shown in the next screenshot where you could pursue how the agent performs and other details. You may need a good knowledge of SQL Agent to pursue further. It is recommended that you do not modify the SQL Server Agent job of the alert.

Editing Data Alerts

If you need to change the alert for any reason, perhaps you want to use a different SMTP server, add a few more people to the e-mail recipient list, and so on, you can edit the alert as well. It is very easy to edit.

1. Click on the handle of the `TestSP` report to display the drop-down menu (the handle becomes visible when you hover over it).

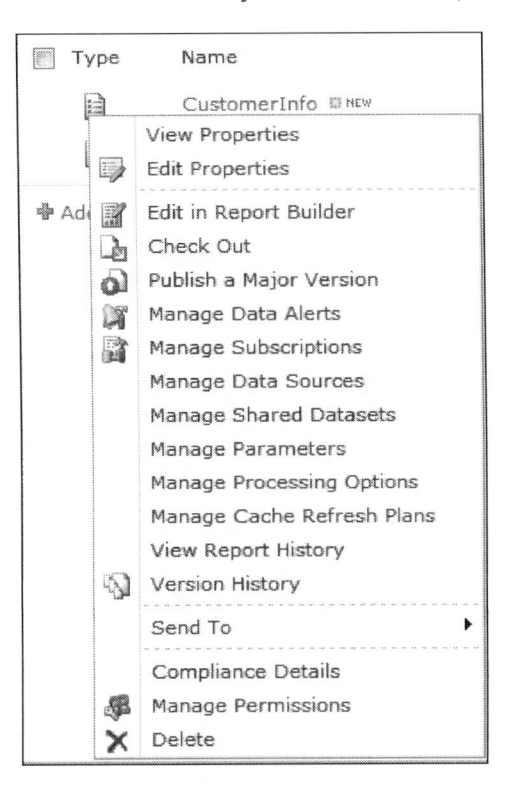

Using this menu, you can do most of the things you accomplished using Report Manager for a Reporting Services server installed in the native mode.

2. Click on **Manage Data Alerts**. The Data Alert Manager is displayed as shown in the following screenshot:

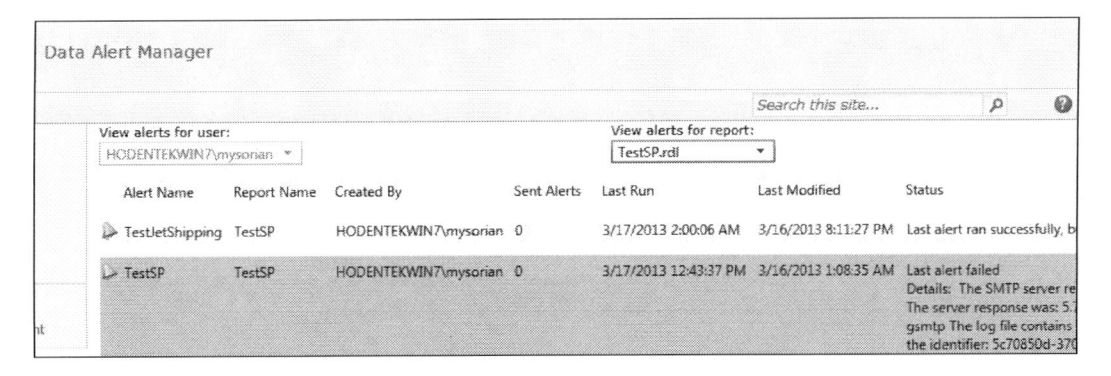

Self-service Data Alerts in SSRS 2012

Notice that the `TestJetShipping` alert ran successfully but no alert was sent. Another `TestSP` alert failed.

Let us edit the **TestJetShipping** to see the conditions we set up and the schedule. Change them if necessary.

3. Right-click the alert to display the drop-down list.

   The choices are **Edit, Run,** and **Delete**. The choice **Run** is good as it immediately runs irrespective of the schedule that you have set up. The **Edit** option will bring up the Alert Designer.

4. Click on **Edit**. The **Edit Data Alert** window comes up as shown in the following screenshot:

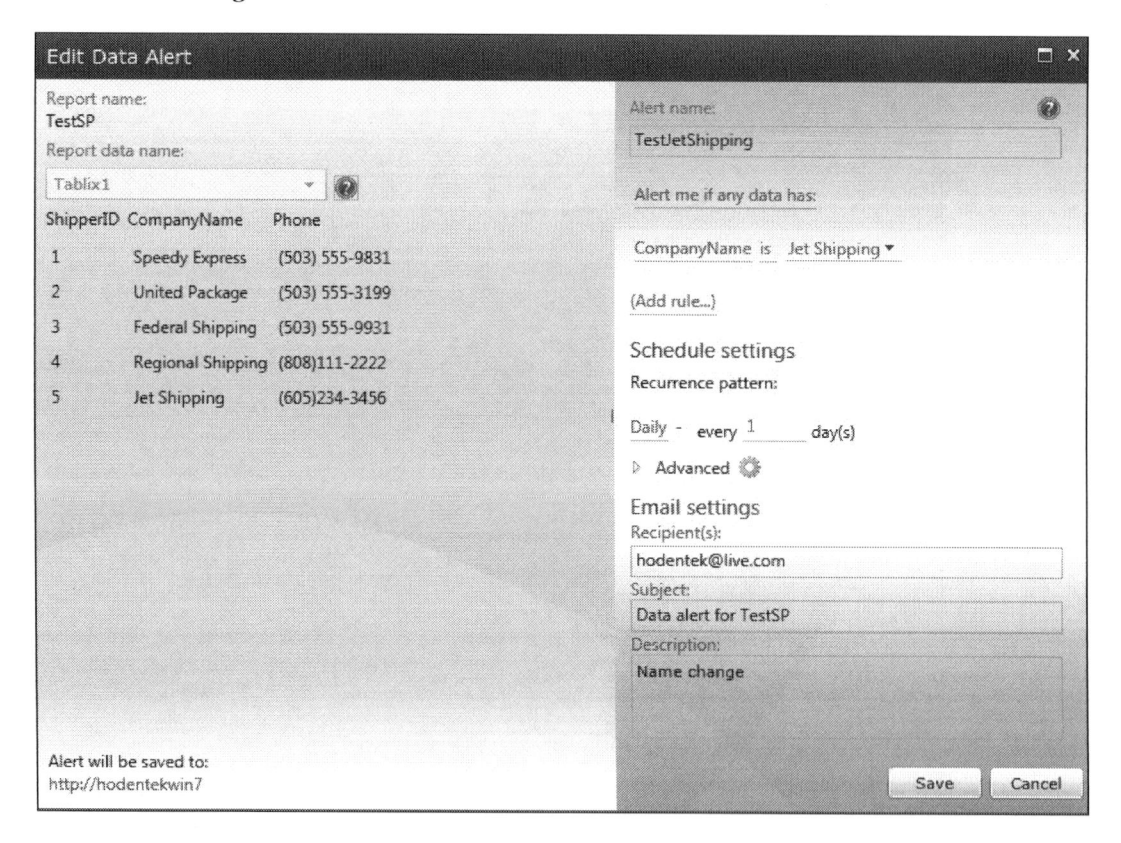

[400]

You will notice a new column in the data feed. This was created to test the alert by editing the `Shippers` table in SQL Server Management Studio.

ShipperID	CompanyName	Phone
1	Speedy Express	(503) 555-9831
2	United Package	(503) 555-3199
3	Federal Shipping	(503) 555-9931
4	Regional Shippi...	(808)111-2222
5	Jet Shipping	(605)234-3456
*	NULL	NULL	NULL

When the alert was run the first time using the SMTP server of a Web e-mail service such as `gmail.com` or `live.com`, the alert succeeded but failed to deliver the message. The alert failed due to a lack of communication with the e-mail server as shown here.

> *The SMTP server requires a secure connection or the client was not authenticated. The server response was; 5.7.0 Must issue a STARTTLS command first. qb10sm17574274pbb.43-gsmtp. the log file contains detailed information about the error. Refer to the log entry with the identifier:066bbfba-5fa9-4ade-89a1-c4a67abb7518.*

The reason this failed to send an e-mail is because our **E-mail Settings** (**SMTP Server** and the **From** address) are not correctly configured with Web e-mail settings. The correct e-mail settings are the settings of your Internet service provider if you are a home user like the author or, the enterprise's SMTP server as mentioned earlier.

When the correct e-mail setting is used the alerts run successfully as shown here:

| TestSP | TestSP | HODENTEKWIN7\mysorian | 2 | 5/4/2013 5:05:41 PM | 5/4/2013 5:04:53 PM | Last alert ran successfully and the alert was sent. |

The alert is sent to the designated recipient as shown in the following screenshot:

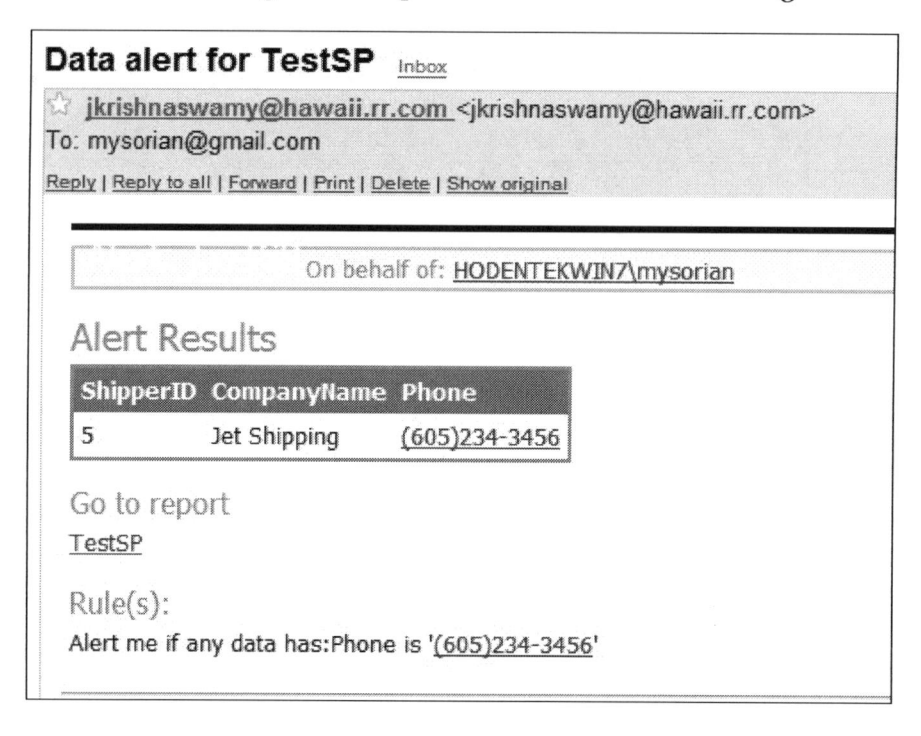

Data alert for TestSP Inbox

jkrishnaswamy@hawaii.rr.com <jkrishnaswamy@hawaii.rr.com>
To: mysorian@gmail.com
Reply | Reply to all | Forward | Print | Delete | Show original

On behalf of: HODENTEKWIN7\mysorian

Alert Results

ShipperID	CompanyName	Phone
5	Jet Shipping	(605)234-3456

Go to report
TestSP

Rule(s):
Alert me if any data has:Phone is '(605)234-3456'

You can access the report by clicking on the link. When the `TestSP` link is clicked by the recipient, a connection will be established to the site to run the report.

Troubleshooting

This is an important part of your learning experience and is also important for getting something done successfully.

Reporting Services service events are logged in SharePoint's **Unified Logging Service (ULS)** trace log beginning with SQL Server Reporting Services 2008 R2. The trace log location is `%CommonProgramFiles%\Microsoft Shared\Web Server Extensions\14\LOGS\`. Reporting Services-related specific categories are available from the SharePoint Central Administration by first bringing up the **Monitoring** page as shown:

Chapter 7

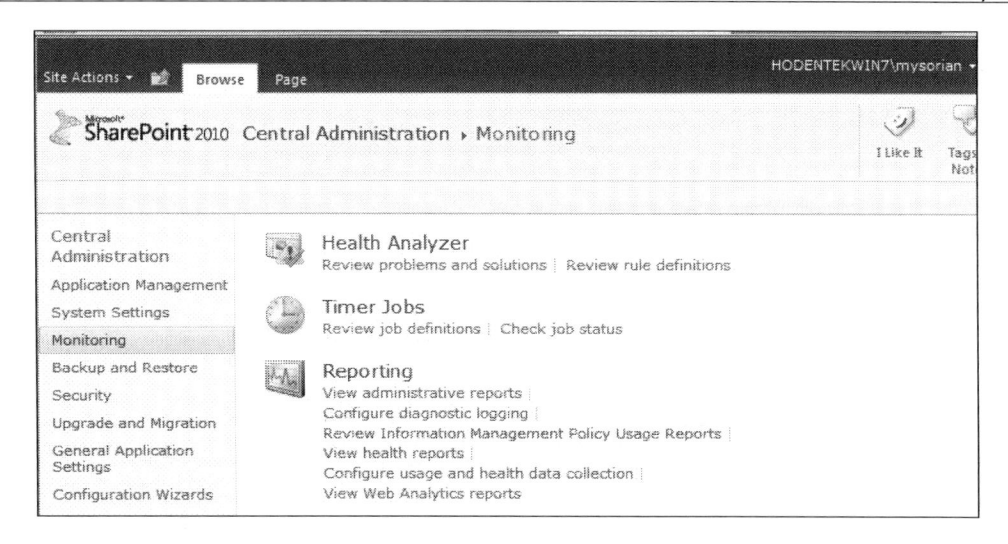

And when you click on **Configure diagnostic logging**, the following page is displayed:

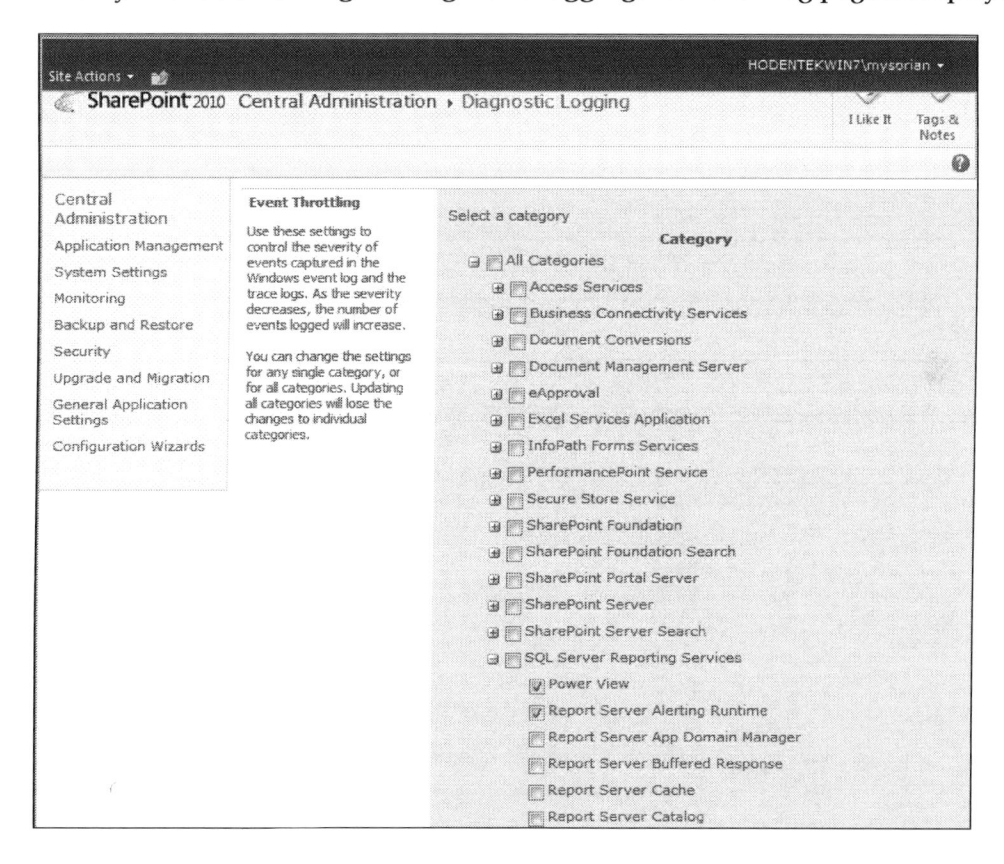

You can enable the ones you want logged here as shown for **Power View** and **Reporting Server Alerting Runtime**. At the bottom of this page you can configure the following as well:

- Enable event log flood protection to detect repeating events in Windows events
- Find the trace log path in the filesystem
- Number of days to store trace logs
- Restrict trace log disk space

> One of the problems you may run into is that the logs are created incessantly unless you take action as shown before to restrict the frequency with which these files (these are hefty!) are written to your filesystem. Also, these files are usually very large. Keep a watch on this folder here:
>
> C:\Program Files\Common Files\Microsoft Shared\Web Server Extensions\14\LOGS

You may keep the more recent and get rid of the older ones. The default says you can keep it for 14 days, but you can change this default. In any case, it is not necessary to keep all of them.

Using PowerShell to review the logfile

The log file contains many categories and you can filter them with the following PowerShell (this will be described fully in *Chapter 8, Reporting Services and Programming*) cmdlet:

```
Get-content -path "C:\Program Files\Common Files\Microsoft Shared\Web Server Extensions\14\LOGS\Hodentekwin7-20130505-1506.log" | select-string "sql server reporting services
```

The log file was created on May 5, 2013 and PowerShell filters the log file for SQL Server Reporting Services. This is very useful when you want to find a pin in a haystack. A sample output is shown here:

```
/--Sample result of running the above code--/

PS C:\Users\mysorian> Get-content -path "C:\Program Files\
Common Files\Microsoft Shared\Web Server Extensions\14\LOGS\
Hodentekwin7-20130505-1506.log" | select-s

tring "sql server reporting services"
```

```
05/05/2013 15:08:44.66     w3wp.exe (0x1C30)
0x3324    SQL Server Reporting Services     Report Server Alerting
Runtime    0000    Medium
Executed AlertingEventQueueWorker.CleanInactiveRows()

05/05/2013 15:12:06.94     w3wp.exe (0x1C30)
0x43C4    SQL Server Reporting Services     Report Server Catalog
0000    Medium
RenderForNewSession('http://hodentekwin7/Documents/May4.rdl')
1cb08bfa-e39b-4d40-bd7a-dcbf6460b733

05/05/2013 15:12:07.57     w3wp.exe (0x1C30)
0x43C4    SQL Server Reporting Services     Report Server WCF Runtime
0000    Medium
Processed report. Report='http://hodentekwin7/Documents/May4.rdl',
Stream=''    1cb08bfa-e39b-4d40-bd7a-dcbf6460b733

05/05/2013 15:12:11.84     w3wp.exe (0x1C30)
0x1044    SQL Server Reporting Services     Report Server Catalog
0000    Medium
Call to GetSystemPropertiesAction().    ec6cfc58-2aba-4ef6-ac1d-
3be95e19309e

05/05/2013 15:12:11.88     w3wp.exe (0x1C30)
0x1044    SQL Server Reporting Services     Report Server Catalog
0000    Medium
Call to GetPropertiesAction(http://hodentekwin7/Documents/May4.rdl,
PathBased).    ec6cfc58-2aba-4ef6-ac1d-3be95e19309e

05/05/2013 15:13:44.63     w3wp.exe (0x1C30)
0x40F8    SQL Server Reporting Services     Report Server Catalog
0000    Medium
Call to CleanBatch()

05/05/2013 15:13:44.81     w3wp.exe (0x1C30)
0x40F8    SQL Server Reporting Services     Report Server Catalog
0000    Medium
Cleaned 0 batch records, 0 policies, 0 sessions, 0 cache entries, 0
snapshots, 0 chunks, 0 running jobs, 0 persisted streams, 0 segments, 0
segment mappings, 0 edit sessions.

05/05/2013 15:13:44.81     w3wp.exe (0x1C30)
0x40F8    SQL Server Reporting Services     Report Server Catalog
0000    Medium
Call to CleanBatch() ends
```

```
05/05/2013 15:13:46.94     w3wp.exe (0x1C30)
0x1044    SQL Server Reporting Services      Report Server Catalog
0000      Medium    RenderForNewSession('http://hodentekwin7/Documents/
May4.rdl')     d3149a5d-607f-49f1-858b-de198a2a5df3

05/05/2013 15:13:47.39     w3wp.exe (0x1C30)
0x1044    SQL Server Reporting Services      Report Server WCF Runtime
0000      Medium
Processed report. Report='http://hodentekwin7/Documents/May4.rdl',
Stream=''      d3149a5d-607f-49f1-858b-de198a2a5df3

05/05/2013 15:13:50.82     w3wp.exe (0x1C30)
0x4EC8    SQL Server Reporting Services      Report Server Catalog
0000      Medium
Call to GetSystemPropertiesAction().     c0fa693e-16f3-4a30-bb22-
c252915e38b5
```

Alert logs and alerting database

Reporting Services provides logs while running data alert definitions. There are three logs associated with Data Alerts: alert execution log, Report Server execution log, and Report Server trace log. The alerting database has a `ExecutionLogViewTable` table, which can be queried or one of several stored procedures can be run to get more detailed diagnostic of how the alert functioned. You can also carry out management using the stored procedures. You will find these in the alerting database shown here in SSMS:

Chapter 7

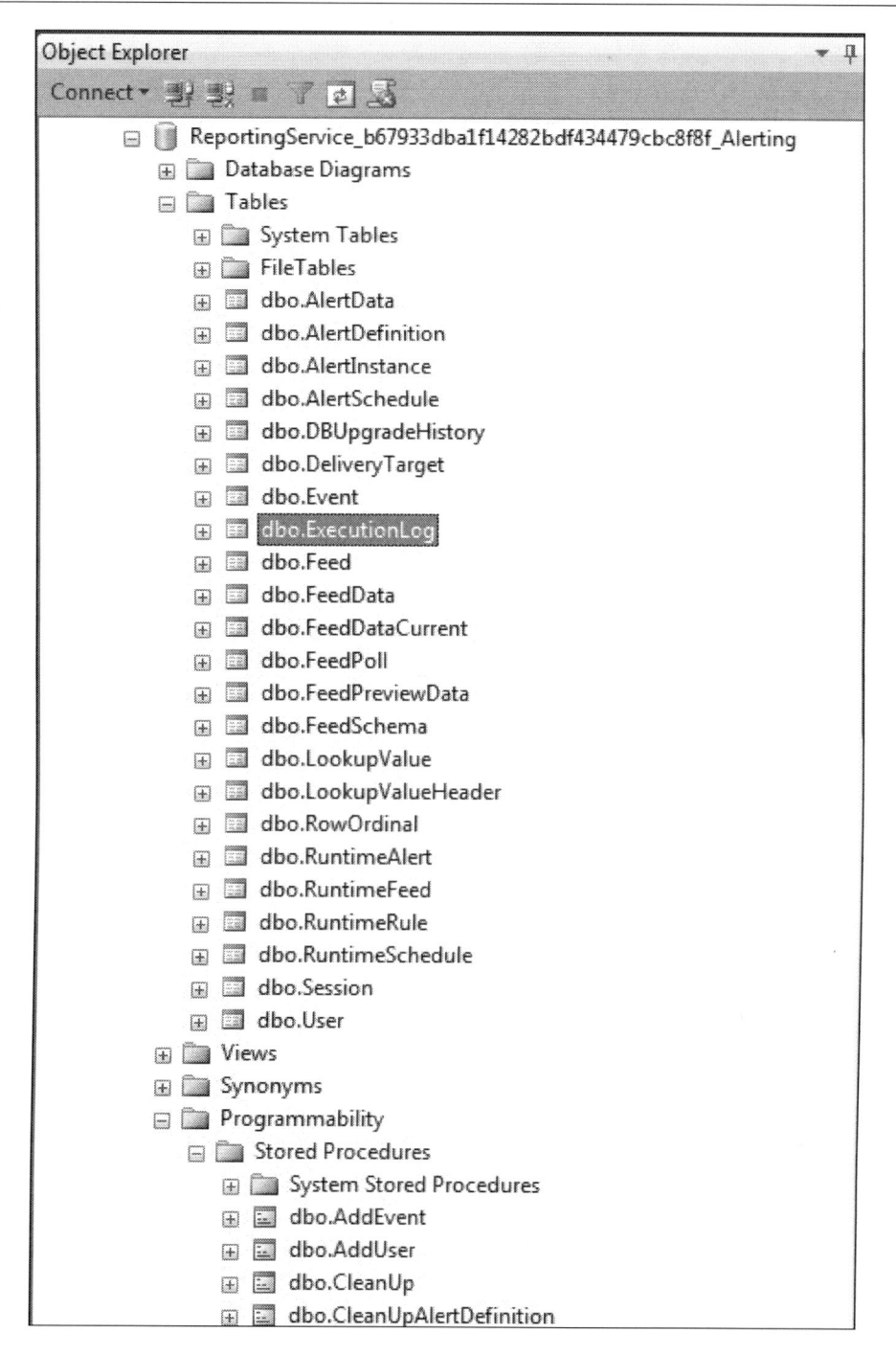

Self-service Data Alerts in SSRS 2012

The following query running on SSMS in the alert database displays the execution result of Data Alerts:

```
SELECT * FROM dbo.ExecutionLogView
```

Summary

In this chapter, Data Alerts, the new feature in SQL Server 2012 Reporting Services, was described. The hands-on exercises give a flavor of tasks that you can work on and the troubleshooting gives you a practical way of looking at the alerts you create and how they were processed. Since you create data alerts in SharePoint server, it is very important to configure the duo, SharePoint Server/Report Server, correctly.

In the next chapter, we will look at some of the programming interfaces available to work with Reporting Services in both modes. For Report Server Management in SharePoint integrated mode, Power Shell appears to be well positioned.

8
Reporting Services and Programming

In this chapter, we will be looking at a number of programming interfaces available to work with SQL Server Reporting Services 2012, both in the Native mode and in SharePoint Server 2010 Integrated installation mode; see *Chapter 1, Overview and Installation – SQL Server Reporting Services 2012*. A number of utilities and interfaces are discussed in this chapter to work with RS. These tools and interfaces help in the maintenance of Reporting Services installed to support both modes of installation as well as working with Reporting services.

> In the first edition of the book, *Learning SQL Server Reporting Services 2008, Chapter 8, Programming Interfaces to Reporting Services*, some of the interfaces were also discussed, and in *Chapter 10, On Programmatically Creating a SSRS Report*, report generation using code in Visual studio 2008 was described.

Overview of programming interfaces and utilities

The programming interfaces and utilities explored in this chapter are listed as follows:

- URL access
- ReportViewer control
- The Reporting Server Web Services API

- PowerShell for Report Server in the Native mode
- PowerShell for Report Server Integration with SharePoint Server
- Windows Management Instrumentation
- Reporting Services utilities
- Incorporating custom code into report

URL access

One way to access the Report Server, Native or SharePoint Integrated, is by sending a URL request. This is quite useful in the absence of the report manager. Sending a request to the URL allows you to customize the rendering of the report in both modes of Report Server installations. You can customize the report by utilizing specific `prefixes` and `parameter` information, together with the URL request. This not only gives specific features of the report, but also the format in which you want the report to be rendered. Once you have fashioned the URL request string, all you need to do is just e-mail it or paste it as a link to a Web page, so that others can also access the report (assuming they have access to the Report Server). URL access allows you to carry out the following actions on the server:

- Interact with the HTML viewer by sending commands to tweak
- Give access to folder contents
- Get the XML of an item on the server
- Render a snapshot in report history
- Report session management

The syntax for URL access is as follows:

```
rswebserverurl?reportpath[&prefix:param=value]...n]
```

The basic information you need to provide to carry out any of the preceding action is by using the URL access information you find at, http://msdn.microsoft.com/en-us/library/1c3e680a-83ea-4979-8e79-fa2337ae12a3.

Here is a summarized list of the prefixes (prefix in the syntax above and within parentheses below) available:

- HTML Viewer commands (`rc:`)
- Report Server commands (`rs:`)
- ReportViewer Web commands (`rv:`)

Each prefix has a number of parameters (`param` in the preceding syntax), which help with looking deeper into the server, or help in rendering a report. In the previous version, there were two other prefixes, **DSU** and **DSP**, and they have been deprecated. Review http://social.msdn.microsoft.com/Forums/en-US/sqlreportingservices/thread/72f83019-9d2b-4ede-a526-e096a0cabc5b/.

Hands-on exercise 8.1 – URL access, Native mode Report Server

In this section, it is assumed that you have a number of items on your Report Server, as shown, when you access the Report Server Web service URL. The items in your server are created by you, and when you access the Report Server, you see those items arranged. They need not be the same ones (will not be, unless you recreate) but then you need to make appropriate changes to the code. There are folders, folders within folders, reports, report parts, report models, and data sources. In the hands-on exercise, you will be looking at a number of prefixes and parameters to access the Report Server.

hodentekwin7/ReportServer_HI - /

Thursday, March 28, 2013 3:52 PM	<dir>	Data Sources
Thursday, March 28, 2013 3:29 PM	24215	EmployeeMarch28
Thursday, March 28, 2013 2:10 PM	28738	EmployeeSales
Thursday, March 28, 2013 4:33 PM	<dir>	Flower
Thursday, March 28, 2013 3:38 PM	<ds>	March28_1
Tuesday, March 26, 2013 5:39 PM	<dir>	Report Parts
Thursday, March 28, 2013 4:01 PM	26794	RepShr
Tuesday, March 26, 2013 6:06 PM	33878	Shadow Simple
Thursday, March 28, 2013 3:52 PM	<dir>	ShrdData
Tuesday, March 26, 2013 10:42 AM	50398	Simple Parameter

Microsoft SQL Server Reporting Services Version 11.0.2100.60

Accessing the Report Server

If there are no problems and the Report Server is working correctly, and if it has already started, then enter the following URL in the address of the IE Browser, http://hodentekwin7/ReportServer_HI.

The browser should bring up the page, as shown in the preceding screenshot, with a number of items shown in the previous screenshot.

Reporting Services and Programming

Listing contents of a folder

The structure of the site is folder-based. Report parts store parts of a report. In the case of embedded data sources, the report parts will not contain the data source separately; it will, however, be present in the part that is saved.

Enter the following in the address of the IE Browser (note that `rs:` is the Report Server command):

`http://hodentekwin7/ReportServer_HI?/Report+Parts&rs:Command=ListChildren`

The following page will be displayed (it is `Report+Parts`):

```
hodentekwin7/ReportServer_HI - /Report Parts

[To Parent Directory]
        Tuesday, March 26, 2013 5:39 PM        30175 Chart2
        Thursday, March 28, 2013 2:30 PM       32928 Tablix2
        Tuesday, March 26, 2013 5:39 PM        33984 Tablix6

Microsoft SQL Server Reporting Services Version 11.0.2100.60
```

Accessing a component in report parts

Report parts store parts of a report that can be re-used by the creator or others who have the permission to do so.

Enter the following URL address in the IE browser: `http://hodentekwin7/ReportServer_HI?/Report+Parts/Tablix6&rs:Command=GetComponentDefinition`

The IE browser will display the report part definition; in this case, Tablix6's XML definition. *Chapter 5, Working with Report Builder 3.0* has a section named *Report Parts*; please review that section.

```xml
<?xml version="1.0" encoding="utf-8" ?>
- <ComponentItem xmlns:rdl="http://schemas.microsoft.com/sqlserver/reporting/2010/01/reportdefinition"
    xmlns:rd="http://schemas.microsoft.com/SQLServer/reporting/reportdesigner" Name="Tablix6"
    xmlns="http://schemas.microsoft.com/sqlserver/reporting/2010/01/componentdefinition">
  + <Properties>
  + <RdlFragment>
  </ComponentItem>
```

Rendering a report

In addition to the name of the report and the folder in which it is found, you need to additionally provide device information to render the report.

Enter the following in the address of the browser: `http://hodentekwin7/ReportServer_HI?/Shadow+Simple&rs:Command=Render&rs:Format=HTML4.0&rc:Toolbar=False`

While `rs:` targets Report Server, `rc:` supplies a rendering extension with specific device information settings. The report will be rendered as follows:

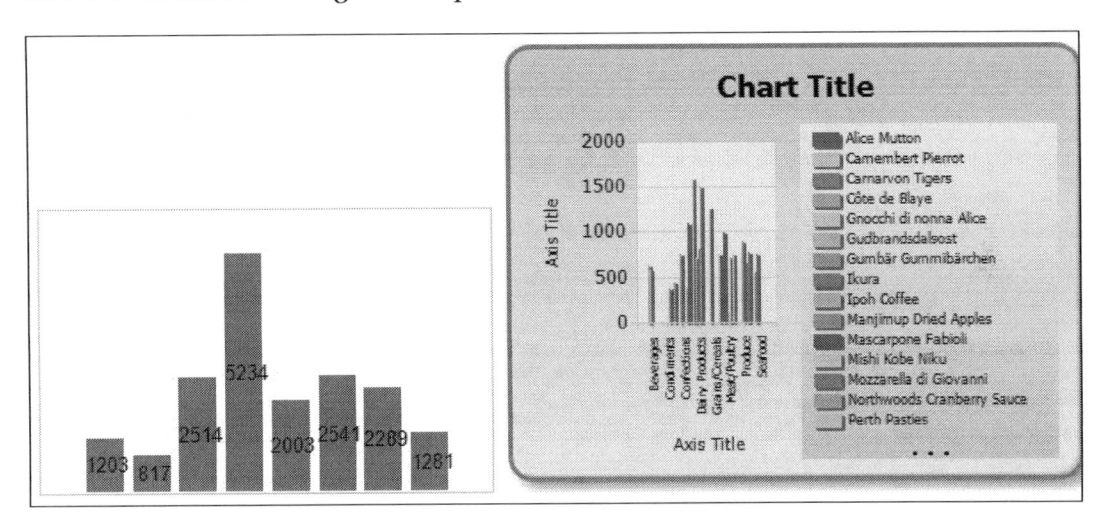

> If you try HTML5.0 (which has become very popular), you would get an `rsRenderingExtensionNotFound` error, and an explanation that it is not supported in this edition.

Accessing the contents of a data source

The data sources folder on the Report Server contains all the shared data sources.

Enter the following in the URL address of the browser:

`http://hodentekwin7/ReportServer_HI?/Data+Sources/ShrSrc&rs:Command=GetDataSourceContents`

The following XML definition will be displayed:

```xml
<DataSourceDefinition>
  <Extension>SQL</Extension>
  <ConnectString>Data Source=HODENTEKWIN7\NJ;Initial Catalog=Northwind</ConnectString>
  <UseOriginalConnectString>False</UseOriginalConnectString>
  <OriginalConnectStringExpressionBased>False</OriginalConnectStringExpressionBased>
  <CredentialRetrieval>Integrated</CredentialRetrieval>
  <Enabled>True</Enabled>
</DataSourceDefinition>
```

Exporting to supported formats

A simple command sent to the URL address can export reports in a couple of supported formats.

Enter the following in the URL address of the browser:

`http://hodentekwin7/ReportServer_HI?/Shadow+Simple&rs:Format=PDF`

After some processing, you will get the following message at the bottom of the browser window:

Do you want to open or save **Shadow Simple.pdf** from **hodentekwin7**?   Open   Save ▼   Cancel   ×

Rendering a report with the report parameter

You can also send a report parameter with a request to render a report. The `report Simple Parameter` on the Report Server has a parameter called `OrderDate`, and this will be accessed.

Enter the following in the URL address of the browser:

`http://hodentekwin7/ReportServer_HI?/Simple Parameter&OrderDate=1/1/1997&rc:Toolbar=false`

The browser displays the Simple Parameter report for the date 1/1/1997, and will not show the toolbar, as in the following image:

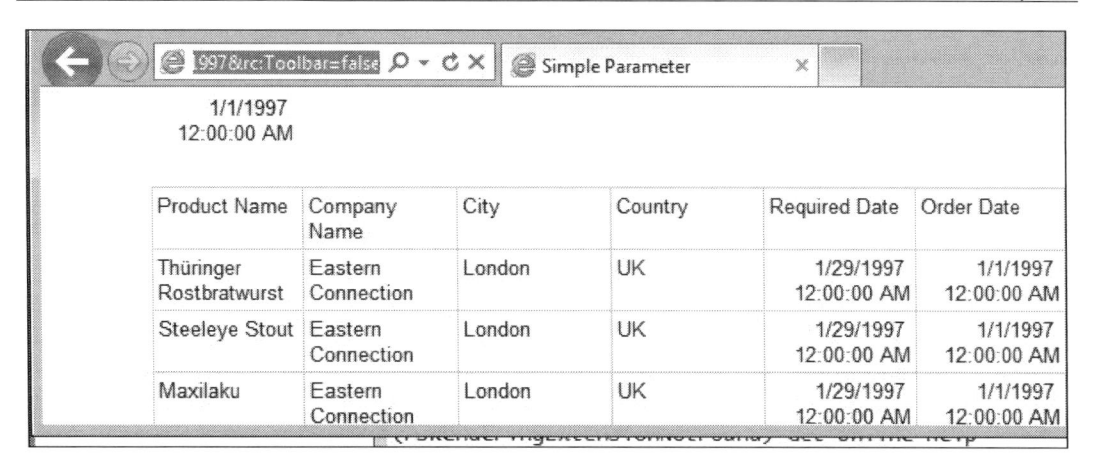

	1/1/1997 12:00:00 AM					
	Product Name	Company Name	City	Country	Required Date	Order Date
	Thüringer Rostbratwurst	Eastern Connection	London	UK	1/29/1997 12:00:00 AM	1/1/1997 12:00:00 AM
	Steeleye Stout	Eastern Connection	London	UK	1/29/1997 12:00:00 AM	1/1/1997 12:00:00 AM
	Maxilaku	Eastern Connection	London	UK	1/29/1997 12:00:00 AM	1/1/1997 12:00:00 AM

Hands-on exercise 8.2 – URL access and SharePoint Integrated mode Report Server

In order to access URL reports on a SharePoint site, route the HTTP request through the Reporting Services proxy at the SharePoint site integrated with reporting services.

The syntax from `http://msdn.microsoft.com/en-us/library/ms153586.aspx` is as follows:

```
http://myspsite/subsite/_vti_bin/reportserver.
```

In the next subsection, we will access the SP site created for this book.

In the next subsections, we will look at only two examples. You may use this basic syntax to get an experience for accessing other Report Server items.

Accessing the Report Server in SP-integrated implementation

Accessing the Report Server in SP-integrated implementation is a normal thing that you will start with before accessing reports, data sources, report parts, and so on, to verify that you can successfully access the Report Server.

Type the following string in the URL address of the browser:

```
http://HodentekWin7/_vti_bin/reportserver
```

Reporting Services and Programming

> Make sure you use _vti_bin to route the request through the reporting services HTTP proxy via SharePoint.

You should see the following response:

hodentekwin7/ - /   http://hodentekwin7/_vti_bin/reportserver

```
Sunday, March 10, 2013 11:05 AM      <dir> http://hodentekwin7
Sunday, March 10, 2013 11:07 AM      <dir> http://hodentekwin7/my
```

Microsoft SQL Server Reporting Services Version 11.0.2218.0

Accessing a report on the Report Server in SP-integrated implementation

We will access the `EmployeesSales.rdl` report in the `Documents` folder on the SP site, `HodentekWin7`.

Type the following string in the URL address of the browser:

```
http://hodentekwin7/_vti_bin/reportserver?http://hodentekwin7/Documents/EmployeesSales.rdl&rs:Command=Render
```

As soon as you enter this in the URL, it changes to the following:

```
http://hodentekwin7/_layouts/ReportServer/RSViewerPage.aspx?rv:RelativeReportUrl=%2fDocuments%2fEmployeesSales.rdl
```

The rendering is via **ReportViewer**. When you display the page, you will see the report as follows:

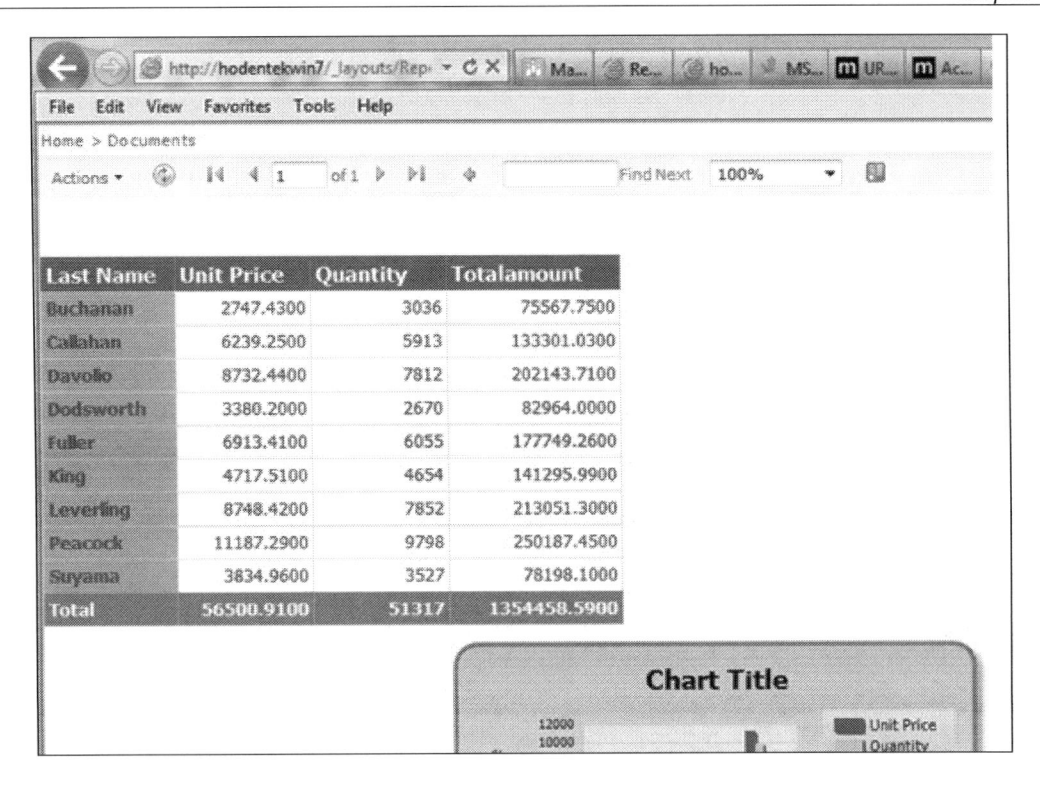

ReportViewer control

In *Chapter 2, SQL Server Reporting Services 2012 Projects with Visual Studio 2012*, we have seen the use of ReportViewer controls—one for the Web and the other for the desktop implemented to display reports that were processed locally as well as remotely on the Report Server. However, we just made use of the graphic user interface of the ReportViewer. In the *Hands-on exercise 8.3 – using URL access and ReportViewer controls with web applications* section, we will write the code to one of them. The code for ReportViewer for Windows forms follows similar lines.

The last section of the code in the *Hands-on exercise 8.3 – using URL access and ReportViewer controls with web applications* section uses a ReportViewer control to display a report. You will also need to add a ScriptManager control to make use of the ReportViewer control, as Silverlight is used in displaying the report.

We have used `ReportViewer1.Visible` to display the ReportViewer with the report, but we can include many other properties of the ReportViewer control as in this intellisense drop-down menu (or alternately from Visual Studio's object browser).

Reporting Services and Programming

> To access ReportViewer properties, just place a dot (.) after **ReportViewer1**, for example, in the code URLaccess.aspx.vb, and the intellisense drop-down will be displayed. You can make a choice from the drop-down list, for example, the visibility property of **ReportViewer1**. The object browser can be accessed from the view menu where you search for **ReportViewer1**. Intellisense is also available in SSMS for T-SQL coding.

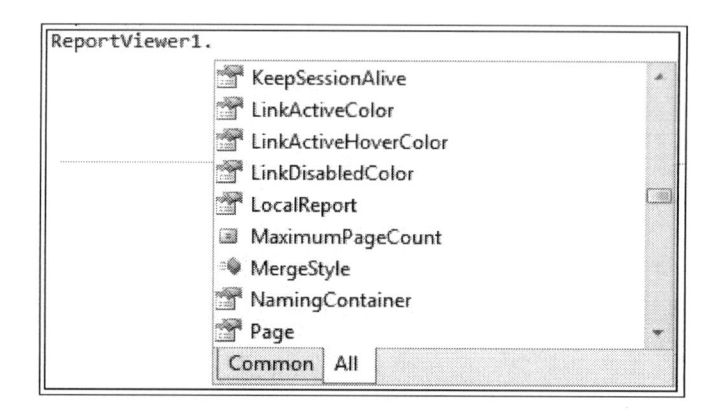

```
ReportViewer1.
              KeepSessionAlive
              LinkActiveColor
              LinkActiveHoverColor
              LinkDisabledColor
              LocalReport
              MaximumPageCount
              MergeStyle
              NamingContainer
              Page
   Common  All
```

After working on this hands-on review, follow these links. http://reportviewer.codeplex.com/ and http://msdn.microsoft.com/en-us/library/microsoft.reporting.winforms.createstreamcallback.aspx links to get a more detailed experience of ReportViewer programming, covering the following topics:

- Microsoft.Reporting.WebForms Namespace and the classes
- Microsoft.Reporting.WinForms Namespace and the classes
- Microsoft.Reporting.WebFormsClient Namespace

Hands-on exercise 8.3 – using URL access and ReportViewer controls with Web applications

In a previous hands-on exercise, we just typed in the URL into the address of an IE Browser. The URL access can also be incorporated into ASPX and HTML pages.

The ASPX page in this hands-on exercise is created assuming that we are looking at the same Report Server in the Native mode. It uses hyperlinks, IFrame tags, and a form Post method to display items on the Report Server.

The last section of the code uses a ReportViewer control and the button click event provides the code for ReportViewer to display a report on the report server. The code incorporates all the methods in one Web form:

1. Start Visual Studio 2010 (here, the Ultimate Evaluation was used).
2. Create an ASP.NET Web Forms application with the name `WebRepView`.
3. The project is created with the standard template structure.
4. Add a new page named `URLAccess.aspx`, as follows:

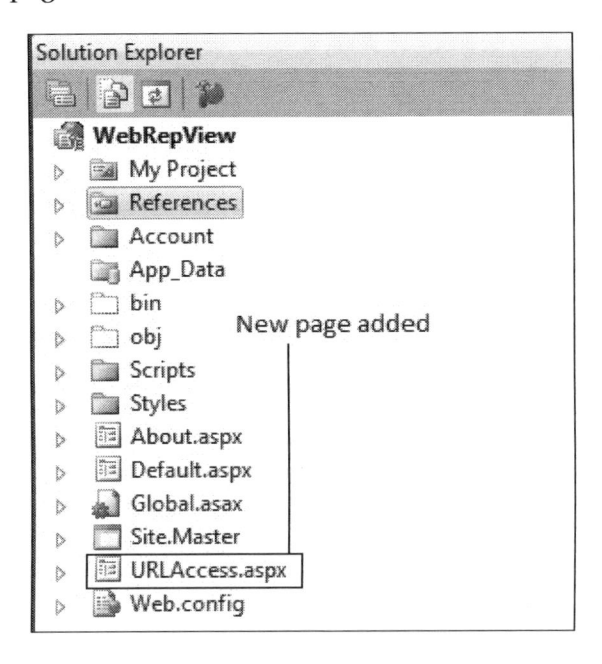

5. Drag-and-drop a **ReportViewer** control and a **ScriptManager** control you find under Ajax Extensions from **Toolbox** on to the Web page (this is very similar to what you did in *Chapter 2, SQL Server Reporting Services 2012 Projects with Visual Studio 2012*).
6. Replace the source code of the page with the following (make sure that the asp.net controls are not duplicated):

```
<%@ Page Language="vb" AutoEventWireup="false"
CodeBehind="URLAccess.aspx.vb" Inherits="WebRepView.URLAccess" %>

<%@ Register Assembly="Microsoft.ReportViewer.WebForms,
Version=10.0.0.0, Culture=neutral, PublicKeyToken=b03f5f7f11d50a
3a"
```

```
            Namespace="Microsoft.Reporting.WebForms" TagPrefix="rsweb" %>

<!DOCTYPE html PUBLIC "-//W3C//DTD XHTML 1.0 Transitional//EN"
"http://www.w3.org/TR/xhtml1/DTD/xhtml1-transitional.dtd">

<html xmlns="http://www.w3.org/1999/xhtml">
<head runat="server">
    <title></title>
</head>
<body>
<h2>URL access with a link</h2>
<a href="http://hodentekwin7/ReportServer_HI?/Shadow+Simple&rs:Com
mand=Render&rs:Format=HTML4.0&rc:Toolbar=False" target="_self">
Shadow Simple Report</a>
<h2>URL Access in a iframe </h2>
<iframe id="main" width="80%" height="500"
src="http://hodentekwin7/ReportServer_HI?/Shadow+Simple&rs:Command
=Render&rs:Format=HTML4.0&rc:Toolbar=False"></iframe>
<h2>URL access in a Post Method of a form</h2>
    <form id="form1" runat="server" action="http://HodentekWin7/
ReportServer_HI?/Report+Parts">
    <input type="hidden" name="rs:Command" value="ListChildren" />
    <input type="submit" value="Get Folder Contents" />
    <div>
    <p>Integrating a report on Report Server with a ReportViewer
Control</p>
    <asp:ScriptManager ID="ScriptManager1" runat="server">
    </asp:ScriptManager>
    <asp:Button
            ID="Button1" runat="server" Text="Show Report in
ReportViewer" />
        <rsweb:ReportViewer ID="ReportViewer1" runat="server">
        </rsweb:ReportViewer></p>
        <p> </p>
     </div>
    </form>
</body>
</html>
```

For URLaccess.aspx.vb, use the following code:

```
Public Class URLAccess
    Inherits System.Web.UI.Page
```

```
    Protected Sub Page_Load(ByVal sender As Object, ByVal e As
System.EventArgs) Handles Me.Load

    End Sub

    Protected Sub Button1_Click(sender As Object, e As EventArgs)
Handles Button1.Click
        ReportViewer1.ProcessingMode = Microsoft.Reporting.
WebForms.ProcessingMode.Remote
        Dim srvReport As Microsoft.Reporting.WebForms.ServerReport
= ReportViewer1.ServerReport
        srvReport.ReportServerUrl = New Uri("http://hodentekWin7/
ReportServer_HI")
        srvReport.ReportPath = ("/Repshr")
        ReportViewer1.Visible = True

    End Sub
End Class
```

7. While writing the preceding code, make full use of intellisense (see the next tip) as shown for an element of code here:

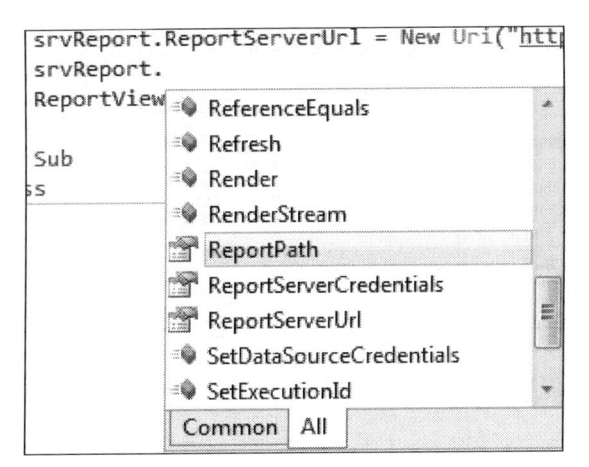

> After typing in ReportViewer1, you can type a dot(.) or hit *Ctrl* + *J* to bring up the intellisense drop-down menu, shown in the preceding screenshot, and can set the level of the details you need to see, by going to **Edit** | **Intellisense** and choosing the options. Intellisense is also available in SSMS, and is helpful while writing the T-SQL Code.

Reporting Services and Programming

When you browse to the page `URLAccess.aspx`, you should be able to do the following:

- Click on the hyperlink **Shadow Simple Report**, and display the report
- See the report displayed in `<iFrame/>` without a toolbar
- When you hit the **Get Folder Contents** button, you should see the contents of the folder
- When you hit the **Show Report in ReportViewer** button, the report should open in the same page

In order for this to happen, you should have your report server (in **Control Panel**) as well as the Reporting Services database (in SQL Server 2012 Management Studio) started, as discussed in *Chapter 1, Overview and Installation – SQL Server Reporting Services 2012*.

Report Server Web Services API

Objects on the Report Server are managed (with the Report Server Web Service) using what are called **Management Endpoints** (basically URLs). In SQL Server 2012, there are three important management endpoints. Review `http://msdn.microsoft.com/en-us/library/ms155398.aspx`.

- ReportServer2005 (for Native mode)
- ReportServer2006 (for SharePoint Integrated mode)
- ReportServer2010 (for both the modes, including both 2005 and 2006)

In Windows or Web applications, we interact with the endpoints via Web proxies. In addition to the management endpoint, there is also the `ReportExecution2005` endpoint for processing and rendering reports; review `http://msdn.microsoft.com/en-us/library/ms154052.aspx`.

While using these APIs, you need to exercise care and use the appropriate API, as shown in the following tip, from the MSDN documentation mentioned previously.

> When a Report Server is configured for the SharePoint integrated mode, the `ReportService2005` APIs will return an `rsOperationNotSupportedSharePointMode` error. If the Report Server is configured for the Native mode, the `ReportService2006` APIs will return an `rsOperationNotSupportedNativeMode` error. Similarly, when mode-specific APIs in `ReportService2010` are used on unintended modes, the APIs will return the respective errors.

The `ReportService2005` and `ReportService2006` are deprecated, and are still available in the present edition (but are not supported by Microsoft), but will be removed from future editions. `ReportingService2010`, while not described in this book (two projects using ReportService 2010 can be downloaded from the Packt website), provides access to both the Native and SharePoint modes of implementation by using the following `.asmx` files. The procedure to develop using the API is no different from the ones discussed earlier:

- **Native mode**: `http://hodentekwin7/ReportServer_HI/ReportService2010.asmx?wsdl`
- **SharePoint Integrated mode**: `http://hodentekwin7/_vti_bin/ReportServer/ReportService2010.asmx?wsdl`

Please review the code download; projects `2010Endpoint` and `2010Endpoint_SP`:

In the following hands-on exercise, we review the usage of the Execution Management endpoint `ReportExecution2005`. `ReportExecution2010` should also be available when you install SQL Server 2012, but it was not found on the author's machine.

Hands-on exercise 8.4 – rendering a report on the Native mode Report Server into different formats

We have seen that reports can be rendered into different formats in the report manager as well as by using URL access. Using the `ReportExecution2005` service, the same can be carried out programmatically. In particular, you will be using the `Render()` method to render a report on the Report Server in Word, PDF, and Excel formats. The WORD and EXCEL reports result in files that you download and save, whereas a report rendered in PDF is displayed in the browser.

Here are the arguments for the `Render()` method:

```
Public Function Render(Format As String, DeviceInfo As String,
ByRef Extension As String, ByRef MimeType As String, ByRef Encoding
As String, ByRef Warnings() As RSExecSVC.ExecSVC.Warning, ByRef
StreamIds() As String) As Byte()
```

Now, carry out the following steps:

1. Launch Visual Studio 2010 Ultimate (you can also use Visual Studio 2008). Display a report and render the report to another format.

Reporting Services and Programming

2. Create an ASP.NET Web application (RSExecSVC) by using the ASP.NET Web application template in Visual Studio 2010 Ultimate, as shown. The target is .NET 3.5:

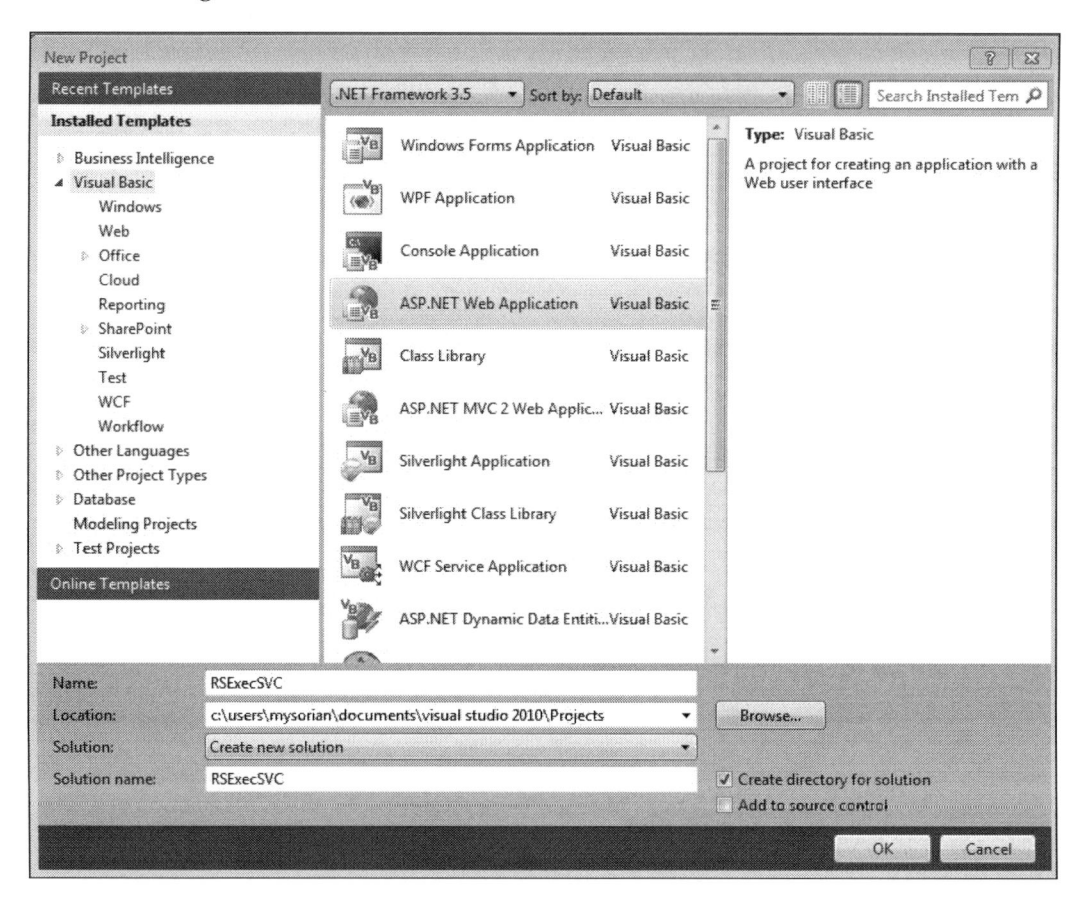

The project will be created with a folder structure, as follows:

3. Right-click on **RSExecSVC** to display the drop-down menu:

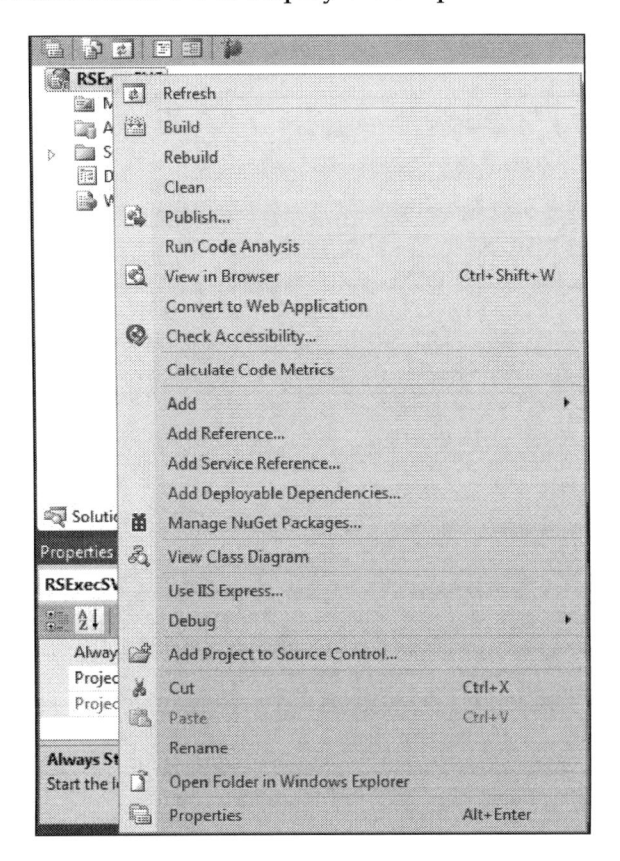

4. Click on **Add Service Reference....**

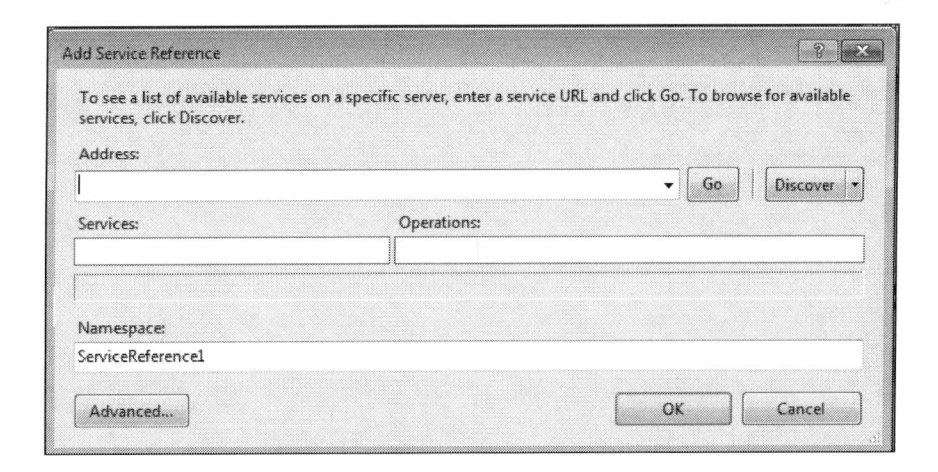

5. In the **Add Service Reference** window that was displayed, click on **Advanced...**.

6. The **Service Reference** Settings page will be displayed:

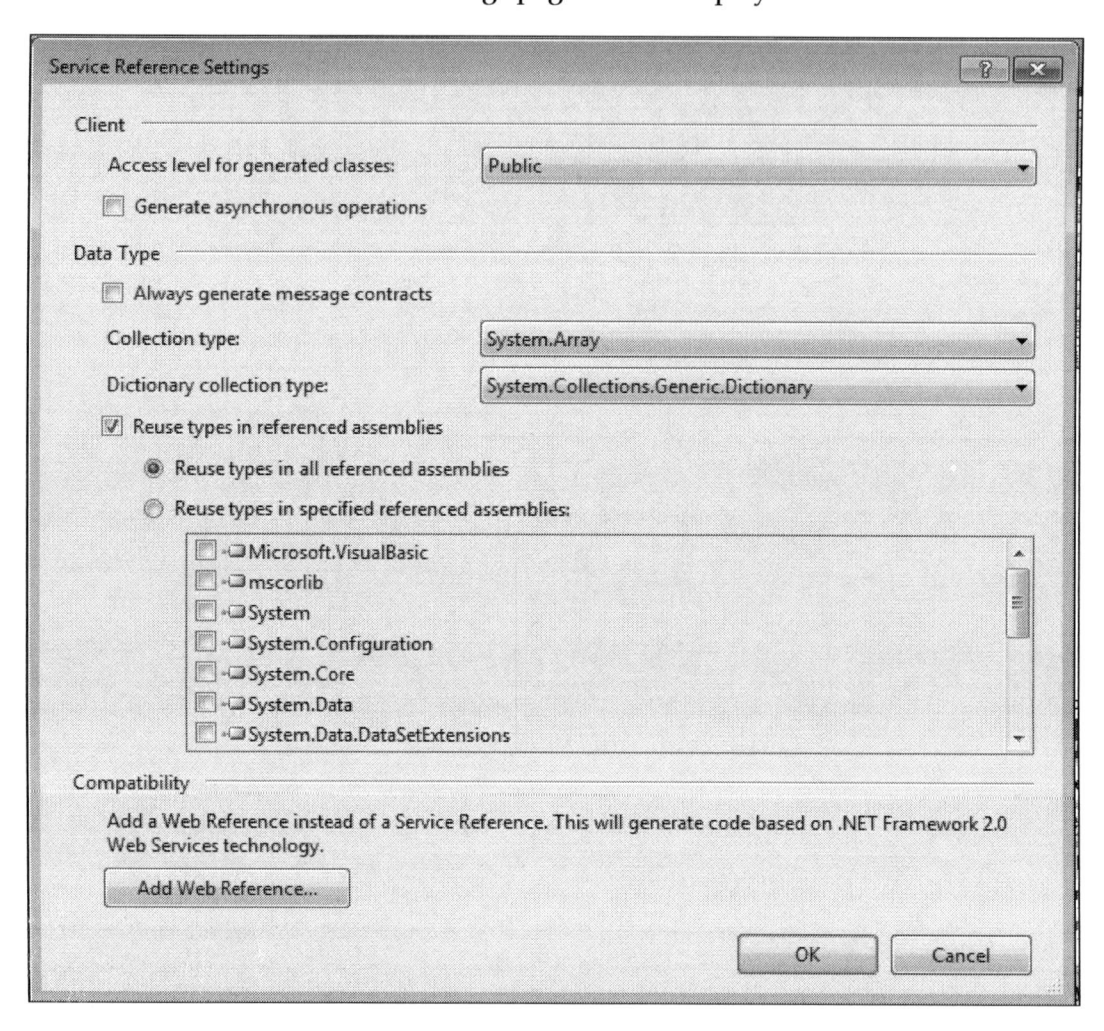

7. Click on the **Add Web Reference...** button.

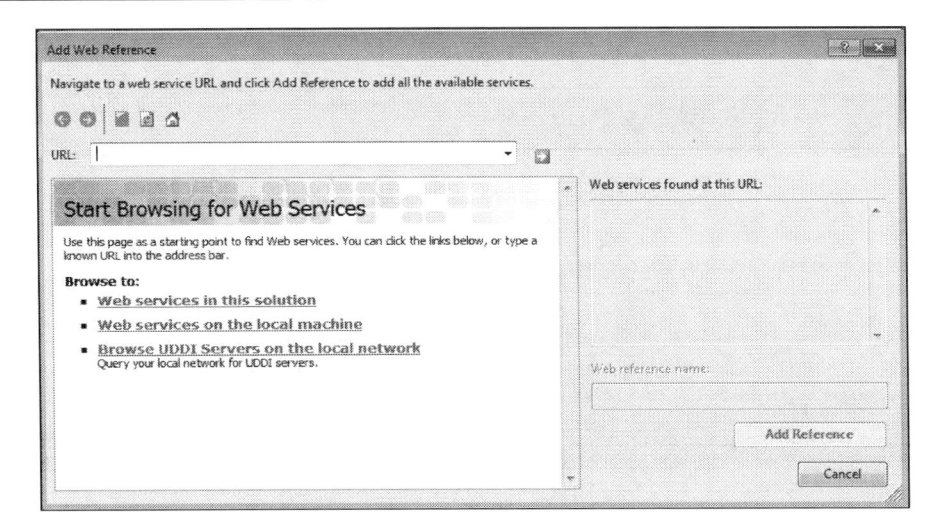

8. In the URL of the **Add Web Reference** window, type-in the following: `http://hodentekwin7/ReportServer_HI/ReportExecution2005.asmx?wsdl`, and click on the green arrow.

   The program processes this information and if the service exists or is found, the `ReportExecutionService` description is displayed as shown. The documentation inside the window lists all the methods that are exposed by this service:

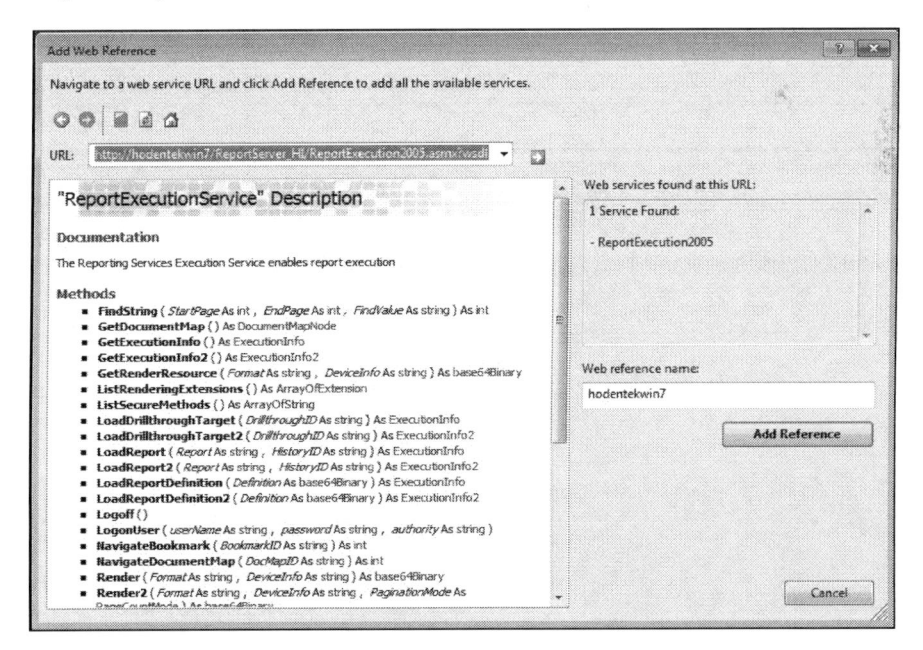

Reporting Services and Programming

9. Change the Web reference name to ExecSVC, and click on the **Add Reference** button.

10. The project gets updated as follows:

11. Drag-and-drop a button control on to the Default.asmx page.

12. Set up the code for the button click event, as follows:

```
Imports RSExecSVC.ExecSVC
Imports System.IO
Public Class _Default
    Inherits System.Web.UI.Page

    Protected Sub Page_Load(ByVal sender As Object, ByVal e AsSystem.EventArgs) Handles Me.Load

    End Sub

    Protected Sub Button1_Click(sender As Object, e As EventArgs) Handles Button1.Click
        Dim svc As New ReportExecutionService
        'set up authorization
        svc.Credentials = System.Net.CredentialCache.DefaultCredentials
        'set up arguments for the Render () method
        Dim repPath As String = "/Shadow Simple"
        Dim historyID As String = Nothing
        Dim extensio As String = ""
```

Chapter 8

```
        Dim result As Byte() = Nothing
        'Dim format As String = "PDF"
        'Dim format As String = "EXCEL"

        Dim format As String = "WORD"
        Dim encoding As String = ""
        Dim mimetype As String = ""
        Dim warnings As Warning() = Nothing
        Dim streamIDs As String() = Nothing

        'declare ExecuteHeader and ExecuteInfo
        Dim executeinfo As New RSExecSVC.ExecSVC.ExecutionInfo
        Dim executeHeader As New RSExecSVC.ExecSVC.ExecutionHeader
        'load report for execution
        executeinfo = svc.LoadReport(repPath, historyID)
        Dim SessionID As String = svc.ExecutionHeaderValue.
ExecutionID
        'coding the Render() method
        result = svc.Render(format, Nothing, extensio, mimetype,
encoding, warnings, streamIDs)
        'clear the response
        Response.ClearContent()
        'add header
        Response.AppendHeader("Content-length", result.Length.
ToString)
        'set up type of content
        'Response.ContentType = "application/pdf"
        'Response.ContentType = "application/vnd.ms-excel"
        Response.ContentType = "application/msword"
        Response.BinaryWrite(result)
        Response.Flush()
        Response.Close()
    End Sub
End Class
```

13. Build the project and browse to the **Default.aspx** page.
14. `Default.aspx` will be displayed in the browser.
15. Click on the button on this page.

Reporting Services and Programming

When you export the report in the PDF format, the report appears in the browser in PDF format. If you are trying to export it to Excel, you get the following message in the IE. This will appear differently in other browsers:

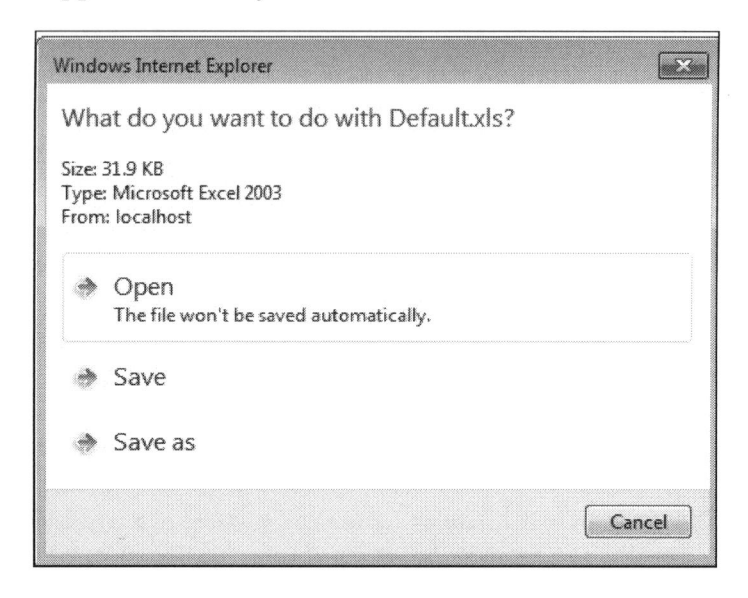

On the other hand, if it is in the Word format, you will get the following message at the bottom of the browser screen. You need to remove appropriate comments in the code for rendering into the desired format.

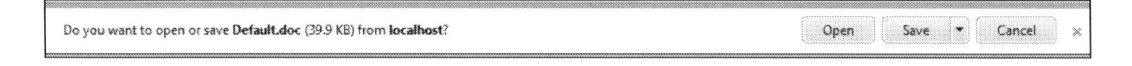

This completes the exercise to invoke the `ReportExecution2005` API to export a report to a different format.

Reporting Services in SharePoint Integrated mode

In the SharePoint Integrated mode with the Reporting Services add-in installed, a set of proxies are installed on the SharePoint Server. These endpoints are the primary APIs for developing reporting services solutions. The add-in manages the exchange of credentials between SPS and the RS in a trusted authentication mode. The following table taken from Microsoft documentation (`http://msdn.microsoft.com/en-us/library/ms155398.aspx`) lists the SharePoint proxy endpoints:

[430]

Proxy Endpoint	Description
ReportService2006	Provides the APIs for managing a report server that is configured for SharePoint integrate mode. **Note** This endpoint is deprecated in SQL Server 2008 R2.
ReportService2010	Provides the APIs for managing a report server that is configured for either native or SharePoint integrated mode.
ReportExecution2005	Provides the APIs for running and navigating reports.
ReportServiceAuthentication	Provides the APIs for authenticating users against a report server when the SharePoint Web application is configured for Forms Authentication.

Hands-on exercise 8.5 – accessing SharePoint management endpoints

There are two management endpoints for SharePoint 2010 — `ReportService2006` exclusively for SharePoint and `ReportService2010` for both the modes of Reporting Services installation. In this hands-on exercise, we will access the `ReportService2006` endpoint and write some simple code to look at the Report Server on SharePoint using the methods:

1. Create an ASP.NET project (**Target Framework 3.5**) with the name `RS-SPExecution` in Visual Studio (here, Visual Studio 2010 Ultimate evaluation was used).

   The project is created, as shown, except for the node **Web References**. This reference will be added in the next few steps:

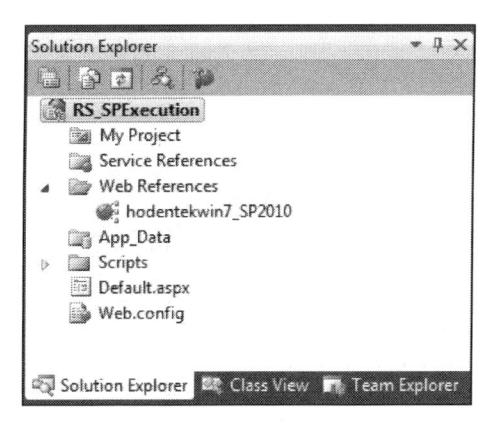

Reporting Services and Programming

2. Right-click on **RS-SPExecution** and then on **Add Service Reference**. The **Add Service Reference** page will be displayed.

3. Click on **Advanced**. The **Service Reference Settings** page will be displayed

4. Click on **Add Web Reference...**.

5. Type the following in the empty box named **URL** `http://hodentekwin7/_vti_bin/ReportServer/ReportService2006.asmx?wsdl`.

6. Click on the green arrow next to where you typed.

7. After some search the **ReportingService2006 Description** page will be displayed. In addition, the Web reference name `hodentekwin7` will be added.

8. Change it to `hodentekwin7_SP2010`:

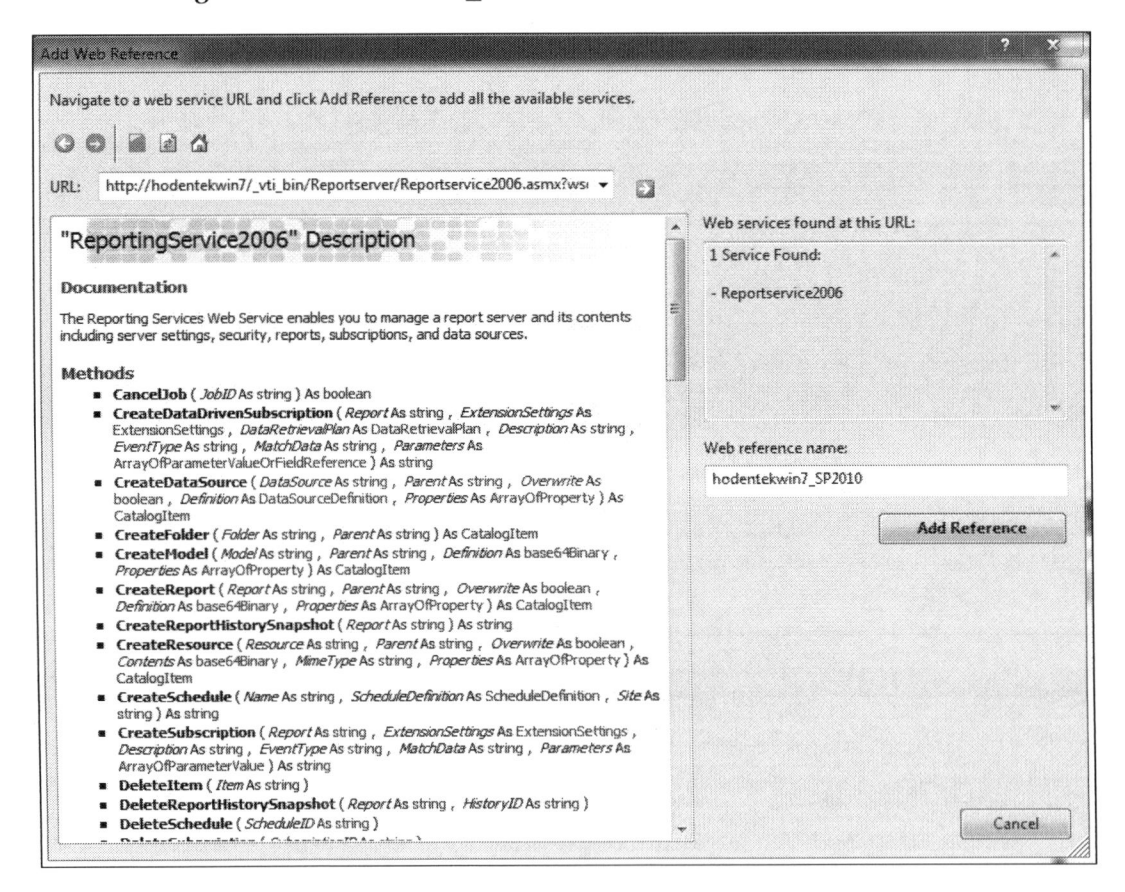

We will look at some simple methods and properties.

Chapter 8

9. Place two buttons (with texts `Create Folder` and `List Folder Contents`) on `Default.aspx`, and add the following code to `Defautl.aspx`:

```
Imports RS_SPExecution.hodentekwin7_SP2010
Imports Microsoft.SqlServer.Server
Imports System.Web.Services.WebService
Public Class _Default
    Inherits System.Web.UI.Page
    'declare items for referencing
    Dim folder As New hodentekwin7_SP2010.CatalogItem
    Dim svc As New ReportingService2006
    Protected Sub Page_Load(ByVal sender As Object, ByVal e As System.EventArgs) Handles Me.Load

    End Sub

    Protected Sub Button1_Click(sender As Object, e As EventArgs) Handles Button1.Click
        'creates a new folder in the Documents folder on the site, hodentekwin7
        svc.CreateFolder("April3", "http://HodentekWin7/Documents/FirstFolder")
    End Sub

Protected Sub Button2_Click(sender As Object, e As EventArgs) Handles Button2.Click
        'some folder properties are explored
        svc.Credentials = System.Net.CredentialCache.DefaultCredentials
        folder.Path = "http://HodentekWin7/Documents/FirstFolder"
        'number of folders in FirstFolder
        Dim i As Int16 = svc.ListChildren(folder.Path).Count
        MsgBox(i)
        'names of last and first folders and a date
        MsgBox(svc.ListChildren(folder.Path).Last.Name & vbCrLf & svc.ListChildren(folder.Path).First.Name & vbCrLf & svc.ListChildren(folder.Path).First.CreationDate)

    End Sub
```

10. Build the project. Right-click on `Default.aspx` and then **View in Browser**.

Reporting Services and Programming

11. In the displayed page, if you click on **button1**, you will be creating a folder in **FirstFolder** on the SharePoint Site. When you click **button2**, a pop-up message will display the folder details (first line in the image), as follows:

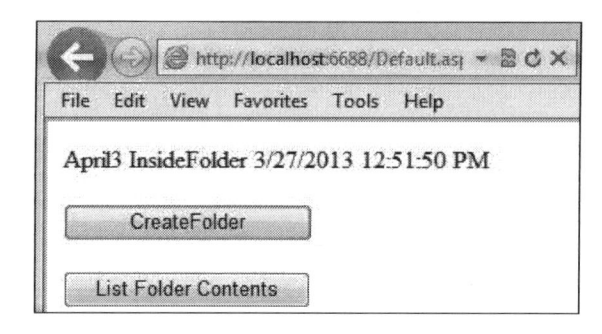

Review the following link if you would like to explore `ReportingService2006` when RS is SharePoint integrated:

`http://technet.microsoft.com/en-us/library/reportservice2006.reportingservice2006`

PowerShell

PowerShell is Microsoft's automation framework to carry out tasks in Windows OS and is used extensively by administrators. It has largely overcome the limitations of the previously used command-line languages, such as Command.com, cmd.exe, VBScript, and MSh. It is being increasingly integrated with various Microsoft Products such as Exchange server, SQL Server, and Microsoft SharePoint Server. PowerShell comes loaded with the OS for both Windows 7 and Windows Server 2008 R2.

> If for some reason you don't find PowerShell, it can be downloaded from (Windows Management Framework 3.0) `http://www.microsoft.com/en-us/download/details.aspx?id=34595`, and cheat-sheets (a good name for it is quick reference) for PowerShell are found at `http://www.microsoft.com/en-us/download/details.aspx?id=30002`.
>
> While installing SharePoint Server 2010, this PowerShell script will be of a considerable value, as it gets all the prerequisites to a folder you designate; see `http://gallery.technet.microsoft.com/scriptcenter/bcf3332d-f726-4ac7-b01a-eeda4b7ece8e`.

In this section, we will have a quick review of PowerShell, followed by how it is used in Reporting Services 2012 in both the modes of installation.

Hands-on exercise 8.6 – a quick review of basics

This section will help in getting started with PowerShell (assumes PowerShell is installed):

1. Type `cmd` in **Start | Search Program and File**.
2. Right-click on `cmd` in **Programs** and click on **Run as Administrator** as some programs require it.
3. Type in `PowerShell` in the command prompt, as shown, to start using PowerShell:

```
Microsoft Windows [Version 6.1.7601]
Copyright (c) 2009 Microsoft Corporation.  All rights reserved.

C:\Windows\system32>cd\

C:\>PowerShell
Windows PowerShell
Copyright (C) 2009 Microsoft Corporation. All rights reserved.

PS C:\>
```

4. Type `$PSversionTable` and press *Enter* to get the version of PowerShell, as follows:

```
PS C:\> $PSversionTable

Name                           Value
----                           -----
CLRVersion                     2.0.50727.5466
BuildVersion                   6.1.7601.17514
PSVersion                      2.0
WSManStackVersion              2.0
PSCompatibleVersions           {1.0, 2.0}
SerializationVersion           1.1.0.1
PSRemotingProtocolVersion      2.1
```

So far, we have directly to run the code in the command prompt of PowerShell; we can also submit a program in a file with the extension `*.ps1`. This works in a similar way to the `*.bat` file in the DOS environment. We shall see examples of this later in the *Hands-on exercise 8.8 – exploring Native mode Reporting Services* section.

Reporting Services and Programming

When you install SharePoint Server 2010, one of the installed programs is Microsoft SharePoint Management Shell, shown here:

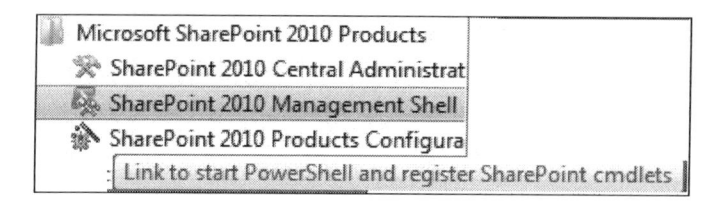

Right-click on **SharePoint 2010 Management Shell** and choose **Run As Administrator**:

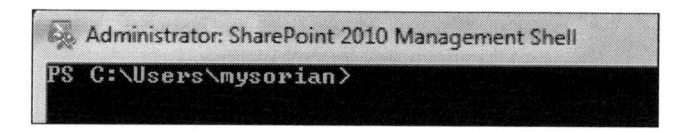

This (the above command prompt) is the entry to PowerShell. There is also a graphic user interface available described in the next step.

5. Go to **Start | Search**, and type `powershell_ise.exe`.

   The graphic user interface known as the PowerShell **Integrated Scripting Environment (ISE)** will be launched:

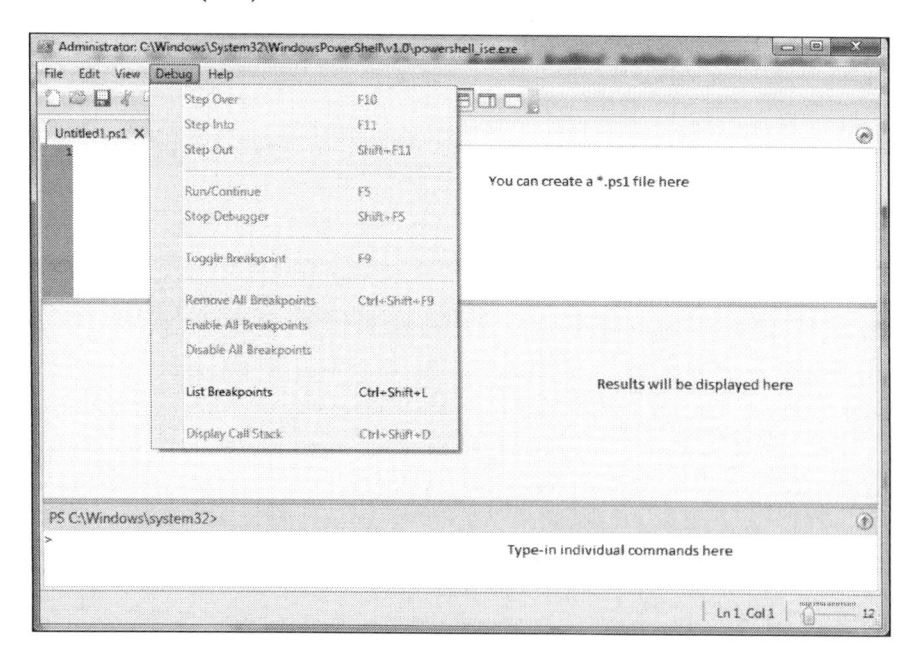

[436]

The shell environment will run most of the locally run programs and only signed programs downloaded from the Internet. The default policy is therefore set to be **Remote Signed,** and you can find it by typing `Get-ExecutionPolicy` when you are in PowerShell. If it is not, you can set the execution policy by typing `Set-ExecutionPolicy RemoteSigned` in the `cmdlet`.

When you use PowerShell for managing SQL Server, it is easier to start PowerShell from **SQL Server Management Studio**.

6. Right-click on the SQL Server Instance, then click on **Start PowerShell** in the drop-down list:

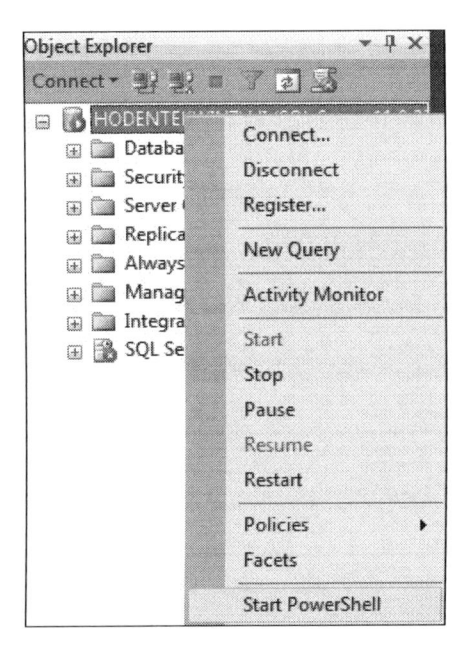

PowerShell and reporting services with SharePoint Integration

When reporting services 2012 is installed in SharePoint Integrated mode, there are basically two ways you can administer. You can administer reporting services directly from the Central Administration Site of SharePoint (parts of which are covered in *Chapter 6, Power View and Reporting Services* and *Chapter 7, Self-Service Data Alerts in SSRS 2012*), or by using PowerShell. In this section, we will look at some of the administration-related features using PowerShell.

As mentioned, you can run PowerShell commands from the **C:** prompt by typing in **C:\PowerShell**, which changes the prompt to **PS C:**. If you want to continue from here, to look at the Report Server SharePoint Integrated items you need to add in the SharePoint Power snap-in, by using the following command:

```
PS C:\Add-PSSnapIn Microsoft.SharePoint.PowerShell
```

The other option is to use the SharePoint 2010 Management Shell, described earlier; in this case, you do not need the add-in. You may also use the Graphic User Interface mentioned earlier.

Hands-on exercise 8.7 – exploring reporting services in SharePoint Integrated mode

In the following series of instructions, you will be starting PowerShell in one of the ways described earlier and type in and hit the *Enter* key.

Getting help about help

PowerShell also comes with help files like Man in Unix Systems and begins with the cmdlet Get-Help, and comes in three different renderings—examples, detailed, and full. The last item displays a comprehensive help file.

Type Get-Help Get-Help when you are in PS C:\.

You should get help about how to use help. In the remarks column, you will see the three types of displayed information you would get.

Application server of the Reporting Services Service Application

HODENTEKWIN7 is the application server where you access the reporting services application. You can find it as shown here.

Type Get-SPRSServiceApplicationServers and hit *Enter*.

```
PS C:\> Get-SPRSServiceApplicationServers
```

You will get the following reply:

```
Address
-------
HODENTEKWIN7
```

Finding all cmdlets related to Reporting Services SharePoint Integration

The following command gives a list of all the cmdlets that you can use while exploring the RS Integration with SharePoint 2010.

Type `Get-Command -noun *SPRS*` and hit *Enter*.

This will give a list of cmdlets that you can use with SharePoint Integration of RS. Notice that some of them (verbs) are `Get` and others are `install`, `restore`, `set`, `mount` and `update`.

```
PS C:\> Get-command -noun *SPRS*

CommandType     Name                              Definition
-----------     ----                              ----------
Cmdlet          Backup-SPRSEncryptionKey          Backup-SPRSEncryptionKey ...
Cmdlet          Dismount-SPRSDatabase             Dismount-SPRSDatabase -Id...
Cmdlet          Get-SPRSDatabase                  Get-SPRSDatabase [-Identi...
Cmdlet          Get-SPRSDatabaseCreationSc...     Get-SPRSDatabaseCreationS...
Cmdlet          Get-SPRSDatabaseRightsScript      Get-SPRSDatabaseRightsScr...
Cmdlet          Get-SPRSDatabaseUpgradeScript     Get-SPRSDatabaseUpgradeSc...
Cmdlet          Get-SPRSExtension                 Get-SPRSExtension -Identi...
Cmdlet          Get-SPRSProxyUrl                  Get-SPRSProxyUrl [-Proxy ...
Cmdlet          Get-SPRSServiceApplication        Get-SPRSServiceApplicatio...
Cmdlet          Get-SPRSServiceApplication...     Get-SPRSServiceApplicatio...
Cmdlet          Get-SPRSServiceApplication...     Get-SPRSServiceApplicatio...
Cmdlet          Get-SPRSSite                      Get-SPRSSite [-Off] [-Ass...
Cmdlet          Install-SPRSService               Install-SPRSService [-Uni...
Cmdlet          Install-SPRSServiceProxy          Install-SPRSServiceProxy ...
Cmdlet          Mount-SPRSDatabase                Mount-SPRSDatabase -Name ...
Cmdlet          New-SPRSDatabase                  New-SPRSDatabase [-Name <...
Cmdlet          New-SPRSExtension                 New-SPRSExtension -Identi...
Cmdlet          New-SPRSServiceApplication        New-SPRSServiceApplicatio...
Cmdlet          New-SPRSServiceApplication...     New-SPRSServiceApplicatio...
Cmdlet          Remove-SPRSDatabase               Remove-SPRSDatabase -Iden...
Cmdlet          Remove-SPRSEncryptedData          Remove-SPRSEncryptedData ...
Cmdlet          Remove-SPRSExtension              Remove-SPRSExtension -Ide...
Cmdlet          Remove-SPRSServiceApplication     Remove-SPRSServiceApplica...
Cmdlet          Restore-SPRSEncryptionKey         Restore-SPRSEncryptionKey...
Cmdlet          Set-SPRSDatabase                  Set-SPRSDatabase -Identit...
Cmdlet          Set-SPRSExtension                 Set-SPRSExtension -Identi...
Cmdlet          Set-SPRSServiceApplication        Set-SPRSServiceApplicatio...
Cmdlet          Update-SPRSEncryptionKey          Update-SPRSEncryptionKey ...
```

In fact, while configuring the Reporting Services for the SP integration, the two `Install` commands were used. While this gives a nice list, if you want the complete text of each of the line items, you should request to produce a list of the items, as shown in the next step.

Proxy URL of the Report Server

Type `Get-SPRSProxyURL|Format-List` when you are in the shell, and hit *Enter*.

You will get the following result:

```
PS C:\> Get-SPRSProxyURL | Format-List

Url  : http://hodentekwin7:80/_vti_bin/ReportServer
Zone : Default
```

This is the URL of the Report Server for a SharePoint integrated RS.

SP service application pool

SP service application pool is an important item that you will need for configuring the Reporting Services service application in SharePoint 2010 (see the screenshot in step 3 of the *Creating the Reporting Services Service application* section in *Chapter 1, Overview and Installation – SQL Server Reporting Services 2012*, and http://hodentekhelp.blogspot.com/2013/04/how-do-you-make-changes-to-application.html.

Type `Get-SPServiceApplicationPool`, and hit *Enter*.

The following information will be displayed:

```
PS C:\> Get-SPServiceApplicationPool

Name                                    ProcessAccountName
----                                    ------------------
SecurityTokenServiceApplicationPool     HodentekWin7\mysorian
SharePoint Web Services Default         HodentekWin7\mysorian
SharePoint Web Services System          HodentekWin7\mysorian
```

Note that `AccountName` is that of the administrator and when it was `NetworkService` or `LocalService`, the RS integration failed (it was directly changed later in IIS). You will find the same in your IIS 7.5.

Review the following link to get a deeper understanding of PowerShell as applied to Reporting Services Integration with SharePoint Server 2010, categorized as follows:

- Shared service cmdlets
- Service application cmdlets
- Reporting services functionality-related cmdlets

http://msdn.microsoft.com/en-us/library/gg492249.aspx

PowerShell and Native mode Reporting Services 2010

For the Native mode installation of Reporting Services in 2012, **Windows Management Instrumentation (WMI)** provides the API. Programming languages can be used to manage Windows programs through the API.

The Reporting Services WMI provider exposes two WMI classes for developers to administer the Native mode Report Server. They are as follows:

- `MSReportServer_Instance`: Namespace:root\Microsoft\SqlServer\ReportServer\RS_<EncodedInstanceName>\v11
- `MSReportServer_ConfigurationSetting`: Namespace:root\Microsoft\SqlServer\ReportServer\RS_<EncodedInstanceName>\v11\Admin

These can be used by both Microsoft and third-party programs to administer Reporting Services. The latter needs administrator privileges.

Hands-on exercise 8.8 – exploring Native mode Reporting Services

We will look at the Report Server properties in this section by using PowerShell.

The Native mode Report Server

The PowerShell code can be used to get at the properties of the RS instance(s) and the configuration(s) by performing the following steps:

1. Type the following code in a notepad, and save it as `RS1.ps1` in the `C:\` drive, where you can run PowerShell:

    ```
    $computer = "LocalHost"
    $namespace = "root\Microsoft\SqlServer\ReportServer\RS_HI\V11"
    Get-WmiObject -class MSReportServer_Instance -computername $computer -namespace $namespace
    ```

2. Open the command prompt and start PowerShell.

3. Type in .\RS1.ps1 in the PowerShell prompt and hit the *Enter* key. You will get the following response related to the instance:

```
PS C:\> .\rs1.ps1

__GENUS                 : 2
__CLASS                 : MSReportServer_Instance
__SUPERCLASS            :
__DYNASTY               : MSReportServer_Instance
__RELPATH               : MSReportServer_Instance.InstanceName="HI"
__PROPERTY_COUNT        : 6
__DERIVATION            : {}
__SERVER                : HODENTEKWIN7
__NAMESPACE             : root\Microsoft\SqlServer\ReportServer\RS_HI\V11
__PATH                  : \\HODENTEKWIN7\root\Microsoft\SqlServer\ReportSer
                          ver\RS_HI\V11:MSReportServer_Instance.InstanceNam
                          e="HI"
EditionID               : 610778273
EditionName             : ENTERPRISE EVALUATION EDITION
InstanceID              : MSRS11.HI
InstanceName            : HI
IsSharePointIntegrated  : False
Version                 : 11.0.2218.0
```

> You can create the file in the PowerShell integrated environment described earlier, where you can run, save, and debug the code. Debugging is similar to that in Visual Studio.

Native mode Report Server configuration

Native mode configuration was described in *Chapter 1*, *Overview and Installation – SQL Server Reporting Services 2012*, which is manipulated by using the configuration manager. It can also be managed programmatically by using WMI. Here, we will explore using PowerShell:

1. Type the following code in a notepad and save it as RS2.ps1 in the C:\ drive, where you can run PowerShell:

   ```
   $computer = "LocalHost"

   $namespace = "root\Microsoft\SqlServer\ReportServer\RS_HI\V11\Admin"

   Get-WmiObject -class MSReportServer_ConfigurationSetting
   -computername $computer -namespace $namespace
   ```

2. Type .\RS2.ps1 in the PowerShell prompt and hit the *Enter* key.

Chapter 8

You will get an output similar to the following screenshot:

```
PS C:\> .\rs2.ps1


__GENUS                          : 2
__CLASS                          : MSReportServer_ConfigurationSetting
__SUPERCLASS                     :
__DYNASTY                        : MSReportServer_ConfigurationSetting
__RELPATH                        : MSReportServer_ConfigurationSetting.Ins
                                   tanceName="HI"
__PROPERTY_COUNT                 : 29
__DERIVATION                     : {}
__SERVER                         : HODENTEKWIN7
__NAMESPACE                      : root\Microsoft\SqlServer\ReportServer\R
                                   S_HI\V11\Admin
__PATH                           : \\HODENTEKWIN7\root\Microsoft\SqlServer
                                   \ReportServer\RS_HI\V11\Admin:MSReportS
                                   erver_ConfigurationSetting.InstanceName
                                   ="HI"
ConnectionPoolSize               : 768
DatabaseLogonAccount             :
DatabaseLogonTimeout             : -1
DatabaseLogonType                : 2
DatabaseName                     : ReportServer$HI
DatabaseQueryTimeout             : 120
DatabaseServerName               : HODENTEKWIN7\HI
ExtendedProtectionLevel          : Off
ExtendedProtectionScenario       : Proxy
InstallationID                   : {c53748ce-6c5c-4404-8128-c8dee817450e}
InstanceName                     : HI
IsInitialized                    : True
IsReportManagerEnabled           : True
IsSharePointIntegrated           : False
IsWebServiceEnabled              : True
IsWindowsServiceEnabled          : True
MachineAccountIdentity           :
PathName                         : c:\Program Files\Microsoft SQL Server\M
                                   SRS11.HI\Reporting Services\ReportServe
                                   r\RSReportServer.config
SecureConnectionLevel            : 0
SenderEmailAddress               : hodentek@live.com
SendUsingSMTPServer              : True
ServiceName                      : ReportServer$HI
SMTPServer                       : smtp.live.com
UnattendedExecutionAccount       :
Version                          : 11.0.2218.0
VirtualDirectoryReportManager    : Reports_HI
VirtualDirectoryReportServer     : ReportServer_HI
WindowsServiceIdentityActual     : NT Service\ReportServer$HI
WindowsServiceIdentityConfigured : NT Service\ReportServer$HI
```

The preceding window provides all the details of the Report Server configuration settings.

[443]

Extensions supported on a Windows Forms ReportViewer

Reporting services ships with two ReportViewer controls—one for Windows Forms and another for Web forms. There are supported extensions that you find in configuration files. You can get to display them by using PowerShell:

1. Create an `RSExtensions.ps1` file by using the following code in a notepad and saving it to the `C:\` drive:

   ```
   [System.Reflection.Assembly]::Load("Microsoft.ReportViewer.
   WinForms, Version=11.0.0.0, Culture=neutral, PublicKeyToken=89845d
   cd8080cc91") | Out-Null
     $ReportServer = "http://HodentekWIn7/ReportServer_HI"
   $rv = New-Object Microsoft.Reporting.WinForms.ReportViewer
   $rv.ProcessingMode = "Remote"
   $rv.ServerReport.ReportServerUrl = $ReportServer
   $rv.ServerReport.ListRenderingExtensions()
   ```

   In the first line of code, the assembly for `WinForms` related ReportViewer is loaded. This is followed by indicating the Report Server, initiating a new ReportViewer, and setting up its properties. The last line gets a list of rendering extensions that are supported. The details for the Web form ReportViewer are different.

   > The version and `PublicKeyToken` of ReportViewer can be found by placing a control in SSDT (Windows form/Web form) and looking at the code on the page.

2. Start PowerShell as described earlier, type `.\RSExtensions.ps1`, and hit the *Enter* key.

   The list of extensions, visible/hidden, will be displayed as shown. The visibility can be changed within the configuration file:

```
PS C:\> .\RSExtensions.ps1
Name                    LocalizedName                Visible
----                    -------------                -------
XML                     XML file with report ...     True
NULL                    NullRenderer                 False
CSV                     CSV (comma delimited)        True
ATOM                    Data Feed                    False
PDF                     PDF                          True
RGDI                    Remote GDI+ file             False
HTML4.0                 HTML 4.0                     False
MHTML                   MHTML (web archive)          True
EXCEL                   Excel 2003                   False
EXCELOPENXML            Excel                        True
RPL                     RPL Renderer                 False
IMAGE                   TIFF file                    True
WORD                    Word 2003                    False
WORDOPENXML             Word                         True
```

Word renderer, compatible with Word 2007-2010 and Word 2003, and Microsoft Excel renderer, compatible with Excel 2007-2010 and Excel 2003, are new in Report Builder 3.0 for SQL Server 2012. These, however, require the installation of Microsoft Office Compatibility Pack for Word, Excel, and PowerPoint. Follow this link for more details: http://msdn.microsoft.com/en-us/library/dd239307.aspx#RendererTypes

Windows Management Instrumentation

WMI is the tool of choice to manage the Reporting Services server in the Native mode. It is also a generic tool for Windows management. It is especially indicated for management of not only Windows, but also other Windows-based applications.

> Follow http://msdn.microsoft.com/en-us/library/aa719480.aspx to learn about the System.Management namespace for accessing management objects in .NET Framework. Note that the System.Management and System.Management.Instrumentation namespaces can both be used for finding information, although System.Management has a wider scope.
>
> Also note that the Reporting Services Configuration Manager requires that the WMI service must be enabled and running.

Reporting Services and Programming

Hands-on exercise 8.9 – exploring the Native mode Report Server programmatically

We will be using some VB.Net code with Visual Studio 2010 Ultimate; the code should work in VS 2008 as well.

Providing access permission to WMI

As the owner of the computer, you may have permission to access information via WMI, but a user may in general need access permission to WMI:

1. Click on **Start** and type Computer Management in the **Search** programs and files box. In the open window, access WMI, as follows (expand the **Services and Applications** node):

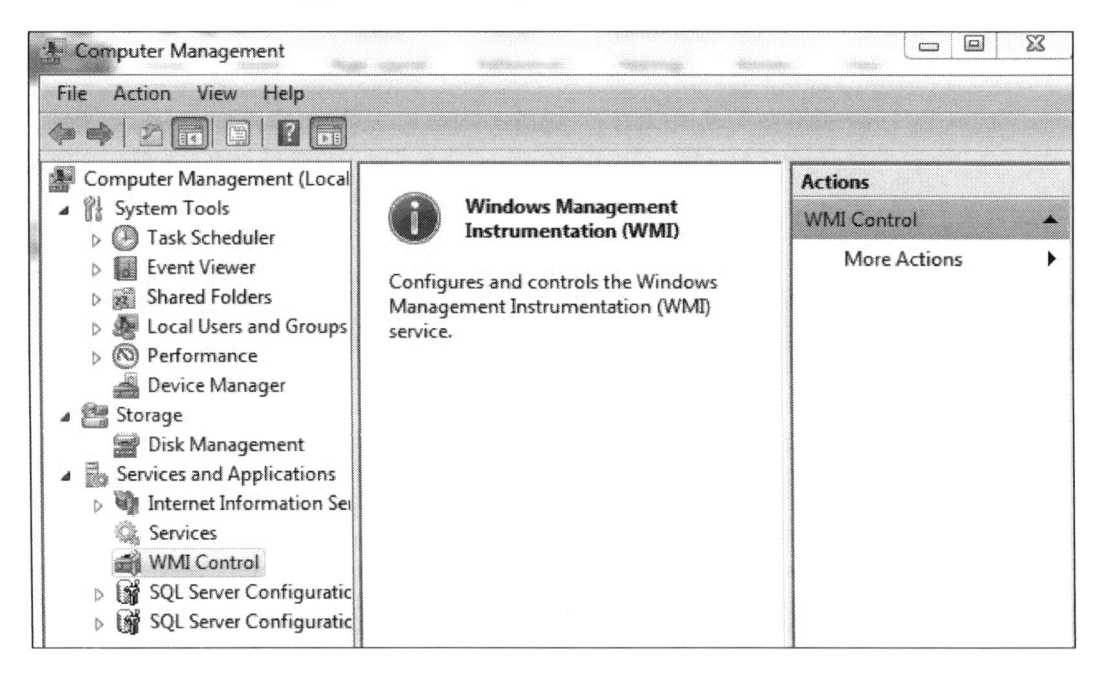

2. Click on **More Actions** and then on **Properties**. The **WMI Control Properties** window will be displayed:

3. In the **Security** tab, highlight RS_HI under **Microsoft | SQL Server**, as follows:

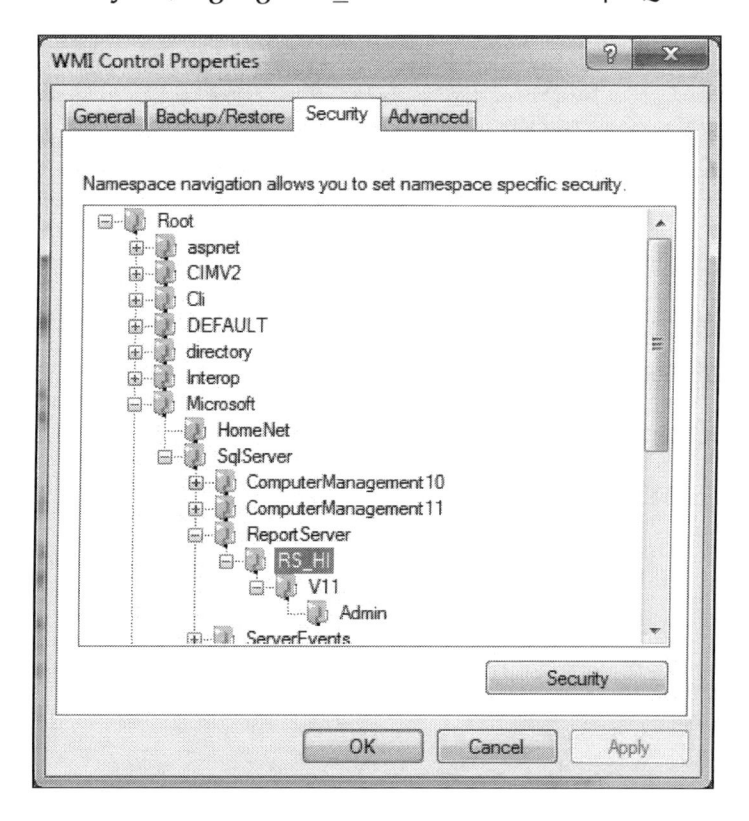

Reporting Services and Programming

4. Click on Security and the **Security for RS_HI** window will open, where you can provide the security. You can also check the admin's permissions for WMI (RS_HI is used in the place of RS_Kailua, both are Native mode).
5. Close all the open windows.

Report Server properties using WMI

We will use VB.NET and use the System.Management namespace with its Management classes to access the properties of the Report Server, http://hodentekwin7/ReportServer_HI, on the computer.

1. Create an ASP.NET Web application called WMI_RS for the .NET 4.0 target framework–you can see the target under **Project Properties | Compile | Advanced Compile Options...**.
2. Drag a button (text property set to **Get RS Configuration Details**), a listbox, and a label controls on to the Default.aspx page. The project folder is shown in the next image:

3. Add the following code to the click event of the button on the Default.aspx.vb page; make sure the namespaces are referenced:

```
Imports System.Management
Imports System.IO
Imports System
```

Chapter 8

```vb
Public Class _Default
    Inherits System.Web.UI.Page

    Protected Sub Page_Load(ByVal sender As Object, ByVal e As System.EventArgs) Handles Me.Load

    End Sub

    Protected Sub Button1_Click(sender As Object, e As EventArgs) Handles Button1.Click
        Dim WmiNamespace As String = "\root\Microsoft\SqlServer\ReportServer\RS_HI\v11\Admin"
        Dim WmiRSClass As String = "\root\Microsoft\SqlServer\ReportServer\RS_HI\v11\admin:MSReportServer_ConfigurationSetting"
        Dim serverClass As New System.Management.ManagementClass

        Dim scope As ManagementScope
        scope = New ManagementScope(WmiNamespace) 'Connect to the Reporting Services namespace.
        scope.Connect() 'Create the server class.
        serverClass = New ManagementClass(WmiRSClass) 'Connect to the management object.
        Try
            serverClass.Get()
        Catch ex As Exception
            MsgBox(ex.ToString)
        End Try

        If serverClass Is Nothing Then Throw New Exception("No class found")


        Dim instances As ManagementObjectCollection = serverClass.GetInstances()
        Dim instance As New ManagementObject
        For Each instance In instances
            Label1.Text = ("Number of Instances detected:" & instances.Count)
            Dim instProps As PropertyDataCollection = instance.Properties
            '[The following code or similar code can be used for
            'modifying the instance properties:]
```

[449]

Reporting Services and Programming

```
                'If instProps.Item("isReportManagerEnabled").Value =
    False Then  'instProps.Item("isReportManagerEnabled").Value = True
                'End If
                Dim prop As PropertyData
                For Each prop In instProps

                    Dim name As String = prop.Name
                    Dim val As Object = prop.Value
                    ListBox2.Items.Add("Property Name: " + name & ":"
    & "Property Value: " + val.ToString())
                Next
            Next
        End Sub
End Class
```

4. Build the project and browse to the `Default.aspx` page.
5. In the browser, click on the button with the text **Get RS Configuration Details** on the page.

    If there are no errors, you should see the following displayed:

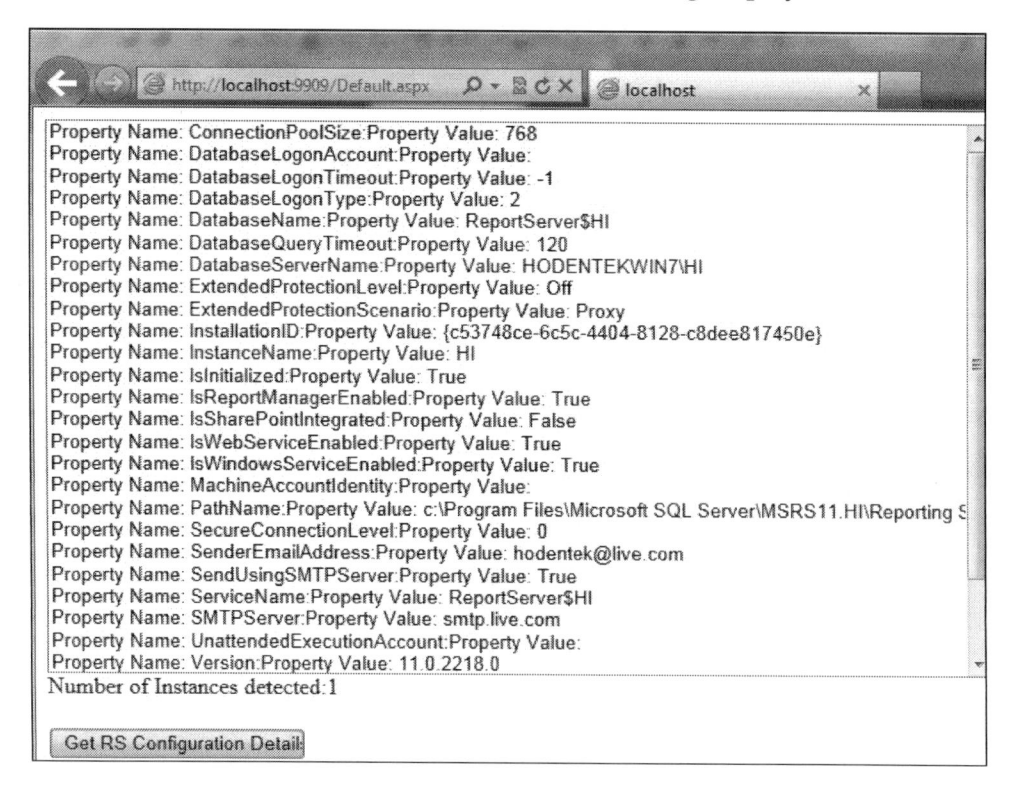

```
Property Name: ConnectionPoolSize:Property Value: 768
Property Name: DatabaseLogonAccount:Property Value:
Property Name: DatabaseLogonTimeout:Property Value: -1
Property Name: DatabaseLogonType:Property Value: 2
Property Name: DatabaseName:Property Value: ReportServer$HI
Property Name: DatabaseQueryTimeout:Property Value: 120
Property Name: DatabaseServerName:Property Value: HODENTEKWIN7\HI
Property Name: ExtendedProtectionLevel:Property Value: Off
Property Name: ExtendedProtectionScenario:Property Value: Proxy
Property Name: InstallationID:Property Value: {c53748ce-6c5c-4404-8128-c8dee817450e}
Property Name: InstanceName:Property Value: HI
Property Name: IsInitialized:Property Value: True
Property Name: IsReportManagerEnabled:Property Value: True
Property Name: IsSharePointIntegrated:Property Value: False
Property Name: IsWebServiceEnabled:Property Value: True
Property Name: IsWindowsServiceEnabled:Property Value: True
Property Name: MachineAccountIdentity:Property Value:
Property Name: PathName:Property Value: c:\Program Files\Microsoft SQL Server\MSRS11.HI\Reporting S
Property Name: SecureConnectionLevel:Property Value: 0
Property Name: SenderEmailAddress:Property Value: hodentek@live.com
Property Name: SendUsingSMTPServer:Property Value: True
Property Name: ServiceName:Property Value: ReportServer$HI
Property Name: SMTPServer:Property Value: smtp.live.com
Property Name: UnattendedExecutionAccount:Property Value:
Property Name: Version:Property Value: 11.0.2218.0
Number of Instances detected:1

[Get RS Configuration Details]
```

> The `Try...Catch()` part of the code will catch errors, if any. `WmiNamespace`, and `WmiRSClass` are strings, and if they are not correctly formatted, they will throw exceptions

Reporting Services command prompt utilities

The following are the available command prompt utilities in SQL Server 2012 (see *Chapter 1, Overview and Installation–SQL Server Reporting Services 2012*:

- The RSS utility (`rs.exe`) supported on both the Native mode and SharePoint Integrated mode servers helps to write scripts to carry out operations such as copy data between Report Servers, publish reports, and other deployment and administrative tasks.
- `Rsconfig` (`rsconfig.exe`) is used to configure and manage a Report Server connection in the Native mode to the Report Server database.
- `Rskeymgmt` utility (`rskeymgmt.exe`) is supported in the Native mode only, `Rskeymgmt` utility manages encryption keys. Associated tasks such as backup, restore, apply, and recreate symmetric keys are also handled. `Rskeymgmt` is also used for database recovery tasks. You can also delete encrypted content and recreate new ones, and so on.
- PowerShell cmdlets used exclusively with SharePoint Integrated installations were explored in an earlier section of this chapter.

Three of the above are found in the SQL Server `installation` folder (`C:\Program Files (x86)\Microsoft SQL Server\110\Tools\Binn`), as follows:

RSKeyMgmt	2/11/2012 10:10 AM	Application	112 KB
RSConfigTool	6/12/2012 10:22 PM	Application	1,315 KB
rsconfig	2/11/2012 10:11 AM	Application	104 KB
rs	2/11/2012 10:11 AM	Application	812 KB

The RSS utility

The help for rs.exe is obtained by typing the following in the command prompt:

`C:\Program Files(x86)\Microsoft SQL Server\110\Tools\Binn>rs /?`

The result of this is as follows:

```
C:\Program Files (x86)\Microsoft SQL Server\110\Tools\Binn>rs /?
Microsoft (R) Reporting Services RS
Version 11.0.2100.60 x86
Executes script file contents against the specified Report Server.
RS -i inputfile -s serverURL [-u username] [-p password]
   [-l timeout] [-b] [-e endpoint] [-v var=value] [-t]

         -i  inputfile    Script file to execute
         -s  serverURL    URL (including server and vroot) to execute
                          script against.
         -u  username     User name used to log in to the server.
         -p  password     Password used to log in to the server.
         -e  endpoint     Web service endpoint to use with the script.
                          Options are:
                          Exec2005 - The ReportExecution2005 endpoint
                          Mgmt2005 - The ReportService2005 endpoint
                          Mgmt2006 - The ReportService2006 endpoint
                          Mgmt2010 - The ReportService2010 endpoint
         -l  timeout      Number of seconds before the connection to the
                          server times out. Default is 60 seconds and 0 is
                          infinite time out.
         -b               Run as a batch and rollback if commands fail
         -v  var=value    Variables and values to pass to the script
         -t  trace        Include trace information in error message
```

What can rs.exe do?

The RSS utility can do a lot of heavy work such as the examples listed here:

- Install Reporting Services
- Configure the service account
- Configure the Report Server Web Service and Report Manager URLs
- Create the Report Server database
- Configure the Report Server database connection
- Configure a scale-out deployment
- Back up encryption keys
- Configure Report Server e-mails
- Configure the unattended execution account
- Deploy the existing content on another Report Server, including the folder hierarchy, role assignments, reports, subscriptions, schedules, data sources, and resources.

Chapter 8

The `rss` extension is not unique, in that it is used in contexts other than Reporting Services (see http://en.wikipedia.org/wiki/RSS_(disambiguation)), including the most popular Web feed format RSS (**Really Simple Syndication**). If you need to debug, you need to use VS 2010.

Hands-on exercise 8.10 – creating a data source on the Report Server using rs.exe and a script file

We will prepare a script file, which provides the code to create a data source taking data on a SQL Server. The script file is then provided as an input file to the `rs.exe` program, as shown in the invocation line. This creates a data source called `rsCreated` in the `Data Sources` folder on the Native Report Server:

1. Copy the following code in a notepad and save it as `rsDataSource.rss` to `C:\`. Make sure it is not saved as a text file, with the extension (.txt).

   Here is the code to use (purposely inserted in a column):

   ```
   '--------------------------------------
   ------File name: rsDataSource.rss------
   '------Demo of rs.exe utility----------
   '------the i switch requires an input file
   ------ -the s switch points to the Report Server url
   ----invocation as in C:\>rs -i 'rsDataSource.rss 'http://
   HodentekWin7/ReportServer_HI'------------------------------------
   ----

   Public Sub Main()
       'provide credentials
       rs.Credentials= System.Net.CredentialCache.DefaultCredentials
       'call up the procedure
       CreateSampleDataSource( )
   end sub

   Public Sub CreateSampleDataSource( )
       'Define the data source definition.
       Dim definition As New DataSourceDefinition()

   Dim dsname as string
   dsname="rsCreated"
   ```

```
    dim parentPath as string
    parentPath="/Data Sources"

    dim extension as string="SQL"
        definition.CredentialRetrieval =  CredentialRetrievalEnum.
Integrated
        definition.ConnectString ="DataSource=HODENTEKWin7\NJ;Initial
Catalog=Northwind;Integrated Security=True"
        definition.Enabled = True
        definition.EnabledSpecified = True
        definition.Extension = extension
        definition.ImpersonateUser = False
        definition.ImpersonateUserSpecified  = True
        'Use the default prompt string.
        definition.Prompt = Nothing
        definition.WindowsCredentials =  False

    Try
        rs.CreateDataSource(dsname,parentPath, False, definition,
Nothing)
        Console.WriteLine("Data source {0}  created successfully",
dsname)

    Catch e As Exception
        Console.WriteLine(e.Message)
    End Try

    This is the data source created on the Report Server.
    End Sub
```

2. pen the command prompt and type the following:

    `C:\rs -i rsDataSource.rss -s "http://hodentekwin7/ReportServer_HI`

3. Open a command prompt and type the following:

    `C:\rs -i rsDataSource.rss -s "http://hodentekwin7/ReportServer_HI`

Here is the result of running the code from command-line prompt:

```
C:\>rs -i rsDataSource.rss -s http://HodentekWin7:80/ReportServer_HI
The specified script failed to compile with the following errors:
C:\> "C:\Windows\Microsoft.NET\Framework\v2.0.50727\vbc.exe" /t:exe /main:M
ainModule /utf8output /R:"System.dll" /R:"System.Xml.dll" /R:"System.Web.Se
rvices.dll" /R:"C:\Program Files (x86)\Microsoft SQL Server\110\Tools\Binn\
rs.exe" /out:"C:\Users\mysorian\AppData\Local\Temp\b4qxdijp.exe" /debug-   "
C:\Users\mysorian\AppData\Local\Temp\b4qxdijp.0.vb" "C:\Users\mysorian\AppD
ata\Local\Temp\b4qxdijp.1.vb"

Microsoft (R) Visual Basic Compiler version 8.0.50727.5420
for Microsoft (R) .NET Framework version 2.0.50727.5466
Copyright (c) Microsoft Corporation.  All rights reserved.

C:\Users\mysorian\AppData\Local\Temp\b4qxdijp.1.vb(16) : error BC30203: Ide
ntifier expected.                ── Error corrected and submitted again

    rs.Credentials= _  System.Net.CredentialCache.DefaultCredentials
                    ~

C:\>rs -i rsDataSource.rss -s http://HodentekWin7:80/ReportServer_HI
Data source rsCreated  created successfully
The command completed successfully
```

Here is the data source on the Report Server:

hodentekwin7/ReportServer_HI - /Data Sources

[To Parent Directory]
Thursday, April 04, 2013 10:07 PM   <ds> rsCreated
Thursday, March 28, 2013 3:52 PM   <ds> ShrSrc

Microsoft SQL Server Reporting Services Version 11.0.2218.0

The Rskeymgmt utility

The Rskeymgmt utility is another very useful utility while working with the Report Server. Although you may not create a key for testing, it is recommended that you create one as you may not know when a malware hits your computer, and you may need to restore. Make sure you keep the key and the credentials to use it again.

Here is the help menu for `Rskeymgmt`:

```
C:\>rskeymgmt /?
Microsoft (R) Reporting Services Key Manager
Version 11.0.2100.60 x86

Performs key management operations on a local report server.

    -e  extract            Extracts a key from a report server instance
    -a  apply              Applies a key to a report server instance
    -s  reencrypt          Generates a new key and reencrypts all encrypted
                           content
    -d  delete content     Deletes all encrypted content from a report server
                           database
    -l  list               Lists the report servers announced in the report server
                           database
    -r  installation ID    Remove the key for the specified installation ID
    -j  join               Join a remote instance of report server to the
                           scale-out deployment of the local instance
    -i  instance           Server instance to which operation is applied;
                           default is MSSQLSERVER
    -f  file               Full path and file name to read/write key.
    -p  password           Password used to encrypt or decrypt key.
    -m  machine name       Name of the remote machine to join to the
                           scale-out deployment
    -n  instance name      Name of the remote machine instance to join to the
                           scale-out deployment
    -u  user name          User name of an administrator on the machine to join
                           to
                           the scale-out deployment. If not supplied, the current
                           user is used.
    -v  password           Password of an administrator on the machine to join
                           to
                           the scale-out deployment
    -t  trace              Include trace information in error message

To create a back-up copy of the report server encryption key:
RSKeyMgmt -e [-i <instance name>] -f <file> -p <password>

To restore a back-up copy of the report server encryption key:
RSKeyMgmt -a [-i <instance name>] -f <file> -p <password>

To reencrypt secure information using a new key:
RSKeyMgmt -s [-i <instance name>]

To reset the report server encryption key and delete all encrypted content:
RSKeyMgmt -d [-i <instance name>]
```

Rsconfig

In *Chapter 1, Overview and Installation – SQL Server Reporting Services 2012*, the Report Server configuration was carried out by using the Reporting Services Configuration Manager. Report Servers can also be configured by using the command line with correct arguments. Here is the argument list for SQL Server 12.0 by invoking help for the `rsconfig` file:

```
C:\>rsconfig /?
Microsoft (R) Reporting Services RSConfig
Version 11.0.2100.60 x86

Sets configuration information for the specified report server.

RSConfig {-e | -c} [-m machinename] [-i instancename] [-s servername] [-d databasename] [-a authmethod] [-u username] [-p password] [-t]

        -c  connection          Sets the connection information to the report
                                server database
        -e  executionaccount    Sets the Unattended Execution Account used by
                                the report server when executing reports
        -m  machinename         optional, UNC to machine to configure, default
                                is localhost
        -i  instance name       Name of the Reporting Services instance,
                                default is MSSQLSERVER, which corresponds to
                                the default instance
        -s  servername          Name of SQL Server (including instance, if
                                applicable) that hosts the report server
                                catalog.
        -d  databasename        Name of SQL Server catalog database.
        -a  authmethod          Authentication type used to connect to the
                                Report Server catalog. Can be SQL or Windows.
        -u  username            User name used to connect to the server. May
                                be SQL user or Windows user as DOMAIN\UserName.
                                Optional for Windows Authentication.
        -p  password            Password used to connect to  the server. May
                                be a SQL or Windows password. Optional for
                                Windows authentication.
        -t                      Include trace information in error messages.
```

If you configure the reporting services URL, you may need to specify a number of items. You will know what those are by reading *Chapter 1, Overview and Installation – SQL Server Reporting Services 2012*, where the configuration used the Reporting Services Configuration Manager. Before you start the configuration by using `rs.exe`, review http://msdn.microsoft.com/en-us/library/bb630447.aspx. This link describes the following tasks in detail:

- Creating a URL for the Report Server Web Service
- Creating a URL for Report Manager
- Defining additional URLS using advanced settings

Incorporating custom code into reports

Providing custom code support empowers reports to work with the following

- Custom constants
- Complex functions
- Functions that are used in more than one place of the report

Custom code can be new constants, variables, functions, and subroutines.

Report Designer (SSDT) is preferred for coding custom code and Report Builder through valid expressions, or including references to custom assemblies on the Report Server is chosen to include/embed code. Custom code assemblies support keeping code in one place and sharing with multiple reports.

Using expressions is one way of incorporating aggregate functions. You can also use the custom code to incorporate into reports. Here, you will learn to incorporate custom code.

Hands-on 8.11 – inserting custom code into a report

You will create a report by using the `Northwind` database on your SQL Server 2012 instance using Report Builder. The design and fields inserted into the report design are as follows:

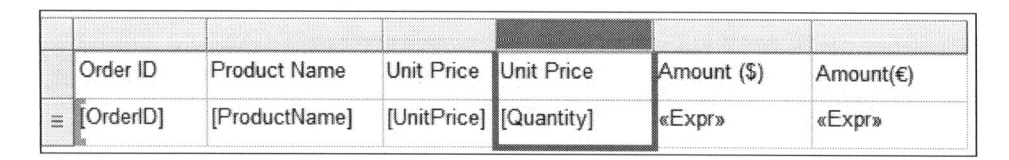

Order ID	Product Name	Unit Price	Unit Price	Amount ($)	Amount(€)
[OrderID]	[ProductName]	[UnitPrice]	[Quantity]	«Expr»	«Expr»

The last two columns are the total sales amount, one in US Dollars and the other in Euros. The first one is calculated by creating an expression using the expression builder, as follows:

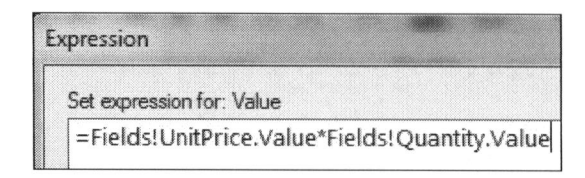

```
Expression
Set expression for: Value
=Fields!UnitPrice.Value*Fields!Quantity.Value
```

Now, we will write the custom code to insert the value into the last column (in Euros):

1. Right-click outside the design layout area to bring up the drop-down menu, as follows:

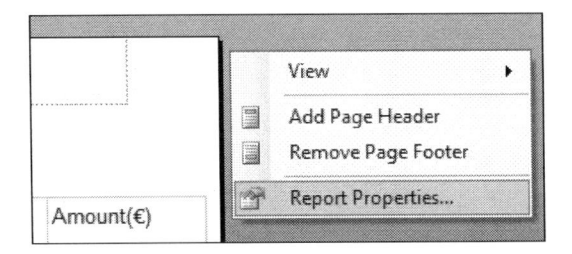

2. Click on **Report Properties** and write the code, as follows:

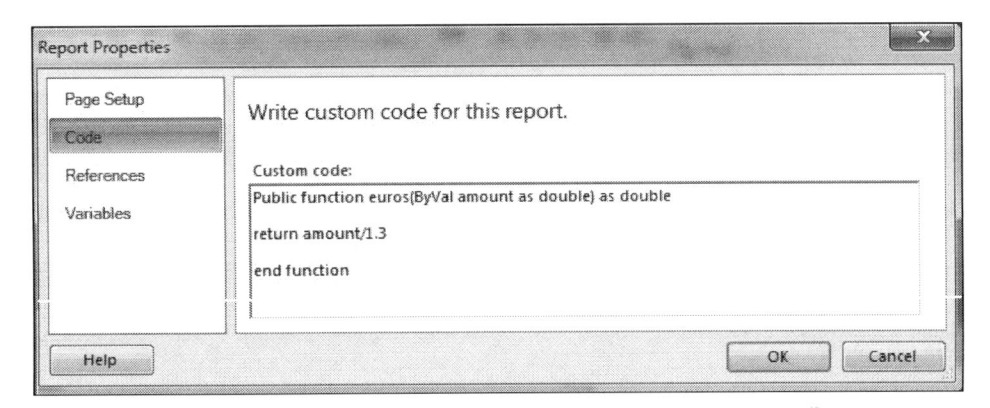

   ```
   Public function euros(ByVal amount as double) as double
   return amount/1.3
   end function
   ```

3. Click on **OK**.

4. In the last column in the cell under **Amount (€)**, bring up the expression builder and write the code, as shown, using the fields in the bottom panel:

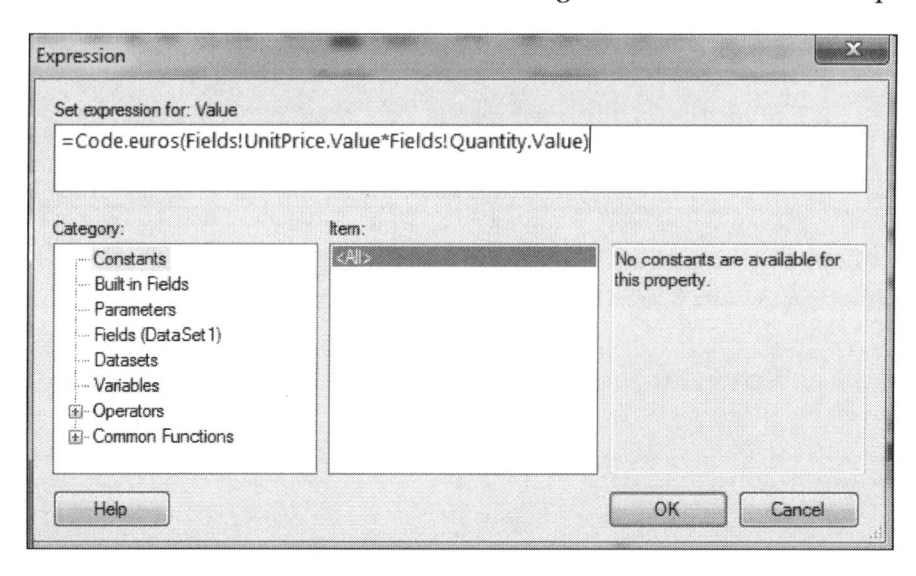

5. Click on **OK** and run the report.

   The last column should display the amount in Euros.

> To learn more about writing custom code, follow
> http://msdn.microsoft.com/en-us/library/ms156028.aspx

Summary

A number of programs to manage and probe reporting services in both native and SharePoint Integrated modes were described. URL access, displaying reports in ASP.NET page, using Reporting Server Web Services in both native and SharePoint Integrated implementations, PowerShell scripting to manage SharePoint and WMI namespaces, programmatic access to Reporting services WMI objects, the Reporting Services utility programs, and incorporating custom code into reports are all described with a number of hands-on exercises.

In the next chapter, we will deviate somewhat to describe the Windows Azure SQL Reporting Services-SQL Server Reporting Services hosted on the Windows Azure Platform. We will describe, starting from scratch, how to create reports by using the SQL Azure Database Service to create reports and host them in the Cloud.

9
Windows Azure SQL Reporting

What was announced as SQL Azure Reporting Services in the fall of 2010 became Windows Azure SQL Reporting, making it available in June 2012. It is just like Reporting Services implemented in Native mode except that the platform is Windows Azure. This means it uses two of the following Microsoft technologies:

- Windows Azure Platform
- SQL Server Reporting Services

In this chapter, you will be introduced to Cloud-based Microsoft Reporting Services and learn to carry out the following:

- How to begin working with Windows Azure Cloud Services
- Create an account to work with Windows Azure Cloud services and how to log in to the Windows Azure portal
- Create a SQL database in the Cloud and create a table
- Connect to the Windows Azure Cloud-based SQL database and populate the table from SSMS
- Create a SQL Reporting Service in Windows Azure
- Create a report based on the Windows Azure SQL database
- Deploy report to the SQL Reporting Services on Windows Azure
- View reports on the SQL Reporting Web server
- Create a shared data source in the Windows Azure portal
- Learn to manage users and user permissions

What is Windows Azure SQL Reporting?

Windows Azure SQL Reporting may be called SQL Server Reporting Services hoisted in the Cloud. You can use this to publish, view, as well as manage reports based on SQL Azure database sources. It also has a robust API for programmatic support.

What you get out from this for the enterprise is enormous. You get the most flexible set of resources that you can access from world-wide data centers, with rock solid security features and scalability. You will be creating reports in record short time, with no hardware to bother about. These claims are not special to the Microsoft Azure platform, but are true for all Cloud services in general.

- The agility, flexibility, and ease of creating Cloud-based services are well known
- The existence of enormous data centers dispersed world-wide is an established fact

Data can exist locally or dispersed worldwide and reports can be generated in one geographical location and accessed in another.

Although you can do most of the reporting tasks, there are certain limitations listed here. This is because the two platforms are not exactly the same.

- The only type of data source that you can use with **Windows Azure SQL Reporting (WASR)** is Windows Azure SQL databases.
- Report Management and rendering reports to multiple formats in WASR is through the Windows Azure Management portal and reports can be viewed by using browsers, and using ASP.NET and Windows Forms with ReportViewer controls. There is no Report Manager as in Native SSRS.
- Extensions are not supported in this release and may be supported in the future releases.
- Windows Azure SQL database password authentication and permissions to reports is through roles.
- Creating semantic report models (creating files with extension `.smdl`) is not supported.
- SOAP Application Programming Interfaces as well as WMI are not supported.

Please review limitations at `http://msdn.microsoft.com/en-us/library/windowsazure/gg430132.aspx`.

It is not only for the Cloud, but you can also include on-premise resources for your reporting needs. The tools are already familiar, such as **Business Intelligence Development Studio (BIDS)**, Report Builder, and **SQL Server Data Tools (SSDT)**.

Readers who are not familiar with Windows Azure Services will want to know how to access the portal to Windows Azure Services. Windows Azure SQL Reporting is one of the services. The next hands-on exercise using a number of screenshots shows how to set up an account and get into the Windows Azure portal. Except for Internet connection and a browser, you need no other hardware or software to install.

Hands-on exercise 9.1 – accessing the Windows Azure portal

Windows Azure is a Web-based service, which means you pay for what you use. Of course, there are different payment options but for the purposes of this book, readers can get it free (at the time of this writing) and use it for 90 days.

1. Go to the Azure Free site at https://www.windowsazure.com/en-us/pricing/free-trial/, which takes you to the page displayed in the following screenshot:

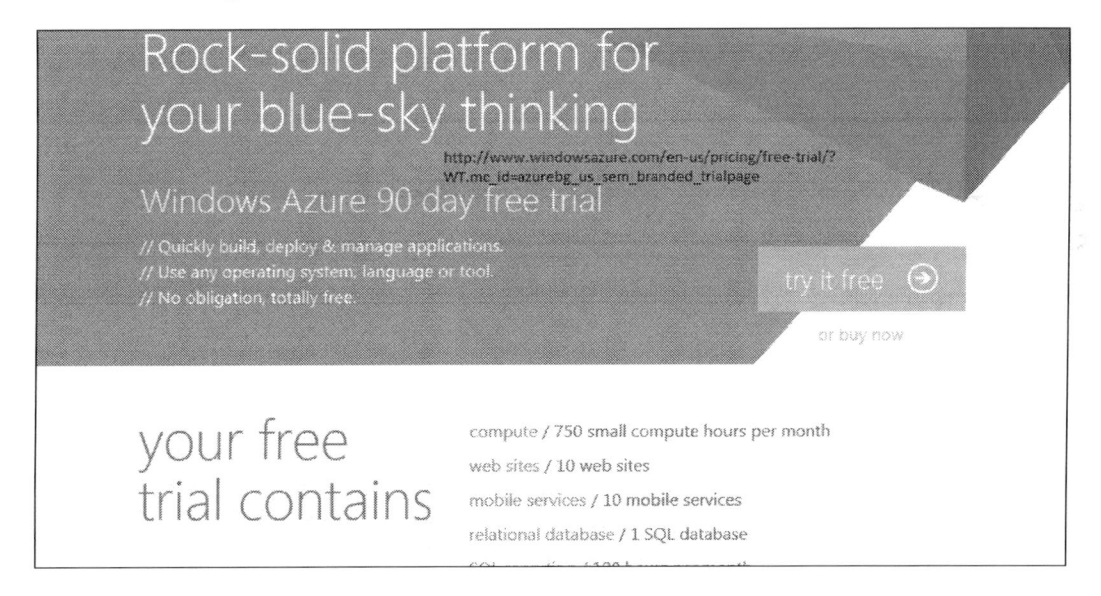

2. Click on **try it free** and follow the instructions. If you already have a `live.com` or `hotmail.com` account, you may be asked to log in, if you do not, you may need to register and get one.

3. Provide the Hotmail (Outlook) or Windows live credentials.

> It is recommended to get a `Live.com` or `hotmail.com` ID (Hotmail has moved to Outlook.com) if you do not have one, as it makes it easier to work with Windows Azure. The added benefit is that you will get access to some of the Office components and storage, free of cost on SkyDrive, which can be accessed from the desktop or the Web or handhelds such as Slate or iPad.

If you already have an account like the author, you will not be eligible for the free service. For pricing information, review the following (reported in one of the forums at `http://social.msdn.microsoft.com/Forums/en-US/ssdsgetstarted/thread/fecb288a-d1a8-4eda-b6f7-85f6dc1e4b4e`):

> *Reporting instance hours are charged only when your service is deployed. A customer is billed a minimum of $0.88 per hour (a "Reporting Instance Hour") while they have SQL Reporting deployed. This base charge covers up to 200 reports each clock hour. During each clock hour that you generate more than 200 reports, you will be billed another Reporting Instance Hour at $0.88 per hour for each additional block of 200 reports, rounded up.*
>
> *For example, if you deployed 1 reporting instance for 1 day during the billing cycle and during that 1 day you stayed within 200 reports per hour except for one hour, where you initiated 250 reports, you would pay $22.00. Below are the calculations:*
>
> *• ($0.88 per hour x 24 hours) + ($0.88 per hour x 1 hour) = $22.00*

This may change, and readers should look up to the link at `http://www.windowsazure.com/en-us/pricing/details/`.

After the trial period, if you desire to continue, this may be the option for you:

Pay-As-You-Go

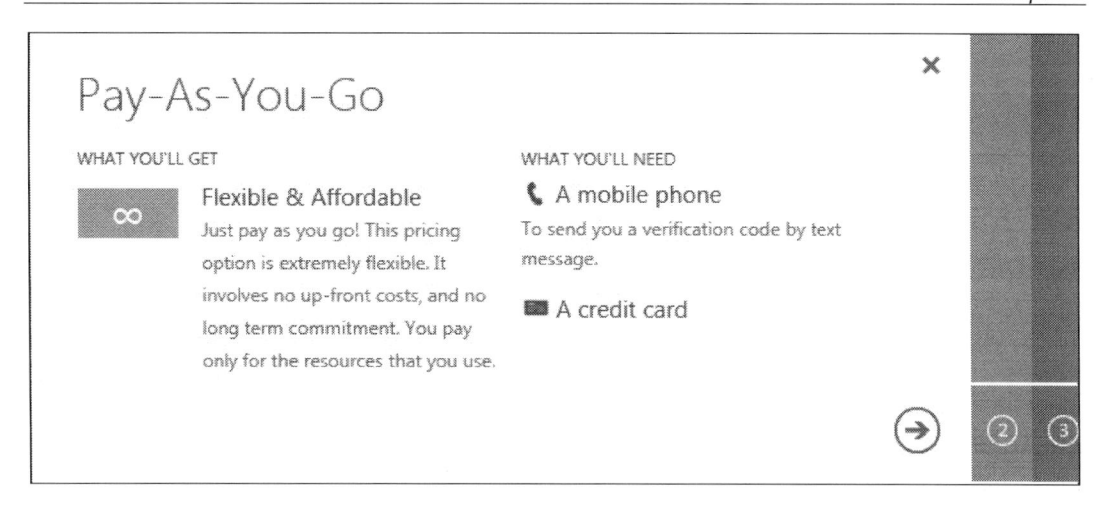

WHAT YOU'LL GET

∞ **Flexible & Affordable**
Just pay as you go! This pricing option is extremely flexible. It involves no up-front costs, and no long term commitment. You pay only for the resources that you use.

WHAT YOU'LL NEED

📞 A mobile phone
To send you a verification code by text message.

💳 A credit card

Continuing the instructions, you will be asked to provide your credentials, credit card number, expiration date, and so on. After this, you will be able to begin using the service. Finally, you will arrive at the following window:

> Even though your credit information is collected, you will not be charged if it is in the free period.

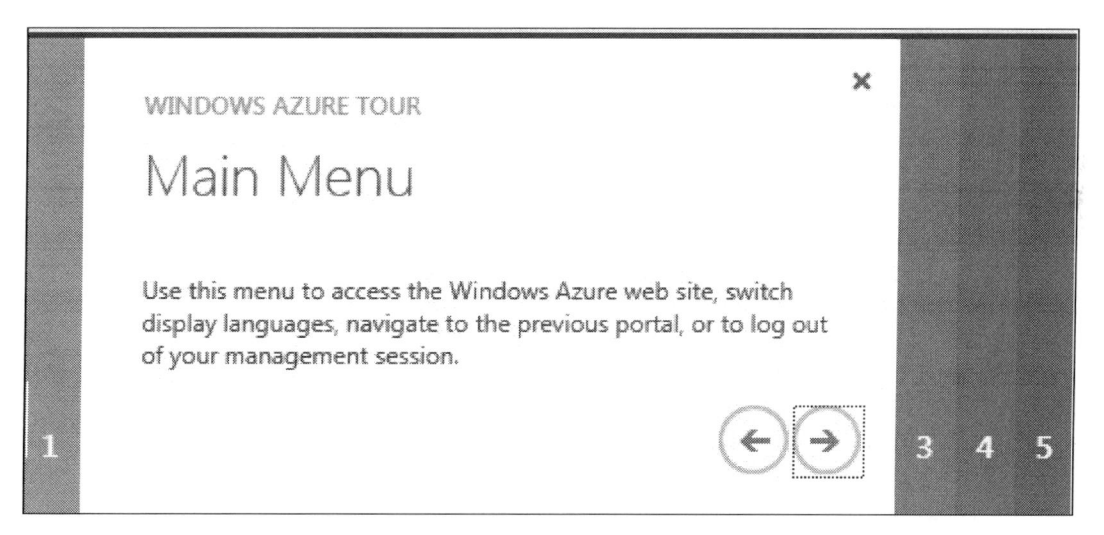

WINDOWS AZURE TOUR

Main Menu

Use this menu to access the Windows Azure web site, switch display languages, navigate to the previous portal, or to log out of your management session.

Windows Azure SQL Reporting

4. Click on the arrow under the rectangle, and you will be taken to the third screen:

Everything that you can create in this site is on the page in the background, shown on the left.

5. Click on the arrow pointing to the fourth page. You will be taken to page four of the **Windows Azure Tour** GUI:

The preceding commands come in very handy to work with the items on Windows Azure.

6. Click on the arrow to the fifth page.
7. You have to look out for information regarding the status. You can also access **Help**:

Chapter 9

WINDOWS AZURE TOUR

Notifications

The notifications area provides you with status updates for active commands and service health, as well as quick access to Help

1 2 3 4

8. Click on the tick (✓) symbol, and you will be allowed to the portal, with the top-right showing your login ID, as follows:

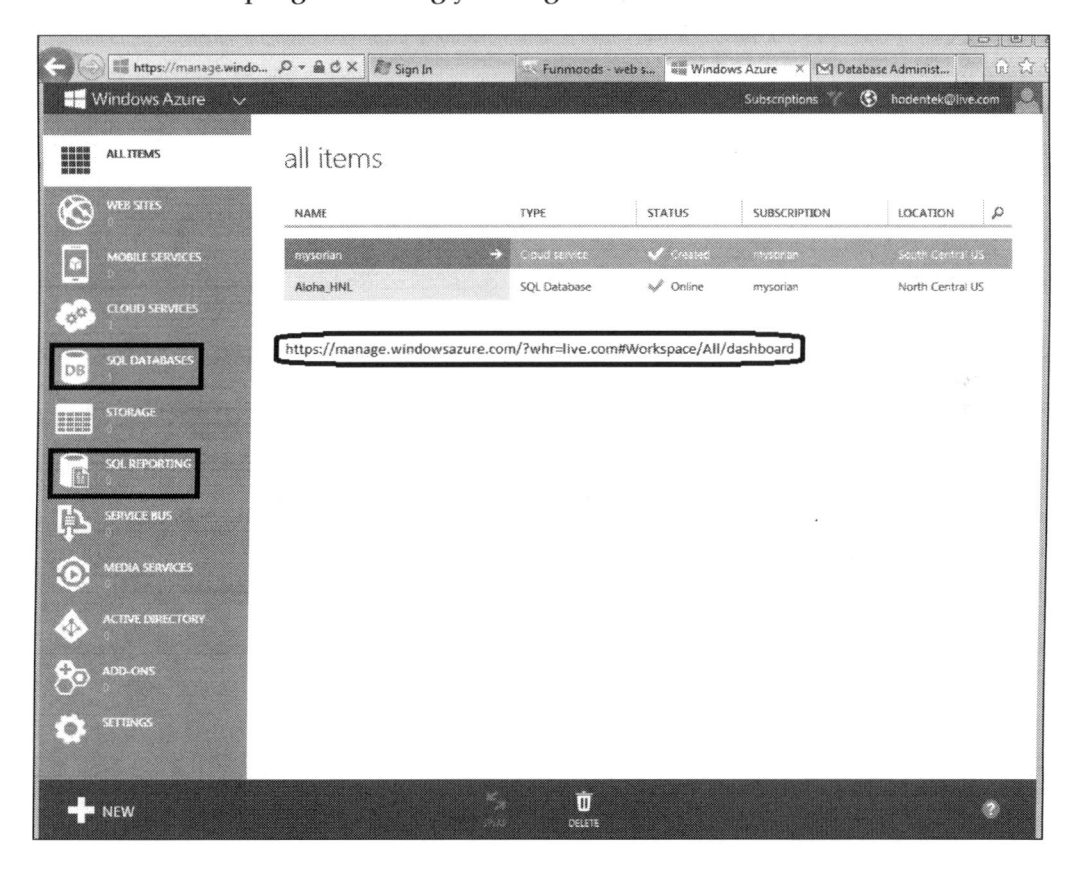

[467]

The secure Internet address in the center is that of the **Windows Azure** portal, which you enter after accessing your Live.com ID account. The left-hand side navigation is your link to the various items on Windows Azure. In our exercises, we will be using the Windows Azure SQL Reporting Services as well as Microsoft Azure SQL databases. If you are going to host a Web application, you may have to add in Cloud services and storage as well. The Cloud service (**mysorian**) and the SQL database service (**Aloha-HNL**) here are the old accounts the author had. These will be deleted and new services will be established. Getting a subscription and entering the portal has become a lot easier compared to when Windows Azure began its operation.

As we saw earlier, it is not necessary to work with any hardware; all you need is a browser and access to the Internet. This is because the Azure platform does the business of maintaining all the servers, hardware, and software needed, for maintaining them. All you need to do is author your reports and publish.

Creating content for reports and viewing them

You will be using tools that you are already familiar with. These are the same tools you used in *Chapter 2, SQL Server Reporting Services 2012 Projects with Visual Studio 2012* and *Chapter 5, Working with Report Builder 3.0*, to author and deploy reports. One limitation with Windows Azure SQL Reporting at present is that you cannot use linked external images.

Preparing to author reports

The following list is assumed to be complete, or is already present before you start authoring reports:

- Internet connection.
- Windows Azure account.
- Authoring tools (if you do not have them, you can download from a link in the portal).
    - Report Builder 3.0.
    - SSDT.
- SQL Server Management Studio (optional but highly desirable).

- Sample data or your actual data (you may need to migrate it to SQL Azure). Reports can be written only for data on the Microsoft SQL Azure database. Please review the last hands-on exercise for moving some data to SQL Azure (*Hands-on exercise 9.4 – migrating a table on an on-premise SQL Server 2012 to Windows Azure SQL Database*)

Hands-on exercise 9.2 – creating a report using SSDT and deploying it to the Windows Azure Reporting on the Cloud

In this hands-on exercise, we will create an SQL Azure database using the SQL Database service, and populate the database with some data. We will create a report using SSDT and deploy it to SQL Reporting. We will also view this report on SQL Reporting.

Creating a SQL database on Windows Azure

First, we need to log in to the portal to access the services (`https://manage.windowsazure.com/?whr=live.com#Workspaces/All/dashboard`). We will then create a SQL Server database and add a table to the database.

1. Enter the portal after providing the login information. The following Web page will be displayed (`https://manage.windowsazure.com/#Workspace/All/dashboard`):

Windows Azure SQL Reporting

2. Click on **SQL DATABASES** on the left.
3. The following page will be displayed:

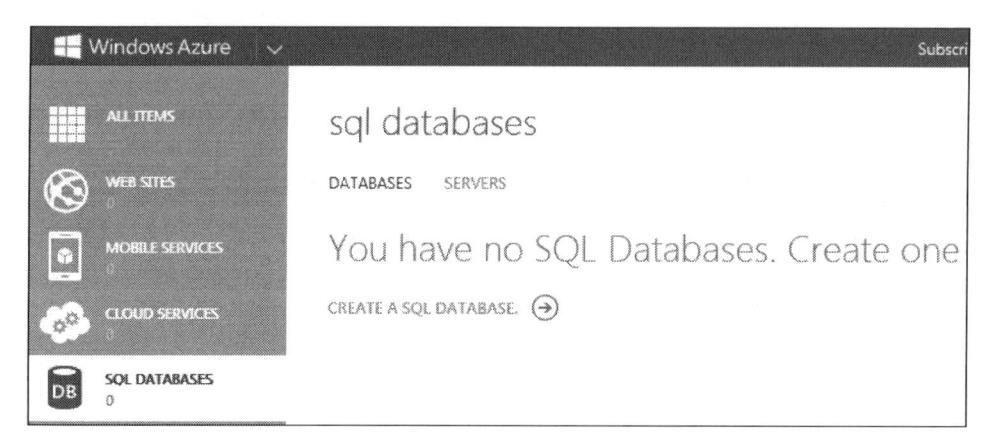

4. Click on **CREATE A SQL DATABASE**.
5. The **Specify database settings** page will be displayed. Provide a name of your choosing (herein `Skyblue`) and select **New SQL database server** in **SERVER**.

    You may change some of the settings by using the drop-down menu. Keep in mind that the price is related to the database size:

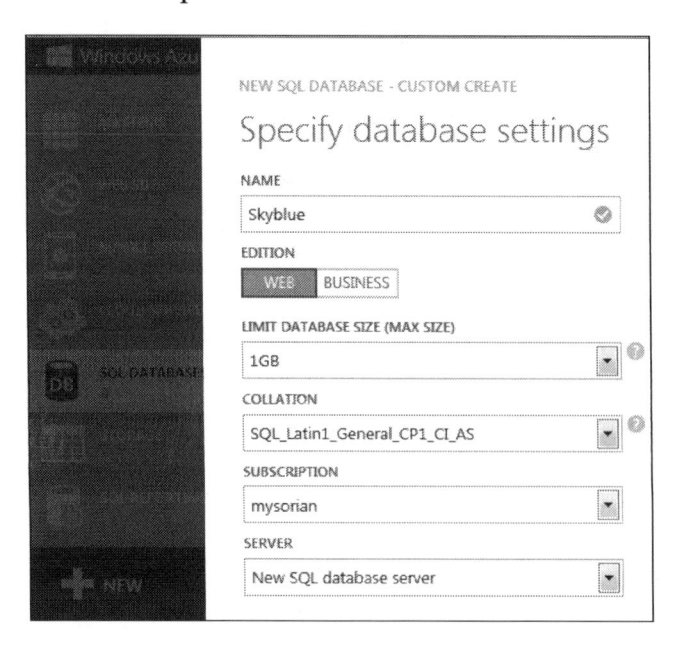

Chapter 9

> The **WEB** database is **1 GB** and the **BUSINESS** database is **10 GB**. There is a large selection for **COLLATION** (click on the handle to find out).

6. Click on the arrow at the bottom to move to page two. The SQL database server settings page will be displayed, where you need to create a login for the server. The password you create is very important; it has got to be strong, and should adhere to the following:

```
Password must be between 8 and 128 characters in length.
The password must meet the following requirements:
Does not contain all or part of the login name
Contains characters from at least three of the following categories:
-English uppercase characters (A through Z)
-English lowercase characters (a through z)
-Base 10 digits (0 through 9)
-Non-alphanumeric characters (for example: !, $, #, %)
```

7. The **SQL database server settings** page after providing details for **LOGIN NAME** and **LOGIN PASSWORD** is as shown in the next screenshot. Note that the **ALLOW WINDOWS AZURE SERVICES TO ACCESS THE SERVER** checkbox is selected:

NEW SQL DATABASE - CUSTOM CREATE

SQL database server settings

LOGIN NAME

june10

LOGIN PASSWORD

••••••••••••

LOGIN PASSWORD CONFIRMATION

••••••••••••

REGION

North Central US

☑ ALLOW WINDOWS AZURE SERVICES TO ACCESS THE SERVER.

[471]

Windows Azure SQL Reporting

> The value for **LOGIN PASSWORD** used was `@#MountEtna9$`. As this will have been removed by the end of this day, it matters little to mention it. This is a strong password.

8. Click on the tick mark at the bottom. Presto! You have a 1 GB server at your disposal:

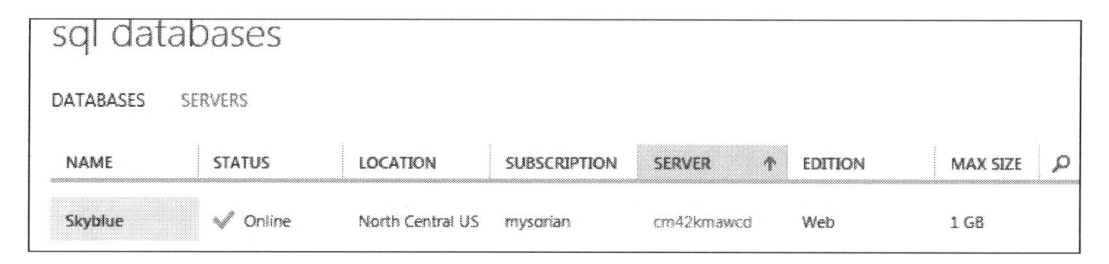

sql databases

DATABASES   SERVERS

NAME	STATUS	LOCATION	SUBSCRIPTION	SERVER	EDITION	MAX SIZE
Skyblue	Online	North Central US	mysorian	cm42kmawcd	Web	1 GB

It is ready to use (**Online**) and the server is named **cm42kmawcd** and it is located at Microsoft's **North Central US** data center. The name of this subscription is **mysorian**.

9. Click on **Skyblue** in the preceding image. The **Skyblue** server page will be displayed. Note down the Web address of the server at the bottom:

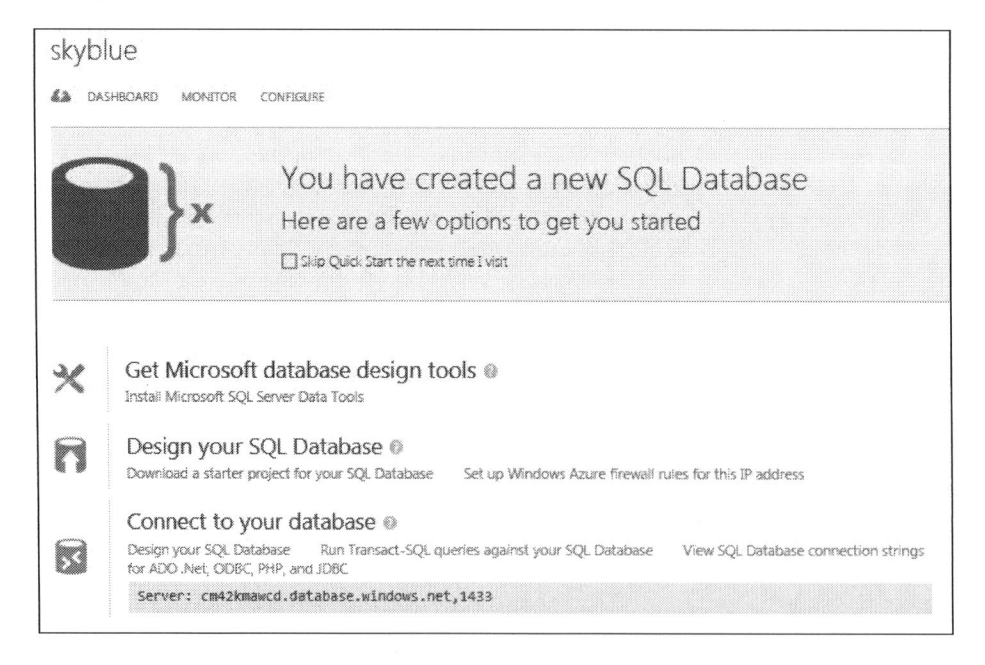

skyblue

DASHBOARD   MONITOR   CONFIGURE

You have created a new SQL Database
Here are a few options to get you started
☐ Skip Quick Start the next time I visit

Get Microsoft database design tools
Install Microsoft SQL Server Data Tools

Design your SQL Database
Download a starter project for your SQL Database   Set up Windows Azure firewall rules for this IP address

Connect to your database
Design your SQL Database   Run Transact-SQL queries against your SQL Database   View SQL Database connection strings
for ADO .Net, ODBC, PHP, and JDBC

Server: cm42kmawcd.database.windows.net,1433

[472]

SQL Server Data Tools was described and used in *Chapter 2, SQL Server Reporting Services 2012 Projects with Visual Studio 2012*. The database we are creating on this server will be protected by Firewall and will be configured now.

10. Click on **Set up Windows Azure firewall rules** for this IP address. The following window will appear in the status line. You may get a different message depending upon your IP address. Please do what is suggested by the message:

11. Click on **YES**.
12. Click on **Design your SQL Database**. The login screen will appear as follows:

13. Enter the login information you created earlier and click on **Log on**.

[473]

Windows Azure SQL Reporting

You have succeeded in creating the Skyblue database, as shown in the next screenshot. Now, you can create tables, views, and stored procedures. At the very top, we have the breadcrumbs, `cm42kmawcd.database.windows.net -> [Skyblue] - >Tables`. You can upload files and run the queries as well:

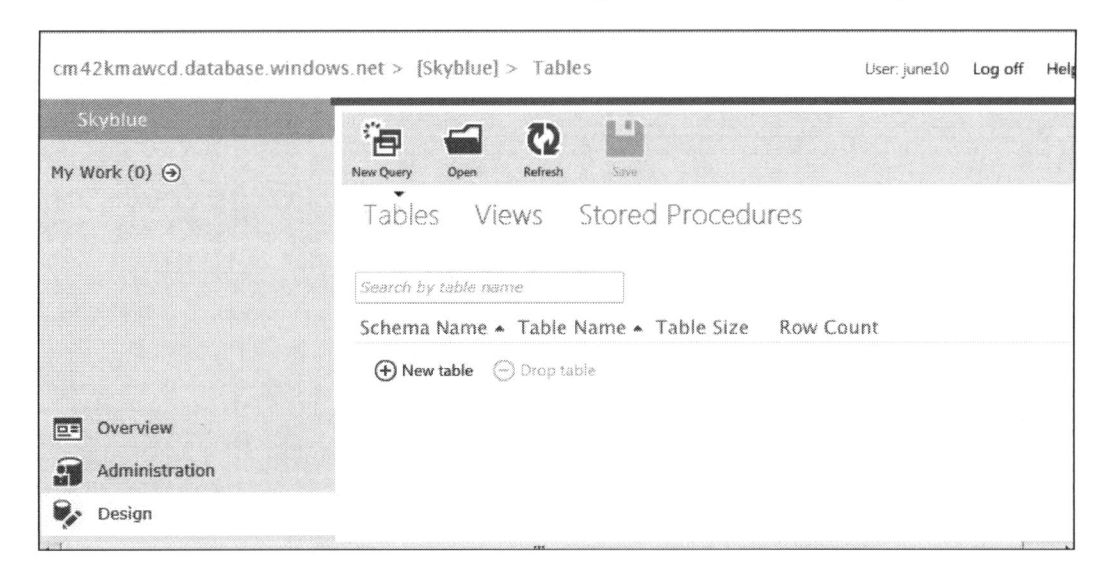

Now that we have a database, we can create a table that contains the data used in the report. The database table can be created either in the portal or in a client like SQL Server Management Studio. Here, we will use the Windows Azure platform to create a table.

Creating a table for the report

We will use the Windows Azure platform to create a table. In the previous page we have an option to create a New Table.

1. Click on **New Table**. After some processing, you will have a table design with an **ID** column and two other columns, as follows:

Chapter 9

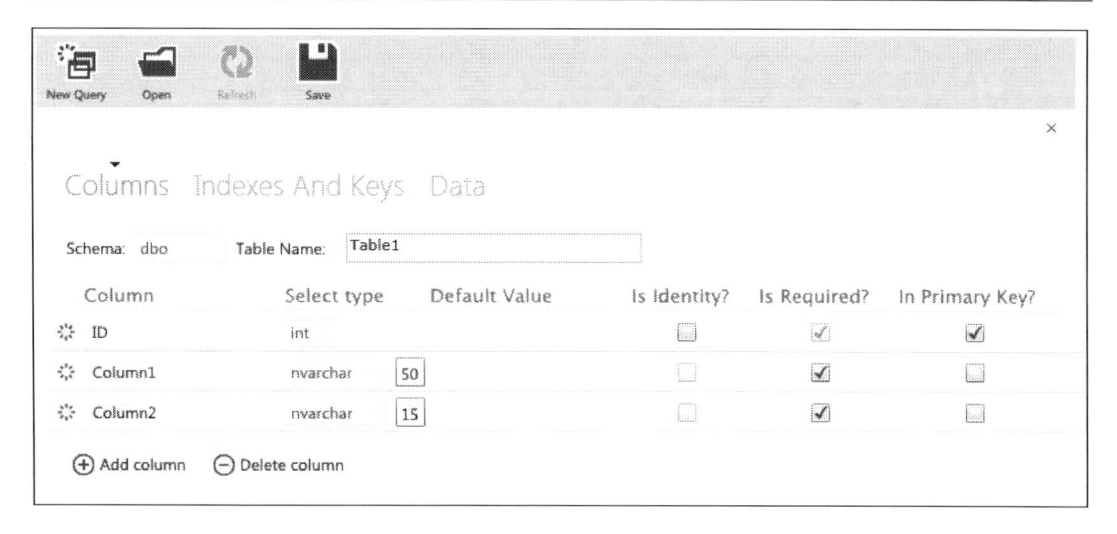

2. Modify the table columns, as shown. You can click on **Column** and overwrite **FName**, and so on. Add an extra column for **Age**. The **ID** column is the primary key:

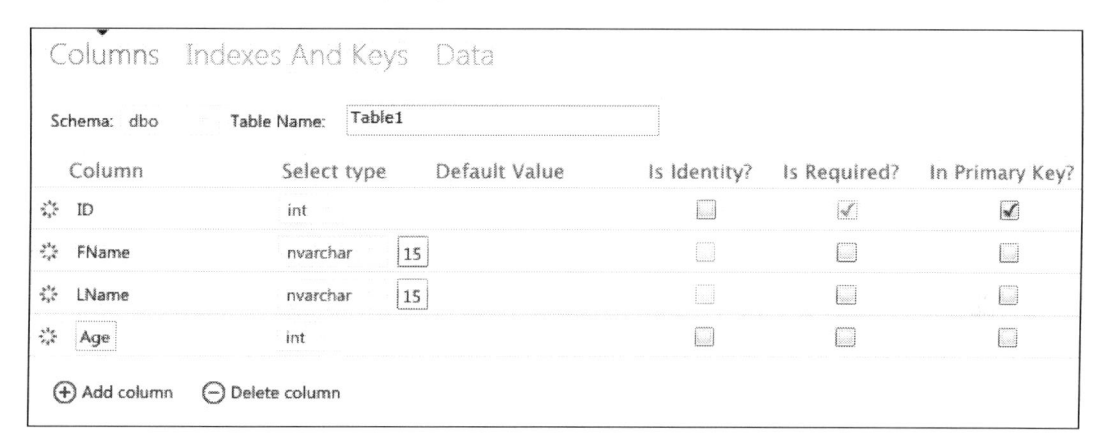

The created table will have four columns, one of which is **ID**, the primary key and the others are an **Age** column with data type `int` and two `nvarchar` datatype columns for **FName** and **LName**, and none of these are required. All datatypes available on premises are also available on SQL Azure databases.

Windows Azure SQL Reporting

3. Click on **Save** at the top of the page to save the table. After some processing, the page comes back asking to name the table. Here, **CloudT** is the name given to the table. The server gets updated as follows:

Now that the table is created in the Windows Azure SQL database, we can populate the table with data. This can be carried out by using a query on Windows Azure's SQL Azure database or in the on-premises SQL Server after connecting to the SQL Azure database.

Populating the table in SSMS

This section of the hands-on exercise shows how you may populate the table using SSMS. Using SSMS, we first establish a connection to the SQL Azure database:

1. Launch SSMS as administrator.
2. Click on **File | Connect Object Explorer...**.
3. The **Connect to Server** window will be displayed. Fill in the details from your notes taken during setting up the database on Windows Azure. The data center automatically recognizes that the request is coming from an allowed IP address.

> When you create a SQL Azure database, the portal discovers your IP address so that it can honor requests from your clients as shown in step 10 of the *Creating a SQL database on Windows Azure* section.

[476]

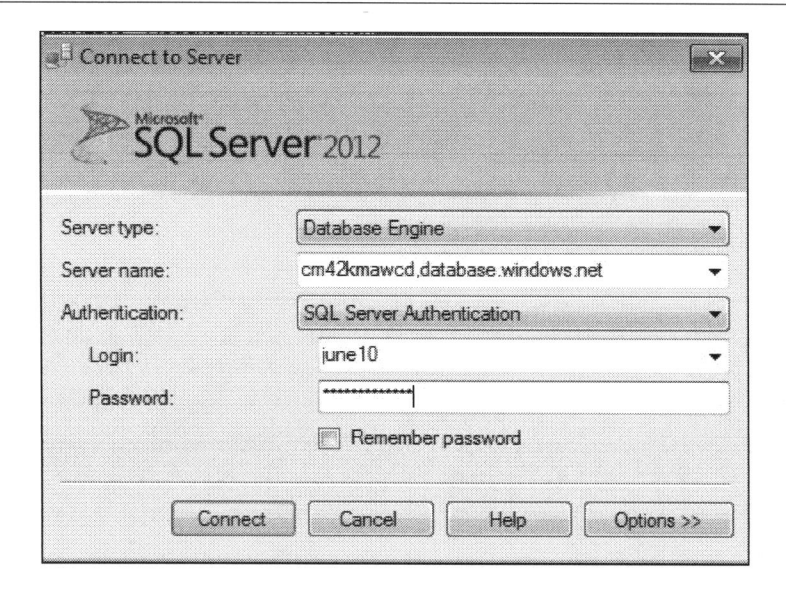

4. Click on **Connect**. You will be connected to the server, as follows, provided there are no errors in the information you supplied:

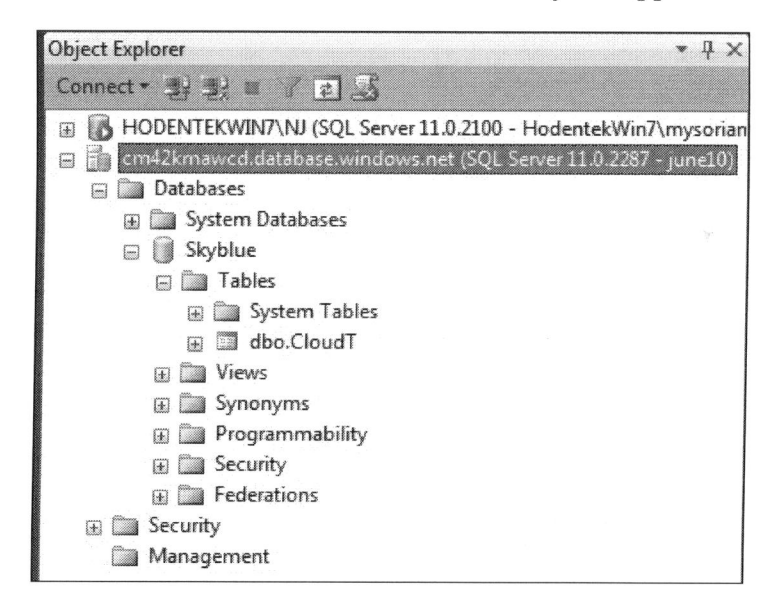

Right-click on the server and then on **New Query**. The query window will be displayed.

Windows Azure SQL Reporting

Run the following query in the window to populate the table:
```
insert into CloudT(id,FName,LName, Age)
values(1, 'Kris', 'Jay', 50), (2,'Julia','Adams', 35),(3, 'Sonia',
'Braga', 70)
```

5. Run the following query to verify that your table has three rows of data:
```
SELECT * FROM CloudT
```

We now have a SQL Azure database with a table, which has been populated. In the next step, we will first create a SQL Reporting Service in Windows Azure, after which we will use the data in the table CloudT to create a report using the SQL Reporting Service.

Creating a SQL Reporting Service in Windows Azure

We will first set up a SQL Reporting Service on Windows Azure:

1. In the portal, click on **SQL Reporting**, as shown.

> You can type in WindowsAzure.com in the browser, which will take you to the gatekeeper; sign in page for the portal. Only after you log in, will you get to see the display of the portal.

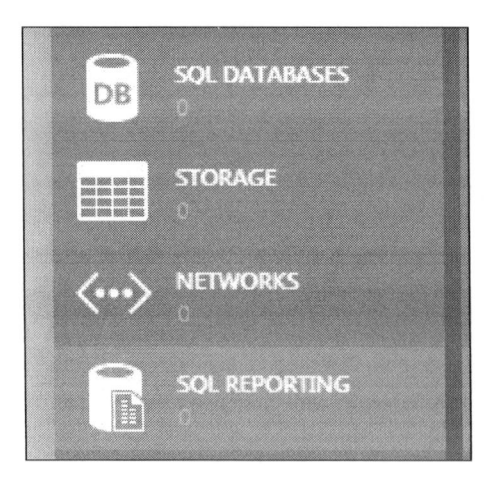

[478]

You will get a message as follows:

> reporting services
>
> You have no reporting services. Create one to get started.
>
> CREATE A REPORTING SERVICE →

2. Click on **CREATE A REPORTING SERVICE**.
3. The **NEW** page for the service (**DATA SERVICES**) will be displayed, as follows:

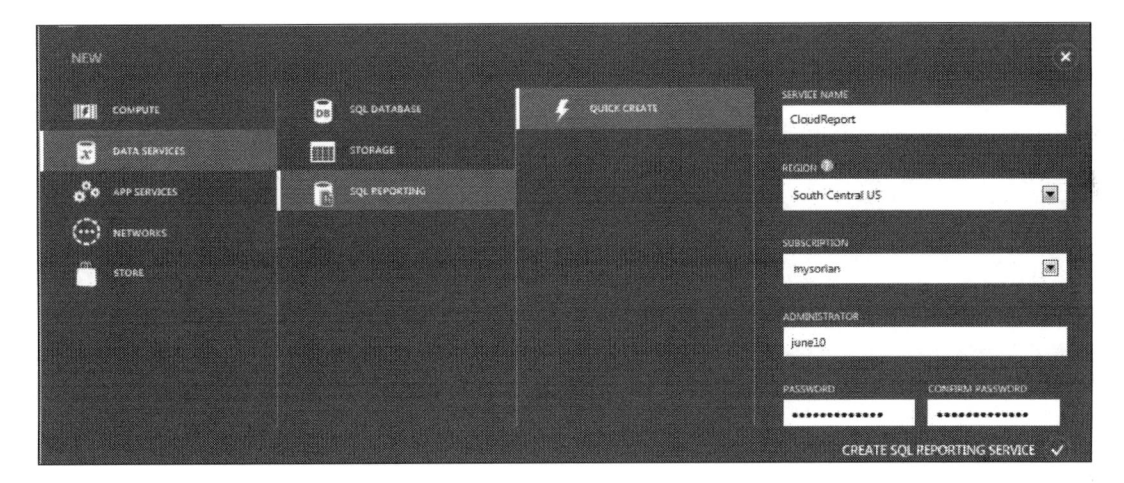

4. Fill in the information, as shown in the preceding screenshot, and click on the tick mark at the bottom.
5. You have succeeded in creating a Reporting Service named **CloudReport**, as follows:

NAME	STATUS	SUBSCRIPTION	LOCATION	ADMINISTRATOR	WEB SERVICE...
CloudReport	✓ Started	mysorian	South Central US	june10	https://1rhqjih70m.r...

The Web service address is the name of the Report Server's Web address on Windows Azure Reporting; hover over it and verify in the status line at the bottom of screen.

6. Click on the link and provide the credentials (`june10`, `password`) and you will see the following window displayed:

1rhqjlh70m.reporting.windows.net/ReportServer - /

Microsoft SQL Server Reporting Services Version 11.0.1722.19

It is very similar to the Native mode Report Server. Presently, there are no reports or data sources or other objects on the database. The version is `11.0.1722.19`, which means it is a SSRS 2012 Report Server.

We have now succeeded in creating a Report Server on the Windows Azure platform. In the next section, we will create a report using the `CloudT` table on `Skyblue` and create a report. After creating the report using SSDT, we will deploy it to the Report Server we created earlier.

Creating a report based on the Skyblue database on the Windows Azure Platform

We start with SSDT (or even Report Builder 3) on the computer to create a report based on the Skyblue database on the `cm42kmawcd` server:

1. Launch SSDT with administrator privileges.
2. Create a Report Server project, `RPCloud`.
3. Create a new data source using a Microsoft SQL Azure type of database.
4. For the connection string, fill in details as shown here. Use the following in the **Connection Properties** window:
   - **Server name**: `cm42kmawcd.database.windows.net`
   - **User name**: `june10`
   - **Password**: `password`
   - **Select or enter a database name**: `Skyblue`
5. Test the connection using the **Test Connection** button:

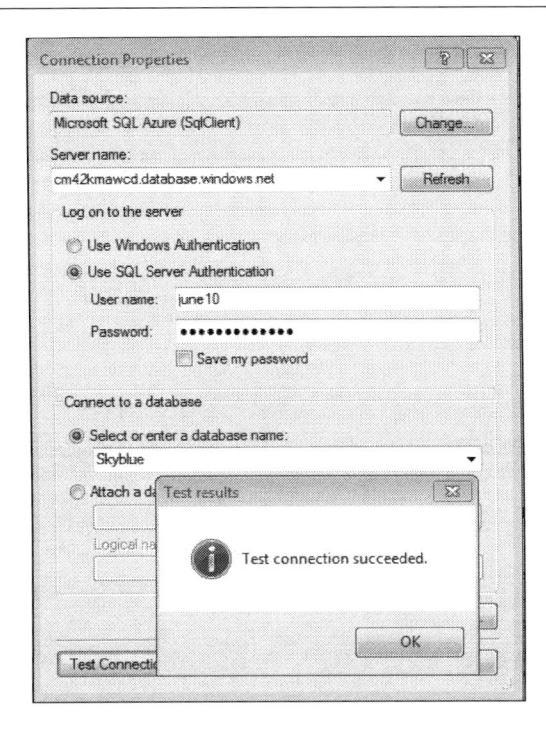

6. Click on **OK** and again on **OK**.
7. Provide a name for the data source. Your data source will look similar to the following screenshot:

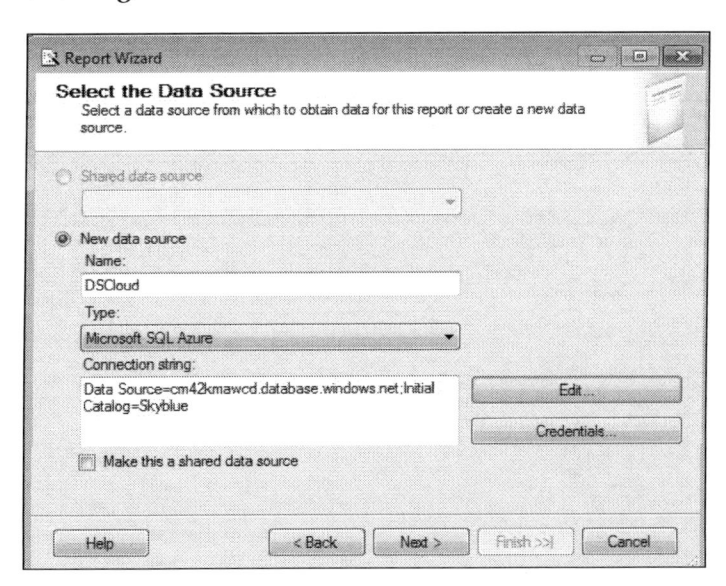

Windows Azure SQL Reporting

8. Click on **Next** and enter the credentials.
9. In the **Design the query** page, enter the following statement:
   ```
   SELECT * FROM CloudT
   ```
10. Click on **Next**.
11. In **Select Report Type** select **Tabular**.
12. Click on and transfer all the items in **Available** pane to the **Displayed** fields.
13. When you are done, the **Design the Table** page will be displayed as follows:

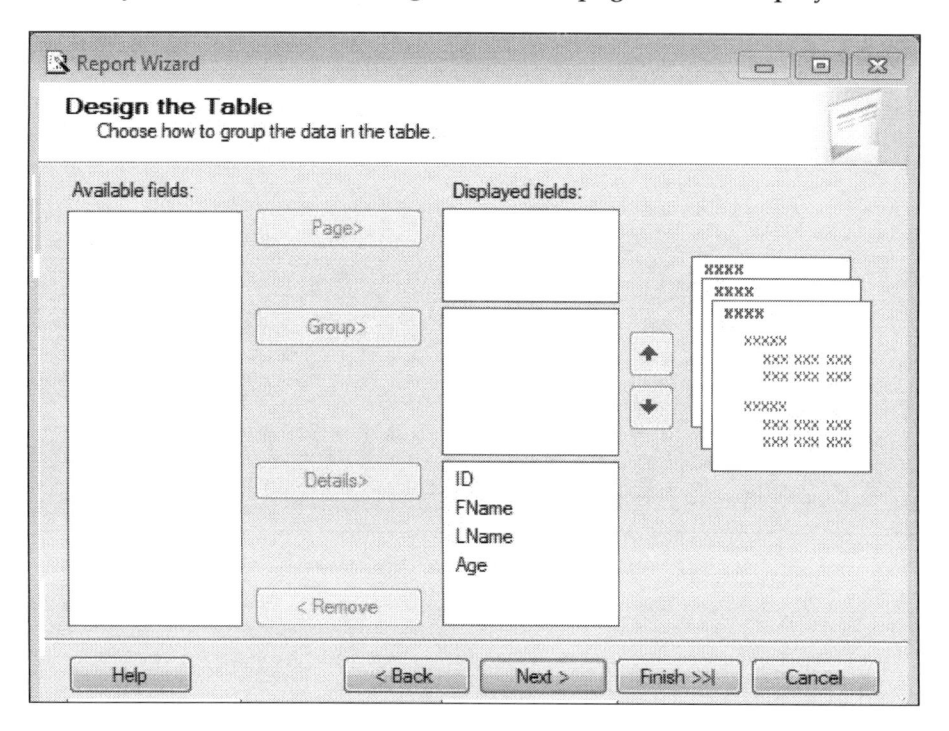

14. Click on **Next** and choose the **Forest** style.
15. Click on **Next**. Change the report name to `Skyblue_Report`, and click on **Finish**.
16. The `SKyBlue` report will appear in the design window, as follows:

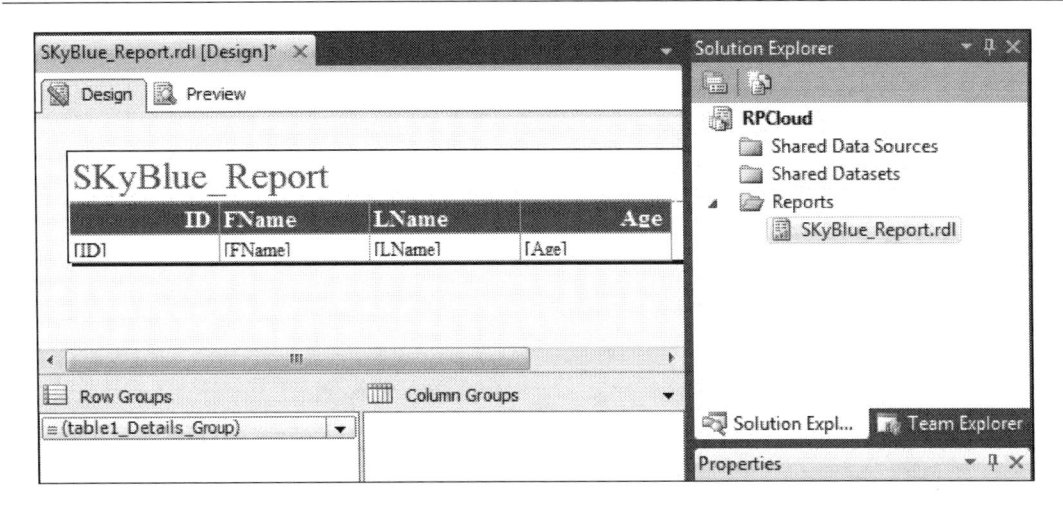

17. Click on **Preview**.
18. Enter the credentials in **Preview,** as follows:

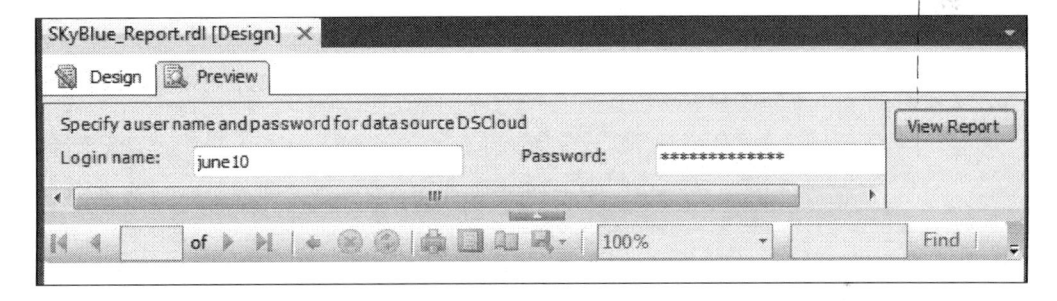

19. Click on **View Report**. The report will appear in the SSDT UI, as follows:

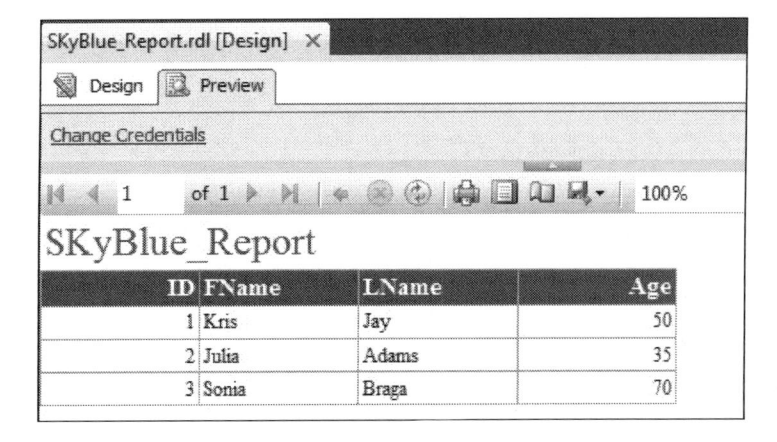

Windows Azure SQL Reporting

The preceding report is in the SSDT's IDE, although the database used for the report is on the Windows Azure SQL Azure database. In the following section, we will deploy it to the SQL Reporting Services on Windows Azure.

Deploying the report to the SQL Reporting Services on Windows Azure

Now that the report is designed we will deploy it to the SQL Reporting Service on Windows Azure. We can do this from SSDT, as seen earlier:

1. Click on **Project** and open the **RPCloud Property** pages as shown. Fill in the value for **TargetServerURL**, as follows:

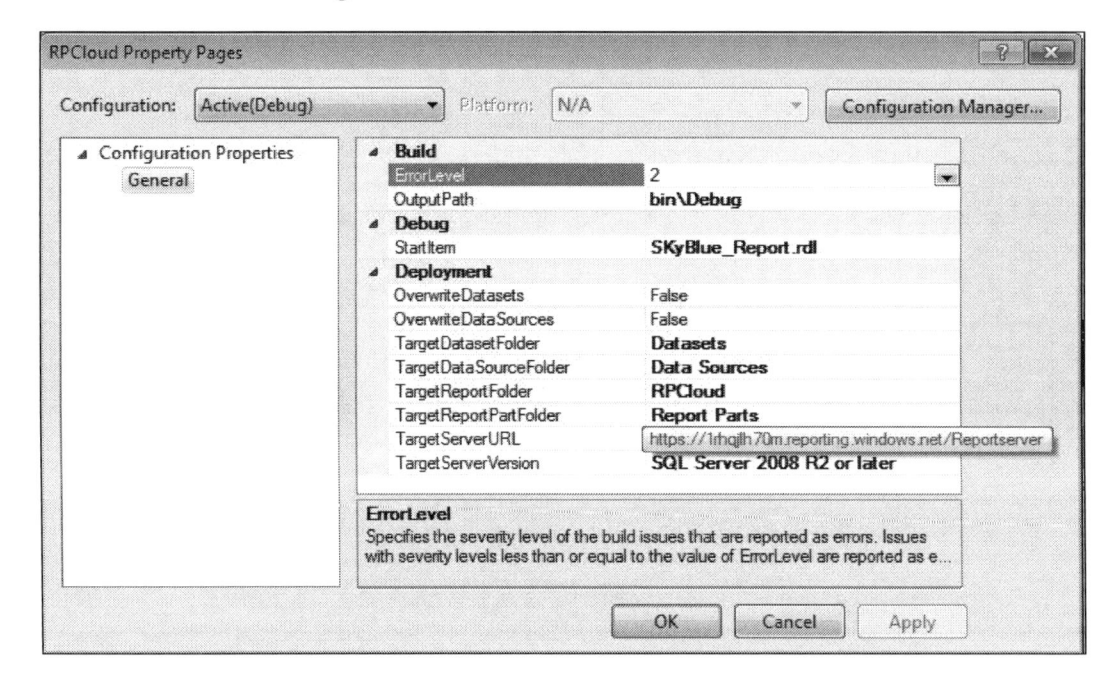

2. Click on **Apply**, then on OK.
3. Right-click on the `RPCloud` project in **Solution Explorer**, then click on **Deploy**.
4. The **Report server Login** page will appear. Enter the credentials. Click on **OK**.
5. The **Output** window will show that the report has been deployed:

[484]

Chapter 9

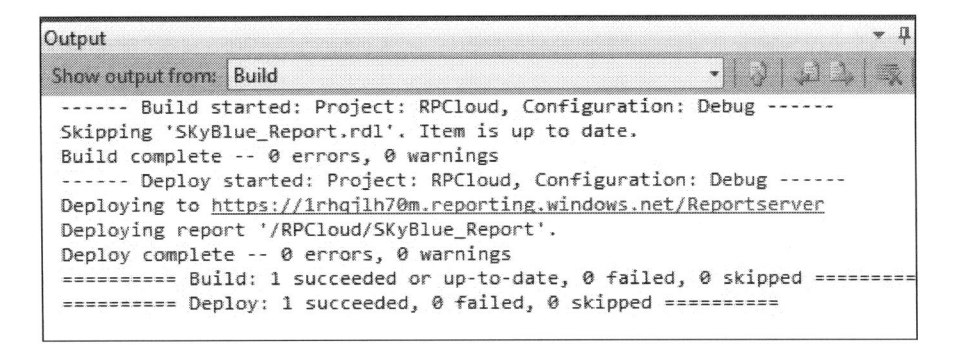

```
------ Build started: Project: RPCloud, Configuration: Debug ------
Skipping 'SKyBlue_Report.rdl'. Item is up to date.
Build complete -- 0 errors, 0 warnings
------ Deploy started: Project: RPCloud, Configuration: Debug ------
Deploying to https://1rhqjlh70m.reporting.windows.net/Reportserver
Deploying report '/RPCloud/SKyBlue_Report'.
Deploy complete -- 0 errors, 0 warnings
========== Build: 1 succeeded or up-to-date, 0 failed, 0 skipped ==========
========== Deploy: 1 succeeded, 0 failed, 0 skipped ==========
```

The report is now on the Windows Azure SQL Reporting services Report Server.

6. Verify by clicking on the link in the preceding output.
7. The link displays the Windows Azure SQL Report Server URL (you may have to go through one more authentication event):

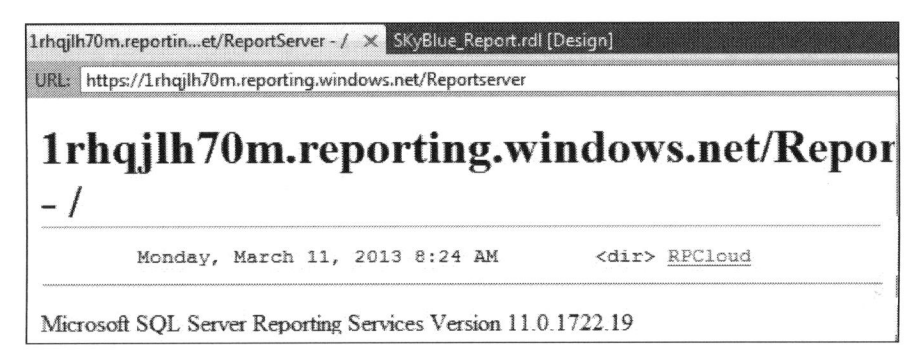

URL: https://1rhqjlh70m.reporting.windows.net/Reportserver

1rhqjlh70m.reporting.windows.net/Repor - /

Monday, March 11, 2013 8:24 AM <dir> RPCloud

Microsoft SQL Server Reporting Services Version 11.0.1722.19

8. Access the portal and verify that there is a report in SQL Reporting, as follows:

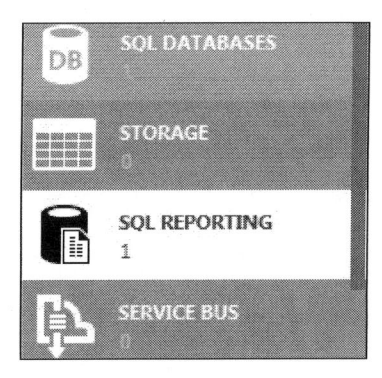

- SQL DATABASES
- STORAGE 0
- SQL REPORTING 1
- SERVICE BUS 0

Windows Azure SQL Reporting

Viewing the report on the SQL Reporting Web server

Once the report is on the Web server it is very easy to access and view the report.

1. In the dashboard, you will find the **CloudReport** project on the Report Server, as follows:

2. Click on the hyperlink under the **WEB SERVICE** column.
3. You will get to the Report Server URL as seen earlier.
4. Click on **RPCloud**.
5. You will see the report in the project `CloudReport`, as follows:

6. Click on the **Skyblue_Report** link in the preceding screenshot.
7. The UI for report display is as follows:

Chapter 9

8. Enter the credentials and click on **View Report**. The report will appears as follows:

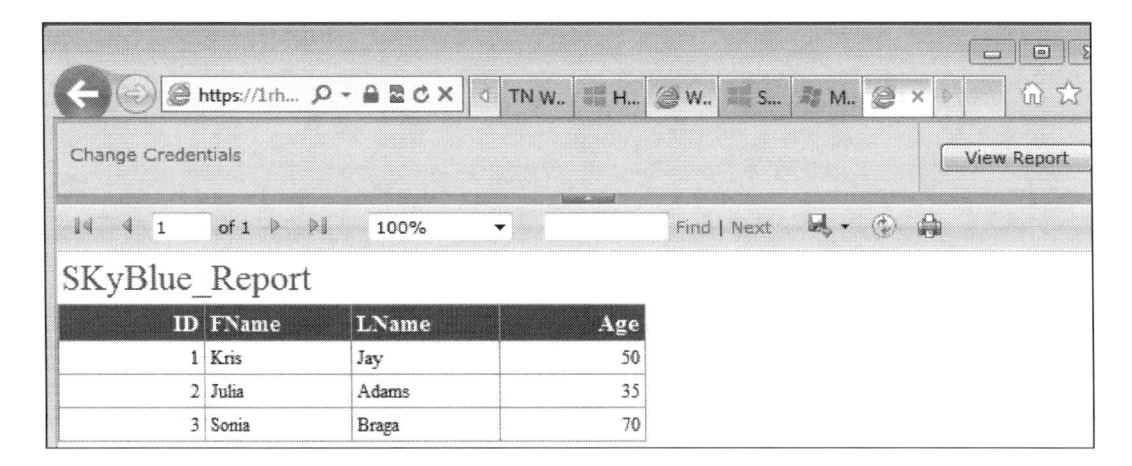

SKyBlue_Report

ID	FName	LName	Age
1	Kris	Jay	50
2	Julia	Adams	35
3	Sonia	Braga	70

9. Log off from the SQL database.

cm42kmawcd.database.windows.net > [Skyblue] > Tables >   User: june10   Log off   Help

10. Sign out of the portal as shown here:

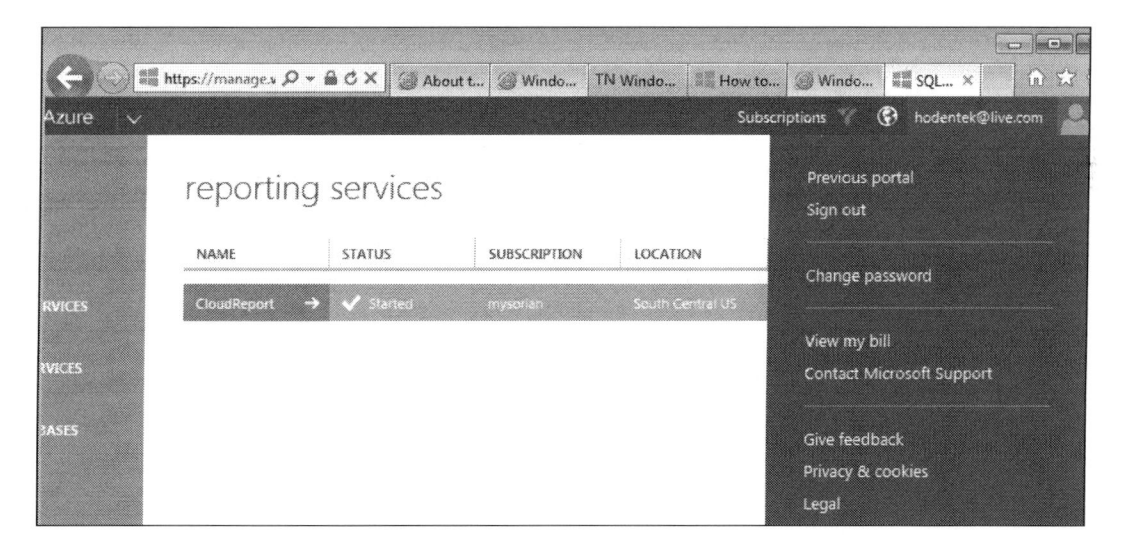

reporting services

NAME	STATUS	SUBSCRIPTION	LOCATION
CloudReport	Started	mysorian	South Central US

Previous portal
Sign out

Change password

View my bill
Contact Microsoft Support

Give feedback
Privacy & cookies
Legal

We have finished creating a report and viewing it on the Windows Azure SQL Reporting Services. As mentioned previously, for the Windows SQL Azure SQL reporting, the portal provides interfaces similar to Report Manager in Native mode reporting. This means you can create `shared data sources`, create `folders`, create `Report Parts`, upload reports, and so on. In the next hands-on, we will create a shared data source

Hands-on exercise 9.3 – using the Windows Azure SQL Reporting Services to create folders, share data sources, and upload reports

Windows SQL Azure Reporting has three menu items:

- **DASHBOARD**
- **USERS**
- **ITEMS**

> The person who creates the service is the administrator of the service and he is the only user to start with. He creates other users.

The **ITEMS** menu supports the following:

- **CREATE A FOLDER**
- **UPLOAD A REPORT**
- **CREATE A DATA SOURCE**

Creating a folder and uploading a report are very easy. For the folder, you need to give a folder name (the folders `Equinox` and `Report Parts` on this server were created by using this menu item). For uploading a report, click on the link that gives access to your computers folders/filesystem. You can successfully upload a report definition file. The report that you upload should be based on the Microsoft SQL Azure database, otherwise you will get an error message from the server.

Creating a shared data source in the portal

We created a SQL Azure database and using this database, we will now create a data source that can be shared:

1. Click on **CloudReport** in the previous image to open the SQL Reporting, to display your project as follows:

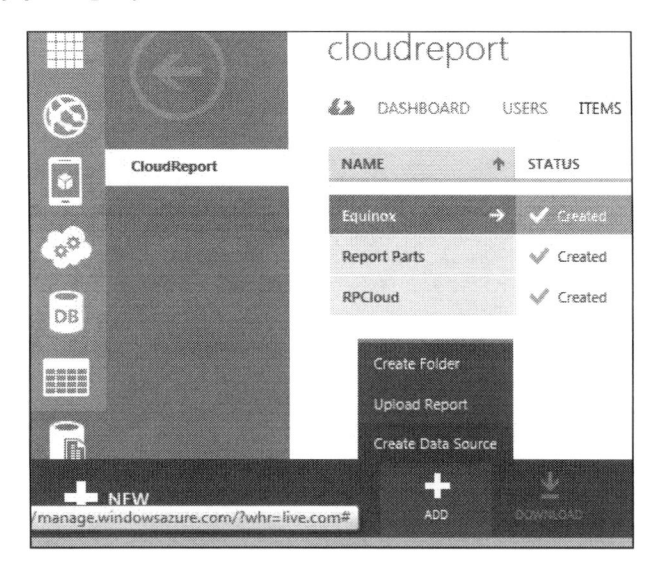

2. In the **ADD +** item, click on **Create Data Source** to open the **CREATE DATA SOURCE** page:

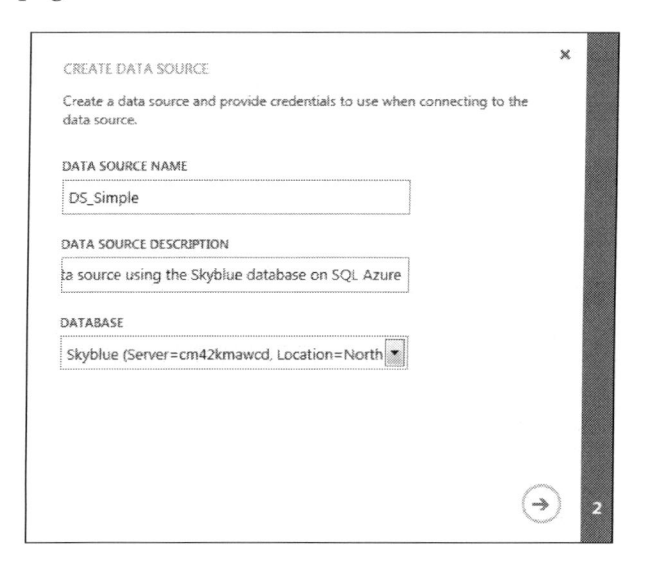

3. Fill in information as shown. `DS_Simple` is the name provided for the shared data source. The **DATABASE** information comes up by itself. Click on the arrow at the bottom. Page 2 opens up as follows:

4. Accept the defaults and click on the tick mark at the bottom. The data source gets created as follows:

Now, you can use it as a shared data source. The next screenshot shows how we are going to use it as shared data source to create a report using Report Builder. In the Report Builder, as described in *Chapter 5, Working with Report Builder 3.0*, you can connect to a shared data source, as shown in the two screenshots in montage:

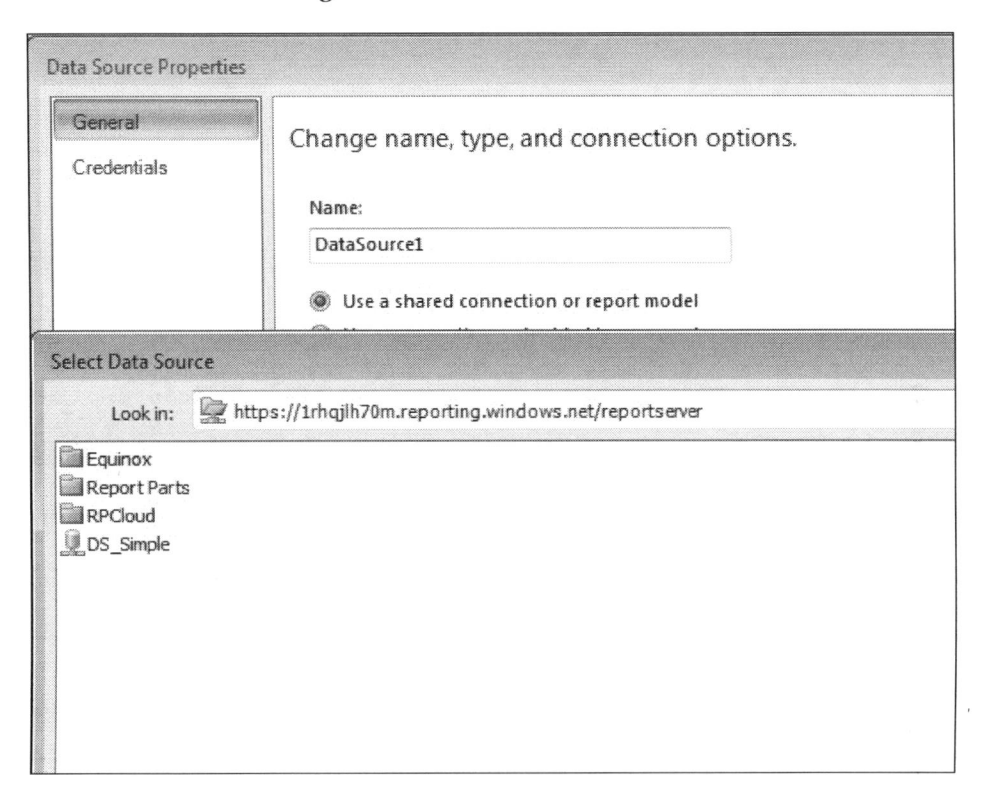

Managing your reports and users is easy

The jobs you do typically are as follows:

- Create and manage report content
- Configure data sources; shared or otherwise
- Use the Report Server Web Service API to create and manage users and their permissions
- Use a GUI to manage users utilizing the Windows Azure portal user interface

Windows Azure SQL Reporting

Managing users

After you bring up your project, as shown in the next image, you can create users very easily:

Clicking on **CREATE** at the bottom of the page in the preceding screenshot will bring the **Create a new user** window, as follows:

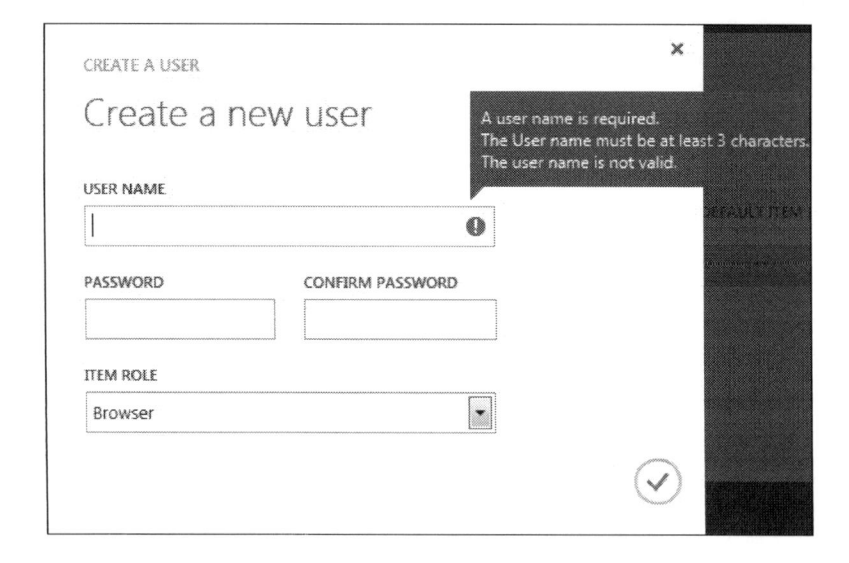

Stringent rules, listed previously, must be followed for passwords and **ITEM ROLE** is the same one as in *Chapter 4, Working with Report Manager*, as shown in the next screenshot, from the drop-down list. The new user you create can view the report and make changes to the content, but the user should also have permissions to the data source. These can be carried out in the SQL databases service we used earlier:

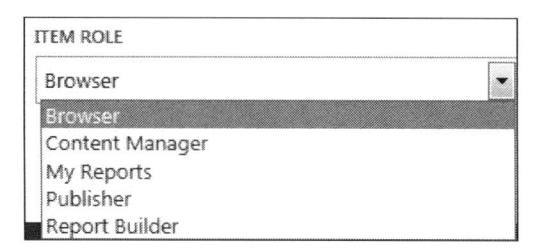

Managing reports

Click on **ITEMS** in the **cloudreport** page to bring up the items in the project, as follows:

By clicking on **ADD**, you can carry out a number of item management tasks, as follows:

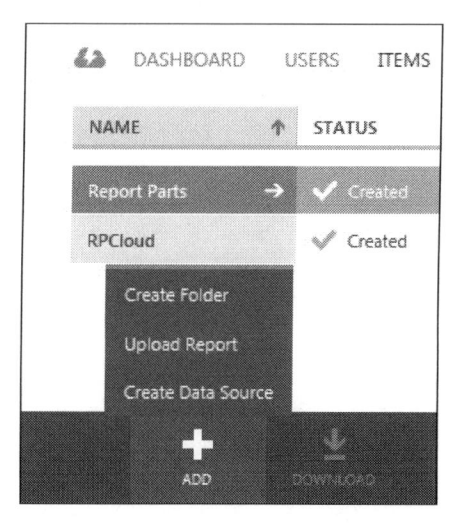

Windows Azure SQL Reporting

The Windows Azure SQL Reporting's project page is very similar to the Report Manager interface in SQL Server Reporting Server in the Native mode. Most of the activities of the previous chapter can be carried out here as well.

Managing the report Dashboard

The users and items were explored previously. The **Dashboard** provides a global view of the service (a quick glance shows all the important details such as the region where the Report Server is located, the name of the Windows Azure subscription, the Web server URL where you can access the report, and the status besides the chronological data about reports processed), as shown in the following screenshot:

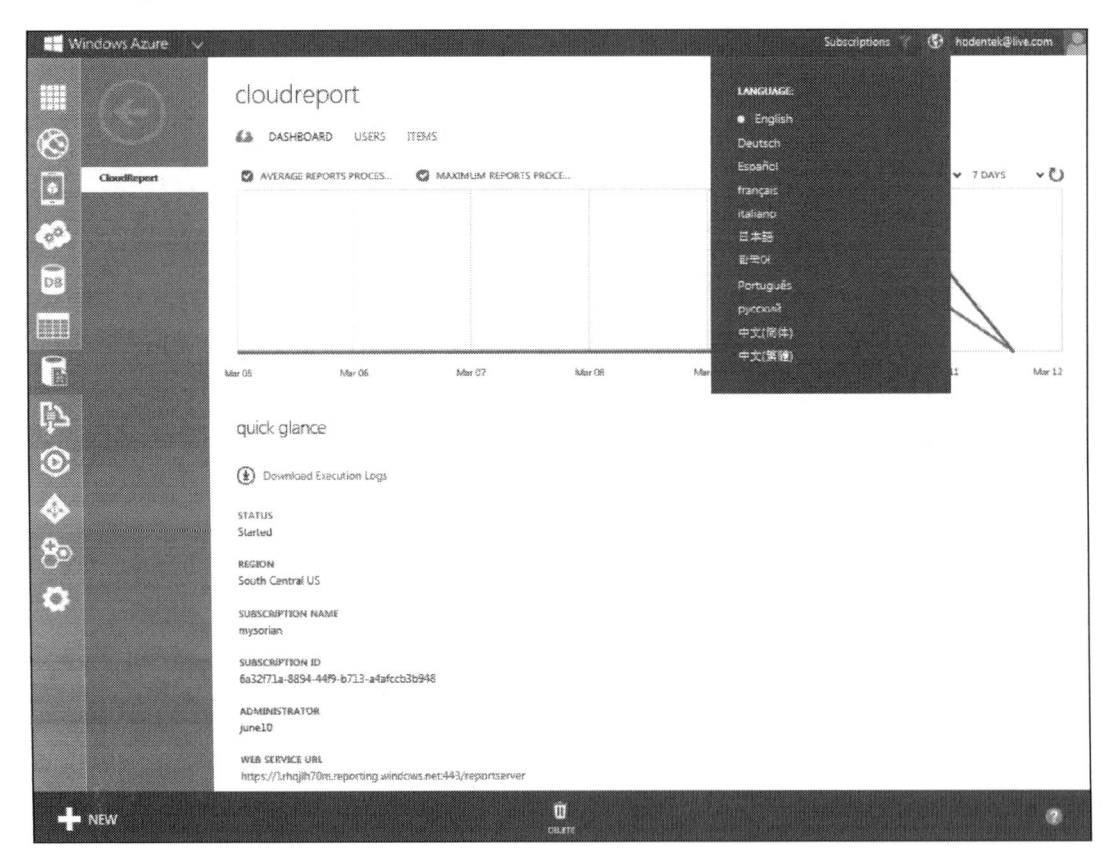

This can be displayed in several languages and gives access to the URL of the Web service at the bottom of this page, as well as the processing activities. You can also access the execution logs of the report processed. A sample screenshot is as follows:

[494]

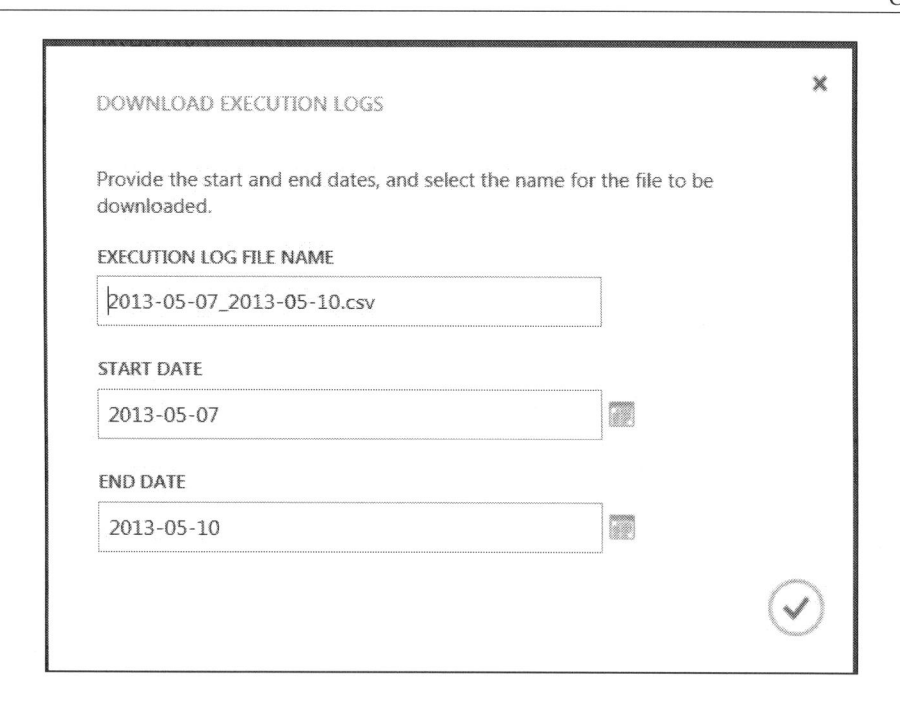

Status of activities

As you carry on various management activities, you should pay attention to the status information at the bottom of the screen, as shown in the next image. It is displaying that a new user was created and a new folder was created. You can work with this accordion control by clicking on the down arrow head at the extreme right, below the **Search** button:

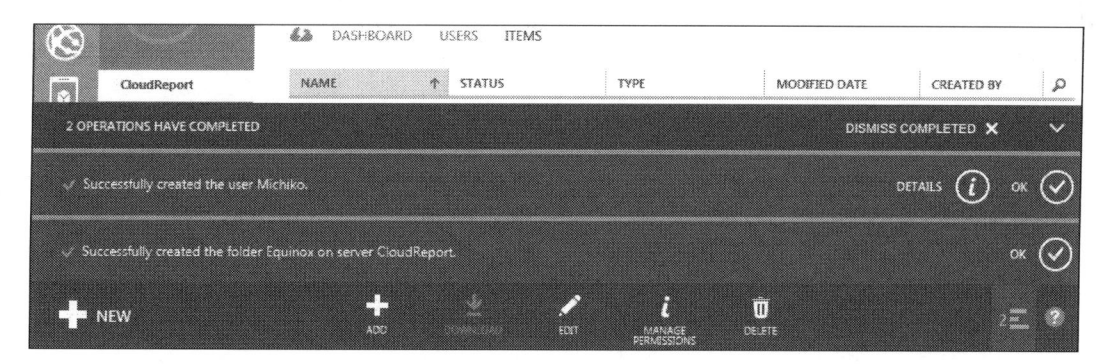

Managing permissions

In the `CloudReport` folder seen earlier, there were two folders and another was added. Highlighting the Report Parts and clicking on **MANAGE PERMISSIONS** at the bottom of the screen brings up the **Manage Permissions** window. The choices are also similar to what you saw in Report Manager in a Native mode installation of Reporting Services 2012:

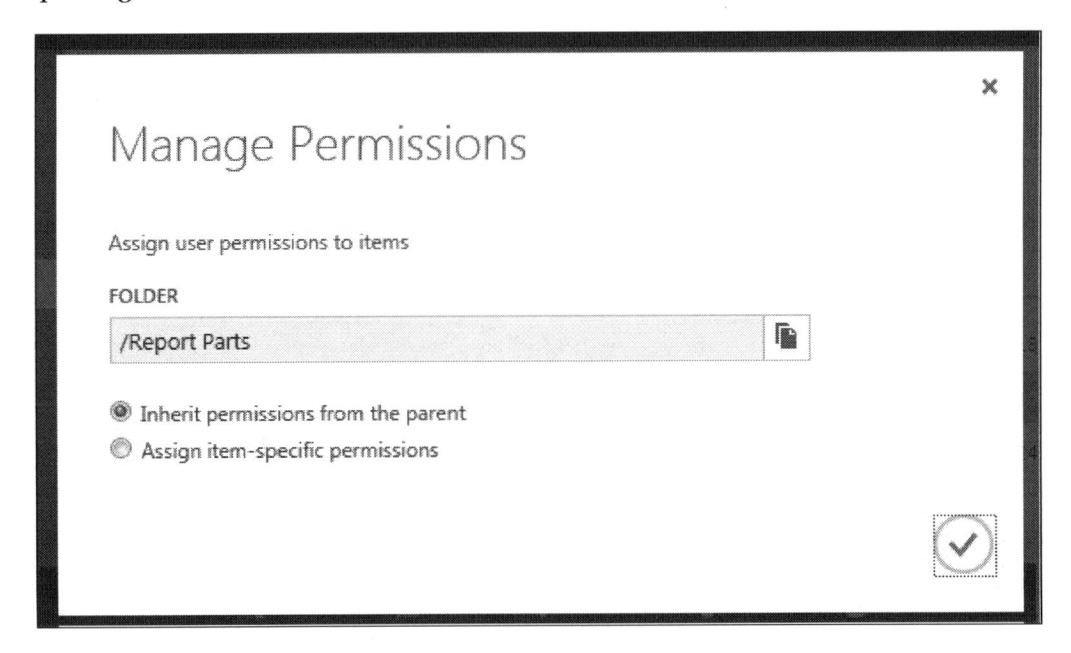

This completes the task of managing users, permissions, and reports.

Report viewing

You can view reports on the Windows Azure Reporting site in three ways:

- Use a Web browser to view hosted reports (also review, accessing Report Server URLs in a WPF Project in the next Chapter)
- On-premise applications with embedded Report Viewer controls
- Windows Azure hosted applications with embedded Report Viewer controls

Everything you learnt in *Chapter 2* can be used for this chapter. You can use all the report layout controls, as well as view reports in various formats.

Using Report Builder to view reports

Earlier, we saw how reports on the Windows Azure SQL Reporting's Web services can be accessed to view reports. There are other ways of viewing reports as well.

Report Builder 3.0 can be used to view and manipulate reports as well. Normally, Report Builder would either connect to a Report Server in the Native mode or during content creation in a SharePoint Server using its **ClickOnce** avatar.

If Windows Azure SQL Reporting is the only accessible Report Server, then one can install a Report Builder with the option of not choosing a default Web server. After launching the Report Builder, point it to the Web Azure Reporting Services Web server by providing the credentials.

At the start up, the Report Builder is not connected to any Report Server, as shown:

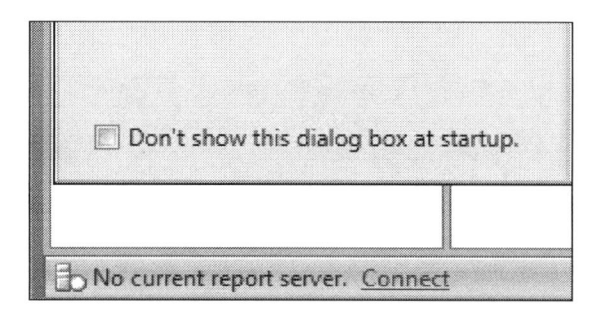

Clicking on the **Connect** hyperlink will bring up the **Connect to Report Server** window, as follows:

> This came up without logging in because it was accessed once before. Normally, a login window will show up and only after entering the credentials, can you get connected to the server.

You will notice at the status line of **Report Builder** that you are now connected to the Report Server.

Now, when you try to open an existing report, you get the familiar window. But it will now be connected to the Windows Azure Reporting Services Web server, as follows:

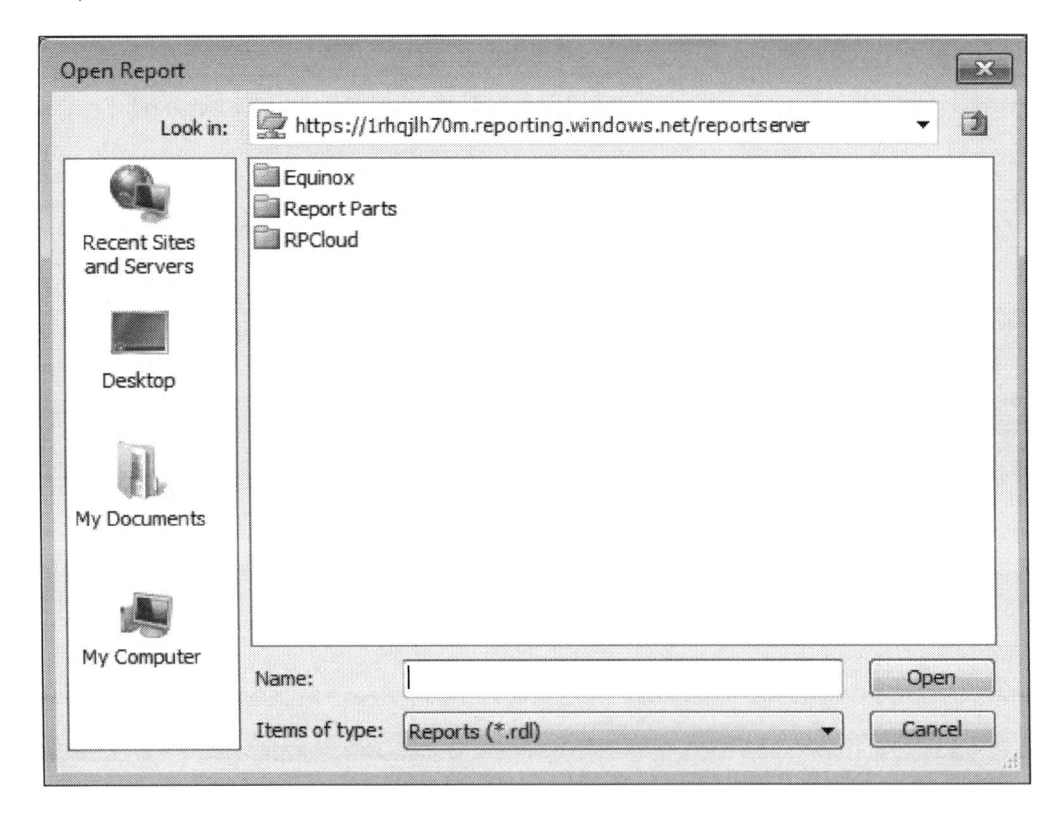

Now, you can get the report you hosted on the Report Server by choosing **RPCloud** and opening it. The report will be opened in Report Builder's design view, as follows:

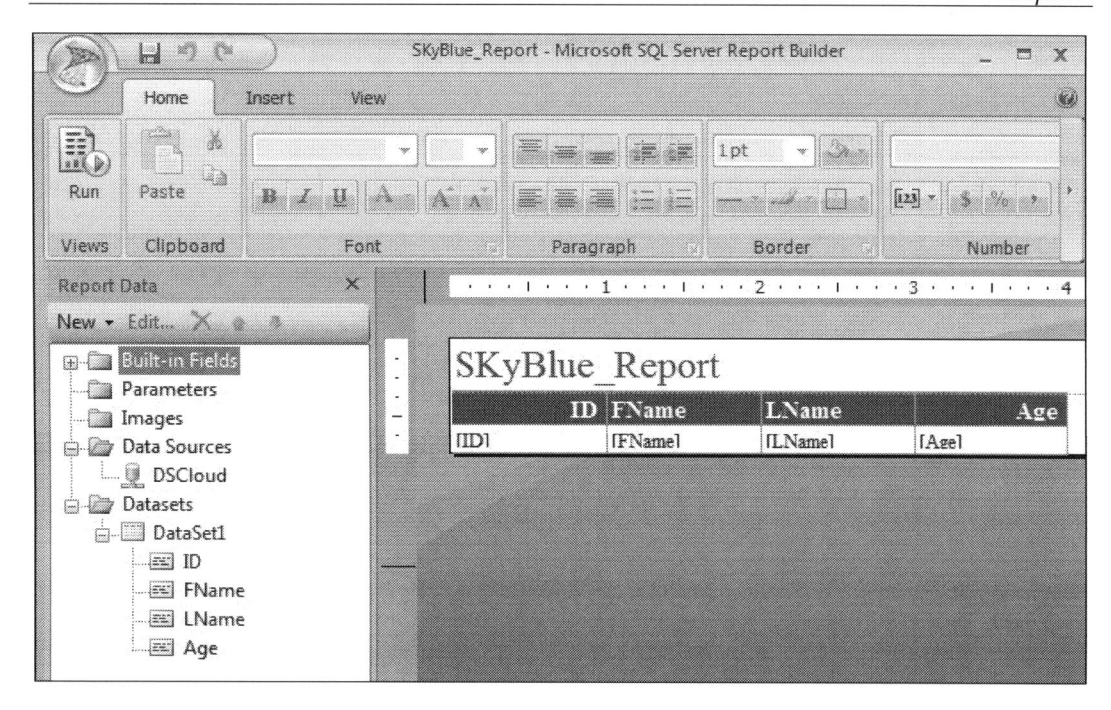

When you try to run the report, you will need to provide the credentials, after which it opens, as follows:

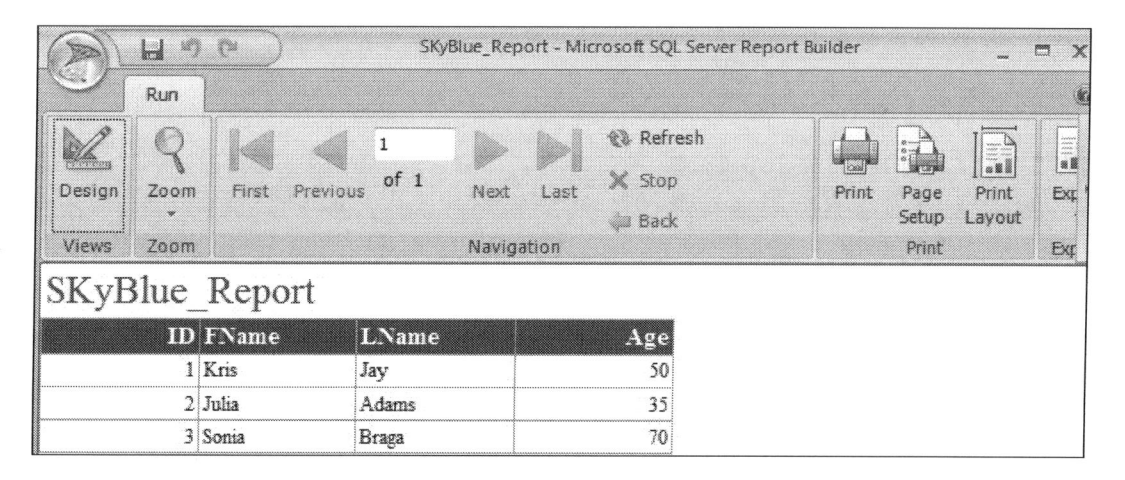

Making changes to the report and placing it on the Report Server

Report data and even the metadata may change over time. However, Report Builder as well as SSDT can make changes to the report and put it back on the Report Server. While using Windows Azure SQL Reporting, it is advisable to observe the following:

- As there are costs involved in storage, bandwidth, and hosting you will have to make the decision to optimize the data used in the reports as well as the uptime of the report on the server.
- Unless your business warrants it, locate all report-related items in the same data center (for example, the data center `Northeast`). This reduces the latency in report rendering, as well as better performance.
- Get only the data you need for the report to reduce traffic and storage.

Let us modify the preceding report by adding a column to the right of **Age**, and create an expression for that column, as shown in the following screenshot:

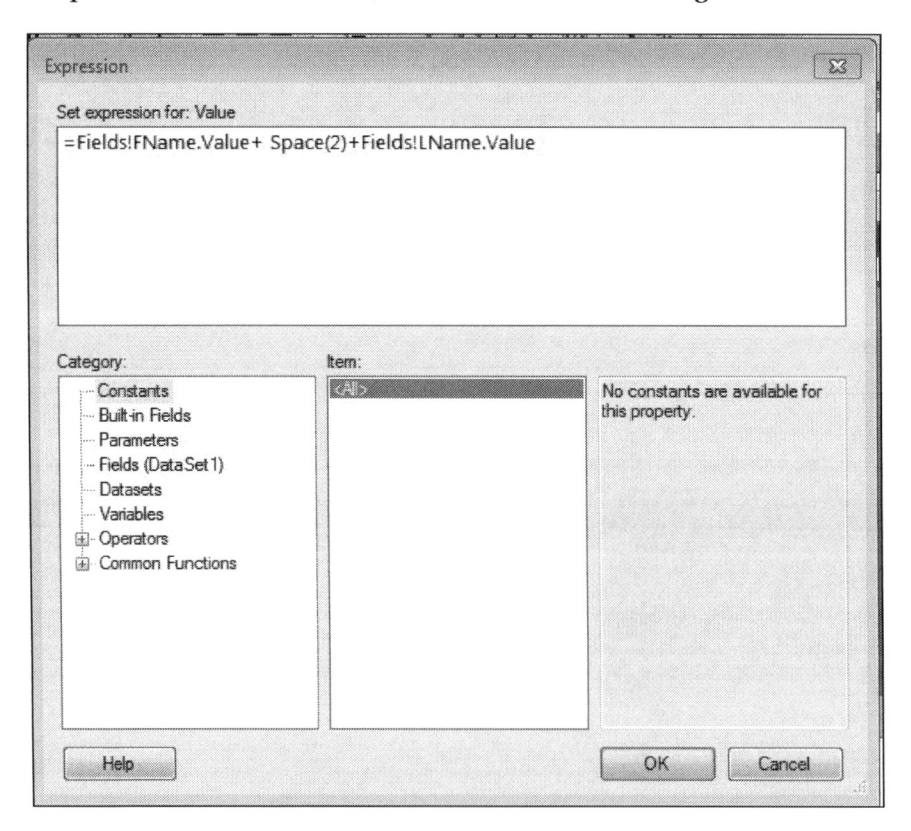

After the design change, if you run the report, you will see the following output:

SKyBlue_Report				
ID	FName	LName	Age	Full Name
1	Kris	Jay	50	Kris Jay
2	Julia	Adams	35	Julia Adams
3	Sonia	Braga	70	Sonia Braga

Now, you can save this back to the Report Server with a different name, as follows:

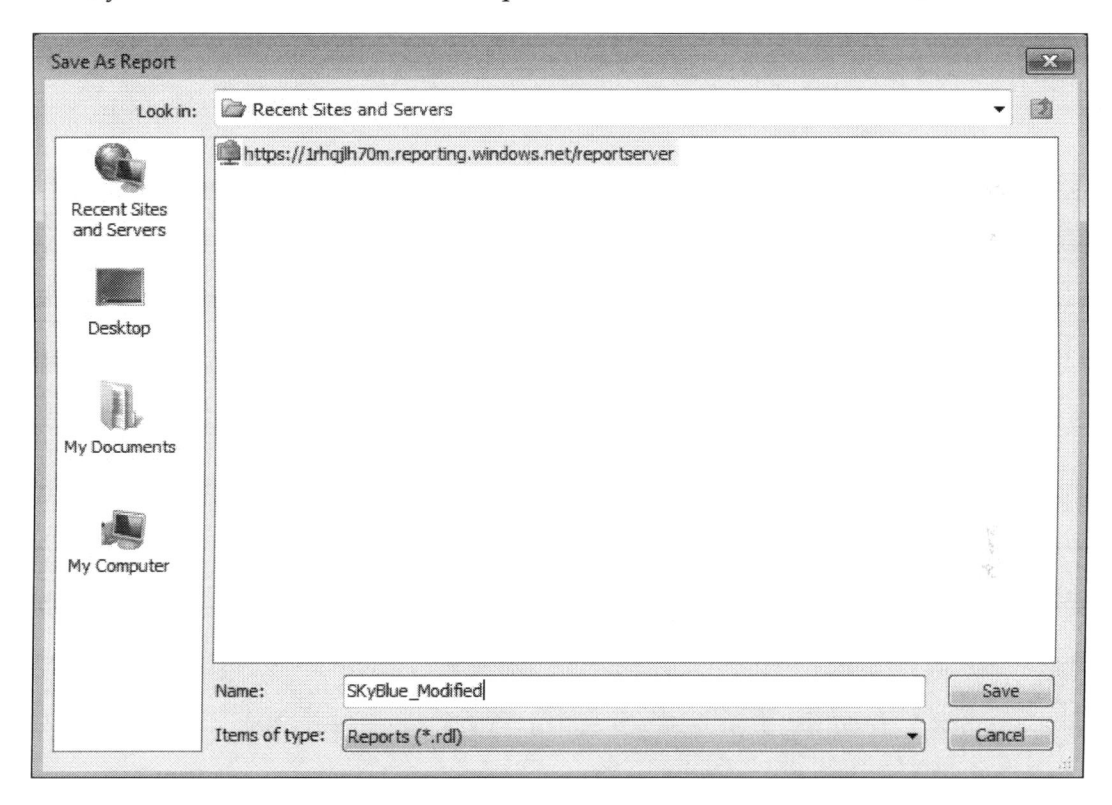

When this is saved, it can be accessed on the Report Server, as follows:

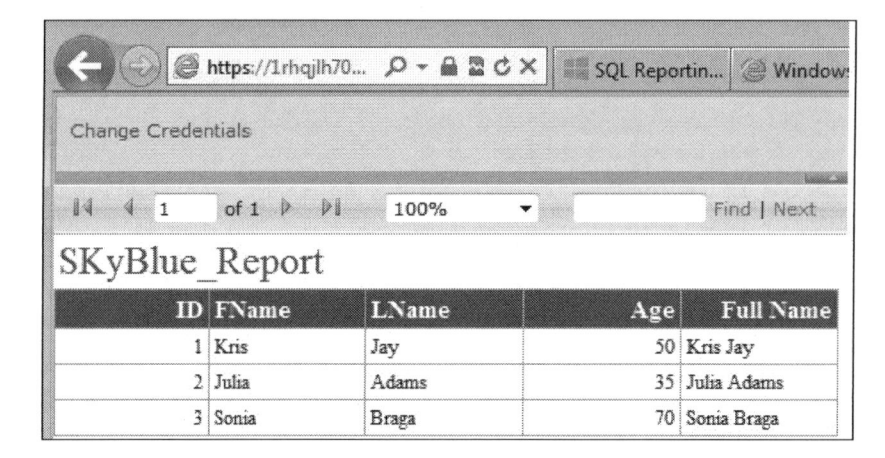

URL access to reports on the Report Server

Web Services URL is a convenient place to access your reports on the Report Server. *Chapter 10, Applications Accessing Report Servers*, describes a WPF application accessing the reports using a Web Browser control. In *Chapter 8, Reporting Services and Programming*, we see many examples of URL access.

Accessing the server and running a report

With the following steps, you can access the Report Server and run a report (display it):

1. Open a browser and enter (type in) the URL of the Report Server.
2. In the examples we have covered this, `https://1rhqjlh70m.reporting.net/Reportserver`.
3. In the **Windows Azure SQL Reporting Login** window, enter the credentials.
4. In the Web server, choose the folder that contains the report you wish to see.
5. Click on the report; you may need to enter credentials again.
6. The report will be displayed.

Do gadgets like indicators and data bars work?

The example report created is rather simple. However, complex reports built using Report Builder as in *Chapter 5, Working with Report Builder 3.0*, can easily create reports for Windows Azure SQL Reporting Services as well, as long as the limitations are duly accepted.

The datatypes (35 types including the spatial data types) are common to both SQL Server as well as the SQL Azure databases and the authoring tools are the same, and you do not need special skills to create a report for Windows Azure SQL Reporting.

The complexity of a report can arise out of interactivity that you want for the report, such as creating charts—use of gadgets, and interactive sorting. When you develop reports, you should look and verify whether the Cloud-hosted service renders them as well.

For example, data bar does not work. When rendered, data bars are replaced by plain text, whereas data indicators work as expected. In a simple test of the idea, the report was rendered as shown in the Report Builder. Note that the processing was on the Report Server:

SKyBlue_Report

ID	FName	LName		Full Name	
1	Kris	Jay	50	Kris Jay	○
2	Julia	Adams	35	Julia Adams	●
3	Sonia	Braga	70	Sonia Braga	●

While Windows Azure SQL Reporting has all the flexibility of reporting services, it still falls short of the capabilities that one finds in Reporting Services implemented in Native mode.

SQL Server 2012 Reporting Services – Known Issues

Like most software, SSRS 2012 is also a work in progress. The best source of information is to visit the *MSDN*(http://social.msdn.microsoft.com/Forums/en-US/category/windowsazureplatform)/*TECHNET*(http://social.technet.microsoft.com/Forums/en-US/ssdsgetstarted/threads) forums to see the issues and workarounds. These are some issues, but they will be fixed in future updates like in other software products:

- **Portal** is a very useful user interface for everything connected to Windows Azure, but at present, you can navigate to the root plus one level and no further. However, it can be done if you connect to an older version of the portal. Review the link on old/new portals at http://www.windowsazure.com/en-us/home/features/portals/.

- Testing for data source connectivity is not available in the new portal, but available in the older version of the portal. The new portal is still a work in progress!
- As compared to an on-premise hardware deployed report, a similar one on Windows Azure SQL Reporting is inferior in terms of performance.
- Unless optimized for the fastest possible rendering, reports that take more than four minutes to render may not complete when accessed by a URL or programmatically using SOAP endpoints.
- Atom feed document (.atomsvc) cannot be used in as a source for PowerPivot.
- There may be sort order problems in reports.
- There may be printing issues.
- Linked images cannot be used.
- Timeout problems while administering users.

Please make sure you look up this page for Known Issues related to this Windows Azure service at http://msdn.microsoft.com/en-us/library/windowsazure/hh667464.

> If you need an in-depth exposure to the SQL Azure platform, you need not go further than reading the author's hands-on book, *Microsoft SQL Azure: Enterprise Application Development*, ISBN 9781849680-80-6, Packt Publishing, 2010.

In the next hands-on exercise, we will learn the process of taking data from an on-premise SQL Server 2012 to Windows Azure SQL Database. This is meant for readers to begin creating reports immediately.

Hands-on exercise 9.4 – migrating a table on an on-premise SQL Server 2012 to the Windows Azure SQL database

It is assumed that you have created a SQL Azure Server instance, but have not created a table. It is also assumed that you are using data from your sample on the on-premise SQL Server 2012:

1. Access SSMS and connect to the SQL Server 2012 instance.
2. Click on **Tools** | **SQL Server Object Explorer** | **Scripting**.
3. Under **General scripting options**, change the option **for Script for database engine type** from default to **SQL Azure Database**.
4. Right-click on the table you want to take to Windows Azure and then click on **Tasks**.
5. Click on **Generate Scripts...** in the drop-down list.
6. In the **Generate and Publish Scripts** dialog box, read the introduction and choose **Objects** from the database you want.
7. In the **Set Scripting Options** page, click on the **Advanced** button after choosing a location for the script to be saved.
8. In the **Advanced Scripting Options** page, change the option **Schema only for Types of data to script** to **Schema and data**. Make sure you read the other options on the **Set scripting Options** page.
9. Click on **Next** or **Finish**.

The generated script file will be saved to the location of your choice in the previous screen. You can upload this file to the Windows Azure SQL database service (see the screenshot in step 1 of *the Creating a table for the report* section). Run the query in the portal (see the screenshot in step 1 of *the Creating a table for the report* section), and you will recreate the database (table) with data. You can now use this data to create reports.

This completes the hands-on to transfer sample table (database) to SQL Azure database.

Summary

Windows Azure SQL Reporting Service on the Windows Azure platform was described in considerable detail—how to start a subscription to the service: how to access the portal: how to create a SQL Azure database: once in the portal, how to create a table and populate it: and how to use it to create a report. Also discussed were many of the management tasks that one can undertake as well methods to view reports created on this server were described. The interaction of Report Builder, SSDT, and Visual Studio were also described.

In *Chapter 10, Applications Accessing Report Servers*, three applications that access the report server are described. Reports that need to be distributed may have to be displayed by using customized programs and *Chapter 10, Applications Accessing Report Servers*, shows some of the possibilities. The Windows Azure SQL Reporting services reports may be accessed from a hosted service by using ASP.NET or Windows Forms applications. While this is not described here, the readers may find examples in the author's book mentioned earlier. In this chapter, you will find the example of SharePoint Web parts accessing the Native mode report server, a Windows Presentation Foundation project accessing reports on report servers, and SQL Server Integration Services project accessing the Report Server.

10
Applications Accessing Report Servers

Reports on the Report Server are accessed by three methods namely, Report Viewer Controls, URL Access, and Report Manager.

In *Chapter 2, SQL Server Reporting Services 2012 Projects with Visual Studio 2012*, applications accessing Report Servers with Windows Forms applications and Web-facing applications using Report Viewer Controls were described. In *Chapter 8, Reporting Services and Programming*, the process of accessing reports using the URL was described. In *Chapter 4, Working with Report Manager*, Report Manager was described, which is a Web-based report access and administration frontend of the Report Server.

In this chapter, some examples of applications accessing reports on the Report Server are explored. All the examples involve one or the other of Microsoft programs. **SQL Server Reporting Services (SSRS)** reports can also be accessed from JAVA and RUBY applications and the easiest implementation is based on URL access. Another approach would be to use the Reporting Services APIs.

Extract, **Transform**, **Load** (**ETL**) is the first step in integrating data from different sources, which is then cleansed and a single version of data is created. This becomes the feed of reporting services to generate reports. ETL in Microsoft Technology takes the form of SQL Server Integration Services, another major **Business Intelligence** (**BI**) component of SQL Server. The first hands-on exercise shows how reporting services can be accessed using **SQL Server Integration Services** (**SSIS**) should a situation require calling up the service. In this example the Web Service Task, one of the tasks in the SSIS toolbox, is used.

Applications Accessing Report Servers

The second example uses the URL access method but instead of an ASP.NET application or HTML application looking up the URL, a **Windows Presentation Foundation (WPF)** application is described. A Web Browser control in the WPF application makes the URL access at runtime. The control is set to accept the URL that the user types in it and is not hard-coded. WPF application is similar to Windows application and it is declarative with rich styling and themes.

The third application is relevant when the Report Server is created in the SharePoint Integrated mode. It is as if the key feature of report creation and report viewing is transported to the SharePoint Site from where you can access the Native mode Report Server. You cannot only create reports using the Report Builder, which is called up by a link on the SharePoint Site, but they can also be viewed and the folders on the Report Manager can be traversed on the site.

Hands-on exercise 10.1 – accessing the Native mode Report Server using SSIS

In *Chapter 8, Reporting Services and Programming*, in *Hands-on exercise 8.8 – exploring Native mode Reporting Services*, we worked with the Report Server Web Services using Visual Studio. In this section, we will access the Report Server using a Web Service Task in a SSIS Package as follows:

1. Launch **SQL Server Data Tools (SSDT)** and create an SQL Server Integration Services Project using the template shown in the following screenshot:

2. Provide a name (**RS_Project**) for the project as shown in the following screenshot:

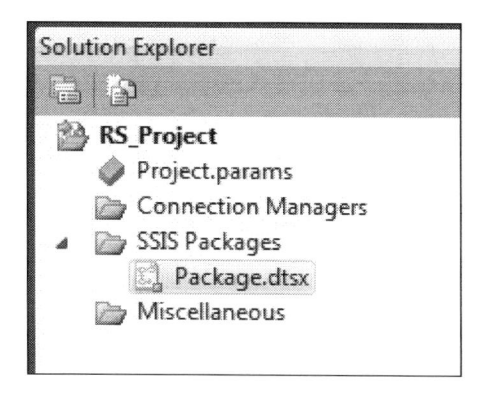

3. Click on the **Package.dtsx** tabbed page and it has several tabs. Click on the **SSIS Toolbox** toolbar item, which you will find on the extreme right.

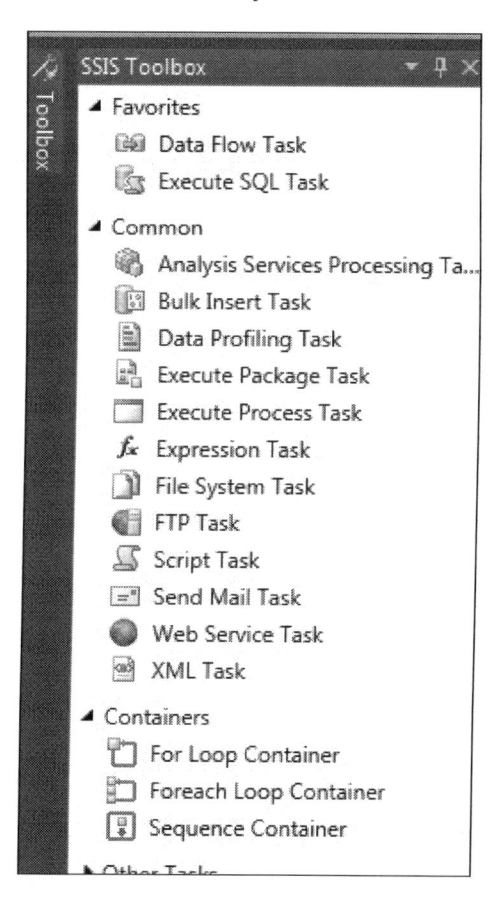

Applications Accessing Report Servers

4. Drag-and-drop the **Web Service Task** on to the **Control Tasks** pane as shown in the following screenshot:

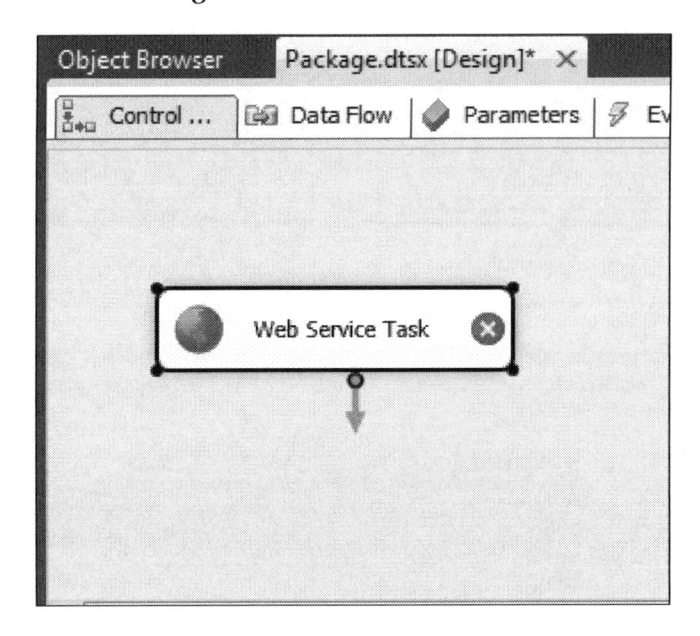

5. Right-click anywhere inside the **Web Service Task** and from the pop-up menu, click on **Edit**. The **Web Service Task Editor** will be displayed. The next screenshot shows the items to be configured to work with this task (the full window is not shown):

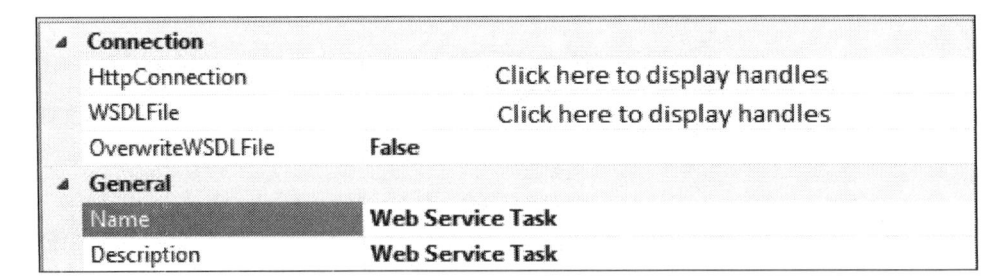

▲ Connection	
HttpConnection	Click here to display handles
WSDLFile	Click here to display handles
OverwriteWSDLFile	False
▲ General	
Name	Web Service Task
Description	Web Service Task

6. Click on the **HttpConnection** in the previous window to display the handles.
7. Click on the handle and then click on **<New Connection...>**.

8. In the **HTTP Connection Manager Editor** window that gets displayed, type in the details shown in the following screenshot:

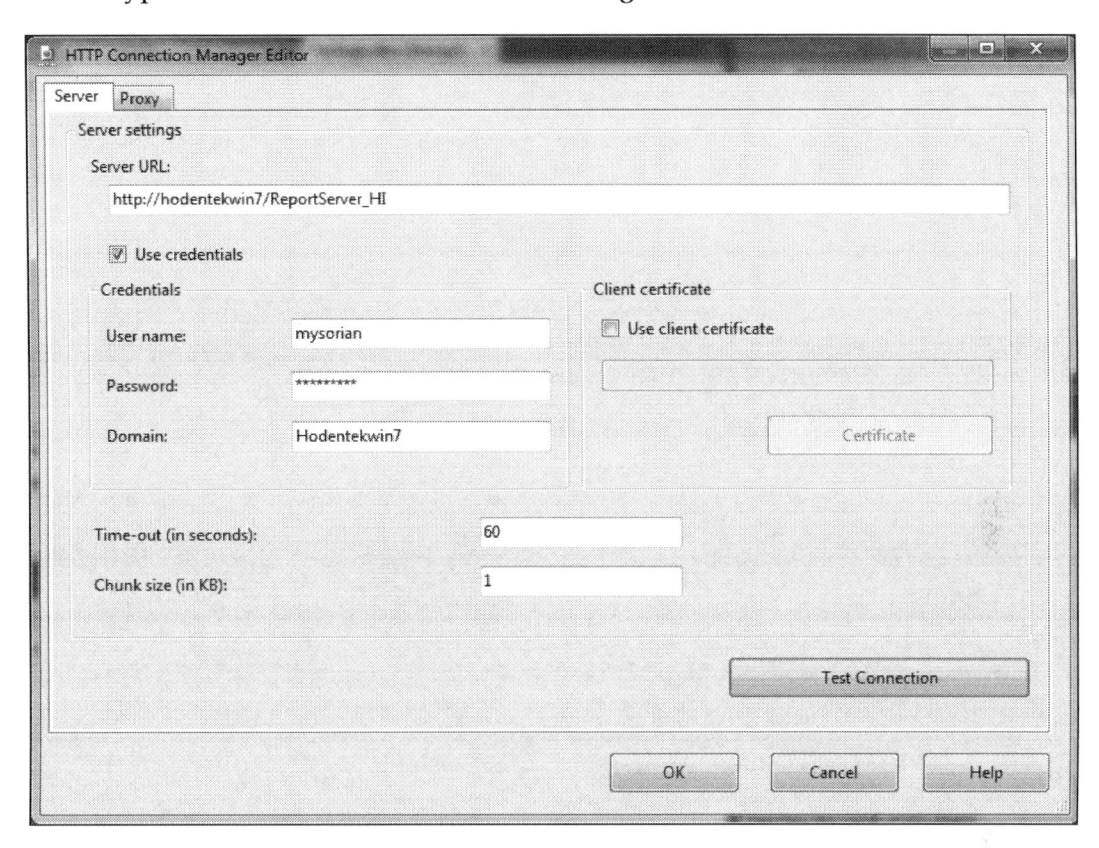

Default values were accepted for the others. The **Time-out** is connecting to the Web server, the default is supposed to be 30 sec (but it came out as 60 sec) and the **Chunk size** is writing a file and is 1 KB. Depending on the data to be written to the filesystem and the accessibility of the Report Server, one has to play with these numbers.

9. In the **Proxy** tabbed page fill in the details shown in the following screenshot:

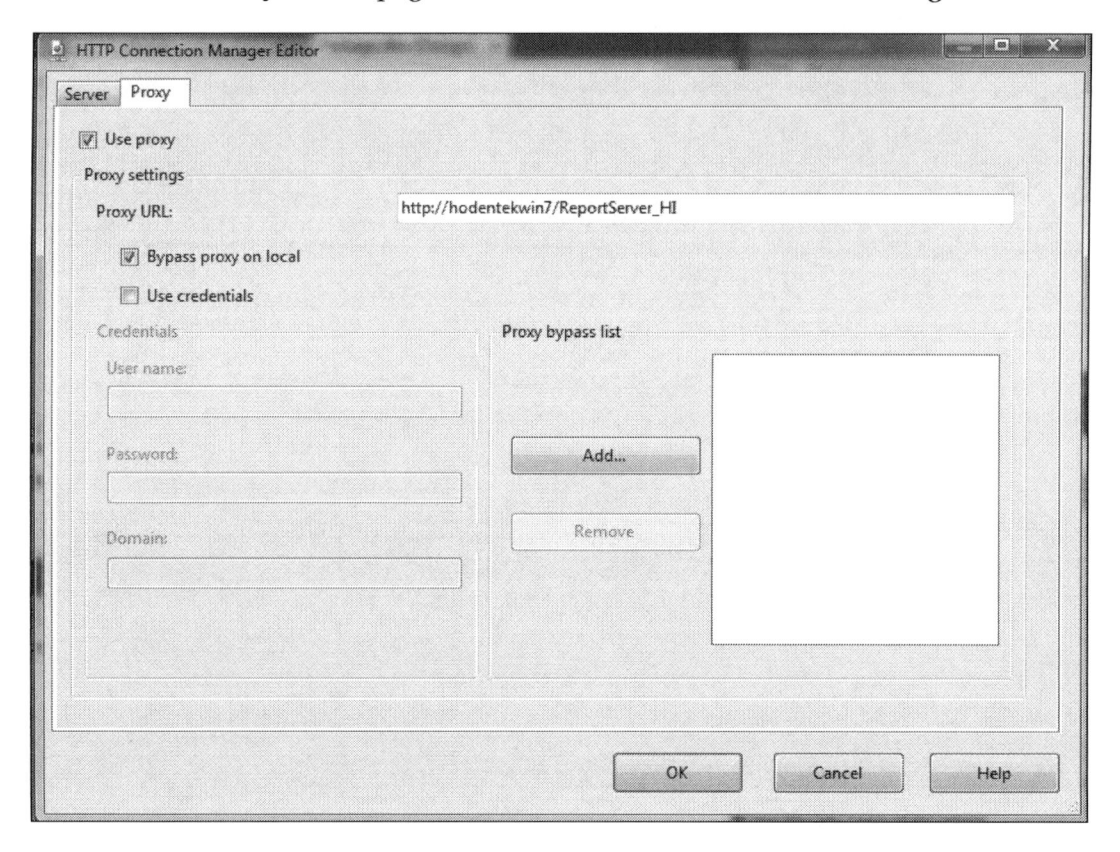

[HTTP Connection Manager Editor — Proxy tab: Use proxy checked; Proxy URL: http://hodentekwin7/ReportServer_HI; Bypass proxy on local checked; Use credentials unchecked]

10. Click on **OK**. In the bottom of **Control Flow** tabbed page of designer, a **HTTP Connection Manager** will be added to the **Connection Managers** tabbed pane.

A Web Service Task as we shall see soon requires not only a connection to the Report Server, but also a reference to the **Web Services Description Language (WSDL)** file, which describes the capabilities of the Web service. In this section we have just completed the connectivity to the Report Server. The WSDL file is created in the next section.

Creating the Report Server Web Service WSDL file

Perform the following steps:

1. Copy the display of `http://hodentekwin7/ReportServer_HI/ReportService2005.asmx` in the browser to a text editor such as Notepad.

   This should be an XML file.

2. Save the text file as `RsExec2005.wsdl`. The extension is important and make sure it is not saved as `.txt` file.

Providing the WSDL file to the Web Service Task

Perform the following steps:

1. On the **Web Service Task Editor** page, click on the ellipsis button (if it is not displayed click on an empty area in that textbox) along the WSDL file to provide the WSDL file you created by browsing to it as shown in the following screenshot:

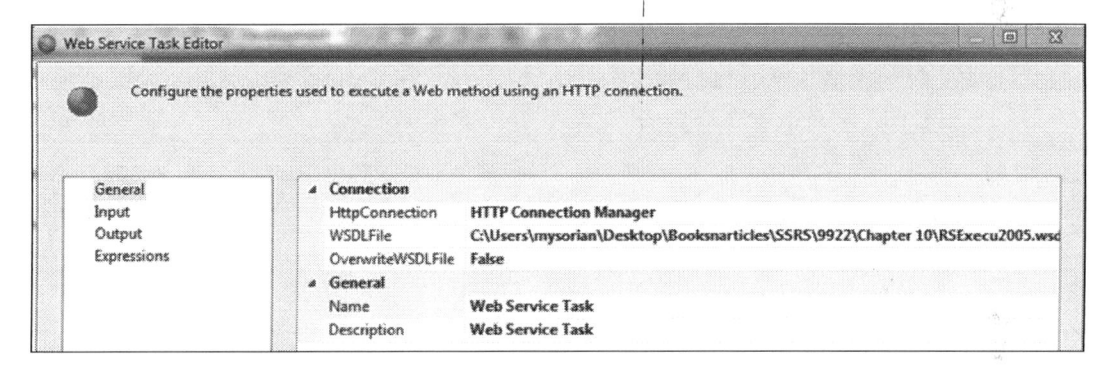

General	▲ **Connection**	
Input	HttpConnection	**HTTP Connection Manager**
Output	WSDLFile	C:\Users\mysorian\Desktop\Booksnarticles\SSRS\9922\Chapter 10\RSExecu2005.wsd
Expressions	OverwriteWSDLFile	False
	▲ **General**	
	Name	**Web Service Task**
	Description	**Web Service Task**

2. Click on **OK** at the bottom of the screen.
3. You have just finished configuring the **General** tabbed page of the Web Service Task.
4. Click on the **Input** tabbed page of the **Web Service Task Editor**.

5. On the **Input** page that is displayed, choose using handles that appear when you click on corresponding areas to configure as shown in the next screenshot. Of the many methods available in the dropdown, we are choosing the option to **ListRenderingExtensions** to get to view the rendering extensions in SQL Server 2012.

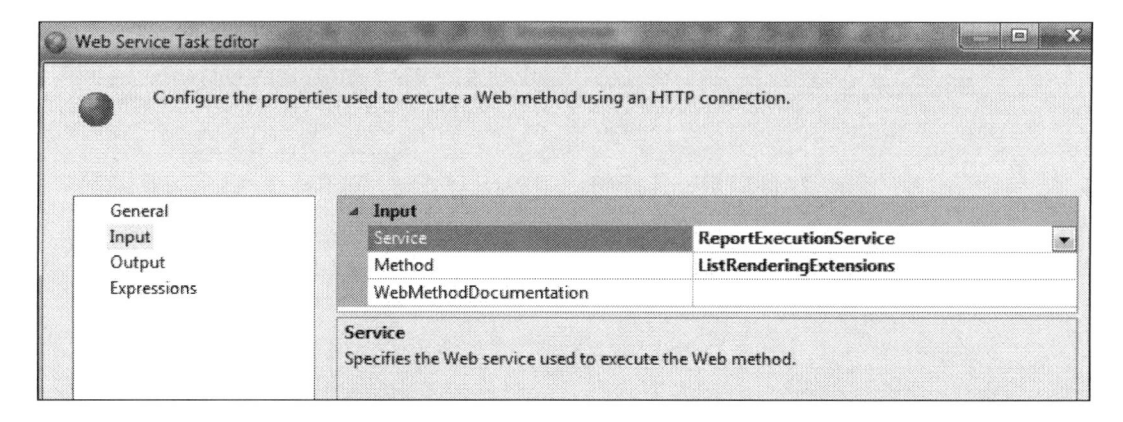

Web Service Task Editor

Configure the properties used to execute a Web method using an HTTP connection.

Service	ReportExecutionService
Method	ListRenderingExtensions
WebMethodDocumentation	

Service
Specifies the Web service used to execute the Web method.

6. Click on **Output** in the **Web Service Task Editor** to bring up the corresponding page of the **Web Service Task Editor** as shown in the following screenshot. Provide a name for the file.

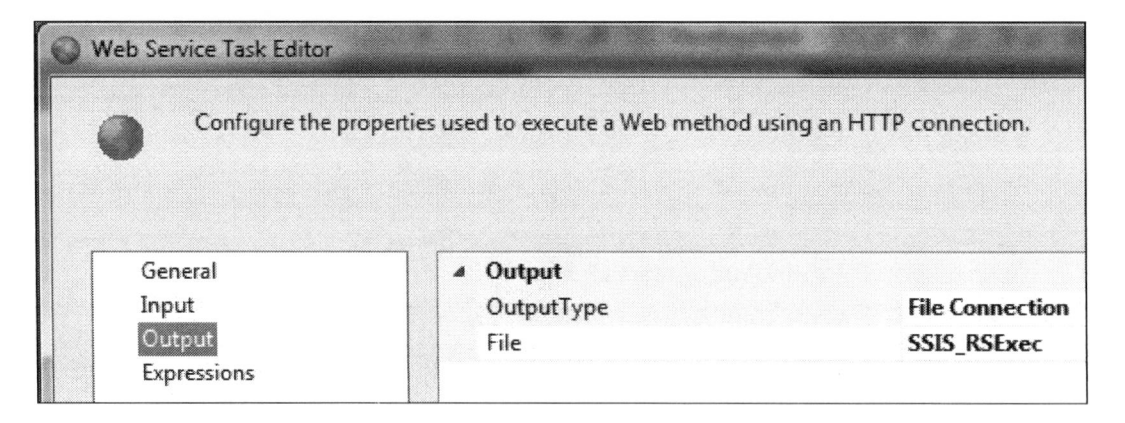

Web Service Task Editor

Configure the properties used to execute a Web method using an HTTP connection.

OutputType	**File Connection**
File	**SSIS_RSExec**

7. Click on **OK**.

The Web Service Task is now complete and it generates a file called `SSIS_RSExec`, which can be found in the `Projects` folder as well as in the Package Explorer of the SSIS Package.

[514]

Adding a File System Task to the Control Flow page

The result of running the Web Service Task will now be directed to the File System Task to create a file. First add a File System Task and perform the following steps:

1. Drag-and-drop a **File System Task** from **SSIS Toolbox** and drop it below the **Web Service Task** and extend the dangling green line to connect with the **File System Task**.

2. Double-click on the **File System Task** to display the **File System Task Editor** page which you will configure next.

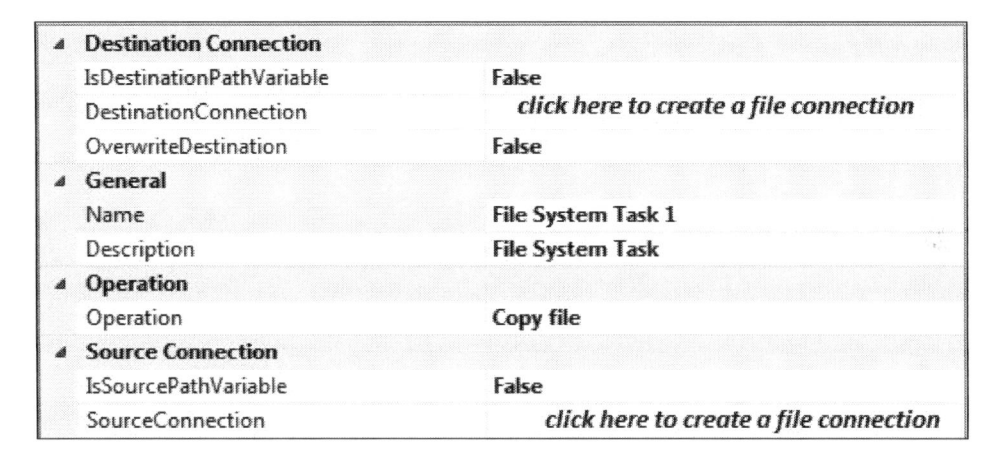

▲ **Destination Connection**	
IsDestinationPathVariable	False
DestinationConnection	*click here to create a file connection*
OverwriteDestination	False
▲ **General**	
Name	File System Task 1
Description	File System Task
▲ **Operation**	
Operation	Copy file
▲ **Source Connection**	
IsSourcePathVariable	False
SourceConnection	*click here to create a file connection*

3. Click on the area related to **DestinationConnection** and in the displayed page use the **Browse** button to locate a directory where you want the file to be saved as shown in the next screenshot. You need to provide a name for the file and it should be a **Create file** option as shown in the following screenshot:

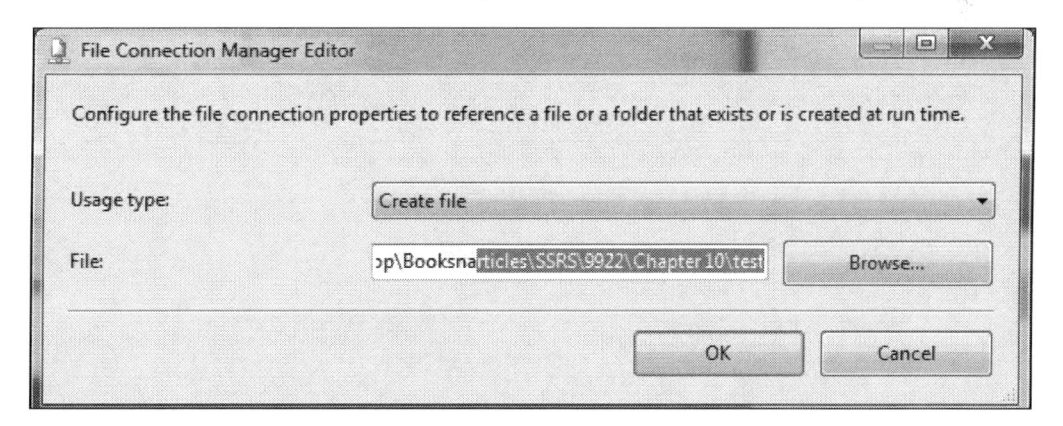

File Connection Manager Editor

Configure the file connection properties to reference a file or a folder that exists or is created at run time.

Usage type: Create file

File: op\Booksna rticles\SSRS\9922\Chapter 10\test   Browse...

OK   Cancel

4. Click on the area related to **SourceConnection**, browse to the `Projects` folder and locate the output file as shown in the next screenshot. (You will find the source location in the property window of the Web Service Task, herein `SSIS_RSExec`).

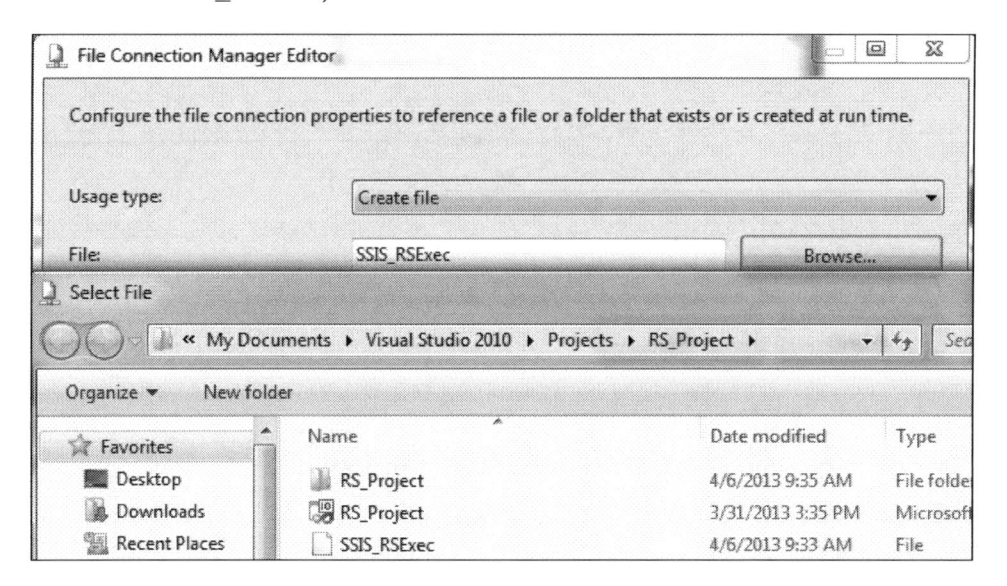

5. Build and run the project (right-click on **Package.dtsx** and choose **Execute Package**). After the processing of the project you will get a green signal as shown in the following figure, and if there are errors you will get a message. Depending on the message, you may have to take corrective measures.

> For example, it could be that the connection properties are not correctly set, the WSDL file is not found in the location indicated, and so on. Unless the errors are corrected the package may not execute.

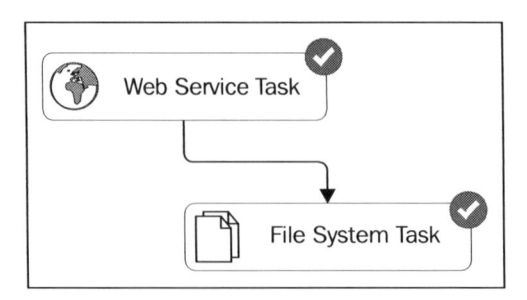

6. Locate the `test.txt` file in the destination folder and review the contents.

   The next code chunk shows the first few lines of this rather long file (`C:\Test.txt`).

   ```xml
   <?xml version="1.0" encoding="utf-16"?>
   <ArrayOfExtension
     xmlns:xsi="http://www.w3.org/2001/XMLSchema-instance"
     xmlns:xsd="http://www.w3.org/2001/XMLSchema">
     <Extension>
       <ExtensionType
         xmlns="http://schemas.microsoft.com/sqlserver/
         2005/06/30/reporting/reportingservices">Render
         </ExtensionType>
       <Name
   xmlns="http://schemas.microsoft.com/sqlserver/
         2005/06/30/reporting/reportingservices">XML</Name>
       <LocalizedName
         xmlns="http://schemas.microsoft.com/sqlserver/
         2005/06/30/reporting/reportingservices">XML file with
         report data</LocalizedName>
       <Visible
         xmlns="http://schemas.microsoft.com/sqlserver/
         2005/06/30/reporting/reportingservices">true
         </Visible>
       <IsModelGenerationSupported
         xmlns="http://schemas.microsoft.com/sqlserver/
         2005/06/30/reporting/reportingservices">false
         </IsModelGenerationSupported>
     </Extension>
   ```

> You can come up to speed rapidly on using SSIS with the Author's book published by Packt, *SQL Server Integration Services Using Visual Studio 2005*, ISBN:9781847193315, 2007.

Accessing reports from a Windows Presentation Foundations classes project

Windows projects entered a new phase with the introduction of **Windows Presentation Foundation (WPF)** classes. WPF applications use vector graphics (you zoom-in or zoom-out, the resolution does not get affected) much like Scalable Vector Graphics, which is resolution independent with crisp images. The use of **Extensible Markup Language (XML)** with highly developed tool and the Expression Studio now called Blend lends itself to creating highly interactive rich Internet applications.

Applications Accessing Report Servers

Regarding user experience, the WPF declarative language based tool is far ahead of the Windows Forms applications. The Presentation Core and Presentation Framework bring in innumerable class library support to make this possible. For more information, see the link `http://msdn.microsoft.com/en-us/library/bb546194(v=vs.90).aspx`.

In this section, we will create a WPF project and embed a Web Browser control. Hosting Web Browser control in an application makes it for in-situ linking of Web documents with the greatest ease as the control provides the ability to navigate a Web document, set up history, and help creating favorites in addition to rendering and parsing of HTML. Web Browser control is implemented through the `shdocvw.dll` and in turn hosts the `mshtml.dll` (rendering and parsing of HTML). Web Browser control is hosted in `IEXPLORE.EXE`, the internet explorer. Read more on this control at `http://msdn.microsoft.com/en-us/library/system.windows.controls.webbrowser.aspx`.

Hands-on exercise 10.2 – accessing Report Server URLs in a WPF project

We will create a WPF project and embed a Web Browser control as follows:

1. Launch Visual Studio 2010 Ultimate (or equivalent).
2. Click on **File** and then click on **New Project...**.
3. Click on **WPF Application** in the templates. Provide a name for the project, herein `WpfRep`.

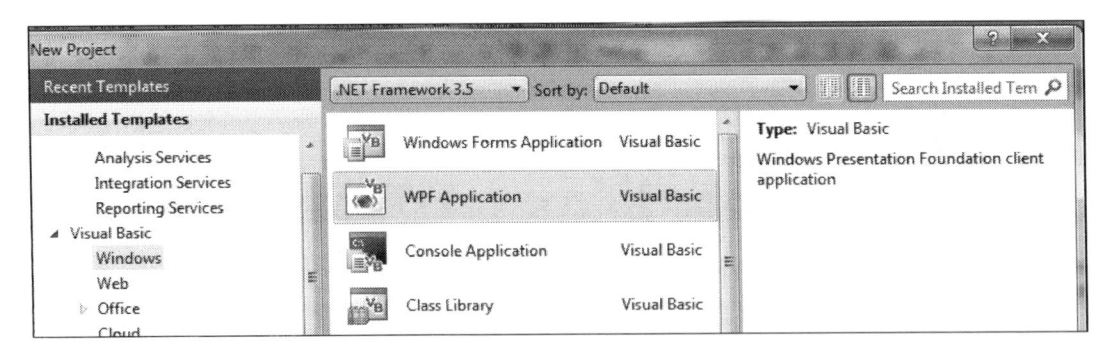

The project is created and you will find the project's folder as shown in the **Solution Explorer**.

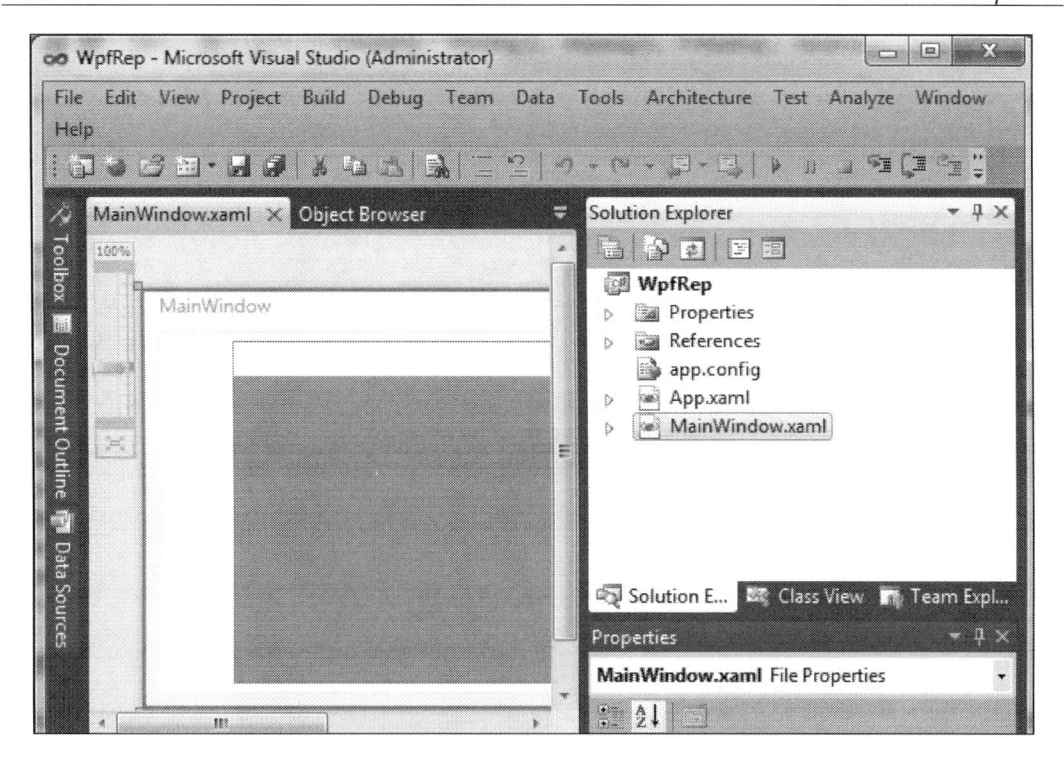

4. In the **Toolbox | All WPF Controls**, find **WebBrowser** as shown in the following screenshot:

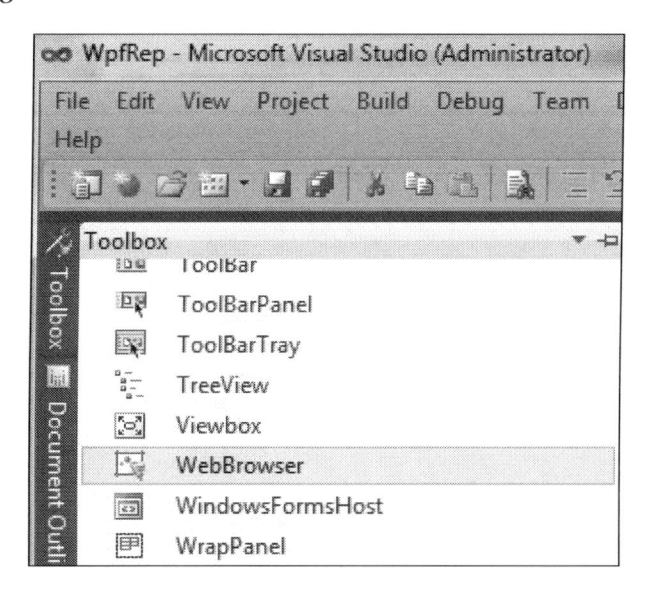

Applications Accessing Report Servers

5. Drag-and-drop the Web Browser control to the **Design** view of the **MainWindow.xaml** page as shown in the following screenshot:

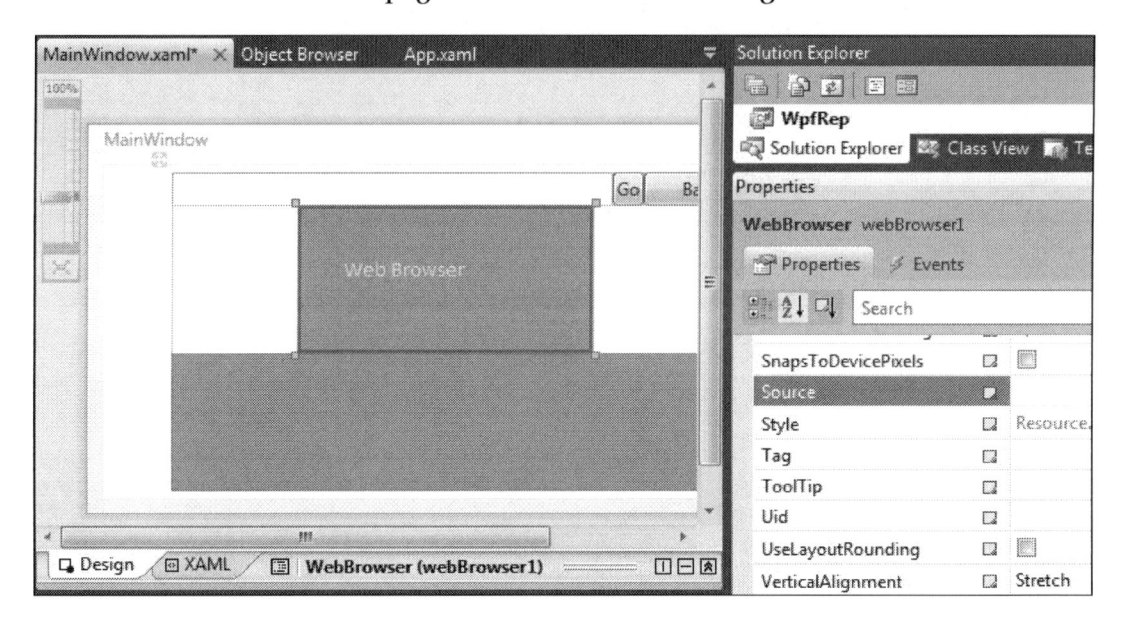

> The **MainWindow.xaml** presents a tabbed and split pane, which can display both the **Design** and **XAML** view of the design with an additional control that can interchange the **Design** and **XAML** views of the page.

Here is the XAML view of the design, which also shows two buttons and a textbox added to the design:

```
<Window x:Class="WpfRep.MainWindow"
  xmlns="http://schemas.microsoft.com/winfx/2006/
  xaml/presentation"
  xmlns:x="http://schemas.microsoft.com/winfx/2006/xaml"
  Title="MainWindow" mc:Ignorable="d"
  xmlns:d="http://schemas.microsoft.com/expression/blend/2008"
  xmlns:mc="http://schemas.openxmlformats.org/markup-compatibility
  /2006" Height="266" Width="488">
  <StackPanel Height="217" Width="374">
    <StackPanel Orientation="Horizontal">
      <TextBox x:Name="addressTextBox" Width="300" />
      <Button Click="goNavigateButton_Click">Go</Button>
      <Button Content="Back" Height="23" Name="button1" Width="75"
        Click="button1_Click" />
```

[520]

```
      </StackPanel>
      <WebBrowser Height="100" Name="webBrowser1" Width="200" />
      <WebBrowser x:Name="myWebBrowser" Width="640" Height="300"
        ToolTip="Requested URL"/>
    </StackPanel>
  </Window>
```

Some of the sizes of the objects have been set to get a reasonable display, but you may have to adjust them to the size of your screen. These can be incorporated into the XAML code or to the objects (Web browser, textbox, and the buttons) property windows.

> Using Property window is easier if you are not familiar with XAML. Right-click on an element and pick up a property to open its property window where you can make changes.

The textbox is where you will type-in the address of the Report Server, Report Manager, SharePoint Server site, or other URL.

We will be using the Web Browser's `Navigate ()` method to access the URL (Review the link `http://msdn.microsoft.com/en-us/library/system.windows.forms.webbrowser.navigate.aspx`).

> You can find the Web Browser's properties and methods in the **Object browser** as shown in the next screenshot:

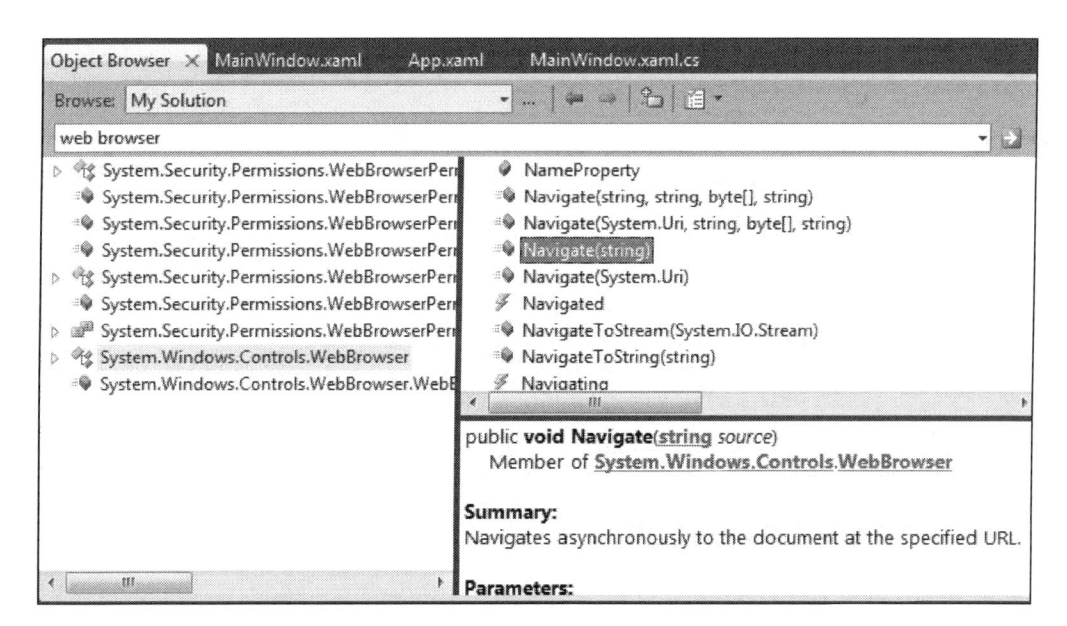

Applications Accessing Report Servers

You will be coding some basic functionality, but as you can notice from the rich properties and methods of this object, you can do a lot more.

The code you will be writing to the buttons' click events is actually taken from Microsoft's documentation for the `Navigate ()` method of the control. The code is put together to arrange for going back in history as well by adding code to the second button:

1. Double-click on the first button and paste the code so that the **Mainwindow.Xaml.cs** code page has the following code:

```
using System;
using System.Collections.Generic;
using System.Linq;
using System.Text;
using System.Windows;
using System.Windows.Controls;
using System.Windows.Data;
using System.Windows.Documents;
using System.Windows.Input;
using System.Windows.Media;
using System.Windows.Media.Imaging;
using System.Windows.Navigation;
using System.Windows.Shapes;

namespace WpfRep
{
  /// <summary>
  /// Interaction logic for MainWindow.xaml
  /// </summary>
  public partial class MainWindow : Window
  {
    public MainWindow()
    {
      InitializeComponent();
    }

    private void goNavigateButton_Click(object sender,
      RoutedEventArgs e)
    {
      // Get URI to navigate to
      Uri uri = new Uri(this.addressTextBox.Text,
        UriKind.RelativeOrAbsolute);
```

```
      // Only absolute URIs can be navigated to
      if (!uri.IsAbsoluteUri)
      {
        MessageBox.Show("The Address URI must be absolute eg
           'http://www.microsoft.com'");
        return;
      }
      // Navigate to the desired URL by calling the .Navigate
method
        this.myWebBrowser.Navigate(uri);
    }

    private void button1_Click(object sender, RoutedEventArgs e)
    {
      // Navigate to the previous HTML document, if there is one
      if (this.myWebBrowser.CanGoBack)
      {
        this.myWebBrowser.GoBack();
      }
    }
  }
}
```

2. Build the project and click on the **Start Debugging** (press *F5* key) button in the menu at the top.
3. The project runs and the following window forms will be displayed.

   A window with the title **MainWindow** will be displayed with a textbox (herein you write the URL of the Report Server, Report Manager, SharePoint Server, and so on) and two buttons, **Go** and **Back**.
4. Type in the URL of the Native Report Server and click on **GO**. The Report Server Site appears in the **MainWindow** as shown in the following screenshot:

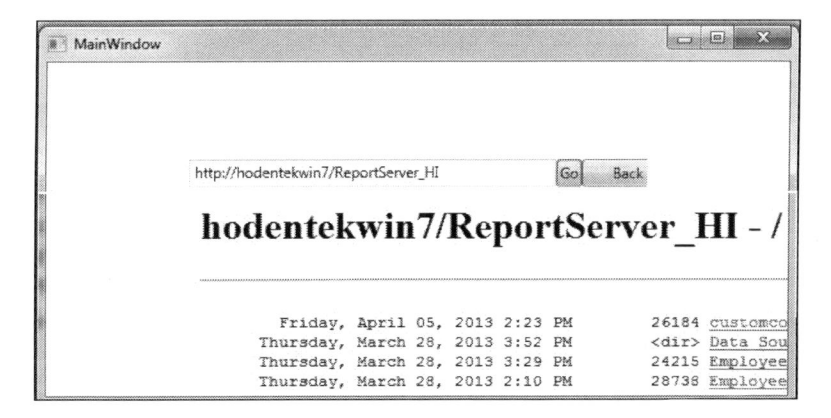

The same window can be used to view Report Manager and SharePoint Server as well.

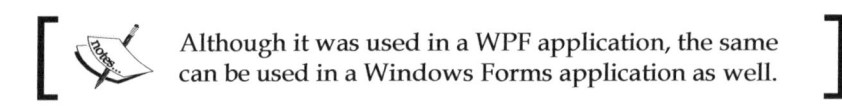

> Although it was used in a WPF application, the same can be used in a Windows Forms application as well.

Accessing Native Report Server reports from SharePoint Web parts

Report Explorer and Report Viewer have long history going back to the SQL Server 2000 Reporting Services service. It is also available in the SQL Server 2012 version. These Web parts will be useful if you want to bring up reports on the Native Mode Report Server in a SharePoint Site. The reports can be viewed and the Report Server hierarchy can be traversed using these Web parts.

Report Explorer (SPExplore.dwp) connects to the Report Manager of the Native mode Report Server. The Report Explorer shows the contents of the Report Manager URL. If you have permissions to Report Builder (as Administrator you already have) you can launch Report Builder as well from Report Explorer. The Report Explorer provides the HTML viewer with some of the toolbar controls.

Report Viewer (SPViewer.dwp) displays the report and all the associated controls to work with reports.

It is assumed that all of the following requisites are available (*Chapter 1, Overview and Installation – SQL Server Reporting Services 2012*) to work with these Web parts:

- The Report Server installed in Native mode (Report Server HI or Report Server Kailua in this book) and Report Manager enabled
- SharePoint Server 2010

Hands-on exercise 10.3 – viewing reports on the Native mode Report Server using SharePoint Web parts

In order to work with the Web parts they must first be installed. When you install SQL Server, the Web parts are installed as RsWebParts.cab (24 KB) file as shown in the directory C:\Program Files (x86)\Microsoft SQL Server\110\Tools\Reporting Services\SharePoint

You can install them using Power Shell or through command lines as follows:

1. Bring up the Power Shell prompt (refer to section on Power Shell in *Chapter 8, Reporting Services and Programming*) and run the following command:

   ```
   Install-SPWebPartPack -LiteralPath "C:\Program Files
       (x86)\Microsoft SQL Server\110\Tools\Reporting
       Services\SharePoint\RSWebParts.cab" -GlobalInstall
   ```

2. For the question, **Are you sure you want to perform this action**, click on **Yes**.

Another method is to use `STSADM.exe` found at `%CommonProgramFiles(x86)\Microsoft Shared\Web Server Extensions\14\BIN`.

Accessing the Web parts

The Web parts will be available on the SharePoint Site. Perform the following steps:

1. Open the site at `http://hodentekwin7` (this is not the Central Administration site, but a site installed for keeping Report Server reports).
2. Click on **Site Actions** (top-left) and click on **Edit a page**. The page sections of the ribbon are displayed.
3. Click on **Add a Web Part** and click on **Miscellaneous** category item as shown in the following screenshot:

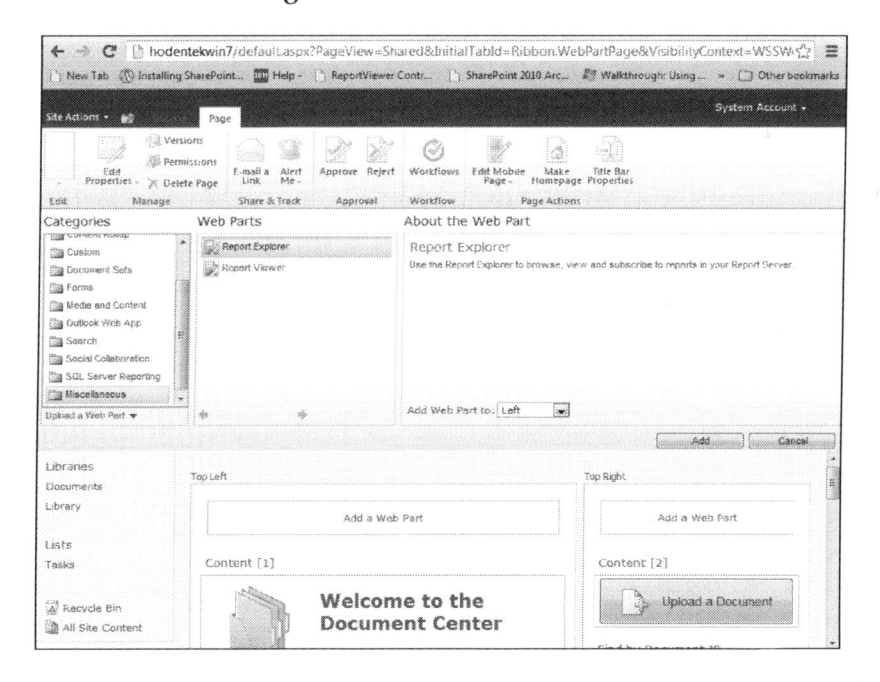

Applications Accessing Report Servers

Notice that the two Web parts mentioned earlier are both available.

4. Click on **Report Viewer** and click on Add. **Report Viewer** is added to the left section as shown in the following screenshot:

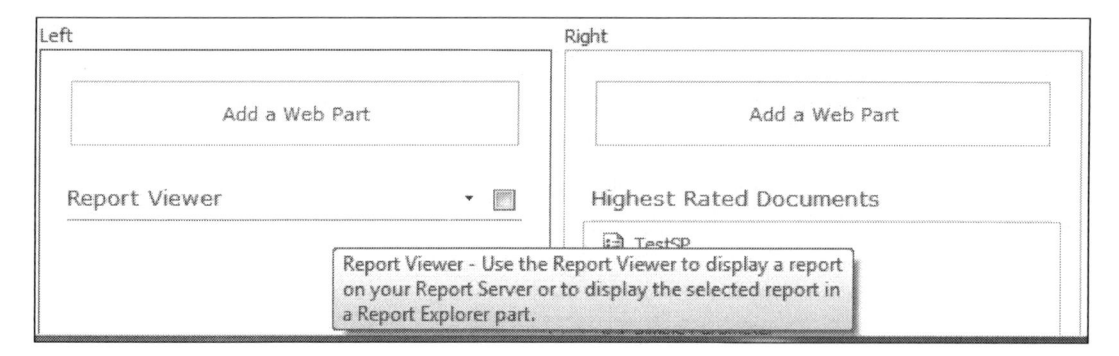

5. Click on the **Report Viewer** handle and click on **Edit Web Part**.

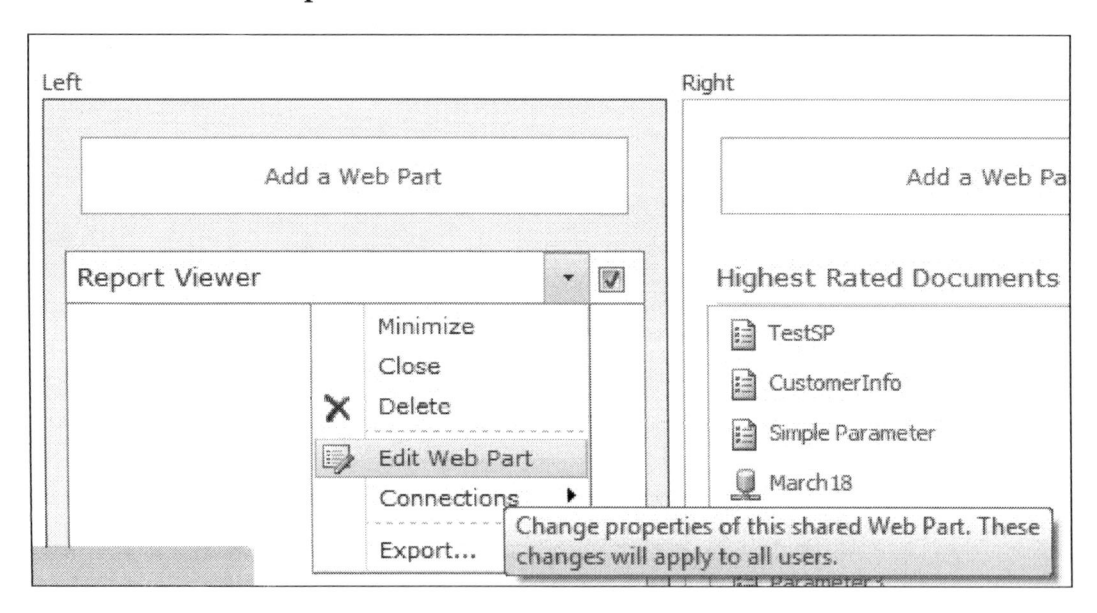

The **Report Viewer** edit page is displayed as shown in the following screenshot:

6. Enter the Report Manager URL and the report path to one of the reports (**Shadow Simple**) on the Report Manager in the following screenshot:

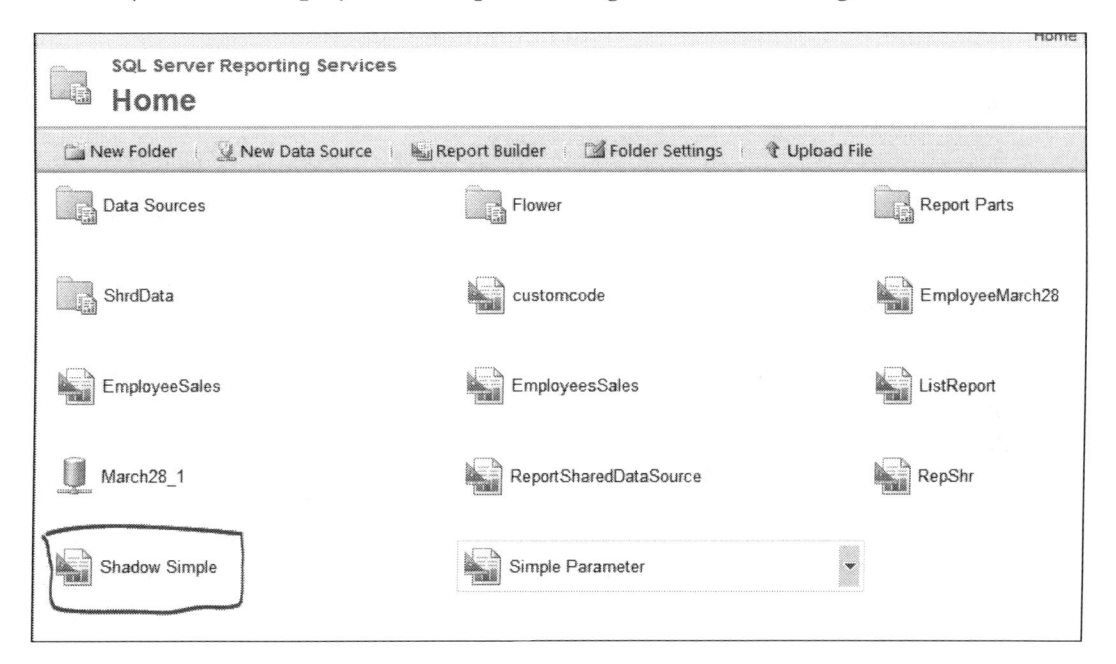

Applications Accessing Report Servers

7. Specifically enter the path to the report **Shadow Sample** on Report Manager as shown in the following screenshot:

8. After typing in the information shown in the previous screenshot, click on **Apply** and then click on **OK**. The report appears as shown in the **Report Viewer Web** Part.

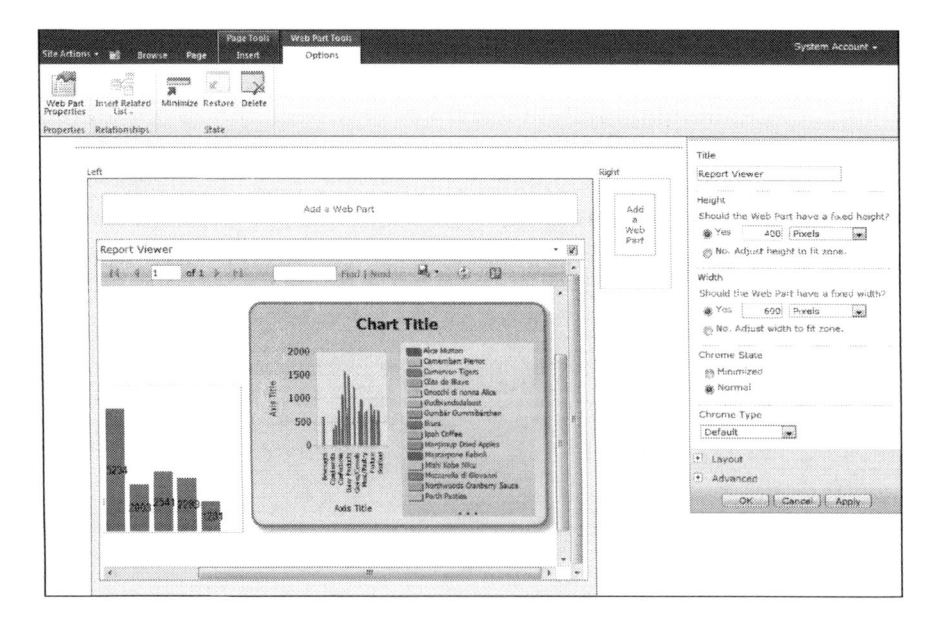

[528]

Chapter 10

9. In the **Top Left**, click on **Add Web Part** and again from the **Miscellaneous** category, locate **Report Explorer** as shown in the following screenshot:

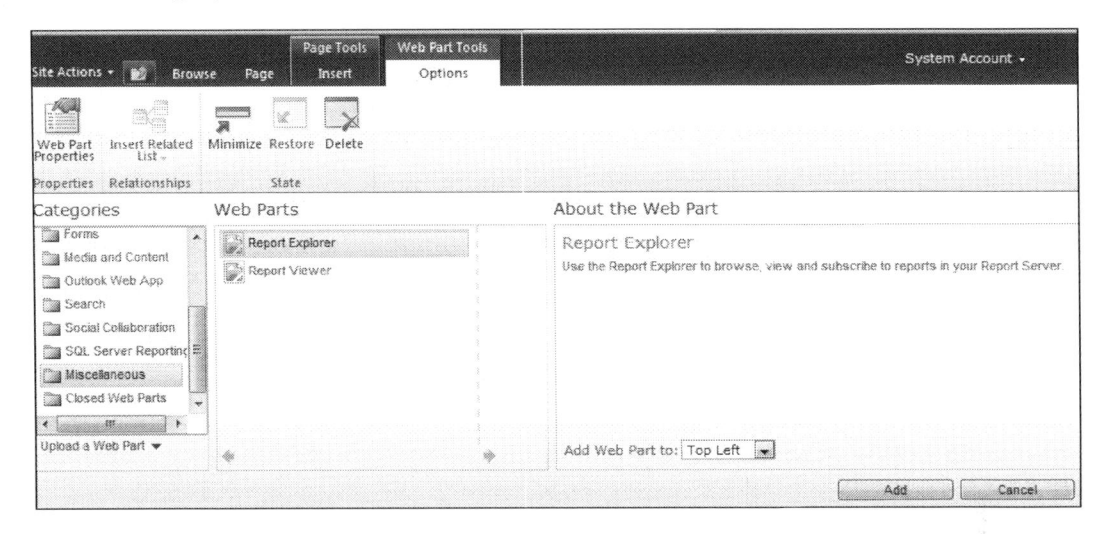

10. Click on **Report Explorer** and click on **Add**. The **Report Explorer** will be added to the **Top Left** as shown in the following screenshot:

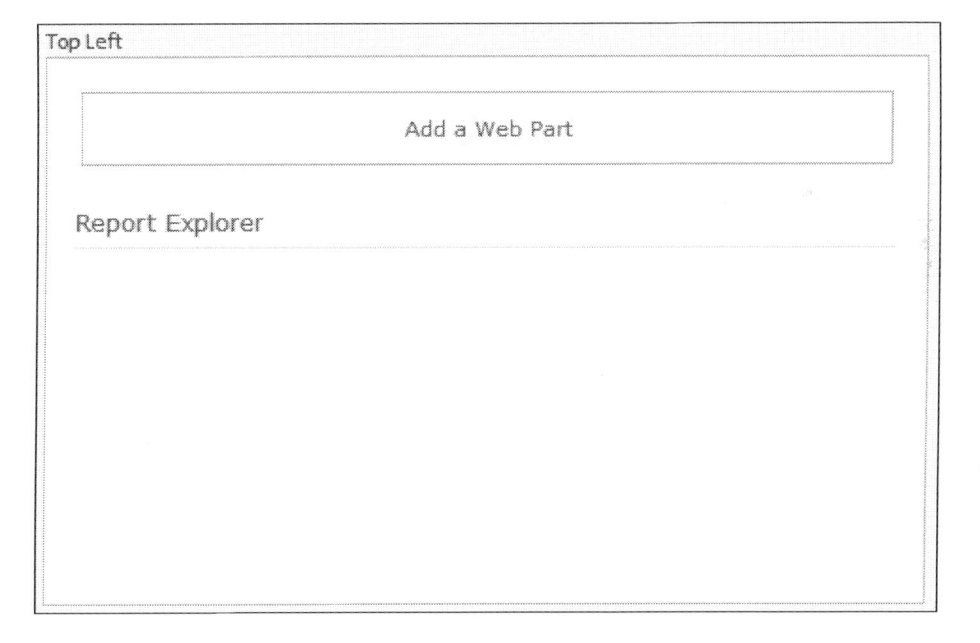

Applications Accessing Report Servers

11. Click on the handle for **Report Explorer** to bring up the menu as shown in the following screenshot:

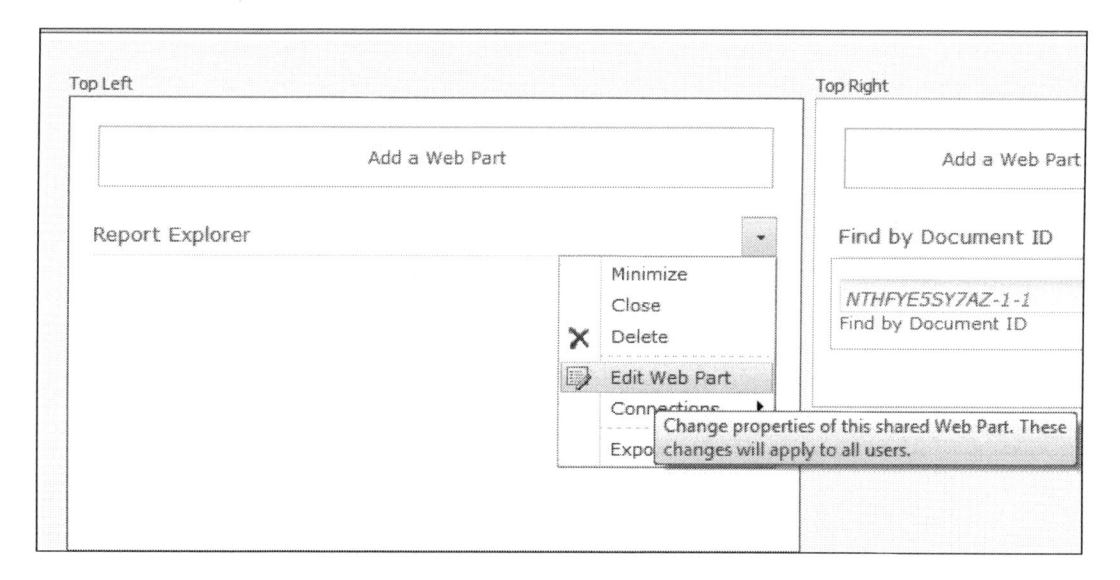

12. Click on **Edit Web Part**.
13. **Report Explorer** window is displayed on the extreme right as shown in the following screenshot:

14. Enter **Report Manager URL** and **Start Path** (herein **Home**) as shown in the following screenshot. Also choose **List** for **View Mode**.

15. Click on **OK**. The **Home** page of Report Manager appears as shown in the following screenshot:

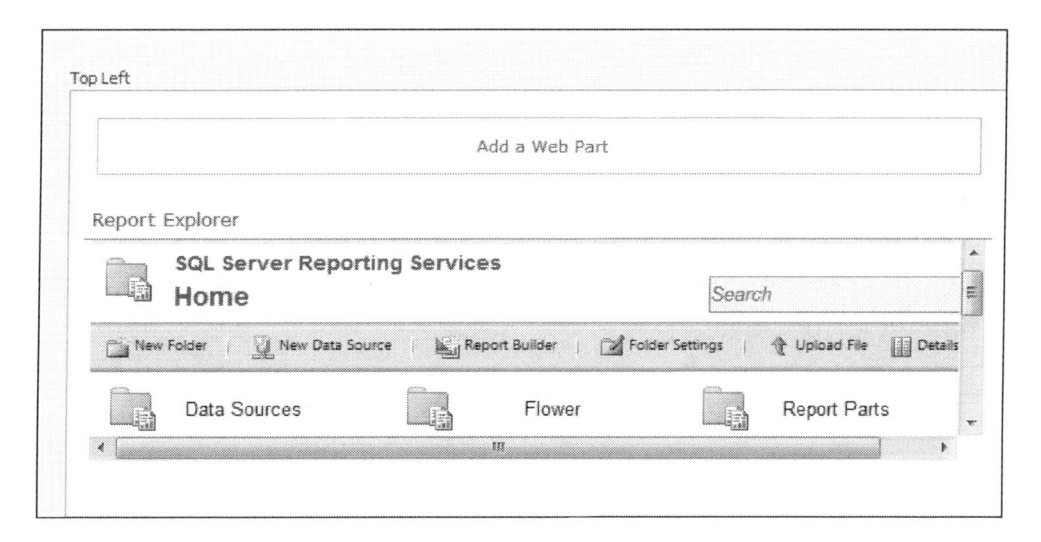

16. Click on **Report Builder** in the **Report Explorer** and verify that it can launch the Report Builder.

Summary

In this chapter, we looked at accessing Report Servers from three different kinds of applications, namely, SSIS, WPF Application, and SharePoint Site. SQL Server Integration Services can be used to look at Report Servers using the Web Service Task but still some of the parts are hard to configure. The Windows Presentation Foundation class project as well as the Windows Forms project can make use of a Web Browser control to access Report Servers useful for developers desiring to integrate reports with desktop/Web applications. Finally, reports on a Native mode Report Server can be brought into folder, traversed and viewed by using SharePoint Web parts, the Report Explorer, and the Report Viewer.

While SQL Server 2012 marked the beginning of Reporting Services 2012 integration with SharePoint 2010, there are still many folks using the SQL Server 2008 R2. The reporting services integration for those servers works differently from that of SQL Server 2012. With the release of SQL Server 2012 SP1 and the SharePoint 2013, reporting services gets turbocharged especially for Power View.

In conclusion, the book provides a complete reference to SSRS 2012 covering both modes of implementation, Native and SharePoint Integrated mode. In the introductory chapters, the installation, configuration of SQL Server 2012, the SharePoint 2010, and the sample databases are covered followed by details of reporting services Native mode components and report authoring tools, the Report Builder 3.0, and the SSDT. Creating reports using the tools and managing the reports from the Report Manager frontend is covered, all of which by way of exercises the users can run through guided by numerous screenshots. Two new features that were introduced with RS 2012 with SharePoint Integration, namely Power View and self service Data Alerts, are covered in two separate chapters, *Chapter 6*, *Power View and Reporting Services* and *Chapter 7*, *Self-Service Data Alerts in SSRS 2012*. Configuring RS in SharePoint Integrated mode using Power Shell, including a section on *Power Shell* as a tool, are described. Programmatic access to reporting services, cloud-based Windows Azure SQL Reporting, application access to reports using SSIS, WPF, and SharePoint Web Parts accessing Native mode reporting services completes the picture.

Index

Symbols

@CategoriesCategoryID parameter 269

A

Advanced... button 44
advanced filtering techniques 365
AlwaysOn Failover Cluster 10
AlwaysOn feature 10
authentication
  about 166, 169
  Custom type 169
  RSWindowsBasic type 168
  RSWindowsKerberos type 168
  RSWindowsNegotiate type 167
  RSWindowsNTLM type 167
authorization
  about 170
  Browser Role 170
  Content Manager Role 170
  My Reports Role 170
  Publisher Role 170
  Report Builder Role 170
  System Administrator Role 170
  System User Role 170

B

BI 11, 73, 507
BIDS 73, 463
BISM 11, 75, 326
Browse button 318
bubble charts 366
BUILTIN\Administrators 195
Business Intelligence. *See* BI
Business Intelligence Development Studio.
  See BIDS
Business Intelligence Semantic Model.
  See BISM

C

card 360
CatSales 318
Chart Tools option 356
Cloud service (mysorian) 468
collation 28
configuration file modifications,
      in native mode
  about 143
  Report Manager, on/off action 145
  Report Server Web service, on/off
      actions 144, 145
  scheduled events, on/off actions 145
Connect to Report Server window 320, 387
custom code
  incorporating, into reports 458-460

D

data
  displaying, as card 360-362
  highlighting 360
Data Alert Designer
  data alert, creating 394-398
Data Alerts
  about 373
  creating 393
  creating, in Data Alert Designer 394
  editing 398-402
  requirements 373, 374

starting with 374-376
working with, permission grant 377, 378, 384, 385
Data Alerts. Power View 11
Data Analysis Expression. *See* **DAX**
data-driven report subscription
creating 229-237
Subscribers database, creating in SQL Server 230
table, populating in Subscribers database 230
Data Manager window 398
data source
creating, model as source used 347-349
Data Source Properties page 260, 309
DAX 337
default field set 337
Distributed Replay tool 10
document map
adding, to report 280
drill-down report
about 288
creating 289, 290
drill-through report
about 285
action, setting up 287, 288
creating 285
destination report 286
source report 285
DSP 411
DSU 411

E

Edit Data Alert window 400
Edit Role Assignment page 200
ErrorLevel property 157
ETL 507
Extensible Markup Language. *See* **XML**
Extract, Transform, Load. *See* **ETL**

F

Feature Selection page 24
features, Reporting Services 2012
about 147
report authoring tools 174

report content management tools 174
report customization 154
report definition 148
report, deploying 155
Reporting Services extensions 172
Reporting Services tools 173
report part reusability 153
report, saving 155
Report Server administration tools 173
reports, managing 158
reports, viewing 157
report validation 156
RS2012 SharePoint Integrated 162
security implementation 166
URL access 171
files, downloading from Report Server to file system
about 217
on computer 217
report definition file, downloading 218-220
report definition file, reviewing 218-220
steps 217, 218
Find tool 211
folder
creating 185-189
deleting 185
item, moving into 190, 191
navigating 186
subfolder, creating 187-189
foreign key 288
FromSSDT-OrderDetails report 218

G

Geographic Information System. *See* **GIS**
Getting Started screen 270
GIS 158
group
adding, to data 277-279
setting up 276
Group Properties windows 281

H

hardware
configuration 17

hardware requirements
  data file storage 16
  DVD drive 16
  hard disk space requirement 16
  memory 16
  monitor and pointing device 16
  processor speed 16
  processor type for a 64-bit processor 16
HighTemp indicators 306
Home page 531
HTTP Connection Manager Editor window 511

I

indicators
  about 304
  used, for report creation 304-306
item-level roles 180
ITEMS menu 488

K

Key Performance Indicator. *See* **KPI**
KPI 339

L

linked reports
  about 291
  creating 291, 292
  creating, in France folder 292
Local Mode 100

M

MainWindow.xaml 520
Management Endpoints 422
Manage Report History 242
Manage Reporting Services Application page 70
master database 378
measures
  about 339
  adding 339
Microsoft Report Viewer Runtime
  2008 129
  2010 129
  2010 SP1 129
  2012 129
  about 129
Microsoft SQL Server Data Tools-Database projects 76
model
  deploying 340
MSDN 503

N

Native mode installation
  major components 134, 135
Native mode Reporting Services
  exploring 441
  Native mode report server 441, 442
  server configuration 442, 443
  Windows Forms ReportViewer, supported extensions 444
  Windows Management Instrumentation 445
Native mode Report Server
  about 410, 411
  accessing, SSIS used 508-512
  access permission, to WMI 446-448
  actions 410
  data source content, accessing 413
  exploring 446
  folder contents, listing 412
  report part component, accessing 412
  report, rendering 413
  report rendering, with report parameter 414
  report server, accessing 411
  supported formats, exporting 414
Native mode Report Server access
  File System Task, adding to Control Flow page 515, 516
  Report Server web service WSDL file, creating 513
  WSDL file, providing to Web Service Task 513, 514
Native Report Server reports
  accessing, from SharePoint web parts 524
  report viewing, SharePoint web parts used 524

Navigate () method 522
New Role Assignment page 197

O

Office Open XML 248
Operating System (OS) 194
operating system requirements (64-bit) 15

P

parameter
  removing 276, 277
parameterized reports 267
permission
  granting, to report 389
  updating, ways 377-385
PowerShell
  about 434
  and Native mode Reporting
      Services 2010 441
  basic review 435-437
  Native mode Report Server, exploring 446
  reporting services , exploring in SharePoint
      Integrated mode 438
  reporting services, with SharePoint
      Integration 437, 438
  Report Server properties, WMI used 448, 451
  using, for log file review 404
Power View
  about 325, 326
  creating 344
  data source creation, using model as
      source 347-349
  development environment, points 327
  model, connecting to 347
  report creation, data source used 349, 350
  report, exploring 350
  resources 326, 327
Power View report
  advanced filtering techniques 365
  animation 368, 369
  authoring, need for 327
  bubble chart 366-368
  data, displaying as card 360-362
  data, highlighting 360

  data, slicing 363, 364
  exploring 350, 351
  first view, creating 351-354
  refresh button 370
  sales order shipped chart,
      modifying 355-357
  save button 370
  saving, to Saving to PowerPoint 371
  scatter chart 366-368
  second view, adding 357-360
  tiles, using 362
  undo button 370
  views, navigating 370
primary key 288
programming interfaces
  overview 409
Project RSPW2012
  report, modifying 96-99
Publish Report Parts window 316

R

RDLC
  converting, to RDL file 123-128
Reading Mode 371
Remote Mode 100
Remove Field 354
report
  bringing up 276, 277
  control, granting to user 390-393
  creating 150, 385
  creating, embedded data source
      used 249-259
  creating, from shared data source 259-263
  creating, indicators used 304
  creating, in Report Builder 386-389
  creating, Report Server Project Wizard
      used 79-87
  creating, SSDT Report wizard used 90-96
  creating, SSDT used 469
  creating, Visual Studio 2012 used 100
  creating, with embedded maps 307-313
  creating, XML data sources used 293
  customizing 154
  data 151, 152
  data feed format 215
  defining 148

deploying 155
deploying, step 181
deploying, to Report Server 87-89
document map, adding 280
drill-down report 288
drill-through reports 285
format, changing 213, 214
formats, in Report Server Reports 98, 99
freeform report, adding 270-272
groups 275
interactive sorting, adding 282-284
List report, creating 263-267
main report, creating 270
managing 158, 493
maps, using 307
modifying, in Project RSPW2012 96-98
new toolbox items, in Report Builder 3 153
page breaks, configuring 281, 282
parts 314
permissions, granting 389
printing 211, 213
saving 155
saving, as report parts 315, 316
saving, to Documents library 386
saving, to Report Server 385, 386
saving, to SharePoint site 387-389
searching 211
subreport 268
subreport, embedding 272-275
table, creating for 474, 476
validating 157
viewing 157, 211, 212
viewing, on SQL Reporting
   web server 486, 487
report authoring
  about 248
  key considerations 248
report authoring, tools
  Report Builder 174
  Report Designer 174
  SharePoint Site for Power View 174
Report Builder
  downloading 246
  installing 246
  report authoring 246

report authoring 246
report changes, making 500-502
report, creating 386
standalone version, files 246
user interface 248
using, for report viewing 497-499
Report Builder 3
  enhancements 13
Report Builder 3.0. *See* **Report Builder**
Report Builder installation
  requirements 247
report caching
  about 237, 238
  cache refresh plan, creating 240, 241
  refresh options 239
  report processing options 238, 239
report content
  author reports, preparing 468
  creating 468
report content management, tools
  Report Manager 174
  Report Server Web Service 174
  RS Utility-RS Server Command Prompt 174
**report, creating for Windows Form
   application**
  Report Viewer Control, using 101-115
report creation, Visual Studio 2012 used
  hardware requirements 100
  RDLC, converting to RDI FILE 123-128
  Report Viewer Control, using in remote
     mode 121, 122
  software requirements 100
  Web Report Viewer Control, using 115-120
report creation, XML data sources used
  about 293
  data displaying, sparklines used 297, 300
  data display, with data bars 297
  data display, with indicators 297
  data display, with maps 297
  data highlighting, with data bars 297-299
  sparklines, inserting 302-304
  sparklines, using 301, 302
  well-formed XML data, creating 294-296
Report Dashboard
  managing 494
Report Data pane 78

Report data sources
  about 202
  embedded data source 202, 203
  shared data source 203
report definition
  Power View report contents 150
  XML-based report definition (.rdl file) 148, 149
Report Explorer 524
Reporting Service, in SSM
  turning on/off 146, 147
Reporting Services
  extensions 172
  overview 131
  tools 173
Reporting Services 2012 installation, in SharePoint Integrated mode
  Reporting Services Add-in 61, 62
  SharePoint Service, installing 62
  types 60
Reporting Services command prompt utilities
  about 451
  data source creating, rs.exe used 453-455
  Rsconfig 457
  rs.exe 452, 453
  Rskeymgmt utility 456
  RSS utility 452
Reporting Services Configuration
  about 139
  configuration file, modifying in native mode 143
  native mode 139
  Reporting Service, turning on/off 146, 147
  SharePoint Integrated mode 142, 143
Reporting Services extensions
  tasks 172
  types 172
Reporting Services, in SharePoint Integrated mode
  about 438
  application server 438
  Reporting Services SharePoint Integration related cmdlets 439
  report server, proxy URL 440
  SP service application pool 440

Reporting Services (RS) 78, 374
Reporting Services Service application
  creating 65-71
Reporting Services SharePoint Service
  installing 63
  Power View Site Collection feature, activating 71, 72
  Reporting Services Service application, creating 65-71
Reporting Services SharePoint Service installation
  about 63
  service, starting 64, 65
Reporting Services tools 173
report management
  delivery 160
  delivery Extension 162
  report scheduling 158, 159
  subscriptions 160
  subscriptions, requirements 161
Report Manager
  about 177
  customizing 185
  permission, creating to specific report 200, 201
  permissions, configuring from 191, 192
  starting 179
  starting, for URL 180
  tasks, performing 178
  user access 180
  user, assigning to custom role 198, 199
  user interface 182
  users, assigning to Item-Level roles 196, 197
  users, reviewing on reporting services database 198
Report Manager user interface
  about 182
  customizing 182-184
  folders, creating 185
  folders, deleting 185
  folders, modifying 185
  folders, moving 185
  role based security, configuring 192
  Windows user, assigning to System Administrator role 193

Report Part Gallery 321
report parts
  about 153, 314
  creating 314, 315
  items, reusing 319-321
  reusing 153, 154
report-related projects
  in Visual Studio 2012 99
Report Server
  accessing 502
  data bar 503
  indicator 503
  report access, methods 507
  report, deploying to 87-89
  report, running 502
  report, saving to 385, 386
  SQL Server 2012 Reporting
    Services 503, 504
Report Server administration, tools
  Reporting Services Configuration
    Manager 173
  RSConfig Command line Utility 174
  Rskeymgmt Utility 174
  SQL Server Configuration Manager 174
  SQL Server Management Studio 173
  Windows Management Instrumentation
    (WMI) Classes 174
Report Server Catalog 52
Report Server Project Wizard
  used, for report creating 79-87
Report Server Web Services API
  about 422, 423
  report, rendering on native mode report
    server 423-430
  SharePoint Integrated mode 430
  SharePoint management endpoints,
    accessing 431-434
Report subscription
  about 220
  data driven report subscription,
    creating 229
  Data Driven, types 221
  defining 220
  delivering, types 221
  event driven report subscription,
    creating 222-229

  standard, types 221
Report Viewer 524
Report Viewer Control
  about 417
  used, for Web report creating 115-120
  used, for Windows Form application
    report creation 101-113
  using, in Remote mode 121, 122
  using with URL access and web
    applications 418-422
Report wizard
  used, for report creation in SSDT 90-96
RM. See Report Manager
roles, tabular model
  administrator 341
  none 341-343
  process 341
  read 341
  Read and Process 341
RS2012
  about 14
  features 147
  installing, in SharePoint Integrated
    mode 60
RS2012 SharePoint Integrated
  Data Alerts 164, 165
  features 162
  Power View 163, 164
Rsconfig 457
rs.exe
  tasks 452
Rskeymgmt utility 456
RSS utility 452

S

SAAS 327
sample databases installation
  about 55
  files, downloading 55
  scripts, running 55
scatter charts 366, 367
search feature
  about 215
  using, within report 216

using, within Report Manager site 216
Search icon 320
security implementation
  about 166
  authentication 166
  authentication, types 167-169
  authorization 170
self-service alerts. *See* **Data Alerts**
Service Applications page 70
Service Principal Name 51
Service Reference Settings page 426
Setup Support Rules page 22
shared data source
  about 203
  creating, on Report Manager 203-205
  data model, creating from data source 206-210
SharePoint environment
  overview 132-134
  SharePoint Integrated mode 136
SharePoint Integrated mode
  about 136
  diagram explanation 137, 138
  elements 136, 137
  reporting services, exploring 438
SharePoint Integrated mode report server
  about 415
  accessing, in SP-integrated implementation 415, 416
SharePoint management endpoints
  accessing 431-433
SharePoint Server 2010
  model, connecting from 344-347
SharePoint Server 2010 Enterprise Edition
  about 56
  installing 56-59
SharePoint site
  report, saving 387, 388
SharePoint web parts
  accessing 525-531
  Native Report Server reports, accessing 524
  used, for Native Report Server reports view 524
Show Filters icon 353
Simple Mail Transfer Protocol. *See* **SMTP**

Skyblue database based report
  creating, on Windows Azure 480-483
Slicer 363
SMTP 47
snapshot
  about 242
  creating 242
  history 242
  history, creating 242, 243
Snapshot Options
  history, creating 243
software installation 14
software requirements 16, 17
SQL database
  creating, on Windows Azure 469-474
SQL database service (Aloha-HNL) 468
SQL Reporting web server
  report, viewing 486, 487
SQL Server
  Native mode installation 132-134
SQL Server 2012
  highlights 10
SQL Server 2012 installation
  requirements 15
  source file, downloading 18
  steps 18-33
  verifying 33-36
SQL Server 2012 installation, requirements
  hardware requirements 16
  operating system requirements (64-bit) 15, 16
  software requirements 16, 17
SQL Server 2012 installation verification
  about 33-36
  choices 37
  notes 37
SQL Server 2012 Reporting Services 503, 504
SQL Server 2012 Reporting Services Native mode
  configuring 38-50
  Report Server, configuration options 50-54
SQL Server Analysis Services. *See* **SAAS**
SQL Server Data Tools. *See* **SSDT**
SQL Server Integration Services. *See* **SSIS**

SQL Server Management Studio. *See* SQL
SQL Server Reporting Services. *See* SSRS
SQL Server Reporting Services Application 66
SQL servers structural design
  overview 132
SSDT
  about 74-76, 463, 508
  BI Projects 77
  Report Server Project 78
  Report Server Project Wizard 78
  used, for report creating 79
SSDT ribbon
  review 330
SSIS
  about 507
  used, for Native mode Report Server access 508-512
SSMS
  about 145
  Reporting Service, turning on/off 146, 147
  table, populating 476-478
SSRS
  about 11, 507
  configuring 37
  data sources 12
  enhancements 11
  overview 11-13
subreport
  about 267
  alternate row background color, setting 269, 270
  creating 268, 269
Subscriptions page 222
system-level roles 180

T

table
  populating, in SSMS 476-478
table behavior 337
tabular data model. *See* TDM
tabular model
  about 328
  connecting, to Northwind database 331, 332
  creating 328, 329
  default field set 337
  deploying 340
  measures, adding 339
  permissions 341
  roles 341
  SSDT ribbon review 330
  table behavior 337, 338
  tables, obtaining from database 332-336
TargetServerURL 484
TDM 325
TECHNET 503
TestSP link 402
tiles
  using 362
troubleshooting
  about 402, 404
  alert logs 406
  database alerting 408
  PowerShell used, for log file review 404

U

ULS 402, 404
Unified Logging Service. *See* ULS
URL access 171
user access, Report Manager
  granting, considerations 180
  item-level roles 180
  system-level roles 180
user interface, Report Builder 248
users
  managing 492
utilities
  overview 409

V

View Report 487
View Report History 242
Visibility property 290
Visual Studio 2012 (VS2012)
  about 74
  report-related projects 99
  used, for report creation 100

W

WASR
  about 462
  limitations 462, 463
  portal, accessing 463-468
Web Services Description Language.
  See **WSDL**
Web Services URL 502
Windows Azure
  report, deploying to SQL Reporting
    Services 484, 485
  SQL database, creating 469-474
  SQL Reporting Service, creating 478-480
Windows Azure HDInsight 331
Windows Azure Platform
  Skyblue database based report, creating
    480-484
Windows Azure SQL Database
  table, migrating to on-premise
    SQL Server 2012 505
Windows Azure SQL Reporting. *See* **WASR**
Windows Azure SQL Reporting Services
  activity status 495
  ITEMS menu 488
  menu items 488
  permission, managing 496
  Report Dashboard, managing 494
  reports, managing 491-494
  reports, viewing 496
  shared data source, creating 489-491
  users, managing 492

Windows Management Instrumentation.
  See **WMI**
Windows Presentation Foundation.
  See **WPF**
**Windows Presentation Foundations
  classes project**
  reports, accessing 517
  Report Server URLs, accessing in WPF
    project 518-524
Windows user
  creating 193, 194
  RSMax, assigning to RS System
    Administrator role 195, 196
WMI
  about 441
  used, for Report Server properties 448-451
WPF 508
WSDL 512

X

XML 517
XML data sources
  used, for report creating 293

[PACKT] PUBLISHING enterprise
professional expertise distilled

Thank you for buying
Learning SQL Server Reporting Services 2012

About Packt Publishing

Packt, pronounced 'packed', published its first book "Mastering phpMyAdmin for Effective MySQL Management" in April 2004 and subsequently continued to specialize in publishing highly focused books on specific technologies and solutions.

Our books and publications share the experiences of your fellow IT professionals in adapting and customizing today's systems, applications, and frameworks. Our solution based books give you the knowledge and power to customize the software and technologies you're using to get the job done. Packt books are more specific and less general than the IT books you have seen in the past. Our unique business model allows us to bring you more focused information, giving you more of what you need to know, and less of what you don't.

Packt is a modern, yet unique publishing company, which focuses on producing quality, cutting-edge books for communities of developers, administrators, and newbies alike. For more information, please visit our website: www.packtpub.com.

About Packt Enterprise

In 2010, Packt launched two new brands, Packt Enterprise and Packt Open Source, in order to continue its focus on specialization. This book is part of the Packt Enterprise brand, home to books published on enterprise software – software created by major vendors, including (but not limited to) IBM, Microsoft and Oracle, often for use in other corporations. Its titles will offer information relevant to a range of users of this software, including administrators, developers, architects, and end users.

Writing for Packt

We welcome all inquiries from people who are interested in authoring. Book proposals should be sent to author@packtpub.com. If your book idea is still at an early stage and you would like to discuss it first before writing a formal book proposal, contact us; one of our commissioning editors will get in touch with you.

We're not just looking for published authors; if you have strong technical skills but no writing experience, our experienced editors can help you develop a writing career, or simply get some additional reward for your expertise.

Learning Highcharts

ISBN: 978-1-849519-08-3 Paperback: 362 pages

Create rich, intuitive, and interactive JavaScript data visualization for your web and enterprise development needs using this powerful charting library — Highcharts

1. Step-by-step instructions with real-live data to create bar charts, column charts, and pie charts, to easily create artistic and professional quality charts

2. Learn tips and tricks to create a variety of charts such as horizontal gauge charts, projection charts, and circular ratio charts

3. Use and integrate Highcharts with jQuery Mobile and ExtJS 4, and understand how to run Highcharts on the server side

QlikView 11 for Developers

ISBN: 978-1-849686-06-8 Paperback: 534 pages

Develop Business Intelligence applications with QlikView 11

1. Learn to build applications for Business Intelligence while following a practical case -- HighCloud Airlines. Each chapter develops parts of the application and it evolves throughout the book along with your own QlikView skills

2. The code bundle for each chapter can be accessed on your local machine without having to purchase a QlikView license

3. The hands-on approach allows you to build a QlikView application that integrates real data from several different sources and presents it in dashboards, analyses and reports

Please check **www.PacktPub.com** for information on our titles

[PACKT] enterprise
professional expertise distilled

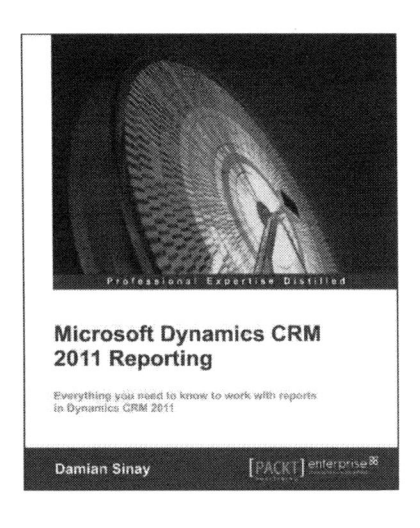

Microsoft Dynamics CRM 2011 Reporting

ISBN: 978-1-849682-30-5   Paperback: 305 pages

Everything you need to know to work with reports in Dynamics CRM 2011

1. Create reports with SQL Reporting Services for CRM
2. Empower your reports with the different Report Wizards and dashboards
3. Troubleshoot and optimize your reports for better performance

FusionCharts Beginner's Guide: The Official Guide for FusionCharts Suite

ISBN: 978-1-849691-76-5   Paperback: 252 pages

Create interactive charts in JavaScript (HTML5) and Flash for your web and enterprise applications

1. Go from nothing to delightful reports and dashboards in your web applications in super quick time
2. Create your first chart in 15 minutes and customize it both aesthetically and functionally
3. Create a powerful reporting experience with advanced capabilities like drill-down and JavaScript integration
4. Integrate the charts with PHP, ASP.NET, Java or other server-side scripts pulling data from databases

Please check www.PacktPub.com for information on our titles

Made in the USA
San Bernardino, CA
16 January 2016